Graphics **Interface** 2014

Montreal, Quebec, Canada
7 - 9 May 2014

Proceedings

Edited by
Paul G. Kry
Andrea Bunt

ISSN: 0713-5424
ISBN: 978-1-4822-6003-8

Proceedings Graphics Interface 2014, Paul G. Kry and Andrea Bunt (Program Chairs), Montreal, Quebec, Canada, 7 - 9 May 2014. Published by the Canadian Human-Computer Communications Society / Société canadienne du dialogue humain-machine and CRC Press.

Graphics Interface is sponsored by:
The Canadian Human-Computer Communications Society / Société canadienne du dialogue humain-machine (CHCCS/SCDHM)

Membership Information for CHCCS/SCDHM is available from:
    Canadian Information Processing Society (CIPS)
    5090 Explorer Drive, Suite 801
    Mississauga, Ontario L4W 4T9
    Canada
    Telephone: (905) 602-1370
    Fax: (905) 602-7884
    Web: http://www.cips.ca/

Additional copies of the proceedings are available from:
    CRC Press
    Taylor & Francis Group
    6000 Broken Sound Parkway NW, Suite 300
    Boca Raton, FL 33487-2742
CRC Press is an imprint of Taylor & Francis Group, an Informa business.

Published by the Canadian Human-Computer Communications Society / Société canadienne du dialogue humain-machine and CRC Press.
Distributed by CRC Press.
Available online through the Association for Computing Machinery (ACM) Digital Library.
Editorial and production support by Meghan Haley at Junction Publishing.
Printed in the USA by The Printing House Inc.

Contents

Invited Paper

Papers

Session: Physics and Collision
Session Chair: Christopher Batty

Session: Input Techniques
Session Chair: Michael McGuffin

President's Welcoming Letter

 Canadian Human-Computer Communications Society /
Société canadienne du dialogue humain-machine

Paul G. Kry
School of Computer Science
McGill University, Canada

The Canadian Human-Computer Communications Society (CHCCS) / Société Canadienne du Dialogue Humaine Machine (SCDHM) is a non-profit organization dedicated to advancing research and education in computer graphics, visualization, and human-computer interaction. CHCCS/SCDHM is a Special Interest Group within the Canadian Information Processing Society (CIPS).

The primary activity of CHCCS/SCDHM is sponsoring the annual Graphics Interface conference, the longest-running regularly scheduled conference on interactive computer graphics. In most years, Graphics Interface is held as part of a larger suite of conferences. This year the AI/GI/CRV 2014 conference, encompassing Artificial Intelligence and Computer and Robotic Vision along with Graphics Interface, is located in Montreal, Quebec. The conference promises to be an excellent event, with a selection of high quality papers in computer graphics, visualization, and human-computer interaction, accompanied by a lively posters and demo session featuring late breaking ideas and work in progress.

In addition to its annual conference, CHCCS/SCDHM sponsors several awards. The annual Michael A.J. Sweeney Award recognizes best student papers presented at the conference. The annual Alain Fournier Dissertation Award and the Bill Buxton Dissertation Award recognize the best Ph.D. dissertations awarded in Canada during the previous year for computer graphics and human-computer interaction, respectively. The annual CHCCS/SCDHM Achievement Award is presented to a Canadian who has made substantial research contributions to computer graphics, visualization, or human-computer interaction. Finally, the CHCCS/SCDHM Service Award is presented to a Canadian who has rendered substantial service contributions to the society or to the research community.

Each year the Awards Committee receives nominations and selects a winner of the Achievement Award and, from time to time, a winner of the Service Award. The current committee is chaired by Marilyn Tremaine, Rutgers University, and has as members Kellogg Booth, University of British Columbia, and Brian Wyvill, University of Bath. I thank the Awards committee for their efforts in finding a very well-deserving recipient. Nominations for the Alain Fournier Award and Bill Buxton Award are due mid-February of each year, and the winners are selected by independent committees coordinated by Pierre Poulin. I am very grateful to Pierre and the members of the respective committees for their work in identifying the top dissertations of 2013. Finally, the Michael A.J. Sweeney Award winners are selected by the program cochairs in consultation with the program committee.

The Annual General Meeting of CHCCS/SCDHM is held every year during the Graphics Interface conference, to review the previous year's activities and elect the executive committee. Current members of the executive committee are

- Paul G. Kry, McGill University, president
- Pierre Poulin, Université de Montréal, vice president
- Michael McGuffin, École de Technologie Supérieure, treasurer
- William Cowan, University of Waterloo, past president
- Derek Reilly, Dalhousie University, editor-in-chief
- James Stewart, Queen's University, web master

All Graphics Interface attendees are invited to attend the General Meeting, or to contact any member of the executive committee about CHCCS/SCDHM. I encourage everyone interested in the future of Graphics Interface to attend and get involved. Recent activities of CHCCS/SCDHM include scanning old proceedings to build an archive going back to 1971, and correcting inconsistencies in the ACM Digital Library for proceedings dating back to 2002. Since 2012, top graphics papers at Graphics Interface have been invited to submit extended versions to a special section of Computers & Graphics, and there are ongoing efforts to find a journal with which we can do the same for the top papers in the area of human-computer interaction.

On behalf of the society, and of all those who have worked to put on this year's conference, I extend a warm welcome to all the attendees of AI/CRV/GI 2014. I am pleased to serve a cochair of this year's conference, and wish to thank cochair Andrea Bunt, along with the committee members and referees for all their hard work in creating the conference program. And most important, I wish to thank all the authors who submitted their research. Without their commitment there would be no conference.

Preface

A Message from the Program Chairs

GRAPHICS COCHAIR
Paul G. Kry
McGill University, Canada

HCI COCHAIR
Andrea Bunt
University of Manitoba, Canada

You are holding the proceedings for Graphics Interface 2014. Now in its 40th year, Graphics Interface is the oldest continuously-scheduled conference in computer graphics and human-computer interaction; the conference dates back to 1969, when it was the "Canadian Man-Computer Communications Seminar", changing its name in 1982 to Graphics Interface. This year, Graphics Interface takes place in Montreal, Quebec from May 7th to May 9th.

The program for Graphics Interface 2014 features 28 papers. We received 40 (HCI) + 36 (Graphics) submissions. We have roughly equal numbers of papers for both tracks, with acceptance rates of 38% for the HCI track and 36% for the Graphics track.

The program committee comprised 29 experts from Graphics and HCI. Each paper was formally reviewed by two committee members, at least two external reviewers, and often received informal reviews from more. A fully double-blind reviewing process was used: the identity of the paper authors was known only to the program committee chairs and to the primary committee member assigned to the submission. We thank the program committee and the external reviewers for ensuring rigor and integrity in the reviewing process.

The Michael A. J. Sweeney Award will be awarded at the conference to the best student papers in graphics and HCI. This year, NVIDIA has kindly sponsored Graphics Interface by donating GTX780 graphics cards as prizes. The posters session is also an important part of the conference, featuring late breaking research and work in progress. Best posters in graphics and HCI will be recognized at the conference, and Intel has kindly sponsored Graphics Interface this year by donating Bay Trail powered Windows tablets as prizes.

Since 2012, authors of selected top papers in graphics have be invited to submit extended and revised manuscripts to be considered, with partial reviewer continuity, for journal publication in a special section of Computers & Graphics. We look forward to seeing the final extended versions of these selected papers later this year in the special section on graphics interaction, while we also continue efforts to find a journal with which we can do the same for the top papers in HCI.

We are proud to include keynote talks from two invited speakers, one Achievement Award winner, and two dissertation award winners. The two invited speakers, Elizabeth Churchill, eBay Research Labs, and Matthias Müller, NVIDIA are both well known for their exemplary contributions to their disciplines. Our congratulations to Eugene Fiume, University of Toronto, this year's recipient of the recipient of the CHCCS/SCDHM Achievement Award. We also congratulate the two dissertation award winners, Hua Li, University of North Carolina, Wilmington (2013 Alain Fournier Dissertation Award winner), and Xing-Dong Yang, University of Calgary (2013 Bill Buxton Dissertation Award winner).

We would like to thank various people who contributed to the behind-the-scenes conference organization, especially Pierre Poulin, Kelly Booth, Michael McGuffin, Derek Reilley, and Meghan Haley. Thanks also go out to Christopher Batty, the poster chair, Atefeh Farzindar, the AI/GI/CRV general chair, and local organizers Philippe Langlais and Guillaume-Alexandre Bilodeau. Lastly, we owe a great debt to James Stewart and Precision Conference Solutions for handling the electronic submission and review system; James's patience and responsiveness made the process run as smoothly as we could have hoped.

For further information about the conference series, you can visit the official web site, http://www.graphicsinterface.org

Organization

PROGRAM COCHAIRS

Paul G. Kry
McGill University, Canada

Andrea Bunt
University of Manitoba, Canada

POSTERS CHAIR

Christopher Batty
University of Waterloo, Canada

Program Committee

Usman Alim
University of Calgary, Canada

Lisa Anthony
University of Florida, USA

Scott Bateman
University of Prince Edward Island,
Canada

Stephen Brooks
Dalhousie University, Canada

Marie-Paule Cani
Grenoble Institute of Technology /
INRIA, France

Christopher Collins
University of Ontario Institute of
Technology, Canada

Eugene Fiume
University of Toronto, Canada

Alain Forget
Carnegie Mellon University, USA

Baining Guo
Microsoft Research Asia, China

Carl Gutwin
University of Saskatchewan,
Canada

Manfred Lau
Lancaster University, UK

Michael McGuffin
École de Technologie Supérieure,
Canada

Karyn Moffatt
McGill University, Canada

Torsten Möller
University of Vienna, Austria

David Mould
Carleton University, Canada

Lennart Nacke
University of Ontario Institute of
Technology, Canada

Derek Nowrouzezahrai
University of Montreal, Canada

Eric Paquette
École de Technologie Supérieure,
Canada

Pierre Poulin
University of Montreal, Canada

Jaime Ruiz
Colorado State University, USA

Faramarz Samavati
University of Calgary, Canada

Karan Singh
University of Toronto, Canada

Ian Stavness
University of Saskatchewan,
Canada

Anthony Tang
University of Calgary, Canada

Michael Terry
University of Waterloo, Canada

Daniel Vogel
University of Waterloo, Canada

Emily Whiting
ETH Zürich, Switzerland

James Young
University of Manitoba, Canada

Richard Zhang
Simon Fraser University, Canada

Reviewers

Glen Anderson
Sheldon Andrews
Francesco Banterle
Markus Billeter
Elizabeth Bonsignore
Sebastian Boring
Adrien Bousseau
Christopher Brooks
Stefan Bruckner
Erin Carroll
Guillaume Caumon
Jiawen Chen
Nuttapong Chentanez
Fanny Chevalier
Jason Chuang
Patrick Coleman
Jeremy Cooperstock
Carlos Correa
Joao Costa
Anind Dey
Fabian Di Fiore
Timothy Edmunds
Oskar Elek
Mark Eramian
Petros Faloutsos
Deborah Fels
Elsa Flechon
Eelke Folmer
Jodi Forlizzi
Dustin Freeman
Aaron Genest
Kathrin Gerling
Benjamin Gilles
Markus Hadwiger
Michael Haller
Mark Hancock
Khalad Hasan
Padraic Hennessy
Sébastien Hillaire
Juan David Hincapié-Ramos
Ken Hinckley
Hui Huang
Jeff Huang
Samuel Huron
Junko Ichino
Pourang Irani
Wojciech Jarosz
Bo Jiang
Pushkar Joshi
Ricardo Jota
Marcelo Kallmann
Shaun Kane
Bill Kapralos

ChangHun Kim
Theodore Kim
Søren Knudsen
Paul G. Kry
Pierre-Yves Laffont
Jochen Lang
Edward Lank
Hyun-jean Lee
Sungkil Lee
Christian Lessig
Bruno Levy
Honghua Li
Hua Li
Wilmot Li
Libin Liu
Ligang Liu
Xiaopei Liu
Noah Lockwood
Hugo Loi
Hao Lu
Rui Ma
Joao Madeiras Pereira
Oliver Mattausch
Victoria McArthur
James McCrae
Amon Millner
Jeremy Mogk
Sarah Morrison-Smith
Tomer Moscovich
Ahmed Mostafa
Cosmin Munteanu
Suraj Musuvathy
Miguel Nacenta
Kumiyo Nakakoji
Matei Negulescu
Ulrich Neumann
Joerg Niesenhaus
Chris North
Jan Novak
Makoto Okabe
Hirotaka Osawa
Cengiz Oztireli
Romain Pacanowski
Jia Pan
Alexander Pasko
Andriy Pavlovych
Evan Peck
Matthieu Perreira Da Silva
Emmanuel Pietriga
Jeff Pool
Tiberiu Popa
Gonzalo Ramos
Adrian Reetz

Christian Richardt
Tobias Ritschel
Daisuke Sakamoto
Antonio Sanchez
Daisuke Sato
Christopher Scaffidi
Erik Scheme
Christian Schumacher
Jack Snoeyink
Cyril Soler
Milos Sramek
Ben Steichen
Elizabeth Stobert
Tanasai Sucontphunt
Kazuki Takashima
Kenshi Takayama
Robert Teather
Jacob Tholander
Joelle Thollot
Melanie Tory
Zachary Toups
Theophanis Tsandilas
Fereydoon Vafaei
Radu-Daniel Vatavu
Vinayak Vinayak
Bruce Walter
Yang Wang
Li Wei
Andy Wilson
Brian Wyvill
Guofu Xie
Xing-Dong Yang
Koji Yatani
Shumin Zhai
Lei Zhang

Michael A. J. Sweeney Award 2014

 Canadian Human-Computer Communications Society /
Société canadienne du dialogue humain-machine

The CHCCS/SCDHM honours the memory of Michael A. J. Sweeney through an annual award to the best student papers presented at each year's Graphics Interface conference. The winning papers selected by the program committee, one graphics paper and one HCI paper, are chosen from among accepted papers that have a student as lead author and for which one or more student authors are presenting the paper.

Best Student Papers 2014

In Memory
Michael A. J. Sweeney, 1951-1995

Graphics 2014 Award Winner

"Interactive Light Scattering with Principal-Ordinate Propagation" by Oskar Elek, Tobias Ritschel, Carsten Dachsbacher, and Hans-Peter Seidel.

BIOGRAPHIES

Oskar Elek received his M.S. degree in 2011 at the Charles University, Prague, and is currently pursuing a Ph.D. at the Max Planck Institut (MPI) Informatik and the Multimodal Computing and Interaction Cluster of Excellence (MMCI) of the Saarland University, Saarbruecken. His main research interests include efficient physically-based rendering and simulation of light scattering in participating media.

Tobias Ritschel is a senior research group leader at the MPI Informatik and the MMCI Saarbruecken. His interests include interactive and non-photorealistic rendering, human perception and data-driven graphics. He received the Eurographics Ph.D. dissertation award in 2011.

Carsten Dachsbacher is a full professor at the Karlsruhe Institute of Technology (KIT) and the head of the Institute for Visualization and Data Analysis at KIT. His research focuses on high performance graphics, (interactive) global illumination, scientific visualization and perceptual rendering.

Hans-Peter Seidel is the scientific director and chair of the Computer Graphics Group at the MPI Informatik and a professor of computer science at Saarland University. In 2003, he received the Leibniz Preis, the most prestigious German research award, from the German Research Foundation (DFG). He is the first computer graphics researcher to receive such an award.

HCI 2014 Award Winner

"Experimental Study of Stroke Shortcuts for a Touchscreen Keyboard with Gesture-Redundant Keys Removed" by Ahmed Sabbir Arif, Michel Pahud, Ken Hinckley, and Bill Buxton.

BIOGRAPHIES

Ahmed Sabbir Arif is a Ph.D. candidate at York University, Canada in the Department of Computer Science & Engineering. His primary research interests are in the area of human-computer interaction. As a researcher he has worked on a wide-range of projects, both independently and in collaboration with academic and industrial research labs.

Michel Pahud has a Ph.D. in parallel computing from the Swiss Federal Institute of Technology. He has won several prestigious awards including the Logitech prize for an innovative industrially-oriented multiprocessors hardware/software project. He joined Microsoft in 2000 to work on different projects, including videoconferencing. More recently, he has been focusing on human-computer interaction at Microsoft Research. His research includes seamless collaborative technologies, bimanual interactions, and haptics.

Ken Hinckley is a Principal Researcher at Microsoft Research, where he has spent the last 17 years investigating novel input devices, device form-factors, and modalities of interaction. Ken is perhaps best known for his work on sensing techniques, cross-device interaction, and pen computing. He has published over 75 academic papers and is a named inventor on upwards of 150 patents. Ken holds a Ph.D. in Computer Science from the University of Virginia, where he studied with Randy Pausch.

Bill Buxton is a principal researcher at Microsoft Research. His focus for over 35 years has been in improving user experience through design, and improved theories, technology and techniques of interaction.

Alain Fournier Award 2013

 Canadian Human-Computer Communications Society /
Société canadienne du dialogue humain-machine

On August 14th, 2000, Dr. Alain Fournier passed away. He was a leading international figure in computer graphics, and a strong and frequent contributor to the Graphics Interface conference. His insights, enthusiasm, wisdom, vast knowledge, humour, and genuine friendship touched everyone he met.

The "Alain Fournier Memorial Fund" was created to celebrate his life, to commemorate his accomplishments, and to honour his memory. It rewards an exceptional computer graphics Ph.D. dissertation defended in a Canadian University over the past year. The winning dissertation is selected through a juried process by a selection committee consisting of accomplished researchers in computer graphics.

For more information about the "Alain Fournier Memorial Fund", and information about donation, please visit http://www.cs.ubc.ca/~fournier.

Hua Li
University of North Carolina,
Wilmington, USA
CHCCS/SCDHM Alain Fournier
Award Recipient 2013

This year, Dr. Hua Li is the recipient of the Alain Fournier Ph.D. Dissertation Award. Her dissertation, entitled *Perception-Motivated High Quality Stylization*, made several outstanding research contributions to non-photorealistic image stylization.

Her central observation approached image stylization from the angle of priority, where local greedy algorithms are tuned to achieve great results by properly structuring how local operations are ordered and applied. She applied her priority-based approach to automatic halftoning, stippling, and line art, where her algorithms always delivered very beautiful results. In fact, her stippling results are today considered the state-of-the-art. Her work and expertise also extend to image filtering, procedural image synthesis, non-photorealistic rendering, and human-subject evaluations of non-photorealistic images.

Hua completed her B.Eng. in Mining Engineering and her M.Eng. in Control Theory and Control Engineering, both at the University of Science and Technology in Beijing, and her Ph.D. in Computer Science at Carleton under the supervision of Professor David Mould.

She has co-authored a paper at Eurographics, two at Graphics Interface (one of which received the best student paper in graphics), two at NPAR, one at ARTECH (honorable mention), as well as other publications; a number of her contributions have appeared as extended versions in journals. She has been a regular reviewer in Graphics Interface and other top computer graphics conferences and journals. She is now a faculty member at the University of North Carolina, Wilmington.

For more information, please visit: http://people.uncw.edu/lihua/

Bill Buxton Dissertation Award 2013

 Canadian Human-Computer Communications Society /
Société canadienne du dialogue humain-machine

The award is named in honour of Bill Buxton, a Canadian pioneer who has done much to promote excellence, both within Canada and internationally, in the field of Human-Computer Interaction. Bill truly advocates HCI. He challenges how academics and practitioners think, and inspires them to do things differently. This is why we are proud to name this award after him.

The winning dissertation is selected through a juried process by a selection committee consisting of accomplished researchers in Human-Computer Interaction.

Xing-Dong Yang

iLab
University of Calgary, Canada
CHCCS/SCDHM Alain Fournier
Award Recipient 2013

The recipient of the 2013 award for the best doctoral dissertation completed at a Canadian university in the field of Human-Computer Interaction is Dr. Xing-Dong Yang.

In his dissertation, *Blurring the Boundary Between Direct and Indirect Mixed Mode Input Environments*, he introduces and studies how direct and indirect input modes can co-exist and improve our digital interactions. His dissertation breaks new ground by demonstrating that input methods need not be confined to only one type, but can instead be designed to cleverly shift across different modes. His work is exemplary in showing how to build and study not one, but several prototypical systems and on diverse platforms, from the desktop to wearables, which encapsulate the concepts promoted in his thesis.

Through four carefully designed systems, Xing-Dong's dissertation examines how mixed input modes can be implemented through software and hardware innovations and then leveraged for common, everyday computing tasks. In one example, the Magic Finger, he exposes the ability to turn the finger into a very precise pointer. In another example, he transforms the ubiquitous desktop mouse, known for its ability to select pixel-size objects, into an input device suitable for coarse and direct manipulation. The performance of the proposed systems was evaluated from various perspectives through a set of carefully designed user and system evaluations.

Xing-Dong earned his Ph.D. in Computer Science with a specialization in Human-Computer Interaction from the University of Alberta, where he worked under the supervision of Dr. Pierre Boulanger. He has generated a large number of publications, many in top-tier venues for HCI research, including the ACM Conference on Human Factors and Systems (ACM CHI) and the ACM Conference on User Interfaces and Technology (ACM UIST). He has over twenty publications in the fields of HCI, mobile computing, wearable technology and haptic interfaces. His work has also been recognized through best paper nominations at ACM CHI and ACM MobileHCI, featured in the public press through Discovery News, NBC, and New Scientist, and has led to five US patent applications filed between 2010 and 2013. He is currently a Postdoctoral Fellow in the iLab, at the University of Calgary, where he works with Dr. Tony Tang and Dr. Saul Greenberg.

For more information, please visit: http://webdocs.cs.ualberta.ca/~xingdong/

Achievement Award 2014

 Canadian Human-Computer Communications Society /
Société canadienne du dialogue humain-machine

The CHCCS/SCDHM Achievement Award is presented periodically to a Canadian researcher who has made a substantial contribution to the fields of computer graphics, visualization, or human-computer interaction. Awards are recommended by the CHCCS/SCDHM Awards Committee, based on nominations received from the research community. The 2014 members of the Awards Committee are Kellogg Booth, Marilyn Tremaine, and Brian Wyvill.

The 2014 CHCCS/SCDHM Achievement Award of the Canadian Human Computer Communications Society is presented to Eugene Fiume of the University of Toronto.

Eugene Fiume
University of Toronto, Canada
CHCCS/SCDHM Achievement
Award Recipient 2014

Eugene is Professor and past Chair of the Department of Computer Science at the University of Toronto. He directs the Masters of Science in Applied Computing programme and has long been a member of the Dynamic Graphics Project. After earning a B.Math. degree in 1981 at the University of Waterloo and M.Sc. and Ph.D. degrees from the University of Toronto in 1983 and 1986, respectively, he became an NSERC Postdoctoral Fellow and Maitre Assistant at the University of Geneva, Switzerland. He was then awarded an NSERC University Research Fellowship in 1987 and returned to the University of Toronto where he has held a faculty position ever since. During that time, Eugene has made fundamental contributions to the field of computer science, primarily in the area of computer graphics, where he specializes in modelling and rendering. These are two of the core problems that define the essence of computer graphics. The models used in computer graphics are often ad hoc and based on convenient approximations that lack rigorous theoretical justification. Sometimes it is possible to do better. Eugene's work is distinguished by formal, mathematical frameworks through which a deeper understanding of objects and their behaviours at various levels of complexity supports more efficient and accurate rendering.

This focus on mathematical precision arose from his early theoretical training. His doctoral research presented a mathematical formalization of raster graphics that provided a framework within which a number of problems could be understood and solutions compared. The importance of this and much of the subsequent work by Eugene has been his insistence on establishing a sound theoretical basis for all aspects of computer graphics. In this endeavour he has been extremely successful, as evidenced by the quantity and the quality of his publications in leading journals and the most prestigious international conferences. His research over more than thirty years spans most aspects of realistic computer graphics, including computer animation, modelling of natural phenomena, and illumination algorithms, as well as strong interests in imaging, software architectures, and parallel algorithms. He has written two books and authored or co-authored over 130 papers on these topics. Fourteen doctoral students and 45 masters students have graduated under his supervision.

His work on various problems related to the modelling and rendering of natural phenomena is particularly noteworthy. These solutions are inspired by the techniques of control theory, applied mathematics and physics, but they frequently are subject to a different set of constraints from similar problems found in the other mathematical sciences. In mathematical simulations, such as those conducted in computational fluid dynamics, the traditional goal is to accurately represent aggregates of energy and mass transported over time. Good numerical solutions may not lead directly to realistic or aesthetically pleasing depictions. For example, a fluid flow model might accurately predict the volume of water that flows through a river channel, but it might not provide the depictions of surface details of the waves and eddies that are of most interest in a computer animation. Eugene and his students have looked at techniques that balance the need for both visually interesting and physically plausible depictions that are computationally feasible. This has led to many notable breakthroughs and helped launch the careers of some of the current leaders in the field. Twenty years ago, with Michiel van de Panne (1993), and concurrent work by Ngo and Marks, he introduced neural networks to computer graphics. Work with Jos Stam (1995) in simulating wind, smoke, clouds and fire has set the standard for future efforts in this area and led to successful commercial deployment in hundreds of films requiring the realistic simulation and control of natural phenomena. The "wire" deformation technique, developed with Karan Singh (1998), is now ubiquitous in practical geometric modelling and animation. Michael McCool and Eugene created a simple, often-used poisson-disk sampling algorithm (1990). With George Drettakis, he developed an early penumbral shadow rendering algorithm (1994). With Victor Ng-Thow-Hing, he developed an early volume preserving skeletal muscle model

For more information, please visit: http://www.dgp.toronto.edu/~elf/

(2003); indeed, his interest in biomechanical and biomedical simulation continues to this day in his collaborations with Sami Siddique and Dongwoon Lee. Derek Nowrouzezahrai and Eugene have contributed to data-driven animation and fast rendering for animated characters. With Tyler de Witt and Christian Lessig (2011-present), he developed very efficient real-time control techniques for the artistic animation of fluids as well as fast algorithms for the rotation of signals on the sphere. His work with Lessig continues on the mathematical characterization of light transport, the development of spherical orthogonal wavelets, as well as the introduction of reproducing kernel Hilbert spaces to computer graphics. Alain Fournier was his most frequent collaborator, and together they made many contributions to sampling, filtering and rendering problems.

Eugene has contributed to the computer graphics and digital media communities in many other ways. He has won two teaching awards at the University of Toronto, as well as Innovation Awards from the Information Technology Research Centre of Ontario (ITRC) for research in computer graphics, an award from Burroughs-Wellcome for biomedical research, and an NSERC Synergy Award for innovation and industrial collaboration in visual modelling with Dr. Gordon Kurtenbach of Autodesk (2012). He served as the papers chair for SIGGRAPH 2001, chair of the ACM SIGGRAPH Awards Committee (2003-2008) and the ACM Paris Kanellakis Awards Committee (2011), and general cochair of the ACM Symposium for Computer Animation (2008) and Pacific Graphics (2011). He has served on numerous scientific and corporate boards both within Canada and internationally. He has also contributed to the industrial practice of computer graphics through his role as Research Scientist and then Director of Research and Usability Engineering at Alias|wavefront (now part of Autodesk) from 1995 to 1999. He has also served on many industrial and academic boards.

Eugene is currently Principal Investigator for a $6M Canada Foundation for Innovation/Ontario Research Fund project for the construction of a digital media and systems lab. He has been selected to serve as the next Scientific Director of the Graphics, Animation and New Media Network of Centres of Excellence (GRAND), beginning in 2015. He has the distinction of having been (co-)supervised by three previous CHCCS/SCDHM Achievement Award winners: Kellogg Booth (bachelor's paper), Bill Buxton (master's thesis), and Alain Fournier (doctoral dissertation).

Graphics Keynote Speaker

Physics in Games

Matthias Müller
NVIDIA, Switzerland

ABSTRACT

Physical simulations have a long history in engineering and have been successfully used to complement real world experiments. Main advantages computer simulations have over real experiments are the ability to study extreme conditions and the analysis of very small time intervals. With this in mind, the accuracy of the models and the results are central to engineering applications.

For more than three decades, physical simulations have also been used in computer graphics in order to increase the realism of animations and to free artists from animating secondary motion by hand. The two main applications are special effects in movies and physical effects in computer games. Here, accuracy is important to the extent that plausible behavior is generated. There are, however, additional requirements not present in the engineering world that are more important than accuracy. One such requirement is controllability: movie directors and game developers want to be able to control how a building collapses or what path a flood wave takes in order to create the desired effect or to make sure game play does not get blocked. Another aspect that plays a major role, especially in games, is stability. The simulations need to be unconditionally stable even in unphysical situations such as characters turning 180 degrees in a single time step.

These new requirements are the reason why physically based simulation in computer graphics has become an important research field separate from scientific computing. In my talk I will present a variety of simulation methods we have developed to meet these requirements, while still producing plausible physical behavior. Examples are approaches to simulate soft bodies, clothing, destruction and liquids.

BIOGRAPHY

Dr. Matthias Müller is Research Lead of the PhysX SDK team at NVIDIA. PhysX is a GPU accelerated physically based simulation engine for computer games. His research interests include the development of methods for the simulation of rigid bodies, fracture, soft bodies, cloth and fluids that are fast, controllable and robust enough to be used in game environments. He is a pioneer in the field of position based dynamics and has been contributing to this and other fields via numerous publications in the major computer graphics conferences and journals. Position based dynamics has become the standard for the simulation of soft bodies and cloth in computer games and has been adopted by the film industry as well.

Matthias Müller received his Ph.D. from ETH Zürich for his work on the atomistic simulation of dense polymer systems. During a two year post-doc with the computer graphics group at MIT he changed his research focus from atomistic offline simulations to macroscopic real time simulation in computer graphics. In 2002 he co-founded Novodex, a company that developed a simulation engine for computer games. In 2004 Novodex was acquired by AGEIA which, in turn, was acquired by NVIDIA in 2008.

For more information, please visit: http://www.matthiasmueller.info

HCI Keynote Speaker

Foundations for Designing User Centered Systems:
A framework and some case studies

Elizabeth Churchill
eBay Research Labs, USA

ABSTRACT

Interactive technologies pervade every aspect of modern life. Web sites, mobile devices, household gadgets, automotive controls, aircraft flight decks; everywhere you look, people are interacting with technologies. These interactions are governed by a combination of: the users' capabilities, capacities, proclivities and predilections; what the user(s) hope to do and/or are trying to do; and the context in which the activities are taking place. From concept to ideation to prototype and evaluation, when designing interactive technologies and systems for use by people, it is critical that we start with some understanding of who the users will be, what tasks and experiences are we are designing to support; and something about the context(s) of use. In this talk, I will discuss a framework for thinking about design, the ABCS. Using examples from my own work, I will illustrate how this framework has been explicitly and/or tacitly applied in the design, development and evaluation of interactive, multimedia systems.

BIOGRAPHY

Dr. Elizabeth Churchill is an applied social scientist working in the area of social media, interaction design and mobile/ubiquitous computing. She is currently Director of Human Computer Interaction at eBay Research Labs (ERL) in San Jose, California. She was formerly a Principal Research Scientist at Yahoo! Research, where she founded, staffed and managed the Internet Experiences Group. Originally a psychologist by training, throughout her career Elizabeth has focused on understanding people's social and collaborative interactions in their everyday digital and physical contexts. She has studied, designed and collaborated in creating online collaboration tools (e.g. virtual worlds, collaboration/chat spaces), applications and services for mobile and personal devices, and media installations in public spaces for distributed collaboration and communication.

Elizabeth has a B.Sc. in Experimental Psychology, an M.Sc. in Knowledge Based Systems, both from the University of Sussex, and a Ph.D. in Cognitive Science from the University of Cambridge. In 2010, she was recognised as a Distinguished Scientist by the Association for Computing Machinery (ACM). Elizabeth is the current Executive Vice President of ACM SigCHI (Human Computer Interaction Special Interest Group). She is a Distinguished Visiting Scholar at Stanford University's Media X, the industry affiliate program to Stanford's H-STAR Institute.

For more information, please visit: http://elizabethchurchill.com

Visual Models and Ontologies

Eugene Fiume*

Dynamic Graphics Project, Department of Computer Science
University of Toronto

For Alain Fournier

ABSTRACT

Realistic computer graphics will change the way people think and communicate. Achieving deeper success as a ubiquitous medium will require a more resonant understanding of visual modelling that must embrace mathematical, philosophical, cultural, perceptual and social aspects. With an interleaved understanding, people will be able to create visual ontologies that better align to their expressive needs. In turn, this will naturally lead to ubiquitous supporting technologies. First we need good visual models. A model induces an ontology of things that inevitably omits aspects of the phenomenon, whether desired or not. Thus modelling a model's incompleteness is crucial, for it allows us to account for artifacts, errors, and ontological surprises such as the "uncanny valley". Over the years, my choice of tools to model models has been mathematics. In this paper, I will speak to how little progress we have made and how much broader our investigation must be.

1 *"One must imagine Sisyphus happy."*
– Albert Camus

Ever since I encountered it as a teenager, I have routinely returned to Camus' luminous essay, "The Myth of Sisyphus", and dwelt on its resonant concluding sentence. In five words, Camus compels us to think of an absurd possibility as real. It is a bracing exercise in modelling, imagination, and metaphor. We visualise Sisyphus rolling a rock up a hill, we momentarily inhabit his body as he heaves the rock upward, and we feel the perpetual agony of watching it roll back down the hill. If there are gaps in our imagined mythology, we suspend disbelief and fill them in as needed, just as we scan an impossible object. But Camus pushes us further: he insists we imagine this imaginary person would find equanimity in his imaginary, pointless effort. For good measure, we cannot help but wrap another model around the myth that casts it into a parable for human struggle, or closer to the current discussion, a long research career in computer graphics! Five simple words elicit a cascade of interacting models. This marvellous enterprise of imagination constantly engages our senses, intuitions and understanding, even though nothing "real" has happened beyond some neurochemical reactions costing about three Calories. Five words to induce a thousand pictures.

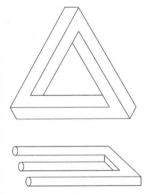

---

*e-mail: elf@dgp.toronto.edu

The realities we construct through computer graphics are much the same. Researchers create abstractions of appearance, and develop ways to transform them into computational representations. Engineers embed implementations of them into software that allows users to create stories through visual illusions. There is an implicit relationship between tool makers and tool users. I could be just as well be speaking about the coupling of the science and engineering of paints, media and paint brushes to the process of an artist creating a painting. In this paper, I'll stick to what I know.

One thing that distinguishes our endeavours as researchers in computer graphics and human-computer interaction is that we are on the verge of creating technologies that will allow ubiquitous, computationally *sustained* narratives. In all artistic expression, the medium of the expression is a conduit linking a presumed mental state of its creator to that of an observer. The difference in our field is that we are moving to a computationally enhanced reality in which we will be embedded in continuous narratives. Computational reality will interleave with external physical reality. The persistence of computational illusions will one day take us into a place that is different from painting, sculpture, theatre or film.

I am guilty of having spent a good deal of time trying to model how computers can be used to make images [3]. I have used the language of mathematics to do so, not from some dogmatic position of the superiority of mathematics, but because there is no real alternative. When done well, the use of mathematical methods also allows us to define assumptions and limits. My goal, then, has been to make precise the mappings $\mathbf{R}$ that take scenes $\mathbf{S}$ to images $\mathbf{I}$. Along the way I have also spent time on computational models of specific visual phenomena, such as light transport, fluid flow, muscle models, shadow computation, and many others. These can be seen as components of $\mathbf{R}$. This is a paper about models, so let me describe one non-mathematically (as I do in most of the paper).

What is an *image I*, in $\mathbf{I}$? In most of my work, it is the mathematical equivalent of a camera's light sensor. It represents a simulated measurement of light energy impinging on a region of interest at a given time of interest. We often think of this region as composed of a set of pixels that are individual measurements of light energy. This descriptive model allows us to understand how we might sample the physical processes that participate in the distribution of light into a dynamic environment. It is an incomplete model, and as it stands we have made remarkably little progress in actually saying when a specific mapping R taking a scene S to I is adequate. I will first motivate some important things we usually leave out of models in $\mathbf{R}$. Then I will talk about how badly we do even with what we have left in. Lastly, I will argue that the evolution of interactive computer graphics into a ubiquitous medium of visual expression is fundamentally impeded both by what we leave out, and by how poorly we understand what we leave in.

2 MODELS AND PHENOMENOLOGY

Science may well be the antidote to anecdote, but I will start with a story anyway. My family originates from the remote south of Italy where it is difficult to distinguish dwellings from rocks; the dialect had no place for words like *computer*, *model* or *simulation*. It is a dialect rooted in the tangible and the real. My grandmother was the

matriarch of our family. Her dominant presence belied her almost total lack of facility in English. I was named after her husband, which may have explained her life-long curiosity with what I did. As a young researcher in computer graphics, however, most of my time was spent thinking about **R**–hardly a great conversation starter.

My Ph.D. thesis had exactly one picture in it, and that was only because I thought it odd to not have a picture in a thesis about making pictures. It may not be surprising that describing what I did would typically invoke more bemusement than interest. One day, however, I had a chance to change things. A Ph.D. student at the time, Jos Stam, who did the hard work, and I had been working on the computational physics underlying the appearance of smoke, mist, clouds and fire. We had a little breakthrough and were able to simulate these phenomena efficiently. It was Christmas-time in the early 90s, a couple of years before the first full-length computer animated feature, Pixar's *Toy Story*, would appear. Realistic computer graphics was just emerging as a research area, and our techniques and those of many others would come to be used in just about every film, game or animation requiring realistic simulation of "natural phenomena". But at the time I was only thinking that with many imminent family gatherings, and with videotape evidence in hand, I finally was in a position to explain to my family what I did!

So I played animations of computer generated smoking cigarettes, wispy clouds, and flickering fire. Satisfying sounds of appreciation came from my some in my family. I then spoke to my grandmother in dialect. "So, what do you think?", I asked.
"What do you mean? I see a cigarette smoking", she said.
"But it's not a real smoking cigarette", I respond.
"What do you mean, not real? There is smoke coming from a cigarette."
"Well, you know that thing I work on called a 'computer'? It creates pictures of a smoking cigarette."
"Where?"
"In the 'computer'."
"So there is a cigarette smoking in the 'computer' and it takes pictures of the smoking?"
"Sort of, but there is no real cigarette. The computer pretends to make it smoke."

"I don't understand. I see a cigarette. I see smoke. I do not see a cigarette pretending to smoke. I see a cigarette smoking. And why do you want to pretend to smoke cigarettes anyway?"

I was defeated. Shouldn't I just have been gratified that she could not tell the difference between an approximation and the real thing? In the world of my grandmother, as fashioned by post-war austerity, there seemingly were no illusions. Everything is real. A character in a movie is real. Souls and spirits and angels are material. Her *ontology* of physical reality, namely those things that exist through her model of reality, is complicated by few abstractions. Here I was trying to explain that a piece of mathematics made feasible by an algorithm was brought to life–i.e., animated–by a program running on a computer. Her ontology of reality was different from mine.

We (post-)postmoderns are not so gullible. We maintain an ironic distance between message and meaning. We consciously distinguish reality and illusion: if we cry at the end of *Old Yeller*, or the "mad elephant" mother's caress of Dumbo, it is because we choose to suspend disbelief, consciously allowing an emotional engagement tempered by an acute awareness that we are in control.

Really? While we do have control over what we see, it is a mistake to think we have full control over our visual ontologies. Even the partial control we do have can be eroded in many ways. About the best we can expect is to limit vigilantly the erosion of whatever control we do have. A danger in the argument in this paper that we need to model our models is that the insights gained could be turned against us to make it even more difficult to exert personal control.

Like Camus' visualisation of Sisyphus, we know from computer graphics, photography and fine art that images can be used to invoke realities that can depart arbitrarily from real life.[1] We need to understand these processes to enhance visual communication. Modelling is key to how we make computational or artistic depictions of the world. It is also key to making sense of the world, to understanding the words, images, actions and indeed the thoughts of others. We do not just sense the world: we make sense of the world, and we do so by modelling. We do not precisely file our sense data in mental folders and recall it exactly. We actively retrieve, refresh, reconstruct, reconnect data through the use of models. All of this is particularly true of how we understand images, but we must appreciate that understanding is based on models, and that models induce an ontology of things that are consistent with that model. Different models give different meaning to the same phenomenon.

Sight is not merely light. While vision science is providing us with clues as to the operation of our visual processing systems, one of the frustrating aspects in my work is that these processes 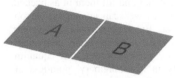 do not harmonise with my mappings **R**. In Ted Adelson's classic study [1], consider the two parallelograms above labelled A and B. Their interiors both are, and appear to be, of the same luminance. Now, let us position A and B in a checkerboard in which the region B is in slight shadow, and A is not. Suddenly B appears to be considerably lighter in shade than A. Why? There is no difference in the light energy radiated by A and B in the two images, so the discrepancy is not an intrinsic physical property of light.[2]

A model induces an ontology of phenomena that are consistent with that model. But why should the brain stop at one? It would be more robust to have myriad models available that "run" in parallel (in this case a model that takes 3D environments and shadowing into account, and one that works in flatland) and then choose the

---

[1] A beautiful reflection on this is John Berger's "Ways of Seeing", a 1972 BBC documentary archived at www.youtube.com/watch?v=LnfB-pUm3eI.

[2] Similar effects have long been known for colour. Beau Lotto interactively demonstrates some lovely examples of colour "illusions" in www.ted.com/talks/lang/eng/beau_lotto_optical_illusions_show_how_we_see.html.

Edward H. Adelson

one that provides the most convincing, surprise-minimising interpretation. It is easy to see, then, how different ontologies can be induced from the same physical conditions. Moreover, our visual systems may consistently sacrifice accurate perception of physical quantities for a more efficacious phenomenology.

The neural processing of visual signals is the object of considerable modern scientific attention. Our recognition of shape, hue, contrast, saturation, are certainly not linear processes. These effects have been known to artists for centuries. *Chiaroscuro*, or the enhancement of features through the interplay of light/dark contrast, has long been in the artistic vocabulary. The virtuosic use of contrast and dark in Rembrandt's *Nightwatch* evokes brightly lit faces and uniforms of three central characters in sunlight–a brightness that would be otherwise unrepresentable within the physical gamut of oil paints under normal illumination. In the restored painting shown above, almost all of it, indeed over 95% of the image, is "dark" in the sense of being lower than $\frac{1}{16}$ of the maximal luminance elsewhere in the image. I thresholded the image so as to depict in white the areas that are in the upper half of the luminance range and in black otherwise; we see just how dark the painting is. Rembrandt pulled out all the stops to amplify and focus attention.

Humans recognise faces with great efficiency, but it is another example of how models induce ontology. Unlike the world of seals or dolphins, but like most apes, we tend to see others in a cylindrical panorama with a clear sense of "up". Thus we expect to see faces in a preferred orientation: upright and eyes above the mouth. Consider the photograph on the next page (left) of a strikingly handsome lad

in need of a shave. To illustrate that we have a preferred orientation for recognising faces, I made a few minor changes to this image and inverted it (centre). At first blush it appears to pass muster as an acceptable face. However, upon setting the modified image upright (right), we see that it is a grotesque distortion.

This famous effect, now immortalised as "Thatcherisation" in honour of its first victim, was first documented by Peter Thompson, and has spawned much discussion [7].[3] An aspect of the Thatcher illusion I find noteworthy is the reaction of disgust that often arises in the distorted upright image. Admittedly, I chose a photograph with a big smile because the resulting upturned teeth seem to strengthen the effect. While the brain clearly employs models that select for orientation, the discomfort elicited from distorted facial images is an acute, disproportionate response to the violation of a "low-surprise" threshold. This appears to extend to other primates, as evidenced by a macaque study[2]. I personally have little regard for the "uncanny valley", but I would be willing to argue that what we call the "uncanny valley" is but one instance of an exaggerated ontological gap between our expectations of an external model and the internal mental models we use to assess its outcomes. As we can see, we do not need computers or robots to elicit this effect. As a further thought experiment, imagine the neutral emotionless face of actor Bill Murray and compare it to the blank-stare of Christopher Walken. Both are neutral faces, and yet we tend fill Murray's face with imputed meaning while we are creeped out by Walken. This curious effect is an instance of "Fundamental Attribution Error", which is beginning to get further attention [6].

Note that the famous "moon illusion" is also highly orientation dependent. The interested reader is invited to discover the embarrassing posture he or she can employ to eliminate this effect.

Why is the sky blue? The common explanation to this age-old question is "Hey bud, it's late. Go to sleep." A slightly better one goes like this. Sunlight is composed of a distribution of electromagnetic waves of various frequencies. When sunlight enters our atmosphere, shorter wavelengths (and thus higher frequencies) are uniformly scattered more than longer wavelengths. The former correspond to the colour blue, while the latter correspond to other colours such as green and red. Thus longer wavelengths pass through the atmosphere and hit the earth while the shorter wavelengths bounce about more in the atmosphere, giving it a blue hue in a clear daytime sky. Even when more physical language is wrapped around

---

[3] An excellent popular discussion can be found in the BBC article www.bbc.co.uk/bang/article_thatcher.shtml.

 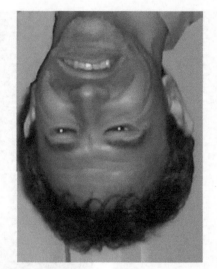 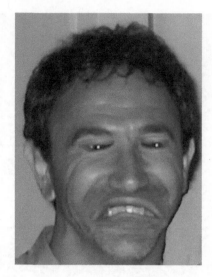

is just as much violet as blue in atmospheric sunlight, so the sky should be violet because the largest proportion of scattering occurs in wavelengths corresponding to violet. The sky is indeed "violet",

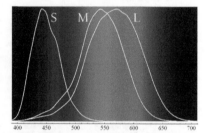

but it does not appear so, because our retinal spectral sensitivity has a sharp fall-off below 420nm. Because our sensitivity in violet is so much lower than blue, we see the sky as blue. I am omitting here the increased likelihood that violet will scatter sooner than blue as sunlight passes through the atmosphere.

So the sky appears blue, but even taking into account that most camera sensors are also blue-violet insensitive, notice that if I boost the violet signal in top part of the sky at left by a modest amount, we suddenly see violet. But for a small difference in the colour sensitivity of our retinas, a beautiful blue sky would be a vibrant violet. This model also accounts for the yellowish appearance of the sun at ground level, since the original white light of the sun is filtered by what amounts to a low-pass filter.

A good model just keeps on giving: because of variable sensitivities of our visual system to the different visible wavelengths of light, two colours may *look* the same but actually have different spectral power distributions under certain illumination conditions. Such colours are called *metamers*, and by playing around a bit, one can easily construct examples. Metamers are a bane to our existence when we discover that a paint chip looks great in the paint store but terrible in our kitchens.

In providing an incrementally better model for the colour of our sky, we have unearthed a vein of discussion regarding model construction, how in some cases we accept poor ones that do not make appropriate predictions, the importance of skepticism, and the need to revise and refine models. We have also indirectly challenged the very idea that colour and shade even exist independent of the human observer. It is fair to say that the very idea of *colour* is not a physical entity, but in fact exists only in our minds. And yet we have sufficient consensus both on the qualities of colour and agree on names for them, despite their apparent contingency. Many of our the concepts we think of as extrinsic and objective are in fact the product of emergent social consensus. This makes systematic modelling very difficult.

this explanation, it is at best one-third correct, making it a poor model for a visual phenomenon [5].

We can do a bit better. The visible spectrum of light occupies a sliver of electromagnetic radiation of about 350-750 nanometres (nm) in wavelength. Shorter wavelengths perceptually correspond to violet and blue, with longer wavelengths attributed to green, yellow, orange and red. About two-thirds of the energy emitted from the sun that irradiates our upper atmosphere falls within the visible spectrum, and just as it enters the atmosphere, all wavelengths within that spectrum are about equally represented. Most of our atmosphere consists of nitrogen (N_2, 78%) and oxygen (O_2, 21%). These are small molecules with a gas, so we can imagine them as well spaced, tiny particles that are far smaller in diameter than the wavelengths present in the sunlight radiating through the gas. These small particles are more likely to interact with waves that wiggle more finely, so such waves have higher frequencies or shorter wavelengths. The propensity for light-particle interaction is called *scattering* and the particular variety that applies here is *Rayleigh* scattering. I'll draw attention to only one aspect: the likelihood of scattering varies with λ^{-4}, where λ is the wavelength of that component of light. This term increases quickly as λ decreases. Now, "blue" is around 475nm and "red" near 700nm. Since blue light is about 2/3 the wavelength of red, it is $(2/3)^{-4}$ or five times more likely than red to be scattered. Thus the sky is blue. We're done! Aren't mathematical models great?

Not so fast. The wavelength of violet is about 400nm, so it is *ten* times more likely to scatter than red, and twice that of blue. There

3 A Science of Ubiquitous Realistic Graphics

Since before my grandmother's reaction to second-hand synthetic cigarette smoke, I have been interested in *realistic computer graphics*. My one-time supervisor, long-time collaborator and departed friend, Alain Fournier, was my inspiration[4]. The long-term goal of the field is to give expression to those wishing to create virtual worlds for the purposes of recreation, education, exploration and communication. Its mathematical core has facilitated some early visible progress, but the problems are boundless and difficult, and I believe we require new approaches. This field has already extended well beyond entertainment-based applications to design, biomedicine, surgery, anatomy, biomechanics, and physics. This is all more reason to ensure we understand what we are doing!

Our earlier discussion suggests that many things we see are difficult to model. This does not invalidate a mathematical programme, but it does point to gaps in understanding. Tools for visual expression should enable effective, reproducible results of all manner of visual phenomena as users explore ways to express themselves. A deep obstacle we face is that the mundane actions of human characters, such as facial expression, body language, diction and prosody, personality, emotional intent, natural motion, and indeed just about every definable human quality, are elusive challenges to computational depiction. Likewise, we have a long way to go on modelling natural materials in plausible physical environments. We have partitioned solutions into specific phenomena that do not easily interact with others. For example, we have cloth models, friction models for various surfaces, geometric and physical models of individual components of, say, the utensils on a kitchen table. And yet we cannot accurately simulate the magician's trick of balancing friction and inertia in pulling a virtual tablecloth from under plates and cutlery without tipping over or breaking them.

While we have made some practical progress in visual modelling, I will restate more starkly some of our shortcomings. We have no objective understanding of when an image or animation is "good" enough. We cannot define *natural* or *expressive* motion. We have few tools to create emotive animation. We have virtually no *a priori* error bounds on our computations. We cannot prescribe effective resource bounds such the running time of global illumination implementations. We presume that a bounded, finite set of samples will be sufficient for the signals we are trying to represent. We do not understand how to develop provably good sampling processes on non-rectangular manifolds (such as spheres or other interesting surfaces). Like the tablecloth analogy, we are unable to bind nontrivial models in one domain, such as fluid flow, to another, say a biomechanical model, to yet another, say light transport, to create a fully coupled model of hydrodynamically plausible swimming in which the motion of the water and the swimmer is exploited to inform and accelerate the light-transport solution. A huge amount of insight (to be distinguished from mere data) is available from one process, and yet we are unable to exploit those insights in coupled systems. This is a very small subset of the incompleteness of our models. Notice that the problems can be both mathematical and behavioural.

Let us begin with a basic question about realistic graphics.

Q1: Since artists and technologists have demonstrated that with sufficient effort virtually any phenomenon can be convincingly depicted, and virtually any narrative effectively told, do any scientific questions remain?

This is a fair question, since for practical purposes we could employ, as is done in movies or games, dozens of people to touch up an arbitrary number of pixels in an animation by hand if necessary to get the right look. But is visual modelling something to be done only by experts or those with big budgets? Lurking in here somewhere is an important scientific agenda of how to minimise the human effort needed to maximise the effectiveness of a visual narrative. The unsurprising answer to Q1 is that we have barely started asking the right scientific questions, let alone answer most of them. Rather than make a tool for the few as we once did, we should be more interested in ubiquity. Hence a refinement of Q1.

Q2: Can we make computational visual depiction sufficiently good, fast and ubiquitous to allow non-experts to express themselves visually as easily as in other media?

If the answer to Q1 is an emphatic yes, a positive answer to Q2 seems dubious. Although there are positive signs in the open-source movement, there is little positive evidence for Q2, and most attempts to allow non-experts to do realistic graphics have not gained traction. This is a serious problem. An archeologist wishing to visualise ancient ceramics, a paleontologist wanting to model a vanished hominid, an oncologist visualising a tumour, or someone wanting to put together an animation for his or her family, should not need to endure a long learning curve to achieve a specific task.

This dismal situation has emerged because the dominant application area of realistic computer graphics has been that of high-production value entertainment and industrial design, and most workflows have adapted to their high-touch content-generation pipelines. Note that I could make similar observations on other applications of computer-aided visual communication, such as scientific visualisation, information visualisation, and visual analytics. However, more usable tools are now emerging to support these applications. Realistic graphics is still making very small steps through the emergence of display software such as WebGL, new (often proprietary) games engines, and open versions of complex graphics systems. So far, very little is addressed to the novice user.

Q1 implicitly assumed a target of expert users who have a well developed visual sense. Like professional photographers, they are embedded in the culture and aesthetics of their craft, and they know when a creation is "good". While this is a slowly growing set of users, what of non-experts? Surely they are in the vast majority and may have interesting visual narratives to convey. Let us suppose we continue to include non-expert users with appropriate workflow constraints, and that our goal is to allow them to use realistic computer graphics to create effective, emotive visual communication. Q2 might then become a very long sentence with a scientific aim:

Q3: Is it possible to develop models that would allow anyone to create convincing graphical depictions, expending a level of effort that is commensurate with their expressive goals, as one would expect with other forms of communication such as playing a musical instrument at a novice level, singing a song, or writing a poem?

Science is about *possibility*, so this is an appropriate question. Leaving undefined terms like "convincing" and "commensurate", the answer to to Q3 in the short term is "no". Current computer-aided graphical tools require a learning curve that far exceeds, for example, that of learning to play a three-chord song on guitar, and their lack of integration with immersive virtual environments renders them almost useless to non-experts. I am, however, optimistic about the long term. Indeed, while expert photographers may disagree, it is fair to say that most of us take much better photographs than we were able to even a decade ago. Digital photography has achieved ubiquity, and new technologies have emerged to allow its users to become more expressive and tell more interesting stories with photographs. Realistic computer graphics has similar, as yet unrealised, potential. Geometry is all around us, and input techniques for this geometry are becoming commonplace, including range and time of flight scanners, photogrammetry, laser scanners, and structured light. Likewise new output devices such as 3D printers are making considerable inroads. One does get the feeling that we are on the verge of a new chapter in graphical computing, but I do worry that we are becoming a society of copiers, not creators.

Let us look forward and think about the new science and technology that we will need to achieve ubiquitous visual modelling. New ways of looking at the problem are required, since the reduction of complexity of creating visual models cannot be accomplished just by improving interfaces, workflows and input devices. This will simply give us more ways of making copies of more existing geometric and appearance models. We need insight into how to help fashion effective visual narratives.

We will need to expand our research agenda in three ways. First, we will need more precise and general mathematical models for visual phenomena. Second, we need a strong contribution of empiricism. Third, taking the first two into account, we need to develop systematic tools for constructing visual narratives. We will need to augment our traditional synthetic computational mathematical approaches with *observation*. I believe we will gain insight into "seeing is believing" by "looking at looking". Specifically, we should explore and characterise how people apprehend visual phenomena. The examples of the previous section led us to unanticipated models of visual processing. We should work with researchers in applied perception to create a more inclusive models. For example, we can employ high scan rate eye-tracking technology to gather data on how people scan emotional faces, bodies, human and animal motion, and complex imagery. Where do people look? How do they scan? How quickly? How often? The hope here is that by observing observers, we can both define better workflow for non-experts and create a bridge between phenomenology and the mathematical foundations of realistic depiction. This of course has been a tenet of human-computer interaction since its inception, and the fact that computer graphics forums chased away HCI and usability researchers (with the exception of the present forum), may well be one of the reasons for the difficulty of seeing past expert users.

I hypothesise that by calibrating how people scan synthetic and natural visual depictions in various domains we will add to our understanding of "good enough", from which I believe we we can develop better measures. Most of the mathematical models underlying realistic depiction have high computational complexity and thus in practice they must be approximated by simpler models. By employing systematic empirical methods, I believe we willll discover simpler models that are demonstrably "good enough". The idea of examining human behaviour and performance is certainly not new, but it is remarkably under-used in validation studies for realistic computer graphics. Empirical observation adds a new dimension to assessing human performance and capacity, and it will help us in areas that in which synthetic methods do not do particularly well.

Observation is only part of the battle. Advances in workflow, human factors and human-computer interaction, story-telling tools, script construction, speech synchronisation, and sound synthesis are also important components. I will let experts in these areas tackle these problems. That said, it is clear that, just as we must appeal to perception scientists to understand how people look at things, we need to work with artists to understand how people may express things.

Returning to mathematical aspects, we are faced ultimately with the immensely difficult problem of the computational complexity of computational reality: scale. Physical simulation is remarkably complex, and as we couple physical models, the computations will become more brittle. I can propose only a small first step toward the resolution of this immensely challenging problem: by defining a new problem! Consider a model replacement strategy based on the following question: when does a replacing something complicated by something simple give about the same result? More precisely, I will expand the notion of **R** that I mentioned earlier.

Model replacement. *Suppose we have a graphical representation S consisting of various geometric/volumetric models* **M**, *light sources* **L**, *camera attributes, etc., all a function of time. Let a rendering R map S into a rendered image I. Further suppose S′ is evolved from S with the replacement of, say, one model M_i in* **M** *by M_i'. Then under what conditions would a rendering $I = R(S)$ be the* same *as a rendering $I' = R(S')$?*

Here, M' could replace an object, a moving character, indeed any phenomenon we wish. Likewise we could replace light sources in **L** that may have the same visual effect. Each class of replacements is likely a field of study in itself. Notice as well that I did not write $I = I'$. I wrote the *same*, recognising that numerical equality might not be achievable or desirable. For example, we may find through perceptual studies that humans place a much higher precedence on the consistency of shadows than on geometric shadow accuracy. Systematically finding new replacement strategies of M' for M in different domains will require new techniques and it will be daunting. We will require models of models, since in some cases we may determine that small changes in a model M may be imperceptible (e.g., when M is travelling in shadow), but in other cases the opposite might be true (e.g., when M moves in or out of shadow). Again, this is not a new agenda: there is a large literature, for example, on heuristic pre-computation of images, reflectance, motion, etc., for synthetic computations. I am searching here for mathematically and empirically sound ways to carry out such replacements so that we can make some rigorous statements about their efficacy. Model replacement may derive from machine learning, or more likely from advances in perceptual studies indicate situations in which simpler models can stand in for complex ones. If successful, they will provide ways to accelerate realistic visual depictions and make them accessible to non-experts as well.

A "science of computational depiction" will thus consist of several interleaved modelling agendas: a synthetic agenda involving *a priori* mathematical models, an analytic agenda involving *a posteriori* observational models, and a behavioural agenda involving new workflow. After all this discussion, we have arrived at the most basic of starting points: computational depiction is a natural science, a mathematical science, a social science and a humanity. It is a cascade of interacting models and a work of imagination. It will be a pleasure to work alongside colleagues from many disciplines on our Sisyphean task!

ACKNOWLEDGEMENTS

My many students and colleagues have done an awful lot of the heavy lifting in "my" research; thank you one and all. I have been funded by various agencies, but the most consistent and crucial funding has been from the Natural Sciences and Engineering Research Council of Canada: starting with NSERC post-graduate scholarships, a post-doctoral fellowship, a University Research Fellowship, numerous Operating and Discovery Grants, and a Synergy Award. Thank you! More recently, funding from the GRAND NCE has been most welcome and is gratefully acknowledged.

REFERENCES

[1] E. Adelson. Perceptual organization and the judgment of brightness. *Science*, 262:2042–2044, 1993.

[2] C. Dahl, N. Logothetis, H. Bulthoff, and C. Wallraven. The Thatcher illusion in humans and monkeys. *Proc. R. Soc. B*, pages 1–10, 2010.

[3] E. Fiume. *The Mathematical Structure of Raster Graphics*. Academic Press Professional, Inc., San Diego, CA, USA, 1989.

[4] E. Fiume. Alain Fournier, 1943-2000: An appreciation. *ACM Trans. Graph.*, 19(4):243–245, Oct. 2000.

[5] G. Smith. Human color vision and the unsaturated blue color of the daytime sky. *American Journal of Physics*, 73(7):590–597, 2005.

[6] N. Tal-Or and Papirman. The fundamental attribution error in attributing fictional figures characteristics to the actors. *Media Pychology*, 9:331–345, 2007.

6

[7] P. Thompson. Margaret Thatcher: A new illusion. *Perception*, 9:483–484, 1980.

IMAGE CREDITS

1. Impossible figures: Derrick Coetzee, Wikimedia Commons, en.wikipedia.org/wiki/File:Impossible_objects.svg.

2. Image of Cleto, Italy: Eugene Fiume.

3. Fire and cigarette: Jos Stam.

4. Checkerboard and shadow illusion: Edward Adelson, by permission, web.mit.edu/persci/people/adelson/checkershadow_illusion.html.

5. Original Rembrandt image: Wikimedia Commons, en.wikipedia.org/wiki/File:The_Nightwatch_by_Rembrandt.jpg. Thresholded image: Eugene Fiume.

6. Faces, photo and treatments: Eugene Fiume.

7. Cotopaxi Volcano in blue sky, Lion Hirth, Wikimedia Commons, commons.wikimedia.org/wiki/File:Cotopaxi_blue_sky_2007.jpg

8. Spectral retinal sensitivity: Ben Rudiak-Gould, Wikimedia Commons, en.wikipedia.org/wiki/File:Cone-fundamentals-with-srgb-spectrum.png.

I place the images created by me in the public domain.

Task Efficient Contact Configurations for Arbitrary Virtual Creatures

Steve Tonneau*
IRISA

Julien Pettré†
Inria

Franck Multon‡
Univ. Rennes 2 - M2S
IRISA

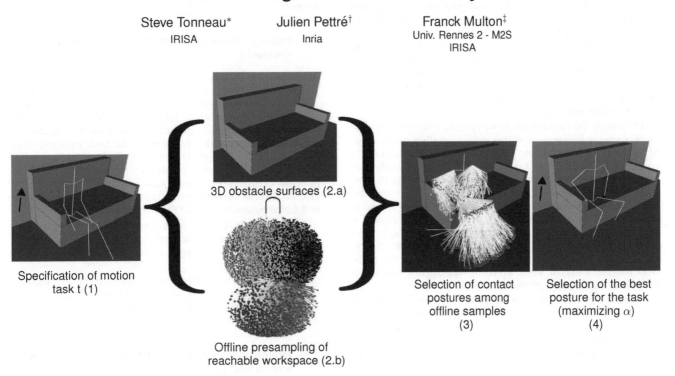

Figure 1: Online step request. Given the task of getting up (1), We transpose the samples from our database into the local environment (2), and select the configurations in contact with the environment (3). Among these candidates, we select the collision-free configurations that maximize the heuristic α (4). For clarity the creature and samples are shown in a wireframe form.

ABSTRACT

A common issue in three-dimensional animation is the creation of contacts between a virtual creature and the environment. Contacts allow force exertion, which produces motion. This paper addresses the problem of computing contact configurations allowing to perform motion tasks such as getting up from a sofa, pushing an object or climbing. We propose a two-step method to generate contact configurations suitable for such tasks. The first step is an offline sampling of the reachable workspace of a virtual creature. The second step is a run time request confronting the samples with the current environment. The best contact configurations are then selected according to a heuristic for task efficiency. The heuristic is inspired by the force transmission ratio. Given a contact configuration, it measures the potential force that can be exerted in a given direction. Our method is automatic and does not require examples or motion capture data. It is suitable for real time applications and applies to arbitrary creatures in arbitrary environments. Various scenarios (such as climbing, crawling, getting up, pushing or pulling objects) are used to demonstrate that our method enhances motion autonomy and interactivity in constrained environments.

Index Terms: I.3.7 [Computer Graphics]: Three-Dimensional

---

*stonneau@irisa.fr

†jpettre@inria.fr

‡fmulton@irisa.fr
Graphics Interface Conference 2014
7-9 May, Montreal, Quebec, Canada

Graphics and Realism—Animation

1 INTRODUCTION

Research in computer animation is motivated by the need to provide virtual creatures with an increased autonomy of motion in 3D environments. Such improvements allow to propose new forms of gameplay in video games, or to validate ergonomic designs.

In this work we are interested in the contacts created between a creature and the environment: contacts allow to efficiently exert the force necessary to perform motion tasks (such as getting up, climbing or pulling). For instance in Figure 9, several contacts are created between the end-effectors of a virtual insect and the books composing the environment.

Motion capture methods are inherently limited in such a constrained context: addressing various tasks and environments for different creatures requires the creation of prohibitively large motion databases. Therefore, a common approach is the decomposition of the motion into a sequence of contact configurations between a virtual creature and the environment. The notion of configuration is central in motion planning [11]. Such planners often use randomly generated configurations [29], and select those preserving static stability [10]. However, they lack heuristics to determine if those configurations are suited for the task in terms of force exertion. In the rest of the paper such configurations are called *task efficient*. Dynamic simulations use predefined configurations as inputs to motion controllers, but show little adaptation to the environment [37].

Thus, motion planners and dynamic controllers could benefit from a method to generate appropriate contact configurations. This is our problem statement, formalized in Section 3.

The key idea: The environment as a mean to exert a force
Contacts allow force exertion, which in turn produces the motion. Therefore to select a contact configuration, it is important to make sure it will allow to perform the task. For this reason we need heuristics to measure the compatibility of a contact configuration with a translational motion task. Examples of such tasks are pushing, pulling, standing up, or climbing. This set of motions is commonly needed by interactive simulations (such as videogames). They could benefit from our method to introduce more variety in the environments and interactions they propose. Rotational tasks will be addressed in future works.

To measure the task efficiency, we propose a heuristic inspired by the force transmission ratio [7]. It defines the efficiency of a configuration as the potential force it allows to exert in the direction of a translational task, as detailed in Section 3.4. It is traditionally used to optimize the configuration of a robotic arm, but requires to know in advance the future position of the end-effector. To overcome this issue, we combine our heuristic with a random sampling approach, independent from the environment (Section 4). The sampling is performed offline to ensure good performances. Then the samples are filtered online to select configurations in contact with the environment, and free of collisions. This approach is similar to the work introduced in [20], where a precomputed dynamic roadmap is updated as the environment changes.

Therefore the contribution of this paper is a method for the real time, automated computation of task efficient contact configurations for arbitrary creatures. As shown in Section 5, it can be applied to various motions tasks in arbitrary environments. We discuss the limitations of our method, potential applications and future works in Section 6.

2 RELATED WORK

The issue of creating contact configurations has been addressed in different ways: Example-based methods use motion clips as references for motion (Section 2.1); Biomechanical and robotical approaches define relevant contact configurations by quantifying them in terms of force exertion (Section 2.2); Motion planning and optimization methods focus on contact configurations that preserve balance (Section 2.3).

2.1 Example-based methods for constrained environments

To improve the natural aspect of an animation, a common method consists in using motion clips, either created by an artist or obtained through motion capture. Effective methods exist to adapt those clips to the constraints of the environment such as external force pressure [9] or locomotion on uneven terrain [18, 27]. Similarly foot-step planning techniques proposed hybrid approaches to address this issue [8, 22].

Motion graphs [23, 25] or precomputed search trees [24] can be used for acyclic motions, and be adapted for contact interaction in constrained environments.

Other methods address acyclic motions such as reaching and manipulating tasks [35, 21], or close contact interaction motions [16].

However, methods based on motion capture do not easily apply to arbitrary virtual creatures.

Another drawback is that although motion adaptation is possible (for instance through inverse kinematics), the adaptation of a motion clip is limited to a motion including the same end-effectors in contact. This is problematic when the environment differs too much from the one used in the reference motion. To provide such methods with rich contact interactions for complex environments would require to be able to produce the animations corresponding to each possible interaction and appropriately choose between them at run time.

Conversely the generality of our method covers a large set of tasks, applies to any kind of virtual creature and adapts to the environment.

2.2 Inverse kinematics and manipulability for virtual creatures

The issue of optimizing a contact configuration for a task has been widely studied. Inverse kinematics methods exploit the redundancy of kinematic trees to optimize secondary objectives [2]. Yoshikawa presented the manipulability measure for quantifying the ability of robotic mechanisms in positioning and orienting end-effectors [38]. Based on this work, Chiu proposed the force transmission ratio, another index for optimizing a manipulator pose relatively to a specific task [7]. Several manipulability-based methods have since been proposed to either optimize a configuration [31] or a trajectory [13, 33]. Recent works in biomechanics tend to show the relevance of the manipulability measure for human beings [17].

Those methods require *a priori* knowledge of the target that an end-effector must reach. They only solve half of our problem because we need to know where a contact must be created to find a suitable configuration.

Conversely, our method extends the force transmission ratio and uses it along with a random sampling approach. This allows us to address simultaneously the issues of finding a contact position and a task efficient configuration.

2.3 Motion planning and optimization for constrained environments

The advantage of procedural methods over example-based ones is that they are not limited by a motion database. Recently Wampler et al. proposed a method to automatically synthesize gaited motion for arbitrary creatures [34].

Contact interactions have been considered for grasping tasks [36, 12], or for motion planning problems. Hauser et al. introduced the *Contact before motion* approach [15], used in several other contributions [19, 10, 3]. A common drawback of this approach is that it requires prior discretization of possible contact positions in the environment. Also, task efficiency is not always considered in the process of finding contact configurations.

In the continuity of those works, Mordatch et al. proposed the Contact-Invariant Optimization (CIO) term [30]: contact positions and trajectory are planned simultaneously in the same optimization loop. Along the process, an end-effector is guided towards the nearest surface satisfying dynamic constraints. Al Borno et al. proposed a full-body trajectory optimization method that does not require explicit contact definition, but still requires to specify with which obstacle an effector should be in contact [1].

However, to get up from a chair in the environment shown in Figure 5, a human would more likely put his hand on the table than on the chair, even if the table is farther away. Those methods cannot achieve this without requiring the user to explicitly define the table as an input of the problem (Figure 5). Another drawback of those approaches is that, as for other planning methods, the computation time is too long for interactive simulations.

Other contributions in robotics have considered the quality of the contact configurations in their approach [14]. In particular Bretl et al. proposed a heuristic similar to the manipulability measure as a criteria for contact creation [4].

Our method lies in the continuity of these procedural approaches. It does not address the planning issue, rather the problems of automatically finding better task efficient contact positions and configurations, while offering more flexibility than example-based methods [6].

3 PROBLEM STATEMENT

In this section we give several mathematical definitions to formulate our issue: How to rapidly compute a limb contact configuration, efficient for performing a given task? Figure 2 provides an illustration for such definitions.

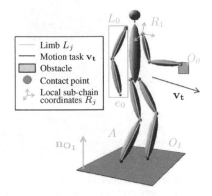

Figure 2: Virtual human composed of 4 limbs. 3 end-effectors are in contact with 2 obstacles.

3.1 Kinematic representation of a virtual creature.

A virtual creature is described by a kinematic structure A, with m end-effectors. We decompose A to treat each limb separately.

Definition of a limb. A limb $L_j, 0 \leq j \leq m - 1$ is a kinematic sub-chain of A, comprising n rotational joints, and exactly one end-effector e_j (Figure 2 – blue rectangle). R_j denotes the 4×4 transformation matrix attached to L_j's root joint.

Limb configuration. A configuration Θ_j is a set of n angle values for each joint of the limb L_j. $p(\Theta_j) = \begin{pmatrix} x_j & y_j & z_j \end{pmatrix}^T$ gives the position of the end-effector e_j for the configuration Θ_j, in world coordinates.

Jacobian matrix of a configuration. $J(\Theta_j)$ is the $3 * n$ Jacobian matrix of L_j in the configuration Θ_j. $J(\Theta_j)^T$ is its transposed matrix. If $\theta^i, i = 1...n$ are the joint values of the configuration Θ then the Jacobian is defined as follows (the $_j$ indices are removed for clarity):

$$J(\Theta) = \begin{pmatrix} \frac{\partial x}{\partial \theta^1} & \cdots & \frac{\partial x}{\partial \theta^n} \\ \frac{\partial y}{\partial \theta^1} & \cdots & \frac{\partial y}{\partial \theta^n} \\ \frac{\partial z}{\partial \theta^1} & \cdots & \frac{\partial z}{\partial \theta^n} \end{pmatrix} \quad (1)$$

$J(\Theta_j)$ is computed using the method given in [5]. We also define $J_p(\Theta_j) = J(\Theta_j) * J(\Theta_j)^T$ as the product of the jacobian by its transpose; We call sample a the triplet $< p(\Theta_j), \Theta_j, Jp(\Theta_j) >$.

3.2 Environment and contact interactions

The virtual creature moves in an environment W. W is composed of obstacles with which the creature interacts.

The environment as a set of obstacles. An obstacle is a planar surface $O \in W$ defined in the 3-dimensional Euclidian space (orange surfaces in Figure 2). This definition of an obstacle is not restrictive since any complex three-dimensional object can be decomposed into a set of obstacles. $\mathbf{n_O}$ is the obstacle normal unit vector (orange arrow in Figure 2).

Contact between a limb and the environment. We say that a configuration Θ_j is in contact regarding an obstacle set $E \subset W$ if

$$\exists O \in E, D(x_O, p(\Theta_j)) < \epsilon$$

where: x_O is the orthogonal projection of $p(\Theta_j)$ onto the obstacle O; D returns the Euclidian distance between two points; $\epsilon \in \mathbb{R}$ is small (red cylinders in Figure 2).

3.3 Objective formulation

The motion task is expressed as a **unit** vector $\mathbf{v_t} \in \mathbb{R}^3$, expressed in R_j coordinates (black arrow in Figure 2) for a limb L_j. $\mathbf{v_t}$ expresses a translational motion task for the root of the creature. Rotational tasks are not discussed in this work.

Task efficient configuration. We want to compute a configuration Θ_j with the three following properties: Θ_j is in contact with an obstacle O_i of W; Θ_j is collision-free (no interpenetration) and does not violate eventual joint limits; Θ_j is suitable for the task $\mathbf{v_t}$, according to a heuristic α that must be provided. Computation time should be compatible with real time interactive simulations.

3.4 A heuristic for task efficient contact configurations

We want a heuristic α to answer the following question: How appropriate is a configuration Θ_j regarding $\mathbf{v_t}$? We make the hypothesis that for a subset of the possible motions, $\mathbf{v_t}$ will be satisfied more easily if the end-effector can exert a high force in the direction of $\mathbf{v_t}$. This makes sense for the tasks we are addressing, such as pushing a cupboard, which might require an important effort. We propose to use that potential force as a heuristic for task compatibility. Previous works in robotics [7] showed that this potential force can be quantified by computing, for a given configuration, the force transmission ratio f_T regarding $\mathbf{v_t}$:

$$f_T(\Theta_j, \mathbf{v_t}) = [\mathbf{v_t}^T(J(\Theta_j)J(\Theta_j)^T)\mathbf{v_t}]^{-\frac{1}{2}} \quad (2)$$

The force manipulability ellipsoid provides an intuitive representation of the different values taken by the force transmission ratio, as shown in Figure 3 [38]. The value $f_T(\Theta_j, \mathbf{v_t})$ corresponds to the length of the ellipsoid in the direction $\mathbf{v_t}$. According to f_T in those two examples it appears that the lower obstacle is more suited for a horizontal task, when the upper obstacle is more suited for a vertical task.

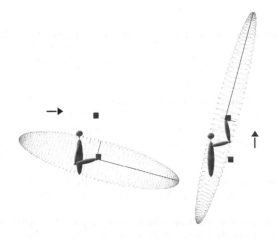

Figure 3: The force manipulability ellipsoid for two different configurations. A longer axis means that a more important force can be exerted in the direction of the axis.

We extend the force transmission ratio to use it as a heuristic for contact location. We consider that Θ_j is in contact with an obstacle

O_i. We weigh f_T with the dot product between the task $\mathbf{v_t}$ and the normal $\mathbf{n_{Oi}}$ of O_i.

$$\alpha(\Theta_j, \mathbf{v_t}) = f_T(\Theta_j, \mathbf{v_t})\mathbf{v_t} \cdot \mathbf{n_{Oi}} \qquad (3)$$

If we maximize α, obstacles with normals collinear to the motion task will be advantaged for contact creation. This is coherent with our problem because it verifies that force exertion is actually applied against the obstacle, as shown in Figure 5.

Also, we can see that α can take negative values. This is interesting especially for pushing and pulling tasks, as shown in Section 5.2.

In the results shown in this paper α is the only heuristic used. Its integration with other heuristics is discussed in Section 6.

With our new heuristic α and those definitions in mind we can describe our contribution.

4 COMPUTATION OF TASK EFFICIENT CONTACT CONFIGURATIONS

The definitions given in Section 3 allow us to describe our method in mathematical terms. Our contribution lies in the proposition of a method to generate and compare contact configurations according to a motion task. For efficiency reasons, the algorithm is decomposed in two steps:

Offline sampling step. The first step is independent from the environment. A large set of arbitrary configurations Q_j is randomly generated for each limb L_j (Figure 4). Precomputation is made for each configuration to accelerate run time performance.

Online request step. The second step consists in a request performed on the configuration set Q_j. The configurations that, in the current situation, are in contact with the environment W, will be selected as potential solutions. Among those we select the configuration for which our heuristic α gives the highest score (Figure 1).

4.1 Offline generation of random limb configurations

This step is independent from the environment, and thus only has to be run once for each limb L_j composing our creature A. Figure 4 illustrates the sample configuration generation process. As inputs, we take a number of samples N and a limb L_j. We fill a sample container Q_j with the sample configurations of L_j by repeating N times four steps:

Random generation of a configuration Θ_j (Figure 4 – middle left). This is done by independently generating a random angle value for each joint of L_j, comprised between the joint boundary limits.

Computation of the jacobian product $Jp(\Theta_j)$. The jacobian matrix $J(\Theta_j)$ is computed and multiplied by its transpose $J(\Theta_j)^T$ to obtain $Jp(\Theta_j)$. $Jp(\Theta_j)$ is needed for the run time computation of the extended force transmission ratio α. Storing it reduces the online computation of α to two simple matrix products.

Computation of $p(\Theta_j)$ (Figure 4 – middle left). The end-effector position $p(\Theta_j)$ is expressed in the limb coordinates R_j.

Insertion of the resulting sample in Q_j (Figure 4 – right). We create the sample denoted by the triplet $< p(\Theta_j), \Theta_j, Jp(\Theta_j) >$, and store it into the sample container Q_j.

As stated earlier, the generation of sample configurations has to be performed for every limb composing our creature A. For instance, for a virtual human, we would end up with four sample containers (one for each arm, and one for each leg). We cannot use

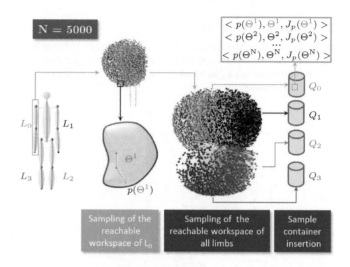

Figure 4: Illustration of the environment-independent offline sampling for $N = 5000$, for the right arm first, then for all the limbs. A sample container is created for each limb. An entry contains a configuration Θ, and its jacobian product J_p. Entries are indexed by the end-effector position $p(\Theta)$. For clarity the samples are shown in a wireframe form.

a single tree for both arms because the joint limits differ symmetrically in our model.

The appropriate value for N is discussed Section 5.4. The sampling method is discussed in Section 6.

4.2 Online computation of task efficient contact configurations

We consider the motion task $\mathbf{v_t}$ –Figure 1 (1): *the black arrow indicates the task of getting up*–. To find a contact configuration for a limb L_j that is efficient for $\mathbf{v_t}$, we proceed in four steps:

Identification of the reachable obstacles. We retrieve the obstacle set $E \subset W$ of obstacles potentially reachable by the limb L_j –Figure 1 (2.a): *the sofa, the ground and the wall*–.

Selection of the samples in contact. We request Q_j for all the samples that are in contact with an obstacle of E –*Figure 1 (2.b)*–. The result of the query is a list of limb configurations $Q_j^{contact} \subset Q_j$ –Figure 1 (3): *Selection of configurations in contact with the sofa and the ground*–.

Ordering of the candidate samples. We sort the samples of $Q_j^{contact}$ using our heuristic $\alpha(\Theta_j, \mathbf{v_t})$. This means that the first sample of $Q_j^{contact}$, that we call Θ_j^{max}, verifies:

$$\forall \Theta_j \in Q_j^{contact}, \alpha(\Theta_j, \mathbf{v_t}) <= \alpha(\Theta_j^{max}, \mathbf{v_t}).$$

This is the configuration that is the most appropriate for the task regarding the extended force transmission ratio.

Selection of the best collision-free sample. We perform a collision check between the environment and Θ_j^{max}. If Θ_j^{max} is free of collision, it is returned as the solution configuration. Otherwise, we keep iterating through the sorted configurations of $Q_j^{contact}$ until we find a configuration free of collisions. If all the configurations of $Q_j^{contact}$ are colliding, no configuration is returned –Figure 1 (4): *our method places the right hand on the armchair, both feet on the ground, close to the root, and the left hand on the sofa*–.

By decomposing our method into an offline and an online step, we are able to generate task efficient configurations within time limits acceptable for real time applications. Both steps are automatic and do not require manual editing.

5 RESULTS

We designed several scenarios to demonstrate the benefits of our method, through the variety of creatures and environments that were designed. In this section we give implementation details on those scenarios. We then detail each scenario and comment the results obtained. The section is concluded with a performance analysis.

5.1 Implementation details

In order to allow for a fast and efficient search among the configurations, we implemented Q_j as an octree data structure that offers support for spatial queries. The position of the end-effector $p(\Theta_j)$ is used as an index in Q_j.

The test application was developed using the C++ language. One limitation of our current implementation is that collision checks are only tested against the environment and not between limbs. This is not a limitation of the method and will be corrected in future work.

Environments are described in the obj format, while virtual creatures and scenarios are described using custom xml files. Rendering is achieved using the OpenGl API. No other third-party libraries were used. We performed the runs on a laptop with an Intel Core i7-2760QM 2.40GHz processor and 4 GB of memory. The application is not multi-threaded.

5.2 Test scenarios

We consider a virtual creature in a constrained environment. Six coordinates describe the position and orientation of its root. By default the chosen initial limb configuration is the reference posture of the creature (as shown for instance in Figure 6). We consider a directional task, and one or several limbs of the creature. We then use our method to compute a task efficient contact configuration. Each scenario is also illustrated in the companion video.

Standing up (Figure 1 and Figure 5 – right). The environment is composed of a sofa, or a chair and a table. The creature is a virtual human (Figure 2). In the initial configuration the human is sitting on a sofa or a chair. We formulate the task of getting up as a vertical vector. These examples show the adaptability of our method: the same task in different environments results in different configurations that take advantage of it.

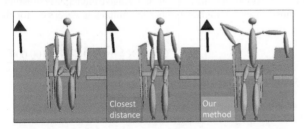

Figure 5: Our method (right) is compared with the closest distance heuristic (middle) in this example of getting up from a chair. In the latter case, the left hand position (on the side of the table) is not suitable to generate a vertical effort.

Multi-limb creatures in constrained environments (video). The environment is composed of a challenging set of books placed on a bookshelf. The creature is an insect with six limbs (Figure 6). The input is a forward directional task. This example shows that our method is generic and can be applied to arbitrary creatures, as opposed to example-based approaches.

Figure 6: An insect composed of 6 limbs. Each limb is composed of 5 degrees of freedom.

Pushing and pulling objects (Figure 7 and Figure 8 – right). The environment is composed of a cupboard and the ground. In variations of the scenario it is also composed of a rope attached to the cupboard, and a small wall. The creature is a virtual human. The task consists in pulling (pushing) the cupboard. We formulate the task as a horizontal vector, and compute task efficient configurations for the arms and the left leg of the human. The right foot is already in contact. To push objects it is preferable to create contacts on surface the normals of which are opposite to the pushing direction. Therefore in this case we use a different heuristic $\alpha_{push}(\Theta_j, \mathbf{v_t}) = -\alpha(\Theta_j, \mathbf{v_t})$. These examples show that our method can be applied to pushing and pulling tasks, enhancing the autonomy of motion of our virtual characters.

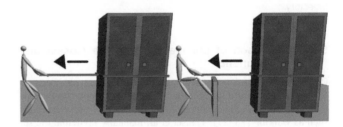

Figure 7: Configurations found for a pulling task. In the right figure, our creature uses the pink wall as a better support for the foot. The asymmetry between the arm configurations is induced by the sampling phase.

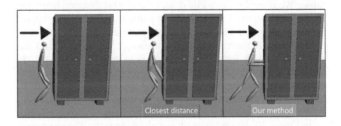

Figure 8: Our method (right) is compared with the closest distance heuristic (middle) in this example of pushing a cupboard. The closest distance heuristic places the hands and left feet at locations close to their original positions (left) while our method places the end-effectors in configurations relevant for the pushing task.

Computation of a sequence of task efficient contact configurations (Figure 9 + climbing example in video). A virtual creature is set in an environment in its reference configuration. Given a trajectory for the creature root, we use our method to compute a configuration sequence along the trajectory. The first configuration computed is given as an input to compute the second one, and so on. These examples show how a simulation can interact with our method to obtain target configurations and eventually synthesize motion.

Figure 9: Configuration sequence for an insect with 6 limbs crossing a bookshelf. Task efficient contact configurations are found along the trajectory.

5.3 Comparison of our method with the closest distance heuristic

Comparing the results obtained by our method is not trivial because few methods perform the real time automatic computation of contacts: Several previous contributions only address cyclic motions such as walking [18, 27]. Hauser et al. manually predefine the set of possible contacts [15]. Bretl et al. use a form of manipulability integrated in a motion planner [4]. Mordatch et al. use a closest distance approach as part of an optimization loop that takes several minutes to compute a result [30]. Therefore we choose to compare the results we obtained with this closest distance heuristic.

In Figure 5 the environment consists of a chair, the ground and a table. We compare our method with the closest distance heuristic. The configuration of the left arm in particular seems more appropriate to generate a vertical effort with our method.

In Figure 8 the environment consists of a cupboard and the ground. The task for a virtual human is to push the cupboard. In the middle we can see that the results provided by the closest distance heuristic are highly determined by the original location of the end-effectors. Our method, on the other hand, creates contact configurations relevant for the pushing task.

In Figure 10 the environment is a climbing wall. The creature is a virtual human (Figure 2). The initial configuration is the reference posture (Figure 10 – right – middle). The task consists in navigating along the wall in arbitrary directions. This example shows the advantage of our method over heuristics such as the closest distance, because the selected configurations vary according to the motion task.

5.4 Performances

Three parameters play a role in the performances offered by our method: the number N of samples generated during the offline step, the number of obstacles reachable by the limb when the method

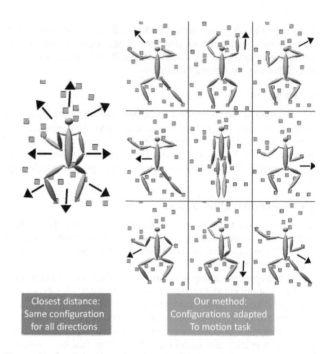

Figure 10: Configurations for a humanoid on a climbing wall. Left: the closest distance heuristic does not consider the motion task, therefore it always computes the same configuration. Right: From the same initial root location (position and orientation), different configurations are computed depending on the task (black arrow).

is called at run time, and the number m of limbs composing our creatures.

We only have control over the number of samples N, so we focus on this variable. We are interested in finding a value for N that will be as low as possible while maintaining an acceptable quality in the results obtained.

We have observed that in our scenarios, the number of samples N has a limited influence on the average maximum value of α. Therefore the main variables of interest are the number N of samples generated and the number of candidate configurations found consequently. Table 1 shows the time spent for one call to our method. Table 2 presents the average number of contact candidates returned by a spatial request.

Except for the climbing scenario, the computation time is short for $N \leq 10000$, and the number of average candidates is satisfying in those cases. A higher number of samples is necessary for the

	N = 1 000	N = 10 000	N = 100 000
Climbing	**1** (3)	**2** (6)	**3** (30)
Getting up	**4** (7)	**5** (60)	**154** (856)
Insect locomotion	**1** (4)	**8** (40)	**55** (370)
Pushing / pulling	**1** (1)	**5** (6)	**34** (70)

Table 1: **Average time** (worst time) (in ms) spent for a call to our method relative to the scenario and the number of samples N.

	N = 1 000	N = 10 000	N = 100 000
Climbing	0	1	26
Getting up	41	49	3442
Insect locomotion	20	312	2553
Pushing / pulling	13	142	1387

Table 2: Average number of contact configurations found relative to the scenario and the number of samples N.

climbing scenario. This is because the environment is composed of a small set of small obstacles.

Looking at the worst performances, we observe a correlation between the time spent in the method and the maximum number of hits obtained. This is explained by the growing number of requests that must be made. For the getting up scenario for instance, setting $N = 1000$ is a reasonable choice, where a value of $N = 100000$ seems more appropriate in the climbing scenario. This can be explained by the limited range of motion of the insect limbs, so that a smaller amount of samples is necessary to cover correctly the reachable workspace of the limb.

Under the appropriate conditions on the number of samples, we observed that the framerate never went below 52 fps even in the worst case scenarios.

Finally, we observe that the memory occupation grows linearly with the number of samples, and remains in reasonable ranges (from 2 MB for 10 000 samples to 166 MB for 1 000 000 samples).

6 DISCUSSION

In this section we review the main limitations of our method and future work, before concluding.

6.1 Limitations

The method is not probabilistically complete. The method generates N samples offline used as inputs for the contact queries. Due to this approach, the method is not probabilistically complete. Maintaining this property would involve performing regularly new sampling steps at run time. We choose to lose this property in favor of real time performance.

The method does not integrate dynamic constraints. The method assumes a non-dynamic environment. For instance linear and angular velocities are not taken into account, nor are gravity and balance. To extend the method to a wider range of motions, additional efforts will be necessary to integrate those parameters. This would make it possible to predict the future positions of moving objects and create contacts with them.

However, we believe that even though our method does not integrate physical parameters yet, interactive applications such as video games can already benefit from it, in a way similar to the locomotion system proposed in [18].

Performance issues. As the complexity of the environment rises, performance can become an issue because of the important number of requests that must be run. Fortunately, as seen in Section 5.4 it is possible to adjust the number of samples N to reduce the number of requests. However, if there are too many obstacles a trade-off between accuracy and abstraction of the environment should be found to maintain a reactive simulation.

6.2 Future work

Our next step is to integrate the method within existing solutions to farther demonstrate its interest. We are also working on several improvements on the method itself.

Dynamic simulation integration. The method can be integrated within an existing physical animation framework, as a complementary tool used only to handle constrained situations. In open situations classical controllers could still be used in this hybrid system. To automatically determine if the local environment is too constrained for a classical approach, we could use a measure such as the one suggested by [32].

Motion planner integration. Offline motion planners can benefit from the method to avoid the manual description of potential contact points. They can also use it as an additional term

to an optimization problem, allowing better results in terms of task compatibility at a small cost.

Global posture computation. As of today, in our method the motion task is the same for every limb. However, designing a high level controller to decompose a global motion task into subtasks for each limb would allow us to obtain more accurate results.

Also, currently we do not integrate the fact that actuating several limbs at the same time could result in undesired torques on the body in the case of a dynamic simulation. Therefore we want to combine the method with a complementary global posture optimization technique [28]. Doing this would allow us to optimize the whole body according to the computed limb configurations, and produce more natural results.

Validating the extended force transmission ratio. The method uses the extended force transmission ratio, based on the manipulability measure. A biomechanical study showed that it is effectively optimized by humans performing grasping tasks with their upper limbs [17]. However, this cannot be demonstrated for all the possible motion tasks, or for non human morphologies. We would like to experimentally validate the application of our heuristic to arbitrary limbs. To do so we intend to conduct a perception study to determine if the results produced by our method are perceived as natural by users.

We also want to improve the heuristic. Several options exist: Treating rotational efforts would allow us to address a larger number of tasks; We would also like to integrate more complex contact and friction models; Lastly, combining the method with other classic ones such as dynamic balance will allow us to obtain more natural results.

A smarter sampling step. The configuration samples of a limb are generated randomly in its reachable workspace. Uniform sampling did not allow us to obtain better results. As explained in Section 5, reducing the number of samples could be interesting for performance. If the task is known, a possible improvement is to design a "task-oriented" sampling that would generate more samples around configurations known to be "good" for a task, in a way similar to [26]. This would probably reduce the number of samples necessary because it would limit the generation of samples in uninteresting areas.

6.3 Conclusion

In this paper we introduced a method to compute task efficient contact configurations for arbitrary creatures in 3D environments. It combines a sampling approach with a heuristic to evaluate the relevance of a configuration for a task. The sampling step is performed offline for enhancing performance, is automatic and independent from the environment. The method is designed to provide contact configurations to motion planners and animation frameworks. It is suitable for real time applications.

Experimental results show that the method can successfully address a large variety of tasks in various constrained environments. Thus it enhances the autonomy of motion and the interactivity proposed by simulations.

Future work will focus on integrating the method within existing frameworks.

ACKNOWLEDGEMENTS

The authors wish to thank Fabrice Lamarche for his help on the octree implementation.

REFERENCES

[1] M. Al Borno, M. de Lasa, and A. Hertzmann. Trajectory Optimization for Full-Body Movements with Complex Contacts. *IEEE transactions on visualization and computer graphics*, pages 1–11, Dec. 2012.

[2] P. Baerlocher and R. Boulic. An inverse kinematics architecture enforcing an arbitrary number of strict priority levels. *The Visual Computer*, 20(6), June 2004.

[3] K. Bouyarmane and A. Kheddar. Multi-Contact Stances Planning for Multiple Agents. In *ICRA'11: International Conference on Robotics and Automation*, pages 5353–5546, Shanghai International Conference Center, Shanghai, Chine, 2011.

[4] T. Bretl, S. Rock, J.-C. Latombe, B. Kennedy, and H. Aghazarian. Free-climbing with a multi-use robot. In M. H. A. Jr. and O. Khatib, editors, *ISER*, volume 21 of *Springer Tracts in Advanced Robotics*, pages 449–458. Springer, 2004.

[5] S. R. Buss. Introduction to Inverse Kinematics with Jacobian Transpose , Pseudoinverse and Damped Least Squares methods. pages 1–19, 2009.

[6] A. J. Champandard. Procedural Characters and the Coming Animation Technology Revolution. *http://aigamedev.com/open/editorial/animation-revolution/*, 2012.

[7] S. Chiu. Control of redundant manipulators for task compatibility. In *Robotics and Automation. Proceedings. 1987 IEEE International Conference on*, volume 4, pages 1718–1724, 1987.

[8] M. G. Choi, J. Lee, and S. Y. Shin. Planning biped locomotion using motion capture data and probabilistic roadmaps. *ACM Transactions on Graphics*, 22(2):182–203, 2003.

[9] S. Coros, A. Karpathy, B. Jones, L. Reveret, and M. van de Panne. Locomotion Skills for Simulated Quadrupeds. *ACM Transactions on Graphics*, 30(4):Article TBD, 2011.

[10] A. Escande, A. Kheddar, S. Miossec, and S. Garsault. Planning Support Contact-Points for Acyclic Motions and Experiments on HRP-2. In O. Khatib, V. Kumar, and G. J. Pappas, editors, *ISER*, volume 54 of *Springer Tracts in Advanced Robotics*, pages 293–302. Springer, 2008.

[11] C. Esteves, G. Arechavaleta, J. Pettré, and J.-P. Laumond. Animation planning for virtual characters cooperation. *ACM Transactions on Graphics*, 25(2):319–339, 2006.

[12] C. Goldfeder, M. Ciocarlie, H. Dang, and P. Allen. The columbia grasp database. In *Robotics and Automation, 2009. ICRA '09. IEEE International Conference on*, pages 1710–1716, May 2009.

[13] L. Guilamo, J. Kuffner, K. Nishiwaki, and S. Kagami. Manipulability optimization for trajectory generation. In *Robotics and Automation, 2006. ICRA 2006. Proceedings 2006 IEEE International Conference on*, pages 2017–2022, 2006.

[14] K. Hauser, T. Bretl, K. Harada, and J.-C. Latombe. Using motion primitives in probabilistic sample-based planning for humanoid robots. In S. Akella, N. M. Amato, W. H. Huang, and B. Mishra, editors, *WAFR*, volume 47 of *Springer Tracts in Advanced Robotics*, pages 507–522. Springer, 2006.

[15] K. Hauser, T. Bretl, and J.-C. Latombe. Non-gaited humanoid locomotion planning. In *Humanoid Robots, 2005 5th IEEE-RAS International Conference on*, pages 7–12, 2005.

[16] E. S. Ho and T. Komura. Indexing and retrieving motions of characters in close contact. *IEEE Transactions on Visualization and Computer Graphics*, 15(3):481–492, 2009.

[17] J. Jacquier-Bret, P. Gorce, and N. Rezzoug. The manipulability: a new index for quantifying movement capacities of upper extremity. *Ergonomics*, 55(1):69–77, Jan. 2012.

[18] R. S. Johansen. *Automated Semi-procedural Animation for Character Locomotion*. Aarhus Universitet, Institut for Informations Medievidenskab, 2009.

[19] M. Kalisiak and M. van de Panne. A grasp-based motion planning algorithm for character animation. *The Journal of Visualization and Computer Animation*, 12(3):117–129, July 2001.

[20] M. Kallman and M. Mataric. Motion planning using dynamic roadmaps. In *Robotics and Automation, 2004. Proceedings. ICRA '04. 2004 IEEE International Conference on*, volume 5, pages 4399–4404 Vol.5, April 2004.

[21] M. Kallmann, A. Aubel, T. Abaci, and D. Thalmann. Planning Collision-Free Reaching Motions for Interactive Object Manipulation and Grasping. *Computer graphics Forum (Proceedings of Eurographics'03)*, 22(3):313–322, 2003.

[22] O. Kanoun, J.-P. Laumond, and E. Yoshida. Planning foot placements for a humanoid robot: A problem of inverse kinematics. *Int. J. Rob. Res.*, 30(4):476–485, Apr. 2011.

[23] L. Kovar, M. Gleicher, and F. Pighin. Motion graphs. In *ACM Transactions on Graphics*, volume 21, pages 473–482, New York, NY, USA, 2002. ACM.

[24] M. Lau and J. J. Kuffner. Precomputed search trees: planning for interactive goal-driven animation. In *Symposium on Computer Animation*, pages 299–308, 2006.

[25] J. Lee and K. H. Lee. Precomputing avatar behavior from human motion data. In *Proceedings of the 2004 ACM SIGGRAPH/Eurographics Symposium on Computer Animation*, SCA '04, pages 79–87, Aire-la-Ville, Switzerland, Switzerland, 2004. Eurographics Association.

[26] P. Leven and S. Hutchinson. Using manipulability to bias sampling during the construction of probabilistic roadmaps. *Robotics and Automation, IEEE Transactions on*, 19(6):1020–1026, Dec 2003.

[27] S. Levine and J. Popovic. Physically Plausible Simulation for Character Animation. In *Symposium on Computer Animation*, pages 221–230, 2012.

[28] M. Liu, A. Micaelli, P. Evrard, and A. Escande. Task-driven posture optimization for virtual characters. In *Proceedings of the ACM SIG-GRAPH/Eurographics Symposium on Computer Animation*, SCA '12, pages 155–164, Aire-la-Ville, Switzerland, Switzerland, 2012. Eurographics Association.

[29] T. Lozano-perez. Spatial Planning : A Configuration Space Approach. c(2), 1983.

[30] I. Mordatch, E. Todorov, and Z. Popović. Discovery of complex behaviors through contact-invariant optimization. *ACM Transactions on Graphics*, 31(4):43:1—-43:8, 2012.

[31] N. Naksuk and C. S. G. Lee. Zero moment point manipulability ellipsoid. In *ICRA 2006 Proceedings*, pages 1970–1975, 2006.

[32] J. Pan, L. Zhang, M. C. Lin, and D. Manocha. A hybrid approach for simulating human motion in constrained environments. *Computer Animation and Virtual Worlds*, 2010.

[33] B. Siciliano, L. Sciavicco, L. Villani, and G. Oriolo. *Robotics: Modelling, Planning and Control*. Springer Publishing Company, Incorporated, 1st edition, 2008.

[34] K. Wampler, J. Popović, and Z. Popović. Animal Locomotion Controllers From Scratch. *Computer Graphics Forum*, 32:153–162, May 2013.

[35] K. Yamane, J. Kuffner, and J. K. Hodgins. Synthesizing Animations of Human Manipulation Tasks. *ACM Trans. on Graphics (Proc. SIGGRAPH 2004)*, 2004.

[36] Y. Ye and C. K. Liu. Synthesis of detailed hand manipulations using contact sampling. *ACM Transactions on Graphics*, 31(4):1–10, 2012.

[37] K. Yin, K. Loken, and M. van de Panne. Simbicon: Simple biped locomotion control. *ACM Transactions on Graphics*, 26(3):Article 105, 2007.

[38] T. Yoshikawa. Analysis and Control of Robotics Manipulators with Redundancy, 1984.

Seamless Adaptivity of Elastic Models

Maxime Tournier
INRIA
LIRMM-CNRS
Université Montpellier 2

Matthieu Nesme
INRIA
LJK-CNRS
Université de Grenoble

Francois Faure
INRIA
LJK-CNRS
Université de Grenoble

Benjamin Gilles
INRIA
LIRMM-CNRS
Université Montpellier 2

(a) Rest state   (b) Compressing   (c) Equilibrium   (d) Decompressing

Figure 1: Deformable Christmas tree with adaptive velocity field. (1a): One frame is sufficient in steady state. (1b): When ornaments are attached, additional frames are activated to allow deformation. (1c): The velocity field can be simplified again when the equilibrium is reached. Note that our method can simplify locally deformed regions. (1d): Once the branches are released, the velocity field is refined again to allow the branches to recover their initial shape.

ABSTRACT

A new adaptive model for viscoelastic solids is presented. Unlike previous approaches, it allows seamless transitions, and simplifications in deformed states. The deformation field is generated by a set of physically animated frames. Starting from a fine set of frames and mechanical energy integration points, the model can be coarsened by attaching frames to others, and merging integration points. Since frames can be attached in arbitrary relative positions, simplifications can occur seamlessly in deformed states, without returning to the original shape, which can be recovered later after refinement. We propose a new class of velocity-based simplification criterion based on relative velocities. Integration points can be merged to reduce the computation time even more, and we show how to maintain constant elastic forces through the levels of detail. This meshless adaptivity allows significant improvements of computation time.

Index Terms: I.3.5 [Computer Graphics]: Computational Geometry and Object Modeling—Physically based modeling; I.3.7 [Computer Graphics]: Three-Dimensional Graphics and Realism—Animation;

1 INTRODUCTION

The stunning quality of high-resolution physically based animations of deformable solids requires complex deformable models with large numbers of independent Degrees Of Freedom (DOF) which result in large dynamics equation systems and high computation times. On the other hand, the thrilling user experience provided

by interactive simulations can only be achieved using fast computation times which preclude the use of high-resolution models. Reconciling these two contradictory goals requires adaptive models to efficiently manage the number of DOFs, by refining the model where necessary and coarsening it where possible. Mesh-based deformations can be seamlessly refined by subdividing elements and interpolating new nodes within these. However, seamless coarsening can be performed only when the fine nodes are back to their original position with respect to their higher-level elements, which happens only in the locally undeformed configurations (*i.e.* with null strain). Otherwise, a popping artifact (*i.e.*, an instantaneous change of shape) occurs. This not only violates the laws of Physics, but it is also visually disturbing. Simplifying objects in deformed configurations, as demonstrated in Fig. 1c, has thus not been possible with previous adaptive approaches, unless the elements are small or far enough. This may explain why extreme coarsening has rarely been proposed, and adaptive FEM models typically range from moderate to high complexity.

We introduce a new approach of adaptivity to mechanically simplify objects in arbitrarily deformed configurations, while exactly maintaining their current shape and controlling the velocity discontinuity, which we call seamless adaptivity. It extends a frame-based meshless method and straightforwardly derives from the ability of attaching frames to others in arbitrary relative positions, as illustrated in Fig. 2. In this example, a straight beam is initially animated using a single moving frame, while another control frame is attached to it. We then detach the child frame to allow the bending of the beam. If the deformation of the beam becomes constant, its *velocity* can again be modeled using a single moving frame, while its *shape* can be frozen in a deformed state by applying an offset to its reference position with respect to the active frame. Setting the offset to the current relative position removes mechanical DOFs without altering the current shape of the object. This deformation is reversible. If the external loading applied to the object changes, we can mechanically refine the model again (*i.e.* activate the passive frame) to allow the object to recover its initial shape or to undergo

Figure 2: Seamless coarsening in a deformed state. Left: reference shape, one active frame in black, and a passive frame in grey attached using a relative transformation (dotted line). Middle: activating the frame allows it to move freely and to deform the object. Right: deactivated frame in a deformed configuration using an offset δx.

new deformations. The ability to dynamically adapt the velocity field independently of the deformation is the specific feature of our approach which dramatically enhances the opportunities for coarsening mechanical models compared with previous methods.

Our specific contributions are (1) a deformation method based on a generalized frame hierarchy for dynamically tuning the complexity of deformable solids with seamless transitions; (2) a novel simplification and refinement criterion based on velocity, which allows us to simplify the deformation model in deformed configurations, and (3) a method to dynamically adapt the integration points and enforce the continuity of forces across changes of resolution.

The remainder of this article is organized as follows. We summarize the original frame-based simulation method and we define some notations in Section 3. An overview of our adaptive framework is presented in Section 4. We discuss our strategy for nodal adaptivity in Section 5. The adaptivity of the integration points is then introduced in Section 6. We discuss results in Section 7 and future work in Section 8.

2 RELATED WORK

The simulation of viscoelastic solids is a well-studied problem in computer graphics, starting with the early work of Terzopoulos et al. [29]. A survey can be found in [24]. Frame-based models have been proposed [20, 22, 9, 7], and the impressive efficiency of precomputed reduced models has raised a growing interest [17, 2, 3, 15, 11, 12], but run-time adaptivity remains a challenge. The remainder of this review focuses on this issue.

Hutchinson et al. [13] and Ganovelli et al. [8] first combined several resolutions of 2D and 3D solids dynamically deformed by mass-springs. Cotin et al. [5] combined two mechanical models to simulate various parts of the same object. Most adaptive methods are based on meshes at multiple resolutions. Mixing different mesh sizes can result in T-nodes that are mechanically complex to manage in the Finite Element Method (FEM). Wu et al. [32] chose a decomposition scheme that does not generate such nodes. Debunne et al. [6] performed the local explicit integration of non-nested meshes. Grinspun et al. [10] showed that hierarchical shape functions are a generic way to deal with T-nodes. Sifakis et al. [26] constrained T-nodes within other independent nodes. Martin et al. [21] solved multi-resolution junctions with polyhedral elements. Several authors proposed to generate on the fly a valid mesh with dense and fine zones. Real-time remeshing is feasible for 1D elements such as rods and wires [18, 27, 25] or 2D surfaces like cloth [23]. For 3D models, it is an elegant way to deal with cuttings, viscous effects and very thin features [4, 31, 30]. A mesh-less, octree-based adaptive extension of shape matching has been proposed [28]. Besides all these methods based on multiple resolutions, Kim and James [16] take a more algebraic approach, where the displacement field is decomposed on a small, dynamically updated, basis of orthogonal vectors, while a small set of carefully chosen integration

points are used to compute the forces. In constrast to these works, our method relies on velocity field adaptation and a meshless discretization.

Numerous error estimators for refinement have been proposed in conventional FEM analysis. For static analysis, they are generally based on a precomputed stress field. This is not feasible in real time dynamics, where the current configuration must be used. Wu et al. [32] proposed four criteria based on the curvature of the stress, strain or displacement fields. Debunne et al. [6] considered the Laplacian of the displacement. Lenoir et al. [18] refined parts in contact for wire simulation. These approaches refine the objects where they are the most deformed, and they are not able to save computation time in equilibrium states. The problems relative to the criterion thresholds are rarely discussed. The smaller the thresholds, the smaller the popping artifacts, but also the more difficult to simplify thus the less efficient.

3 FRAME-BASED SIMULATION METHOD

In this section we summarize the method that our contribution extends, and we introduce notations and basic equations. The method of [7] performs the physical simulation of viscoelastic solids using a hyperelastic formulation. The control nodes are moving frames with 12 degrees of freedom (DOF) which positions, velocities and forces in world coordinates are stored in state vectors $\mathbf{x}$, $\mathbf{v}$ and $\mathbf{f}$. The world coordinates of frame i are the entries of the 4×4 homogeneous matrix $\mathbf{X}_i$, while $\mathbf{X}_i^j$ denotes its coordinates with respect to frame j. These nodes control objects using a Skeleton Subspace Deformation (SSD) method, also called *skinning* [19]. We use Linear Blend Skinning (LBS), though other methods would be suitable (see e.g. [14] for a discussion about SSD techniques). The position of a material point i is defined using a weighted sum of affine displacements:

$$\mathbf{p}_i(t) = \sum_{j \in \mathcal{N}} \phi_i^j \mathbf{X}_j(t) \mathbf{X}_j(0)^{-1} \mathbf{p}_i(0) \qquad (1)$$

where $\mathcal{N}$ is the set of control nodes, and ϕ_i^j is the value of the shape function of node j at material position $x_i(0)$, computed at initialization time using distance ratios as in [7]. Spatially varying shape functions allow deformations. Similarly with nodes, the state of all skinned points are stored as vectors: $\mathbf{p}$, $\dot{\mathbf{p}}$, and $\mathbf{f_p}$. By differentiation of Eq. (1), a *constant* Jacobian matrix $\mathbf{J}_p$ can be assembled at initialization, relating control node and points: $\mathbf{p} = \mathbf{J}_p \mathbf{x}$, $\dot{\mathbf{p}} = \mathbf{J}_p \mathbf{v}$.

External forces can be applied directly to the nodes, or to the contact surface of the object. One can show using the Principle of Virtual Work that the skin forces $\mathbf{f_p}$ can be converted to nodal forces as: $\mathbf{f} = \mathbf{J}_p^T \mathbf{f_p}$. A generalized mass matrix for nodes can thus be assembled at initialization based on scalar masses of skinned particles $\mathbf{M}_p$: $\mathbf{M} = \mathbf{J}_p^T \mathbf{M}_p \mathbf{J}_p$. As shown in [9], differentiating Eq. (1) with respect to material coordinates allows the mapping of deformation gradients instead of points. By mapping deformation gradients to strains (such as Cauchy, Green-Lagrange or corotational), and applying a constitutive law (such as Hooke or Mooney-Rivlin), we can compute the elastic potential energy density at any location. After spatial integration and differentiation with respect to the degrees of freedom, forces can be computed and propagated back to the nodes.

We use different discretizations for visual surfaces, contact surfaces, mass and elasticity (potential energy integration points). Masses are precomputed using a dense volumetric rasterization, where voxels are seen as point masses. Deformation gradient samples (*i.e.* Gauss points) are distributed so as to minimize the numerical integration error (see Sec. 6)). For each sample, volume

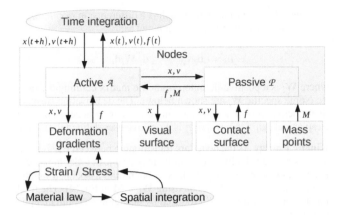

Figure 3: Kinematic structure of the simulation. Our adaptive scheme splits the control nodes into active (*i.e.* independent) nodes and passive (*i.e.* mapped) nodes.

moments are precomputed from the fine voxel grid and associated with local material properties.

The method is agnostic with respect to the way we solve the equations of motion. We apply an implicit time integration to maintain stability in case of high stiffness or large time steps [1]. At each time step, we solve a linear equation system

$$\mathbf{A}\Delta\mathbf{v} = \mathbf{b} \tag{2}$$

where $\Delta\mathbf{v}$ is the velocity change during the time step, matrix $\mathbf{A}$ is a weighted sum of the mass and stiffness matrices, while the right-hand term depends on the forces and velocities at the beginning of the time step. The main part of the computation time to set up the equation system is proportional to the number integration points, while the time necessary to solve it is a polynomial function of the number of nodes (note that $\mathbf{A}$ is a sparse, positive-definite symmetric matrix).

4 ADAPTIVE FRAME-BASED SIMULATION

Our first extension to the method presented in Sec. 3) is to attach some control nodes to others to reduce the number of independent DOFs and deformation modes. This amounts to adding an extra block to the kinematic structure of the model, as shown in Fig. 3. The independent state vectors are restricted to the active nodes. At each time step, the dynamics equation is solved to update the positions and velocities of the active nodes, then the changes are propagated to the passive nodes, then to the skin points and the material integration points. The forces are propagated the other way round. When a node i is passive, its matrix is computed using LBS as

$$\mathbf{X}_i(t) = \sum_{j\in\mathscr{A}} \phi_i^j \mathbf{X}_j(t)\mathbf{X}_j(0)^{-1}\mathbf{X}_i(0) \tag{3}$$

where $\mathscr{A}$ is the set of active nodes and ϕ_i^j is the value of the shape function of node j at the origin of $\mathbf{X}_i$ in the reference, undeformed configuration. The point positions of Eq. (1) can be written in terms of active nodes only:

$$\mathbf{p}_i(t) = \sum_{j\in\mathscr{A}} \psi_i^j \mathbf{X}_j(t)\mathbf{X}_j(0)^{-1}\mathbf{p}_i(0) \tag{4}$$

$$\psi_i^j = \phi_i^j + \sum_{k\in\mathscr{P}} \phi_k^j \phi_i^k \tag{5}$$

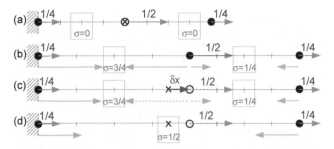

Figure 4: Refinement and simplification. Red and green arrows denote external and internal forces, respectively. Plain circles represent active nodes, while empty circles represent passive nodes attached to their parents, and crosses represent the positions of passive nodes interpolated from their parents positions. Dashed lines are used to denote forces divided up among the parent nodes. Rectangles denote integration points, where the stresses σ are computed. (a): A bar in reference state undergoes external forces and starts stretching. (b): In rest state, 3 active nodes. (c): With the middle node attached with an offset with respect to the interpolated position. (d): After replacing two integration points with one.

where $\mathscr{P}$ is the set of passive nodes. These equations straightforwardly generalize to deformation gradients. This easy composition of LBS is exploited in our node hierarchy (Sec. 5.2)) and our adaptive spatial integration scheme (Sec. 6)). At any time, an active node i can become passive. Since the coefficients used in Eq. (3) are computed in the undeformed configuration, the position $\bar{\mathbf{X}}_i$ computed using this equation is different from the current position $\mathbf{X}_i$, and moving the frame to this position would generate an artificial instantaneous displacement. To avoid this, we compute the offset $\delta\mathbf{X}_i = \bar{\mathbf{X}}_i^{-1}\mathbf{X}_i$, as illustrated in Fig. 2. The skinning of the frame is then biased by this offset as long as the frame remains passive, and its velocity is computed using the corresponding Jacobian matrix:

$$\mathbf{X}_i(t) = \sum_{j\in\mathscr{A}} \psi_i^j \mathbf{X}_j(t)\mathbf{X}_j(0)^{-1}\mathbf{X}_i(0)\delta\mathbf{X}_i \tag{6}$$

$$\mathbf{u}_i(t) = \mathbf{J}_i\mathbf{v}(t) \tag{7}$$

Our adaptivity criterion is based on the comparison of the velocity of a passive node attached to nodes of $\mathscr{A}$, with the velocity of the same node moving independently; if the difference is below a threshold the node should be passive, otherwise it should be active.

One-dimensional Example

A simple one-dimensional example is illustrated in Fig. 4. A bar is discretized using three control nodes and two integration points, and stretched horizontally by its weight, which applies the external forces $1/4$, $1/2$ and $1/4$, from left to right respectively. For simplicity we assume unitary gravity, stiffness and bar section, so that net forces are computed by simply summing up strain and force magnitudes. At the beginning of the simulation, Fig. 4a, the bar is in reference configuration with null stress, and the middle node is attached to the end nodes, interpolated between the two. The left node is fixed, the acceleration of the right node is 1, and the acceleration of the interpolated node is thus $1/2$. However, the acceleration of the corresponding *active* node would be 1, because with null stress, it is subject to gravity only. Due to this difference, we activate it and the bar eventually converges to the equilibrium configuration shown in Fig. 4b, with a non-uniform extension, as can be visualized using the vertical lines regularly spaced in the material domain.

Once the center node is stable with respect to its parents, we can simplify the model by attaching it to them, with offset δx. External and internal forces applied to the passive node, which balance each other, are divided up among its parents, which do not change the net force applied to the end node. The equilibrium is thus maintained. The computation time is faster since there are less unknown in the dynamics equation. However, computing the right-hand term remains expensive since the same two integration points are used.

Once the displacement field is simplified, any change of strain due to the displacements of the two independent nodes is uniform across the bar. We thus merge the two integration points to save computation time, as shown in Fig. 4d.

Section 5 details node adaptivity, while the adaptivity of integration points is presented in Section 6.

5 ADAPTIVE KINEMATICS

5.1 Adaptivity Criterion

At each time step, our method partitions the nodes into two sets: the *active* nodes, denoted by $\mathscr{A}$, are the currently independent DOFs from which the *passive* nodes, denoted by $\mathscr{P}$, are mapped. We further define a subset $\mathscr{A}\mathscr{C} \subset \mathscr{P}$ to be composed of nodes candidate for activation. Likewise, the deactivation candidate set is a subset $\mathscr{P}\mathscr{C} \subset \mathscr{A}$. To decide whether candidate nodes should become passive or active, we compare their velocities in the two cases and change their status when the velocity difference crosses a certain user-defined threshold η discussed below. At each time step, we thus compare the velocities in the three following cases:

1. with $\mathscr{A} \setminus \mathscr{P}\mathscr{C}$ active and $\mathscr{P} \cup \mathscr{P}\mathscr{C}$ passive (coarser resolution)

2. with $\mathscr{A}$ active and $\mathscr{P}$ passive (current resolution)

3. with $\mathscr{A} \cup \mathscr{A}\mathscr{C}$ active and $\mathscr{P} \setminus \mathscr{A}\mathscr{C}$ passive (finer resolution)

We avoid solving the three implicit integrations, noticing that cases 1 and 3 are only used to compute the adaptivity criterion. Instead of performing the implicit integration for case 1, we use the solution given by 2 and we compute the velocities of the frames in $\mathscr{P}\mathscr{C}$ as if they were passive, using Eq. (7). For case 3, we simply use an explicit integration for the additional nodes $\mathscr{A}\mathscr{C}$, in linear time using a lumped mass matrix. In practice, we only noticed small differences with a fully implicit integration. At worse, overshooting due to explicit integration temporary activates too many nodes.

Once every velocity difference has been computed and measured for candidate nodes, we integrate the dynamics forward at current resolution (*i.e.* using system 2), then we update the sets $\mathscr{A}, \mathscr{P}, \mathscr{P}\mathscr{C}, \mathscr{A}\mathscr{C}$ and finally move on to the next time step.

Metrics

For a candidate node i, the difference between its passive and active velocities is defined as:

$$\mathbf{d}_i = \mathbf{J}_i(\mathbf{v} + \Delta\mathbf{v}) - (\mathbf{u}_i + \Delta\mathbf{u}_i) \tag{8}$$

where $\mathbf{J}_i$ is the Jacobian of Eq. (7), and $\Delta\mathbf{v}, \Delta\mathbf{u}_i$ are the velocity updates computed by time integration, respectively in the case where the candidate node is passive and active. Note that for the activation criterion computed using explicit integration (case 3), this reduces to the generalized velocity difference $\mathbf{d}_i = \mathbf{J}_i\Delta\mathbf{v} - dt\tilde{\mathbf{M}}_i^{-1}\mathbf{f}_i$ where $\tilde{\mathbf{M}}_i$ is the lumped mass matrix block of node i, $\mathbf{f}_i$ its net external

force and dt is the time step , which is a difference in *acceleration* up to dt. A measure of $\mathbf{d}_i$ is be computed as:

$$\mu_i = ||\mathbf{d}_i||_{\mathbf{W}_i}^2 := \frac{1}{2}\mathbf{d}_i^T \mathbf{W}_i \mathbf{d}_i \tag{9}$$

where $\mathbf{W}_i$ is a positive-definite symmetric matrix defining the metric (some specific $\mathbf{W}_i$ are shown below). The deactivation (respectively activation) of a candidate node i occurs whenever $\mu_i \leq \eta$ (respectively $\mu_i > \eta$), where η is a positive user-defined threshold.

Kinetic Energy As the nodes are transitioning between passive and active states, a velocity discontinuity may occur. In order to prevent instabilities, a natural approach is to bound the associated kinetic energy discontinuity. We do so using $\mathbf{W}_i = \mathbf{M}$ in Eq. (9). The total kinetic energy difference introduced by changing k candidate node states is:

$$\mu_{total} = \Big|\Big|\sum_i^k \mathbf{d}_i\Big|\Big|_{\mathbf{M}}^2 \leq \sum_i^k ||\mathbf{d}_i||_{\mathbf{M}}^2 = \sum_i^k \mu_i \tag{10}$$

Thus, placing a threshold on each individual μ_i effectively bounds the total kinetic energy discontinuity. The criterion threshold η can then be adapted so that the upper bound in Eq. (10) becomes a small fraction of the current kinetic energy.

Distance to Camera For Computer Graphics applications, one is usually ready to sacrifice precision for speed as long as the approximation is not visible to the user. To this end, we can measure velocity differences according to the distance to the camera of the associated visual mesh, so that motion happening far from the camera will produce lower measures, thus favoring deactivation. More precisely, if we call $\mathbf{G}_i$ the kinematic mapping between node i and the mesh vertices, and $\mathbf{Z}$ a diagonal matrix with positive values decreasing along with the distance between mesh vertices and the camera, the criterion metric is then given by:

$$\mathbf{W}_i = \mathbf{G}_i^T \mathbf{Z}\mathbf{G}_i \tag{11}$$

In practice, we use a decreasing exponential for $\mathbf{Z}$ values (1 on the camera near-plane, 0 on the camera far-plane) in the spirit of the decreasing precision found in the depth buffer during rendering. The two metrics can also be combined by retaining the minimum of their values: simplification is then favored far from the camera, where the distance metric is always small, while the kinetic energy metric is used close to the camera, where the distance metric is always large.

5.2 Adaptive Hierarchy

In principle, we could start with an unstructured fine node discretization of the objects and at each time step, find the best simplifications by considering all possible deactivation and activation candidates. To avoid a quadratic number of tests, we pre-compute a node hierarchy and define candidate nodes to be the ones at the front between passive and active nodes.

Hierarchy Setup Our hierarchy is computed at initialization time, as illustrated in Fig. 5. At each level, we perform a Lloyd relaxation on a fine voxel grid to spread new control nodes as evenly as possible, taking into account the frames already created at coarser levels. Before updating the shape functions, we interpolate the weights ϕ_j^i at the origin of each new node j, relative to the nodes i at coarser levels. For each non-null weight, an edge is inserted in the dependency graph, resulting in a generalized hierarchy based on a Directed Acyclic Graph.

Hierarchy Update The candidates for activation are the passive nodes with all parents active. Conversely, the candidates for deactivation are the active nodes with all children passive, except the root

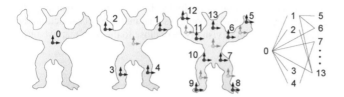

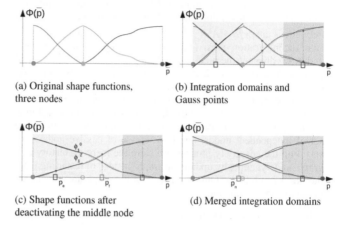

(a) Original shape functions, three nodes

(b) Integration domains and Gauss points

(c) Shape functions after deactivating the middle node

(d) Merged integration domains

Figure 7: Adaptive integration points in 1D. Disks denote control nodes while rectangles denote integration points.

Figure 5: Reference node hierarchy. From left to right: the first three levels, and the dependency graph.

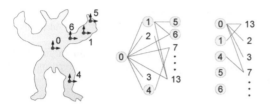

Figure 6: Mechanical hierarchy. Left: active nodes $0, 1, 4, 5, 6$ at a given time. Middle: Reference hierarchy; nodes $2, 3, 7$ are activation candidates; nodes $4, 5, 6$ are deactivation candidates. Right: the resulting two-level contracted graph to be used in the mechanical simulation.

of the reference hierarchy. In the example shown in Fig. 6, nodes $4, 5, 6, 1$, and 0 shown in the character outline are active. As such, they do not mechanically depend on their parents in the reference hierarchy, and the mechanical dependency graph is obtained by removing the corresponding edges from the reference hierarchy. For edges in this two-levels graph, weights are obtained by contracting the reference hierarchy using Eq. (4) and similarly for the different sets of passive/active nodes discussed in the beginning of this section

6 ADAPTIVE SPATIAL INTEGRATION

6.1 Discretization

The spatial integration of energy and forces is numerically computed using Gaussian quadrature, a weighted sum of values computed at integration points. Exact quadrature rules are only available for polyhedral domains with polynomial shape functions (e.g. tri-linear hexahedra). In meshless simulation, such rules do not exist in general. However, in linear blend skinning one can easily show that the deformation gradient is uniform (respectively linear) in regions where the shape functions are constant (respectively linear). As studied in [7], uniform shape functions can be only obtained with one node, so linear shape functions between nodes are the best choice for homogeneous parts of the material, since the interpolation then corresponds to the solution of static equilibrium. One integration point of a certain degree (*i.e.* one elaston [20]) is sufficient to exactly integrate polynomial functions of the deformation gradient there, such as deformation energy in linear tetrahedra. We leverage this property to optimize our distribution of integration points. In a region $\mathcal{V}_e$ centered on point $\bar{\mathbf{p}}_e$, the integral of a function g is given by:

$$\int_{\bar{\mathbf{p}} \in \mathcal{V}_e} g \approx \mathbf{g}^T \int_{\bar{\mathbf{p}} \in \mathcal{V}_e} (\bar{\mathbf{p}} - \bar{\mathbf{p}}_e)^{(n)} = \mathbf{g}^T \bar{\mathbf{g}}_e \quad (12)$$

where $\mathbf{g}$ is a vector containing g and its spatial derivatives up to degree n evaluated at $\bar{\mathbf{p}}_e$, while $\mathbf{p}^{(n)}$ denotes a vector of polynomials of degree n in the coordinates of $\mathbf{p}$, and $\bar{\mathbf{g}}_e$ is a vector of polynomials

integrated across $\mathcal{V}_e$ which can be computed at initialization time by looping over the voxels of an arbitrarily fine rasterization. The approximation of Eq. (12) is exact if n is the polynomial degree of g. Due to a possibly large number of polynomial factors, we limit our approximation to quartic functions with respect to material coordinates, corresponding to strain energies and forces when shape functions are linear and the strain measure quadratic (*i.e.* Green-Lagrangian strain).

Since the integration error is related to the linearity of shape functions, we decompose the objects into regions of as linear as possible shape functions at initial time, as shown in Fig. 7a and Fig. 7b. We compute the regions influenced by the same set of independent nodes, and we recursively split these regions until a given linearity threshold is reached, based on the error of a least squares linear fit of the shape functions. Let $\phi_i(\bar{\mathbf{p}})$ be the shape function of node i as defined in Eq. (1), and $\mathbf{c}_i^{eT} \bar{\mathbf{p}}^{(1)}$ its first order polynomial approximation in $\mathcal{V}_e$. The linearity error is given by:

$$\varepsilon(\mathbf{c}) = \int_{\mathcal{V}_e} (\phi_i(\bar{\mathbf{p}}) - \mathbf{c}^T \bar{\mathbf{p}}^{(1)})^2 \quad (13)$$

$$= \mathbf{c}^T A^e \mathbf{c} - 2\mathbf{c}^T B_i^e + C_i^e \quad (14)$$

$$\text{with: } A^e = \int_{\mathcal{V}_e} \bar{\mathbf{p}}^{(1)} \bar{\mathbf{p}}^{(1)T} \quad (15)$$

$$B_i^e = \int_{\mathcal{V}_e} \phi_i(\bar{\mathbf{p}}) \bar{\mathbf{p}}^{(1)} \quad (16)$$

$$C_i^e = \int_{\mathcal{V}_e} \phi_i(\bar{\mathbf{p}})^2 \quad (17)$$

We solve for the best least squares coefficients $\mathbf{c}_i^e$ minimizing ε: $\mathbf{c}_i^e = (A^e)^{-1} B_i^e$. The region with largest error is split in two until the target number of integration points or an upper bound on the error is reached.

6.2 Merging Integration Points

At run-time, the shape functions of the passive nodes can be expressed as linear combinations of the shape functions of the active nodes using Eq. (5). This allows us to merge integration points sharing the same set of active nodes (in $\mathscr{A} \cup \mathscr{A}\mathscr{C}$), as shown in Fig. 7c. One can show that the linearity error in the union of regions e and f is given by:

$$\varepsilon = \sum_i (C_i^e + C_i^f) - \sum_i (B_i^e + B_i^f)^T (A^e + A^f)^{-1} \sum_i (B_i^e + B_i^f)$$

If this error is below a certain threshold, we can merge the integration points. The new values of the shape function (at origin) and its derivatives are: $\mathbf{c}_i^n = (A^e + A^f)^{-1}(B_i^e + B_i^f)$. For numerical precision, the integration of Eq. (12) is centered on $\bar{\mathbf{p}}_e$. When merging e and f, we displace the precomputed integrals $\bar{\mathbf{g}}_e$ and $\bar{\mathbf{g}}_f$ to a central position $\bar{\mathbf{p}}_n = (\bar{\mathbf{p}}_e + \bar{\mathbf{p}}_f)/2$ using simple closed form polynomial expansions. Merging is fast because the volume integrals of the new integration points are directly computed based on those of the old ones, without integration across the voxels of the object volume. Splitting occurs when the children are not influenced by the same set of independent nodes, due to a release of passive nodes. To speed up the adaptivity process, we store the merging history in a graph, and dynamically update the graph (instead of restarting from the finest resolution). Only the leaves of the graph are considered in the dynamics equation.

When curvature creates different local orientations at the integration points, or when material laws are nonlinear, there may be a small difference between the net forces computed using the fine or the coarse integration points. Also, since Eq. (4) only applies when rest states are considered, position offsets $\delta\mathbf{X}$ on passive nodes create forces that are not taken into account by coarse integration points. To maintain the force consistency between the different levels of details, we compute the difference between the net forces applied by the coarse integration points and the ones before adaptation. This force offset is associated with the integration point and it is added to the elastic force it applies to the nodes. Since net internal forces over the whole object are necessarily null, so is the difference of the net forces computed using different integration points, thus this force offset influences the shape of the object but not its global trajectory. In three dimension, to maintain the force offset consistent with object rotations, we project it from the basis of the deformation gradient at the integration point to world coordinates.

7 RESULTS

7.1 Validation

To measure the accuracy of our method, we performed some standard tests on homogeneous Hookean beams under extension and flexion (see Fig. 8). We obtain the same static equilibrium solutions using standard tetrahedral finite elements and frame-based models (with/without kinematics/integration point adaptation). In extension, when inertial forces are negligible (low masses or static solving or high damping), our adaptive model is not refined as expected from the analytic solution (one frame and one integration point are sufficient). In bending, adaptivity is necessary to model non-linear variations of the deformation gradient. At equilibrium, our model is simplified as expected. Fig. 9 shows the variation of

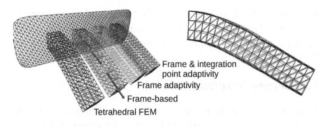

Figure 8: Four cantilever beams at equilibrium with the same properties and loading (fixed on one side and subject to gravity).

the kinetic energy (red curves). As expected, energy discontinuities remain lower than the criterion threshold when adapting nodes and integration points (green and blue curves), allowing the user to

control maximum jumps in velocity. Because there is also no position discontinuities (no popping) as guaranteed by construction, the adaptive simulation in visually very close to the non-adaptive one.

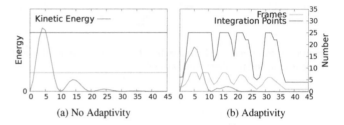

(a) No Adaptivity (b) Adaptivity

Figure 9: Kinetic Energy (red) Analysis with varying number of frames (green) and integration points (blue) over time (cantilever beam under flexion).

7.2 Complex Scenes

We demonstrate the genericity of our method through the following example scenes:

Christmas Tree A Christmas tree (Fig. 1) with heterogeneous material and rigid ornaments is subject to gravity. Initially, only one node is used to represent the tree. As the ornament falls, the branches bend and nodes are automatically active until the static equilibrium is reached and the nodes become passive again. The final, bent configuration is again represented using only one control node.

Elephant Seal A simple animation skeleton is converted to control nodes to animate an elephant seal (Fig. 10) using key-frames. Adaptive, secondary motions are automatically handled by our method as more nodes are added into the hierarchy.

Figure 10: 40 adaptive, elastic frames (green=active, red=passive) adding secondary motion on a (on purpose short) kinematic skeleton corresponding to 12 (blue) frames.

Bouncing Ball A ball is bouncing on the floor with unilateral contacts (Fig. 11). As the ball falls, only one node is needed to animate it. On impact, contact constraint forces produce deformations and the nodes are active accordingly. On its way up, the ball recovers its rest state and the nodes are passive again. This shows that our method allows simplifications in non-equilibrium states.

Elastic Mushroom Field In Fig. 12a, simplification allows all the mushrooms to be attached to one single control frame until a shoe crushes some of them. Local nodes are then activated to respond to shoe contacts or to secondary contacts. They are deactivated when the shoe goes away.

Deformable Ball Stack Eight deformable balls (Fig. 13) are dropped into a glass. From left to right: (a) A unique node is necessary to simulate all balls falling under gravity, at the same speed. (b) While colliding, nodes are activated to simulate deformations.

Scene	Timing including collisions	#Steps (dt)	#Frames total	min	max	mean	#Integration Points total	min	max	mean	Speedup including collisions
Christmas Tree (Fig. 1)	5-270 ms/frame	380 (0.04s)	36	1	31	9	124	124	124	124	×1.5
Cantilever Beam (Fig. 8)	<1-110 ms/frame	370 (0.5s)	15	1	15	1.8	164	3	164	20	×2
Mushroom Field (Fig. 12a)	75-200 ms/frame	200 (0.1s)	156	1	11	5.4	251	78	88	84	×2.1
Armadillo Salad (Fig. 12b)	650-1,200 ms/frame	1,556 (0.01s)	1,800	18	1,784	365	27,162	108	27,086	5,011	×3
Ball Stack (Fig. 13)	100-250 ms/frame	20 (0.1s)	50	1	38	11.5	407	70	360	178	×1.7

Table 1: Adaptivity performances and timings.

Figure 11: A falling deformable ball with unilateral contacts.

(a) Crushing elastic mushrooms   (b) 18 Armadillos falling in a bowl

Figure 12: Selected pictures of complex scenes where only a subset of the available frames and integration points are active.

(c) Once stabilized, the deformed balls are simplified to one node. (d) Removing the glass, some nodes are re-activated to allow the balls to fall apart. (e) Once the balls are separated they are freely falling with air damping, and one node is sufficient to simulate all of them.

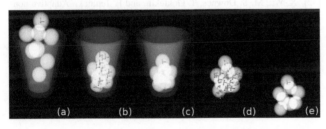

Figure 13: Eight deformable balls stacking up in a glass, which is eventually removed.

Armadillo Salad A set of Armadillos (Fig. 12b) is dropped into a bowl, demonstrating the scalability and robustness of our method in a difficult (self-)contacting situation.

7.3 Performance

In the various scenarios described above, our technique allows a significant reduction of both kinematic DOFs and integration points, as presented in Table 1. Speedups are substantial, even when collision handling is time consuming. It is worth noting that, for a fair comparison with the non-adaptive case, our examples exhibit large, global and dynamical deformations.

In order to evaluate the gain of adaptivity regarding the scene complexity, we throw armadillos in a bowl, at various resolutions. The speedups presented in Table 2 show that scenes resulting in larger systems give better speedups since the complexity of solving the system increases along with the number of DOFs. The algorithmic complexity of solving deformable object dynamics generally depends on three factors: the number of DOFs, the computation of elastic forces and, in the case of iterative solvers, the conditioning of the system. By using fewer integration points, our method is able to compute elastic forces in a much faster way. In the case of badly conditioned systems, as for instance tightly mechanically coupled system (*e.g.* stacks), iterative methods need a large number of iterations and thus the number of DOFs becomes critical. The dependency on the number of DOFs is even larger when using direct solvers. Thus, our method is particularly interesting in such cases and allow for significant speedups compared to the non-adaptive case. For instance: 6.25 when the balls are stacked into the glass (see Fig. 13c).

We noticed that the overhead due to adaptivity is moderate compared to the overall computational time (typically between 5% and 10%), since adaptivity is incremental for both nodes and integration points between two consecutive time steps. The dense voxel grid is visited only once at initialization to compute shape functions, masses, and integration data. Note that the cost of our adaptivity scheme is independent from the method to compute shape functions (they could be based on harmonic coordinates, natural neighbor interpolants, etc.).

Nb Armadillos	Max Nodes / Integration Points per Armadillo		
	10 / 49	100 / 1509	250 / 3953
1	×1.75	×3.3	×12
18	×1.5	×3	×3.1

Table 2: Speedups for a salad of one and 18 armadillos at various maximal resolutions (including collision timing)

8 CONCLUSION AND PERSPECTIVES

We introduced a novel method for the run-time adaptivity of elastic models. Our method requires few pre-processing (few seconds) contrary to existing model reduction techniques based on modal analysis and system training. Nodes are simplified as soon as their velocities can be described by nodes at coarser levels of details, otherwise they are made independent. Linear interpolation is particularly suited for linear materials and affine deformations as it provides the static solution; therefore no refinement occurs except if inertia produces large velocity gradients. In non-linear deformation such as bending and twisting, new nodes are active to approximate the solution in terms of velocity. Using frames as kinematic primitives allows simplifications in deformed configurations based on local coordinates, which is not possible in traditional Finite Element or particle-based techniques. Various distance metrics can be easily implemented to tune the adaptivity criterion depending on the simulation context (*e.g.* physical, visual precision). Reducing the number of independent DOFs speeds up the simulation, although the factor depends on the choice of the solver (*e.g.* iterative/direct solver, collision response method), and on the simulation scenario (*e.g.* presence of steady states, local/global, linear/non-linear deformations, mass distributions). In addition to kinematical adaptivity, we presented a method to merge integration points to speed up the computations even more of elastic internal forces. Force offsets are used to remove discontinuities between the levels of detail.

In future work, we will address the question of stiffness discontinuities and the design of scenario-dependent frame hierarchies.

ACKNOWLEDGEMENTS

The authors would like to thank Laura Paiardini for her much appreciated artistic work (modeling, rendering) and the Sofa team (http://www.sofa-framework.org) for the great simulation library. This work was partly funded by the French ANR SoHusim.

REFERENCES

[1] D. Baraff and A. Witkin. Large steps in cloth simulation. In *Proceedings of the 25th annual conference on Computer graphics and interactive techniques (SIGGRAPH)*, pages 43–54. ACM, 1998.

[2] J. Barbič and D. L. James. Real-time subspace integration for St. Venant-Kirchhoff deformable models. *ACM Transactions on Graphics (Proc. SIGGRAPH)*, 24(3):982–990, Aug. 2005.

[3] J. Barbič and Y. Zhao. Real-time large-deformation substructuring. *ACM Trans. on Graphics (Proc. SIGGRAPH)*, 30(4):91:1–91:7, 2011.

[4] A. W. Bargteil, C. Wojtan, J. K. Hodgins, and G. Turk. A finite element method for animating large viscoplastic flow. In *ACM Transactions on Graphics (Proc. SIGGRAPH)*, volume 26, 2007.

[5] S. Cotin, H. Delingette, and N. Ayache. A hybrid elastic model allowing real-time cutting, deformations and force-feedback for surgery training and simulation. In *The Visual Computer*, volume 16, 2000.

[6] G. Debunne, M. Desbrun, M.-P. Cani, and A. H. Barr. Dynamic real-time deformations using space and time adaptive sampling. In *Proc. ACM SIGGRAPH*, 2001.

[7] F. Faure, B. Gilles, G. Bousquet, and D. K. Pai. Sparse Meshless Models of Complex Deformable Solids. In *ACM Transactions on Graphics (Proc. SIGGRAPH)*, volume 30, 2011.

[8] F. Ganovelli, P. Cignoni, and R. Scopigno. Introducing multiresolution representation in deformable object modeling. In *ACM Spring Conference on Computer Graphics*, 1999.

[9] B. Gilles, G. Bousquet, F. Faure, and D. Pai. Frame-based Elastic Models. In *ACM Transactions on Graphics*, volume 30, 2011.

[10] E. Grinspun, P. Krysl, and P. Schröder. Charms: a simple framework for adaptive simulation. In *ACM Transactions on Graphics (Proc. SIGGRAPH)*, volume 21, 2002.

[11] F. Hahn, S. Martin, B. Thomaszewski, R. Sumner, S. Coros, and M. Gross. Rig-space physics. In *ACM Transactions on Graphics (Proc. SIGGRAPH)*, volume 31, 2012.

[12] K. Hildebrandt, C. Schulz, C. von Tycowicz, and K. Polthier. Interactive spacetime control of deformable objects. In *ACM Transactions on Graphics (Proc. SIGGRAPH)*, volume 31, 2012.

[13] D. Hutchinson, M. Preston, and T. Hewitt. Adaptive refinement for mass/spring simulations. In *Eurographics Workshop on Computer Animation and Simulation*, pages 31–45, 1996.

[14] L. Kavan, S. Collins, J. Žára, and C. O'Sullivan. Skinning with dual quaternions. In *Proceedings of the ACM symposium on Interactive 3D graphics and games*, 2007.

[15] J. Kim and N. S. Pollard. Fast simulation of skeleton-driven deformable body characters. *ACM Transactions on Graphics*, 30, 2011.

[16] T. Kim and D. L. James. Skipping steps in deformable simulation with online model reduction. In *ACM Transactions on Graphics (Proc. SIGGRAPH Asia)*, volume 28, 2009.

[17] P. G. Kry, D. L. James, and D. K. Pai. Eigenskin: real time large deformation character skinning in hardware. In *Proc. ACM SIGGRAPH/Eurographics Symposium on Computer animation*, pages 153–159, 2002.

[18] J. Lenoir, L. Grisoni, C. Chaillou, and P. Meseure. Adaptive resolution of 1d mechanical b-spline. In *Proc. ACM GRAPHITE*, 2005.

[19] N. Magnenat-Thalmann, R. Laperrière, and D. Thalmann. Joint dependent local deformations for hand animation and object grasping. In *Graphics interface*, pages 26–33, 1988.

[20] S. Martin, P. Kaufmann, M. Botsch, E. Grinspun, and M. Gross. Unified simulation of elastic rods, shells, and solids. In *ACM Transactions on Graphics (Proc. SIGGRAPH)*, volume 29, 2010.

[21] S. Martin, P. Kaufmann, M. Botsch, M. Wicke, and M. Gross. Polyhedral finite elements using harmonic basis functions. In *Proc. Eurographics Symposium on Geometry Processing*, 2008.

[22] M. Müller and N. Chentanez. Solid simulation with oriented particles. In *ACM Transactions on Graphics (Proc. SIGGRAPH)*, volume 30, 2011.

[23] R. Narain, A. Samii, and J. F. O'Brien. Adaptive anisotropic remeshing for cloth simulation. In *ACM Transactions on Graphics (Proc. SIGGRAPH Asia)*, volume 31, 2012.

[24] A. Nealen, M. Müller, R. Keiser, E. Boxerman, and M. Carlson. Physically based deformable models in computer graphics. In *Computer Graphics Forum*, volume 25, 2006.

[25] M. Servin, C. Lacoursière, F. Nordfelth, and K. Bodin. Hybrid, multiresolution wires with massless frictional contacts. In *IEEE Transactions on Visualization and Computer Graphics*, volume 17, 2011.

[26] E. Sifakis, T. Shinar, G. Irving, and R. Fedkiw. Hybrid simulation of deformable solids. In *Proc. ACM SIGGRAPH/Eurographics Symposium on Computer Animation*, 2007.

[27] J. Spillmann and M. Teschner. An adaptive contact model for the robust simulation of knots. In *Computer Graphics Forum (Proc. Eurographics)*, volume 27, 2008.

[28] D. Steinemann, M. A. Otaduy, and M. Gross. Fast adaptive shape matching deformations. In *Proc. ACM SIGGRAPH/Eurographics Symposium on Computer Animation*, 2008.

[29] D. Terzopoulos, J. Platt, A. Barr, and K. Fleischer. Elastically deformable models. In *Proc. ACM SIGGRAPH*, 1987.

[30] M. Wicke, D. Ritchie, B. M. Klingner, S. Burke, J. R. Shewchuk, and J. F. O'Brien. Dynamic local remeshing for elastoplastic simulation. In *ACM Transactions on Graphics (Proc. SIGGRAPH)*, volume 29, 2010.

[31] C. Wojtan and G. Turk. Fast viscoelastic behavior with thin features. In *ACM Transactions on Graphics (Proc. SIGGRAPH)*, volume 27, 2008.

[32] X. Wu, M. S. Downes, T. Goktekin, and F. Tendick. Adaptive nonlinear finite elements for deformable body simulation using dynamic progressive meshes. In *Computer Graphics Forum (Proc. Eurographics)*, volume 20, 2001.

Efficient Collision Detection While Rendering Dynamic Point Clouds

Mohamed Radwan*   Stefan Ohrhallinger†   Michael Wimmer‡

Vienna University of Technology, Austria

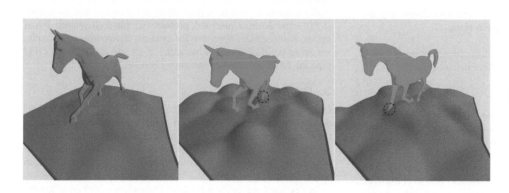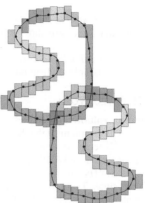

Figure 1: Left: Subsequent snapshots of an animated HORSE traversing continuously oscillating ground. Collisions between those two dynamic point clouds are marked by circles and HORSE is shaded red. Right: TLDIs of two objects. Colliding extents are shaded red.

ABSTRACT

A recent trend in interactive environments is the use of unstructured and temporally varying point clouds. This is driven by both affordable depth cameras and augmented reality simulations. One research question is how to perform collision detection on such point clouds. State-of-the-art methods for collision detection create a spatial hierarchy in order to capture dynamic point cloud surfaces, but they require $O(NlogN)$ time for N points. We propose a novel screen-space representation for point clouds which exploits the property of the underlying surface being 2D. In order for *dimensionality reduction*, a 3D point cloud is converted into a series of *thickened layered depth images*. This data structure can be constructed in $O(N)$ time and allows for *fast surface queries* due to its increased compactness and memory coherency. On top of that, parts of its construction come for free since they are already handled by the rendering pipeline. As an application we demonstrate online collision detection between dynamic point clouds. It shows *superior accuracy* when compared to other methods and *robustness to sensor noise* since uncertainty is hidden by the thickened boundary.

Index Terms: Computer Graphics [I.3.5]: Computational Geometry and Object Modeling—Hierarchy and Geometric Transformations Image Processing and Computer Vision [I.4.8]: Scene Analysis—Surface Fitting

1 INTRODUCTION

This paper proposes a novel accelerated approach for constructing and querying the underlying surface of dynamic point clouds.

---

*e-mail: radwan@cg.tuwien.ac.at

†e-mail:ohrhallinger@cg.tuwien.ac.at

‡e-mail:wimmer@cg.tuwien.ac.at
Graphics Interface Conference 2014
7-9 May, Montreal, Quebec, Canada

When those point clouds are rendered, calculations from the point-based rendering (PBR) pipeline are reused in the surface construction for the points inside the view frustum.

Collision detection requires determining the distance from the shape boundary of the object. For point clouds, especially noisy ones, reconstructing the surface as a triangulated mesh is a tedious process which currently is not feasible to do online. Applications where collision detection between dynamic point clouds is relevant include moving and posing of objects, as well as touch and grip. Such point clouds are dynamically changing environments, e.g., acquired by sensors attached to drones in a disaster scenario as simultaneous location and mapping (SLAM), human avatars captured by a Kinect, or deforming virtual objects for augmented-reality applications. Physically remote point clouds may be transposed into a common coordinate system to allow for interaction. Finally, user interaction can lead to non-rigid deformation or fragmentation.

We target medium-to-large and possibly noisy point clouds which are dynamic in the sense of having little or no temporal coherence. Constructing a spatial hierarchy for geometry, e.g., bounding volume hierarchies (BVH) [12], or tree structures [20], adds a logarithmic time factor to collision processing with respect to the number of handled points. This setup time is amortized only for static point clouds. Using a BVH allows for deformations and local rigid transformations, but not for entirely dynamic point sets. With interactive applications, the interest is often concentrated inside the view frustum, since it determines what the viewer can see and manipulate.

Our main goal is to enable online processing of medium-to-large dynamic point clouds without temporal coherence, such as Kinect input. We achieve this by avoiding construction of spatial hierarchies altogether and instead discretize the surface underlying the points into a screen-space grid. This two-dimensional structure reduces the dimensionality of the grid and thus results in more compact storage and faster intersection testing. The advantages of using a grid remain, namely that construction and evaluation can be parallelized well on the GPU.

Our contributions are:

- *Efficient reconstruction of connectivity* for point clouds where an estimation of local sampling density is available, even in the presence of noise.

- *Compact boundary discretization* of point clouds by extending layered depth images with range, adapted to screen space.

- *Reuse of parts of the rendering pipeline* for constructing the boundary data structure for the point cloud.

- *Precise and online collision detection of dynamic point clouds* as an example application for surface distance queries.

2 RELATED WORK

Bounding volume hierarchies (BVHs). These are spatial object representation structures that have been widely used in many applications. Different volume types are used to bound the geometric primitives, such as AABBs [2], OBBs [8], DOPs [13], and convex hulls [5]. BVHs are efficient in processing proximity queries, with $O(logN)$ time. Their construction of $O(NlogN)$ is also considered efficient, since for static objects the structure is constructed only once at set up. However, updating a BVH of an entirely dynamic data set is also of $O(NlogN)$ time. Therefore, for data sets with continuous temporal updates as we consider in this paper, BVHs suffer from inefficiency, whether they are updated or constructed from the start with every update.

Voxelization. Our work is related to scene voxelization approaches. Eisemann and Decoret [6] utilized the capabilities of the GPU to construct voxel-based representations which need not be aligned in one (i.e., the view) axis but are restricted to a fixed number of constant-size intervals, while Hinks et al. [11] use a similar representation to construct solid models for computational modeling. An older approach [4] also reconstructs a sampled surface implicitly at grid cells using a signed distance function. We compute discrete screen-space aligned layers instead, each layer represented by non-aligned depth ranges.

Image-based techniques for collision detection. Such techniques [14, 9, 10] do not require any pre-processing, and thus are appropriate for dynamically deforming objects. In [10], layered depth images (LDI) are computed for both objects, then volume representations are constructed and compared to find intersection regions. The algorithm, and almost all image-based collision detection (CD) algorithms as well, targets triangulated meshes. To our knowledge, only one approach [1] uses image space to detect collision between point clouds, but is restricted to movement in 2.5D space. They divide the space into slices and compute a height map for each. The approach assumes that obstacles are nearly parallel to YZ plane and perpendicular to XY plane, and uses these assumptions to infer obstacle information and save them with each pixel.

Static point-cloud collision detection. The most important approach [12] is both robust to noise and fast (interactive if need be, depending on the time budget). They construct a BVH and use a collision probability measure between pairs of nodes, in order to traverse the two objects' hierarchies ordered by priority. In the second stage, they sample the implicit surface at the leaf nodes to measure separation distance. However, as mentioned before, construction of a BVH is slow and can be memory-intensive, and the entire data needs to reside in memory as well. Thus it is impractical for large point sets and even detrimental to build such a structure for points sets which change dynamically and are not queried often enough to amortize its building cost. Our approach targets different application scenarios, but it surpasses the accuracy achieved by Klein's algorithm [12], as is shown in Section 7. Pan et al. [16] robustly detect collisions between noisy point clouds by defining the

detection as a two-class classification problem and estimate collision probability with support vector machines, but runtime is comparatively slow. Our approach hides sensor noise by querying a thickened boundary.

Dynamic point-cloud collision detection. A very recent paper [17] uses BVHs and/or octrees to detect collisions and compute distances between sensor-captured point clouds. They propose two ideas, one is appropriate for static environments and the other for dynamic ones. For dynamic environments, they propose to mutually traverse an octree (environment point cloud) and an AABB (robot), and do an unspecified, probably simple collision test at leaf nodes. Although this approach for dynamic environments is simple, we avoid building a spatial hierarchy at all and can keep the GPU pipeline more occupied by streaming coherent data.

3 OVERVIEW

Our input data are *unstructured points*. We assume that the rendering pipeline has already culled points against the view frustum (or respective bounding box) and projected them into screen space. Further we assume that the *sampling density* for the individual input points is given, either globally uniform or, e.g., estimated from sensor device properties.

In Section 4 we define a *thickened boundary* which envelops the implicit surface of the point cloud, provided that the sampling is sufficiently dense. We then transform it into projected space and finally discretize it in screen space, adapted to the view point. Based on this representation, we show how the contained implicit surface can be queried quickly. Then we explain in Section 5 how we efficiently construct this boundary representation in parallel as a *thick layered depth image* extended with depth range (TLDI). For this we show reuse of several parts of a standard point-based rendering pipeline. We describe in Section 6 that detecting collisions by querying the surface in this TLDI data structure is straightforward to do. In Section 7 we compare our collision detection algorithm with sampled meshes as ground truth and show that it is significantly more precise than prior methods, robust in the presence of noise and fast enough to handle dynamic point clouds at *interactive frame rates*. We give concluding arguments in Section 8 along with an outlook to the extensions we are currently working on.

4 SURFACE DEFINITION

Our goal is to determine the distance of a point $p \in \mathbb{R}^3$ to the manifold, possibly bounded surface Σ that is implicitly defined by a set of points S, sampled on or close to it. All distances are in the Euclidean sense, unless otherwise noted. Since Σ is not known, we first define a *thickened boundary* Ω that contains such a surface near S, similar to an adaptive *spherical cover* as proposed in [15]. For precise evaluation of proximity queries to Σ we require that Ω bounds it as closely as possible, but also want to avoid holes in Ω that are not present in S. Evaluating the distance $\|p, \Omega\|$, which in turn allows us to approximate $\|p, \Sigma\|$, requires representation of Ω by a discrete spatial structure. Our design requirements are that it is compact and can be both constructed and evaluated quickly.

4.1 Spherical Cover Ω Containing the Surface Σ

First, we want to define a volume Ω which covers the surface Σ underlying the samples so that we can perform distance queries to Σ. Let $B_i(s_i, r_i)$ be the balls centered at samples $s_i \in S$ in $\mathbb{R}^3$ with radii r_i chosen such that Σ is enclosed entirely in the union of balls Ω (see Figure 2a):

$$\Omega = \bigcup_{i=0}^{N} B_i(s_i, r_i)$$

If S is sampled non-uniformly densely, balls which are close but from geodesically remote parts of the surface may merge in Ω, and then Ω is not homeomorphic to Σ. This is not a problem for our

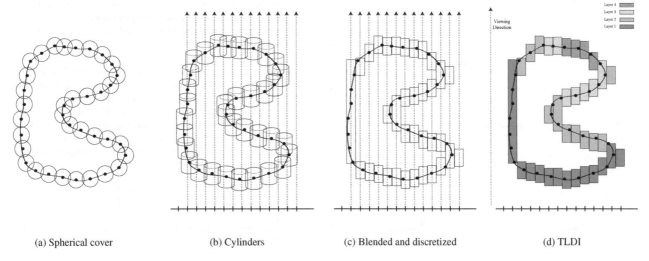

(a) Spherical cover	(b) Cylinders

(c) Blended and discretized	(d) TLDI

Figure 2: Representations of the volume bounding the surface Σ: a) Union of balls Ω centered at samples. b) Projected onto the view plane as cylinders in object space Ω'. c) Blended depth intervals $\hat{\Omega}$. d) TLDI shaded per layer.

use case, since determining the distance from a point $p \in \mathbb{R}^3$ to a surface neither requires that surface to be manifold nor orientable.

If the radii r_i associated with the samples are just sufficiently large with respect to local sampling density, the B_i will overlap such that Σ is entirely contained in Ω. We assume r_i either to be a global constant, estimated from range image properties or determined in preprocessing, as for out-of-core huge point clouds [19]. Alternatively, r_i could be estimated locally by determining k-nearest neighbors in screen space, as shown in [18]. Note that real holes in the surface which are smaller than r_i could disappear in the representation.

Since Ω consists of balls, its thickness perpendicular to Σ will be large and oscillate considerably between samples. Determining the connectivity between samples would allow us to blend their balls and result in a more equally thickened boundary. As mentioned above, inserting the balls into a spatial hierarchy in $\mathbb{R}^3$ to recover the connectivity is slow because we have to sort in three dimensions. Instead, we show how to achieve this more efficiently in projected (2-dimensional) space, which has something in common with splat rendering, as described next.

4.2 Blending Cylinders in Projected Space

We define samples in S as connected if their balls overlap. Now we want to locate the connectivity between the samples so that we can blend their associated balls for neighbors to equalize boundary thickness. This is easier if we project them from $\mathbb{R}^3$ onto a plane. Then we just need to locate overlapping disks in that plane and check if they also overlap in depth with their radii, similar to rendering view-plane aligned splats. In object space this represents testing plane-parallel cylinders which contain the balls and are of minimum size (see Figure 2b). We name the union of cylinders Ω'.

Each point $\hat{\mathbf{x}}$ in the projection plane (i.e., the view plane) represents a view ray in object space and may intersect Ω' multiple times. Therefore each $\hat{\mathbf{x}}$ maps to a set of depth ranges (entry-exit point pairs of Ω') which we call its *layers*, represented by the function $F_i(\hat{\mathbf{x}})$ for layer i:
$$F_i(\hat{\mathbf{x}}) = \{d_{i,near}, d_{i,far}\}$$
We want to equalize the boundary thickness of Ω' since its associated values of $F(\hat{\mathbf{x}})$ change discretely at cylinder boundaries. So we blend its values (both *near* and *far*) for the N connected samples $\mathbf{s}_i$ whose cylinders overlap with the corresponding entry-exit

pair along the view ray of $\hat{\mathbf{x}}$ as follows:
$$\hat{F}_i(\hat{\mathbf{x}}) = \sum_{i=1}^{N} d_i r(\|\mathbf{x} - \mathbf{s}_i\|)$$
where $r(x) = e^{x^2}$. We call $\hat{\Omega}$ the volume defined by the depth range layers of $\hat{F}$.

In regions where the surface is mostly parallel to the view plane, the set of cylinders intersected by a view ray in one layer is such that each cylinder overlaps with each other in that set. Where the surface is oblique, this may not hold because the depth range of a layer becomes large. We call such a set of cylinders containing non-overlapping subsets as *stacked*. For such stacks, we blend the frontmost cylinder only with its overlapping cylinders in the stack to get $d_{i,near}$, and similar for the backmost cylinder to get $d_{i,far}$. Figure 3 explains the two cases.

Σ is not known but implicitly assumed through its set of samples S. Nevertheless, we would like Σ to be bound by $\hat{\Omega}$, so we attempt to define it to lie centered in $\hat{\Omega}$. The way in which Σ approximates S can then be thought of as similar as a blended surface of splats. Our results in Section 7 confirm that $\hat{\Sigma}$ is reasonably close to S.

We would like to define $\hat{\Sigma}$ as the set of centers of maximum balls contained in $\hat{\Omega}$ which touch both sides of its boundary. However, boundary sides of $\hat{\Omega}$ are not clearly defined, but shooting view rays through it results in entry/exit pairs. Based on that information we can define $\hat{\Sigma}$ as the set of centers of maximum balls contained in $\hat{\Omega}$ which are centered along a view ray and growing monotonically either from its entry or exit point. A view ray then contains for each layer $\hat{F}_i$ either one or two balls. $\hat{\Sigma}$ is similar to a subset of the medial axis [3] of $\hat{\Omega}$ as the maximizing of balls along the view ray prunes spurious branches in that direction. However, it may contain spurious branches in the other axes.

4.3 Discretization of $\hat{\Omega}$ in Screen Space

For efficient spatial sorting, we discretize $\hat{\Omega}$ into a 2D grid with screen-space resolution. This data structure is well suited to parallel processing as the point primitives are streamed onto the GPU and connectivity has local extent in screen space so there is not much interdependency.

The result is a kind of non-aligned voxelization, since each pixel can reference multiple layers in $\hat{F}$, but their depth range does not

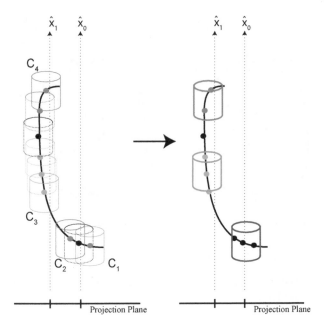

Figure 3: Left: This figure shows blending at stacked ($\hat{x}_1$) and non-stacked ($\hat{x}_0$) view rays. Frontmost (cyan) and backmost cylinders (red) are drawn with continuous lines, other cylinders as dashed. View ray $\hat{x}_0$ enters the layer at cylinder C_1 and leaves at C_2, intersecting three cylinders in total which all overlap and thus are blended together to a single d_i. View ray $\hat{x}_1$ on the other hand intersects a stack of cylinders, C_3 in the front and C_4 at the back. $d_{i,near}$ is then the result of blending C_3 with its overlapping (light cyan) cylinders and $d_{i,far}$ similar for C_4. Right: the result of blending are the cylinders drawn with thick stroke.

correspond between pixels (see Figure 2c). A closely related concept are *layered depth images* (LDI), which are typically used to peel off surface layers from a mesh as shown in [7]. In our case, layers represent depth ranges instead of scalar values, so we extend the depth of an LDI with a second value to represent the near (entry) and far (exit) intersection of the thickened boundary. We name this a *thickened LDI* (TLDI).

5 CONSTRUCTION OF TLDI

Constructing the TLDI for a point cloud peels off layers similar as does depth peeling for a mesh (see Figure 2d). Since operations such as visibility culling, blending and normalization are involved, we can partially reuse work already done in the standard PBR pipeline which processes the points sequentially:

The Standard Three-Pass PBR Pipeline. The common pipeline of surface splatting employed by PBR algorithms is generally composed of three shader passes:

- *Visibility Pass:* All splats are simply rendered, depth culled, leaving only the front-most fragments in the output buffer.

- *Blending Pass:* Fragments of the splats that are within a certain threshold from the front depth values are rendered to accumulate the weighted colors and the weights themselves.

- *Normalization Pass:* The accumulated weighted colors value is divided by the accumulated weights value to get the blended depth.

For the blending and normalizing passes, we simply replace values of color with depth (front and back values respectively).

Modifications for TLDI layer computation:

For constructing a layer of the TLDI, we insert three passes between the visibility and blending pass:

- *Stacking Pass:* Since points are not processed in order, cylinders in a stack may occur after each other such that they do not overlap. We maintain a zero-initialized bit array for an assumed optimal stack size of size 128 bits, 32 bits for each one of the RGBA channels, quantized by the radius of the first encountered point. Subsequent cylinders encountered at that pixel and inside its range fill up the bits corresponding to their depth (see Figure 4).

- *Counter Pass:* The number of contiguous filled bits is determined, starting from the first filled bit.

- *Back Visibility Pass:* The previous count determines the backmost cylinder in that stack and also in the current layer.

The two pipelines are displayed in Figure 5. For each pixel in the TLDI, a pair of depth values (d_{near}, d_{far}) is output. In our implementation, we actually store their average d_{avg} along with half their distance, because for non-stacked pixels, d_{avg} already represents Σ.

In our experiments, we managed to capture all layers entirely within our assumed stack size of 128 bits. However it is important to note that layers exceeding this size would simply be split up into two, adding another layer to the data structure but not changing the underlying representation. We expect this to minimally decrease performance, but accuracy would not be affected.

We execute the above pipeline for each layer of the point cloud, however the collision detection application that we present next often terminates already after a single layer has been constructed.

6 COLLISION DETECTION AS AN APPLICATION

We now present collision detection as one application of querying the TLDI representation of the implicit surface of S. We show that it can be implemented efficiently by merging TLDI construction and collision testing into an existing PBR pipeline.

Simply put, collisions are detected by intersecting view rays from the camera for each pixel with the TLDI for each point cloud and testing if their depth ranges along that ray (since close to $\hat{\Sigma}$) intersect. For non-colliding point clouds, this also infers the separation distance in view direction, which especially makes sense for an object moving with the camera, such as an avatar. We describe next how the two point clouds' collision and distance queries are processed.

6.1 TLDIs Comparison

Comparisons between layers are performed pixel wise. A collision is detected if at a pixel the depth ranges for layers from two objects overlap. Since the boundary is thickened, we expect a number of false positives, i.e., $\hat{\Omega}_0, \hat{\Omega}_1$ of the point clouds intersect while the actual surfaces $\hat{\Sigma}_0, \hat{\Sigma}_1$ do not. In our experiments we discovered that we could compress the thickness of $\hat{\Omega}$ in view direction by a significant factor in order to eliminate most false positives while keeping the number of false negatives small. Since $\hat{\Omega}$ is projected in view direction, thinning it in this axis does not affect the general observations made in Section 4, in fact it approximates Σ more closely.

Since a collision may already be detected in the first layer (which terminates our method), we do not have to construct all layers of the object and compare them against each layer of the other object. Instead, we compute them in depth order on demand as long as no collision is detected, as outlined below. This limits the number of

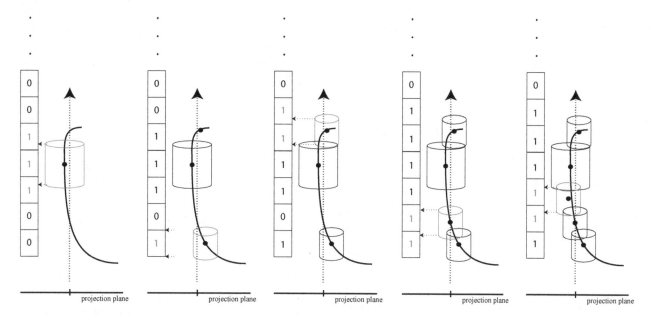

Figure 4: The figure demonstrates how the connectivity of a stack inside a layer is tracked by a bit array in the *stacking pass*. Depth is quantized into segments, where each segment is of height equal to the diameter of the first encountered cylinder in the initial *visibility pass*, and the first segment aligned to its lower disc. In the subsequent *stacking pass*, cylinders of encountered points are projected to gain occupancy information, as shown in order. Each cylinder fills the segments in the buffer bit that intersects with its cylinder depth interval. The order in which points are projected is assumed to be random, and cylinders in the figure are not all the same size.

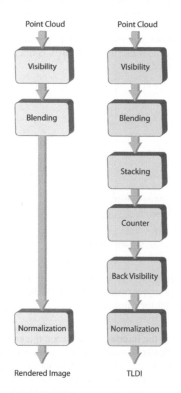

Figure 5: For TLDI construction we insert three additional passes into a standard PBR pipeline.

depth comparisons by the number of layers per object, corresponding to its view-dependent depth complexity.

Let there be two point clouds O_0, O_1. For O_0, the first and second layers – $l_{0,0}$ and $l_{0,1}$ – are computed. Then we consider the subset of O_1 which is clipped by the depth range of – and between – $\hat{\Omega}$ of $l_{0,0}$ and $l_{0,1}$, construct its layers and compare it against those of O_0. The clipping is repeated similar between subsequent layer pairs $l_{0,i-1}, l_{0,i}$, for $i \geq 2$, until the backmost layer of O_0 has been reached or a collision is detected.

6.2 Early Rejection Test

Since entire TLDIs have to be constructed in case of non-collision, we add a quick rejection test in the beginning, where we simply compare the front layer of O_0 to the back layer of O_1, and vice versa. Since the front layer is the closest to the camera, a non-collision is reported if for all pixels d_{near} of the front layer of O_0 is greater than d_{far} of the back layer of O_1. If the depth intervals of those layers intersect, a collision is detected early as well. This test can be performed quickly inside the standard PBR pipeline, as only one depth interval is required to be blended. If the test does not deliver any result, we continue the normal procedure of comparing the layers, in which the already computed layers can be reused.

6.3 Integration into Existing PBR Pipeline

The overlap between the standard PBR pipeline and TLDI construction suggests an integration between those two. The early rejection test already uses the same standard pipeline of rendering to create the two front layers. In fact, the only difference is what is being blended, color or depth. However, in rendering the two objects are processed and z-culled together, while TLDI construction processes one object at a time. The preferred integration scenario is to blend both colors and depth while creating the front TLDIs of O_0 and O_1. While the TLDIs are used for collision detection, the two frames with the blended colors can be merged into one by performing z-culling at each pixel using the corresponding TLDIs to choose which color value is copied to the merging frame pixel.

We note that TLDI construction profits from the reuse of PBR pipeline calculations for point-cloud data located inside the view frustum. For many application scenarios, only these data are of interest anyway, e.g., an avatar moving with the camera.

Point clouds are almost always perspectively projected onto the screen by rendering pipelines, whereas the cylinders in sections 4, 5, 6 are assumed to be orthogonally projected. The integrated pipeline has to use the same projection for both rendering and TLDI and so we use perspective projection in our experiments. This results in perspective foreshortening of the cylinders and thus turns them into truncated cones. However, since the resulting surface is only an approximation, accuracy is not affected significantly as the results in Section 7 confirm.

6.4 Distance Queries

In addition to collision queries, our method can also incidentally answer distance queries in case of non-collision. Since we do not consider $\hat{\Sigma}$ as orientable, the distance function we calculate with respect to it is unsigned. We can therefore not decide if the distance between two objects is one of separation or of penetration. When layers $l_{0,i}, l_{1,j}$ are compared to determine a collision, their absolute depth difference per pixel is calculated as follows:

$$d(\hat{\mathbf{x}}) = min(|\hat{F}_i(near) - \hat{F}_j(far)|, |\hat{F}_j(near) - \hat{F}_i(far)|)$$

We keep track of $d_{min}(\hat{\mathbf{x}})$ at each pixel and then report its overall minimum in case of non-collision, which yields the separation distance in view direction.

7 RESULTS

The algorithm is implemented in C++, OpenGL and GLSL. Tests were run on Core2 Quad processor, 2.4 GHz, with 4 GB RAM, and GeForce GTX 680 graphics processor.

We used the benchmark proposed by [21] for testing, in which two copies of the same model are tested for collision against each other. Both objects are normalized to fit in a 2^3 cube. The center of one object is positioned at the origin, and the center of the second is positioned at a distance d_0 from the origin along the +x direction. The second object is compositely rotated about the y-axis and the z-axis, with a number of small steps. The composite rotations are iteratively repeated, each iteration starting from a position at a distance $d_i = d_0 - i\Delta d$ from the origin. We initialized d_0 with 3.0, 31 iteration/distance, and 30 steps per rotation, which makes 900 cases per iteration/distance, and 27900 total cases. The camera is positioned at coordinates $(0,0,+4)$, and facing the origin. Point clouds are perspectively projected with view angle $90°$ at planes $z = +1$ and $z = +6$ from the camera position.

Accuracy and runtime results are computed for each distance by averaging the results of all steps in the corresponding rotation. Accuracy tests are performed by comparing our outcomes with those of an exact mesh collision procedure. We call this percentage the accuracy error, but it should be noted that *it is not actually an error*. The polygonal mesh of a point cloud is an approximation of the surface, but not the surface itself. So, we consider the mesh collision test results as an *approximation of the ground truth*.

Four models were used for testing: Stanford BUNNY, ARMADILLO, DRAGON, and HAPPY polygonal models. For each model, the point set has been extracted from the mesh and the r_i for its points determined by kNN with $k = 7$ for testing purposes, where r_i is set to 0.65 of the computed distance. An efficient screen-space method to determine a radius containing kNN has been demonstrated in [18]. They project cylinders onto a rather large frame, 1024×1024, to achieve accurate results.

Besides synthetic models, we also tested collision detection between the huge data set of the houses of EPHESUS ($> 5M$ points) captured by a laser scanner (see Figure 6), and a single HAPPY model. We tried to imitate an interactive navigation experience by considering the HAPPY model a human discovering the big model.

Figure 6: The houses of EPHESUS. Left: View from above of the point cloud. Right: Closer view with splat rendering.

Table 1: The percentages of false negatives and false positives with various compression ratios ρ for: BUNNY, ARMADILLO, DRAGON, HAPPY.

ρ	false negatives (%)				false positives (%)			
	B	A	D	H	B	A	D	H
1.0	0	0	0	0	0.92	0.47	0.47	0.12
0.5	0	0	0	0	0.68	0.29	0.29	0.08
0.25	0	0	0	0	0.52	0.23	0.21	0.03
0.1	0	0.1	0.01	0	0.43	0.18	0.15	0.02
0.05	0	0.01	0.02	0.01	0.39	0.17	0.14	0.02
0.01	0.01	0.03	0.05	0.05	0.33	0.16	0.13	0.01
0.005	0.05	0.04	0.06	0.06	0.3	0.16	0.13	0.01

The same benchmark described above is used, where EPHESUS keeps its size, HAPPY scaled to the size of a human – relative to EPHESUS – and the view emanates from the eyes of HAPPY and directed forward. HAPPY is initially positioned at coordinates $(0,0,+D)$, where D is the x-extent of the EPHESUS bounding box. Number of iterations and number of steps per iteration are the same as above. A polygonal mesh of EPHESUS is not available, so only runtime is measured.

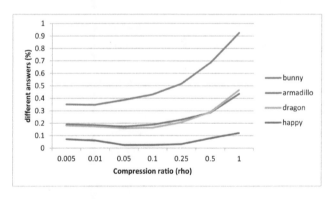

Figure 7: Accuracy error of collision detection compared with the sampled mesh as approximate ground truth. Based on these results we chose $\rho = 0.05$ for subsequent tests.

When querying the intersection between thickened bounding intervals as an indicator of collision, we have encountered very few cases of false negatives in our experiments (none for most object pairs tested), but the ratio of false positives is rather high (see Table 1). Compressing the intervals as mentioned in Section 6.1 with a factor ρ decreases this number effectively while yielding only an insignificant number of false negatives. The accuracy resulting from different compression values is plotted in Figure 7, which shows that accuracy peaks for ρ between 0.01 and 0.05. Smaller values of ρ yield less false negatives, but more false positives, which results in less overall accuracy. Based on that, we chose $\rho = 0.05$ for all

Table 2: Point clouds with total TLDI construction time (in millisec). CD runtime, time overlap with rendering, and error from mesh ground truth are averaged following the benchmark of Section 7.

Model	Size	TLDI	CD	Render	Error
Bunny	36k	13.9	2.2	0.9	0.39 %
Armadillo	173k	43.7	8.1	3.1	0.18 %
Dragon	438k	122.5	15.8	6.7	0.16 %
Happy	544k	134.9	18.3	8.2	0.03 %

following tests, to maximize accuracy (= minimizing sum of false negatives and false positives).

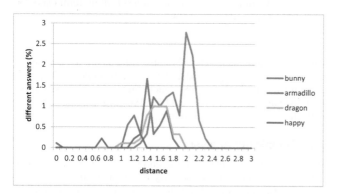

Figure 8: Accuracy error vs distance for all models.

Accuracy

Figure 8 shows a plot of accuracy error against distance d_i. For all models, the error is zero when the two objects centers are either far or close, and increases in between, where the object surfaces collide. The accuracy error stays below 3% for all models for any distance. Table 2 shows accuracy error averaged over distances, and is always below 0.4%. Note that false negatives result from $\hat{\Omega}$ not covering $\hat{\Sigma}$ entirely. This can occur if either ρ is too small, overly compressing $\hat{\Omega}$, or if radii are estimated too small.

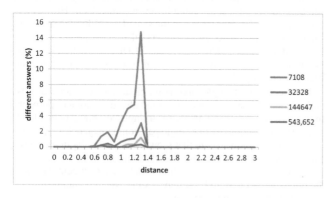

Figure 9: Accuracy error for different resolutions of HAPPY.

We are particularly satisfied by the accuracy results of our method. In Figure 10, [21] showed accuracy error of different resolutions of HAPPY. We reproduce this plot based on the same benchmark in Figure 9, albeit with the different resolutions of HAPPY which were available to us. Interestingly their accuracy do not improve much when increasing sampling density (always < 7%). Our results improve significantly with increasing sampling density as we expect the TLDI to approximate the surface better, down to < 0.3% for the original resolution.

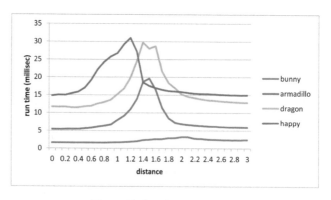

Figure 10: Runtime vs distance.

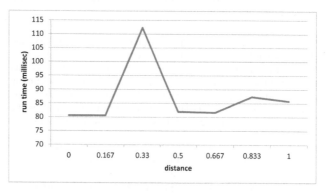

Figure 11: Runtime for colliding large EPHESUS (5M points) with HAPPY averaged over different distances (using benchmark). The numbers on the x-axis are the distances normalized to $[0, 1]$.

Runtime

The result of the benchmark shows that runtime increases approximately linearly with point cloud size (see Table 2). The same table also shows the large overlap of collision detection with the rendering pipeline: about 40% of collision detection runtime is removed if the point clouds are rendered as well. Colliding the large EPHESUS model with HAPPY is still possible at interactive frame rates (see Figure 11). Similar to accuracy, runtime also decreases for near or far object centers and increases in between where surfaces collide, as Figure 10 demonstrates.

Figure 12 confirms that the early rejection test outlined in Section 6.2 reduces runtime significantly as well.

The runtime of TLDI construction is directly proportional to point cloud size, and number of captured layers, whereas the number of layers in turn depends on how tight the TLDI is. The more the TLDI adheres to the actual surface, the more layers are captured and the longer the construction time. TLDI tightness is controllable via scaling the splats radius and the frame resolution. For collision detection, it is necessary to construct a tight TLDI to achieve accurate results, but this is balanced by the fact that it is not necessary to construct the whole TLDI as explained in Section 5. For other applications where the TLDI functions as a bounding volume rather than a surface estimator, the construction time can be traded off with the tightness level. Table 3 shows the runtime of full TLDI construction for HAPPY and DRAGON models, against different frame resolutions and splat scales. The table shows the accuracy error values as well. The smallest error is achieved by a radius scale of 1.0 and frame resolution of 1024×1024. There is no specific rule how accuracy error changes with the two parameters, but the trend is that it decreases as the radius scale increases.

Comparing the runtime of our method to others, e.g. [21], is of

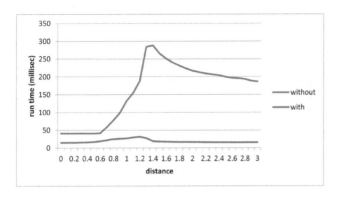

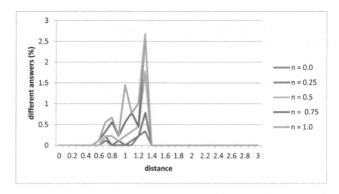

Figure 12: Runtime for HAPPY (using benchmark), without (blue) and with (red) the early rejection test. It clearly shows that it increases efficiency significantly.

Table 3: The average TLDI construction time for HAPPY and DRAGON models at different frame resolutions and splat scales. Average number of captured layers are denoted inside brackets, and accuracy error values are denoted below in italic. The values on top of the columns indicate the scaling value of the splat radius. The numbers show how the TLDI construction time decreases as the frame resolution decreases and the splat radius scale increases.

Model	Resolution	1.0	3.0	5.0
Happy	1024×1024	134.9(10.4)	88.2(6.9)	67.5(5.4)
		0.16%	*0.79%*	*1.9%*
	512×512	121.8(9.5)	85.3(6.8)	68.6(5.6)
		0.18%	*0.67%*	*1.7%*
	256×256	113.4(9.0)	75.9(6.2)	63.2(5.1)
		0.71%	*0.57%*	*1.4%*
Dragon	1024×1024	122.5(11.5)	98.2(9.1)	93.4(6.4)
		0%	*0.20%*	*0.24%*
	512×512	116.2(11.1)	94.2(9.0)	64.6(6.2)
		0.16%	*0.19%*	*0.63%*
	256×256	108.3(10.1)	89.9(8.7)	62.5(6.2)
		0.67%	*0.25%*	*0.42%*

limited usefulness. Their algorithm was designed for static objects, as the underlying structure takes considerable time to construct. For those pre-processed data structures it performs collision queries faster than ours (being of $O(logN)$ versus our $O(N)$ complexity), but for dynamically changing objects, hierarchy construction time needs to be added to each query, and for that our algorithm is faster by orders of magnitude, even considering that they were measured on older hardware. The construction of their underlying BVH may become faster if parallelized and performed on modern hardware. The tested models contain about 1M points. For objects of that size, a BVH-based algorithm of $O(NlogN)$ complexity would require an extra time factor $O(logN)$ of 20, which is quite large.

Robustness to Noise

Since the boundary of Ω is thickened to the extent of sampling density, we expect it to smooth noise up to a similar level. We tested the robustness of our approach by adding Gaussian noise with different σ to HAPPY, the most densely sampled synthetic model used in our tests. We set $\sigma = nr_{avg}$, where r_{avg} is the average over r_i, and random $n = [0, 1]$. Runtime did not change significantly and accuracy error was always below 3% (see Figure 13).

Real Data and Dynamic Simulation

Point clouds captured with the Kinect often exhibit noise and holes, as ROOM (300k points, captured by Kinect) shown in Figure 14a. Figures 14b-d show snapshots of collision detection between BUNNY and ROOM. Collisions are robustly detected near

Figure 13: Accuracy error for different levels of uniform Gaussian noise ($\sigma = nr_{avg}$) added to HAPPY.

flat surfaces and small holes. We also simulated a dynamic environment of an animated model (HORSE) (10 frames, 8.5k points each) traversing the EPHESUS model. Figure 15 shows snapshots from the simulation. BUNNY and HORSE are rendered as meshes in the figures for visual plausibility.

7.1 Complexity Analysis

Worst-case time complexity between pairs of objects occurs only if there is no collision and the early rejection test does not detect that. An example is an object that is partially obscured from the view point by a concavity in the other object. This requires construction of all TLDIs per point cloud and comparing all of those for one point cloud against the subsets of TLDIs clipped between them. TLDI construction is linear in the size of the point clouds, with the added factor of depth complexity, as points are processed in order for each layer and therefore $O(LN)$. The collision test is output-sensitive with $O(LXY)$ for screen space resolution $X \times Y$ and scales with the depth complexity of the point cloud being clipped.

For collision detection among a set of more than two point clouds, using the proposed algorithm would make the overall runtime (both construction and collision detection) quadratic, as the construction of a cloud TLDI is dependent on the other cloud TLDI and thus would be reconstructed for each comparison. However, if the number of clouds is large and the size of each cloud is relatively small, we could also construct the TLDI of each point cloud just once and separately. The then linear TLDI construction time has the trade-off that the previously linear time of collision detection becomes $O(L_1 L_2 XY)$.

If we compare a single large point cloud (environment) against multiple small ones (avatars), we could also use another approach. In that case, all avatars are treated as a single combined point cloud, and the same complexity of a single pair comparison holds. Increasing the number of avatars in that scenario increases N_2 in the above expression, and therefore construction time increases linearly. In order to know which avatars collide with the environment, labels at the points would have to be stored as well, which would result in a small increase in memory storage.

8 CONCLUSION AND FUTURE WORK

We have proposed a novel data structure for representing the surface of dynamic point clouds. We show that it can be constructed efficiently and reuse computation from an existing PBR pipeline. As an application we have demonstrated online collision detection for large models. Our results show that our surface extraction is significantly more precise than for a previous method [12], especially where points are densely sampled, and that it is also robust to noise since the surface underlying the points is thickened.

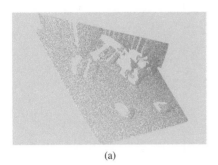

(a)　　　　　　　　(b)　　　　　　　　(c)　　　　　　　　(d)

Figure 14: Collision detection between BUNNY and the (a) Kinect captured ROOM. BUNNY is blue in cases of non collision, and turns red in cases of detected collisions. (b) shows BUNNY near a flat surface, and crosses it in the next frame (c). Both cases are correctly detected. BUNNY passes through a wide hole in (d) which is not recognized as part of the surface, and thus no collision is detected.

Figure 15: Animated HORSE inside EPHESUS, passing through a column.

We are currently working to improve our data structure in terms of compactness and efficiency of construction and traversal. Implementation of the more exact surface extraction for stacks would even further increase accuracy, since we currently simply assume the center of the depth range of a layer along a view ray to be the surface intersection. We think that augmenting the TLDI with data from sampling such as normals and uncertainty information could permit even more precise surface extraction. TLDI could also be used instead of a voxelization as a more compact representation, for example to accelerate global illumination computations.

ACKNOWLEDGEMENTS

This research was supported by the EU FP7 project HARVEST4D (no. 323567).

REFERENCES

[1] R. K. Anjos, J. M. Pereira, and J. F. Oliveira. Collision detection on point clouds using a 2.5+d image-based approach. *J. of WSCG*, 20(2):145–154, 2012.

[2] G. V. D. Bergen. Efficient collision detection of complex deformable models using AABB trees. *J. of Graphics Tools*, 4(2):1–14, 1997.

[3] H. Blum. A Transformation for Extracting New Descriptors of Shape. In W. Wathen-Dunn, editor, *Models for the Perception of Speech and Visual Form*, pages 362–380. MIT Press, Cambridge, 1967.

[4] B. Curless and M. Levoy. A volumetric method for building complex models from range images. *Proc. SIGGRAPH*, pages 303–312, 1996.

[5] S. A. Ehmann and M. C. Lin. Accurate and fast proximity queries between polyhedra using convex surface decomposition. *cgforum*, 20:500–510, 2001.

[6] E. Eisemann and X. Dècoret. Fast scene voxelization and applications. *ACM SIGGRAPH Symp. on Interactive 3D Graphics & Games*, pages 71–78, 2006.

[7] C. Everitt. Interactive order-independent transparency. Technical report, NVIDIA, 2001.

[8] S. Gottschalk, M. Lin, and D. Manocha. OBB-tree: A hierarchical structure for rapid interference detection. *SIGGRAPH 96 Conf. Proc.*, pages 171–180, Aug 1996.

[9] N. K. Govindaraju, M. C. Lin, and D. Manocha. Fast and reliable collision culling using graphics hardware. *Vis. and Computer Graphics, IEEE Trans. on*, 12(2):143–154, Mar-Apr 2006.

[10] B. Heidelberger, M. Teschner, and M. H. Gross. Detection of collisions and self-collisions using image-space techniques. In *J. of WSCG*, volume 17, pages 145–152, 2004.

[11] T. Hinks, H. Carr, L. Truong-Hong, and D. Laefer. Point cloud data conversion into solid models via point-based voxelization. *Surveying Engineering*, 139(2):7283, 2013.

[12] J. Klein and G. Zachmann. Point cloud collision detection. In *Eurographics 2004*, volume 23, pages 567–576, Sep 2004.

[13] J. T. Kloswski, M. Held, J. S. B. Mitchell, H. Sowrizal, and K. Zikan. Efficient collision detection using bounding volume hierarchies of k-dops. *IEEE Trans. on Vis. & Com. Graphics*, 1(4):21–36, Jan 1998.

[14] D. Knott and D. K. Pai. Cinder: Collision and interference detection in real-time using graphics hardware. In *Graphics Interface*, pages 73–80, May 2003.

[15] Y. Ohtake, A. Belyaev, and H.-P. Seidel. An integrating approach to meshing scattered point data. In *Proc. of 2005 ACM symp. on Solid & physical modeling*, pages 61–69. ACM, 2005.

[16] J. Pan, S. Chitta, and D. Manocha. Probabilistic collision detection between noisy point clouds using robust classification. *Int. Symp. on Robotics Research*, 2011.

[17] J. Pan, I. A. Sucan, S. Chitta, and D. Manocha. Real-time collision detection and distance computation on point cloud sensor data. In *IEEE Int. Conf. on Robotics & Automation*, pages 3593–3599, 2013.

[18] R. Preiner, S. Jeschke, and M. Wimmer. Auto splats: Dynamic point cloud visualization on the gpu. In H. Childs and T. Kuhlen, editors, *Proc. of Eurographics Symp. on Parallel Graphics & Vis.*, pages 139–148. Eurographics Association 2012, may 2012.

[19] C. Scheiblauer and M. Wimmer. Out-of-core selection and editing of huge point clouds. *Computers & Graphics*, 35(2):342–351, Apr 2011.

[20] D. Steinemann, M. Otaduy, and M. Gross. Efficient bounds for point-based animations. *Symp. Point-Based Graphics*, pages 57–64, 2007.

[21] G. Zachmann. Minimal hierarchical collision detection. In *ACM Symp. on Vir. Reality Software and Tec.*, pages 121–128, Nov 2002.

Signed Distance Fields for Polygon Soup Meshes

Hongyi Xu*   Jernej Barbič†

University of Southern California

ABSTRACT

Many meshes in computer animation practice are meant to approximate solid objects, but the provided triangular geometry is often unoriented, non-manifold or contains self-intersections, causing inside/outside of objects to be mathematically ill-defined. We
describe a robust and efficient automatic approach to define and
compute a signed distance field for arbitrary triangular geometry.
Starting with arbitrary (non-manifold) triangular geometry, we first
define and extract an offset manifold surface using an unsigned
distance field. We then automatically remove any interior surface
components. Finally, we exploit the manifoldness of the offset surface to quickly detect interior distance field grid points. We prove
that exterior grid points can reuse a shifted original unsigned distance field, whereas for interior cells, we compute the signed field
from the offset surface geometry. We demonstrate improved performance both using exact distance fields computed using an octree,
and approximate distance fields computed using fast marching. We
analyze the time and memory costs for complex meshes that include
self-intersections and non-manifold geometry. We demonstrate the
effectiveness of our algorithm by using the signed distance field for
collision detection and generation of tetrahedral meshes for physically based simulation.

Index Terms: Computer Graphics [I.3.5]: Computational Geometry and Object Modeling—Geometric algorithms, languages, and
systems

1 INTRODUCTION

Given a collection of 3D triangles and a query 3D location x, there
exists some triangle (and a feature on this triangle) closest to x. *Distance field* is a scalar function that gives the minimum distances for
points x from some region of space, such as a bounding box enclosing the triangular geometry. Distance fields sampled on regular
3D grids are a popular datastructure in computer graphics [21], and
have been used in many applications, such as collision detection
and morphing. Distance fields can be signed or unsigned. Signed
distance fields store the sign specifying whether the query point is
inside/outside of the object. Sign is only meaningful, however, if
the input mesh is a watertight mesh with manifold geometry. If the
input is a general "triangle soup", the sign is not well-defined and
in principle only an unsigned distance field can be computed.

We present an approach to both *define* and *compute* a signed distance field for any input triangular geometry, including geometry
containing self-collisions, gaps, holes or inconsistently oriented,
disconnected, non-closed, noisy or duplicated geometry (see Figure 2). Such geometry is very common in computer graphics practice, for example, with 3D characters, mechanical components, and
surgery simulation. Unlike most signed distance field computation
methods that assume a well-defined watertight manifold input mesh
and then optimize the distance field computation, we address the
problem of how to first define the sign for any triangular geometry,

---

*e-mail: hongyixu@usc.edu

†e-mail:jnb@usc.edu

Graphics Interface Conference 2014
7-9 May, Montreal, Quebec, Canada

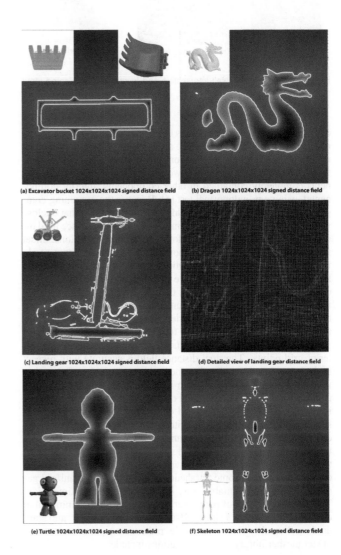

(a) Excavator bucket 1024x1024x1024 signed distance field   (b) Dragon 1024x1024x1024 signed distance field

(c) Landing gear 1024x1024x1024 signed distance field   (d) Detailed view of landing gear distance field

(e) Turtle 1024x1024x1024 signed distance field   (f) Skeleton 1024x1024x1024 signed distance field

Figure 1: Signed distance fields for non-manifold geometry.

and then compute the signed distance field efficiently. Our approach
is not specific to any distance field computation method. We define
and rapidly compute exact signed distance fields using an octree,
and approximate distance fields using fast marching [39]. Exact
signed distance fields are useful, for example, in collision detection,
where inexact signed distance fields will lead to missed collisions
if the distance field is queried against a bounding volume hierarchy.
Fast marching only gives approximate distance fields, and is advantageous for speed, especially with geometrically complex meshes.

Our method first computes an unsigned distance field to the input
geometry. It then extracts a *manifold* offset isosurface, using the
marching cubes algorithm with topological guarantees [26]. The
offset surface distance σ is the only parameter that the user needs
to adjust. This parameter has an intuitive meaning: geometry im-
perfections smaller than σ are considered "noise" and are automati-

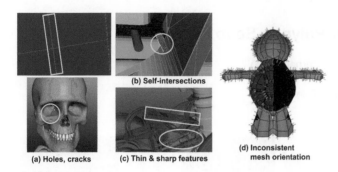

(b) Self-intersections

(a) Holes, cracks

(c) Thin & sharp features

(d) Inconsistent mesh orientation

Figure 2: Non-manifold, self-intersecting and inconsistently oriented input meshes.

cally fused together, whereas gaps larger than σ are above the "engineering tolerance" and contribute to the signed distance field. The resulting isosurface in general consists of several disjoint (potentially nested) components, and we automatically remove components completely contained in other components (interior components), using a pseudonormal test [5]. Because the remaining components form non-nested manifold watertight surfaces that enclose well-defined solids, one could compute the signed distance field directly from their geometry [6]. However, at high resolutions, offset surfaces usually contain many more triangles than the input mesh, which results in signed computations much slower than unsigned field computation. We accelerate the signed computation by two orders of magnitude by proving that the exterior signed distance field is simply a shifted original unsigned distance field, which can therefore be re-used in the exterior region. We exploit the manifoldness of the offset surface to quickly identify the interior grid points, and then compute the signed distance field only for the interior grid points. The final distance field is accurate with respect to the isosurface geometry. Our method is very efficient for meshes where the exterior space is much larger than the interior space, as is the case with many mechanical components, characters and medical meshes. We use our signed distance fields to perform collision detection between objects with non-manifold triangular geometry. Our signed distance fields can also serve as input to isosurface meshers that require well-defined inside/outside of objects, such as those available in the CGAL library [1]. This makes it possible to create quality anisotropic tetrahedral meshes for non-manifold geometry (Figure 9), suitable, say, for physically based simulation. The required number of parameters for such meshing is minimal in our method: we need a single offset surface parameter σ, and standard mesh quality (minimum angle, radius, etc.) parameters of the 3D tet mesher library. Our contributions include:

- an efficient approach to *both* define and compute a signed distance field for arbitrary input geometry,

- algorithm for removing nested interior isosurfaces,

- mathematical proof that the distance field of an offset surface equals to a shifted distance field of the original (non-manifold) surface,

- rapid global sign determination via S-shaped traversal.

2 RELATED WORK

Many efficient algorithms are available to compute unsigned and signed distance fields for *manifold watertight* meshes; see, for example, the survey [21]. To accelerate distance computation, hierarchical data structures can cull branches that cannot contain the shortest distance [17, 45]. Fuhrmann [16] computed distance fields

by analyzing prisms emanating from each triangle along the normal direction. Similarly, the characteristic/scan conversion (CSC) method [28] computes the exact distance field up to some maximum value by scan converting distance fields of individual vertices, edges and faces. The [15, 43] accelerate the CSC method with an efficient GPU implementation. To speed up the hardware-assisted distance field computation, [47, 48] explores a Voronoi-based culling and clamping algorithm and [46] presents an interactive algorithm for surface distance maps with the affine transformation. Based on GPU, distance fields can also be computed on adaptive grids [8, 34], or on local narrow bands for complex geometry [12]. Fast marching method, a propagation method that numerically solves the Eikonal equation, updates the distance voxel-by-voxel with increasing distance [39, 40]. Linear computational complexity for the fast marching method has been demonstrated by [13, 49]. Similarly, jump flooding algorithms can compute approximate distances in constant time for an input set of seeds [36]. Several robust algorithms have been proposed to determine the sign for triangular *manifold* surfaces [2, 5, 43]. All of these algorithms, however, require the input mesh to be manifold and watertight for the sign to be defined. In our work, we address the problem of how to *define* the sign for non-manifold or non-closed geometry, and then rapidly compute the resulting signed distance field.

For "polygon soup" geometry, [32] determines the sign at each grid point with ray stabbing and voting. However, ray stabbing is a global operation and could assign incorrect signs in regions where the surface has high variation or self-overlaps. This problem can be partially overcome by observing that the grid points far from the surface exhibit less sign variation [44]. Similarly, [30] determines the sign by counting the intersections of voxel edges with the geometry, to successfully resolve self-intersections of closed manifold meshes. Robustness can also be improved using ray voting against ε-bands of the unsigned distance field [29]. Ray voting methods in general, however, have difficulties handling structured outliers in the geometry. Space can also be partitioned into polyhedral regions and then the interior solid region is determined based on region adjacency [31]. However, unlike our work, this method does not support open objects (shells) or intersecting solid objects.

Another approach is to create manifold surface with surface repair methods which try to resolve artifacts of the input surface meshes. The mesh-based methods repair the input surface by removing gaps [11, 35] and filling holes [24, 25, 41]. In practice, however, the input geometry may consist of several (non-manifold) surfaces that intersect or are in close proximity, as is the case with mechanical components (landing gear), or 3D characters (turtle). In such cases, it is difficult to apply the above geometric mesh-repair mechanisms to extract a single well-defined manifold mesh, requiring user interaction to resolve ambiguities. Volume-based methods usually can resolve more general complex configurations, but they usually also introduce distortion in trouble-free parts [10, 22]. The input mesh can be modified only locally within the neighborhood of undesired configuration [4]. CAD models can be repaired while avoiding the global sampling problems of the volume base method [9]. This method, however, requires the input geometry to consist of triangular manifold meshes; we make no such assumption. Similarly, the method of [42] requires the input triangle orientation to be consistent; otherwise, suboptimal results are produced (see Section 3.3 in [42]).

Several methods have been proposed to reconstruct surfaces from implicit functions [19, 42, 50]. Robustness to noisy data [23] and unoriented data [3] has been improved. Implicit functions are commonly used to track fluid surfaces [7, 30]. The goal of these methods is accurate reconstruction of surfaces, and therefore these methods generally employ implicit functions in narrow bands around the surface. In our work, we compute global signed distance fields, both inside and outside the object, sampled on regular

3D grids. Global signed distance fields can be computed directly from isosurfaces of unsigned distance fields [6]. We greatly accelerate such global signed distance field computation by proving that the distance field can be re-used in the exterior region. We also give an efficient algorithm to remove interior nested isosurface components (Section 3.1), as well as an S-shaped traversal algorithm (Section 3.3) to rapidly determine the sign globally, with a minimal number of pseudonormal tests.

Given a distance field, the marching cubes algorithm [26, 27], or *dual* methods [38] can robustly extract a closed, manifold and intersection-free triangulated surface. Unless the distance field is signed, this surface will contain interior components, which may not be desirable. The resulting mesh is also typically high resolution and follows a regular pattern. If such a surface is used to create a 3D tetrahedral mesh directly (e.g., using TetGen [18]), one typically obtains a highly detailed tet mesh whose resolution cannot be easily adjusted. Our signed distance fields can serve as input to anisotropic tet meshers that mesh the volume enclosed by an isosurface, such as those implemented in the CGAL [1] library. This makes it possible to create "cage" tet meshes enclosing input *non-manifold* geometry, useful, e.g., for level-of-detail simulation, or the multigrid method [33].

Recently, Jacobson et. al [20] presented a robust approach to compute tetrahedral meshes for "polygon soup" input geometry, using generalized winding numbers and constrained Delaunay triangulation. Although the method is robust to many polygon soup geometries and can preserve the input mesh, it requires consistent orientation of the input triangles whereas our method does not. Duplicated geometry will result in incorrect winding numbers and may cause ambiguities. The most important difference, however, is that the winding number field is *not* a signed distance function to any particular geometry. Multiplying an unsigned distance field with the winding number (or its sign) does not give a signed distance field. The resulting function is not even continuous: it has, for example, a discontinuity when leaving the open container in Figure 7 (b). As such, this method does not address our problem (signed distance field computation). Our implicit functions are *signed distance fields* with respect to some meaningful geometry (the isosurface), with all the resulting benefits: continuity, unit gradient, and the field absolute values are exact distances to some meaningful geometry (the isosurface). We compare our method to [20] in Section 4.

3 COMPUTING THE SIGNED DISTANCE FIELD

Given the input "triangle soup" geometry Ω, a box where the distance field is to be computed, and grid resolutions in x, y, z, we first compute the unsigned distance field. Our implementation is accelerated using an octree and multiple cores for exact computation, and uses the fast marching method for approximate distance field computation. In exact computation, we compute exact distance to the nearest triangle. The octree in the exact method only serves to accelerate the distance queries. The octree and fast marching are orthogonal to our method; we apply them equally to unsigned and signed distance field computation.

3.1 Offset surface and removal of interior components

We proceed by defining an offset surface of the unsigned distance field

$$S_\sigma = \left\{ X \in \mathbb{R}^3 \,|\, d_U(X, \Omega) = \sigma \right\}, \qquad (1)$$

where the function $d_U(X, \Omega)$ returns the unsigned distance from point X to geometry Ω, and $\sigma \geq 0$ is an offset. Typically, we set $\sigma = 3h$, where h is the distance field grid spacing, but other values can be chosen to preserve or remove local detail. We then extract a triangular mesh of S_σ, by applying the marching cube algorithm [26] to the unsigned distance field. This algorithm is guar-

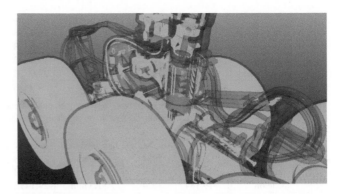

Figure 3: Offset surface S_σ for the Boeing 777 landing gear. Interior components (848 total) are shown green.

anteed to generate a manifold offset surface for any input. We observe that the offset surface in general consists of several *disjoint* connected components, which may be nested:

$$S_\sigma = \left(\amalg_i E_\sigma^i \right) \amalg \left(\amalg_i I_\sigma^i \right), \qquad (2)$$

where E_σ^i are connected components that are not enclosed by any bigger components (*exterior* components), and I_σ^i are all the other components (*interior* components). Note that $\amalg$ denotes the "disjoint union", i.e., set union with the additional understanding that the operands are disjoint. The marching cube algorithm will create both the E_σ^i and I_σ^i surfaces (Figure 3), and we need to remove the latter. We first detect all the connected components of S_σ using a union-find datastructure. For each component, we then efficiently determine if it is of type E or I, as follows. First, compute a tight bounding box for each component, and sort them according to their volumes. Starting from the component with the smallest bounding box volume, we check it against all the other components with a larger bounding box volume (starting from the largest one). If the smaller bounding box is not totally enclosed by the bigger box, there exists a point on the smaller component that is outside the bigger component, and the two components are therefore not nested. Otherwise, we pick a random vertex on the smaller component, and test if it is inside the bigger component. We do so by finding the nearest site on the larger mesh and then perform the pseudonormal test [5]. Testing a single vertex is sufficient because the components are disjoint; they are either nested or enclose disjoint volumes.

Once a surface is known to be of type I, we can remove it from all future pairs. At the end of this process, all surfaces of type E have been identified, and we can define

$$E_\sigma = \amalg_i E_\sigma^i. \qquad (3)$$

The time to compute E_σ was small compared to the signed distance field computation: under 2 minutes in our most complex example (landing gear), and much shorter in the other examples.

We note that the exterior component E_σ could be found using a voxel flood-fill from the bounding box boundary. However, such an approach slows down with increasing resolution. Also, due to geometric detail close to the "surface", multiple components of S_σ may intersect the same surface voxel (landing gear), so decomposition into connected components and determination which are interior is still needed. Our proposed method is very fast: for each component, only a single vertex must be tested (single pseudonormal test).

3.2 Unsigned distance field re-use

Our ultimate goal is to compute the signed distance field for the input mesh Ω. Currently, we have the manifold exterior offset surface

	#tri	resolution	unsigned field	memory	#isosurface tri	#interior components	naive signed field	signed field
excavator bucket	12,825	1024^3	12 min	26.4 GB	4,826,772	4	576 min	9 min
dragon	871,414	1024^3	103 min	27.0 GB	2,532,564	27	354 min	7 min
skeleton	379,184	1024^3	86 min	14.1 GB	812,572	119	116 min	1 min
landing gear	1,847,976	1024^3	53 min	29.0 GB	4,167,414	848	290 min	11 min
turtle	3,654	1024^3	6 min	24.9 GB	3,145,624	268	393 min	11 min

Table 1: **Distance field computation performance.** "Naive signed field" refers to computing the signed field directly from E_σ [Barbič and James 2008], whereas "signed field" refers to our method, which can be seen to be significantly faster. Time to construct E_σ is included. All computations use eight cores.

	#tri	resolution	unsigned field	memory	#isosurface tri	#interior components	naive signed field	signed field
excavator bucket	12,825	1024^3	68.5 min	29.1 GB	4,857,930	73	94.5 min	8.1 min
dragon	871,414	1024^3	85.1 min	30.0 GB	2,597,974	37	89 min	4.6 min
skeleton	379,184	1024^3	81.5 min	29.1 GB	844,394	138	81.9 min	1.7 min
landing gear	1,847,976	1024^3	73 min	30.4 GB	4,199,760	746	90.1 min	8 min
turtle	3,654	1024^3	83 min	29.1 GB	2,930,126	272	96 min	4.9 min

Table 2: **Distance field computation performance with the fast marching method.** The time to initialize marching via exact distance field computation in a narrow band around E_σ is included. All computations use a single core.

E_σ, and the unsigned distance field for Ω. One could now compute a signed distance field for E_σ, using an octree and the pseudonormal test [5], or using fast marching [39]. However, we observed that such an approach is computationally slow in practice, significantly slower than the unsigned computation (see Tables 1 and 2, "naive signed field"). Instead, we prove the following lemma.

Lemma 3.1 *If X is a point in the* exterior *region of E_σ, then the signed distance d_S equals*

$$d_S(X, E_\sigma) = d_U(X, \Omega) - \sigma \geq 0. \qquad (4)$$

Let Z and P' be the closest sites to X on surfaces E_σ and Ω, respectively. Let P be the closest site to Z on Ω. Because E_σ is manifold, XP' intersects E_σ; let Z' be any intersection point.

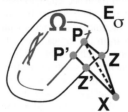

Figure 4: Proof illustration

Proof: Triangle inequality gives

$$d_S(X, E_\sigma) \geq |XP| - |ZP|$$
$$\geq d_U(X, \Omega) - \sigma. \qquad (5)$$

Suppose $d_S(X, E_\sigma) > d_U(X, \Omega) - \sigma$. Then we have

$$|XZ| > |XP'| - |ZP| = |XZ'| + (|Z'P'| - |ZP|). \qquad (6)$$

Because $Z' \in E_\sigma$, we have $|Z'P'| \geq \sigma = |ZP|$. Therefore, $|XZ| > |XZ'|$, contradicting that Z is closest to X on E_σ. ∎

Therefore, in the exterior region of E_σ, we can simply re-use our previously computed unsigned distance field $d_U(X, \Omega)$, leading to large computational savings (two orders of magnitude, see Tables 1 and 2, "signed field").

We also tried extending Equation 4 into the interior of E_σ (or at least into a narrow band on the interior side of E_σ), but discovered a counter-example. Figure 5 gives a counter-example where $\sigma > 0$ and $0 < a < 2\sigma$ are arbitrary, and $\varepsilon = \sqrt{\sigma^2 - a^2/4}$. The point X can be made arbitrarily close to E_σ ($\varepsilon > 0$ can

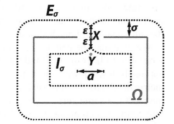

Figure 5: Counter-example

be made arbitrarily small), yet $d_S(X, E_\sigma) \neq d_U(X, \Omega) - \sigma$. This example also rules out another seemingly "intuitive" equality, as we have $|d_S(X, E_\sigma)| \neq d_U(X, \Omega) + \sigma$.

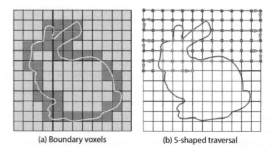

(a) Boundary voxels   (b) S-shaped traversal

Figure 6: **Fast inside/outside determination using boundary voxels.** Left: voxelized mesh and the boundary voxels (red). Right: "snake"-like traversal.

Therefore, we cannot re-use the unsigned field in the interior of E_σ, and must recompute it. In determining the sign, we can, however, use the following lemma to accelerate the computation.

Lemma 3.2 *If a point X satisfies $d_U(X, \Omega) < \sigma$, then X must be in the interior of E_σ.*

Proof: Suppose X is exterior to E_σ. Then by Lemma 3.1, we have

$$d_S(X, E_\sigma) = d_U(X, \Omega) - \sigma < 0, \qquad (7)$$

which contradicts the assumption that X is exterior to E_σ. ∎

Lemma 3.2 makes it possible to avoid a pseudonormal test for any grid point with $d_U(X, \Omega) < \sigma$, which applies to approximately half of the boundary voxel grid points during the S-shaped traversal (Section 3.3). Note that the pseudonormal test can be replaced with any other test to determine the sign, e.g. using winding number [20]; this is orthogonal to our method. In any case, Lemma 3.2 makes it possible to decrease the number of sign computations. We also note that the converse of Lemma 3.2 is not true. The counter-example is shown in Figure 5, where $d_U(Y, \Omega) \geq \sigma$, but Y is in the interior of E_σ.

3.3 Sign determination and interior distance field

Our remaining task is to compute the signed distance field in the interior region of E_σ. We first efficiently compute the sign for all the grid points. To do so, we first voxelize E_σ, and tag all the distance field voxels which intersect E_σ as *boundary* (Figure 6, left). We then compute unsigned distances and closest features (vertex, edge, or face) on E_σ for all the vertices of the boundary voxels. For exact distance field computation, we do so by computing an octree to E_σ, and then use it to compute distances and closest features. For fast marching, we compute the exact distance not just for boundary voxel vertices, but also for vertices of neighboring voxels (call this set of vertices $\mathcal{I}$), so that marching (below) can be properly initialized. We do so by traversing all the triangles of E_σ. To ensure correct 3D instances everywhere on $\mathcal{I}$, we "rasterize" [28] the distance function of each triangle to the vertices of intersecting voxels, their neighbors and neighbor's neighbors, storing the minimum distance.

Next, we perform a S-shaped traversal (Figure 6, right) over all the grid points to determine the sign. For multicore computation, we divide the grid into distinct (and equal in size, modulo #cores) slices, based on the z-coordinate, and process each slice on an individual core. During the traversal, we maintain a boolean flag that corresponds to whether the currently visited grid point is inside or outside of E_σ. The traversal starts at the distance field box corner, and the flag is initialized to *outside*. When a grid point is visited, we need to update the flag. However, if the grid point does not belong to a boundary voxel, the line segment joining the previous and current grid point cannot intersect E_σ, otherwise, the current grid point would belong to a boundary voxel. Therefore, in this case, we can keep the old flag value (whether *outside* or *inside*), without explicitly performing an inside-outside test. If the grid point belongs to a boundary voxel, we first check the condition $d_U(X, \Omega) < \sigma$ of Lemma 3.2. If satisfied, the grid point is in the interior of E_σ. Otherwise, we perform the inside/outside test by using the previously computed nearest site on E_σ and the pseudonormal test [5]. We update the boolean inside/outside flag accordingly.

At the end of the S-shaped traversal, the sign is known for all the grid points. Finally, we compute the distances for interior points. For fast marching, we do so by initializing the marching using the distances and sign computed in the narrow band in the first step above, and then march into the interior. For exact distance fields, we perform another S-shaped traversal, skipping the exterior points and computing the distances for the interior points using the octree. S-shaped traversal order is beneficial so that we can use the triangle inequality to provide a good initial upper bound on the distance for the octree traversal, $|d_S(X + H, E_\sigma) - d_S(X, E_\sigma)| \le |H|$, where $H \in \mathbb{R}^3$ is an arbitrary vector. In our S-shaped traversal, X and $X + H$ are adjacent grid points.

After we compute the signed distance field for E_σ, we can offset it by $-\sigma$, producing the final signed distance field. We note that this last offsetting step is optional (Figure 10), and works best when the input non-manifold surface is intended to approximate a closed mesh. If the input surface is a non-manifold shell, E_σ enlarges it into a volume with a manifold boundary; this is useful, e.g., to define a collision volume with well-defined repulsive normals.

4 Results

Our experiments were performed on an Intel Xeon 2.9 GHz CPU (2x8 cores) machine with 32GB RAM, and an GeForce GTX 680 graphics card with 2GB RAM. Table 1 gives the performance of our signed distance field computation on five non-manifold meshes. All exact signed distance field examples use eight cores for both unsigned and signed distance fields, whereas fast marching uses a single core. Figure 1 shows the distance field results for the five models. The Boeing 777 landing gear, the turtle and the skeleton have self-intersections in the input mesh. The triangles of the turtle and skeleton were not consistently oriented in these meshes which we downloaded from the Internet, which is not a problem for our method as consistent input mesh orientation is not required. Our distance field plausibly resolves non-manifold geometric detail and thin features. Table 3 analyzes scalability under increasing resolutions. In Figure 11, we give an example illustrating a plausible signed distance field computed for non-manifold input geometry.

We have applied our distance field computation algorithm to collision detection and tetrahedral mesh computation. Figure 8 illustrates collision detection performed by testing one object's

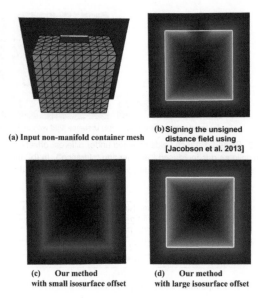

(a) Input non-manifold container mesh

(b) Signing the unsigned distance field using [Jacobson et al. 2013]

(c) Our method with small isosurface offset

(d) Our method with large isosurface offset

Figure 7: **Comparison to generalized winding numbers.** Input mesh (a) is a box with a square hole cut from the top face. The field obtained by multiplying the unsigned distance field by the sign of the thresholded generalized winding number [20] is not continuous across the opening of the box (b). We can treat the box as open space by setting the offset surface value smaller than half of the width of the hole (c), or closed space otherwise (d).

pointshell against the signed distance field of the other object [6]. Figure 9 demonstrates the tetrahedral mesh computed for the turtle model, by using our signed distance field as the input to the anisotropic mesher in CGAL [1]. As commonly done in computer graphics, the original non-manifold triangle mesh geometry can then be animated by performing a FEM deformable object simulation on the tetrahedral mesh.

We compare our signed function to a modified algorithm of [20] in Figure 7. The input mesh is a 3D box with a square hole cut from its top face. The size of the hole a is adjustable. Jacobson et. al [20] computes the inside-outside segmentation based on a graph-cut over the generalized winding number, which here is greater than 0.5 everywhere inside the box, regardless of a. Therefore, the entire box is assigned the interior sign. Our method, however, treats the gap a as either a genuine gap or an artifact, depending on the value of the isosurface input parameter σ relative to a. If σ is small, our method will treat the gap as genuine and the box as open; if σ is large, the box will be closed. Our method therefore provides control (via parameter σ) over what features are considered too small and can be neglected, versus features that are above the "engineering tolerance" σ. It is not easily possible to convert the winding number field into a signed distance field. Because the sign of the thresholded generalized winding number is not continuous, the implicit function obtained by signing the unsigned distance field with the sign of the thresholded generalized winding number is not continuous (Figure 7, b). Similarly, multiplying the winding number field with the signed distance field, or using the winding field directly, gives an implicit function that does not have unit gradient and whose values are not distances to some geometry; it is therefore not a signed distance function.

Performance for exact signed distance fields computed using the octree is provided in Table 1. Our method is not limited to octree-based distance field accelerations, but can be used with any uniform-grid distance field computation method. Regardless of what algorithm is used to compute the unsigned distance field, we can always use Equation 4 to avoid recomputing the distance field outside of the manifold offset surface. This speedup also applies

    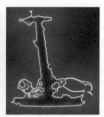

(a) Input landing gear mesh   (b) Distance field with σ=2h   (c) Distance field with σ=3h   (d) Distance field with σ=7h   (e) Distance field with σ=10h

Figure 10: Signed distance fields obtained under different offsets σ, followed by a shift-back by −σ. It can be seen that the method progressively treats larger voids as solid as σ is increased ("engineering tolerance"). In (b) and (c), observe that the walls of the main vertical landing gear support structure (green in (a)) remain equally thin. In (e), σ is so large that the entire interior of the hollow support structure is filled.

resolution	time (unsigned)	time (signed)
128x128x128	2.25 min	0.05 min
256x256x256	5.42 min	0.15 min
512x512x512	22 min	1.5 min
1024x1024x1024	105 min	9 min

Table 3: Computation times (dragon) vs distance field resolution.

Figure 8: **Collision detection using the computed signed distance fields.** Sixteen non-manifold dragons falling onto the ground. Distance field resolution is 1024x1024x1024.

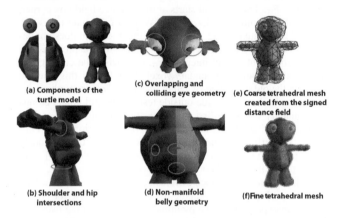

(a) Components of the turtle model   (c) Overlapping and colliding eye geometry   (e) Coarse tetrahedral mesh created from the signed distance field

(b) Shoulder and hip intersections   (d) Non-manifold belly geometry   (f) Fine tetrahedral mesh

Figure 9: Tetrahedral meshes created from a signed distance field computed from non-manifold self-intersecting geometry.

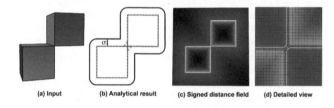

(a) Input   (b) Analytical result   (c) Signed distance field   (d) Detailed view

Figure 11: **Signed distance field for non-manifold input.** (a) Two boxes share an edge. (b) Blue: input geometry. Black: analytical offset surface at offset σ. Dashed red: manifold surface obtained by shifting the black offset surface by −σ (our result). It can be seen that this surface matches input geometry, but regularizes it in the vicinity of the non-manifold "pinch" geometry. (c) and (d): Computed signed distance field (resolution is $256 \times 256 \times 256$).

to approximate distance field computation methods such as vector distance transform [37] and fast marching transform [40]. Table 2 provides computation times for fast marching with second-order finite difference approximations to the partial derivatives, computed using the publicly available implementation of [14]. The marching times are dominated by maintaining a priority queue of grid points, largely depend on grid resolution, and are less dependent on input geometry complexity than the octree exact implementation (see "unsigned field" column in Tables 1 and 2). Our method yields a substantial speedup in the computation of the signed field, both for exact computation and fast marching, because we can avoid traversing the exterior space of E_σ. Parameter σ can be used to provide a cut-off for the geometric size that is deemed significant (Figure 10).

5 CONCLUSION

We presented a simple and robust approach to define and compute a signed distance field for non-manifold input geometry. Our approach is compatible with any uniform-grid distance field computation method. Compatibility with adaptive-grid distance field method needs future investigation. Our distance field is accurate with respect to the offset isosurface. The interior signed distance field is computed from the polygonal offset surface computed using marching cubes, which is an approximation to the analytical offset surface, and may introduce a small amount of discretization error in the distance field. Our method has a single parameter: the isosurface σ value. Small and large values of σ will result in loss of geometric detail. If an automated choice of σ is desired, $\sigma = 3h$ produced good results in practice. A single global parameter σ may fuse geometrically close parts, despite them being semantically dis-

tant. We resolve the problem with careful σ tuning (see legs of turtle in Figure 1(e)), which fortunately is very fast in practice since the isosurface can be recomputed and visualized rapidly before computing the signed distance field. In our work, we remove the interior components I_i, but if the intent is to model hollow objects, interior components can be kept. Only a trivial change is required: perform pseudonormal tests at voxels intersecting interior geometry. Adaptive σ based on the local features of the geometry could be useful future work. We applied our method to polygonal input; but our method could also be applied to more general input, such as point clouds, polygonal lines or parametric curves.

Acknowledgments: This research was sponsored in part by the National Science Foundation (CAREER-53-4509-6600), USC Annenberg Graduate Fellowship to Hongyi Xu, and a donation of two workstations by the Intel Corporation. We thank the Boeing Company for the landing gear model.

REFERENCES

[1] CGAL, Computational Geometry Algorithms Library. http://www.cgal.org.

[2] H. Aanæs and J. A. Bærentzen. Pseudo-normals for signed distance computation. In *Proc. of Vision, Modeling and Visualization*, 2003.

[3] P. Alliez, D. Cohen-Steiner, Y. Tong, and M. Desbrun. Voronoi-based variational reconstruction of unoriented point sets. In *Proc. of Eurographics Symp. on Geometry Processing*, pages 39–48, 2007.

[4] M. Attene. A lightweight approach to repairing digitized polygon meshes. *Vis. Comput.*, 26(11):1393–1406, Nov. 2010.

[5] J. Bærentzen and H. Aanæs. Signed distance computation using the angle weighted pseudo-normal. *IEEE Trans. on Visualization and Computer Graphics*, 11(3):243–253, 2005.

[6] J. Barbič and D. L. James. Six-dof haptic rendering of contact between geometrically complex reduced deformable models. *IEEE Transactions on Haptics*, 1(1):39–52, 2008.

[7] A. W. Bargteil, T. G. Goktekin, J. F. O'Brien, and J. A. Strain. A semi-lagrangian contouring method for fluid simulation. *ACM Transactions on Graphics*, 25(1), 2006.

[8] T. Bastos and W. Celes. Gpu-accelerated adaptively sampled distance fields. In *Shape Modeling and Applications, 2008. SMI 2008. IEEE International Conference on*, pages 171–178, 2008.

[9] S. Bischoff and L. Kobbelt. Structure preserving cad model repair. In *Computer Graphics Forum*, volume 24, pages 527–536. Wiley Online Library, 2005.

[10] S. Bischoff, D. Pavic, and L. Kobbelt. Automatic restoration of polygon models. *ACM Trans. Graph.*, 24(4):1332–1352, Oct. 2005.

[11] P. Borodin, M. Novotni, and R. Klein. Progressive gap closing for mesh repairing. In *Advances in Modelling, Animation and Rendering*, pages 201–213, 2002.

[12] B. Chang, D. Cha, and I. Ihm. Computing local signed distance fields for large polygonal models. *Computer Graphics Forum*, 27(3):799–806, 2008.

[13] F. Chen and Y. Zhao. Distance field transform with an adaptive iteration method. In *IEEE Intl. Conf. on Shape Modeling and Applications*, pages 111–118, 2009.

[14] K. T. Chu and M. Prodanovic. Lsmlib. http://ktchu.serendipityresearch.org/software/lsmlib/.

[15] K. Erleben and H. Dohlmann. Signed distance fields using single-pass gpu scan conversion of tetrahedra. In *GPU Gems 3*, pages 741–763. Addison-Wesley, 2008.

[16] A. Fuhrmann, G. Sobotka, and C. Groß. Distance fields for rapid collision detection in physically based modeling. In *Proc. of GraphiCon 2003*, pages 58–65, 2003.

[17] A. Guezlec. Meshsweeper: dynamic point-to-polygonal mesh distance and applications. *IEEE Trans. on Visualization and Computer Graphics*, 7(1):47–61, 2001.

[18] Hang Si. TetGen: A Quality Tetrahedral Mesh Generator and a 3D Delaunay Triangulator, 2011.

[19] H. Hoppe. *Surface reconstruction from unorganized points*. PhD thesis, Department of Comp. Science and Engineering, University of Washington, 1994.

[20] A. Jacobson, L. Kavan, , and O. Sorkine-Hornung. Robust inside-outside segmentation using generalized winding numbers. *ACM Transactions on Graphics*, 32(4):33:1–33:12, 2013.

[21] M. Jones, J. Bærentzen, and M. Sramek. 3d distance fields: a survey of techniques and applications. *IEEE Trans. on Visualization and Computer Graphics*, 12(4):581–599, 2006.

[22] T. Ju. Robust repair of polygonal models. *ACM Trans. Graph.*, 23(3):888–895, 2004.

[23] M. Kazhdan, M. Bolitho, and H. Hoppe. Poisson surface reconstruction. In *Proc. of Eurographics Symp. on Geometry processing*, 2006.

[24] A. Kumar, A. Shih, Y. Ito, D. Ross, and B. Soni. A hole-filling algorithm using non-uniform rational b-splines. In *Proc. of the 16th Intl. Meshing Roundtable*, pages 169–182, 2008.

[25] B. Lévy. Dual domain extrapolation. In *Proc. of ACM SIGGRAPH 2004*, pages 364–369, 2003.

[26] T. Lewiner, H. Lopes, A. W. Vieira, and G. Tavares. Efficient implementation of Marching Cubes' cases with topological guarantees.

Journal of Graphics Tools, 8(2):1–15, 2003.

[27] W. E. Lorensen and H. E. Cline. Marching cubes: A high resolution 3d surface construction algorithm. *Computer Graphics (Proc. of ACM SIGGRAPH 87)*, 21(4):163–169, 1987.

[28] S. Mauch. *Efficient Algorithms for Solving Static Hamilton-Jacobi Equations*. PhD thesis, California Inst. of Technology, 2003.

[29] P. Mullen, F. De Goes, M. Desbrun, D. Cohen-Steiner, and P. Alliez. Signing the unsigned: Robust surface reconstruction from raw pointsets. In *Computer Graphics Forum*, volume 29, pages 1733–1741, 2010.

[30] M. Müller. Fast and robust tracking of fluid surfaces. In *Symp. on Computer Animation (SCA)*, pages 237–245, New York, NY, USA, 2009. ACM.

[31] T. M. Murali and T. A. Funkhouser. Consistent solid and boundary representations from arbitrary polygonal data. In *Proc. of Symposium on Interactive 3D Graphics*, pages 155–ff., 1997.

[32] F. S. Nooruddin and G. Turk. Simplification and repair of polygonal models using volumetric techniques. *Visualization and Computer Graphics, IEEE Transactions on*, 9(2):191–205, 2003.

[33] M. A. Otaduy, D. Germann, S. Redon, and M. Gross. Adaptive Deformations with Fast Tight Bounds. In *Symp. on Computer Animation (SCA)*, pages 181–190, Aug. 2007.

[34] T. Park, S.-H. Lee, J.-H. Kim, and C.-H. Kim. Cuda-based signed distance field calculation for adaptive grids. In *IEEE Intl. Conf. on Computer and Information Technology (CIT)*, pages 1202–1206, 2010.

[35] P. Patel, D. Marcum, and M. Remotigue. Stitching and filling: Creating conformal faceted geometry. In *Proc. of the 14th Intl. Meshing Roundtable*, pages 239–256, 2005.

[36] G. Rong and T.-S. Tan. Variants of jump flooding algorithm for computing discrete voronoi diagrams. In *Intl. Symp. on Voronoi Diagrams in Science and Engineering*, pages 176–181, 2007.

[37] R. Satherley and M. W. Jones. Vector-city vector distance transform. *Computer Vision and Image Understanding*, 82(3):238 – 254, 2001.

[38] S. Schaefer, T. Ju, and J. Warren. Manifold dual contouring. *IEEE Transactions on Visualization and Computer Graphics*, 13(3):610–619, 2007.

[39] J. A. Sethian. A fast marching level set method for monotonically advancing fronts. *Proceedings of the National Academy of Sciences*, 93(4):1591–1595, 1996.

[40] J. A. Sethian. *Level Set Methods and Fast Marching Methods: Evolving Interfaces in Computational Geometry, Fluid Mechanics, Computer Vision, and Materials Science*, volume 3. Cambridge university press, 1999.

[41] A. Sharf, M. Alexa, and D. Cohen-Or. Context-based surface completion. In *Proc. of ACM SIGGRAPH 2004*, pages 878–887, 2004.

[42] C. Shen, J. F. O'Brien, and J. R. Shewchuk. Interpolating and approximating implicit surfaces from polygon soup. In *Proc. of ACM SIGGRAPH 2004*, pages 896–904, 2004.

[43] C. Sigg, R. Peikert, and M. Gross. Signed Distance Transform using Graphics Hardware. In *Proc. of IEEE Visualization Conference*, pages 83–90, 2003.

[44] J. Spillmann, M. Wagner, and M. Teschner. Robust tetrahedral meshing of triangle soups. In *Symp. on Computer Animation (SCA), Posters and Demos*, pages 1–2, 2006.

[45] J. Strain. Fast tree-based redistancing for level set computations. *J. Comput. Phys.*, 152(2):664–686, 1999.

[46] A. Sud, N. Govindaraju, R. Gayle, E. Andersen, and D. Manocha. Surface distance maps. In *Proc. of Graphics Interface*, pages 35–42. ACM, 2007.

[47] A. Sud, N. Govindaraju, R. Gayle, and D. Manocha. Interactive 3D Distance Field Computation using Linear Factorization. In *Proc. ACM Symp. on Interactive 3D Graphics and Games (I3D)*, 2006.

[48] A. Sud, M. Otaduy, and D. Manocha. DiFi: Fast 3D Distance Field Computation Using Graphics Hardware. *Comp. Graphics Forum*, 23(3):557–556, 2004.

[49] H. Zhao. A fast sweeping method for eikonal equations. *Mathematics of computation*, 74(250):603–627, 2005.

[50] H.-K. Zhao, S. Osher, and R. Fedkiw. Fast surface reconstruction using the level set method. In *Proc. of IEEE Workshop on Variational and Level Set Methods in Computer Vision*, pages 194–201, 2001.

Experimental Study of Stroke Shortcuts for a Touchscreen Keyboard with Gesture-Redundant Keys Removed

Ahmed Sabbir Arif [1,2], Michel Pahud[1], Ken Hinckley[1], and Bill Buxton[1] *

Microsoft Research, Redmond, WA, USA[1] and York University Dept. of Computer Science & Engineering [1,2]

ABSTRACT

We present experimental results for two-handed typing on a graphical QWERTY keyboard augmented with linear strokes for *Space*, *Backspace*, *Shift*, and *Enter*—that is, swipes to the right, left, up, and diagonally down-left, respectively. A first study reveals that users are more likely to adopt these strokes, and type faster, when the keys corresponding to the strokes are removed from the keyboard, as compared to an equivalent stroke-augmented keyboard with the keys intact. A second experiment shows that the keys-removed design yields 16% faster text entry than a standard graphical keyboard for phrases containing mixed-case alphanumeric and special symbols, without increasing error rate. Furthermore, the design is easy to learn: users exhibited performance gains almost immediately, and 90% of test users indicated they would want to use it as their primary input method.

Keywords: multi-touch keyboards; text entry; stroke input

Index Terms: H.5.2 Information Interfaces & Presentation: Input

1 INTRODUCTION

The proliferation of mobiles and tablets has led to widespread use of graphical touchscreen keyboards, and a corresponding user demand for efficient text entry techniques. Researchers have pursued many strategies to improve touchscreen typing, from non-QWERTY key layouts [22,30], to shape-writing entire words in a single stroke [32,33], to approaches that heavily multiplex keys and resolve ambiguous inputs through language models [6].

While such techniques can yield substantial performance advantages, they also often demand substantial investment of skill acquisition from users before performance gains can be realized. In practice, this limits how many users will stick with a new technique long enough to realize such gains.

This paper explores the performance impact of an alternative approach: augmenting graphical touchscreen keyboards with linear stroke shortcuts, i.e. short finger swipes. While we do not expect large performance gains (such as those observed for expert shape-writing users [32]), if stroke-augmented keyboards can offer significant performance benefits while maintaining a high degree of transfer from existing QWERTY touch-typing skills, this complementary approach could represent low-hanging fruit for improving tablet text entry.

Stroke-augmented QWERTY keyboards are well-known, yet nonetheless under-studied in the modern context of touchscreen text entry. While single-point-of-contact stylus input [4,5,13,15] has been widely considered, the performance of linear stroke gestures for two-handed typing on a multi-touch keyboard has not been subjected to experimental scrutiny.

Furthermore, we show that an unusual design decision—that of removing the *Space*, *Backspace*, *Shift*, and *Enter* keys made

---

* {mpahud, kenh, bibuxton}@microsoft.com; asarif@cse.yorku.ca
Graphics Interface Conference 2014
7-9 May, Montreal, Quebec, Canada

redundant by the stroke gestures—can actually lead to superior performance. Although our research unearthed one previous example of such a design in the context of stylus text entry on a handheld [4], to our knowledge the insight that removing four of the most heavily used keys could potentially improve touchscreen text entry has not been anticipated by the literature.

Fig. 1   The stroke-augmented graphical QWERTY keyboard tested in our studies. Note that the keyboard looks familiar despite the absence of the *Space*, *Backspace*, *Shift*, and *Enter* keys.

Likewise, despite previous related studies and examples, the design rationale for linear stroke keyboards (especially with the gesture-redundant keys removed) has not been fully articulated. Thus, in addition to possible time-motion efficiencies of the stroke shortcuts themselves, the design we pursued (*Fig. 1*) yields a number of interesting properties:

- Allowing the user to input stroke gestures for *Space*, *Backspace*, and *Enter* anywhere on the keyboard eliminates fine targeting motions as well as any round-trips necessary for a finger to acquire the corresponding keys.
- Instead of requiring two separate keystrokes—one to tap *Shift* and another to tap the key to be shifted—the *Shift* gesture combines these into a single action: the starting point selects a key, while the stroke direction selects the *Shift* function itself.
- Removing these four keys frees an entire row on the keyboard.
- Almost all of the numeric, punctuation, and special symbols typically relegated to the secondary and tertiary keyboards can then be fit in a logical manner into the freed-up space.
- Hence, the full set of characters can fit on one keyboard *while holding the key size, number of keys, and footprint constant.*
- By having only a primary keyboard, this approach affords an economy of design that simplifies the interface, while offering further potential performance gains via the elimination of keyboard switching costs—and the extra key layouts to learn.
- Although the strokes might reduce round-trip costs, we expect articulating the stroke gesture itself to take longer than a tap. Thus, we need to test these tradeoffs empirically.

Our studies demonstrate that overall the removal of four keys—rather than coming at a cost—offers a net benefit. Specifically, our experiments show that a stroke keyboard with the gesture-redundant keys removed yields a 16% performance advantage for input phrases containing mixed-case alphanumeric text and special symbols, without sacrificing error rate. We observed performance advantages from the first block of trials onward. Even in the case of *entirely lowercase* text—that is, in a context where we would not expect to observe a performance benefit because only the *Space* gesture offers any potential advantage—we found that the design illustrated in *Fig. 1* still performed as well as a standard graphical keyboard. Moreover, users learned the design with remarkable ease: 90% of users wanted to keep using the method, and 80% of test users believed they typed faster than on their current touchscreen tablet keyboard.

Our work thus contributes a careful study of stroke-augmented keyboards, filling an important gap in the literature as well as demonstrating the efficacy of a specific design; shows that removing the gesture-redundant keys is an unexpectedly critical design choice; and that earlier results assessing stroke shortcuts for single-point-of-contact stylus input (e.g. [15]) do not fully translate to the modern touch-typing context. Although our studies focus on the immediate end of the usability spectrum (as opposed to longitudinal studies over many input sessions), we believe the rapid returns demonstrated by our results illustrate the potential of this approach to complement other text-entry techniques.

2 RELATED WORK
Touchscreen text entry is difficult and error prone due to small keys and less salient feedback [22,32,33]. This has led to wide exploration of alternative layouts [21,30], as well as techniques to support many characters on a small number of keys [6,22,25].

Yet, most commodity devices—including the iPad, Android tablets, and Windows 8 tablets—still employ a QWERTY key layout, while relegating numeric keys and most symbols to secondary keyboards or pop-up menus. For example, Fig. 2 illustrates the primary, secondary, and tertiary keyboard layouts on a Windows 8 tablet, which we used as the "Default" keyboard for our study comparisons. The iPad and Android keyboards, while differing in various details, employ similar layout strategies.

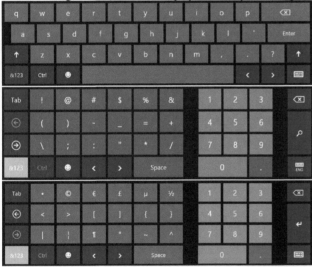

Fig. 2   Default Windows 8 graphical keyboard, with its primary (top), secondary (center) and tertiary (bottom) virtual keyboards.

Stroke-based techniques have often been proposed as alternatives to keyboards. Unistrokes [11], Graffiti [20,26], and EdgeWrite [29] all use a single-stroke shorthand to enter individual characters. Users can quickly achieve high performance with Graffiti [20] because of the similarity its symbols to normal letter-forms. While faster than hand-printing, maximum entry speeds are still typically far slower than multi-finger typing on graphical keyboards (at least for a skilled typist).

Unipad [19] augments single-stroke shorthand with language-based accelerators, including word completion, suffix completion, and frequently-used word prompting. Likewise, many modern touchscreen keyboards include some form of word prediction. Such complementary approaches could enhance stroke keyboards, but here we focus on the influence of the strokes themselves.

The alternate keyboard we study (Fig. 1) falls into a hybrid category of tap + stroke text entry. While our design differs from previous examples in its particulars, the basic concept of using linear strokes is well-known, and even removing the keys made redundant by the gestures has precedent [4]. Our contribution is to revisit this somewhat neglected approach for multi-touch keyboards, as well as to investigate how to fully realize its potential benefits.

Most prior examples emphasize single-point-of-contact graphical keyboards with stylus input. A 1995 patent [5] augments a standard graphical keyboard with linear stroke shortcuts for the *Space*, *Backspace*, *Shift*, and *Enter* keys, but several other systems demonstrate similar gestures [13,14,15,24]. In particular, the Microsoft Windows CE graphical keyboard (circa 2005, in Windows Mobile 5 and 6) supported these linear stroke shortcuts by default, and even provided an option to remove the gesture-redundant keys [4]. However, this was poorly documented, and to our knowledge no studies of the design have ever been published.

Isokoski [15] models a stroke-augmented keyboard, and assesses the model versus expert text entry performance for several keyboard layouts. Isokoski finds that strokes perform significantly slower at first, and only pull even with tap-based stylus entry after 20 experimental sessions. However, this is for stylus input, without the gesture-redundant keys removed, and using alternate keyboard layouts. These (and perhaps other) differences are crucial to study empirically in a more modern context; indeed, our results suggest that, in the right context, strokes can produce performance gains almost immediately.

Shape-writing enables input of words via gestures on top of a QWERTY graphical keyboard [16,31,32,33]. Although it takes practice, the technique is gaining traction commercially [27] because it is fast and easy to learn the most common words.

Techniques such as 1Line [6] and MessageEase [25] use strokes to reduce footprint, whereas our goal is to promote more keys to the primary keyboard. Other techniques extend multi-touch gestures to non-alphanumeric input [8,9] and text editing [10].

Grossman et al. [12] study users' ability to learn and recall keyboard hotkeys: users learn such keyboard shortcuts much faster, and are more likely to use them, after they have trained in a condition where the shortcuts offer the *only* way to select commands from a menu. We explore a similar choice in the context of text entry by assessing performance with or without removing the gesture-redundant keys.

3 DETAILS AND CONSIDERATIONS FOR THE STROKE KEYBOARDS
The aim of our studies was to investigate hybrid tap and stroke keyboards, where the user inputs ordinary alphanumeric characters via taps, and the gestures by short linear strokes.

The specific stroke gestures we employed, designed to maintain stimulus-response compatibility with the corresponding actions, were assigned as follows:

- *Space*– stroke to the right, anywhere on the keyboard;
- *Backspace*– stroke to the left, also anywhere;
- *Enter*– stroke diagonally, again anywhere, down to the left;
- *Shift*– stroke up, starting from the desired key.

Based on pilot study data, we interpreted any finger movement of less than 4.7 mm as a tap. Likewise, to input a stroke gesture, the finger had to slide further than this threshold; we found this cleanly separated taps from strokes.

3.1 Keyboard Variants Implemented for Study
To assess the impact of these strokes, with or without removing the corresponding keys, we implemented the following three keyboard variants in our own instrumented code-base:

- **Default:** First, we implemented a keyboard that conformed pixel-for-pixel to the default Windows 8 keyboard (*Fig. 2*), using identical colors, key sizes, and layouts.
- **Default + Strokes:** Second, we implemented a variant that supported the strokes enumerated above on top of the "Default" keyboard. Visually it looked identical to the Windows 8 keyboard (*Fig. 2*) in all respects, except that swiping a finger produced the desired stroke shortcut.
- **Removed + Strokes:** Third, we implemented the keys-removed design using the layout shown in *Fig. 1*. We maintained a likeness to QWERTY wherever possible. For instance, the ! character appears as the shift symbol on the **1** key, the **:** character appears above the **;** key, and so on.

It is critical to re-emphasize here that these designs—including the *Removed + Strokes* design—all kept the overall keyboard footprint constant. We also kept the standard key sizes absolutely constant. Other details such as key colors and highlight cues (on finger contact) were also identical.

None of the studied keyboards provided auditory click feedback for key presses. Also note that none of them (including the default Windows 8 keyboard) included ESC or CAPS LOCK keys.

Of course, the *Removed + Strokes* design necessitates shifting some keys around to use the freed-up space. We carefully designed and considered the symbol placements and other minor key layout differences. Also note that our current design arranges the keys in rectilinear rows and columns, rather than a more traditional staggered key pattern where alternate rows are shifted slightly (*Fig. 2, top*). This reflects the preliminary nature of our design, rather than any desire on our part to avoid a staggered layout; indeed, as of this writing, we are working on a slightly improved layout that includes staggered keys.

Thus, while removal of the keys is the primary intervention of interest, these various aspects (including but not limited to key removal) may influence its performance. However, since our goal was to empirically test a practical and usable instance of the keys-removed idea, we felt this trade-off would yield the most insightful performance data for such a design.

4 EXPERIMENT 1: STROKES AS ALTERNATIVE VS. KEY REMOVAL

The purpose of our first study was to assess whether it was necessary or desirable to remove the gesture-redundant *Space*, *Backspace*, *Shift*, and *Enter* keys in order for users to achieve the best performance.

As such, Experiment 1 compares the *Default+Strokes* keyboard detailed above to the *Removed+Strokes* design. If the strokes offer significant benefit without having to remove the keys, this would support including them on status quo QWERTY graphical keyboards. If not, it would suggest that the (arguably) counterintuitive step of removing four very frequently used keys might afford superior performance.

At present, our focus is to evaluate how the strokes impact performance, so we simply told users about the presence of the strokes when they first encountered the keyboards, but clearly more sophisticated self-revelation mechanisms for the gestures could be devised (e.g. [3,18]).

For the *Default+Strokes* keyboard, users were free to choose either approach (tapping keys, or making a stroke) when they needed to input *Space*, *Backspace*, *Shift*, and *Enter*.

For the *Removed+Strokes* design, since the corresponding keys were absent, the only option for users was to employ the strokes. However, users clearly recognized the keyboard when they first encountered it; indeed, due to its likeness with normal QWERTY, many users did not notice that the keyboard was "different" until they tried to start typing on it.

4.1 Apparatus – Experiment 1

We used a Samsung Series 7 tablet (11.66″ × 7.24″ × 0.51″, with 1366 × 768 screen resolution at 135 pixels/inch) for our study, running the Windows 8 Release Preview. We placed the device on a desk with a custom stand that tilted the device to a comfortable ~15° typing posture (Fig. 3).

Fig. 3   User typing on a tablet, as presented in all our studies.

4.2 Participants – Experiment 1

Fourteen people participated, from 23-49 years old (average 32). Five were female and two were left-handed. All had at least ten years of experience on QWERTY. Eleven participants used a touch-based device, such as mobile phone, on a regular basis. Eight owned an iPad tablet; three used their device frequently to input text such as emails or notes (almost every day), three used it occasionally (about three days a week), while two used it rarely (once a week or less). All participants were native or fluent speakers of English, and each received a gratuity for participation.

4.3 Design – Experiment 1

The study compared the *Default+Strokes* technique to the *Removed+Strokes* design. We counterbalanced the order of conditions via a standard Latin square, in a design as follows:

    14 participants ×
    2 techniques (*Default+Strokes* vs. *Removed+Strokes*) ×
    3 blocks × 10 phrases
    = 840 phrases in total.

The study included two different types of phrases, *Regular* and *Mixed*, with 5 of each type (in random order) per block.

Regular phrases contained only lowercase letters and spaces, drawn from the MacKenzie-Soukoreff [23] corpus (with all British spellings changed to American usage). We chose this corpus due to its high correlation with English language character frequencies and its wide use in text entry studies.

Mixed phrases included **7%** uppercase characters, **10%** numeric characters, **7%** symbols, with the other **76%** lowercase and spaces, using a custom corpus as further detailed below.

Thus, we carefully bracketed both keyboards' performance by testing with all-lowercase conditions, as well as mixed-case conditions. This therefore gives an honest assessment of how the keyboards perform. In real life scenarios, users often must input such phrases, and the difficulty in entering such symbols is a major shortcoming of present graphical keyboards.

4.4 Procedure – Experiment 1

Participants entered short phrases, which appeared on-screen in a dialog, using the assigned keyboard. We instructed participants to take the time to read and understand the phrases in advance, then to enter them as quickly and accurately as possible. When finished, participants pressed the *Enter* key (or made an *Enter* gesture, based on condition) in order to see the next phrase. All participants used both hands to type, and were allowed to rest between conditions, blocks, or trials.

Direct insertion point control (touch-drag to place the carat or select text) was disabled during the studies, so users had to employ *Backspace*, exclusively, to repair any errors. We instructed participants to correct any errors as soon as they noticed them, but they could ignore ones that were more than 10 characters back. This ensured that participants did not have to delete a lot of text to correct a single mistake.

Although experts notice and correct over 98% of mistakes within five characters [2], less experienced users (such as the ones recruited in this study) might input more characters before noticing an error. Thus, we believe this contributed to the somewhat elevated error rates (in all conditions) reported below. This also motivated us to recruit more experienced touchscreen-typing users for Experiment 2, as discussed later in this paper.

Our custom corpus generated phrases containing uppercase, numeric, and special characters in known patterns, such as URLs, email addresses, phone numbers, and mailing addresses. The corpus placed items from lists of places, addresses, and relationships into the phrases in a meaningful manner, such as: "My **son's** phone number is **+1 (638) 283-9375**". Here, the first bolded fragment was generated from the relationships list, and the latter was produced from the phone-number pattern. The *Mixed* phrases averaged seven words: the average phrase length was 36.81 characters and the average word length was 4.46 characters.

4.5 Results – Experiment 1

Timing started from the finger-down event for the first character and ended with the finger-up event of the last character. We used the standard Words per Minute (WPM) metric for entry speed. We computed Error Rate (ER), which counts only incorrect characters in the transcribed text, as well as Total Error Rate (TER)—which unlike ER also includes corrections of erroneous keystrokes [1]—as our error metrics. (Although not all researchers agree on the utility of TER, we report it here for additional perspective.) Note also that a lowercase character in place of an uppercase was counted as an error. Finally, Operations per Character (OPC) is the average number of actions required to produce one character.

An ANOVA revealed a significant effect of *Technique* on entry speed ($F_{1,13} = 9.44$, $p < 0.01$). For this task *Removed+Strokes* performed significantly faster than *Default+Strokes* with averages of 17.61 WPM ($SE = 0.28$) vs. 15.75 ($SE = 0.25$), respectively.

Removed+Strokes also required significantly fewer Operations per Character than *Default+Strokes* ($F_{1,13} = 36.0$, $p < .0001$), with average OPC of 1.22 ($SE = 0.04$) and 1.51 ($SE = 0.02$), respectively. Hence, removing the keys yielded 11.8% faster text entry with 19.2% fewer actions required of the user, as compared to the *Default+Strokes* keyboard.

There was no significant difference for ER ($F_{1,13} = 0.32$, ns) or of *Technique* × *Block* ($F_{2,26} = 0.81$, ns). On average ER for the *Removed+Strokes* and *Default+Strokes* keyboards were 10.60 ($SE = 5.53$) and 6.92 ($SE = 2.04$), respectively. Similarly, there was no significant difference for the TER metric ($F_{1,13} = 2.93$, $p = 0.1$), nor any significant effect of *Technique* × *Block* ($F_{2,26} = 1.09$, $p = 0.3$). On average TER for the *Removed+Strokes* and *Default+Strokes* keyboards were 10.15 ($SE = 0.52$) and 12.58 ($SE = 0.63$), respectively. However, the disparity between ER (6.92) and TER (12.58) for the *Default+Strokes* keyboard suggests that users committed and corrected more errors with *Default+Strokes* than *Removed+Strokes* (which exhibited similar ER (10.60) and

TER (10.15) metrics). This reflects the fact that only the TER metric takes corrected errors into account [1].

4.5.1 Gesture Use

Further analysis revealed that in cases where gestures could have been used to input characters, on average participants used gestures during the *Default+Strokes* condition only 28.3% ($SE = 5.66$) of the time, ranging from as little as 4% of the time to a maximum of 58% usage. A Kruskal-Wallis test found this to be highly significant ($H_1 = 160.16$, $p < .0001$), as compared to the 100% occurrence of gestures in the *Removed+Strokes* condition.

While strokes were used by necessity in the latter condition, it is noteworthy that users did not complain about having to use the gestures. Rather, they often made positive remarks about them ("the gestures were really intuitive," "once I got a hold of the gestures my typing got really fast").

4.6 Summary of Findings – Experiment 1

This pattern of results strongly suggests that removing the gesture-redundant keys was essential to make stroke shortcuts a worthwhile enhancement to the keyboards we tested. The *Removed+Strokes* design resulted in faster text entry, and about 19% fewer Operations per Character, without any significant difference in error rates.

The *Default+Strokes* participants tended to use the strokes infrequently and achieved little, if any, benefit from them, despite knowing that they were available as an optional shortcut—and their performance suffered for it. We therefore pursued the keys-removed design as the foundation for the stroke keyboard in the main experiment that follows.

5 EXPERIMENT 2: MAIN EXPERIMENTAL STUDY

The purpose of our second experimental study was to evaluate the performance of the *Removed+Strokes* design in comparison to the *Default* keyboard with tap input only (no strokes). The apparatus was exactly as described for Experiment 1.

5.1 Participants – Experiment 2

Twenty participants, none of whom participated in Experiment 1, took part in the study. All had a minimum of 10 years of experience on QWERTY, and all had owned an iPad tablet for at least six months and typed on it frequently, such as to write emails, for at least three hours three times a week.

Note that this is a higher, and more carefully controlled, level of experience than the participants we recruited in the first study. We wanted users more familiar with touchscreen tablet keyboards, and at present, such users are most readily recruited in significant numbers for the iPad. Furthermore, current iPad users are not familiar with the Windows 8 keyboard, and thus come at both the *Default* and *Removed+Strokes* designs with fresh eyes. They also represent the population of users most likely to encounter our proposed technique if it were to be widely deployed.

The participants we recruited were then randomly assigned to the following groups:

- **Default Group:** The ten participants in this group used the *Default* keyboard during the study. Their age ranged from 19 to 49 years (average 39.3). Five were male, one was left-handed.
- **New Group:** Ten participants used the *Removed+Strokes* technique—which for brevity we henceforth call the **New** keyboard. Their age ranged from 26 to 44 years (average 33.6). Six were male and all were right-handed.

We ran Experiment 2 as a **between-subjects study** to allow participants to input as many phrases as possible with each keyboard, while avoiding any possibility of skill transfer or other interference effects between the two conditions.

5.2 Procedure – Experiment 2

Participants entered phrases following the same procedure as Experiment 1. However, in Experiment 2 the *Regular* and *Mixed* phrases were presented in two separate conditions rather than in random order within blocks.

In the first condition users entered *Regular* text (all-lowercase from a standard corpus [23]). Note that this tests the *New* keyboard in a setting where it would have the least possible benefit—that is, for phrases that contain no uppercase or special characters. In the second condition users entered *Mixed* text (from our custom corpus as described in Experiment 1). In addition to the WPM, ER, and TER metrics, participants in Experiment 2 also responded to a questionnaire with 7-point Likert scales for their assigned keyboard.

5.3 Design – Experiment 2

Participants were thus equally divided and assigned to either the *Default* or the *New* group, in an experimental design as follows:

Between-subject group: *New vs. Default* ×
10 participants per group ×
2 conditions (*Regular vs. Mixed text types*) ×
3 blocks × 15 phrases (+ 2 additional practice phrases)
= 1800 phrases per group (excluding practice phrases).

Note that all participants started with *Regular* text, so that we could assess their typing performance with lowercase text first.

5.4 Results – Experiment 2

5.4.1 Text Entry Speed

An ANOVA revealed no main effect of *Keyboard* on entry speed ($F_{1,18} = 0.42$, ns), but the overall means conceal the fact that there was a highly significant effect of *Keyboard × Text Type* ($F_{1,18} = 9.68, p < .01$), which echoes the results found in Experiment 1: the *New* keyboard was faster than the *Default* keyboard, but only for the *Mixed* phrase sets.

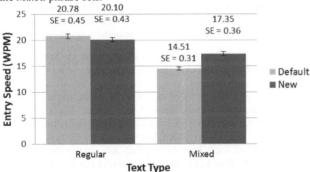

Fig. 4 Keyboard entry speeds for *Regular* vs. *Mixed* text.

Average entry speed for *Default* in the *Regular* and *Mixed* conditions was 20.78 ($SE = 0.45$) vs. 14.51 ($SE = 0.31$) WPM, respectively. By contrast, average entry speed for the *New* keyboard with regular and mixed text were 20.10 ($SE = 0.43$) and 17.35 *WPM* ($SE = 0.36$), respectively (*Fig. 4*). A Tukey-Kramer test (MSE = 396.67, $df = 18$, $z_\alpha = 3.08$) confirmed that inputting *Mixed* phrases was significantly faster with the *New* keyboard than the *Default* one ($p < .05$), but there was no significant difference for *Regular* phrases ($p > .05$).

5.4.2 Errors (ER and TER metrics)

There was no significant effect of *Keyboard* on either ER ($F_{1,18} = 0.89$, ns) or TER ($F_{1,18} = 0.28$, ns). The *Keyboard × Text Type* interaction was also not significant. This confirms the benefits observed for the *New* keyboard did not come at the cost of increased error rates (*Fig. 5*).

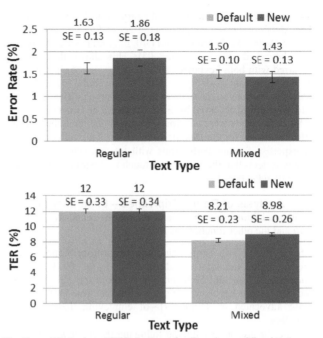

Fig. 5 ER (top) and TER (bottom) for *Regular* vs. *Mixed* text.

5.4.3 Operations per Character

An ANOVA revealed a significant effect of *Keyboard* on OPC ($F_{1,18} = 6.91$, $p < .05$). There was also a significant effect of *Keyboard × Text Type* ($F_{1,18} = 14.63$, $p < .005$). Average OPC with the *Default* keyboard was 1.37 (SE = 0.03) for *Regular* text and 1.42 (SE = 0.03) for Mixed text. By contrast, OPC for the *New* keyboard was 1.33 (SE=0.03) for *Regular* text and 1.21 (SE=0.02) for *Mixed* text. A Tukey-Kramer test (MSE = 0.189, $df = 18$, $z_\alpha = 2.64$) confirmed that the *New* keyboard required significantly fewer OPC than the *Default* keyboard ($p < .05$). There were no significant effects or interactions with *Block* for OPC.

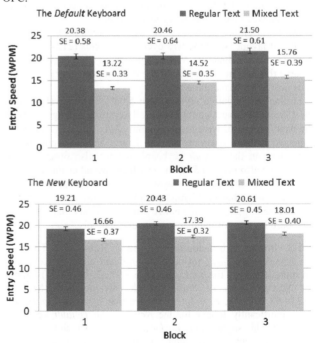

Fig. 6 Entry speeds (WPM) broken out per block.

5.4.4 Learning Effects on Text Entry Speed across Blocks

The ANOVA showed a significant effect of *Block* on entry speed for the *Default* keyboard ($F_{2,9} = 11.40$, $p < .001$) as well as for the *New* keyboard ($F_{2,9} = 4.61$, $p < .05$). This shows that learning occurred with both keyboards across blocks (*Fig. 6*), but the lack of any significant *Text Type × Block* or *Keyboard × Text Type × Block* interactions suggests there was not a strong difference in the rates of learning observed by either *Keyboard* or *Text Type*.

Since our users were all experienced with the iPad, the learning effect observed for the *Default* condition does not reflect any lack of expertise for our participants with touchscreen text entry; it simply reflects that the Windows 8 touch keyboard is not identical to the iPad keyboard.

5.5 Analysis of Round Trip Times – Experiment 2

To gain additional insights, we compared the round-trip costs for *Shift* and the other functions as follows.

5.5.1 Round-Trip Time Including Preparatory Motions

We computed the total round-trip time, T_{round}^t, for the *Space*, *Backspace*, *Enter* and *Shift* functions on both the *New* keyboard and the *Default* keyboard. This considers the "true cost"—in the sense advocated by Dillon [7]—of employing these gestures, including:

- Time for preparatory motion following the *previous* action, up to the onset of finger contact with the screen.
- The time spent with the finger in contact with the screen to input the current gesture (a tap or stroke, depending on the keyboard type of *Default* or *New*, respectively).
- All motion following lift-off, up to the *next* finger contact with the screen.

We accounted for all of these time-motion costs (which might also include hesitations or mental preparation) in the round trip time so that we could be sure to consider any and all impacts of a gesture on the surrounding operations.

5.5.2 Impact of Keyboard Switching on Performance

During the *Mixed* text condition with the *Default* keyboard, our results show that fully 7.79% of all keystrokes served solely to switch between the different keyboard layouts.

On the *Default* keyboard, the average round trip time for keyboard layout swapping was over two seconds (2124.2 ms, *SE* = 33.2), a cost which the *New* design completely eliminates. We believe this is a major source of the performance benefits for the *New* design on *Mixed* phrases.

Further investigation revealed that 5.08% of all keystrokes on the *Default* keyboard, and 9.25% of all keystrokes and gestures on the *New* keyboard, were made to input *Shift*. This was somewhat expected because users always had to use *Shift* to input special characters on the *Default* keyboard, but we also observed that users often also pressed *Shift* to see which special characters were available on the primary layout. Our interpretation of this behavior was that it highlights how difficult it is even for experienced users to memorize the secondary and tertiary keyboard layouts for numbers and special symbols.

5.5.3 Impact of Individual Gestures on Round-Trip Time

An ANOVA on T_{round}^t revealed a significant effect of *Keyboard* on round-trip time for *Backspace* ($F_{1,9} = 97.23$, $p < .0001$) but not for *Space*, *Enter*, or *Shift*. A Tukey-Kramer test (MSE = 78239.63, $df = 18$, $z_\alpha = 2.97$) revealed that T_{round}^t for *Backspace* was significantly longer for the *New* vs. the *Default* keyboard ($p < .05$). This suggests the *Backspace* gesture, which users often apply in rapid succession, could benefit from design improvements to make repeated invocation faster, such as by issuing additional backstrokes in proportion to the stroke length.

Finally, *Block* was also significant for all four keyboard actions, indicating that users' performance was becoming more efficient with *both of the keyboards* over the course of the experiment. These trends are illustrated in *Fig. 7*.

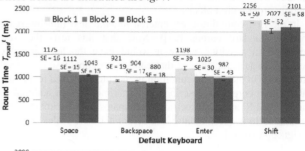

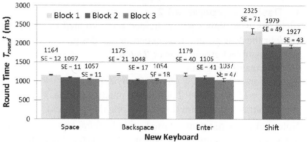

Fig. 7 Per-key round trip times for *Default* (top) vs. *New* (bottom).

5.6 Qualitative Findings

At the conclusion of the experiment, we asked users to compare the keyboard they had just tried—either our facsimile of the standard Windows 8 keyboard in the *Default* condition, or the stroke keyboard with redundant keys removed in the *New* condition—with the touchscreen keyboard on iPad (which all of our recruited participants used heavily). Hence, because the Windows 8 touchscreen keyboard was unfamiliar to all users, both the *Default* and *New* conditions were novel to users in each group.

5.6.1 Keyboard Preference and Willingness to Use

A Kruskal-Wallis test on the questionnaire data indicated significance with respect to user preference across techniques ($H_1 = 18.05$, $p < .05$). 80% of the *New* keyboard users liked the new keyboard, while only 40% of the *Default* keyboard users liked it compared to their existing method for tablet touchscreen text entry (i.e. the iPad graphical keyboard).

We also asked users how willing they were to use the keyboard compared to the iPad keyboard that they were familiar with. Users also responded significantly positively to this question ($H_1 = 7.24$, $p < .05$), with 90% of the *New* keyboard users expressed their interest in using it as their primary input method, while only 50% of the *Default* keyboard users expressed willingness to use it compared to the their existing method.

5.6.2 Overall Experience with the New Keyboard

Users were extremely positive regarding their overall typing experience with the *New* keyboard. All of our participants found the *New* keyboard comfortable to use. They all agreed that the gestures used to replace the *Space*, *Backspace*, *Shift*, and *Enter* keys were intuitive and easy to remember. Interestingly, even though our empirical results showed there was no significant difference in entry speed while inputting lowercase text with the *New* keyboard, 80% of users *thought* their typing speed increased substantially with the *New* keyboard even when typing such text.

Users in the *New* group quickly grew to like the stroke gestures (typical comments were that "it didn't take me much time to learn the gestures," "once I knew them I started using it like a regular keyboard," and "The keyboard was more responsive than my normal tablet keyboard"), although at least one user did verbalize that it "takes time to get used to it."

Users appreciated having a single keyboard (commenting that "I liked the fact that you don't have to swap between different keyboards to enter special characters" and "This is perfect for entering URL's, digits, addresses.") They also found the stroke keyboard comfortable and easy to use ("I liked how it felt under my hands," and "I liked that I could apply the gestures without moving my fingers").

Of course, although the balance of the feedback was positive, some users did comment on issues they encountered. In particular, in the Likert-scale questions, 80% of users had a greater than neutral response when asked if they sometimes triggered unintended gestures by accidentally brushing the screen. Some users commented on this ("I sometimes accidentally performed gestures, which caused errors"). Accidental sliding of the entire tablet if the user applied too much pressure when gesturing was also occasionally an issue. The *Shift* gesture seemed most prone to this issue, e.g. one user commented that "I had difficulties performing the Shift stroke, which made my typing slower."

While we cannot distinguish intentional versus accidental touches in our experimental data, we did *not* observe a statistically significant difference in error rate between the techniques. However, since users did perceive a higher incidence of errors, this is an area of concern that should be examined further in future work. Nonetheless, as reported above, 90% of the *New* keyboard users still expressed interest in using the strokes as their primary input method, and many asked if they could download the *New* keyboard to use on their personal tablet device.

A few users did mention the missing keys ("I missed the space bar, I would have liked an option to enable it") or other functionality absent from our prototype implementation ("It would have been great if the new keyboard augmented word prediction"). Another user observed the difficulty in correcting errors ("Backspace is time consuming, especially when multiple characters needed to be deleted. In a regular keyboard, I can tap-hold the Backspace key to delete multiple characters.") Future studies and design refinements should explore these options and capabilities.

6 DISCUSSION

The results clearly showed that the *New* keyboard provided faster text entry for *Mixed* text phrases, at near-identical error rates, suggesting that the benefits of the design do not come at the cost of a speed-accuracy tradeoff. But just as importantly, even in the case of all-lowercase text where we would not expect the *New* keyboard to offer much benefit, it was statistically equivalent to the status-quo keyboard—from the very first block of trials onward. This emphasizes that Isokoski's findings [15] were in a different context (single-touch stylus input on a handheld, among other differences) that does not fully translate to multi-touch typing on a tablet, at least for the designs we tested.

Likewise, since we observed our results after only three blocks of 15 phrases, it strongly suggests users do not require extensive training to start using the new design and realize performance gains from it.

Although in future work we would like to examine learning trends across a much larger number of trials, our current focus on the immediate end of the usability spectrum acknowledges the practical reality that users are unlikely to adopt a new technique if they do not find it useful in the short term. Even in the limited number of trials examined by our current studies, users adapted to the new technique almost immediately—unlike many alternate keyboard layouts or other text-entry enhancements reported in the literature, the benefits we observed did not require a long period of skill acquisition. This, we believe, further highlights the potential of the approaches we studied. In our study, each user inputted 90 total phrases, which took about an hour including practice and breaks; this was about as long as a single session could go before fatigue effects would start to set in.

Furthermore, our studies demonstrate that even issues as subtle as whether or not the gesture-redundant keys are removed from the keyboard can significantly influence user behavior and success with the technique. Hence our studies also contribute the novel result that the removal of the redundant keys is crucial to the successful realization of linear stroke shortcuts.

6.1 Tapping Rhythm

We acknowledge that the standard tap-tap rhythm of typing cannot be maintained with the *New* keyboard. However, this is not to say that a new and perhaps equally effective typing rhythm cannot be established. In our own use of the keyboard, and in observing a few of the fastest users in Experiment 2, we have noticed a tendency for a rhythm of fast taps and ballistic strokes to emerge. Furthermore, a strategy of entering the *Space* gesture by quickly scrubbing *right* with the thumb of the *left* hand—and *Backspace* using the thumb of the opposite hand—particularly lends itself to such a rhythm. However, more trials (or preferably a longitudinal study) would be necessary to establish whether users naturally pick up such skills. We also plan to study whether performance with the technique might be enhanced by gradually steering users towards this strategy somehow.

6.2 Performance Modeling and the Phrase Corpus

Predicting the performance of a hybrid keyboard, such as the one presented here, is difficult with existing models, as they either focus on one-handed, single point text entry (e.g. with a stylus), or do not account for hybrid tap and stroke inputs [2]. While we chose to start by collecting performance data, it should be possible to devise a model for hybrid designs using KLM or GOMS-style techniques; this would then enable rapid model-based exploration of many additional design permutations.

The choice of corpus is also critical: in our study we used a standard corpus with all-lowercase text, as well as a custom corpus for mixed-case phrases containing symbols and numbers. Another approach would be to employ a corpus of actual mobile email data (e.g. [28]), but one issue with such an approach is that current keyboard designs discourage the entry of special symbols because they are inefficient to enter. Hence one would likely see a corresponding absence of those symbols in such a corpus, due to users' natural tendency to avoid tedious tasks. Thus, a range of approaches seems to be called for in terms of the ideal corpus for studies—as well as deployment and longitudinal evaluation of our keyboard to users for their real work, which we are also pursuing as of this writing.

6.3 Self-Revelation (Learnability) of Stroke Gestures

One key issue with removing the keys, of course, is that if users are confronted by a keyboard with no *Space*, *Backspace*, *Shift*, or *Enter* key—and without any instruction whatsoever—they may quite justly feel uncertain how to proceed. However, in our studies we found that a brief verbal explanation was enough to get users started. Furthermore, a variety of suitable self-revelation techniques appear in the literature [3,17,18]. In our current deployment of a refined version of the keyboard studied here, we have found that a short one-minute video tutorial sufficient to get users started on the stroke shortcuts.

Another approach follows from Grossman et al.'s work on hotkey adoption: *only* offer the shortcut, which forces users to adopt it and learn it quickly [12]. Indeed, this is exactly the approach we follow with the removal of redundant keys. While draconian in one sense, users liked the new approach and clearly performed better when using it, as opposed to a design which left both methods available—and hence implicitly forced people to reflect on and decide which of the two approaches (key press or shortcut gesture) to use while typing—which, by foisting a design choice on the user, is draconian in a different sense. That users failed to adopt the gestures, then, when they were faced with such a choice is perhaps another reminder that sometimes 'less is more,' supported in this case by the clearly superior performance and user preference we observed with redundant keys removed.

However, with perhaps a different technique for self-revelation, it is possible that a linear stroke keyboard design that does *not* remove the redundant keys could still be realized—but we certainly did not discover any support for that in our studies. Furthermore, the rapidity with which users took to the new keyboard, and the preference expressed by many users for the new design after a relatively brief exposure, suggests that it is worth investing further effort in devising ways for the technique to reveal itself to users.

7 CONCLUSION AND FUTURE WORK

Perhaps the primary virtue of the stroke keyboard designs studied in this paper is that they require little change to existing habits of use—even (and perhaps especially) when the *Space*, *Backspace*, *Shift*, and *Enter* keys are removed. As our studies revealed, users benefitted from the latter design almost immediately. While we do not claim linear stroke shortcuts can rival the peak performance expert users might attain with techniques such as shape-writing, linear stroke keyboards are worth studying and understanding as an interesting class in their own right because of the extremely low barrier to entry, which affords a smaller but still significant performance benefit with minimal investment in skill acquisition.

Furthermore, it may be possible to combine linear stroke keyboards and shape gestures in future work (a design path that we are actively exploring), which underscores the need to carefully isolate and analyze the potential contribution of linear stroke shortcuts to the touchscreen text-entry problem.

Finally, by taking the design step of removing the gesture-redundant keys—which while not without precedent [4], has never been quantitatively studied before—the *Removed+Strokes* ("*New*") keyboard design tested here offers a simple, single-level keyboard design that almost entirely eliminates the need to switch to secondary and tertiary virtual keyboards for entering special characters, thus saving keystrokes while also avoiding the visually and cognitively jarring changes of the keyboard context required by touchscreen keyboards in common use today.

Looking forward, our research program aims to further advance this approach. We are currently conducting a longitudinal deployment of a stroke keyboard with the gesture-redundant keys removed in the context of users' day-to-day text entry. Whether stroke-based designs can exhibit advantages in other contexts—such as mobile phones, large-format displays, or one-handed text entry—remains to be demonstrated. We also intend to explore the potential of adding other enhancements, such as word prediction, shape-writing gestures, and integrated text editing and selection techniques [10].

8 REFERENCES

[1] Arif, A.S., Stuerzlinger, W. Analysis of text entry performance metrics. *Proc. IEEE TIC-STH 2009*.

[2] Arif, A.S., Stuerzlinger, W. Predicting the cost of error correction in character-based text entry technologies. *CHI '10*.

[3] Bragdon, A., et al. GestureBar: improving the approachability of gesture-based interfaces. *CHI '09*.

[4] Buxton, B. *Too Hidden Features of the Windows CE Graphical Keyboard*. Sept. 17, 2013. Available from: www.billbuxton.com/Windows%20CE%20Graphical%20Keyboard.pdf.

[5] Buxton, W., Kurtenbach, G., *Graphical keyboard, U.S. Patent 6,094,197*, May 17, 1995.

[6] Chun Yat Li, F., et al. The 1Line Keyboard: A QWERTY Layout in a Single Line. *UIST'11*.

[7] Dillon, R.F., et al. Measuring the True Cost of Command Selection: Techniques and Results. *CHI'90*.

[8] Findlater, L., et al. Beyond QWERTY: augmenting touch screen keyboards with multi-touch gestures for non-alphanumeric input. *CHI '12*.

[9] Findlater, L., et al. Typing on flat glass: examining ten-finger expert typing patterns on touch surfaces. *CHI '11*.

[10] Fuccella, V., et al. Gestures and Widgets: Performance in Text Editing on Multi-Touch Capable Mobile Devices. *CHI'13*.

[11] Goldberg, D., Richardson, C. Touch-typing with a stylus. *CHI '93*.

[12] Grossman, T., et al. Strategies for accelerating on-line learning of hotkeys. *CHI '07*.

[13] Hashimoto, M., Togasi, M. A virtual oval keyboard and a vector input method for pen-based character input. *CHI '95*.

[14] Hot Virtual Keyboard. http://hot-virtual-keyboard.com. 2012.

[15] Isokoski, P. Performance of menu-augmented soft keyboards. *CHI '04*.

[16] Kristensson, P.-O., Zhai, S. SHARK 2: a large vocabulary shorthand writing system for pen-based computers. *UIST'04*.

[17] Kurtenbach, G., Buxton, W. Issues in combining marking and direct manipulation techniques. *UIST'91*.

[18] Kurtenbach, G., et al. Contextual Animation of Gestural Commands. *Proc. Graphics Interface'94*.

[19] MacKenzie, I.S., et al. Unipad: Single-stroke text entry with language-based acceleration. *ACM NordiCHI 2006*.

[20] MacKenzie, I.S., Zhang, S.X. The immediate usability of graffiti. *Proceedings of the conference on Graphics interface '97.*.

[21] MacKenzie, I.S., Zhang, S.X. The design and evaluation of a high-performance soft keyboard. *CHI'99*.

[22] MacKenzie, I.S., et al. Text entry using soft keyboards. Behaviour & Information Technology, 1999. **18**: p. 235-244.

[23] MacKenzie, S., Soukoreff, W., Phrase sets for evaluating text entry techniques. *CHI'03 Extended Abstracts*.

[24] Masui, T. An Efficient Text Input Method for Pen-based Comptuers. *CHI'98*.

[25] MessageEase. *MessageEase keyboard for touch screen devices*. 2012. Available from: www.exideas.com.

[26] Palm Inc. *Getting Started*. 2000. Available from: http://research.microsoft.com/en-us/um/people/bibuxton/buxtoncollection/a/pdf/Palm%20m500%20User%20Manual.pdf.

[27] Swype. http://www.swypeinc.com. 2012.

[28] Vertanen, K., Kristensson, P.O. A Versatile Dataset for Text Entry Evaluations Based on Genuine Mobile Emails. *MobileHCI'11*.

[29] Wobbrock, J., et al. EdgeWrite: A Stylus-based text entry method designed for high accuracy and stability of motion. *UIST'03*.

[30] Zhai, S., et al. The Metropolis keyboard - an exploration of quantitative techniques for virtual keyboard design. *UIST'00*.

[31] Zhai, S., Kristensson, P.O. Shorthand writing on a stylus keyboard. *CHI '03*.

[32] Zhai, S., Kristensson, P.O., The word-gesture keyboard: reimagining keyboard interaction. Commun. ACM, 2012. **55**(9): p. 91-101.

[33] Zhai, S., Kristensson, P.O., Appert, C., Andersen, T.H., Cao, X., Foundational Issues in Touch-Surface Stroke Gesture Design - An Integrative Review. Foundations and Trends in Human-Computer Interaction, 2012. **5**(2): p. 97-205.

Position vs. Velocity Control for Tilt-Based Interaction

Robert J. Teather*

McMaster University

I. Scott MacKenzie**

York University

ABSTRACT

Research investigating factors in the design of tilt-based interfaces is presented. An experiment with 16 participants used a tablet and a 2D pointing task to compare position-control and velocity-control using device tilt to manipulate an on-screen cursor. Four selection modes were also evaluated, ranging from instantaneous selection upon hitting a target to a 500-ms time delay prior to selection. Results indicate that position-control was approximately 2× faster than velocity-control, regardless of selection delay. Position-control had higher pointing throughput (3.3 bps vs. 1.2 bps for velocity-control), more precise cursor motion, and was universally preferred by participants.

Keywords: Fitts' law, pointing, position-control, velocity-control.

Index Terms: H.5.2. Information interfaces and presentation (e.g., HCI): User Interfaces – evaluation/methodology.

1 INTRODUCTION

Tilt control is now available in virtually all mobile devices and tablets, and in many game controllers. The ubiquity of this technology arises from the low cost of accelerometers coupled with the interaction possibilities afforded by the technology. Most mobile devices change their display orientation upon rotating the device. Many mobile games are tilt-based, for example, racing games where the player tilts the device like a steering wheel, and "marble maze" games where tilting rolls a ball to simulate gravity.

Although tilt control intuitively *seems* natural for the above examples, it tends to underperform relative to direct touch [2, 11, 30], another universal technology. One wonders if game developers might intentionally choose tilt to *increase* game difficulty. It is possible that minor changes to the control scheme such as using position instead of velocity control could offer better user performance. To assess this hypothesis, we used a widely accepted paradigm of pointing device evaluation to assess tilt performance in a general interaction task.

Our research focuses on an on-going investigation of human performance aspects of tilt control as an interaction primitive. Motivated by our previous work [17], the major objective of this work is to compare different control modes and different selection modes. Specifically, the research described herein is the first to compare position-control and velocity-control for tilt-based input in a pointing task.

We also expand our previous work [17] which only compared two selection modes: immediate selection when the cursor enters the target, and delayed selection after a 500-ms dwell time upon target entry. The rationale for the delay is that in any real user interface, target disambiguation is required. However, the delay duration limits the upper bound of performance. Hence, we look at several selection delays to determine a setting that minimally impacts performance and does not interfere with the user's subjective impression of the system.

* teather@mcmaster.ca

** mack@cse.yorku.ca

2 RELATED WORK

2.1 Tilt-Based Interaction

Tilt control has long been of interest to HCI researchers. We present previous work in several areas. See Table 1.

2.1.1 UI Tasks

Early tilt research focused on list/menu navigation [21], scrolling [1, 6, 19, 24], document browsing [3], and changing display orientation [9]. The cited papers all present implementation *examples*; performance was not quantified. Here, we focus on user performance for basic input control using tilt for target selection.

Wang et al. [27] used vision-based motion tracking instead of an accelerometer for tilt control. They proposed several tasks using tilt, including a pointing task, game control, and text entry. The pointing task, which used Fitts' law [4], is the closest to our evaluation. However, they only investigated 1D cursor control in four directions, possibly due to sensor imprecision. Performance as indicated by Fitts' throughput was about 1 bps. The authors speculated that accelerometer-based tilt control may offer better performance due to lower processing requirements. Other work confirms that tilt-based pointing and scrolling conform to Fitts' law, but did not report pointing throughput [22]. Later research [17] using accelerometer-based tilt control indicates that, for multi-directional pointing, throughput is as high as 2.5 bps.

2.1.2 Text Entry

Several researchers investigated tilt for text entry [13, 20, 23, 28]. Wigdor and Balakrishnan [28] used device tilt to disambiguate letter selection and reported that their technique was faster but more error-prone than MultiTap. Unigesture [23] partitioned letters into seven "zones" corresponding to seven tilt directions, with an eighth zone for SPACE. Like T9, Unigesture uses dictionary-based disambiguation to determine the word the user is entering. GestText [13] is similar as it partitions text into zones. Two options for partitioning were examined, with a matrix-based layout (like Unigesture) found to be superior. TiltType [20] is also similar, but accesses letter groups via physical buttons and uses tilt to disambiguate. The technique was not evaluated, though. While these studies suggest promise in tilt-based text entry, how well the results generalize to other tasks is unclear.

2.1.3 Games

Tilt-controlled games are increasingly common and popular on mobile devices. Tilt offers an alternative to touchscreen-based controls, which perform poorly relative to physical controls [2, 11, 30]. This performance discrepancy is largely attributed to the absence of tactile feedback in touchscreens [29].

Much of the work on tilt control for games is qualitative, for example, looking at user experience [5, 26]. However, there is also quantitative work [2, 18]. Browne and Anand [2] compared tilt to touchscreen controls for a shooting game on an Apple iPod Touch. Participants could play the game significantly longer with tilt than with touch controls. However, this was in part because the virtual buttons did not support multi-touch; i.e., participants could not move and shoot simultaneously, unlike with tilt.

51

First Author	Tilt Control	Device	Task	Main Findings
Browne [2]	Velocity	Smartphone	2D shooter game	Tilt performed better and more preferred than swiping or on-screen buttons
Gilbertson [5]	Velocity	Mobile Phone	3D tunnel game	Participants had higher scores with tilt than keypad
Henrysson [7]	Velocity	Mobile Phone	3D rotation	Tilt slower than device motion and keys
Henrysson [8]	Velocity	Mobile Phone	3D rotation	Tilt faster than touchscreen, slower than keys
Hynninen [11]	Velocity	Smartphone	First-person shooter games	Tilt performed worse than virtual joystick controls on touchscreen
Jones [13]	Position (gestures)	Wiimote	Text entry	Entry speed of around 5 wpm after four days with two difference soft keyboard layouts
MacKenzie [17]	Velocity	Tablet	ISO pointing task	Tilt conforms to Fitts' law, lower performance than mouse
Medryk [18]	Velocity	Smartphone	Pong-like game	Touchscreen (swiping) faster and higher scores than tilt
Oakley [19]	Velocity and position	Handheld computer	Menu Navigation	Tilt using position control faster than velocity control
Sad [22]	Position	PDA with tilt sensor	Scrolling, pointing	Tilt control in both tasks conforms to Fitts' law
Sazawal [23]	Position	Custom	Text entry	Mainly qualitative, error counts also reported
Valente [26]	Position	Mobile Phone	Navigation via audio	Tilt control feasible for non-visual games
Wang [27]	Velocity	Mobile Phone, tilt from camera	Multiple tasks, pointing	Fitts' pointing throughput of about 1.1 bps, differences based on motion direction
Wigdor [28]	Position	Mobile Phone	Text entry	TiltText 23% faster, about 2x as error prone as multitap

Table 1: Overview of empirical performance studies on tilt control.

Other researchers report contradictory results. Medryk and MacKenzie [18] found tilt was inferior to touchscreen control: Participants had worse game scores and accuracy, and took longer to complete levels in a *Pong*-like game. This may be due to the nature of the touch-control. Instead of displaying virtual joysticks and buttons, the game was controlled with swipe gestures. Similarly, Hynninen [11] found that tilt-control was inferior to touch-based virtual joystick control in a first-person shooter game.

The results on tilt-based gaming are mixed and difficult to generalize due to the complexity of the game tasks. The effectiveness of tilt control may thus be task-dependent.

2.1.4 Mobile Augmented Reality

The power, portability, and availability of multiple sensors (including cameras) make smartphones an interesting platform for mobile augmented reality (AR). Several studies investigated the use of tilt for object manipulation in a phone-based AR system. These systems typically use the device's accelerometers, but sometimes instead use the camera to detect device motion [27].

Henrysson et al. [7] used phone tilt to control 3D object rotation, comparing four techniques for single-axis rotation. The techniques included two using phone tilt, one using phone displacement, and one using keys. They found that the tilt methods were slowest. A later study on object rotation [8] compared tilt to key/joystick and touchscreen input. Consistent with earlier results, the authors found key-based input superior to tilt. However, tilt outperformed the touchscreen method, suggesting positive benefits in using tilt for input control.

Other researchers [10] report that moving objects in an AR environment using the movement/tilt of the device was faster than direct or indirect touch-based interfaces. Selection was slower using tilt than direct touch, however.

2.1.5 Summary

Of the studies cited above, only Oakley et al. [19] compared velocity and position tilt control. They used a menu navigation task. We seek to better understand these two control types in more general tilt-based interaction. Overall, few studies seem to consider position-control at all, likely because velocity-control is a more reality-founded control style. Our work is motivated on the hypothesis that position-control will offer better performance and could be employed in new or re-imagined tilt-based designs.

2.2 Fitts' Law and Pointing

Our evaluation employs Fitts' law [4], which models the speed-accuracy tradeoff in rapid aimed movements. The prediction form of Fitts' law is

$$MT = a + b \times \log_2\left(\frac{A}{W} + 1\right) \quad (1)$$

where MT is movement time. The constants a and b are empirically derived via linear regression. The log term is the index of difficulty (ID, in bits) where A and W are the amplitude (distance to the target) and width (target size), respectively. Essentially, the model implies that far, small targets are harder to hit than near, large targets. Harder tasks take longer, as reflected by MT. This has been formalized in an international standard for pointing device evaluation, ISO 9241-9 [12]. Figure 1 depicts the standard's 2D pointing task.

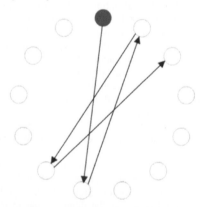

Figure 1: ISO 9241-9 2D tapping task with 13 circles (12 targets). Arrows indicate the first five targets.

The standard suggests using "effective" measures for width and amplitude to better account for user performance. This offers some advantages [15, 25], but effective measures are not used in the current study because the task precludes missing targets. Consequently, and similar to previous work [17], we instead calculate throughput using presented ID and average MT as

$$TP = \frac{ID}{MT} \quad (2)$$

Figure 2: Samsung *Galaxy Note 10.1* tablet running the experimental software.

Finally, while throughput quantifies performance, it does not explain performance differences. Hence, we also employ accuracy measures (target re-entries, movement variability, and errors) [16] to help explain performance differences.

3 POSITION- AND VELOCITY-CONTROL

The main factor studied in our experiment is control mode. We investigated two options: position-control and velocity-control. Both use the tablet tilt but result in dramatically different experiences. Velocity-control is reminiscent of marble-maze games, as the cursor (a ball) increases its movement speed based on the amount of device tilt. Position-control is quite different: The farther the device is tilted, the farther from center the cursor is positioned. There is a direct correspondence between tilt angle and cursor position. Upon leveling the device, the cursor returns to the display center. The algorithms to determine ball position in each control mode are explained in the Apparatus section.

Previous work has shown that position-control affords higher performance than velocity-control in a tele-manipulation task [14]. Also, tilt-based position-control was superior to velocity-control for menu selection [19] on a mobile phone. There appears to be no prior empirical evaluation comparing tilt-based velocity- and position-control in general point-select tasks, though.

4 METHODOLOGY

4.1 Participants

Sixteen participants (8 male) took part in the study. Ages ranged from 18 to 47 ($\mu = 25$, $\sigma = 7.3$ years). All were undergraduate students enrolled in an introductory computer course. Participants were not regular tilt users – on a five point scale (1 meaning they never used tilt control and 5 meaning they used it every day), the mean response was a 3.1 ($SD = 1.4$).

4.2 Apparatus

The experiment was conducted on a Samsung *Galaxy Note 10.1* tablet with Google's *Android 4.1.2 (Jelly Bean)* OS. See Figure 2. The display resolution was 1280 × 800 pixels and measured 260 mm (10.1") diagonally. Pixel density was 149 pixels/inch.

Software was developed in Java using the Android SDK. Tilt control used the device's orientation sensor, fusing data from the accelerometer, gyroscope, and magnetometer. The sensor sample rate was 100 Hz. Two different methods were used to convert device pitch and roll to tilt magnitude and tilt angle, resulting in the two control modes investigated.

4.2.1 Calculating Ball Position[1]

Both control modes computed tilt magnitude and angle as:

$$tiltMag = \sqrt{pitch^2 + roll^2} \qquad (3)$$

$$tiltAngle = \operatorname{asin}\left(\frac{roll}{tiltMag}\right) \qquad (4)$$

These data controlled the ball direction and speed in velocity-control mode, and the ball position in position-control mode. In velocity-control mode, the ball "rolled" according to the tablet tilt. The ball velocity (v, in pixels/second) was a linear function of tilt magnitude and a programmable tilt gain setting:

$$v = tiltMag \times tiltGain \qquad (5)$$

With each sample, the ball displacement ($dBall$, in pixels) was calculated as the product of the velocity and time since the last sample (dt, in seconds):

$$dBall = dt \times v \qquad (6)$$

As an example, if the tilt magnitude was 3° and tilt gain was set at 50, then velocity was 3 × 50 = 150 pixels per second. If the sample occurred 20 ms after the previous sample, the ball was moved 0.02 × 150 = 3.0 pixels in the direction of the tilt angle. Based on previous results [17], tilt gain was fixed at 100.

The second control mode used position- or absolute-control, and behaved somewhat like an isotonic joystick. The farther participants tilted the tablet, the farther the ball was positioned from the home position. "Centering" the tablet – setting it down, or otherwise positioning it flat – re-centered the ball. Ball position was determined according to the following equations:

$$dBall = tiltMag \times tiltGain \qquad (7)$$

$$offset = (dBall * \sin(tiltAngle), dBall * \cos(tiltAngle)) \qquad (8)$$

$$ballPos = center + offset \qquad (9)$$

The *offset* vector was added to the center position to determine the ball position. Tilt gain for position-control was fixed at 20. This resulted in a reasonable or nominal user experience, comparable to velocity-control with a tilt gain setting of 100.

4.2.2 Task and Target Parameters

The software implemented a variation on the ISO 9241-9 [12] 2D targeting task. See Figure 3. The task required tilting the tablet to hit the highlighted target with the 20-pixel diameter ball. Three target amplitudes (A) were used: 131, 263, and 526 pixels. Three target sizes (W) were used: 42, 63, and 105 pixels. See Figure 4. Note that the targets were effectively smaller, since the ball had to be completely inside the target for selection. Consequently, we subtract the ball diameter from the target diameter in the calculation of *ID*.

The *A-W* conditions yielded nine combinations of *ID* calculated according to Equation 1 and subject to the modification discussed above. *ID*s ranged from 1.35 to 4.64 bits. For each condition, there were 13 targets (12 selections), yielding 12 recorded trials per sequence. Each trial ended upon successful selection of the target, hence missing targets was impossible. In addition to the two control modes detailed above, four target selection delays were studied. The first was 0 ms delay. In this mode, selection occurred as soon as the ball was completely inside the target. The remaining selection modes required keeping the ball (completely) inside the target for a specified duration. Extending previous work [17], we used three non-zero levels of selection delay: 500, 400, and 300 milliseconds.

---

[1] These equations are a fast and accurate simplification of the exact equations, which require converting Euler angles to an axis-angle representation. The error is < 1 degree for all tilt angles < 45 degrees, which is well within the range of angles used.

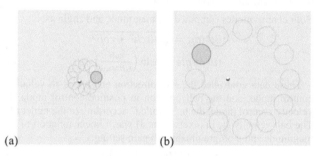

(a)   (b)

Figure 3: The task performed by participants. (a) *A* = 131 pixels, *W* = 63 pixels. (b) *A* = 526 pixels, *W* = 105 pixels.

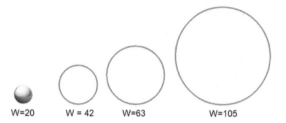

W=20   W = 42   W=63   W=105

Figure 4: The user-controlled ball (cursor) relative to the three target sizes used in the experiment.

4.3   Procedure

After giving informed consent, the procedure and software were demonstrated to participants. The study was performed seated, and participants held tablet however they felt comfortable. See Figure 5. At the start of the experiment, participants were given 12 practice trials with each of the extreme selection delays (i.e., 0 ms and 500 ms) in the starting control mode. At the halfway point the control mode changed, and participants were given the same number of practice trials with the same selection delays.

Participants completed a questionnaire after the experiment. This included questions on control smoothness, mental and physical effort, and general preference of selection delay.

4.4   Design

The experiment used a repeated-measures design with the following independent variables and levels:

Control mode:	Position, Velocity
Selection delay:	0, 300, 400, and 500 ms
Target amplitude:	131, 263, 526 pixels
Target width:	42, 63, 105 pixels

Half of the participants started with position-control, and the other half started with velocity-control. Control mode switched at the halfway point. Selection delay was counterbalanced within control mode according to a balanced Latin square.

The dependent variables were movement time, target re-entries (for non-zero selection delays), movement variability, maximum tilt angle, and throughput. Results of the post-experiment questionnaire are also presented.

Overall, the experiment took about one hour per participant. Each participant completed 2 control modes × 4 selection delays × 3 amplitudes × 3 widths × 12 selections = 864 trials total, or 13,824 trials over all 16 participants.

5   RESULTS

Statistical reports for movement time (*MT*), throughput (*TP*), target re-entries (*TRE*), movement variability (*MV*), movement error (*ME*), and maximum tilt (*MaxTilt*) are shown in Table 2.

Figure 5: Participant performing the selection task.

5.1   Movement Time

The grand mean for movement time was 2325 ms. There was a significant main effect on movement time for both control mode and selection delay. See Table 2. Overall, movement times were 1555 ms for position-control and 3095 ms for velocity-control; i.e., movement time was about 50% lower for position-control than for velocity-control. A Tukey-Kramer post hoc test indicated that 0 ms selection delay was significantly faster than all others, while the 300 and 400 ms delays were significantly faster than the 500 ms delay. See Figure 6.

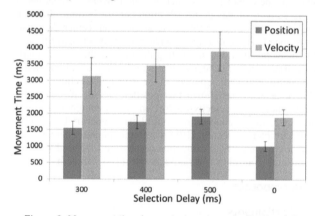

Figure 6: Movement time by control mode and selection delay. Error bars show ±1 *SE*.

There was also a significant interaction effect between control mode and selection delay on movement time. The difference in movement time with the 0 ms delay was more substantial for velocity-control than for position-control.

5.2   Throughput

Throughput was calculated according to Equation 2. As mentioned earlier, effective width and amplitude were unavailable since the task precluded missing the targets.

The main effects and interaction effect for control mode and selection delay were significant. See Table 2. Throughput scores are shown in Figure 7. Position-control with 0 ms selection delay had the highest throughput, at 3.3 bps. For comparison, most ISO-conforming pointing studies on desktop systems report mouse throughput of around 4 to 5 bps [25, Table 4]. Thus, throughput for position-controlled tilt input is about 25% lower than for mouse input. Conversely, velocity-control had an overall

Effect		MT		TP		TRE		ME		MV		MaxTilt	
Name	df	F	p	F	p	F	p	F	p	F	p	F	p
(C)ontrol Mode	1,15	230.7	*	1115.2	*	30.9	*	53.9	*	23.7	*	1409.1	*
(S)election Delay	3,15	78.3	*	207.2	*	25.2	*	84.5	*	36.7	*	35.9	*
C × S	3,45	24.7	*	55.3	*	3.1	.06	23.3	*	15.2	*	48.3	*

Table 2: Statistical effects for accuracy measures. Control mode and selection delay are main effects, while C × S is the interaction. Significant effects are indicated with * for $p < .0001$.

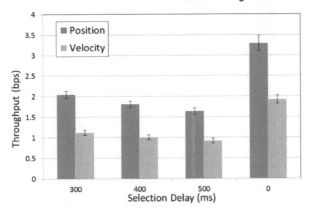

Figure 7: Throughput by control mode and selection delay. Higher is better. Error bars show ±1 *SE*.

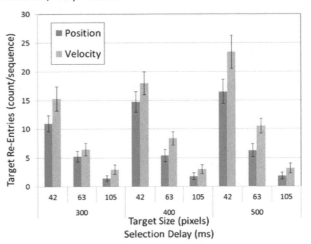

Figure 8: Target re-entries by control mode, selection delay, and target size. Lower is better. Error bars show ±1 *SE*.

throughput of 1.2 bps which was significantly lower than position-control (and about 70% lower than mouse throughput).

Unsurprisingly, throughput is lower for higher selection delays. The worst condition was velocity-control with 500 ms selection delay. Even the 300 ms delay was substantially worse than the 0 ms delay. This suggests that alternative target disambiguation techniques may fare better than the delayed timeout used. These delays may also be too short for UIs with distracter targets.

5.3 Accuracy

Since all trials ended with selection of the target, error rates were unavailable for the study. Instead, we examined other accuracy measures (target re-entries, movement variability, and movement error) which correlate with pointing performance [16]. Statistical data for these metrics are reported in Table 2.

5.3.1 Target Re-Entries (TRE)

Target re-entries is the count (averaged per 12 selections) of how frequently the cursor left and then re-entered the target. In a "perfect" selection task, *TRE* is 0, i.e., there is one target entry. *TRE* gives an indication of control problems, and may be more pronounced for smaller targets. See Figure 8 for *TRE* scores.

Aside from the results shown in Table 2, there were significant interaction effects between control mode and target size ($F_{2,30} = 13.1$, $p < .0001$) and between selection delay and target size ($F_{4,60} = 18.0$, $p < .0001$) (not given in Table 2). Evidently, participants had a much harder time selecting the smallest targets with velocity-control than with position-control, and also with longer selection delays. The worst overall score resulted from the combination of velocity-control, a 500 ms selection delay, and a 42-pixel target. *TREs* for this condition exceeded 20 per sequence of 12 selections.

5.3.2 Movement Variability and Movement Error

In a perfect selection task, the cursor would move in a straight line to the target, irrespective of the actual distance along the task axis (the line between subsequent targets). Movement variability (*MV*)

represents this path straightness; the lower the score, the straighter the path. Movement error (*ME*) is the average distance of the motion path from the task axis, and may reflect difficulty in maintaining an optimal path. Control mode and selection delay had significant main effects on both *MV* and *ME*. The interaction effects were also significant. See Table 2.

Both movement variability and error were lower with position-control than velocity-control. Interestingly, velocity-control with 0 ms delay had the highest scores for both movement variability and error. While this suggests participants had more difficulty moving the ball in a straight line in this condition, reckless tilting of the tablet may be a better explanation. This is discussed further in the motion analysis section below. This path inefficiency is reflected in the overall higher movement times and lower throughput scores reported above. Conversely, position-control with 0 ms selection delay was not significantly worse than with other selection delays. See Figures 9 and 10.

Overall, position-control offered superior handling. Participants had difficulty keeping the ball close to the task axis with velocity-control, especially with the 0 ms delay. Motion path analysis (see below and Figure 13) corroborates this result.

5.3.3 Maximum Tilt

The degree to which participants tilted the tablet was also recorded. Note that position-control *required* a certain amount of tilt, as determined by the target distance (relative to the center of the tablet) and the tilt gain. With velocity-control, however, the amount of tilt depends on the user's *strategy* – greater tilt yields higher ball velocity. The main effects and interaction effect of control mode and selection delay on maximum tilt were both statistically significant. See Table 2.

Tilt angles were significantly and substantially lower for velocity-control than for position-control. See Figure 11. Velocity-control with 0 ms selection delay exhibited significantly larger tilt angles than all other delays for that control mode.

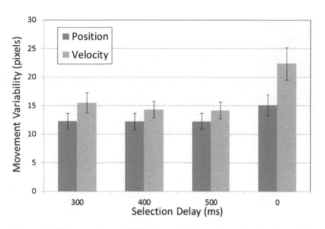

Figure 9: Movement variability by control mode and selection delay. Error bars show ±1 *SE*.

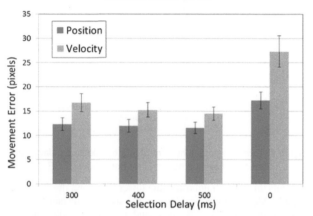

Figure 10: Movement error by control mode and selection delay. Error bars show ±1 SE.

Position-control required approximately twice as much tilt as velocity-control. The maximum tilt for position-control across selection delays was essentially flat. As noted above, maximum tilt with position-control is determined more by target location than by user strategy. Despite requiring greater degrees of tilt, position-control also offered higher performance. This suggests that the degree to which participants tilted the device was not directly linked to performance. This is likely linked to the tilt gain setting.

5.3.4 Motion Path

Figure 13 depicts typical motion paths of the ball in four conditions (0 ms and 500 ms selection delays for both control modes). Red dots indicate where selections occurred, and the blue line indicates the cursor/ball motion path. Velocity-control yielded erratic motion, with large target overshoots and corrections. This is supported by higher *MV* and *ME* scores and overall worse performance. Conversely, motion is fairly accurate with position-control; this likely explains the higher overall performance.

Line thickness in Figure 13 increases with the amount of tilt (i.e., thick lines indicate more tilt than thin lines). With position-control (Figure 13c and d), lines are thicker farther away from the center, as greater tilt is required to position the ball farther from the tablet center. Conversely, for velocity-control the lines are thinner near targets. Participants were more careful upon approaching the target, and reduced the tablet tilt to slow the ball movement, improving control for the feedback-guided selection. Conversely, when moving the ball between targets, they would tilt the tablet to greater degrees to traverse the distance more quickly.

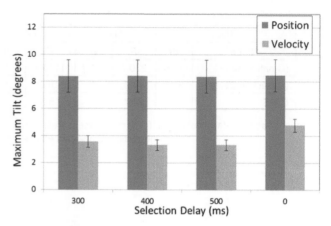

Figure 11: Maximum tilt angle by control mode and selection delay. Error bars show ±1 *SE*.

Figure 13b (velocity-control with 0 ms selection delay) shows the most erratic motions, and are typical of the condition. Participants would recklessly tilt the device to quickly traverse the distance between targets. This behaviour is especially evident in the line thickness near the center of Figure 13b. The movement appears somewhat ballistic and frequently resulted in the ball moving *through* the target, followed by a correction to adjust the ball's direction for the next target.

5.3.5 Subjective Questionnaire Results

Participants also completed a questionnaire, the results of which were compared using *t*-tests. Position-control scored significantly higher in all questions, see Figure 12. These results indicate that position-control was also preferred by the study participants.

Participants also provided comments on the experimental conditions. One participant reported that their lower arms were more tense while using the velocity mode and that the position mode was more relaxing. Another noted, "If I had to use velocity-control for any real task, I would stop using that app". These comments help explain the difference in participant preference for the two control modes, while underlining the measured performance differences.

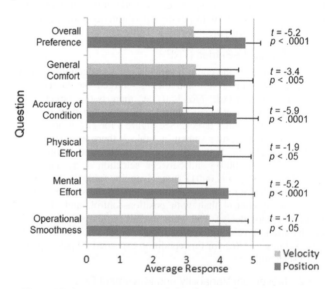

Figure 12: Survey responses and statistical reports by question. Higher scores are more favorable. Error bars show ±1 *SD*.

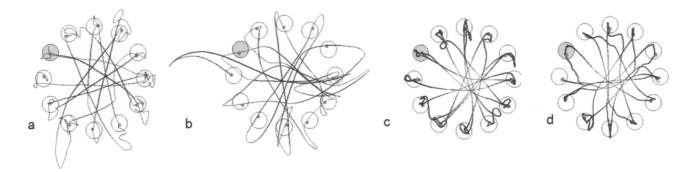

Figure 13: Motion paths for (a) velocity-control with 500 ms delay, (b) velocity-control with 0 ms delay, (c) position-control with 500 ms delay, and (d) position-control with 0 ms delay.

The survey also asked participants for their selection delay preference. Eleven preferred no selection delay, four preferred a 300 ms delay, and one preferred a 400 ms delay. It is likely that the strong preference for instantaneous selection is simply due to the higher performance it offers. Of course, this selection mode is not always feasible (e.g., in the presence of distracter targets)..

6 DISCUSSION AND LIMITATIONS

Our results suggest that, in applications where there is a choice, position-control tilt input is preferred. Overall, participants performed better with and generally preferred position-control over velocity-control. This may be due to the higher attention demand in the velocity-control mode, where constant visual attention is required to adjust the ball's motion. Conversely, in position-control, attention demand is somewhat lower as participants can leverage proprioception without worrying that the ball will venture off-course. This is reflected in the analyses of motion, movement variability, and error. Attention demand differences are also reflected in participants' assessment of higher mental effort with velocity-control.

It is worth noting that position-control is unsuited to situations with unbounded scrolling, for example, map or document navigation. Position-control is thus dependent on the control range. This can be mitigated by increasing the tilt gain or through clutching. Of course, after a point the screen simply tilts out of a viewable range. Velocity-control does not have this limitation.

Participants also tended to prefer shorter selection delays. Of course, this result is contingent with the task. Typical UIs include multiple targets yielding the possibility of selecting the wrong target. Our study did not include distracter targets. While performance was highest with a 0 ms delay, such a technique is clearly impractical for real-world use. Similarly, the some selection delays (e.g., 300 ms) may be too short to avoid accidental selections. We plan to study this further in an experiment that includes distracter targets.

Finally, we also acknowledge that touch-control is the predominant control style on mobile devices. Tilt control is typically used only in limited situations, or in conjunction with touch. As we did not directly compare these two control styles, we can only speculate on performance differences in selection tasks. It is likely that touch control would offer superior performance to tilt control for the most common interactions in mobile user interfaces. That said, we believe that the present investigation indicates that position-controlled tilt is worth further consideration. It would be interesting to implement position-control for games which commonly use velocity-control and compare scores between these. We are also considering other possible uses of position-control tilt, including phone dialers and text entry. These are topics for future study, however.

7 CONCLUSIONS

We presented a study investigating important aspects of tilt-based interaction. This study represents (to our knowledge) the first comparison between position- and velocity-control for general tilt-based interaction. Results indicate that although it required greater amounts of tilt, position-control offered significantly better performance than velocity-control and was also strongly preferred by participants. Not only was this mode faster and yielded higher throughput, it also offered much smoother control as indicated by the analysis of several motion metrics.

The results also indicate that instant selection upon entering a target (i.e., 0 ms selection delay) afforded better performance than a delayed selection. While this is not surprising, such a selection mode is not always practical. For example, some means of target disambiguation is required if the cursor must cross other targets to reach the intended target. While the selection delays studied here suggest faster delays offer better performance, we note again that these results must be considered in light of the fact that no actual distracter targets were present in our study.

7.1 Future Work

The study used nominal gain settings chosen from pilot testing. This is one obvious parameter to evaluate further in future work. In particular, and as suggested by participants, a dynamic gain level is worth considering.

A long term objective is to further investigate what kinds of tasks benefit more from velocity tilt control versus position tilt control. For example, one might consider a marble-maze style game using position-control, and compare this to velocity-control.

ACKNOWLEDGEMENTS

Thanks to the anonymous reviewers for their helpful suggestions on improving the paper. This work was supported by NSERC.

REFERENCES

[1]   J. F. Bartlett, Rock'n'Scroll is here to stay, *IEEE Computer Graphics and Applications*, 20, 2000, 40-45.

[2]   K. Browne and C. Anand, An empirical evaluation of user interfaces for a mobile video game, *Journal of Entertainment Computing*, 3, 2012, 1-10.

[3]   P. Eslambolchilar and R. Murray-Smith, Tilt-based automatic zooming and scaling in mobile devices – a state-space implementation, *Proceedings of Human Computer Interaction with Mobile Devices and Services - MobileHCI 2004*, (Berlin: Springer, 2004), 120-131.

[4] P. M. Fitts, The information capacity of the human motor system in controlling the amplitude of movement, *Journal of Experimental Psychology*, *47*, 1954, 381-391.

[5] P. Gilbertson, P. Coulton, F. Chehimi, and T. Vajk, Using "tilt" as an interface to control "no-button" 3-D mobile games, *Computers in Entertainment (CIE)*, *6*, 2008, 38.

[6] B. L. Harrison, K. P. Fishkin, A. Gujar, C. Mochon, and R. Want, Squeeze me, hold me, tilt me! An exploration of manipulative user interfaces, *Proceedings of the ACM SIGCHI Conference on Human Factors in Computing Systems - CHI '98*, (New York: ACM, 1998), 17-24.

[7] A. Henrysson, M. Billinghurst, and M. Ollila, Virtual object manipulation using a mobile phone, *Proceedings of the International Conference on Augmented Tele-Existence - ICAT 2005*, (New York: ACM, 2005), 164-171.

[8] A. Henrysson, J. Marshall, and M. Billinghurst, Experiments in 3D interaction for mobile phone AR, *Proceedings of the ACM Conference on Computer Graphics and Interactive Techniques in Australia and Southeast Asia - GRAPHITE 2007*, (New York: ACM, 2007), 187 - 194.

[9] K. Hinckley, J. Pierce, M. Sinclair, and E. Horvitz, Sensing techniques for mobile interaction, *Proceedings of the ACM Symposium on User Interface Software and Technology - UIST 2000*, (New York: ACM, 2000), 91-100.

[10] W. Hürst and C. van Wezel, Gesture-based interaction via finger tracking for mobile augmented reality, *Multimedia Tools and Applications*, *62*, 2013, 233-258.

[11] T. Hynninen, First-person shooter controls on touchscreen devices: A heuristic evaluation of three games on the iPod touch, *M.Sc. Thesis, Department of Computer Sciences, University of Tampere, Tampere, Finland*, 2012, 64 pages.

[12] ISO, ISO 9241-9 Ergonomic requirements for office work with visual display terminals (VDTs) - Part 9: Requirements for non-keyboard input devices: International Standard, International Organization for Standardization, 2000.

[13] E. Jones, J. Alexander, A. Andreou, P. Irani, and S. Subramanian, GesText: Accelerometer-based gestural text-entry systems, *Proceedings of the ACM SIGCHI Conference on Human Factors in Computing Systems - CHI 2010*, (New York: ACM, 2010), 2173-2182.

[14] W. S. Kim, F. Tendick, S. R. Ellis, and L. W. Stark, A comparison of position and rate control for telemanipulations with consideration of manipulator system dynamics, *IEEE Journal of Robotics and Automation*, *3*, 1987, 426-436.

[15] I. S. MacKenzie and P. Isokoski, Fitts' throughput and the speed-accuracy tradeoff, *Proceedings of the ACM SIGCHI Conference on Human Factors in Computing Systems - CHI 2008*, (New York: ACM, 2008), 1633-1636.

[16] I. S. MacKenzie, T. Kauppinen, and M. Silfverberg, Accuracy measures for evaluating computer pointing devices, *Proceedings of the ACM SIGCHI Conference on Human Factors in Computing Systems - CHI 2001*, (ACM, 2001), 9 - 16.

[17] I. S. MacKenzie and R. J. Teather, FittsTilt: The application of Fitts' law to tilt-based interaction, *Proceedings of the 7th Nordic Conference on Human-Computer Interaction - NordiCHI 2012*, (New York: ACM, 2012), 568-577.

[18] S. Medryk and I. S. MacKenzie, A comparison of accelerometer and touch-based input for mobile gaming, *International Conference on Multimedia and Human-Computer Interaction - MHCI 2013*, (Ottawa, Canada: International ASET, 2013), 117.1-117.8.

[19] I. Oakley and S. O'Modhrain, Tilt to scroll: Evaluating a motion based vibrotactile mobile interface, *Eurohaptics Conference and Symposium on Haptic Interfaces for Virtual Environment and Teleoperator Systems*, (New York: IEEE, 2005), 40-49.

[20] K. Partridge, S. Chatterjee, V. Sazawal, G. Borriello, and R. Want, TiltType: Accelerometer-supported text entry for very small devices, *Proceedings of the ACM Symposium on User Interface Software and Technology - UIST 2002*, (New York: ACM, 2002), 201-204.

[21] J. Rekimoto, Tilting operations for small screen interfaces, *Proceedings of the ACM Symposium on User Interface Software and Technology - UIST '96*, (New York: ACM, 1996), 167-168.

[22] H. H. Sad and F. Poirier, Evaluation and modeling of user performance for pointing and scrolling tasks on handheld devices using tilt sensor, *Advances in Computer-Human Interactions - ACHI 2009*. (New York: IEEE, 2009), 295-300.

[23] V. Sazawal, R. Want, and G. Borriello, The Unigesture approach: One-handed text entry for small devices, *Proceedings of Human Computer Interaction With Mobile Devices - MobileHCI 2002*, (Berlin: Springer, 2002), 256-270.

[24] D. Small and H. Ishii, Design of spatially aware graspable displays, *Extended Abstracts of the ACM SIGCHI Conference on Human Factors in Computing Systems - CHI '97*, (New York: ACM, 1997), 367-368.

[25] R. W. Soukoreff and I. S. MacKenzie, Towards a standard for pointing device evaluation: Perspectives on 27 years of Fitts' law research in HCI, *International Journal of Human-Computer Studies*, *61*, 2004, 751-789.

[26] L. Valente, C. Sieckenius de Souza, and B. Feijo, Turn off the graphics: Designing non-visual interfaces for mobile phone games, *Journal of the Brazilian Computer Society*, *15*, 2009, 45-58.

[27] J. Wang, S. Zhai, and J. Canny, Camera phone based motion sensing: Interaction techniques, applications and performance study, *Proceedings of the ACM Symposium on User Interface Software and Technology - UIST 2006*, (New York: ACM, 2006), 101-110.

[28] D. Wigdor and R. Balakrishnan, TiltText: Using tilt for text input to mobile phones, *Proceedings of the ACM Symposium on User Interface Software and Technology - UIST 2003*, (New York: ACM, 2003), 81-90.

[29] L. Zaman and I. S. MacKenzie, Evaluation of nano-stick, foam buttons, and other input methods for gameplay on touchscreen phones, *International Conference on Multimedia and Human-Computer Interaction - MHCI 2013*, (Ottawa, Canada: International ASET, 2013), 69.1-69.8.

[30] L. Zaman, D. Natapov, and R. J. Teather, Touchscreens vs. traditional controllers in handheld gaming, *Proceedings of the International Academic Conference on the Future of Game Design and Technology - FuturePlay 2010*, (New York: ACM, 2010), 183-190.

The Performance of Un-Instrumented In-Air Pointing

Michelle A. Brown[1]

York University, Toronto, Canada

Wolfgang Stuerzlinger[2]

York University, Toronto, Canada

E. J. Mendonça Filho[3]

Federal University of Bahia, Brazil

ABSTRACT

We present an analysis of in-air finger and hand controlled object pointing and selection. The study used a tracking system that required no instrumentation on the user. We compared the performance of the two pointing methods with and without elbow stabilization and found that the method that yielded the best performance varied for each participant, such that there was no method that performed significantly better than all others. We also directly compared user performance between un-instrumented in-air pointing and the mouse. We found that the un-instrumented in-air pointing performed significantly worse, at less than 75% of mouse throughput. Yet, the larger range of applications for un-instrumented 3D hand tracking makes this technology still an attractive option for user interfaces.

Keywords: Human-computer interaction, Fitts' law, pointing tasks.

Index Terms: H.5.2. [Information interfaces and presentation]: User Interfaces — Input *devices and strategies (e.g., mouse, touchscreen)*

1 INTRODUCTION

In the everyday world, pointing at objects to reference them is a fundamental task that spans across 2D and 3D selection. When people are using computers with others they will often point to objects visible on screen to indicate them to another person. This suggests that exploring the benefits and trade-offs of in-air pointing as an interaction modality is a worthwhile endeavour.

In-air pointing, especially un-instrumented pointing, promises to be less intrusive and possibly more convenient. We identify characteristics of this technology, measure throughput based on the ISO 9241-9 standard relative to the mouse, identify possible technological improvements, and identify situations where this type of selection method is beneficial.

1.1 Motivation

A number of hand tracking devices have recently appeared on the market and many more have been announced. This includes the Leap Motion, the DUO, the CamBoard pico, the touchless control system by Elliptic Labs, and 3 Gear Systems' hand tracking camera setup. These new devices promise revolutionary and "natural" control of your computer. However, the performance of such in-air un-instrumented hand tracking devices relative to other pointing devices has yet to have been evaluated.

While it is widely assumed that 3D un-instrumented tracking does not perform as well as the mouse, there is no scientific study that quantitatively shows this. Furthermore, the reasons for a

---

[1] brown@cse.yorku.ca

[2] wolfgang@cse.yorku.ca

[3] euclidesmendonca.f@gmail.com

Graphics Interface Conference 2014
7-9 May, Montreal, Quebec, Canada

possibly lower throughput have not been explored. Currently it is unclear whether these systems have a lower throughput due to various human postures, differences in latency, poor click detection methods, sub-optimal tracking algorithms, or potentially even human limitations. As such, it is unclear what developers could do to improve the performance of such systems.

Un-instrumented in-air pointing technologies are ideal in situations when users are concerned with sterility, situations where there is no mouse such as with a laptop or tablet, and situations where smudges are a concern, such as when using a mobile device while cooking. This last scenario occurs when people today consult the Internet to find new recipes for cooking. Instead of printing the recipe, users then bring their laptops, tablets, or phones into the kitchen while cooking. Yet, currently all interaction with the device requires users to first wash their hands or risk getting their device dirty. Un-instrumented in-air pointing avoids this problem and enables simple interaction with scrolling, unit conversions, cooking timers, or the music player. In order for this dream to become a reality, the performance of such systems needs to be evaluated and the benefits and shortcomings clearly understood.

We performed several pilot studies to identify a reasonable in-air tracking system. The first system we considered was 3 Gear Systems' hand tracker version 0.9.22. This Kinect-based system had a very high end-to-end latency of about 170 ms and was found to yield very noisy 3D data. In a pilot study, throughput was estimated to be at best 1:5 bps, with selection through the space bar. We also experimented with 3D tracking systems, but decided not to use these, as they required the user to put on extra equipment to use the system.

In the end, we decided to use the Leap Motion device. It easily affords pixel-accurate pointing, due to its' low noise level. We identified 85 ms of end-to-end latency in our system with this device. As this is reasonably close to the 75 ms reported for a instrumented 3D tracking system in a study of effects of latency on 3D interaction [1], we decided to use this device in our study. In another pilot study we found that only about half of all performed "click" motions, a short up and down of a finger, registered with the version 0.8.0 of the Leap Motion system as a successful "click". This success rate was deemed much too low to be practically competitive as a method to indicate selection. Thus, we did not consider this further in our study and used an alternate selection approach, which relies on the space bar operated with the non-dominant hand.

Before investigating how well un-instrumented 3D pointing works, we first devised user study 1 to determine the best operational method for un-instrumented pointing. This study also explores two possible explanations for a possibly lower throughput: pointing method (finger vs. hand) and the effect of elbow stabilization. Past work has shown that pointing with the finger alone (with the arm immobilized) affords significantly lower throughput compared to the whole hand. Elbow stabilization has the potential to improve performance through better accuracy. We then designed user study 2 to directly compare un-instrumented 3D tracking to the mouse by using the same selection technique for both devices. This second study thus also explores the effect different selection methods have on user performance. The reason we decided to directly compare un-instrumented pointing to the mouse was to enable calibration against other pointing studies, including MacKenzie and Jusoh's work [2].

1.2 Contributions

Our contributions are:

- The first accurate performance measurement for in-air un-instrumented pointing with ISO 9241-9.
- A comparison of two in-air target acquisition methods: finger pointing and whole hand movement.
- An analysis of the effect of elbow stabilization on selection performance.
- An evaluation of the performance benefit of using a ring button vs. selection with the other hand.

1.3 Related Work

Ray pointing is a method for pointing at objects. In this method, the user will move a tracked object, such as a pen or laser pointer, or a tracked arm or finger and orient it in the direction she or he wishes to point to, such that the tracked entity forms a ray toward the desired pointing location. The first object along that ray is then traditionally highlighted and selected when the user indicates selection, e.g., through a button click. Ray pointing remains a popular selection method for large screen and virtual reality systems. Many studies have investigated this technique, including [2]–[14]. All these comparisons used various 3D tracking systems to implement ray pointing. However, users cannot simply walk up to these systems and start using them; they must first put on the proper tracking equipment or grab an instrumented device.

Ray pointing uses 3D input to afford control over a 2D cursor. Effectively users rotate the wrist (or finger) to move the cursor. Balakrishan and MacKenzie quantified the relative bandwidth of the fingers, wrist, and forearm and found that the wrist and forearm afford bandwidth of about 4.1 bits/s, while a finger had only 3.0 bits/sec [15]. Another option for 2D cursor control is to directly map 3D motion to 2D motions by dropping the third degree of freedom recorded by the 3D tracking system. With this input method, the user then has to move her or his whole hand. Moving the finger or the whole hand to control the cursor both afford efficient pointing [16]. However, tracking very small hand rotations with 3D tracking systems with sufficient accuracy is difficult, as any amount of tracking noise is effectively magnified increasingly along the ray. This is the most likely explanation why ray pointing has been identified as inferior to other pointing methods in *desktop* environments, e.g., [17].

Un-instrumented pointing has been studied in the past. Here, the system tracks the hand or finger(s) of the user without instrumentation on the user. Typically this is done with some form of cameras. This body of work also explores gestures as a method of interaction. Yet, ray pointing with the finger or arm is typically used as the main pointing method even in gesture-based systems. Work by Gallo et al. [18] explored the benefits of an un-instrumented hand tracking device in a medical context, where sterility is a major concern. Here contact-less technologies offer clear benefits. In a paper by Kolarié et al., finger pointing was enabled through a two camera stereo setup [19]. Matikainen et al. tracked multiple users and their pointing gestures with a camera system [20]. In another work [21] the authors look at the requirements of an un-instrumented tracking system and present an implementation similar to previous work. The authors developed three sample applications to demonstrate its use: FingerMouse, FreeHandPresent, and Brainstorm. Most relevant to our context is the FingerMouse application, which tracks a user's index finger to position a mouse pointer on screen. In this application, a one second dwell time is used for selection [21]. Song et al. also used finger pointing to select and move virtual objects [22]. None of the above work evaluates the performance of un-instrumented in-air pointing with the ISO standard.

Last, but not least, there has been research into the design and use of wearable digital jewellery, specifically rings. This research looks at creating a device that not only functions well, but is also comfortable and attractive to the user. Many of these rings are made of conventional jewellery materials [23], [24], but some are made of more unconventional materials such as elastic [25] and Velcro [26]. These unconventional materials permit users with different finger sizes to use the same ring. Such rings can be used for 3D selection, in particular for indicating which object to select.

1.4 Fitts' Law and Pointing

Fitts' Law is an empirical model that describes the speed accuracy tradeoff in pointing tasks [27]. It can be used both as a predictive model and as a way to calculate throughput. The model is $MT = a + b \times log_2(D / W + 1)$. In this model, MT is movement time, D is the target distance, W is the target size, and a and b are derived from linear regression. The log term in this model is referred to as the index of difficulty (ID). The ID describes the difficulty of selecting a particular target by combining the distance and the size of the target into a single value. Fitts' law implies that the further away or the smaller a target is, the harder it will be for a user to select. Although Fitts' law was originally developed for one-dimensional pointing tasks, it has been successfully adapted to 2D pointing tasks and can describe even some 3D pointing tasks.

Building on decades of Fitts' law based studies, the ISO 9241-9 standard [28] has been developed to standardize experimental methodologies and to improve the quality of Fitts' law data. In this standard, throughput is the primary measure of performance. Throughput is calculated as $TP = log_2(D_e / W_e + 1) / MT$. In this equation, D_e is the effective distance and W_e the effective width. These effective values measure the task that the user actually performed, not the one that she or he was presented with [27]. This reduces variability in identical conditions, which also facilitates comparisons between different Fitts' law studies.

1.5 Interaction Techniques

We studied two types of interaction techniques in this work (see Figure 1). The first method is the *Whole Hand* method. With this method the user moves her or his dominant hand in space to indicate the area on the screen the cursor should move to. For example, if the user held her or his hand at the bottom left area of the screen the cursor would appear there, if she or he then began moving her or his hand up then the cursor would gradually move with the hand towards the upper left area of the screen. The second is the *Pointing* method, based on ray casting. With this method the user uses her or his index finger of the dominant hand to point to the relative location on the screen that she or he wishes the cursor to move to.

2 METHODOLOGY

For the remainder of this paper in-air will always refer to in-air un-instrumented interaction.

In this section, we describe the two user studies we performed to evaluate in-air performance. In the first study, two in-air methods and the effect of elbow placement were evaluated in terms of throughput. In the second study, in-air is directly compared to the mouse using either a button or the spacebar for target selection.

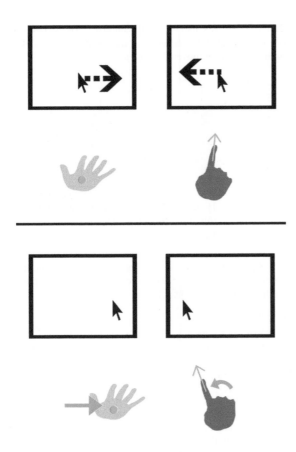

Figure 1: The two interaction methods. The *Whole Hand* method is pictured on the left and the *Pointing* method on the right. The top and bottom frame indicate the cursor position before and after the movement. The green dot and green arrow illustrate what is being tracked by the system.

3 USER STUDY 1

The objective of this study was to determine the interaction method that yields the best throughput for in-air operation. The two compared interaction methods were the *Pointing* interaction method and the *Whole Hand* method (see the section on Interaction Techniques for details). These two interaction styles were tested both with the user's elbow resting on the table and with the user's elbow in the air. When using a mouse, one's hand benefits from the natural stabilization afforded by resting the arm on the desk. We wanted to see if there would be a performance benefit if users grounded their elbows on the table thereby stabilizing their hands and fingers so that they would be less prone to natural hand tremor. On the other hand, grounding the elbow has the potential for restricting the movement over users and thus may also decrease performance from a participant's arm being more constricted in movement by being confined to the surface of the desk. This work is similar to the work by Cockburn et al., except we look at these two interaction methods in a desktop environment [29]. Our participants were seated while using these two methods and the range of motion required was much smaller than in previous work. The range of motion in our experiment was at a comparable level to the range of motion required by a mouse.

3.1 Participants

We recruited 16 participants for this study (mean age 23 years, *SD* 8.5). Seven were female and one was left-handed. None had used in-air devices before to interact with a computer. All users kept

their hands in an open relaxed position when using the *Whole Hand* interaction method.

3.2 Setup

The Leap Motion sensor was placed directly in front of computer display so that it was centered with the middle of the monitor. The sensor was then calibrated to the screen with the default calibration process, which uses a wooden chopstick for a more precise calibration. The Leap Motion device driver and hardware used for this first study was version 0.8.0 respectively v.05. The software used for this Fitts' Law study was FittsStudy [30]. We added support to read data from the LeapMotion to this package.

3.3 Input Conditions

For this user study there were four input conditions for selecting targets. These were the *Whole Hand* method with the participant's elbow supported by the table or by a stack of books (depending on what was more comfortable), the *Whole Hand* method with the participant's elbow raised above the table, i.e., in the air and not supported, the *Pointing* method with the elbow supported, and the *Pointing* method with the elbow unsupported. After targets had been acquired using one of these four methods, targets were selected using the spacebar on a keyboard. The spacebar was operated by the non-dominant hand of the participant and was placed in a comfortable operating position so that the dominant hand used for object acquisition was not obstructed. Figure 2 illustrates the setup. In all these conditions the distance between the participant's hand and the computer was relatively consistent, but an exact distance was not enforced to prevent unnatural poses.

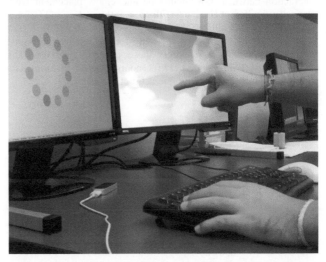

Figure 2: Photo of experimental setup in the condition where users were pointing with the finger and where the elbow was off the table. This user operates the space bar with the left thumb.

3.4 Procedure

First, each participant was given a brief questionnaire about her or his background. The questionnaire recorded gender, age, and handedness. Then, the participant was instructed in the use of one of the four input conditions and was encouraged to practice with this input method until she or he felt comfortable. Once the participant was comfortable with the input method, she or he completed a series of Fitts' law selection tasks using her or his dominant hand to move the cursor to the desired location and operating the spacebar with the other hand for selection. The participant was instructed to select these targets as quickly and accurately as possible. She or he was also instructed that breaks should be taken between circle groups if her or his arm was getting tired. Each such block consisted of 9 Fitts' law "circles", with 13 trials per circle. The 9 circles used all combinations of target widths of 32, 64, and 96 and amplitudes of 256, 384, and 512 pixels, respectively. This smaller range of ID values was chosen, as target widths below 32 pixels would often be missed, not due to participant error, but due to jitter in the tracking system. We wanted to get a good measurement of the achievable performance with a well-operating system and so did not include these targets. Participants were free to move their arm around while using the *Pointing* method and, as such, movement angles and distances would not be consistent across all participants. Consequently, we report ID values in pixels. The participant would then be presented with another "block" for the next input method and the above process would be repeated until all four input conditions had been completed using a Latin square design across all participants. Overall, the study took about one hour per participant.

3.5 Results

Data was first filtered for participant errors, such as hitting the spacebar twice on the same target or pausing in the middle of a circle to focus her or his attention elsewhere. Removing these errors and outliers, i.e., results more than three standard deviations from the mean, amounted to a 3% loss of total data collected.

3.5.1 Throughput

The data were not normally distributed. Also, Levene's test for homogeneity of variance showed no significance for elbow placement ($F_{1,15} = 0.4332$, ns), but movement type and the interaction between movement type and elbow placement were statically significant ($F_{1,15} = 57.708$, $p < .001$ and $F_{3,13} = 27.724$, $p < .001$). This invalidates the assumption of similar differences between groups variances needed for parametric repeated measures ANOVA. To address these concerns, we used the *Aligned Rank Transform (ART)* for nonparametric factorial data analysis in Human-Computer Interaction treatment [31].

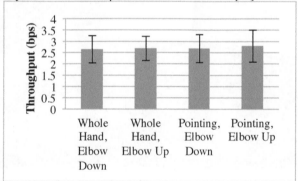

Figure 3: Graph depicting the average throughput (bps) for each condition with error bars. Difference between methods was not significant. Error bars (in this and subsequent figures) show standard deviation.

Overall, there was no significant effect for movement type ($F_{1,15} = 0.52$, ns) or for elbow placement ($F_{1,15} = 0.67$, ns) on (effective) throughput (see Figure 3). There was also no significant effect from the interaction of movement type and elbow placement ($F_{1,15} = 0.44$, ns).

3.5.2 Movement Time

The data were not normally distributed and also failed Levene's test for homogeneity. ART was used again to address this concern.

There was no significant effect on movement time for both movement type ($F_{1,15} = 1.42$, $p > .05$) and elbow placement ($F_{1,15}$

= 0.92, ns). There was also no significant effect for the interaction between movement type and elbow placement ($F_{1,15} = 0.04$, ns). See Figure 4 for mean movement times.

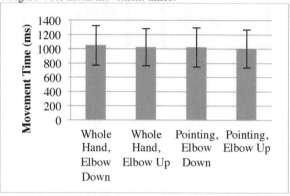

Figure 4: Graph depicting the average effective movement time (bps) for each condition with error bars. Difference between methods was not significant.

3.5.3 Error Rate

The data were not normally distributed and also failed Levene's test for homogeneity. ART was used again to address this concern.

The placement of a participant's elbow had no significant effect on error rate ($F_{1,15} = 0.29$, ns), but the movement type did identify a significant difference ($F_{1,15} = 4.93$, $p < .05$) with the *Whole Hand* method producing fewer errors. Although technically significant, the statistical power of this result is rather low at 0.55, so we cannot claim this to be a strong result.

3.5.4 Index of Difficulty (ID)

There was no significant effect on the interaction between ID and movement type ($F_{1,15} = 1.22$, $p > .05$) or ID and elbow placement ($F_{1,15} = 0.23$, ns) on movement time. See Figure 5 for the data for all conditions. Values for linear trendlines are as follows: *Whole Hand* elbow down: $y = 302.36\,x + 151.97$, $R^2 = 0.986$, *Whole Hand* elbow up: $y = 295.87\,x + 156$, $R^2 = 0.9918$, *Pointing* elbow up: $y = 273.15\,x + 198.42$, $R^2 = 0.9976$, *Pointing* elbow down: $y = 283.81\,x + 190.5$, $R^2 = 0.9742$.

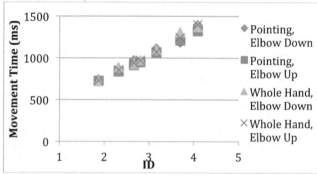

Figure 5: Graph depicting Fitts' law model for input conditions in user study 1.

3.5.5 Learning

As there was only one block per input condition for this experiment it is unclear how strong learning was. Over all participants, no significant learning effects could be detected, but this does not mean that users did not learn. For more information about learning effects with in-air operation see user study 2.

3.5.6 Other Results

We also analyzed in which condition each *individual* participant showed the highest throughput. We classified throughput as being equal if the two throughput values were within 5%, otherwise as different. The results of this analysis identify that the similar results seen for throughput between each method are not due to individual participants performing equally well with each method. Rather, there seems to be a half-half split among the population, both for the question as to which input method is better and if it is better if the elbow is placed on the table or not.

3.6 Discussion

The overall conclusion from this study is that there seems to be no particular method of using in-air devices that works best for all people. As such, we believe that the differences between these methods are not a major contributing factor to lower in-air throughput. Statistical significance between movement types was only found for error rate, but even this significance had low statistical power. These results are in keeping with the results found by Cockburn et al. and show that this trend holds even with modern desktop sensors. Performance for each method was heavily dependent on the individual participant. Some participants exhibited no difference between the methods, while others found that a particular method yielded substantially better results. As such, there seems to be no universal solution that exhibits uniformly high performance. This indicated to us that in-air systems should be configurable to account for different input methods.

The throughput observed for in-air interaction in this study was at best about 2.8 bps, which is lower than the usually observed range of 3.7–4.9 bps for the mouse in Fitts' law studies [32]. With 85 ms end-to-end latency in whole the system, the finger tracking system ranks comparable to other 3D tracking systems in terms of delay (though there are better ones). Even so, 85 ms of latency is much higher than the measured 28 ms of end-to-end latency for the mouse in our setup. While this difference of 57 ms in latency can be expected to have an impact on the performance of in-air interaction, it should decrease throughput by only about 0.3 bps according to previous work on the effects of latency [33]. If this latency were eliminated it would bring the Leap Motion's throughput to about 3.1 bps. This is still not even close to levels that can be easily achieved with a mouse.

4 USER STUDY 2

The purpose of this study was to directly compare in-air interaction with the mouse. The two input methods were compared using the ISO 9241-9 test procedure using both the spacebar and a button click for selection. Both spacebar and button were used in order to determine the effect different click detection methods have on performance. Specifically, we wanted to identify if clicking the left button on the mouse affords an advantage in terms of throughput. The purpose of this study was not to suggest in-air interaction as a mouse replacement, but rather to provide a comparative measurement to the mouse that could be used to calibrate the performance of this system against other systems. This enables comparisons to other hand tracking devices and other input methods.

4.1 Participants

We recruited 16 *different* participants for this within subjects study (mean age 27 years, *SD* 9.5). Six were female and one was left-handed. That participant still preferred to operate the mouse and to point with the right hand. None had used an in-air system before. All users kept their hands in an open relaxed position when using the *Whole Hand* interaction method.

4.2 Setup

The sensor was placed directly in front of computer display so that it was centered at the middle of the monitor and carefully calibrated. The Leap Motion software and hardware used was version 1.0.5+7357, respectively LM-010 (a more up-to-date version relative to user study 1). The measured end-to-end latency of the overall system was 63 ms. The mouse was a Microsoft IntelliMouse Optical set to the default pointer speed in the Windows 7 operating system. The system had an end-to-end latency of 28 ms with the mouse.

We developed a ring button as an alternative method to indicate object selection in the in-air condition. We wanted this button to mimic the left click on the mouse as close as reasonably possible. The ring button consisted of a button glued to a *Hook and Loop* strip. We used a *Hook and Loop* strip to accommodate participants with diverse finger sizes, much as Harrison and Hudson did with their Velcro ring [26]. The button, an Omron B3F-1020 tactile switch, is a 6×6 mm square box, 5 mm tall with a 3.5 mm cylindrical tip. The operating force is specified at 0.98 N and the tip travel during a click is about 0.5 mm. The *Hook and Loop* strip was 20 mm wide and 100 mm long and was glued to the button with a hot-melt adhesive. The button was wired in parallel to the left-button of a desktop mouse. The thin wire connecting the ring to the mouse was held on participants' arms with two 50 mm bands of 3M™ Coban™ Self-Adherent tape in order to prevent the wire from interfering with the arm motions and from possibly confounding the sensor's view. Figure 6 illustrates the ring button, its placement as well as the wire placement. The software used for conducting the Fitts' law tasks was again FittsStudy [30].

Figure 6: Photo of finger ring with the button visible below the users thumb (raised more than normal for illustration). Self adhesive tape was used to keep the cable from interfering with the motions.

4.3 Input Conditions

For this user study there were four input conditions that the participants selected targets with. These were in-air with spacebar selection (using whatever in-air technique the participant preferred), in-air with ring button selection (using the same in-air technique chosen), the mouse with spacebar selection, and the mouse with left mouse button selection. For selection with the spacebar, the keyboard was operated and placed as described in user study 1.

4.4 Procedure

First, each participant was given a brief questionnaire about her or his background. The questionnaire recorded gender, age, and handedness. Then, the participant was introduced to the two different interaction styles for in-air operation, the *Whole Hand* method and the *Pointing* method, as described above under Interaction Techniques. After trying both methods, participants were asked to choose which method they wanted to use. That method was then used for the rest of the experiment. We permitted participants to choose their own in-air method based on the results of our first user study, where different people performed better with different interaction methods. Keeping with the work by Sparrow and Newell [34], we assumed that participants would choose the in-air style that would yield the best throughput through self-optimization. For the same reason, we also did not control for user elbow placement in this study.

Once a particular input method was chosen, participants completed 2 blocks of 9 Fitts' law circles with 11 trials per circle for practice with this method. This practice period accounted for the inexperience of participants with in-air interaction. Our study thus indicates the performance possible in the early adaptation stages of in-air interaction. The performance in these early stages is frequently just as important as potential top performance: if performance is much lower than an alternative method, users will often just give up and use that alternative method even if their performance could ultimately be better by adapting the higher performing method. One well-known example is QWERTY vs. Metropolis for touchscreen keyboards [35].

After the practice period, the participant started with one of the four conditions, and then experienced the others. The presentation order to participants was determined with a Latin square design.

With each given condition the participant completed 3 blocks of 9 Fitts' law circles with 11 trials per circle. Target widths of 32, 64, and 96 and amplitudes of 256, 384, and 512 pixels were used (see user study 1 for an explanation as to why this range of ID values was chosen and why the values were presented this way). Between blocks, participants were encouraged to rest for about a minute before starting the next one. Participants were also instructed that breaks should be taken between "circles" if they experienced fatigue. At the end of all four conditions, participants were given a brief questionnaire about discomfort they might have experienced while using in-air interaction.

4.5 Results

Data were first filtered for participant errors, such as hitting the spacebar twice on the same target or pausing in the middle of a circle. Removing these errors amounted to less than .005% loss of total data collected. There were no outliers.

4.5.1 Throughput

The data for throughput were not normally distributed. Also, the data failed Levene's test for homogeneity. Consequently, we again used the *Aligned Rank Transform (ART)* for nonparametric factorial data analysis [31] and performed a repeated measures parametric ANOVA on the transformed data.

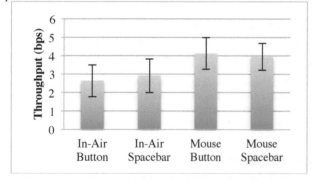

Figure 7: Graph depicting the average throughput (bps) for each condition in the second study with error bars. The difference between methods was significant.

For throughput there was a significant effect of type of device of ($F_{1,15} = 90.76$, $p < 0.0001$), with effect size (η^2) of 0.3 and power ($1-\beta$) of 0.99. There was no significant effect of selection method on throughput ($F_{1,15} = 0.47$, *ns*). There was a significant interaction of selection method and type of device ($F_{1,15} = 17.10$, p

< 0.001), with an effect size (η^2) of only 0.03 and very weak power ($1-\beta$) of 0.07. The mouse exhibited throughput around 4 bps, while the in-air conditions showed less than 3 bps, see Figure 7.

4.5.2 Movement Time

The data for movement time were not normally distributed and also failed Levene's tests for homogeneity. Consequently, we used *ART* again.

For Type of device there was a significant effect on MT_e ($F_{1,15} = 49.66$, $p < 0.0001$), with effect size (η^2) of 0.23, and power ($1-\beta$) = 0.96. There was no significant effect of selection method on movement time ($F_{1,15} = 0.8$, *ns*). Similar to the results for throughput, there was a significant effect for the interaction of Selection Method and Type of device on MT_e ($F_{1,15} = 14.37$, $p < 0.05$), with an effect size (η^2) of only 0.03, and with very weak power ($1-\beta$) = 0.065. See Figure 8 for mean movement times.

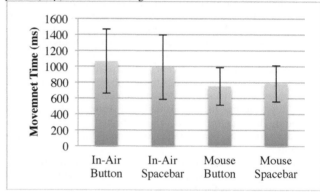

Figure 8: Graph depicting the average effective movement time (milliseconds) for each condition in the second study with error bars. The difference between methods was significant.

4.5.3 Error Rate

We did not find any significant effects in the data for error rates.

4.5.4 Learning

There was no statistically significant difference between blocks on throughput ($F_{1,15} = 0.49$, ns). There was also no statistically significant difference for the interaction of block and selection method on throughput ($F_{1,15} = 0.6$, ns).

4.5.5 Index of Difficulty (ID)

There was no significant effect on the interaction between *ID* and selection method ($F_{1,15} = 2.67$, $p > .05$). See Figure 9 for a depiction of the Fitts' law data for this study.

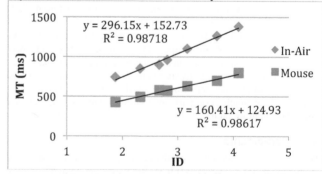

Figure 9: Graph depicting Fitts' law model for in-air interaction in user study 2 and a linear regression

4.6 Discussion

The results of the second user study show that the mouse performs significantly better than in-air interaction, regardless of the target selection method used. The performance of the mouse is around 4 bps, which is in line with other work. The performance of in-air conditions is slightly less than 3 bps, which corresponds (approximately) to our first study and to the results of other recent evaluations of ray pointing techniques [8] with traditional 3D tracking systems. A caveat is that these results are not fully comparable, as our work did not use a stereo display.

One result of this study is that even in a condition designed to be as optimal for in-air interaction as possible, the mouse still outperforms this method by a substantial margin. Moreover, and in all conditions, the selection mechanism (spacebar or ring button) was 100% reliable. Consequently, we are fairly confident in stating that using finger gestures, such as "up-down" click motions, would not improve throughput. The reasoning here is that any inaccuracies in gesture detection will very likely have a negative effect on error rates, as un- or mis-recognized button presses will result either in a "miss" or correction movement. Both alternatives will decrease throughput. Moreover, and even assuming that there is a 100% reliable gesture recognizer, we point out that to make an "up-down" click gesture in free air easily recognizable, the user needs to move the finger a distance that is sufficiently large to be detectable. This distance is likely larger than the small motion needed to operate a mouse or ring button. Consequently, such a motion likely takes longer, which again can only decrease throughput. Other gestures, such as a pinch, making a fist, and closing the gap between the thumb and the side of the hand, suffer from the same problem and are also not likely to exhibit increased throughput.

Moreover, all participants in the study reported some level of fatigue while using the in-air system regardless of whether they were using the *Pointing* or the *Whole Hand* method. All participants reported either 'mild discomfort' or 'discomfort' (values 2 and 3 respectively) on a five-point scale from 'none' to 'pain' with an average reported value of 2.5. There was no correlation between interaction method used and level of fatigue.

To get a better idea of the performance potential of in-air interaction, one would need to run a longitudinal study, where participants get several hours of practice.

5 OVERALL DISCUSSION

In these two studies we largely rule out three potential factors (arm stabilization, cursor control method, and selection method) as potential explanations for the lower throughput observed with un-instrumented tracking systems. This considerably narrows the search space for future research and brings the community closer to tracking down the factor or factors that contribute to the reduced throughput for such systems. We also presented an accurate throughput measurement for in-air interaction using the ISO 9241-9 standard. This enables our research to be easily compared to other future work.

In general, we can state that modern instantiations of in-air interaction can achieve throughput comparable to that of state-of-the-art 3D tracking systems. We are particularly excited about the low level of noise in the system we used. Yet, end-to-end system latency affects throughput and reductions of lag may improve throughput levels even further. Based on previous results around latency, such as [33], the potential for improvement is (only) in the range of 15–20%. Nevertheless, it is good to see that the developers of in-air interaction systems have recognized the issue and are continuously working on improving the latency of their devices. They are now even reaching out to developers to explain the issue and give active advice on how to reduce the latency in a given system [36].

Some of our experiments can be considered a replication of the work by Balakrishnan and MacKenzie [15]. However, our work considers in-air interaction, while their work investigated only interaction on a surface. Yet, the throughput results that we see in our experiments are very similar to the results seen in this previous study. There, the throughput for the finger was reported to be approximately 3.0 bits/s and the throughput of the wrist 4.1 bits/s. Taking into account that the experimental setup in this previous work had lower latency than our system, our measured throughput of approximately 2.8 bits/s is right within the expected range from this study (as our participants were free to use both their fingers and wrists to control the system). This can be interpreted both as a validation of these previous results and of our current user study design.

Based on our results, we cannot recommend un-instrumented in-air hand tracking for user interfaces that require the best possible pointing performance or that need to compete with mice or touch screens. However, un-instrumented hand tracking is attractive for many other applications, such as user interfaces that require the use of multiple fingers at the same time, casual games, bi-manual interaction, gesture-based systems, and applications where the user cannot touch or hold a device.

5.1 Limitations

In order to study in-air device performance it was necessary to choose an un-instrumented system to do this with. In the case of this paper, the Leap Motion was selected. While this is a necessary step, it potentially causes particulars of the selected system to be studied, rather than the class of devices it is meant to represent. While the authors have tried to make this research as device-independent as possible, it is possible that particular aspects that are Leap Motion-specific have exhibited themselves in the results.

6 CONCLUSION

We conducted two studies to explore the performance of un-instrumented 3D tracking for controlling a cursor on a screen. We show that elbow support is not uniformly advantageous for in-air interaction. Likewise, the best method of cursor control, either *Pointing* or *Whole Hand*, varies from one individual to the next. This suggests that one method of operation is not universally beneficial and that multiple methods should be permitted to accommodate different users. This result also indicates that neither arm stabilization nor the cursor control method are likely causes for the decreased throughput of in-air interaction. This finding permits future studies to ignore these two factors when designing experiments.

Our second study provided evidence that un-instrumented, in-air tracking is unlikely to reach levels of throughput equivalent to the mouse, even if the technical implementation had minimum latency. Consequently, we believe that some other factor accounts for the decrease in throughput. We also show that there is no statistically significant benefit to using a button for selection with the same hand that is being used to move the cursor. As such, this is another factor that does not need to be controlled for in future experiments. Furthermore, we found evidence that the left-click on the mouse does not contribute to its higher throughput and that there must be some still untested factor in un-instrumented interaction that is contributing to its lower throughput. Consequently, we suggest using un-instrumented 3D tracking only in situations where interaction would benefit from using a hands-free, sterile, multi-hand, or multi-finger device. In other situations, it is likely that the mouse is still better suited to the task.

6.1 Future Work

We plan to further explore potential causes of the gap between pointing and mouse throughput, such as latency, learning, and sub-optimal tracking algorithms. Ultimately, we hope to explore new realms of computer operation that extend beyond what the mouse is capable of.

6.2 Acknowledgements

We would like to thank the GRAND NCE and York University for supporting this work. CNPq, Brazil supported E. Mendonça.

REFERENCES

[1] R. J. Teather, A. Pavlovych, W. Stuerzlinger, and I. S. MacKenzie, "Effects of tracking technology, latency, and spatial jitter on object movement," in *2009 IEEE 3DUI*, 2009, pp. 43–50.

[2] I. MacKenzie and S. Jusoh, "An evaluation of two input devices for remote pointing," *Eng. Human-Computer Interact.*, vol. 2254, pp. 235–250, 2001.

[3] A. Banerjee and J. Burstyn, "Pointable: an in-air pointing technique to manipulate out-of-reach targets on tabletops," in *ACM Tabletops and Surfaces*, 2011, pp. 11–20.

[4] K. Das and C. W. Borst, "An evaluation of menu properties and pointing techniques in a projection-based VR environment," *2010 IEEE Symp. 3D User Interfaces*, pp. 47–50, Mar. 2010.

[5] R. Jota, M. Nacenta, and J. Jorge, "A comparison of ray pointing techniques for very large displays," in *GI*, 2010, pp. 269–276.

[6] A. Kunert, A. Kulik, C. Lux, and B. Fröhlich, "Facilitating system control in ray-based interaction tasks," in *ACM VRST*, 2009, vol. 1, no. 212, pp. 183–186.

[7] C. Wingrave and D. Bowman, "Baseline factors for raycasting selection," in *Proc. of HCI International*, 2005.

[8] R. J. Teather and W. Stuerzlinger, "Pointing at 3d target projections with one-eyed and stereo cursors," in *ACM CHI*, 2013, p. 159.

[9] D. Vogel and R. Balakrishnan, "Distant freehand pointing and clicking on very large, high resolution displays," in *ACM UIST*, 2005, p. 33.

[10] J. Zigelbaum, A. Browning, D. Leithinger, O. Bau, and H. Ishii, "G-stalt: a chirocentric, spatiotemporal, and telekinetic gestural interface," in *International Conference on Tangible, Embedded, and Embodied iIteraction*, 2010, pp. 261–264.

[11] M. Gokturk and J. L. Sibert, "An analysis of the index finger as a pointing device," in *Extended Abstracts on Human Factors in Computing Systems*, 1999, no. May, p. 286.

[12] I. Oakley, J. Sunwoo, and I.-Y. Cho, "Pointing with fingers, hands and arms for wearable computing," in *Extended Abstracts on Human Factors in Computing Systems*, 2008, no. 3255, pp. 3255–3260.

[13] J. Oh and W. Stuerzlinger, "Laser pointers as collaborative pointing devices," *GI* vol. 2002, pp. 141–149, 2002.

[14] T. Grossman and R. Balakrishnan, "Pointing at trivariate targets in 3D environments," in *ACM CHI*, 2004, vol. 6, no. 1, pp. 447–454.

[15] R. Balakrishnan and I. S. MacKenzie, "Performance differences in the fingers, wrist, and forearm in computer input control," in *ACM CHI*, 1997, pp. 303–310.

[16] R. Balakrishnan, T. Baude, G. Kurtenbach, and G. Fitzmaurice, "The Rockin'Mouse : Integral 3D Manipulation on a Plane," in *ACM CHI*, 1997, pp. 311–318.

[17] R. J. Teather and W. Stuerzlinger, "Pointing at 3D targets in a stereo head-tracked virtual environment," in *2011 IEEE 3DUI*, 2011, no. 1, pp. 87–94.

[18] L. Gallo, A. Placitelli, and M. Ciampi, "Controller-free exploration of medical image data: Experiencing the Kinect," in *Computer-Based Medical Systems*, 2011, pp. 1–6.

[19] S. Kolaric, A. Raposo, and M. Gattass, "Direct 3D manipulation using vision-based recognition of uninstrumented hands," in *X Symposium on Virtual and Augmented Reality*, 2008, pp. 212–220.

[20] P. Matikainen, P. Pillai, L. Mummert, R. Sukthankar, and M. Hebert, "Prop-free pointing detection in dynamic cluttered environments," *Face Gesture*, pp. 374–381, Mar. 2011.

[21] C. von Hardenberg and F. Bérard, "Bare-hand human-computer interaction," *Work. Perceptive user interfaces*, 2001.

[22] P. Song, H. Yu, and S. Winkler, "Vision-based 3D finger interactions for mixed reality games with physics simulation," in *ACM VRCAI*, 2008, vol. 1, no. 212.

[23] C. Miner, D. Chan, and C. Campbell, "Digital jewelry: wearable technology for everyday life," in *Extended Abstracts on Human Factors in Computing Systems*, 2001, pp. 45–46.

[24] D. Ashbrook, P. Baudisch, and S. White, "Nenya: subtle and eyes-free mobile input with a magnetically-tracked finger ring," in *ACM CHI*, 2011, pp. 2043–2046.

[25] S. Rhee, B. Yang, and H. Asada, "Artifact-resistant power-efficient design of finger-ring plethysmographic sensors," *IEEE Trans. Biomed. Eng.*, vol. 48, no. 7, pp. 795–805, 2001.

[26] C. Harrison and S. E. Hudson, "Abracadabra : Wireless , High-Precision , and Unpowered Finger Input for Very Small Mobile Devices," in *ACM UIST*, 2009, pp. 121–124.

[27] I. S. MacKenzie, "Fitts' Law as a Research and Design Tool in Human-Computer Interaction," *Human-Computer Interact.*, vol. 7, no. 1, pp. 91–139, Mar. 1992.

[28] ISO, "9241-9 Ergonomic requirements for office work with visual display terminals (VDTs)-Part 9: Requirements for non-keyboard input devices (FDIS-Final Draft International Standard)," *Int. Organ. Stand.*, 2000.

[29] A. Cockburn, P. Quinn, C. Gutwin, G. Ramos, and J. Looser, "Air pointing: Design and evaluation of spatial target acquisition with and without visual feedback," *Int. J. Hum. Comput. Stud.*, vol. 69, no. 6, pp. 401–414, Jun. 2011.

[30] J. O. Wobbrock, K. Shinohara, and A. Jansen, "The Effects of Task Dimensionality , Endpoint Deviation , Throughput Calculation , and Experiment Design on Pointing Measures and Models," in *ACM CHI*, 2011, pp. 1639–1648.

[31] J. Wobbrock, L. Findlater, D. Gergle, and J. J. Higgins, "The aligned rank transform for nonparametric factorial analyses using only anova procedures," in *ACM CHI*, 2011, pp. 143–146.

[32] R. W. Soukoreff and I. S. MacKenzie, "Towards a standard for pointing device evaluation, perspectives on 27 years of Fitts' law research in HCI," *IJHCS*, vol. 61, no. 6, pp. 751–789, Dec. 2004.

[33] A. Pavlovych and W. Stuerzlinger, "The tradeoff between spatial jitter and latency in pointing tasks," in *ACM EICS*, 2009, pp. 187–196.

[34] W. Sparrow and K. Newell, "Metabolic energy expenditure and the regulation of movement economy," *Psychon. Bull. Rev.*, vol. 5, no. 2, pp. 173–196, 1998.

[35] S. Zhai, M. Hunter, and B. a. Smith, "The metropolis keyboard - an exploration of quantitative techniques for virtual keyboard design," in *ACM UIST*, 2000, vol. 2, pp. 119–128.

[36] R. Bedikian, "Understanding Latency," *Leap Motion Developer Labs*, 2013. [Online]. Available: http://labs.leapmotion.com/post/ 55354675113/understanding-latency-part-1.

A Natural Click Interface for AR Systems with a Single Camera

Atsushi Sugiura*

University of Yamanashi

Masahiro Toyoura[†]

University of Yamanashi

Xiaoyang Mao[‡]

University of Yamanashi

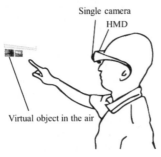

(a) Configuration of the prototype system.

(b) Typing on a virtual keyboard.

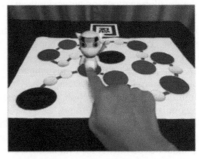

(c) Operating a virtual object by clicking a position in the real world.

Figure 1: Overview of the proposed interface. A user wears a head-mounted display with a single camera. He clicks virtual buttons in the air with his finger.

ABSTRACT

Clicking on a virtual object is the most fundamental and important interaction in augmented reality (AR). However, existing AR systems do not support natural click interfaces, because head-mounted displays with only one camera are usually adopted to realize augmented reality and it is difficult to recognize an arbitrary gesture without accurate depth information. For the ease of detection, some systems force users to make unintuitive gestures, such as pinching with the thumb and forefinger. This paper presents a new natural click interface for AR systems. Through a study investigating how users intuitively click virtual objects in AR systems, we found that the speed and acceleration of fingertips provide cues for detecting click gestures. Based on our findings, we developed a new technique for recognizing natural click gestures with a single camera by focusing on temporal differentials between adjacent frames. We further validated the effectiveness of the recognition algorithm and the usability of our new interface through experiments.

Keywords: Wearable system, Augmented reality, Gesture recognition, Mobile application.

Index Terms: H.5.1 [Information Interfaces and Presentation]: Multimedia Information Systems Artificial, augmented, and virtual realities; I. 2. 10 [Artificial intelligence]: Vision and Scene Understanding Motion

1 INTRODUCTION

In this paper, we propose a natural input interface for AR systems. Figure 1(a) shows the configuration of a prototype system with the proposed interface. It consists of a HMD display and one

* email: g12dhl02@yamanashi.ac.jp

† email: mtoyoura@yamanashi.ac.jp

‡ email: mao@yamanashi.ac.jp

Graphics Interface Conference 2014
7-9 May, Montreal, Quebec, Canada

single camera. The camera is assumed to be installed around the user's eyes and to face outwards along the view direction. A user can use his hand to directly operate a virtual object in the augmented environment shown on the HMD screen. Figure 1(b) is the HMD screen snapshot of the user typing on a virtual keyboard with his finger. Figure 1(c) demonstrates the application of the new interface to a game in which the user can move a virtual object by clicking a position in the real world, which is captured by the camera.

With the widespread adoption of smartphones and other camera-installed mobile devices, AR technology has become an important part of many practical applications and services. Google announced that the long-awaited Google GLASS [1] will become available for sale in early 2014, which is expected to further boost the dissemination of AR devices. Google GLASS provides a see-through display in front of an eye and a camera facing outwards, capturing the real world. However, it relies on voice recognition and a small touch panel input for command execution. A more natural interface for such an AR system would be a gesture-based interface, which would allow the user to interact with a virtual object in a similar way as he or she interacts with objects with using his or her hands in the real world. However, even with the most state-of-the-art AR systems, this kind of true direct manipulation, which is considered vital for the seamless connection between the virtual world shown on the display and the real world captured by the camera, has not been realized. A major factor preventing existing AR systems from supporting gesture-based direct manipulation is the difficulty of recognizing an arbitrary gesture with a single camera, which cannot capture accurate depth information. Although several projects developing wearable display devices with stereo-camera [17] have been reported recently, developing a single-camera-based AR system remains important, especially considering the population of AR applications on compact mobile devices, such as cellphones.

In this work, we aim to recognize natural hand gestures with a single camera. In particular, we focus on click gestures. In a traditional graphical interface, a click refers to the action of placing the cursor on a target and then pressing a button on the mouse to select an object or execute a command. It is the most essential operation. Here, we define a click operation in a VR system as an intuitive gesture a user would make to select a virtual object or execute a graphically represented command. Through a study investigating how subjects perform when they are told to "click" virtual objects with their fingers without any instructions or training, we found that the velocity and acceleration of fingers provide useful cues for detecting click gestures. Based on our findings, we defined a new motion-based model for intuitive click gestures and developed a novel technique for recognizing such gestures with a single camera. Our technique does not assume controllable illuminations or an accurate 3D capturing of hand. Therefore, it can be implemented in any AR system, including those using mobile phones and head-mounted displays (HMDs).

The major contributions of this paper can be summarized as follows:

- Design a novel study for investigating what an intuitive click gesture in an AR system is.
- Introduce a new motion state transition model for recognizing the click gestures.
- Implement two new algorithms for detecting the click gestures in an AR system based on the motion of a finger.
- Conduct experiments for evaluating the new click interfaces in terms of click gesture recognition performance and intuitiveness.

The remainder of the paper is organized as follows: Section 2 introduces the related works. Section 3 describes the study. Sections 4 and 5 present the technical details of the proposed click interface. Section 6 describes the implementation issues and the experiments for evaluating the proposed techniques. Section 7 concludes the paper.

2 RELATED WORKS

The creation of a natural user interface using a single camera is an active research topic in the fields of human computer interaction and computer vision. Projects on tangible interfaces [2-3], tabletop interfaces [4-5], projector-camera systems [6-7], Kinect [8] and the iPad [9] have attracted a great deal of attention. Especially in the case of tabletop interfaces, bare-hand gesture recognition from camera-captured images is often employed as a tool for inputting commands. Attempts to extract hand regions from captured images always face the challenges of self-occlusion, unpredictable illumination, cluttered backgrounds, blurred images, and so on. Attracted by the ease and robustness of recognition, conventional systems employ hand-shape-based command inputs [10] or pinching gesture detection [11], which unfortunately force users to perform predefined gestures rather than intuitive ones.

Although hand gesture recognition is one of classic problems in computer vision, it is still under active research. A survey of state-of-the-art hand recognition techniques can be found in [15]. The difficulty of hand recognition comes from 1) a deformable and flexible object with multiple joints having a high DOF (degree of freedom), 2) self-occlusion caused having by many joints, and 3) skin region extraction under fluctuating illumination.

The problem of estimating a high-DOF hand posture can be solved using textured gloves. Wang et al. [13] introduced a color glove and tried to estimate the posture and position of fingers from the texture of the glove. This work requires wearing textured gloves, which may limit the range of applications.

Self-occlusion caused by multiple joints can be addressed using multiple cameras. Multiple cameras can also reconstruct the 3D shape of a hand, which provides more information about the posture and position of the hand. Lee et al. [12] implemented a system supporting the interaction between virtual objects and a hand. In the system, skin color regions are first extracted from captured images. The stereo cameras provide 3D hand regions and fingertip positions. By computing the collision between the virtual objects and the line defined by using the gravity point and the fingertip position, the object the user is interacting with can be detected. Recently, another research group has begun developing a wearable display device [17] that combines a depth sensor [8] and an HMD to support hand gestures in AR systems. These multiple camera systems require calibration in advance. Furthermore, such systems tend to be bulky in size.

Skin region estimation under fluctuating illumination can be solved by progressively updating observed skin color. Kölsch et al. [18] addressed the accuracy of skin region extraction based on the idea of AR applications. In AR applications, cluttered backgrounds and objects of skin-like color are often observed. Their method can robustly extract hand regions, even in such an environment. The same group has also proposed shape-based hand region extraction [19-20]. Their main targets were static gesture recognition and hand position estimation for a hand. We adopt their intelligent skin color updating technique to detect dynamic clicking gestures.

In this paper, we propose an interaction system with no gloves, a single camera, and dynamic click detection. We identified a unique motion of the fingertip when performing click gestures through a study and developed a robust recognition technique that involves detecting such a motion with a single camera.

3 USER STUDY

We have conducted a study to investigate what a natural click gesture in an AR system is. Twelve subjects of varying ages (four in their 30s, six in their 20s, and one in his or her teens) and varying levels of computer skill participated in the experiment. The subjects sat on a chair, wearing a video-see-through HMD (Vuzix WRAP AR920). The resolution of the monitor is 800x600. It has a dual-channel output, but we only used a single-channel output. The same image is displayed on both monitors. An additional Logicool QCam Pro 9000 camera is installed on the HMD, which captures the video of the operating scene at a resolution of 800x600. For the task, the subjects were asked to "click" each of the virtual buttons once with the pointing finger of their dominant hand (all twelve subjects were right-handed), without any detailed instructions or training. To investigate how 3D positions and the orientation of buttons may affect click gestures, we used two sets of virtual buttons. As shown in Figure 2(a), the first set of buttons consisted of five buttons in a cross-shaped layout, and they were oriented so as to be parallel to the XY plane. The second set, as shown in Figure 2(b), was oriented in the depth (Z) direction. During the operation, the finger is always displayed in front of the virtual buttons. No other visual, aural, or haptic feedbacks were provided for the interaction between the finger and a button. And no haptic feedback forced the subject to stop the movement of their fingers in the air, although most of the subjects commented that it would have been better to provide some feedback indicating that the click was completed. They also found it difficult to place their fingers on a target button in the HMD display.

(a) Buttons parallel to XY plane. (b) Buttons along Z direction.

Figure 2: The arrangement of virtual buttons.

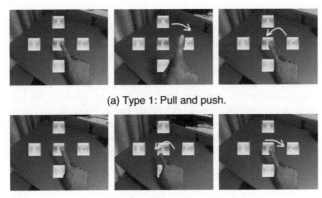

(a) Type 1: Pull and push.

(b) Type 2: Push and pull.

Figure 3: Click gesture by users.

To track the 3D trajectory, velocity, and acceleration of the fingertip, we installed to capture the 3D position of fingertips with a LeapMotion Controller [6] from LEAP Inc. on a table in front of the seat of a user. However, due to the limited observation range, with the radius of 50 centimetres from LeapMotion, we could only obtain the motion data for six out of the twelve subjects. The other six subjects performed partially out of the range during this experiment.

To understand the common patterns involved in a click gesture, we conducted a post-task interview with each subject. Each subject was presented with the video of himself/herself performing the task and asked to explain in detail the motion of his/her finger. Based on the post-task interview and the data from LeapMotion, we observed the following facts to be common to all or the majority of subjects:

1. Based on the post-task interview, we found the subjects trying to confirm that their fingertips were on top of a button before clicking the button. The LeapMotion video also confirmed this statement. Also see the supplemental movie to confirm the gestures.
2. Based on the data tracked by LeapMotion, we found that the depth at which subjects tried to click the buttons varied by subject. Based on the post-task interview, we confirmed that this is because the subjects could not perceive the correct position of the buttons in terms of depth.
3. From the LeapMotion video, we observed that click gestures are similar to but more exaggerated than a general tapping gesture. In the interview, most subjects commented that because there was no haptic feedback for touching a virtual button, they tried to represent the click with an exaggerated gesture. Specifically, they had to stop their fingers to represent the click because there was no haptic feedback upon touching a button. Ten subjects first raised their fingers up, pushed down quickly, and then stopped on the button suddenly (Figure 3(a)). Two subjects pushed their fingers down slowly first and then raised them quickly (Figure 3(b)).
4. By analyzing the data from LeapMotion, we found that the click gesture described in (3), including its 3D motions, varies by subject, as well as by the position of the buttons. In other words, it includes the motion not only in the Z direction but also in the X and Y directions, depending on the relative position of the button and the hand.

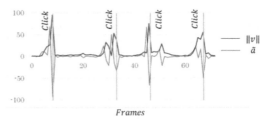

(a) Fingertip's speed and its differential for Subject A.

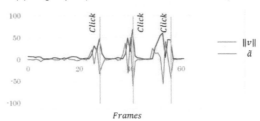

(b) Fingertip's speed and its differential for Subject B.

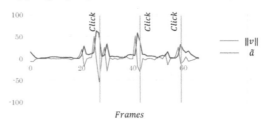

(c) Fingertip's speed and its differential for Subject C.

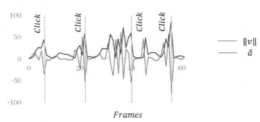

(d) Fingertip's speed and its differential for Subject D.

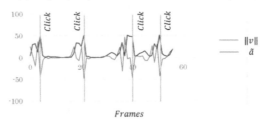

(e) Fingertip's speed and its differential for Subject E.

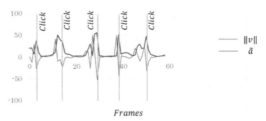

(f) Fingertip's speed and its differential for Subject F.

Figure 4: Fingertip's speed and its differential in click gesture, as tracked with LeapMotion [6].

Facts 1 and 2 suggest the necessity of providing some kind of feedback to the user regarding the pressing of a particular virtual button. As described in Section 1, we provide such feedback by changing the size and color of the button pressed.

Fact 3 suggests that the speed of the fingertip is an important cue for detecting clicks. Figure 4 shows the speed (magnitude of velocity) $\|v\|$ and the differential of speed $\tilde{a}$ for the six subjects' fingertips as tracked by LeapMotion. We observed that, when a click occurred, the differential of speed increased first and then dropped down drastically. We also observed a large peak in speed around the moment of the click. Such a characteristic motion within the gesture will help to distinguish it from other kinds of finger motions. Fact 1 suggests that there was usually a pointing gesture before the clicking gesture. Combining the detection of this pointing gesture has the potential to improve the performance of click gesture detection. Finally, Fact 4 suggests that we should consider the velocity in 3D when computing the speed.

4 HAND AREA EXTRACTION AND FINGERTIP POSITION ESTIMATION

Hand area extraction is necessary both for providing visual feedback to users and for detecting the click gesture. To provide a natural click interface, we should render the operating scene as if the user is operating an object with his/her hand in the real world. For this purpose, we extract the hand area from the image captured by the camera and render it in front of the virtual objects. To track the motion of the fingertip, we need a further estimate of the position of the fingertip.

4.1 Hand area extraction

We extract hand area by assuming it to be the region with skin color. Numerous other projects have already been performed regarding skin color detection and hand region extraction. Nevertheless, they are still problems in such cases. For example, illumination is often uncontrollable, such as in the outdoors or a dark place. Because developing sophisticated skin area detection is not our main focus, we employ a classic method, a Gaussian mixture skin color model [21], for extracting hand regions. The use of more recent tracking-based methods [18] or shape-based methods [20] would improve the accuracy of extracted hand regions. Note that computational cost should remain low when installing such methods into our system.

Assuming skin color can be represented with a single Gaussian model in HSV color space given a representative skin color $S = (h_s, s_s, v_s)$, we compute the distance of each pixel from S and extract all pixels with a distance smaller than a given threshold. In the current implementation, we measure each component of HSV separately. Assuming the thresholds for H, S, and V to be h_{th}, s_{th}, v_{th}, respectively, a pixel $P = (h_p, s_p, v_p)$ is detected to be of skin color if it satisfies all of the following three conditions:

$$h_s - h_{th} \leq h_p \leq h_s + h_{th} \tag{1}$$

$$s_s - s_{th} \leq s_p \leq s_s + s_{th} \tag{2}$$

$$v_s - v_{th} \leq v_p \leq v_s + v_{th} \tag{3}$$

The hand area is then detected as the largest connected component of the extracted skin-colored pixels.

Our system provides a calibration tool that allows a user to interactively specify an initial representative skin color and adjust the threshold using the initial frame captured in the assumed environment. During runtime, the hand area extracted from the previous frame is used as the training data for the next frame.

When the hand region is not detected in a frame, the system abandons and resets the training data. Therefore, if the user is not satisfied with the result of the hand region extraction, he/she can let the algorithm restart from the current frame simply by removing his/her hand from the camera view once and then putting it back. We detect the skin-colored pixels by computing their Mahalanobis distance from the average color of the hand area in the previous frame. Assuming that $\mu = (\mu_h, \mu_s, \mu_v)$ is the average and Σ is the variance-covariance matrix of the color for the hand area extracted in the previous frame, a pixel P of the current frame satisfying the following condition is detected to be of skin color:

$$(P - \mu)^T \Sigma^{-1} (P - \mu) \leq d_{th} \tag{4}$$

The threshold d_{th} is empirically set to 0.5 in our experiment. Using the previous frame as the training data makes the algorithm more robust considering the dynamic changes in lighting conditions.

As shown in Figure 5(a), depending on the lighting conditions, the claw area may not be successfully detected and appear as a hole in the hand area. We fill this potential hole by applying morphological closing operations to the extracted skin-colored area (Figure 5(b)).

4.2 Fingertip extraction

As shown in Figure 5(b), assuming the top-left corner of the captured image as the origin of coordinates, we take the pixel with the smallest y in the hand region as the temporarily assumed fingertip. Such an assumption is rational because the hand is expected to come from the bottom. Then, we draw a circle with the temporarily assumed fingertip as the center and R (given in advance) as the radius. We next perform a distance transformation for the finger region enclosed in the circle (Figure 5(c)). As a result, the pixels on the boundary of the finger region receive 0 as their distance value, and regarding the pixels inside the region, the farther they are from the boundary, the larger distance value they receive. The position of the fingertip is finally estimated as the peak of the parabola fitted curve for the distance values, as shown in Figure 5(d).

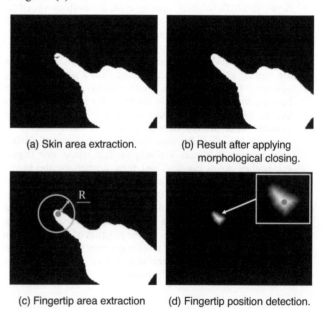

(a) Skin area extraction. (b) Result after applying morphological closing.

(c) Fingertip area extraction (d) Fingertip position detection.

Figure 5: Hand area detection and fingertip position estimation.

5 PROPOSED VIRTUAL CLICK INTERFACE

5.1 Motion-Based Click Model

Based on the observations from the study, we have recognized click gestures by analyzing the motion of the fingertip. We first classify the motion of a fingertip into one of the following four states:

STILL: stop at a position
MOVE: move at a normal speed.
FAST: move quickly
Sudden SD: slow down suddenly

Then, a click gesture can be modeled as the state transition diagram in Figure 6 shows. To perform a click, the user starts by confirming the pointing at a virtual object (STILL or MOVE), quickly raises his/her finger (FAST), and then pushes toward the object. Finally, the speed drops suddenly (Sudden SD) before stopping at the object (STILL).

State transitions can be detected by monitoring the fingertip's speed $\|v\|$ (magnitude of velocity) and the differential of the speed $\tilde{a}$ based on the diagram shown in Figure 7. The transition from STILL to MOVE can be detected by checking whether the current speed is above a given threshold. If both $\|v\|$ and $\tilde{a}$ become large, then a transition from MOVE to FAST has probably occurred. A Sudden SD is detected by checking whether $\tilde{a}$ is smaller than a given negative value. Although the current recognition algorithm relies on choosing an appropriate threshold, it is relative easy to find a robust threshold because $\|v\|$ and $\tilde{a}$ show large peaks around the moment of the click, as confirmed in the study. As mentioned in Section 6, we have implemented a calibration tool for adapting the thresholds to individual users.

From the primary study, we have learned that the most characteristic feature of the click motion is the Sudden SD state, which distinguishes the click from all other motions of the finger. Therefore, we also implemented a simpler but efficient algorithm that recognizes a click gesture simply by detecting the Sudden SD state.

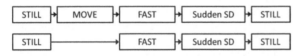

Figure 6: The state transition of the click motion.

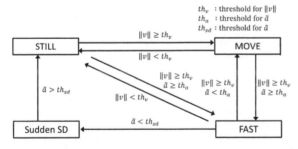

Figure 7: State transition diagram for detecting states of motion

5.2 Motion detection

To recognize the click gesture using the state transition diagram given in Section 5.1, we must compute the speed and the differential of the speed of the fingertip. As observed in the study, a click gesture is a 3D motion that includes the movement not only in the XY plane but also along the Z (depth) direction.

However, because we assume single-camera-based AR systems, it is impossible to track the motion in the depth direction directly. To solve the problem, we use the change in object size due to perspective projection as the cue to estimate the change in the depth direction. In particular, we use the change in finger width to approximate the Z component of the speed and the differential of the speed.

Denoting the position of the fingertip on the XY plane as (x_t, y_t) and the width of the finger as w_t for a frame t, the approximate speed $\|v_t\|$ and the differential of speed $\tilde{a}_t$ of the fingertip for frame t are computed as follows:

$$\|v_t\| = \|(x_t, y_t, w_t) - (x_{t-1}, y_{t-1}, w_{t-1})\| \tag{5}$$

$$\tilde{a}_t = \|v_t\| - \|v_{t-1}\| \tag{6}$$

Note that $\|v_t\|$ and $\tilde{a}_t$ are calculated as the displacement and its differential in a unit of time. Because the acceleration, as the secondary differential of position, is always a positive value and there is no way to distinguish "suddenly slow down" from "suddenly speed up" simply by computing the acceleration, we compute $\tilde{a}_t$ as the differential of speed $\|v_t\|$ instead of the differential of velocity vector v_t and use the sign of $\tilde{a}_t$ to distinguish "suddenly slow down" from "suddenly speed up." "Suddenly slow down" is indicated by a small negative $\tilde{a}_t$. As shown in Figure 8, w_t is computed as the distance between the two intersections of the finger region boundary and a circle centered on the fingertip (x_t, y_t). To make the algorithm more robust, we compute the average of the distance obtained by using five circles of different radii.

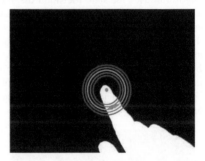

Figure 8: Estimation of finger width.

5.3 Hand and Fingertip Detection

Without haptic feedback, it is very difficult for users to perceive the relative position between their fingertips and virtual objects. As observed in the study, a subject tries to confirm that his/her fingertip is on the top of a button before performing the click. Therefore, providing some kind of feedback to notify the user of whether an object is ready for clicking is very important.

In traditional GUI, changing color is a commonly used approach to providing visual feedback about pointing at an object. In their gaze-based system, Majaranta et al. [23] proposed to change the color of a button when it was gazed at to provide the visual feedback that supports effective text input. Terajima et al. [5] succeeded in providing visual feedback for the touching of a virtual keyboard by changing the size of key buttons. We also employed changing the color and size of a virtual button when it was pointed at, as shown in Figure 9.

Pointing is detected by checking whether the position of the fingertip (x_t, y_t) is within the area of a virtual object for a certain period. Too long a period annoys users attempting to push a button, while too short a period causes a false-positive clickable state for the button, which leads to the Midas touch problem. We empirically set the period to four frames, or 266msec in 15fps, in our current implementation.

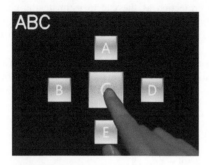

Figure 9: Visual feedback for pointing.

6 EXPERIMENTS

6.1 Implementation

To verify the effectiveness of proposed click interface, we have implemented a prototype system, as depicted in Figure 1. An HMD (Wrap920AR, Vuzix Cooporation) was connected to a laptop PC (OS : Windows 8, CPU: Core i5, CPU: 2.5GHz, MM: 4GB). The HMD originally possessed two VGA (640x480) USB cameras. We used one of the cameras for the experiment. The resolution of the displays was SVGA (800x600).

Two click gesture recognition algorithms are implemented. The first algorithm recognizes a click gesture by detecting a sudden drop-off in speed before stopping at a pointed-at virtual object. The second algorithm uses the state transition diagram based on the click model shown in Figure 7. When using the state-diagram-based method, choosing appropriate thresholds is especially crucial to achieving a high success rate. We have implemented a calibration tool for adapting the thresholds to individual users. Figure 10 shows a screenshot of the tool. The user is asked to click a button a few times, and the system computes the distribution of $\|v\|$ and $\tilde{a}$ and automatically finds the best thresholds for the user.

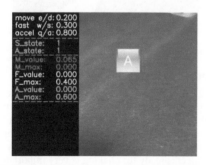

Figure 10: Calibration tool for adapting thresholds to individual users.

6.2 Evaluation

We have tested the effectiveness of the proposed visual feedback and the click gesture detection technique via subject studies. To evaluate the intuitiveness of the proposed click interface, children and seniors were also invited as subjects.

Two sets of virtual buttons are used in the experiment. Because the motion of the finger may vary according to the position relative to the virtual object, the first set of buttons, which is the same as the one used in the study, is designed to test the relative position factor among a virtual object, the finger and the camera.

As shown in Figure 11(a), we use five virtual buttons in a cross-shaped layout for inputting the letters A~E. The size of each button is 80×80 pixels on the screen. The button for the letter C is placed in the center of the screen. The distance from the top and bottom buttons to the center button is 140 pixels, and the distance from the left and right buttons to the center button is 160 pixels. The second set of virtual buttons is designed to investigate whether the proposed detection algorithm is effective even when the virtual buttons are very close to one another. When the buttons are placed very close to one another, a part of the fingertip may overlap with the adjacent buttons and thus may affect the performance of click gesture detection. We expect that the visual feedback involving color and size will not only help user to point at the button more precisely but can also improve the performance of gesture detection. As shown in Figure 11(b), as a potential application, we designed a virtual calculator consisting of 18 squared buttons of 60*60 pixels and two rectangular buttons, "0" and "=," of 60*125 pixels. The distances in both the horizontal and vertical directions between the centers of the two adjacent buttons are 125 pixels. The color of a button changes to orange when a pointing is detected. The color changes to red, and the size changes to 1.5 times the original size if a click is detected.

(a) Character input buttons.　　　(b) Virtual Calculator.

Figure 11: Arrangement of virtual buttons for subject study.

6.2.1 Click gesture recognition

We tested the click gesture recognition algorithms based on sudden speed drop-off detection (Test A) and the state transition model (Test B) and compared the results of the two algorithms. Twenty subjects, including nine males and eleven females in their teens, 20s, and 30s, participated in both tests. To eliminate the learning effect, they were divided into two groups of the same size. The subjects in the first group participated in Test A first and then Test B, while with was reversed in the second group.

For each test, a subject was asked to perform five trials for the character inputting task and ten trials for the calculation task. For each trail of the character inputting task, the subject was asked to input ten characters. For each trial of the calculation task, the subject was asked to input an equation, such as "123+423=", to add, subtract, multiply, or divide two 3-digit numbers. Before starting the trial, each subject was allowed to practice for 1~2 minutes. The reason we allowed the users to practice is that it was the first time most subjects had worn an HMD. As a future project, we plan to use a different task that can help user to get used to the HMD without any learning effect regarding the proposed interface.

6.2.1.1 Test A: by detecting sudden speed drop-off

Performance data in terms of precision (ratio of true clicks over all detected clicks), recall (ratio of detected clicks over all the true clicks), and F-measure for the 20 subjects are presented in Figures 12 and 13. The performance statistics are given in Table 1. As we can see, the averages of the three measures are all above 93%. There are no significant differences between the two tasks. The false detections were mainly caused by the failure of skin area detection, which results in incorrect fingertip position. In the experiment, we observed that slow clicking gestures tend to be missed.

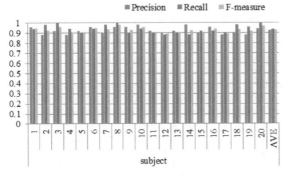

Figure 12: Performance of click gesture detection via sudden speed drop-off of fingertips for the character input task.

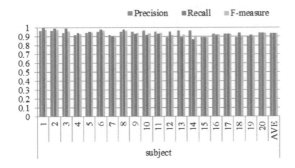

Figure 13: Performance of click gesture detection via sudden speed drop-off of fingertips for the calculation task.

Table 1: Statistics on the performance of click gesture detection via sudden speed drop-off of fingertips.

	Character			Calculator		
	Precision	Recall	F-measure	Precision	Recall	F-measure
AVE	0.93	0.94	0.93	0.93	0.93	0.93
MAX	0.98	1.00	0.98	0.96	1.00	0.98
MIN	0.88	0.88	0.89	0.89	0.86	0.89

6.2.1.2 Test B: by using the state transition model

The results and statistics are shown in Figures 14 and 15 and Table 2. Compared to the results of detecting sudden speed-drop off, all three measures went down. For the character input task, one subject's precision was below 80%. We conducted a T-test to compare the results of the two detection algorithms and found that there were significant differences at P=0.01 for precision, recall, and F-measure.

That is, the method of detecting the sudden speed drop-off outperforms the method using the state transition diagram. The main reason for this is that the latter uses multiple thresholds and it is difficult to find the best values for all the thresholds. However, the state transition diagram is a more general model and can be easily extended to other gestures. We are now improving the implementation of state transition detection by using statistical learning.

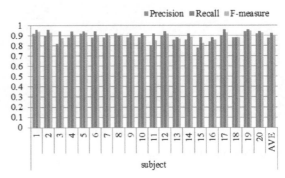

Figure 14: Performance of click gesture detection with the state transition model for the character input task.

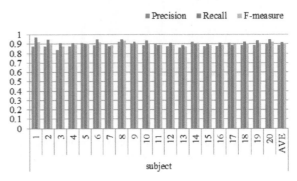

Figure 15: Performance of click gesture detection with the state transition model for the calculation test.

Table 2: Statistics on the performance of click gesture detection with the state transition model

	Character			Calculator		
	Precision	Recall	F-measure	Precision	Recall	F-measure
AVE	0.88	0.93	0.90	0.89	0.92	0.90
MAX	0.94	0.96	0.95	0.93	0.98	0.94
MIN	0.78	0.88	0.83	0.84	0.88	0.87

6.3 Evaluation of the Intuitiveness of the Proposed Interface

To evaluate the intuitiveness of the proposed click interface, we invited seven senior subjects between 60 and 70 years old and six teenagers. None of them were familiar with the computer environment. They were asked to perform three trials for the character input task and five trials for the calculation task.

Figure 16 shows snapshots of the experiment. The performance and the statistics for all subjects are shown in Figure 17, Figure 18, Table 3, and Table 4. Only the sudden-speed-drop-off-based algorithm was tested. The performance of the seniors was lower than that of youth group. As shown by the T-test, there was a significant difference between the senior group and the youth group, and between the teenaged groups and youth group, with p=0.01, but there was no significant difference between the senior group and the teenager group.

Through interviews, we confirmed that it was very easy for senior subjects to learn the interface, even without any computer experience. The visual feedback also contributed largely to the usability of the interface. Some senior subjects reported that they felt like they were pushing a button in the real world and that the highlighting of a button with a different color made them feel the moment of pushing a button.

| (a) A subject in his 70s. | (b) A teenaged subject |

Figure 16: Experimental environment.

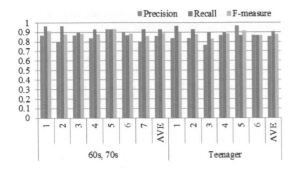

Figure 17: Click gesture detection performance for the senior and teenaged groups for the character input task (via detecting sudden speed drop-off).

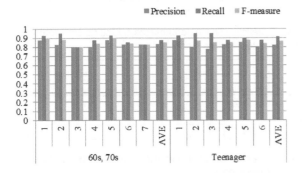

Figure 18: Click gesture detection performance for the senior and teenaged groups for the character input task (via detecting sudden speed drop-off).

Table 3: Statistics on click gesture detection performance for senior subjects.

	Character			Calculator		
	Precision	Recall	F-measure	Precision	Recall	F-measure
AVE	0.86	0.93	0.89	0.83	0.88	0.85
MAX	0.93	0.97	0.93	0.88	0.95	0.90
MIN	0.80	0.87	0.86	0.80	0.80	0.80

Table 4: Statistics on click gesture detection performance for teenaged subjects.

	Character			Calculator		
	Precision	Recall	F-measure	Precision	Recall	F-measure
AVE	0.86	0.91	0.88	0.82	0.91	0.86
MAX	0.97	0.97	0.91	0.88	0.95	0.90
MIN	0.77	0.87	0.83	0.78	0.88	0.84

DISCUSSION

Several subjects reported that the virtual buttons looked like real buttons. Clicking the buttons was fun and enjoyable. Several teenaged subjects became enthusiastic during the experiment because it felt like playing a game. Their comments support the idea that the proposed interface is intuitive for the subjects. On the other hand, several senior subjects claimed that clicking in the air made them tired. Therefore, the current click interface may not be suitable for use over an extended period of time.

Wearing an HMD was a new experience for all the subjects except for a few student colleagues. Nevertheless, most of those subjects did not have any particular difficulties in clicking the buttons displayed in front of them. The buttons were on the HMD coordinates, which makes it difficult to place a real finger on the virtual buttons. The subjects avoided this situation by adjusting their heads during the experiment. The problem can be solved by fixing the buttons to the world coordinates of the environment, which can be realized by using natural feature tracking and creating a 3D environment map.

7 CONCLUDING REMARKS

We have presented a novel click interface for AR systems with a single camera. With the new interface, a user can click an object in an AR environment in the same way he/she interacts with objects in the real world with his/her finger. A primary study was first conducted to build a model for a natural click gesture for AR systems. The effectiveness of the proposed gesture recognition algorithm, as well as the intuitiveness of the interface, was evaluated through subject studies.

The click is the most essential operation of interactive systems, so our system has a large variety of applications. For example, we can allow a user to type on a virtual keyboard or play a game with his/her, finger as shown in Figures 1(b) and (c), respectively. In Figure 1(c), our technique allows the user to click the positions on the papers, which are real objects captured by camera. Because we use a single camera, our technique can be used for building various user-friendly AR systems on compact devices. For example, a doctor can retrieve information about a patient without touching the screen of an iPad during an operation. Another example is that one can select the menu on a cell phone without touching the screen when one's hand is not clean.

As a future project, we would like to design a more elaborate experimental setup to test the effectiveness of our technique for different interface variables. One promising approach is to employ some standard benchmark systems, such as an AR variation of the FittsStudy software (http://depts.washington.edu/ aimgroup/proj/fittsstudy).

The currently implemented skin area defection algorithm may fail to detect the hand area correctly if the background consists of objects of skin-like color. Because the accuracy of the extracted fingertip position is highly dependent on the accuracy of skin region extraction, we need to employ more robust techniques. Recent hand posture estimation methods may contribute to the solution of this problem. Making proper assumptions about the environment, such as use in front of a wall, could be a more practical solution. Currently, we detect the click gesture by either detecting the sudden slowdown or the state transition of the motion. By combing the detection of pointing gestures, we can confirm high performance for both algorithms in the evaluation tests and avoiding the Midas touch problem. However, more experiments are required before we can make broad claims about the effectiveness of the interface. For example, when the users become more familiar with the interface, they may move their fingers more quickly and need less time to confirm pointing. In that case, it may become difficult to distinguish the click gesture from other quick movements. We are now improving the robustness of the gesture detection by constructing a probability model for the state transition of the click model. Currently, our technique only applies to the click gesture performed with a single finger. It will be another interesting future direction to extend the technique to recognizing other kinds of gestures.

Wearing an HMD degrades the intuitiveness of the system. The HMD did not fit well on a small child's head in the experiment. An optical-see-through HMD may provide another solution to enhance the intuitiveness of the system, but it may cause difficulty in registering the positions of a real finger and virtual buttons. We plan to explore the possibility of installing a gaze tracker on an optical-see-through HMD to register the position of a real finger and virtual buttons.

ACKNOWLEDGMENT

We are deeply grateful to Prof. Kwan-liu Ma, Dr. Lichan Hong and anonymous reviewers for the numerous valuable comments and constructive suggestions. This work was supported by JSPS KAKENHI Grant Number 25730120 and 25540045.

REFERENCES

[1] GoogleGlass, Google, http://www.google.com/glass/start/.

[2] L. Taehee, H. Tobias. Handy AR: Markerless Inspection of Augmented Reality Objects Using Fingertip Tracking. *IEEE Wearable Computers, 2007 11th IEEE International Symposium on*, pages 83-90. 2007.

[3] S. Hashimoto, A. Ishida, M. Inami and T. Igarashi. TouchMe: Direct Manipulation for Robot Based on Augmented Reality. *The 21st International Conference on Artificial Reality and Telexistence, Proceedings of ICAT2011*. 2011.

[4] T. Murase, A. Moteki, N. Ozawa, N. Hara, T. Nakai, K. Fujimoto. Gesture Keyboard Requiring Only One Camera. *Proceedings of the 24th annual ACM symposium adjunct on User interface software and technology*, pages 9-10. 2011.

[5] K. Terajima, T. Komuro and M. Ishikawa. Fast finger tracking system for in-air typing interface. *In Proceedings of the 27th international conference extended abstracts on Human factors in computing systems*, pages 3739-3744. 2009.

[6] C. Harrison, H. Benko and A. D. Wilson. OmniTouch: Wearable Multitouch Interaction Everywhere. *Proceedings of the 24th annual ACM symposium on User interface software and technology*, pages 441-450. 2011.

[7] C. Colombo, A. D. Bimbo and A. Valli. Visual capture and understanding of hand pointing actions in a 3-D environment, *Man, and Cybernetics, Part B: Cybernetics. IEEE Transactions on*, volume 33, number 4, pages 677-686. 2003.

[8] Kinect, Microsoft.

[9] iPad, Apple, http://store.apple.com/us.

[10] H. Kim, G. Albuquerque, S. Havemann and W. D. Fellner. Tangible 3D: Immersive 3D Modeling through Hand Gesture Interaction. Proceedings of the 11th Eurographics conference on Virtual Environments, pages 191-199. 2005.

[11] A. Wilson, Robust. Vision-Based Detection of Pinching for One and Two-Handed Input. *UIST*. 2006.

[12] M. Lee, R. Green, and M. Billinghurst. 3D Natural Hand Interaction for AR Applications. *Image and Vision Computing New Zealand 23rd International Conference*, pages.1-6. 2008.

[13] R. Y. Wang, and J. Popovic. Real-Time Hand-Tracking with a Color Glove. *Journal of ACM Transaction on Graphics*, volume 28, number 3. 2009.

[14] A. Akl. A Novel Accelerometer-Based Gesture Recognition System. *Signal Processing, IEEE Transactions on*, volume 59, number 12, pages 6197-6205. 2011.

[15] A. Chaudhary, J. L. Raheja, K. Das, & S. Raheja. Intelligent Approaches to interact with Machines using Hand Gesture Recognition in Natural way: A Survey. *International Journal of Computer Science & Engineering Survey*, volume 2, number 1, pages 122-133. 2011.

[16] Leap Motion, Inc, https://www.leapmotion.com/.

[17] The Only Fully Augmented Reality Glasses, http://www.spaceglasses.com/.

[18] M. Kölsch, M. Turk. Fast 2D Hand Tracking with Flocks of Features and Multi-Cue Integration. *IEEE Workshop on Real-Time Vision for Human-Computer Interaction*, 2004.

[19] M. Kölsch, M. Turk. Analysis of Rotational Robustness of Hand Detection with a Viola-Jones Detector. International Conference on Pattern Recognition, volume 3, papes 107-110. 2004.

[20] T.Lee, T.Höllerer. Initializing Markerless Tracking Using a Simple Hand Gesture. *International Symposium on Mixed and Augmented Reality (ISMAR)*, 2007.

[21] M. J. Jones and J. M. Rehg. Statistical color models with application to skin detection, *CVPR*, pp. 1274-1280, 1999.

[22] R.J.K. Jacob. The Use of Eye Movements in Human Computer Interaction Techniques: What You Look at is What You Get, ACM Transactions of Information Systems, Vol.9, No.2, pp.152-169, 1991.

[23] P. Majaranta, A. Aula, K.J. Raiha, Effects of Feedback on Eye Typing with a Short Dwell Time. ETRA, pp.139-146, 2004.

Using Stochastic Sampling to Create Depth-of-Field Effect in Real-Time Direct Volume Rendering

AmirAli Sharifi*
University of Alberta

Pierre Boulanger†
University of Alberta

ABSTRACT

Real-time visualization of volumetric data is increasingly used by physicians and scientists. Enhanced depth perception in Direct Volume Rendering (DVR) plays a crucial role in applications such as clinical decision making. Our goal is to devise a flexible blurring method in DVR and ultimately improve depth perception in real-time DVR using synthetic depth of field (DoF) effect. We devised a permutation-based stochastic sampling method for ray casting to render images with DoF effect. Our method uses 2D blurring kernels in 3D space for each sample on a ray. Furthermore, we reduce the number of required samples for each kernel of size n^2 from n^2 to only 2 samples. This method is flexible and can be used for DoF, focus-context blurring, selective blurring, and potentially for other photographic effects such as the tilt effect.

Index Terms: I.3.7 [Computer Graphics]: Three-Dimensional Graphics and Realism—Color, shading, shadowing, and texture;

1 INTRODUCTION

Direct volume rendering plays a significant role in 3D medical visualization. Many medical imaging modalities such as Computed Tomography (CT), Magnetic Resonance Imaging (MRI), and echocardiography produce volumetric data that need to be visualized. Visualization of these data sets is required to be correct, informative, and fast. Each of these three properties are vital to any rendering method to enhance clinical decision making through better visualization.

Many none-invasive medical diagnostic systems such as virtual angioscopy almost always rely on Direct Volume Rendering (DVR) despite its high computational cost. This is due to the fact that DVR can use the acquired volumetric data as is to produce more accurate visualizations in comparison with surface extraction and surface rendering methods [10] which tend to produce artifacts.

Despite all benefits of DVR, there are some shortcomings that need to be addressed. Generally in DVR a 3D volumetric data is projected onto a 2D screen. This projection process is a simplified approximation of a photographic system with sensor, lens, and apertures. There are phenomena in a 2D photograph such as DoF effect, which can assist viewers with understanding the spatial arrangement of objects. Such phenomena are not naturally present in volume rendering due to the simplifications and approximations of the imaging process. These missing information can provide vital cues for 3D human perception. Consequently, supplementing DVR-generated images with depth dependent blurring effects can enhance visualization.

In this paper, we propose a method to approximate DoF effect for one of the widely used DVR method, ray casting. The goal of our method is to amplify the effectiveness of volume visualization by improving depth perception in DVR-rendered 2D images

*e-mail:asharifi@ualberta.ca

†e-mail:pierreb@ualberta.ca

Graphics Interface Conference 2014
7-9 May, Montreal, Quebec, Canada

and ultimately enhancing clinical decision making. Moreover, our method has the ability to highlight the edges of the rendered object in blurred areas with no extra computational cost. This capability, which we will discuss later in the paper, has been shown to enhance perception in medical 3D rendering. Although the focus of this paper is on making volume visualization more informative, our method maintains imaging accuracy and provides users with a flexible blurring method that was previously unavailable for DVR, while keeping the extra computational overhead to a minimum.

This paper is organized as follows. Section 2 is a brief review of the related research found in the literature. Section 3 presents the proposed method in detail. Assumptions of the method are discussed in Section 5. Details about our implementation and results are presented in Sections 6 and 7. Finally, in Section 8 we conclude and discuss possible future works.

2 RELATED WORKS

Although there has been a considerable amount of work for simulating DoF for rendering geometry, only a few methods were proposed to tackle this problem in DVR. Many methods have been proposed for DoF simulation in ray-tracing; however, it is not trivial to extend those methods to DVR. Both image-space and object-space methods [1] can potentially be extended to DVR.

Held et al. [11] show previous assumptions about weakness of blur as a depth cue is not correct. Blur can be used to positively affect the perception of size and depth ordering of objects in a scene. It has been shown that a combination of blur and other depth cues can strongly increase the viewer's ability to perceive the absolute or relative distance between objects.

An empirical model of human blur perception is presented by Ciuffreda et al. [4]. This study evaluates blur distinction, discrimination, and depth ordering based on blur. The proposed model suggests that it is possible to clearly distinguish an object of interest surrounded by other objects such as a cup on a crowded table if DoF is employed on a 2D screen.

Boucheny et al. [2] have performed various experiments to evaluate the quality of depth perception for DVR. They identify the problem of depth perception in DVR by arguing that human perception is trained mainly with opaque surfaces rather than with semitransparent ones. Semitransparent objects, which appear regularly in DVR, can mislead human perception in terms of depth in absence of depth cues. They have performed user studies with motion parallax, exaggerated perspective, and light propagation models and found shortcomings in each one of them. Ropinski et al. [22] have evaluated the effect of various depth cues on rendering for angiography. They concluded that DoF is more beneficial in angiography when accompanied with pseudo chroma-depth. A recent study by Grosset et al. [9] evaluates the effect of DoF on depth perception in DVR. They have shown that DoF accompanied by other depth cues improves depth perception in many cases.

Barsky et al. [1] present an informative survey of various techniques to produce DoF effect in different rendering methods. Although some of the suggested approaches such as image-space methods can be extended to DVR, there are no specialized or trivially extendable methods presented to create DoF for DVR. One of the first methods to simulate DoF was proposed by Cook [6]. To determine the color of a pixel many rays are cast for each pixel on the image plane and through various points on the lens. The returned values are then used to simulate an integral of rays with a common origin over the surface of the lens. Despite its good results for ray-tracing, it is virtually impossible to extend such methods to ray-casting due to being computationally very expensive.

Yu *et al.* [26] devised a method to generate DoF in ray-tracing using synthetic light field. Kraus *et al.* proposed an image-space approach using sub-images and depth map to create DoF through post processing of the rendered image [13]. Although this is an image-space technique, it is not trivial to extended this method to ray-casting. Lei *et al.* [16] extended the idea of distributed ray-tracing by reusing the value obtained from each single ray traversed in a pinhole camera model. Also, to compensate for partial occlusion a few additional see-through rays are traced. In this way the DoF effect is approximated for ray-tracing reducing the computational cost. Various techniques for DoF generation mostly in ray-traced scenes have also been surveyed in the literature [7].

There has been very little work on creating DoF effect for DVR. Krivanek [14] presents an algorithm to produce DoF effect for surface splatting. The idea of under-sampling in blurred areas from this paper, which was also emphasized by Barsky *et al.* [1] has inspired us in our method. Schott *et al.* [23] proposed a method to generate DoF for volumetric data in slice-based DVR. The idea of incremental blur [21] was used with slice-based approach to DVR to create this effect. The volume is divided into front, back, and in-focus slices. Each are processed separately into three different buffers and then blended together to create the final image. Our approach, however, does not require using of slice-based, triple buffered, or synchronized incremental blur while providing the user with great flexibility and speed. Our method can blur any portion of any shape of the volume. Parallel computing hardware can be fully utilized in our method since there is no need for synchronization of rays. Finally, our method is compatible with many speed optimization methods for DVR.

3 PROPOSED ALGORITHM

In this section, we present the algorithm that we devised to create DoF effect. Krivanek [14] uses the idea that a high sampling rate of low resolution part of the input signal is not required as long as the Nyquist rate is preserved. Our approach uses this idea to reduce the amount of sampling required for blurring. This minimizes the rendering overhead and boosts the performance of our method.

Traditional ray-casting has an important property that our method exploits. The fact that many equidistant samples are taken along a ray very close to each other is used to produce blur effect. Our method maintains the 6 vital properties that are often seen as the criteria for an acceptable method for simulating DoF [1]. These 6 properties are:

- Choice of Point Spread Function (PSF);

- Per-pixel blur level control;

- Lack of intensity leakage;

- Lack of depth discontinuity artifacts;

- Proper simulation of partial occlusion;

- High performance.

In the following sections, we will discuss our method in detail.

3.1 Simulating Out-of-Focus Blur in 3D

Convolution using averaging kernel (box blur), Gaussian kernels, etc. is one of the popular methods to produce a blurred image. In case of box blur, a square kernel is placed over each pixel of an image. The value of each pixel is then replaced by the average intensity of all the pixels in the kernel to produce the blurred image.

3.1.1 Using 2D Kernels in DVR

There are different approaches to simulate out-of-focus blur in 3D. One way is to place a 2D kernel, parallel to the viewing plane, and centered over each sampling location along each ray. Doing so simulates the physical process by which the light rays from the neighboring out-of-focus points contribute to the final color of the central point on the kernel. The average intensity of all the samples taken on the kernel plane and inside the kernel is calculated and returned as the intensity of the central sample location. The returned intensity is then used by the ray-casting algorithm to determine pixel colors from samples.

Normally in ray-casting one sample is taken on each sampling location along a ray. Instead, one can use a square kernel of size $n \times n$ to sample average kernel intensity at each sampling location. This is computationally very expensive and makes this approach impractical. However, the question is that do we need all these samples when our output is blurred? In this paper, we show that an approximation with much fewer number of samples can be used to create blur. In this method, we will show that only 2 samples per each kernel of size n^2 is needed instead of n^2 samples.

3.1.2 Kernel Sampling

Let us first define a few terms and symbols that will assist us in explaining the process of sampling a kernel.

Definition 1. Let $\vec{r}(x,y,t)$ be the current ray cast towards the volume and started from location $(x,y,0)$ on the image plane.

Definition 2. Let t denote time which starts at 0 and each time we move to the next sampling location on $\vec{r}(x,y,t)$ it is increased by 1. Here t and $t+1$ refer to two consecutive time-steps.

Definition 3. Neighboring rays of $\vec{r}(x,y,t)$ denoted as $\boldsymbol{R}_n(x,y,t)$ refers to all the rays that intersect the kernel that is placed on the ray $\vec{r}(x,y,t)$ at time t. This kernel is parallel to the image plane and centered on $\vec{r}(x,y,t)$.

Definition 4. Let $\boldsymbol{K}(x,y,t)$ be the set of all the n^2 intersection points of $\vec{r}(x,y,t)$ and its neighbors, $\boldsymbol{R}_n(x,y,t)$, with the kernel at time t. Each one of these intersections on the kernel is denoted as $k(i,j,t) \in \boldsymbol{K}(x,y,t)$ where $\boldsymbol{K}$ is defined by:

$$\boldsymbol{K}(x,y,t) = \begin{pmatrix} k(0,0,t) & k(0,1,t) & \cdots & k(0,n-1,t) \\ k(1,0,t) & k(1,1,t) & \cdots & k(1,n-1,t) \\ \vdots & \vdots & \ddots & \vdots \\ k(n-1,0,t) & k(n-1,1,t) & \cdots & k(n-1,n-1,t) \end{pmatrix}$$

A neighboring ray of $\vec{r}(x,y,t)$, denoted by $\vec{r}_n \in \boldsymbol{R}_n(x,y,t)$, that intersects the kernel of size n^2 at $k(i,j,t) \in \boldsymbol{K}(x,y,t)$ can be obtained from $\vec{r}_n(x+i-\frac{n-1}{2}, y+j-\frac{n-1}{2}, t)$. Also, $\vec{r}(x,y,t)$ intersects the kernel at the kernel's central point $k(\frac{n-1}{2}, \frac{n-1}{2}, t)$.

In our method while following $\vec{r}(x,y,t)$ at each t only a single $k(i,j,t)$ is chosen among all n^2 possibilities. The volume is then sampled at the location of the chosen $k(i,j,t)$ instead of sampling all n^2 locations. Figure 1 illustrates this neighborhood sampling scheme with an example for $n = 3$.

The distances between the consecutive sampling locations along $\vec{r}(x,y,t)$ are very small, and a different $k(i,j,t)$ is chosen for each time-step as shown in Figure 1. This results in an approximation of completely calculating the average of n^2 kernel averages (in case of box blur). It is possible to put weights on the different $k(i,j,t)$ in order to approximate other point spread functions using other kernels such as a Gaussian kernel. Also, the shape of the kernel can change from square to other shapes to produce a desired effect.

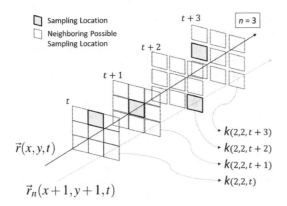

Figure 1: A different sampling location is chosen within a kernel on each time-step. Solid squares show the chosen sampling location on each time-step. Dotted squares show the potential sampling locations within a kernel. The sampled value at these sampling locations are treated and accumulated by the ray-casting algorithm as if they are being read normally on $\vec{r}(x,y,t)$ ray. Divergence of the rays is to demonstrate perspective projection.

3.1.3 Permutation-based Selection of a Single $k(i,j,t)$

Empirically, we found that complete randomness or pseudo-randomness in choosing each single $k(i,j,t)$ does not necessarily produce the desired results. In fact, it produces aliasing and there is a possibility of missing details of the volume. Repeating selection patterns are also not favorable for the same reasons. As a result, we used random permutations of sampling locations inside kernels to solve these two issues. Let us define a few symbols and terms to help us explain the permutation-based sampling scheme.

Definition 5. Let $Z(t_i,n)$ refer to a window on $\vec{r}(x,y,t)$ consisting of n^2 consecutive time-steps associated with a kernel of size n^2 and starting at time t_i. There are exactly n^2 sampling locations in $Z(t_i,n)$. By "associated" we mean a kernel of size n^2 is placed on each of the n^2 different sampling locations within $Z(t_i,n)$. All these kernels are parallel to the image plane and centered on $\vec{r}(x,y,t)$.

Definition 6. Let $Z^*(t_i,n)$ be a window on $\vec{r}(x,y,t)$ associated with a kernel of size n^2. It is similar to $Z(t_i,n)$ except that it consists of less than n^2 time-steps. For brevity, we use Z_i notation when we refer to both $Z(t_i,n)$ and $Z^*(t_i,n)$ at the same time. Also, t_i and t_{i+1} refer to two different starting times and not two consecutive time-steps. $Z(t_i,n)$ and $Z^*(t_i,n)$ are mutually exclusive.

Definition 7. Let Ψ_n be the set of all the permutations of n^2 with $n^2!$ distinct elements. Let $\omega_n \in \Psi_n$ be a single permutation of n^2 distinct elements.

Definition 8. Let $g : \omega_n \to K(x,y,t)$ be an injective map that takes a single element from ω_n and outputs a sampling location $k(i,j,t)$. The map g is defined when ω_n and $K(x,y,t)$ have the same size.

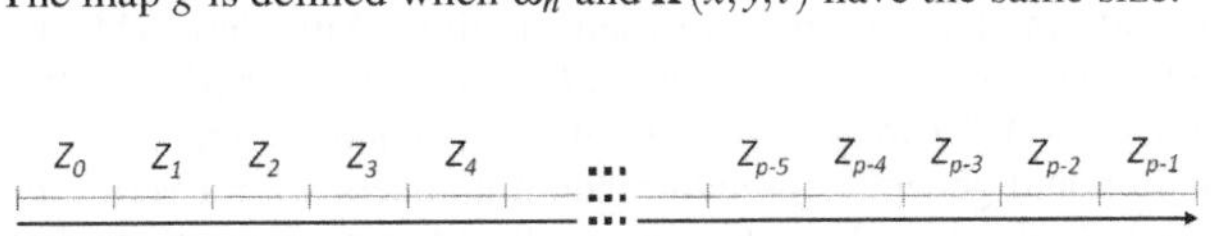

Figure 2 shows a ray that has been divided into p sections called Z_0 to Z_{p-1}. Each different Z_i may have a different associated n based on the desired blur level and consequently a different length. A new permutation $\omega_n \in \Psi_n$ is chosen pseudo-randomly every time we enter a new Z_i associated with a kernel of size n^2.

On each consecutive time-step in Z_i the next unused element in ω_n is used with the mapping g to select a unique $k(i,j,t)$. This permutation-based selected $k(i,j,t)$ is the location on which the volume will be sampled on that time-step. This guarantees that in $Z(t_i,n)$ all the n^2 distinct sampling locations on the kernel are chosen exactly once. It also guarantees that in $Z^*(t_i,n)$ all the chosen $k(i,j,t)$ are different. After entering Z_{i+1} a new permutation ω_n is generated and the algorithm continues in a similar manner.

Our initial single samples on each kernel produce a certain amount of noise in low frequency areas. Although Cook [5] states that human adapts well to noise, we added an additional step to further eliminate the noise.

3.1.4 Central Reflection Sampling

If we take n^2 samples for a kernel of size n^2 and m is the number of samples taken from the volume in Z_i, then m equals n^4 in $Z(t_i,n)$ and $n^2 \leq m < n^4$ in $Z^*(t_i,n)$. By replacing the average of a kernel with a single permutation-based sample on each time-step, we under-sample the kernel by only taking $\frac{m}{n^2}$ samples instead of taking m samples in Z_i.

A kernel can cover a variety of values such as different materials as well as empty space. Using a value as the representative of the kernel's average can contribute to the noisiness of the image if the value is very different from the actual average. It is shown in this paper that using central reflection sampling that we explain here can tackle this problem and considerably reduce the amount of noise in the final image.

On each time-step t the reflection of the chosen sampling location through the central point of the kernel is found and sampled as well. Then the average of the value sampled at the location of the original sample $k(i,j,t)$ and the value sampled at the point reflection of the sample at $k'(i',j',t)$ is calculated and processed as the current sample taken from the volume. This method has shown to greatly reduce the amount of noise. Other methods of blending can also replace averaging of the two samples.

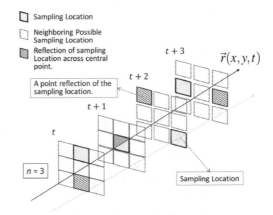

Figure 3: A second sampling location is calculated by finding the point reflection of the stochastic sampling location across the central point of the kernel. Solid squares are the permutation-based sampling locations. Hatched squares are the secondary sampling locations found by central reflection. The final value that will be used by the ray-casting algorithm on each time-step is the average of the two values read on these two locations on the corresponding time-step.

Figure 2: A ray is divided into windows associated with kernels of size n^2. We should note that n can change during traversal of the ray in order to produce different levels of blur. Each Z_i can have a different n associated with it.

Figure 3 illustrates the idea behind central reflection sampling by expanding on our previous example of Figure 1. Solid squares represent our normal stochastic sampling locations chosen based on the current permutation. Diagonally hatched squares show the sampling location, which is the point reflection of the permutation-based sampling location across the central point of the kernel.

3.1.5 Calculating Sampling Locations

We need to find the locations of the stochastic sample $k(i,j,t)$ and its point reflection $k'(i',j',t)$ at each time-step. Having variable kernel sizes make it infeasible to keep all the neighboring sampling locations at all time. As a result, we need to calculate the locations of $k(i,j,t)$ and $k'(i',j',t)$ on each time-step.

By using vector calculations as shown in Figure 4, locations of $\vec{C'} = k(i,j,t)$ and $\vec{E'} = k'(i',j',t)$ are found. Here $\overrightarrow{AB}$ is the ray that is being traversed. Kernel plane K intersects $\overrightarrow{AB}$ at $\vec{A'}$ and $K \parallel$ *Image Plane*. The normal vector of the plane K, denoted as $\vec{h}$, is also the same as the normal vector of the image plane.

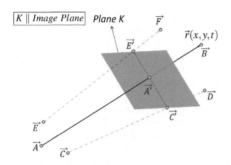

Figure 4: Finding the permutation-based sampling location for $\overrightarrow{AB}$ on its neighboring ray $\overrightarrow{CD}$. $\vec{C'}$ is the stochastically chosen sampling location and $\vec{E'}$ is its point reflection through the central point, $\vec{A'}$.

Equation 1 is the plane equation of K. Equation 2 is the line equation of $\overrightarrow{CD}$. Intersecting plane K and ray $\overrightarrow{CD}$ gives us the α corresponding to our stochastic sampling location $\vec{C'} = k(i,j,t)$ as shown in Equation 3. The location of $\vec{E'} = k'(i',j',t)$ can now be found simply by using symmetry. $\vec{E'}$ is the point reflection of $\vec{C'}$ through $\vec{A'}$.

$$Plane\ K:\ (\overrightarrow{A'C'}) \cdot \vec{h} = 0 \tag{1}$$

$$\overrightarrow{CD}:\ \vec{C'} = \alpha \cdot \vec{l} + \vec{C} \quad \text{where} \quad \vec{l} = \frac{\overrightarrow{CD}}{|CD|} \tag{2}$$

$$\vec{C'} = \frac{\overrightarrow{(CA')} \cdot \vec{h}}{\vec{l} \cdot \vec{h}} \cdot \vec{l} + \vec{C} \tag{3}$$

We should note that although $\vec{E'} = k'(i',j',t)$ is guaranteed to be inside the kernel, it might not exactly fall on one of the $n^2 - 1$ neighboring rays of $\vec{r}(x,y,t)$. This is due to perspective projection and does not cause any problem.

3.2 Fast Sampling of the Permutation Space

In order to accomplish our stochastic sampling without visible aliasing, we used permutations of sampling locations inside a kernel. For each Z_i associated with a kernel of size n^2 we need a pseudo-random permutation ω_n of size n^2 while on each time-step t, we need only one element from ω_n.

Most methods for generating permutations require remembering previously generated elements, which is infeasible due to GPU's hardware limitations such as limited number of registers, slow

global memory, etc. Other methods such as loop-less methods either require calculating $n^2!$ or they are not suitable for real-time rendering [8, 24]. Some methods that use mathematical sequences to generate permutations could have been ideal, however, they generate a single randomized permutation over and over [17].

None of these methods are suitable for our rendering task due to our limited memory and performance requirements. We generate permutations one element at a time for each time-step. We do not need to keep track of the elements we generated so far, and we do not need to calculate $n^2!$. The requirements for our method is to have a seed permutation for different permutation lengths less than or equal to n_{max}^2 where n_{max} is the maximum size of the kernel for maximum desired blur level, a set of prime numbers, a random number generator, and time-step counter t.

3.2.1 Seed Permutations

Generating DoF requires different levels of blur. In our method blur level directly depends on the size of the kernel. As a result, one need to have access to seed permutations of different sizes. A one-dimensional array of size n_{max}^2 can hold all our seed permutations for $n \in [1, n_{max}]$. In our implementation for all $n \in [1, n_{max}]$, the first n^2 elements of the one dimensional seed permutation array contain a permutation of numbers between 1 and n^2. If $\lambda_i \in \mathbb{N}$ is the value at index i of the permutation array, $\mathbf{\Lambda}$, then $\mathbf{\Lambda}$ is defined as follows:

$$\mathbf{\Lambda} = \{\mathbf{\Lambda}_n \mid n \in [1, n_{max}] \in \mathbb{N}\}$$
$$\mathbf{\Lambda}_n = \{\lambda_i \mid i \in \mathbf{I}_n \wedge (n-1)^2 < \lambda_i \leq n^2\}$$
$$\mathbf{I}_n = \{i \mid (n-1)^2 < i \leq n^2\}$$
$$\forall \lambda_i \forall \lambda_p \in \mathbf{\Lambda},\ \lambda_i = \lambda_p \Leftrightarrow i = p$$

3.2.2 Set of Prime Numbers

We store a set of prime numbers with numbers larger than n_{max}^2 in constant memory on GPU. Being larger than n_{max}^2 is important since in this case the largest common multiple of the prime numbers with all the numbers from 1 to n_{max}^2 range is going to be 1. This means that we can use them in the way that we describe in Algorithm 1 to read our seed permutation each time in a different order.

In order to completely eliminate any visible aliasing, we need enough diversity among the permutations that we generate. This diversity depends on the number of elements we keep in our set of prime numbers. Algorithm 1 describes how for a Z_i that is associated with a kernel of size n^2 the remainder of a randomly chosen prime number over n^2 is used. In our implementation, $n_{max} = 30$ and the set of prime numbers contains 732 prime numbers from 1000 to 7000.

3.2.3 Generating Permutations

The current element of permutation ω_n at time t is calculated using Algorithm 1 and denoted as *element*. Moreover, here the seed permutation array is denoted as $\mathbf{S}$ and the set of prime numbers of size N_p is denoted as $\mathbf{P}$. In this algorithm, the fact that single elements of a seed permutation can also be used as a pseudo-random index for the seed permutation itself has also been used to read the seed permutation each time in a different order. In order to generate a pseudo-random number, we used Multiply With Carry (MWC) method proposed by Marsaglia *et al.* [18]. This method, which is denoted as $MWCRand()$ in Algorithm 1, requires minimal computation and generates pseudo-random numbers with a very long period. In this pseudo-code α is an offset to make sure that when a transition between two blur levels happen, a new permutation is started from its beginning.

In summary, although we do not claim that our sampling of permutation space follows a specific distribution, it has proven to be effective in eliminating visible aliasing and moiré patterns to the

Algorithm 1 Generating one pseudo-random element of a permutation at a time inside the ray casting loop.

Input: seed permutation S, set of prime numbers P with size N_p, kernel size n^2

Output: current element in a permutation of size n^2 denoted as *element*

$\alpha \leftarrow 0$
for $t = 0 \rightarrow \infty$ **do**   \\ Loop for casting a single ray
   $\vdots$ \\ Ray casting initializations
   if n has changed **then**   \\ Handling $\boldsymbol{Z}^*(t_i, n)$ transition
      $\alpha \leftarrow t \bmod n^2$
   end if
   if $((t - \alpha) \bmod n^2) = 0$ **then**   \\ New permutation
      $r_1 \leftarrow MWCRand()$
      $r_2 \leftarrow MWCRand()$
      $p \leftarrow \boldsymbol{P}[r_1 \bmod N_P]$
   end if
   $index \leftarrow (\boldsymbol{S}[((t+1) * p) \bmod n^2] + r_2) \bmod n^2$
   $element \leftarrow \boldsymbol{S}[index]$
   $\vdots$
   $t \leftarrow t + 1$ \\ Other ray casting tasks
end for

point that it is undetectable by eye. Figure 7 compares our permutation based sampling results with purely pseudo-random selection of the first sampling location on a kernel. It can be seen in the results that visible aliasing has been removed by using permutation-based sampling.

3.2.4 Transition Between Different Blur Levels

In addition to eliminating aliasing, permutations also helped us guarantee that in each $\boldsymbol{Z}(t_i, n)$ with blur level n, exactly n^2 unique sampling locations are devised in a pseudo-random order. These samples uniformly cover the whole area of the kernel.

In $\boldsymbol{Z}^*(t_i, n)$ where a change in kernel size and consequently a change in blur level occurs, a new permutation is devised and used from the current sampling location and the previous permutation is no longer followed. When a new permutation is devised, it is important to make sure that sampling starts from the beginning of the new permutation. Failing to do so will result in artifacts and errors that can be seen specially when a transition from in-focus to out-of-focus regions happen.

Figure 5 illustrates the process of changing blur levels with an example. Here $\boldsymbol{Z}^*(t_i, n_j)$, $\boldsymbol{Z}(t_{i-1}, n_j)$, and $\boldsymbol{Z}(t_{i-2}, n_j)$ are associated with a kernel of size n_j^2. However, the length of $\boldsymbol{Z}^*(t_i, n_j)$ is shortened due to a change in kernel size from n_j^2 to n_{j+1}^2 where

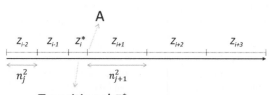

Figure 5: Transition of different blur levels. In this example, all three regions $\boldsymbol{Z}(t_{i-2}, n_j)$, $\boldsymbol{Z}(t_{i-1}, n_j)$, and $\boldsymbol{Z}^*(t_i, n_j)$ are associated with a kernel of size n_j^2. However, a change of blur levels from n_j^2 to n_{j+1}^2 while traversing $\boldsymbol{Z}^*(t_i, n_j)$ resulted in abandoning the rest of $\boldsymbol{Z}^*(t_i, n_j)$ and starting $\boldsymbol{Z}(t_{i+1}, n_{j+1})$ at the point labeled as A.

$n_j^2 \neq n_{j+1}^2$. A new permutation of size n_{j+1}^2 is devised and followed from A before taking all n_j^2 samples in $\boldsymbol{Z}^*(t_i, n_j)$.

3.3 Varying Blur Levels for Depth of Field

In order to simulate the DoF effect, we need to vary the blur level based on the distances from the image and lens planes. The theory of DoF has been discussed in many textbooks and papers so we are not going to go into details of lens theory.

Majority of volume rendering algorithms use thin lens model which implies that the thickness of the lens compared to its focal length is negligible and no light refraction happens inside the lens. It also assumes that entrance and exit pupils of the lens have the same size. This model makes the calculations for ray casting easier.

Light travels from each visible point on an object through the lens. For each point on an object a footprint of light is formed on the image plane. If this footprint is small enough to be perceived as a single point then that point on the object is said to be in focus. In contrast, if the point on the object is not between near and far focus planes, then the light footprint is larger than a point on the image plane. This is called the circle of confusion (CoC). In our system, we used the diameter of CoC in direct correlation with the size of kernel. Although we used square shaped kernels, it is possible to use weighted kernels to simulate circular effect.

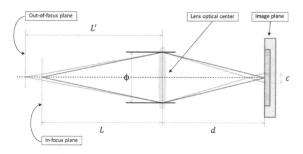

Figure 6: A thin lens model. Here Φ is the aperture diameter. Points on the In-focus plane form points on the image plane while points on the Out-of-focus plane form circles of diameter "c" on the Image plane. Image is taken and modified from [20].

Let f be the focal length of the lens which can be calculated from Equation 4:

$$\frac{1}{f} = \frac{1}{L} + \frac{1}{d} \qquad (4)$$

Equation 5 calculates the diameter of the CoC created by objects at distance L' from the lens' optical center:

$$c = \Phi \frac{|L' - L|}{L'} \frac{f}{L - f} \qquad (5)$$

Equation 5 can be simplified if the magnification m of the lens is known. Lens magnification can be calculated using Equation 6:

$$m = \frac{f}{L - f} \qquad (6)$$

Finally, the diameter of the CoC can be calculated using Equation 7 by knowing the aperture diameter Φ, lens magnification m, focal length f, the distance between optical center of the lens and object plane L', and the distance between optical center of the lens and focus plane L as shown in Figure 6.

$$c = \Phi m \frac{|L' - L|}{L'}. \qquad (7)$$

By knowing the distance that has been traveled from the image plane towards the negative z direction of the camera coordinates (away from camera and towards the volume), it is possible to determine the kernel size at each sampling location during ray traversal. By converting the coordinates of the current sampling location to camera coordinates, current distance from the image plane can be calculated. Also, one can accumulate the distances that the ray travels towards negative z direction for each sample. It is possible to determine the kernel size by using Equation 7 based on the accumulated distance.

4 BLURRED EDGE HIGHLIGHTING

While the average of a sample and its point reflection is calculated, it is possible for either or both of these samples to be taken from the empty space around the volume. This happens around the edges of the rendered object in blurred areas. As a result, a color is assigned to the empty space inside the transfer function. This will facilitate the calculation of the average of the sampled values. In an RGBA color scheme, the value of A, which is reserved for opacity, is used to make the empty space invisible. For example, in a 4 byte RGBA color, a value of $(128, 128, 128, 0)$ can be used as a neutral grey empty space to avoid any color or luminosity shift.

By using different colors assigned to empty space while keeping the opacity 0, the edges of the blurred areas can be highlighted with no extra computation. For example, in the same 4 byte RGBA scheme, assigning $(0, 0, 0, 0)$ would darken the edges or assigning $(255, 255, 255, 0)$ would lighten the edges. Trivially assigning any value with $A \neq 0$ would produce fog. Figure 8 shows the effect of our edge highlighting method applied to the rendering of a cardio-vascular arteries CT data set. Researchers have proposed different methods with extra computational cost to create such volumetric halos and showed that it positively affects perception [3] [25], while in our method this effect exists at no additional cost.

5 DISCUSSION OF THE PROPOSED MODEL

Under-sampling can produce aliasing, noise, and potential missing of details. By using permutations, we have eliminated the visible aliasing that was created by patterns in stochastic sampling. Noise has also been dealt with by using central reflection sampling as discussed in Section 3.1.4.

Since we are not sampling each ray on its own path, someone might argue that it is possible to miss very little details in blurred areas. Permutation-based choosing of the sampling locations inside each kernel forces all neighboring rays of a ray to compensate for what is perceived as a small probability of missing of details in blurred areas in the following manner.

Most of Z_i while traversing a single ray are of the form $Z(t_i, n)$. While sampling $\vec{r}_n(x, y, t)$ it is guaranteed that a single sample on the ray itself will be taken once in each $Z(t_i, n)$. This is also possible on $Z^*(t_i, n)$ but not guaranteed. For all $\vec{r}_n \in R_n(x, y, t)$ it is guaranteed that a stochastic sample from each of the $n^2 - 1$ neighboring rays will be on $\vec{r}(x, y, t)$ in a $Z(t_i, n)$ exactly once. Moreover, in almost all cases the point reflection of a single stochastic sample on each of the neighboring rays will also fall on $\vec{r}(x, y, t)$. The worst case scenario would be that in a single Z_i all n^2 samples of the n^2 rays in the kernel that are supposed to be on ray $\vec{r}(x, y, t)$ happen at the same time. However, using seed-permutations as well as unique seed points for random number generation using MWC for each ray will prevent such events by guaranteeing different permutations for different rays in a single Z_i. As a result, the probability of missing minute details in out of focus areas is extremely low.

6 IMPLEMENTATION

We used CUDA and OpenGL on a laptop with GeForce GTX 680M and an Intel Core i7 running at 2.4GHz. Although it is possible to implement this method with CG or GLSL, we chose CUDA to have more control over the available resources on the GPU. Volumetric data was stored in texture memory while the array of prime numbers and seed-permutations reside in constant memory.

Our method augments ray casting with DoF. Except for early ray termination (ERT), we did not take advantage of any other DVR speed optimization method. Also, shading has not been used in the results that we present here. A single cube containing the entire volume was rendered to two textures to obtain ray start and end coordinates [15]. Moreover, a post-interpolative piecewise linear real-time transfer function has also been used to convert from intensity values to colors and opacities. In our results when no DoF is applied, the DoF calculation is bypassed entirely. This is different than calculating the DoF for a $0mm$ aperture diameter where the overhead of calculating DoF might still slow down the rendering. Also, we have limited the maximum aperture opening to $40mm$ in our implementation.

Finally, our method is compatible with other optimization and enhancement methods for DVR. However, some of these methods might need simple modifications to take advantage of our method. For example, many methods have been devised to improve performance of ray casting by skipping the empty space. In this paper, blurring effect is created by the rays sampling the volume and a subset of rays that are sampling the empty space around the volume. As a result, in order to incorporate empty space skipping it is important not to skip the rays that are contributing to the blur around the volume. If n_{max} is the maximum kernel size, then the rays that are passing into the empty space and no further than $\frac{n_{max}\sqrt{2}}{2}$ from the volume should still be cast. This distance is half of the diagonal of the biggest kernel.

7 RESULTS

The frame rate of a rendering algorithm can vary due to different parameters, data, implementation technique, and hardware. This makes frames per second (FPS) an inaccurate measure of performance to compare methods that are implemented in different settings. However, FPS can provide us with other insights such as whether a method is real-time or not, or the amount of change in rendering speed because of extra computation. The frame rate in our DoF method when a volume is rendered with maximum aperture opening is approximately between 40% to 75% of the frame rate when the same volume is rendered without DoF.

Changes in the frame rate are not solely the result of the DoF calculations. Other factors such as the distance between samples on a single ray also play an important role in how much the frame rate changes. The Nyquist-Shannon sampling theorem states that at least $2 \times f_{max}$ samples should be taken from a signal with maximum frequency f_{max} to avoid aliasing in signal reconstruction. Since we are already under-sampling our kernels, Nyquist sampling rate based on f_{max} of the volume produces noise in the final image. In order to reduce this noise, one can take more samples on each ray in addition to the method discussed in 3.1.4. The adverse effect of sampling $2 \times (2 \times f_{max})$ on performance has already been considered whenever the changes in frame rates are presented in this paper. Also, details of parameters, frame rate, and changes in the frame rate are presented in the captions of the images for the following results.

Figures 8 shows a close up view of the patient's heart. In these images blurred-edge-highlighting capability of our method to highlight blurred arteries is demonstrated. Figure 9 shows a set of 3 images rendered with full aperture opening from the same heart CT data as Figure 8. This set of images present the rendering of cardiovascular system around heart using our DoF method compared to plain rendering without DoF.

Figure 10 shows a set of 6 images produced by our method. Figures 10a, 10b, and 10c are showing both knees of a patient with different aperture openings. These three images aim to illustrate how our method can help separating the interfering background from the foreground.

Figure 11 compares the speed and quality of our stochastic DoF generation with full-kernel sampling as a reference. Full-kernel sampling is to sample all n^2 samples on each individual kernel. This can be seen as a brute force method to perform full sampling over the area of the lens. Figures 11a, 11b, and 11c show in order a scene without DoF, with DoF generated with full-kernel sampling, and with DoF generated by our method. Figures 11d and 11e are 2.5 times magnified crops of the full-kernel DoF compared with our method. Figures 11f, and 11g are 14 times magnified, while Figures 11h, and 11i are 56 times magnified crops of the full-kernel DoF compared with our method.

In the results that are presented here details about the time to generate each frame, size of data, and type of data is given in the caption of the Figures.

8 CONCLUSION AND FUTURE WORK

In this paper, we presented a method to create blur in DVR, and we have used it to render images with DoF. Our main goal is to create a flexible way of incorporating DoF as a depth cue in DVR so it can improve perception of depth in conjunction with other depth cues. The method proposed in this paper satisfies the criteria for an acceptable DoF simulation as mentioned in Section 3 [1].

In this method there is no need for any pre-computation that involves the volumetric data. The only preparation step is to store the array of seed permutations and a subset of prime numbers in memory. It is also possible to hard code both of these arrays. As a result, our algorithm does not limit the developer by introducing extra preprocessing time. The proposed algorithm is compatible with different optimization methods such as empty space skipping and image enhancement methods such as various types of shading.

Previously there was no practical methods of augmenting ray-casting with blur capabilities. Our proposed ray-casting based method operates in parallel at ray level (similar to traditional ray-casting) with no need for any synchronization or dependency among different processes and threads. The slice based approach is not required for our method and consequently it is possible to blur any portion of any extent in the volume, which was unavailable in previously proposed methods.

Although the results presented in this paper only show DoF effect created by our method, in future it is possible to create other effects in DVR using our method since each ray is blurred separately. One of these effects is the tilt effect [11]. In this effect the lens plane is not parallel to the image plane creating a variation of blur levels even on the surfaces parallel to the lens. This effect can change the perception of distance and size [11]. Moreover, the control and flexibility available in this method provide the opportunity for new and novel approaches to enhance perception in direct volume rendering.

In the future, we want to further investigate ways to improve the quality and performance of our algorithm. This would include minimizing the change in the frame rate, and eliminating noise. Other possibility is to experiment with focusing on complex structures and blurring the surroundings to provide context for the viewer. This idea can extend the work of Kosara *et al.* [12]. Another possibility is to modify other depth cues in accordance to special properties of DoF to help DoF to be more effective [22].

REFERENCES

[1] B. A. Barsky and T. J. Kosloff. Algorithms for rendering depth of field effects in computer graphics. In *Proceedings of the 12th WSEAS international conference on Computers*, ICCOMP'08, pages 999–1010, 2008.

[2] C. Boucheny, G.-P. Bonneau, J. Droulez, G. Thibault, and S. Ploix. A perceptive evaluation of volume rendering techniques. *ACM Trans. Appl. Percept.*, 5(4):23:1–23:24, February 2009.

[3] S. Bruckner and E. Gröller. Enhancing depth-perception with flexible volumetric halos. *IEEE Transactions on Visualization and Computer Graphics*, 13(6):1344–1351, November 2007.

[4] K. J. Ciuffreda, B. Wang, and B. Vasudevan. Conceptual model of human blur perception. *Vision Research*, 47(9):1245 – 1252, 2007.

[5] R. L. Cook. Stochastic sampling in computer graphics. *ACM Trans. Graph.*, 5(1):51–72, January 1986.

[6] R. L. Cook, T. Porter, and L. Carpenter. Distributed ray tracing. In *Proceedings of the 11th annual conference on Computer graphics and interactive techniques*, SIGGRAPH '84, pages 137–145. ACM, 1984.

[7] J. Demers. *Depth of Field: A Survey of Techniques*. GPU Gems. Addison-Wesley Professional, 2004.

[8] G. Ehrlich. Loopless algorithms for generating permutations, combinations, and other combinatorial configurations. *J. ACM*, 20(3):500–513, July 1973.

[9] P. Grosset, M. Schott, G.-P. Bonneau, and H. Charles. Evaluation of depth of field for depth perception in dvr. In *IEEE Pacific Visualization 2013*, 2013.

[10] C. D. Hansen and C. R. Johnson, editors. *The Visualization Handbook*. Elsevier, 2005.

[11] R. T. Held, E. A. Cooper, J. F. O'Brien, and M. S. Banks. Using blur to affect perceived distance and size. *ACM Trans. Graph.*, 29(2):19:1–19:16, April 2010.

[12] R. Kosara, S. Miksch, and H. Hauser. Semantic depth of field. In *Proceedings of the IEEE Symposium on Information Visualization*, INFO-VIS '01, pages 97–, 2001.

[13] M. Kraus and M. Strengert. Depth-of-field rendering by pyramidal image processing. volume 26, pages 645–654. Blackwell Publishing Ltd, 2007.

[14] J. Krivanek, J. Zara, and K. Bouatouch. Fast depth of field rendering with surface splatting. In *Proceedings of Computer Graphics International.*, pages 196–201, 2003.

[15] J. Kruger and R. Westermann. Acceleration techniques for gpu-based volume rendering. In *Proceedings of the 14th IEEE Visualization*, VIS '03, pages 38–, 2003.

[16] K. Lei and J. F. Hughes. Approximate depth of field effects using few samples per pixel. In *Proceedings of the ACM SIGGRAPH Symposium on Interactive 3D Graphics and Games*, I3D '13, pages 119–128. ACM, 2013.

[17] N. L. Manev. Sequences generating permutations. *Applied Mathematics and Computation*, 216(3):708–718, 2010.

[18] G. Marsaglia and A. Zaman. Some portable very-long-period random number generators. *Comput. Phys.*, 8(1):117–121, January 1994.

[19] OsiriX. OsiriX DICOM Repository. http://www.osirix-viewer.com/datasets/. Accessed: 2013-07-31.

[20] N. Pears, Y. Liu, and P. Bunting. *3D Imaging, Analysis and Applications*. SpringerLink : Bücher. Springer London, 2012.

[21] P. Rokita. Generating depth-of-field effects in virtual reality applications. *IEEE Comput. Graph. Appl.*, 16(2):18–21, March 1996.

[22] T. Ropinski, F. Steinicke, and K. Hinrichs. *Visually Supporting Depth Perception in Angiography Imaging*, volume 4073 of *Lecture Notes in Computer Science*. Springer Berlin Heidelberg, 2006.

[23] M. Schott, A. V. P. Grosset, T. Martin, V. Pegoraro, S. T. Smith, and C. D. Hansen. Depth of field effects for interactive direct volume rendering. In *Proceedings of the 13th Eurographics / IEEE - VGTC conference on Visualization*, EuroVis'11, pages 941–950. Eurographics Association, 2011.

[24] R. Sedgewick. Permutation generation methods. *ACM Comput. Surv.*, 9(2):137–164, June 1977.

[25] Y. Tao, H. Lin, F. Dong, and G. Clapworthy. Opacity volume based halo generation for enhancing depth perception. In *Computer-Aided Design and Computer Graphics (CAD/Graphics), 2011 12th International Conference on*, pages 418–422, September 2011.

[26] X. Yu, R. Wang, and J. Yu. Real-time depth of field rendering via dynamic light field generation and filtering. *Computer Graphics Forum*, 29(7):2099–2107, 2010.

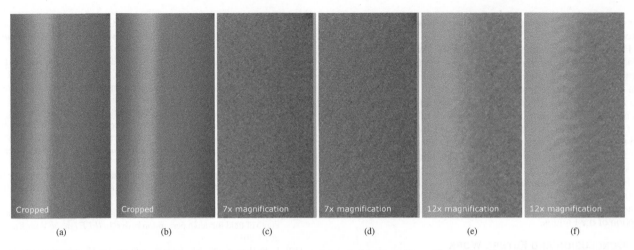

|(a)|(b)|(c)|(d)|(e)|(f)|

Figure 7: Comparison of permutation based sampling with purely pseudo-random sampling. Figures 7a, 7c, and 7e are rendered with our proposed permutation based sampling. Figures 7b, 7d, and 7f are rendered with pseudo-random selection of the first sampling point. Visible aliasing that can be seen in pseudo-random sampling has been removed by the permutation-based sampling.

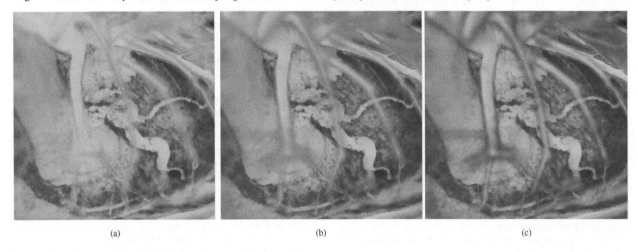

|(a)|(b)|(c)|

Figure 8: For all 3 images the number of rays cast is 512^2 and 1350 samples were taken on each ray while the lens magnification is $m = 2$. Figures 8a, 8b, and 8c show a side view of a $512 \times 512 \times 308$ heart CT data set. All images are rendered at ≈ 3.78 FPS ($264.5ms/frame$). These figures show our method's ability to lighten or darken edges of blurred areas without any additional computation in order to enhance perception. Figure 8b shows the neutral rendering of the edges while in 8a the edges are lightened and in 8c they are darkened.

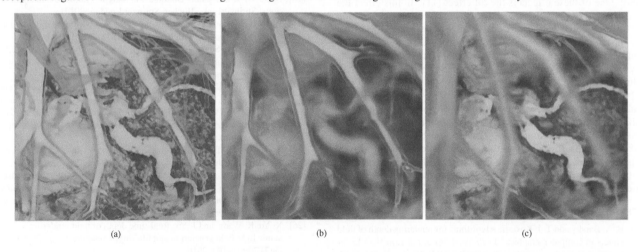

|(a)|(b)|(c)|

Figure 9: For all 3 images the number of rays cast is 512^2 and 1350 samples were taken on each ray while the lens magnification is $m = 2$. Figures 9a, 9b, and 9c show a side view of heart and cardiovascular system from a $512 \times 512 \times 308$ CT data from Osirix [19]. Figure 9a shows the scene without any DoF rendered at ≈ 7.55 FPS ($132.3ms/frame$). Figure 9b has full DoF effect (aperture diameter = $40mm$) and focused on the foreground arteries while rendered at ≈ 3.22 FPS ($310.2ms/frame$ and $\approx 42\%$ of the plain rendering speed). Figure 9c has full DoF effect (aperture diameter = $40mm$) while focused on the background arteries and rendered at ≈ 4.79 FPS ($208.8ms/frame$ and $\approx 63\%$ of the plain rendering speed).

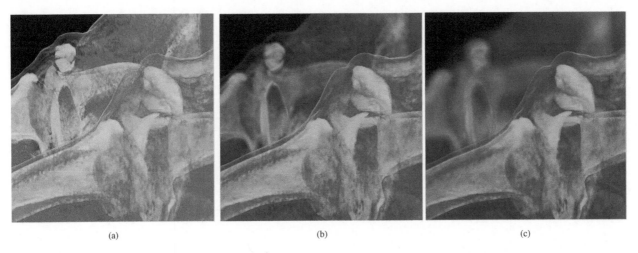

Figure 10: For all 3 images the number of rays cast is 512^2 and 1350 samples were taken on each ray while the lens magnification is $m = 2$. Figures 10a, 10b, and 10c show both knees of a person from a $512 \times 512 \times 912$ CT data from Osirix [19]. Figure 10a shows the scene without any DoF rendered at ≈ 7.7 FPS ($129.87ms/frame$). Figure 10b has moderate DoF effect (aperture diameter = $20mm$) while rendered at ≈ 3.8 FPS ($263.15ms/frame$ and $\approx 48\%$ of the plain rendering speed). Figure 10c has shallower DoF (aperture diameter = $40mm$) and rendered at ≈ 3.1 FPS ($322.58ms/frame$ and $\approx 40\%$ of the plain rendering speed).

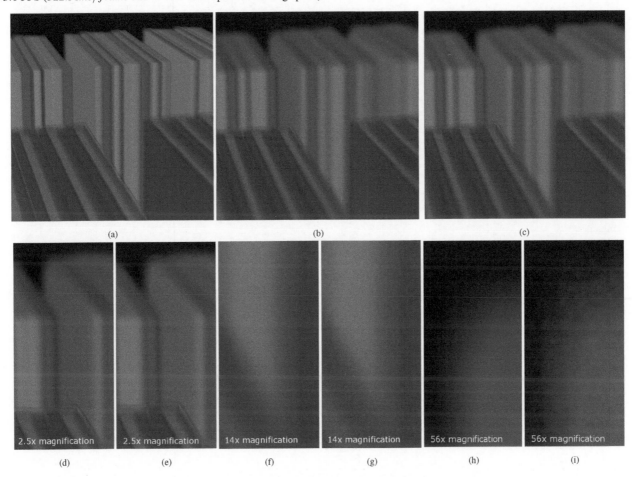

Figure 11: Quality and speed of generating results from our DoF method is compared to full kernel sampling (brute force ground truth) using a 256^3 volume. There are 512^2 rays cast simultaneously and 1350 samples are taken on each ray. Figure 11a shows the plain image with no DoF rendered at ≈ 5.14 FPS ($194.5ms/frame$). Figure 11b shows the results of full kernel sampling (reference) rendered at ≈ 0.01 FPS ($104044.6ms/frame$ or 1 minute and 44 seconds per frame). Figure 11c was rendered at ≈ 2.58 FPS ($387.8ms/frame$) using our stochastic sampling DoF method and same camera setting as Figure 11b. Our method was rendered 268 times faster than full kernel sampling and at 50.1% of the speed of rendering the scene without any DoF. Both Figures 11b and 11c are rendered with aperture diameter of $40mm$. Figures 11d, 11e, 11f, 11g, 11h, and 11i show a comparison between the quality of our method and significantly slower full kernel sampling in pairs of two. Each two similar images have the same magnification factor as well. Figures 11d, 11f, and 11h are magnified from 11b, while Figures 11e, 11g, and 11i are magnified from 11c.

Interactive Light Scattering with Principal-Ordinate Propagation

Oskar Elek [1,2*]   Tobias Ritschel [1,2]   Carsten Dachsbacher [3]   Hans-Peter Seidel [1]

[1] MPI Informatik   [2] MMCI / Saarland University   [3] Karlsruhe Institute of Technology

Figure 1: Dense smoke exhibiting strong multiple anisotropic scattering produced by a steam locomotive under complex environment illumination. Our approach renders it interactively without any precomputations at 10 Hz (NVidia GeForce GTX 485 Mobile).

ABSTRACT

Efficient light transport simulation in participating media is challenging in general, but especially if the medium is heterogeneous and exhibits significant multiple anisotropic scattering. We present a novel finite-element method that achieves interactive rendering speeds on modern GPUs without imposing any significant restrictions on the rendered participated medium. We achieve this by dynamically decomposing all illumination into directional and point light sources, and propagating the light from these virtual sources in independent discrete propagation volumes. These are individually aligned with approximate principal directions of light propagation from the respective light sources. Such decomposition allows us to use a very simple and computationally efficient unimodal basis for representing the propagated radiance, instead of using a general basis such as Spherical Harmonics. The presented approach is biased but physically plausible, and largely reduces rendering artifacts inherent to standard finite-element methods while allowing for virtually arbitrary scattering anisotropy and other properties of the simulated medium, without requiring any precomputation.

Index Terms: I.3.7 [Computer Graphics]: Three-Dimensional Graphics and Realism—Radiosity; I.6.8 [Simulation and Modeling]: Types of Simulation—Parallel

1 INTRODUCTION

Scattering, or translucency, greatly contributes to the appearance of many natural substances and objects in our surrounding. Albeit the problem can be easily formulated as the radiance transfer equation [3,21], computing a solution can be very costly. Consequently, many existing approaches simplify the problem, e. g., by assuming isotropic scattering or homogeneity of the material, to achieve interactive performance.

In this work we propose a novel interactive algorithm for plausible rendering of heterogeneous participating media with arbitrary

*e-mail: {oelek, ritschel, hps}@mpi-inf.mpg.de, dachsbacher@kit.edu

anisotropy. The core of our approach is to propagate light in propagation volumes oriented along the *principal ordinates* of the source illumination. For this we typically use multiple rectilinear grids to propagate environmental (distant) lighting, and spherical grids to account for point light sources. In both cases, one dimension of the grids is aligned with the prominent directional part of the source radiance for which the grid has been created. In contrast to previous methods (e. g., [1, 13]), discretizing the illumination into directional and point light sources enables us to approximately describe the anisotropy (directionality) of light transport by a single scalar value per grid cell. Specifically, this anisotropy value corresponds to a unimodal function implicitly aligned with the respective principal ordinate. In addition to exploiting data locality and the parallelism of GPUs, the benefit of these decisions is a significant reduction of the *false scattering* and *ray effect* artifacts arising in many finite-element methods as a consequence of representing the propagated radiance by, e. g., spherical harmonics or piecewise-constant functions.

Our main contributions can be summarized as follows:

- We introduce a novel approach to finite-element light propagation using implicitly aligned unimodal distributions for regular and spherical grids. This helps reducing propagation artifacts and helps to preserve the directionality of light during the propagation.

- A simplification of lighting by decomposing both environmental and surface illumination (via virtual point lights) into separate principal ordinate grids.

- An observer-centric importance-based selection of principal ordinates and prefiltering for environment lighting, helping to hide its discretized character used in the propagation.

2 PREVIOUS WORK

Offline methods   A range of different approaches has been presented to compute solutions to the radiance transport equation for participating environments [3,21]. However, none of the classic techniques provides a satisfying combination of generality, robustness, and, most importantly in our context, speed. Unbiased Monte-Carlo methods, such as bidirectional path tracing [18] and Metropolis light transport [26] usually require a large number of paths to be traced; in particular in dense media with high scattering anisotropy and albedo (like clouds or milk) the computation time increases tremendously. Caching is often used to speed up the computation, e. g., radiance caching [10], photon mapping [11, 12] or virtual point lights [6].

However, these methods typically do not handle highly anisotropic scattering very well, even with recent improvements [24, 25], and their performance is often far from interactive.

Finite-Element methods Finite-element methods, including volume radiosity [29], the discrete ordinates method (DOM) [3], light diffusion [32], and lattice-Boltzmann transport (LB) [8] handle highly multiple scattering well. However, in practice they allow only isotropic or moderately anisotropic scattering, and usually suffer from false scattering (smoothing of sharp light beams) and ray effects (selective exaggeration of scattered light due to discretized directions). Light propagation maps [7] significantly reduce the artifacts, but are still limited to rather moderate anisotropy. It can therefore be seen that strong scattering anisotropy is one of the main limiting factors for existing methods. This is unfortunate, as most real-world media exhibit relatively high anisotropy (Henyey-Greenstein [9] coefficient $g \approx 0.9$ or more [23]). Although isotropic approximations are acceptable in some cases, this is generally not a valid assumption and one of the primary motivations for our work.

Interactive rendering Numerous works focus on individual optical phenomena to achieve interactive or real-time performance. These phenomena include light shafts [5, 28], volume caustics [17, 19], shadows [20, 30], and clouds [2]. Various approaches can also be found in classic visualization literature, e. g., half-angle slicing [15] which empirically computes forward scattering for volume visualization. Sometimes precomputation is used to speed up the rendering of heterogeneous translucent objects [31, 33] or smoke using compensated ray marching [34]. In contrast, we target general multiple scattering in participating media without any precomputation or focus on a particular phenomenon.

We build on concepts of DOMs and light propagation volumes [1, 13]. These approaches are attractive for interactive applications as their grid-based local propagation schemes allow for easy parallel implementation on contemporary GPUs. Virtually all existing variants of DOM use a single scene-aligned grid, where every grid cell stores a representation of the directional radiance function using spherical harmonics (SH) or piecewise-constant functions. This representation is then used to iteratively calculate energy transfer between nearby cells, typically within a local 18- or 26-neighbourhood. However, this representation is only suited for moderately anisotropic scattering at best; especially for anisotropic media under complex (high-frequency) illumination such approach causes prominent ray effect and false scattering artifacts (see [7]). We take a different approach and propose to identify the most important light propagation directions (principal ordinates) in the scene and then use *multiple propagation grids* aligned with these directions, instead of a single volume. This enables using a unimodal representation of the angular energy distribution around the principal direction in each grid cell.

3 Principal Ordinate Propagation

The core idea of our method is to reduce the main drawbacks of previous grid-based iterative methods, false scattering and ray effects, by using propagation volumes where the propagation domain is explicitly aligned with approximate principal directions of light transport. Furthermore, we use only a single scalar value per grid cell to describe the local anisotropy of the directional light distribution. In our scheme, we use the well-known Henyey-Greenstein (HG) [9] distribution; the aforementioned value, called the *anisotropy coefficient*, is used to parametrize this distribution. Using principal directions implies that for more complex lighting scenarios we have to use multiple grids that sufficiently well approximate their directionality; for local light sources we propose to use spherical grids centred around them.

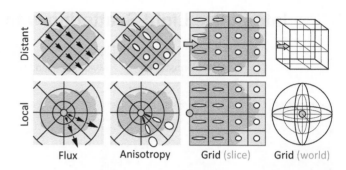

Figure 2: For distant (parallel) light we use rectilinear grids aligned with its principal direction, and spherical grids for point light sources. Every grid cell stores only radiance magnitude and anisotropy. The propagation scheme is almost identical for both cases.

$\mathbf{d}$	(principal) direction
g	scattering anisotropy coefficient
σ_s, σ_a	scattering / absorption coefficient
$\mathbf{x}_i$	location of grid cell i
L_i, a_i	(per-cell) radiance magnitude and anisotropy
$f_{\mathrm{hg}}, F_{\mathrm{hg}}$	HG function and its cumulative distribution
μ	scattering angle cosine
$\mathbf{L}, \mathbf{L}_{\mathrm{acc}}$	propagation and accumulation grid
M, m	number of iterations / iteration index
$L_{\mathrm{in}}(\mathbf{d})$	incident radiance from direction $\mathbf{d}$
$\Delta L_{src \to dst}$	src to dst radiance contribution
$T_i, T_{src \to dst}$	transmittance to cell i and between cells
Ω_i, Ω_n	solid angle subtended by cell i or ordinate n
N, n	number of principal ordinates / ordinate index

Table 1: Table of symbols (in the order of appearance).

These choices assume that the principal directions can be derived from the initial radiance distribution and do not change strongly when light travels through the medium. However, such variation might occur if the density of the simulated medium changes abruptly. Still, as we discuss in Sec. 3.1.5, violating this assumption does not cause our algorithm to fail, but only leads to decreasing its accuracy.

In the following we first detail our concept of principal ordinate propagation for a single directional source (Sec. 3.1). Then we describe how to extend this scheme to environment illumination (Sec. 3.2) and local light sources (Sec. 3.3) by using multiple importance-sampled rectilinear and spherical propagation volumes, respectively. The propagation scheme is explained using radiance as the radiometric quantity; we assume all other quantities (such as irradiance from environment maps or intensity from point lights) to be converted accordingly. All frequently-used notation is summarized in Table 1.

3.1 Regular grids for directional light

The concept as well as the propagation scheme can be best explained for parallel (distant) light travelling along a direction $\mathbf{d}$ through a region in space (Fig. 2, top). For this case we discretize the space into a uniform rectilinear grid similar to DOM; however, we make sure that one of its dimensions is aligned with $\mathbf{d}$. For every grid cell i, we store the directional distribution of light and its magnitude L_i (all computations are performed independently per-wavelength, which is omitted here for brevity). The main difference to DOM is that we represent both the *directional distribution* of light and the *phase function* using the HG distribution implicitly aligned with $\mathbf{d}$. To distinguish radiance anisotropy (directional distributions) from phase functions, we denote the HG parameter for the former as $a_i \in [-1, 1]$, and $g \in [0, 1]$ for the latter (we do not consider negative values of g because of physical implausibility of dominantly-backscattering

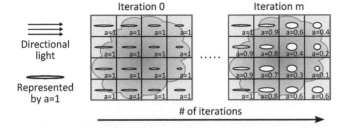

Figure 3: The propagation grid aligned with the direction of incidence is initialized with the attenuated radiance and an anisotropy parameter $a_i = 1$. During the propagation both radiance magnitude and anisotropy change towards lower anisotropy.

media). That is, the directional radiance of a grid cell centred at $\mathbf{x}_i$ is $L(\mathbf{x}_i, \omega) = L_i \cdot f_{\text{hg}}(\mu, a_i)$, where f_{hg} is the HG function and $\mu = \omega \cdot \mathbf{d}$ is the cosine of the angle between a direction ω and the principal light direction $\mathbf{d}$. We assume that the medium is further characterized by its (spatially-varying) scattering coefficient σ_s and absorption coefficient σ_a; these two quantities as well as the spatially-varying anisotropy of the phase function defined by the HG parameter g are wavelength-dependent and stored for every cell of the medium volume (which exists *independently* of the propagation volumes).

Conceptually, two grids are required in the propagation procedure. The first, *propagation grid*, stores the unpropagated (residual) energy; we will denote it as $\mathbf{L}$ and its state at the iteration $m \in \{1..M\}$, where M is the total number of propagation iterations, as $\mathbf{L}^m$. The second, *accumulation grid* $\mathbf{L}_{\text{acc}}$, is needed to accumulate the energy transported through the medium over the course of the computation. Two options are available for implementing $\mathbf{L}_{\text{acc}}$: we could either store the overall radiance distribution that has passed though each cell during the propagation, or alternatively store only the observer-dependent out-scattered radiance at each iteration. We opted for the second approach, because storing the entire directional radiance distribution at each cell is much more expensive than just accumulating the outgoing radiance (which is essentially a single scalar value). Although this of course requires recomputing the solution on every observer position change, it is in agreement with our premise of a fully dynamic algorithm without relying on precomputations.

3.1.1 Grid initialization

At the beginning each propagation grid—which is scaled to span the entire medium (Fig. 2, top)—needs to be initialized by the incident radiance at each cell. As no scattering has been accounted for yet, the anisotropy is set to an HG coefficient of $a_i = 1$, an equivalent to the Dirac function in the direction $\mathbf{d}$ (Fig. 3). The radiance magnitude L_i is set to the incident radiance $L_{\text{in}}(\mathbf{d})$ at $\mathbf{x}_i$, attenuated by absorption and out-scattering. That is, for every cell, we compute the transmittance T_i (from the point where light enters the medium, travelling along $\mathbf{d}$ to $\mathbf{x}_i$) set to $L_i = L_{\text{in}}(\mathbf{d}) \cdot T_i$. Note that this can be efficiently computed using ray marching: as our grid is aligned with $\mathbf{d}$ we can compute the transmittance incrementally along individual 'slices' of the grid along $\mathbf{d}$ in a single pass.

3.1.2 Light energy propagation

In this section, we describe how to iteratively update the grid to simulate the propagation of light. We use a propagation stencil where the radiance of each grid cell is propagated to its 6 direct neighbours in every iteration. More specifically, we perform a gathering-type computation of how much radiance flows *into* each grid cell from its neighbours based on their radiance distributions

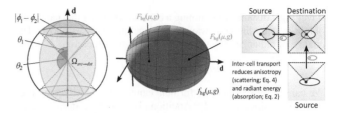

Figure 4: Left: Our polar parametrization of the solid sphere. The coloured patches correspond to the approximate solid angles subtended by the cells next to (green), in front (purple) and behind (orange) *src*. Middle: The HG cumulative function F_{hg} is used to integrate the radiance from the source cell flowing towards the destination cells (depicted as coloured patches of f_{hg}, for $g = 0.5$). Right: On the way the light undergoes scattering and is possibly reduced by absorption.

and then combine these contributions to yield the new distribution at that cell (Fig. 4, right). In the following we denote the neighbouring source cell with index *src*, and the target destination cell with *dst*.

Radiance magnitude contribution   We first need to determine the amount of radiant energy that flows from cell *src* towards *dst* according to the radiance distribution in *src*. To this end, we efficiently compute the integral of $L(\mathbf{x}_{src}, \omega)$ over the solid angle subtended by *dst* (denoted as $\Omega_{src \rightarrow dst}$ below) using the closed form of the cumulative HG function $F_{\text{hg}}(\mu, g) = \int_{-1}^{\mu} f_{\text{hg}}(\mu', g) \, d\mu'$:

$$F_{\text{hg}}(\mu, g) = \frac{1-g^2}{4\pi g} \cdot \left(\frac{1}{(1+g^2-2g\mu)^{1/2}} - \frac{1}{1+g} \right). \quad (1)$$

By this we compute the radiance from *src* travelling towards to *dst* using the transmittance $T_{src \rightarrow dst}$ as

$$\Delta L_{src \rightarrow dst} = L_{src} \cdot T_{src \rightarrow dst} \cdot |\phi_1 - \phi_2|$$
$$\cdot \left(F_{\text{hg}}(\cos \theta_1, a_{src}) - F_{\text{hg}}(\cos \theta_2, a_{src}) \right) \quad (2)$$

using the following approximate parametrization for the subtended solid angle $\Omega_{src \rightarrow dst}$ (depending on mutual positions of *src* and *dst*):

$$(\theta_1, \theta_2, |\phi_1 - \phi_2|) = \begin{cases} (0, \frac{\pi}{4}, 2\pi) & dst \text{ in front of } src \\ (\frac{\pi}{4}, \frac{3\pi}{4}, \frac{\pi}{2}) & dst \text{ next to } src \\ (\frac{3\pi}{4}, \pi, 2\pi) & dst \text{ behind } src \end{cases} \quad (3)$$

(see Fig. 4, left for a sample illustration of the second case of Eq. 3). Since the HG distribution is rotationally-symmetric (Fig. 4, middle) only the absolute value of the difference of the azimuthal angles $|\phi_1 - \phi_2|$ is required. Note that here the transmittance $T_{src \rightarrow dst}$ accounts *just for absorption* that affects the radiance propagation on its way from *src* to *dst*. This is because our scheme treats scattering as a decrease of anisotropy and not as an extinction process, as we show below. In practice, we take the averaged absorption coefficients σ_a at the source and destination cells and the distance between their centres t, and apply the Beer-Lambert-Bouguer law; however, ray-marching with a small number of steps might potentially be required to integrate the absorption coefficient if the resolution of the propagation volume is much smaller than the medium grid.

Radiance anisotropy contribution   Similarly to absorption attenuating the radiant energy flowing between neighbouring cells, the anisotropy of the energy propagated from *src* to *dst* will decrease due to scattering. In agreement with the radiance transfer equation, in our case this can be easily computed exploiting the self-convolution property of the HG distribution [22]: in a medium with scattering anisotropy of g the radiance anisotropy reduces to $a' = a \cdot g^{\sigma_s \cdot t}$ after travelling a distance t (assuming a constant σ_s along this path). We obtain σ_s and t the same way as for computing $T_{src \to dst}$ above. The change of radiance anisotropy from src to dst is therefore

$$\Delta a_{src \to dst} = a_{src} \cdot g^{\sigma_s \cdot t}. \tag{4}$$

We can easily see that this formula cannot lead to an increase of anisotropy, since $g \in [0, 1]$. Additionally, in non-scattering media ($\sigma_s = 0$) the anisotropy will be preserved perfectly.

Combining contributions from neighbours   Updating the radiance distribution at the cell dst entails accumulating the contributions from its six neighbours (indexed by src) as

$$L_{dst} = \sum_{src} \Delta L_{src \to dst}, \tag{5}$$

$$a_{dst} = \frac{\sum_{src} \Delta L_{src \to dst} \cdot \Delta a_{src \to dst}}{\sum_{src} \Delta L_{src \to dst}}. \tag{6}$$

While the radiant energy contributions simply need to be added up, the anisotropy is a weighted average of its neighbours, since the update has to yield an anisotropy value a_{dst} within the valid range. We discuss implications of Eq. 6 in Sec. 3.1.5.

3.1.3   Iterating the solution

The update procedure defined by Eqs. 5 and 6 is performed for every cell of $\mathbf{L}^m$ to yield $\mathbf{L}^{m+1}$ for every iteration m. Implementation-wise, this requires maintaining a second grid identical to the propagation grid and swapping these at each iteration.

Additionally, the results of every propagation iteration need to be accumulated in $\mathbf{L}_{acc}$ by evaluating the updated distributions in $\mathbf{L}^{m+1}$:

$$L_{acc,i}^{m+1} = L_{acc,i}^m + L^{m+1}(\mathbf{x}_i, \mathbf{c} - \mathbf{x}_i) \tag{7}$$

$$= L_{acc,i}^m + L_i^{m+1} \cdot f_{hg}(\mu, a_i^{m+1}) \tag{8}$$

for every cell i. Here $\mathbf{c}$ is the observer position and μ is therefore the dot product of $\mathbf{d}$ and the view direction.

3.1.4   Upsampling and rendering

When the solution has converged after a sufficient number of iterations, using it for rendering is relatively straightforward. We employ ray-marching to integrate the incoming radiance for every camera ray using the common front-to-back emission-absorption model [21]. In this case the emission term corresponds to the scattered radiance accumulated in $\mathbf{L}_{acc}$.

As we discuss in Sec. 4, the typical resolutions used for the propagation grids need to be rather small (in most of our examples 20^3 or less) for performance reasons. In order to improve the rendering quality with such low grid resolutions it is desired to upsample them prior to their visualization. We use a 3D version of the joint bilateral upsampling [16] where the density field of the medium (i. e., the spatially varying scattering coefficient) is used as a guidance signal. Typically, the density field is significantly more detailed than the propagation volumes; this detail is "transferred" to the solution by the upsampling. According to our experiments, low-resolution propagation grids are usually sufficient for plausible results.

3.1.5   Discussion of the propagation scheme

Using the unimodal HG function with a single parameter to represent the directional distributions in light transport obviously means that there are distributions in a cell that cannot be represented well. On the other hand, we compensate for this by using multiple grids

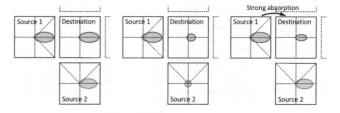

Figure 5: Three examples of the local propagation behaviour. Left: all source cells exhibit strong forward scattering which is well-preserved by our propagation scheme. Centre: radiance anisotropy is reduced due to in-scattering from Source 2 which has isotropic radiance distribution. Right: light from Source 1 to destination is almost entirely absorbed. Light from Source 2 should then be deviated "upwards", which our scheme cannot represent.

(see Sec. 3.2), which in turn can handle anisotropic phase functions significantly better than previous work thanks to the proposed propagation scheme. In comparison, an exceedingly large number of SH coefficients is required to represent highly anisotropic distributions, and this still does not prevent false scattering issues if a local propagation scheme is employed.

In this view the most heuristic step of our scheme is the recombination of reduced anisotropies from the neighbouring cells in Eq. 6. The logic behind this formulation is that the radiance distribution at dst will result from superposing the neighbouring distributions according to how much energy they contribute to dst. The main limitation of this approach lies in the fact that combining multiple HG distributions with different anisotropy values cannot generally be represented by any single HG distribution. Although we have experimented with fitting the resulting HG distribution to the combination of its neighbours in terms of least square error, we found that the simple weighted arithmetic average produces comparable results while keeping the computational cost of this core operation minimal. In addition, Eq. 6 very well preserves the anisotropy of light transported along the principal direction, thus greatly reducing false scattering effects.

Note that there are cases of very heterogeneous media where our approach might locally become too inaccurate (see Fig. 5). If light along the principal direction undergoes strong absorption, while light from other directions does not, the resulting light distribution should possibly become skewed, which cannot be represented within our framework. Although this is obviously a failure case of our representation, occurrences of such strong absorption fluctuations are comparatively rare, and more importantly the resulting radiance magnitude in these cases is typically very small (therefore having little impact on the resulting image). Also note that with multiple propagation volumes we can actually reproduce complex multimodal radiance distributions, despite each grid being composed of unimodal HG distributions.

3.2   Environment lighting: Multiple propagation grids

In the previous section we have described our approach for a single directional light source. In order to account for environmental lighting (typically modelled by an environment map), we need to use multiple grids oriented in different principal directions. In the following we discuss how to choose these directions and, as every grid accounts for light from a finite solid angle, how to prefilter the respective incident radiance to avoid singularity artifacts (see Fig. 6).

Prefiltering   A straightforward approach is importance-sampling the environment map to obtain N directions, $\mathbf{d}_n$, each carrying an

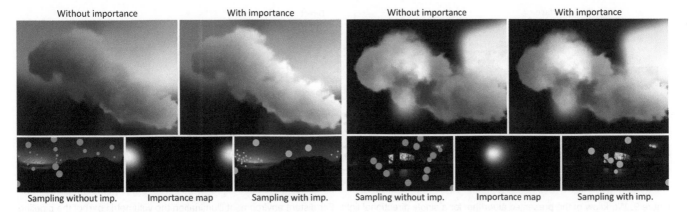

| Without importance | With importance | Without importance | With importance |

Sampling without imp.   Importance map   Sampling with imp.   Sampling without imp.   Importance map   Sampling with imp.

Figure 7: Importance propagation improves overall radiance distribution across the medium and visibility of bright regions behind. This especially holds for high-albedo media with strong scattering anisotropy (here $g = 0.98$) and when using a low number of ordinates (27 here).

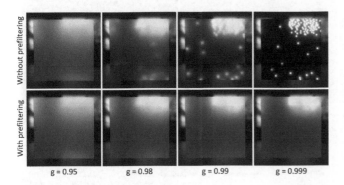

Without prefiltering   With prefiltering

$g = 0.95$ $g = 0.98$ $g = 0.99$ $g = 0.999$

Figure 6: The effect of prefiltered initialization on a thin, strongly-scattering medium with increasing anisotropy (left to right). Without prefiltering (top) the individual ordinates become apparent. Using prefiltering (bottom) the resulting images become much smoother and yield the expected appearance (more anisotropic slabs appear more transparent). Note that our technique is energy-conserving (as opposed to, e. g., singularity clamping in instant radiosity).

Ours ($g = 0$)   Ours ($g = 0.81$)   Ours ($g = 0.7$)   Ours ($g = 0.87$)   Ours ($g = 0.8$)   Ours ($g = 0.92$)   Ours ($g = 0.9$)

Light tracing ($g = 0$)   Light tracing ($g = 0.7$)   Light tracing ($g = 0.8$)   Light tracing ($g = 0.9$)

Figure 8: Comparison of our radial propagation to a Monte-Carlo reference for a uniform spherical medium (radius 2.5 m, $\sigma_s = \{0.8, 1, 1.3\}\,\mathrm{m}^{-1}$ and unit albedo). The resolution of the radial propagation grid was 32^3. Our solution differs from the reference mainly due to low (but for this propagation type still present) false scattering, in particular with low anisotropy values. We found that this can be reduced by artificially increasing g, if a specific appearance is desired.

energy corresponding to its associated portion of the directional domain Ω_n. We can account for the shape of Ω_n when determining the initial directional radiance distributions (parameter a_i in Sec. 3.1.1). Recall that the anisotropy parameter of f_{hg} represents the average cosine of the distribution. We can therefore approximate the initial $a_{n,i} = \int_{\Omega_n} -\mathbf{d}_n \cdot \omega \, d\omega / ||\Omega_n||$, the average cosine between $\mathbf{d}_n$ and the directions in Ω_n and use this value for the grid initialization. In practice, $a_{n,i}$ can be approximated without the integration over Ω_n for each ordinate or without even knowing the shape of Ω_n. As we importance-sample the environment map, the importance of the ordinate n is proportional and (up to a factor) very similar to the actual solid angle of Ω_n. Therefore, we use a heuristic that maps the importance $w_n \in (0, 1)$ to anisotropy as $a_{n,i} = (1 - w_n/N)^\beta$: important ordinates are denser in the directional domain and will have small solid angle and high anisotropy, less important ordinates are more sparse, will have larger solid angles and low anisotropy. The scalar factor $\beta > 0$ defines the proportionality and currently needs to be tuned empirically once for each environment map; from our experiments this is a simple and quick task.

Importance propagation   The described sampling scheme can be further improved by considering how much illumination from different directions actually contributes to the image. To this end, we introduce an additional *importance propagation* step before sampling

the environment map: we use a regular grid (perspective-warped into the camera frustum and oriented along the view direction) and propagate importance from the camera through the medium. Thanks to the duality of light transport this is equivalent to the radiance propagation as described before. The result of this propagation is a directional importance distribution stored in the grid cells. By ray-marching this grid we project the importance into the directional domain and create a directional importance 'map' that aligns with the environment map. We then sample the environment map according to its product with the importance map. We show that in certain situations this step improves the sampling result, especially when a low number of propagation grids is used (see Sec. 4 and Fig. 7). It is also quite cost-effective, since the directional importance function is typically very smooth and therefore only low resolutions for the propagation grid and the directional map are required (all our examples use the resolutions of 16^3 and 32×16 respectively).

3.3   Radial grids for local light sources

In order to extend our method to local light sources, we use spherical grids with two angular coordinates and a radial coordinate which is again aligned with the initial principal directions of the point source (Fig. 2). To obtain more isotropic cell shapes, the spacing of shells along the radial coordinate grows exponentially (in proportion to the radial segment length at a given radius). For parametrizing the spherical domain we use the octahedron parametrization [27] mainly as it is simple, provides reasonably uniform sampling, and above all, it discretizes the domain into a 2D square where every cell has four natural neighbours (plus two along the radial axis), similar to rectilinear grids. The resulting grid is thus topologically equivalent to rectilinear grid and albeit not being uniform, it allows

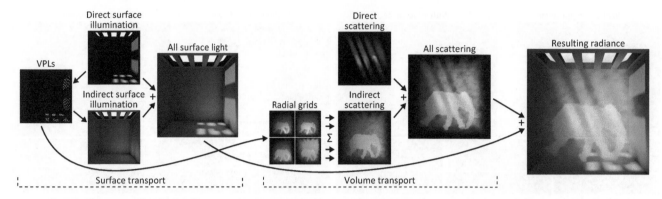

Figure 9: Workflow of the presented algorithm for a single directional light. For distant environment illumination the volumetric part of the pipeline is very similar, with the exception of rectilinear grids being used to propagate illumination from distant ordinates instead of the combination of VPLs and spherical grids.

Figure 10: In media like clouds the scattering anisotropy plays a significant role in their appearance, thus the common assumption of isotropic scattering prevents a believable rendition of such media. The clouds are rendered by the described method at 12 Hz using 64 ordinates and 20^3 grid resolution for each of them, with 15 propagation iterations. The scattering anisotropy was set to $g = 0.96$.

us to approximately treat the space as locally Euclidean and obtain plausible results again using virtually the same propagation scheme as before. The main difference in the propagation is that we have to account for the quadratic fall-off : although we base our propagation on radiance, we have to explicitly compensate for the varying grid cell sizes resulting from the non-uniform shell spacing. To this end, we scale the radiance when propagating along the principal direction in proportion to the radial coordinate spacing. A sample demonstration of this propagation type for a point light in a simple homogeneous spherical medium is shown in Fig. 8.

Instant radiosity Given the ability to use local point lights, we can use instant radiosity [14] methods, which represent complex illumination as a collection of point lights, to simulate surface-to-volume light transport. Normally these VPLs are obtained from random walks through the scene. In our interactive setting, we generate VPLs using a reflective shadow map (RSM) [4] for every primary light. We importance-sample these RSMs according to surface albedo and (attenuated) irradiance, aiming at keeping the total number of VPLs low. The reflected radiance is then used to initialize the radial propagation grids. Prefiltering can be done in the same way as for environment maps: VPLs with a large importance have a high initial anisotropy and vice versa. Similar to surface lighting, we can use clamping to reduce any remaining singularities [6]. Fig. 9 depicts the pipeline of the algorithm when propagating scattering from one directional light and VPLs generated from its RSM.

4 RESULTS

All results were computed on a laptop PC with a 2.0 GHz Intel Core i7 CPU, 16 GB of RAM and an NVidia GeForce GTX 485 Mobile card with 2 GB of VRAM. In all our measurements we use the framebuffer resolution of 800×600 in order to let the computation time be dominated by the propagation rather than ray-marching. Resolutions of the medium density datasets are typically in the order of tens in each dimension (but effectively enhanced by the procedural noise). Although the number of propagation iterations needs to be chosen empirically at the moment, in general we found that amounts similar to the propagation grid resolution along the propagation dimension is sufficient (around 10–20 in our examples). Other specific scene details are provided in the caption of each discussed figure.

We first tested our method for cloudy media with high scattering anisotropy in comparison to their isotropic versions (Fig. 10). It can be seen that our propagation scheme handles both cases well. Interestingly, grid resolutions as well as computation times required to render plausible participating media are rather insensitive to its anisotropy, i.e., anisotropic media render as fast as isotropic media. Although a larger number of ordinates is required to reproduce high-anisotropy effects, this additional effort is usually compensated by a decreased complexity of the spatial radiance distribution, which enables using coarser propagation grids.

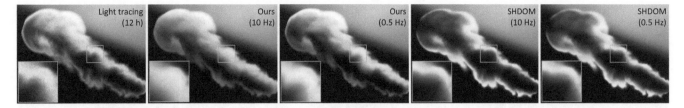

Figure 11: Comparison of our principal ordinates propagation to SHDOM and a Monte-Carlo reference, for a smoke plume 10 m across with $\sigma_s = \{2.9, 3.6, 4.2\}\,\text{m}^{-1}$, $\sigma_a = \{3.4, 3.35, 3.4\}\,\text{m}^{-1}$ and $g = 0.9$ using the "Uffizi" environment map as illumination. For our technique we used 64 and 125 principal ordinates, grid resolutions of 20^3 and 50^3, 10 and 30 propagation iterations, respectively. For SHDOM we have used 5 and 10 bands to represent the directional radiance distribution in each cell and the same grid resolutions. SHDOM required a strong prefiltering to avoid ringing and due to false scattering fails to reproduce the high scattering anisotropy. Our method compares well to the reference solution, and even with low-quality settings it matches the overall appearance.

Next, we compare our approach to an unbiased Monte-Carlo reference, as well as SHDOM, in Fig. 11. It is apparent that the described artifacts prevent SHDOM from handling anisotropic media correctly, despite being theoretically capable to do so.

The effect of using different numbers of principal ordinates is shown in Fig. 12. It can be seen that the discretization becomes apparent only with very few ordinates. The importance propagation usually helps to alleviate this by sampling those directions which will influence the solution most significantly. As Fig. 7 demonstrates, this is most likely the opposite side of the medium, suggesting that a simpler empirical heuristic could potentially work in certain cases.

One of the main shortcomings of the importance propagation is its potential temporal incoherency, mostly manifested by temporal flickering. For this reason we filter the importance map both spatially and temporarily, which, however, mainly distributes the incoherency over time. One of our main targets for future work is therefore improving this by explicitly enforcing temporal coherency when the sampled light sources relocate due to camera movement.

Prefiltering helps to improve the rendering quality in most scenarios and we used it to generate all results throughout the paper. It is particularly indispensable for media with an optical thickness insufficient to blur the sampled illumination, e. g., as in Fig. 6, where singularity-like artifacts would appear otherwise. Prefiltering removes these artifacts but still allows to perceive features of the background illumination, thanks to its adaptivity.

Finally in general, Fig. 1 and Fig. 13 show our propagation scheme for both regular and radial grids used to render multiple scattering effects in the volume stemming from direct illumination (light shafts), environment lighting, and indirect surface illumination (using virtual local light sources) under fully-dynamic conditions.

5 CONCLUSION

We propose a novel discrete ordinates method capable of computing light transport in heterogeneous participating media exhibiting light scattering of virtually arbitrary anisotropy. The method does not require any precomputations, which makes it suitable even for simulating dynamic and evolving media. Our representation also adapts to and prefilters the incident lighting. Radiance is represented by the Henyey-Greenstein distribution, and propagated by our novel scheme in volumes oriented along the principal light directions.

In general the steps of the proposed method are physically-plausible (please refer to the supplementary materials for further details). The employed empirical heuristics introduce a certain bias but allow us to make design decisions that result in a near-realtime performance on contemporary graphics hardware.

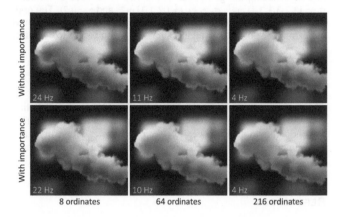

Figure 12: The smoke dataset with an increasing number of ordinates using the "kitchen" environment map ($g = 0.9$, 20^3 grid resolution, 10 propagation iterations). Accounting for importance improves the results, mainly if low numbers of principal ordinates are used. The typical setting we use is shown on the bottom-centre and takes 10 ms for importance propagation, 4 ms for determining the ordinates, 7 ms for grid initialization, 50 ms for propagation, 10 ms for residuum propagation, 3 ms for upsampling and 11 ms for ray-marching.

The decomposition into a finite number of directions for distant light can only be successful if the variation of the initial light distribution is not too high; this however holds for the HDR environment maps we used in our examples. In addition our prefiltered initialization can be used to avoid discretization artifacts in favour of a smooth approximation. Another limitation that we share with most variants of DOM is the handling of (surface) boundaries. In volumes with high density gradients (close to opaque surfaces) the light distribution might not be faithfully reproduced by the HG basis aligned with the initial light direction. Also the resolution of every principal grid is limited and therefore the general limitations of discrete sampling apply: for finer details more resolution is required. Fortunately, the upsampling and prefiltering help to defer this problem and for typical volume data sets moderate propagation grid resolutions of 8^3–20^3 have shown to be sufficient to handle a wide range of illumination conditions and medium properties.

As future work, we would like to extend our propagation to work on hierarchical or nested grids to handle higher details in media as well as illumination. In general, we believe that the effect of complex lighting on dynamic participating media is an exciting visual phenomenon that deserves more dedicated research, e. g., to better understand human perception of volumetric light or the artistic practice applied to depict it.

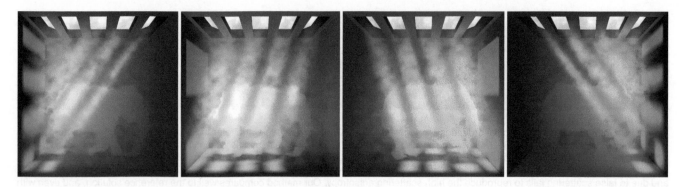

Figure 13: A scene with both animated medium and illumination, combining scattering from directional and local virtual light sources (running at $9\,\mathrm{Hz}$ including the generation of the 125 VPLs used to render indirect illumination from surfaces; the medium has a size of 20^3 m with $\sigma_s = \{3.2, 3.3, 3.4\}\,\mathrm{m}^{-1}$, $\sigma_a = \{1.15, 1.2, 1.3\}\,\mathrm{m}^{-1}$ and $g = 0.7$). The grid size for the directional light is $128^2 \times 16$, with the 16-cell axis oriented along the light shafts (i. e., along the principal ordinate). The radial grids have a resolution of 8^3 each. We use these settings for local light sources in all our examples; note how even this small resolution proves to be sufficient for plausible results.

ACKNOWLEDGEMENTS

We would like to thank Chuong Nguyen, Peter Vangorp and Yulia Gryaditskaya for proofreading, Anton Kaplanyan for discussions, and the anonymous reviewers for their feedback. This work has been supported by the Max Planck Center for Visual Computing and Communication.

REFERENCES

[1] M. Billeter, E. Sintorn, and U. Assarsson. Real-time multiple scattering using light propagation volumes. In *Proc. I3D*, 2012.

[2] A. Bouthors, F. Neyret, N. Max, E. Bruneton, and C. Crassin. Interactive multiple anisotropic scattering in clouds. In *Proc. I3D*, 2008.

[3] S. Chandrasekhar. *Radiative transfer*. Dover Publications, 1960.

[4] C. Dachsbacher and M. Stamminger. Reflective Shadow Maps. In *Proc. I3D*, pages 203–213, 2005.

[5] T. Engelhardt and C. Dachsbacher. Epipolar sampling for shadows and crepuscular rays in participating media with single scattering. In *Proc. I3D*, 2010.

[6] T. Engelhardt, J. Novák, T.-W. Schmidt, and C. Dachsbacher. Approximate bias compensation for rendering scenes with heterogeneous participating media. *Comp. Graph. Forum*, 31(7):2145–2154, 2012.

[7] R. Fattal. Participating media illumination using light propagation maps. *ACM Trans. Graph.*, 28:7:1–7:11, 2009.

[8] R. Geist, K. Rasche, J. Westall, and R. Schalkoff. Lattice-Boltzmann lighting. In *Proc. EGSR*, pages 355–362, 2004.

[9] L. G. Henyey and J. L. Greenstein. Diffuse radiation in the Galaxy. *Astrophysical Journal*, 93:70–83, 1941.

[10] W. Jarosz, C. Donner, M. Zwicker, and H. W. Jensen. Radiance caching for participating media. *ACM Trans. Graph.*, 27:7:1–7:11, 2008.

[11] W. Jarosz, D. Nowrouzezahrai, I. Sadeghi, and H. W. Jensen. A comprehensive theory of volumetric radiance estimation using photon points and beams. *ACM Trans. Graph.*, 30:5:1–5:19, 2011.

[12] H. W. Jensen and P. H. Christensen. Efficient simulation of light transport in scenes with participating media using photon maps. In *Proc. SIGGRAPH*, pages 311–320, 1998.

[13] A. Kaplanyan and C. Dachsbacher. Cascaded light propagation volumes for real-time indirect illumination. In *Proc. I3D*, 2010.

[14] A. Keller. Instant radiosity. In *Proc. SIGGRAPH*, pages 49–56, 1997.

[15] J. Kniss, S. Premože, C. Hansen, and D. Ebert. Interactive translucent volume rendering and procedural modeling. In *Proc. Visualization*, pages 109–116, 2002.

[16] J. Kopf, M. F. Cohen, D. Lischinski, and M. Uyttendaele. Joint bilateral upsampling. *ACM Trans. Graph*, 26(3):96, 2007.

[17] J. Krüger, K. Bürger, and R. Westermann. Interactive screen-space accurate photon tracing on GPUs. In *Proc. EGSR*, 2006.

[18] E. P. Lafortune and Y. D. Willems. Rendering participating media with bidirectional path tracing. In *Proc. EGWR*, pages 91–100, 1996.

[19] G. Liktor and C. Dachsbacher. Real-time volume caustics with adaptive beam tracing. In *Proc. I3D*, 2011.

[20] T. Lokovic and E. Veach. Deep shadow maps. In *Proc. SIGGRAPH*, pages 385–392, 2000.

[21] N. Max. Optical models for direct volume rendering. *IEEE Trans. Vis. and Computer Graphics*, 1:99–108, 1995.

[22] N. Max, G. Schussman, R. Miyazaki, K. Iwasaki, and T. Nishita. Diffusion and multiple anisotropic scattering for global illumination in clouds. *J. WSCG*, 1–3:277–284, 2004.

[23] S. G. Narasimhan, M. Gupta, C. Donner, R. Ramamoorthi, S. K. Nayar, and H. W. Jensen. Acquiring scattering properties of participating media by dilution. *ACM Trans. Graph.*, 25:1003–1012, 2006.

[24] J. Novák, D. Nowrouzezahrai, C. Dachsbacher, and W. Jarosz. Progressive virtual beam lights. *Comp. Graph. Forum*, 31:1407–1413, 2012.

[25] J. Novák, D. Nowrouzezahrai, C. Dachsbacher, and W. Jarosz. Virtual ray lights for rendering scenes with participating media. *ACM Trans. Graph.*, 29(4):60:1–60:11, 2012.

[26] M. Pauly, T. Kollig, and A. Keller. Metropolis light transport for participating media. In *Proc. EGWR*, pages 11–22, 2000.

[27] E. Praun and H. Hoppe. Spherical parametrization and remeshing. *ACM Trans. Graph.*, 22(3):340–49, 2003.

[28] Z. Ren, K. Zhou, S. Lin, and B. Guo. Gradient-based interpolation and sampling for real-time rendering of inhomogeneous, single-scattering media. Technical Report MSR-TR-2008-51, Microsoft Research, 2008.

[29] H. E. Rushmeier and K. E. Torrance. The zonal method for calculating light intensities in the presence of a participating medium. *Computer Graphics (Proc. SIGGRAPH)*, 21:293–302, 1987.

[30] M. Salvi, K. Vidimče, A. Lauritzen, and A. Lefohn. Adaptive volumetric shadow maps. In *Proc. EGSR*, pages 1289–1296, June 2010.

[31] P. Sloan, J. Kautz, and J. Snyder. Precomputed radiance transfer for real-time rendering in dynamic, low-frequency lighting environments. In *ACM Trans. Graph.*, 2002.

[32] J. Stam. Multiple scattering as a diffusion process. In *Proc. EGWR*, pages 41–50, 1995.

[33] Y. Wang, J. Wang, N. Holzschuch, K. Subr, J.-H. Yong, and B. Guo. Real-time rendering of heterogeneous translucent objects with arbitrary shapes. *Comp. Graph. Forum*, 29:497–506, 2010.

[34] K. Zhou, Z. Ren, S. Lin, H. Bao, B. Guo, and H.-Y. Shum. Real-time smoke rendering using compensated ray marching. In *ACM Trans. Graph.*, pages 36:1–36:12, 2008.

Micro-buffer Rasterization Reduction Method
for Environment Lighting Using Point-based Rendering

Takahiro Harada*

Advanced Micro Devices, Inc.

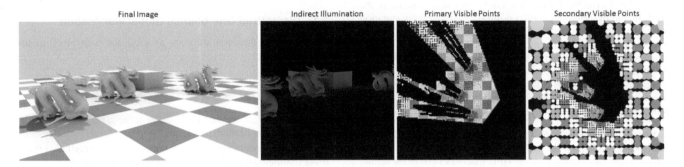

Figure 1: Indirect illumination under environment lighting is calculated by detecting primary visible points, then secondary visible points. Direct illumination on secondary visible points are used to render indirect illumination.

ABSTRACT

This paper proposes a point-based rendering pipeline for indirect illumination for environment lighting. The method improves the efficiency of the algorithm used in the previous studies that calculate direct illumination on all the points in the scene which is prohibitively expensive for environment lighting because it requires a hemispherical integration for each point to compute direct illumination. The proposed rendering pipeline reduces the number of direct illumination computations by introducing approximations and careful selection of points on which indirect illumination is calculated. More specifically, the rendering pipeline first selects primary visible points on which indirect illumination is calculated from the point hierarchy. A micro-buffer is rasterized for each primary visible point to identify secondary visible points whose direct illumination affects indirect illumination of a primary visible point. Dependency of those points is analyzed and approximations are introduced to reduce the number of points on which micro-buffer rasterization is executed to calculate direct illumination. After direct illumination is obtained for those points, direct illumination on all of the primary and secondary visible points is calculated by illumination propagation without rasterizing any micro-buffer. The method can be used for a dynamic scene if it is combined with dynamic point hierarchy update.

Index Terms: I.3.7 [Computer Graphics]: Three-Dimensional Graphics and Realism—Color, shading, shadowing, and texture

1 INTRODUCTION

Point-based global illumination is a technique to compute global illumination widely used in VFX [2]. Recent work studied ways to accelerate it using the computational power of the GPU [12]. Most of this research focused on a closed environment under a few analytic lights. To compute indirect illumination under such conditions, existing works compute direct illumination on all the points

in the scene first; then, those points are used to calculate indirect illumination on the screen. We can use such an approach for this type of scene because direct illumination computation is computationally inexpensive and direct illumination of most of the points can affect indirect illumination of the visible surface in the scene. However, for an open outdoor scene under environment lighting, the situation is different; direct illumination computation is computationally expensive because it requires hemispherical integration, and it is likely that direct illumination on many points will not affect indirect illumination on the visible surface of the scene. Therefore, it is not practical to use the existing approach.

This paper proposes a point-based global illumination rendering pipeline for such a scene that computes at interactive speed one-bounce indirect illumination for environment lighting as shown in Fig. 1. The key of the algorithm and the primary contribution of this paper is reduction of micro-buffer rasterization used for hemispherical integration. As micro-buffer rasterization is computationally expensive, reduction of the operation is important to improve the performance of the rendering. The rendering pipeline does not require precomputation except for point hierarchy generation. Thus, the method is also applicable for a dynamic scene with a dynamic point hierarchy generation technique.

The method first selects primary visible points on which indirect illumination is calculated from the point hierarchy. Secondary visible points whose direct illumination affects indirect illumination of primary visible points are gathered by rasterizing a micro-buffer for each primary visible point. Then dependency among secondary visible points is analyzed to identify points on which direct illumination computation using hemispherical integration is inevitable. Approximations are also introduced to reduce the number of micro-buffer rasterizations.

We apply the proposed rendering pipeline to several scenes and show that the proposed method reduces the number of micro-buffer rasterizations drastically, which is essential to render indirect illumination for environment lighting at interactive speed.

2 RELATED WORKS

Interactive global illumination computation is an active area of research. A complete review can be found in [11]. Recently, methods

---

*e-mail: takahiro.harada@amd.com
Graphics Interface Conference 2014
7-9 May, Montreal, Quebec, Canada

using a hierarchical grid were studied [9] [3]. One advantage of using a grid for global illumination computation is the decoupling of the scene mesh complexity from the computational cost because it does not use scene geometry directly. Those indirect illumination computation methods rely on the computation of direct illumination on reflective shadow maps [4]. Therefore, most of the existing methods compute indirect illumination only from analytic lights but not from an environment light.

Another hierarchical data structure to represent a scene is the point hierarchy. Bunnell started using point-based representation for global illumination effects [1]. They showed that it is possible to compute a high-quality ambient occlusion without any precomputation except for the hierarchy generation. [5] extended the work to consider occlusion of points. They rasterized the point hierarchy to a cube map storing the closest point for each direction. However, because of restriction on the GPU at the time, part of the rendering pipeline was executed on the CPU.

Ritschel *et al.* developed a method to run point-based global illumination entirely on the GPU by implementing point-hierarchy traversal and rasterization on the GPU that was performed on the CPU in the previous work [12] [5]. They also proposed to creating a mapping function for each BRDF that makes it possible to perform an importance sampling, which maximizes the usage of a limited number of texels in a small micro-buffer. All the works discussed so far traverses the point hierarchy for detection of the visible point in a direction; Maletz and Wang introduced a stochastic sampling of points for micro-buffer rasterization [10]. Because this method does not require traversal of the point hierarchy, a micro-buffer rasterization is parallelized. Those optimizations of micro-buffer rasterization are orthogonal to our work which proposes a rendering framework of global illumination under environmental lighting. Therefore, they can be integrated to the proposed method to further accelerate illumination computation.

Wang *et al.* focused on the redundancy of micro-buffer rasterization. They reduced computational cost by clustering visible pixels and execute a rough tree traversal first which is followed by detailed tree traversal for each pixel [16]. Although this work is similar to this paper because it also reduces redundancy of micro-buffer rasterization [16], a major difference between their work and our work is that their method is not reducing any redundant computation on direct illumination while our method does. Therefore, all the examples in their paper is illuminated by analytic lights but no environmental light.

All previous research on the point-based method was for a small closed scene under analytic lights such as point or directional lights. For such a scene, we can first calculate direct illumination on all the points in the scene and then use it to compute indirect illumination. We can use this method because direct illumination computation is computationally inexpensive and direct illumination on most of the points affects indirect illumination on another point; therefore, there is not much unnecessary computation. However, this is not the case for an open outdoor scene in which there could be many points whose direct illumination does not affect illumination on any point. Also, an environment light is often used as well as analytic lights for an open scene. Direct illumination computation from an environment light is not as computationally cheap as computing illumination from analytic lights because it requires hemispherical integration. Therefore, it is not practical to compute direct illumination on all the points in the scene, as most of the previous work did.

This paper proposes a solution to compute at interactive speeds the indirect illumination for an open scene under an environment light.

3 METHOD

In this section, we first give a general description about one-bounce global illumination and discretized form of the rendering equation in Sec. 3.1. Then we describe how one-bounce global illumination is solved using point-based method in Sec. 3.2 in which we also discuss about challenges for a scene lit by an environmental light, and the key ideas about this paper. The detail of the proposed method is described in Sec. 3.3, 3.4, and 3.5.

3.1 Discretized One-bounce Global Illumination

The rendering equation we want to solve for each pixel on the screen is

$$L_o(x^0, \omega_o) = \int_\omega f(x^0) \left(L_i^D(x^0, \omega) + L_i^I(x^0, \omega) \right) \left(n(x^0) \cdot \omega \right) d\omega \tag{1}$$

where x^0, f, L_i^D, L_i^I are surface position at the pixel, BRDF, and direct and indirect illumination terms.

If the hemisphere is split into n non-overlapping regions, Eqn. 1 is approximated with the following discretized equation.

$$\begin{aligned} L_o(x^0, \omega_o) &\approx \sum_{i \in n} f(x^0) L_i^D(x^0, \omega_i) \left(n(x^0) \cdot \omega_i \right) \Delta\omega \\ &+ \sum_{i \in n} f(x^0) L_i^I(x^0, \omega_i) \left(n(x^0) \cdot \omega_i \right) \Delta\omega \end{aligned} \tag{2}$$

If $\Delta\omega$ is small enough, we find point x_i^1, which is visible from x^0 in the direction of ω_i. Therefore, once the set of points $x^1 = \{x_0^1, x_1^1, \cdots, x_{n-1}^1\}$ is found, we can solve the direct illumination term in Eqn. 2 because $L_i^D(x^0, \omega_i) = L_o^D(x_i^1, \omega_i)$ can be sampled from an environment light and mask it $(L_o^D(x_i^1, \omega_i) = 0)$ for the direction where x_i^1 is found.

For the indirect illumination term in Eqn. 2, we need to calculate incoming radiance from x_i^1 in the direction of ω_i. This can be obtained by solving Eqn. 2 at x_i^1. If only one-bounce indirect illumination is considered, the indirect illumination term of Eqn. 2 can be dropped. Thus, the equation we need to evaluate is

$$L_o(x_i^1, \omega_i) \approx \sum_{j \in n} f(x_i^1) L_o^D(x_j^2, \omega_j) \left(n(x_i^1) \cdot \omega_j \right) \Delta\omega. \tag{3}$$

In the same way as finding x^0, we find point x_j^2, which is visible from x_i^1 in the direction of ω_j. Once the set of points x^2 is found, we can evaluate this equation in the same way we did for the direct illumination term in Eqn. 2.

Therefore, the discretized rendering equation can be solved once we found x^1 for all the pixels and x^2 for all x^1.

3.2 Point-based Global Illumination

Point-based global illumination first converts scene geometry to set of points. It uses those points for computation of illumination.

3.2.1 Point Hierarchy

Conversion of scene geometry to points are done by generating points uniformly on the surface of scene geometry. Those points are used to build a point hierarchy in which they are stored as leaf nodes. We used a top down construction in which points are split into two groups at each level. A node of the hierarchy stores references to children, and position, radius, normal vector and cone angle of the point [13].

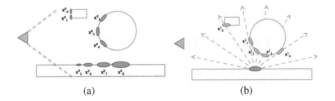

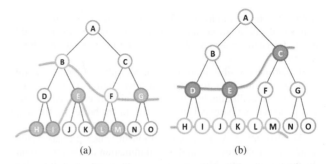

(a)   (b)

Figure 2: (a) Primary visible points. (b) Secondary visible points.

3.2.2 Point-based Hemispherical Integration

Using point hierarchy described in Sec. 3.2.1, point-based global illumination evaluates the discretized hemispherical integration in two steps.

The first step is to find visible points from a surface point for all the discretized directions using micro-buffer rasterization. For point x^i, micro-buffer rasterization finds the set of points $x^{i+1} = \{x^{i+1}_0, x^{i+1}_1, \cdots, x^{i+1}_{n-1}\}$.

Once those points are found, they can be used to compute global illumination at x^i. For instance, indirect illumination at x^i can be calculated as follows once direct illumination on those points are calculated.

$$L_o^I(x^i, \omega_i) = \sum_{j \in n} f(x^i) L_o^D(x^{i+1}_j, \omega_j) \left(n(x^i) \cdot \omega_j \right) \Delta \omega \qquad (4)$$

This process is called evaluation of a micro-buffer.

This equation is identical to the direct illumination term in the discretized rendering equation in Eqn. 2. Therefore, the point-based hemispherical integration can be used to calculate direct illumination.

To evaluate one-bounce indirect illumination, we could apply the brute-force method in which direct illumination is evaluated first for each leaf point and the values then are used to calculate direct illumination of internal points in the point hierarchy by propagating illumination from leaf points. Then a micro-buffer is rasterized for each pixel on the screen. This is the method employed by previous works to calculate indirect illumination using point-based global illumination. However, direct illumination computation is too expensive for an interactive application when hemispherical integration via micro-buffer rasterization is necessary for each point. One-bounce indirect illumination computation under environment lighting is such a case.

The proposed rendering pipeline reduces the number of micro-buffer rasterizations by introducing the following key ideas.

1. There is a dependency of direct illumination on x^1. Therefore, there is a subset of x^1 on which hemispherical integration is inevitable.

2. By selecting x^0, where points on which Eqn.2 is evaluated from the point hierarchy, there is an overlap between x^0 and x^1.

In the following, we call x^0 and x^1 primary and secondary visible points, respectively, because x^0 are points visible from the camera and x^1 are points visible from the camera after one bounce (Fig. 2).

3.3 Direct Illumination on Secondary Visible Points

If we assume that we have selected primary visible points x^0, we can obtain the list of secondary visible points by rasterizing a micro-buffer for each of those points. When indirect illumination is only calculated up to one-bounce effect, all we need is direct illumination on secondary visible points. Direct illumination on a secondary visible point can be calculated by selecting leaf points that have the

(a)   (b)

Figure 3: The green curve is a cut of visible points from a primary visible point. The blue curve is a cut of visible points from the camera (i.e., primary visible points). Points filled with a solid colors are points on which direct illumination needs to be calculated by micro-buffer rasterization. (a) There are two cuts from two primary visible points. Direct illumination on F is obtained from values on L and M; thus F does not require its own micro-buffer. B has a child D on which direct illumination is not calculated. However, the value on D is obtained from H and I; therefore, illumination on B is deduced from its children. (b) Direct illumination on all the secondary visible points in this figure is calculated from values on primary visible points.

point as an ancestor, rasterizing a micro-buffer for each of those leaf points, and averaging values by using areas of points as weights.

However, the amount of direct illumination computation is reduced by introducing an approximation. Secondary visible points are selected from the appropriate level of the point hierarchy so they occupy almost the same solid angle from a primary visible point. Therefore the contributions of illumination from secondary visible points to a primary visible point are almost the same even if the size of the points is different. This means that direct illumination calculation at the resolution of secondary visible points makes uniform the resolution of computation. Therefore, direct illumination is calculated once at the center of the point rather than on all the leaf points that are descendants of the secondary visible point.

By using the dependency among secondary visible points, we reduce the number of micro-buffer rasterization further, while increasing the accuracy of direct illumination computation. If two children of a secondary visible point are included with the secondary visible point, direct illumination is calculated for those child points by hemispherical integration. Then, direct illumination on the secondary visible point parent to those child nodes can be calculated by the weighted average of direct illumination on the children. For example, F in Fig. 3 (a) corresponds to the parent in this case where it has children L and M both of which are included with the secondary visible point. the parent is F and children are L and M. By re-using direct illumination on children, we execute only two micro-buffer rasterizations and the weighted average of illumination values, whereas three micro-buffer rasterizations were necessary when the dependency among them was ignored.

Even if both its direct children are not included with the secondary visible point, direct illumination of the node can be calculated by values on descendants if secondary visible points form a cut of the hierarchy under the point. A secondary visible point on which hemispherical integration is not necessary can be detected by traversing the hierarchy upward from all the secondary visible points. This is illustrated in Fig. 3 (a).

3.4 Selection of Primary Visible Points

An obvious choice for primary visible points is points at which primary rays for pixels hit a scene. However, it requires an additional micro-buffer rasterization for each pixel to identify secondary visible points in the hierarchy. Instead, we select primary visible points from the point hierarchy too. This choice allows us to reduce the number of micro-buffer rasterizations. To find secondary visible points for each primary visible point, micro-buffer rasterization is required.

If a primary visible point is included with a secondary visible point, we do not have to rasterize a micro-buffer for the point to calculate direct illumination because it is already executed to detect secondary visible points. Thus, we have micro-buffer for the point already.

We also introduce an approximation in which primary visible points are small enough that direct illumination on the area around the point is uniform. More specifically, we assume that direct illumination on all of its descendants is equal to the illumination of the point. By using the assumption, direct illumination of a secondary visible point that has a primary visible point as an ancestor does not need to be calculated by micro-buffer rasterization; instead, the value is copied from the value of the ancestor. Those secondary visible points whose direct illumination is obtained from primary visible points are detected by downward traversal of the point hierarchy as illustrated in Fig. 3 (b).

Micro-buffer rasterizations are executed for secondary visible points whose direct illumination is not computed from direct illumination on other secondary visible points and primary visible points. Then direct illumination on those points and primary visible points are propagated in the hierarchy to obtain direct illumination on all the secondary visible points.

3.5 Illumination Calculation on Frame Buffer

Once direct illumination on all the secondary visible points is calculated, indirect illumination is evaluated at primary visible points by Eqn. 2. However, the resolution of indirect illumination calculation is different from screen pixel resolution, i.e., we need to calculate indirect illumination for those primary visible points as well as all the pixels on the screen. Therefore, calculating indirect illumination on primary visible points is not enough.

Instead, primary visible points close to the surface at a pixel are searched for in the object space. Once m nearest primary visible points are found, outgoing radiance at the pixel is calculated by taking a weighted average.

$$L_o(x, \omega) = \sum_{k \in m} w_k \sum_{j \in n} f(x) L_i^i(x_k^0, \omega_j) \left(n(x) \cdot \omega_j \right) \Delta \omega \quad (5)$$

This is essentially the same as a radiance cache in which primary visible points are used as cached location [6].

Direct illumination has to be calculated for each pixel on the screen. However, direct illumination from environment lighting is expensive and low-frequency. Therefore, instead of calculating it on a per-pixel basis, it is also calculated at each radiance cached point or primary visible point at this stage of the pipeline. In this way, direct illumination is calculated almost for free on primary visible points because micro-buffers are already rasterized when secondary visible points are searched for.

4 IMPLEMENTATION DETAILS

The proposed method is implemented on the GPU using OpenCL and OpenGL. Therefore, we are going to use OpenCL terminology for explanation of a parallel implementation. Fig. 4 is an overview of the entire rendering pipeline detailed in this section.

Data structure   Points are generated uniformly on the surfaces of the scene by using a low-discrepancy sequence. Then a binary bounding volume hierarchy is built on those points. Each point in the hierarchy stores position, radius, normal vector, and cone angle of the point [13]. Those data are stored without quantization (i.e., occupying 32 bytes). In addition to those, we allocate two child indices, a skip index that is used for stackless traversal, and a 32bit

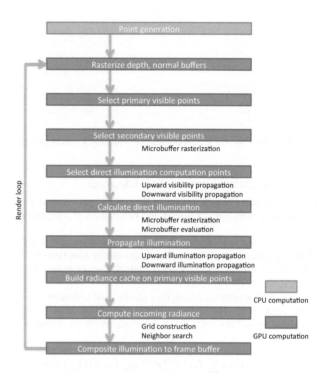

Figure 4: Overview of rendering pipeline.

field that is used for selection of a subset of secondary visible points on which micro-buffer rasterization is executed. Therefore, the size of a point is 48 bytes. Point generation and hierarchy construction are done before the rendering loop starts. This step is the only step executed on the CPU. It took a few seconds for all the examples.

Select Primary Visible Points   To select primary visible points, the point hierarchy is traversed and a cut is defined at the points whose solid angle is below the threshold. Note that we do not collect all the points meeting the criteria which includes most of the leaf points; instead, we collect just a set of points belonging to the cut.

If we select points by checking only the solid angle, it contains a point that has a large cone angle [13]. However, using such a point for a radiance cache increases the error of radiance interpolation. Thus, the cone angle of a point is also compared to the threshold angle. This results in gathering higher-resolution points at a corner of a geometry, which is similar to the strategy of placing cached points for irradiance caching [17].

For a single-threaded implementation, we descend the point hierarchy from the root until we hit a point that satisfies the criteria. For a parallel implementation, a work-item is executed for each point of the hierarchy. It exits if the node does not meet the two criteria. It then checks its two child points. A child point satisfying the conditions is projected into screen space and the depth of the point is compared to the depth stored in the depth buffer at the screen-space position. A point passing the test is appended to the list of primary visible points. The reason we need to check two levels of the hierarchy is because we need to collect points at the cut. In other words, we need to detect the discontinuity of the conditions in the hierarchy.

The left half of Fig. 5 shows the primary visible points selected for a scene. They are different from points stored at the leaf level in the hierarchy shown on the right half of Fig. 5.

Select Secondary Visible Points   Micro-buffer rasterization for primary visible points is implemented in the same way as [12]. A work-item is executed for a primary visible point and it raster-

Figure 5: Left and right halves show primary visible points and points stored at leaf level, respectively.

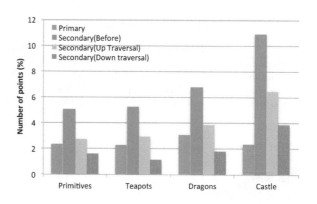

Figure 6: Ratio of the number of points detected as primary and secondary visible points to the number of points generated for each scene.

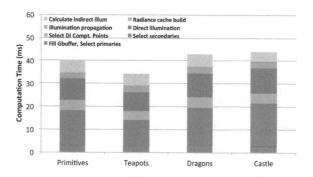

Figure 7: Break down of computation time.

izes a micro-buffer storing depth and point index. Depth and point index are compressed into 8 and 24 bits and packed into a 32-bit value. Micro-buffers are stored in global memory. For all the results shown in Sec. 5, the resolution of micro-buffers was set to 16×16 and 8×8 for rasterization at primary and secondary visible points, respectively. Points are transformed from world space to a micro-buffer using the paraboloid projection [8]. Ray-casting is used to calculate accurate occlusion from leaf points.

After storing point indices in micro-buffers, the indices are used to build a list of secondary visible points.

Select Direct Illumination Computation Points   To select secondary visible points on which micro-buffer rasterization is inevitable, the hierarchy is traversed upward and downward. For upward traversal, a work-item is executed for each leaf point. Each work-item ascends the tree by reading the parent pointer for a point that is computed in advance. Because we use a binary tree, an internal point is always touched twice by work-items processing its children. To compute visibility of the point correctly, visibility on both children must be computed before the point is processed. Therefore, the first work item to visit the point exits the computation and the second work-item processes the point. This guarantees that visibility is propagated to both children when the point is processed. The order of arrival at a point is checked by using an atomic operation on a counter prepared for each point.

Downward propagation is a parallel computation for each primary visible point because they belong to a cut of the point hierarchy that guarantees that a primary visible point does not have any primary visible point as a descendant. Therefore a work-item executed for a primary visible point descends the tree from the point.

Calculate Direct Illumination   Direct illumination from environment lighting is calculated by using a micro-buffer storing a visible node index for each texel to calculate occlusion. Incoming light is accumulated from texels of micro-buffer which does not have a node index. For environmental light, one texture look up for the direction of a texel is executed to obtain incoming light. For secondary visible points, we do not have micro-buffers. Therefore, it must be rasterized and then evaluated. Occlusion from analytic lights such as directional light is calculated by shadow map. At this point, we have direct illumination only on a portion of the secondary visible points. Direct illumination on other points is computed by the following illumination propagation.

Propagate Illumination   Propagation of direct illumination on points is performed in the same way as the selection of direct-illumination computation points. A work-item is executed for a leaf point and a primary visible point on upward and downward propagations, respectively.

Build Radiance Cache   A workgroup is executed for a visible point to convert point index to radiance for each texel in a micro-buffer by looking up illumination on points. After obtaining incoming radiance from all the directions, it is convolved to build a pre-convolved radiance cache [14]. In this work, we created a pre-convolved radiance cache for diffuse BRDF at 5×5 resolution.

Calculate Indirect Illumination   For an efficient neighboring search for radiance caches for a pixel, we build a screen-space two-dimensional grid in which a cell of the grid corresponds to a tile in the screen, as in [7]. The effective radius for each point is defined as a linear function of the radius of a point. Because we chose points with small radius on a surface close to the camera and points with large radius on surface far from the camera, a point close to the camera has a smaller cache footprint while a point far from the camera has a larger cache footprint. A bounding volume for each radiance-cached point constructed in the screen space is used to identify the overlapping cells to which a reference of the point is stored. We store references of a point to all overlapping cells. This increases the memory usage but it simplifies the neighbor search, which is usually more expensive than building a grid. Construction of a grid is implemented in three steps; count number of points in each cell, scan the counts to obtain an offset for each cell, and fill the buffer with references of points. The data of the grid is one dimensional index buffer which is more efficient on query compared to other data structures such as linked list.

After the 2D grid is built, we execute a work-item for a pixel in the screen. A work-item fetches the world position and normal vector of the pixel first and iterates through the list of radiance caches stored in the cell to which the pixel belongs. The weight function proposed in [17], with clamping by maximum angle is used to cal-

Table 1: Test scene data

	Primitives	Teapots	Dragons	Castle
Triangle count	3.67k	3.1k	180.91k	57.13k
Rendering time (ms)	40.00	34.4	42.97	44.09
Primary vis. points	11.72k	11.45k	15.52k	11.72k
Secondary vis. points	8.04k	5.73k	9.14k	19.32k

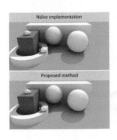

Figure 9: Comparison to the brute-force implementation. Root mean square error (RMSE) is 0.00378. The difference is magnified by 64.

culate a weight from a cache. 2D workgroups are executed in which a workgroup processes pixels in a cell of the 2D grid to increase the coherency of memory access to the radiance cache in a grid cell.

5 RESULTS AND DISCUSSION

We test the proposed method on a system with an AMD Radeon™ R9 290X GPU and an AMD FX-8150 CPU. Test scenes are converted to 500,000 points and rendered under a uniform environment light and a directional light. Therefore, memory footprint for the point hierarchy is 48MB. The scenes are rendered at 1280×720 screen resolution and screenshots of final rendering are shown in the first column of Fig. 1 and Fig. 8. The third column of those figures shows primary visible points rendered from the top of the scenes. We can see that it captures points that are in the view frustum but not occluded by other geometries. We can also see that the size of points increases as the distance from the camera increases. The number of primary visible points for all the test scenes is less than 5% of the number of points generated for the scene (Fig. 6).

We also counted the number of secondary visible points before and after upward and downward hierarchy traversals (Fig. 6). For the scene "Primitives", the number of secondary visible points is reduced from 25.28k to 13.59k after upward traversal. After downward traversal, it is reduced further to 8.04k which is only less than 2% of all the generated points. Also, we can see that the proposed rendering pipeline culled about 70% of the secondary visible points for this scene. The secondary visible points on which direct illumination are computed using micro-buffer rasterizations are visualized at the right-most column of Fig. 1 and Fig. 8. We can see that it does not include points that are in the view frustum except for those which were occluded by a geometry; points in the view frustum are culled because a primary visible point is found as an ancestor. Also, this method does not compute direct illumination on fine resolution at the location far from the camera frustum. From Fig. 6, we can see that the scene "Castle" has more secondary visible points than other scenes. This comes from the nature of the point-based method, which captures more points at a fine level than at a coarse level at a concave edge of a geometry. Because the proposed method culls secondary visible points by traversing upward, it does not reduce points at lower level of the hierarchy. In other words, there is a room for improving the point-reduction algorithm.

The total number of micro-buffer rasterization executed is the number of primary visible points plus remaining secondary visible points after hierarchy traversals; for example, it is 19.76k for the scene "Primitives". For the brute-force implementation, we need to rasterize a micro-buffer for all the points generated on the surface at least (i.e., 500,000 points in those tests). Therefore, our rendering pipeline is rasterizing less than 5% of the brute-force implementation.

Furthermore, if final gathering is performed for each pixel of the screen, we need to execute on the order of another 1 million micro-buffer rasterizations. Thus, the proposed method realizes indirect illumination under an environment light with a fraction of micro-buffer rasterizations compared to the brute-force implementation.

A breakdown of the computation time is measured and shown in Fig. 7. Rendering a frame of those test scenes took from $34ms$ to $44ms$. Computation time is almost irrelevant to the polygon count for the scene although time for selection of secondary visible points that executes micro-buffer rasterization on primary visible points varies slightly. This is because the number of primary visible points is not the same for those scenes. We can also see that the scene "Castle" takes more time for direct illumination which includes micro-buffer rasterization for secondary visible points. This is because the number of points on which direct illumination has to be evaluated for this scene is more than the other scenes (Table 1).

To evaluate the approximation introduced in this work, a rendered image for scene "Primitives" is compared to an image rendered with the brute-force implementation that calculates direct illumination on all the leaf points and is propagated to the entire hierarchy. Although there is error around the small features of teapots, the difference is negligible, as we can see in Fig. 9.

One of the differentiator of the proposed method from existing works is that the proposed method is capable of computing indirect illumination under environmental light. To illustrate it, scenes are rendered only with different environmental lights and shown in Fig. 10.

Multiple Bounces To extend the proposed method to more than one bounce global illumination, we can repeat the step of selection of secondary visible points. However, each step of micro-buffer rasterization finds more points to be illuminated. Thus the difference between the proposed method and the brute-force implementation would get smaller as the number of bounces increases. Therefore, the proposed method would be more effective for a scene with small number of bounces.

Glossy Surface Glossy surface is one of the challenges for point-based global illumination as more micro-buffer resolution has to be allocated for reflection direction [15]. It does apply to the proposed method. All the discussion of this paper is focused on diffuse surface. To apply the method to glossy surface on which outgoing radiance is not constant in direction, we need to store the outgoing radiance on secondary visible points as directional dependent value which can increase the memory usage of the method. A research on an effient representation for it is a future work.

6 CONCLUSION

In this paper, we presented a point-based global illumination rendering pipeline for environment lighting. The proposed rendering pipeline starts with selecting primary visible points which are used to collect secondary visible points from the point hierarchy. After secondary visible points are collected, points on which direct illumination computation using hemispherical integration is inevitable are selected by traversing the point hierarchy. Approximations are introduced to reduce the number of those points.

Experiments showed that the proposed rendering pipeline reduces the number of points on which direct illumination must be calculated by micro-buffer rasterization to $10 - 30\%$ of the secondary visible points. Illumination propagation is also proposed to calculate direct illumination on those culled points from direct

Figure 8: Each column shows one-bounce global illumination under environment lighting, indirect illumination, visualization of primary visible points, and visualization of secondary visible points, respectively.

illumination on points for which micro-buffer rasterization is executed. The proposed rendering pipeline builds a radiance cache on the primary visible points, which then is used to compute indirect illumination on all the pixels on the screen.

There are several avenues for future work, including the further optimizations discussed in Section 5. As there is no precomputation for the proposed rendering pipeline itself, it is straightforward to apply the method to a dynamic scene by adding a fast hierarchy generation method although hierarchy generation on the GPU is still an active research topic. We have studied one-bounce indirect illumination in this paper and we would like to extend the method to support more light bounces and study how the number of direct illumination computation points grows as the number of bounces increases.

ACKNOWLEDGEMENTS

We acknowledge Jason Yang, Karl Hillesland, Jay McKee for useful discussions and comments. We also thank anonymous reviewers for their constructive comments, which helped us to improve the manuscript. HDR environment images are provided by Smart IBL Archive.

REFERENCES

[1] M. Bunnell. Dynamic ambient occlusion and indirect lighting. In M. Pharr, editor, *GPU Gems 2*, pages 223–233. Addison-Wesley, 2005.

[2] P. H. Christensen. Point-based approximate color bleeding. *Pixar Tech. Report*, 2008.

[3] C. Crassin, F. Neyret, M. Sainz, S. Green, and E. Eisemann. Interactive indirect illumination using voxel cone tracing. *Computer Graphics Forum (Proceedings of Pacific Graphics 2011)*, 30(7), 2011.

[4] C. Dachsbacher and M. Stamminger. Reflective shadow maps. In *Proceedings of the 2005 symposium on Interactive 3D graphics and games*, I3D '05, pages 203–231, New York, NY, USA, 2005. ACM.

[5] Z. Dong, J. Kautz, C. Theobalt, and H.-P. Seidel. Interactive global illumination using implicit visibility. In *Proceedings of the 15th Pacific Conference on Computer Graphics and Applications*, PG '07, pages 77–86, Washington, DC, USA, 2007. IEEE Computer Society.

[6] P. Gautron, J. Křivánek, K. Bouatouch, and S. Pattanaik. Radiance cache splatting: A gpu-friendly global illumination algorithm. In *Proceedings of Eurographics Symposium on Rendering*, pages 55–64, 2005.

[7] T. Harada, J. McKee, and J. C. Yang. Forward+: Bringing deferred lighting to the next level. In *Eurographics (Short Papers)*, pages 5–8, 2012.

[8] W. Heidrich and H.-P. Seidel. Realistic, hardware-accelerated shading and lighting. In *Proceedings of the 26th annual conference on Computer graphics and interactive techniques*, SIGGRAPH '99, pages 171–178, New York, NY, USA, 1999. ACM Press/Addison-Wesley Publishing Co.

[9] A. Kaplanyan and C. Dachsbacher. Cascaded light propagation volumes for real-time indirect illumination. In *Proceedings of the 2010 ACM SIGGRAPH symposium on Interactive 3D Graphics and Games*, I3D '10, pages 99–107, New York, NY, USA, 2010. ACM.

[10] D. Maletz and R. Wang. Importance point projection for gpu-based final gathering. In *Proceedings of the Twenty-second Eurographics conference on Rendering*, EGSR'11, pages 1327–1336, Aire-la-Ville, Switzerland, 2011. Eurographics Association.

[11] T. Ritschel, C. Dachsbacher, T. Grosch, and J. Kautz. The state of

One-bounce global illumination   Direct illumination   Indirect Illumination

Figure 10: Scenes with one-bounce global illumination, direct illumination and indirect illumination.

the art in interactive global illumination. *Comput. Graph. Forum*, 31(1):160–188, Feb. 2012.

[12] T. Ritschel, T. Engelhardt, T. Grosch, H.-P. Seidel, J. Kautz, and C. Dachsbacher. Micro-rendering for scalable, parallel final gathering. *ACM Trans. Graph. (Proc. SIGGRAPH Asia 2009)*, 28(5), 2009.

[13] S. Rusinkiewicz and M. Levoy. Qsplat: a multiresolution point rendering system for large meshes. In *Proceedings of the 27th annual conference on Computer graphics and interactive techniques*, SIGGRAPH '00, pages 343–352, New York, NY, USA, 2000. ACM Press/Addison-Wesley Publishing Co.

[14] D. Scherzer, C. H. Nguyen, T. Ritschel, and H.-P. Seidel. Preconvolved Radiance Caching. *Computer Graphics Forum (Proc. EGSR 2012)*, 4(31), 2012.

[15] E. Tabellion. Point-based global illumination directional importance mapping. In *SIGGRAPH Sketch*, 2012.

[16] B. Wang, J. Huang, B. Buchholz, X. Meng, and T. Boubekeur. Factorized point based global illumination. *Computer Graphics Forum*, 32(4):117–123, 2013.

[17] G. J. Ward, F. M. Rubinstein, and R. D. Clear. A ray tracing solution for diffuse interreflection. *SIGGRAPH Comput. Graph.*, 22(4):85–92, June 1988.

Variable-Sized, Circular Bokeh Depth of Field Effects

Johannes Moersch and Howard J. Hamilton

Department of Computer Science, University of Regina, Regina, SK, Canada

ABSTRACT

We propose the Flexible Linear-time Area Gather (FLAG) blur algorithm with a variable-sized, circular bokeh for producing depth of field effects on rasterized images. The algorithm is separable (and thus linear). Bokehs can be of any convex shape including circles. The goal is to create a high quality bokeh blur effect by post processing images rendered in real-time by a 3D graphics system. Given only depth and colour information as input, the method performs three passes. The circle of confusion pass calculates the radius of the blur at each pixel and packs the input buffer for the next pass. The horizontal pass samples pixels across each row and outputs a 3D texture packed with blur information. The vertical pass performs a vertical gather on this 3D texture to produce the final blurred image. The time complexity of the algorithm is linear with respect to the maximum radius of the circle of confusion, which compares favorably with the naive algorithm, which is quadratic. The space complexity is linear with respect to the maximum radius of the circle of confusion. The results of our experiments show that the algorithm generates high quality blurred images with variable-sized circular bokehs. The implemented version of the proposed algorithm is consistently faster in practice than the implemented naive algorithm. Although some previous algorithms have provided linear performance scaling and variable sized bokehs, the proposed algorithm provides these while also permitting more flexibility in the allowed blur shapes, including any convex shape.

Keywords: Depth of field, bokeh, blur, separable algorithm.

1 INTRODUCTION

Despite advances in hardware, today's real-time graphics are still far from photorealistic because geometric data is being drawn in an inaccurate and unconvincing way. Until unbiased path tracing becomes feasible, we will continue to employ shortcuts to maintain real-time speed while increasing realism. One such shortcut is an approximation of the *depth of field* effect, which is caused by the use of a lens with a non-zero aperture. This effect causes blurring of objects that are not on the focal plane. Since an aperture of zero is impossible, even our eyes generate this effect. The larger the aperture of the lens, the greater the effect. Film making and photography use lenses with large apertures, so in these media, the effect can be pronounced.

As shown in Figure 1, light originating from a point lying on the focal plan (solid lines in Figure 1) focuses on a single point in the image plane. In contrast, light originating from a point that does not lie on the focal plane (dashed lines in Figure 1) will not focus on the image plane. Instead, it will focus either in front of or behind the image plane. This results in the light spreading over an area on the image plane, which is called the *circle of confusion*. The radius of this circle (called the *blur radius*) is directly related to the lens size; the larger the aperture, the greater the blur radius.

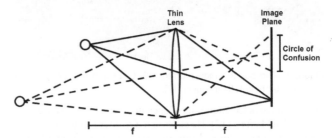

Figure 1: In-focus light (solid lines) and out-of-focus light (dashed).

The depth of field effect has a dramatic impact on the appearance of an image, as can be seen in Figure 2 [18]. This effect is indispensable in non-interactive visual media and its absence has been a barrier to creating compelling cinematic experiences in real-time interactive media. In recent years, a variety of techniques to emulate this effect in screen space have been proposed [5, 6, 8, 10], but most have been lacking either in visual quality or in performance. To improve performance, a standard approach exploits separability. A filtering algorithm is considered *separable* if it breaks the quadratic two dimensional processing into two distinct one dimensional passes, each with linear complexity. Although a rectangular box filter and a circular Gaussian filter are separable, a circular box filter is not.

Figure 2: An image taken with an aperture of f/32 (left) and f/5.6 (right) [18].

Here, we propose the Flexible Linear-time Area Gather (FLAG) blur algorithm with a variable-sized, circular bokeh for producing depth of field effects on rasterized images. The algorithm is separable (and thus linear). Bokehs can be of any convex shape including circles. In Section 2, we review previous work on creating depth of field and bokeh effects. In Section 3, we describe a quadratic-time naive algorithm and our linear-time approach. In Section 4, we show experimental results for these two techniques. Finally, in Section 5, we present conclusions.

2 PREVIOUS WORK

The *blur shape* of a depth of field effect describes the shape and intensity distribution of the region over which each pixel is blurred. As discussed below, many proposed techniques and their early applications in computer games used a Gaussian blur effect, whereby the blur is most pronounced at a central point and then gradually reduces in every direction outward. In reality, the

* {moerschj, hamiltoh}@uregina.ca

Graphics Interface Conference 2014
7-9 May, Montreal, Quebec, Canada

optical effect causes light to spread at a constant intensity. More physically accurate depth of field effects are commonly referred to as *bokeh* depth of field effects. The use of the term "bokeh" implies the blur shape being used is physically plausible. In particular, circular blur shapes, like those in the right side of Figure 3, are physically plausible because they are produced by any optical system with a circular aperture.

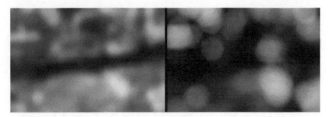

Figure 3: The same image blurred with Gaussian blur (left) and a circular bokeh filter (right) [17].

Demers surveys techniques developed up to 2004 for creating depth of field effects [2]. He states that Z-Buffer Depth-of-Field algorithms are best for real-time use. Wu et al. provide an off-line method for rendering realistic spectral bokeh effects due to chromatic aberration using circles and other shapes [19].

Mulder and van Liere increase the speed of processing by simulating depth of field effects accurately in the centre of attention and less accurately in peripheral areas [12]. The intensity distributions over the circles of confusion at the centre of attention are uniform, but those elsewhere are Gaussian.

Kass et al. give a good description of the problem of real-time computation of blur effects [7]. They devised a linear-time GPU-based algorithm for computing Gaussian blur with tridiagonal matrices [7]. Zhou et al. provide an efficient two-pass algorithm for the task assuming that blurring should fall off with the inverse square of distance [21]. Kraus and Stengert use a GPU-based pyramidal interpolation technique to perform Gaussian blurring [9]. They devised a novel technique that adds the effect of pixels that are invisible in the original image but contribute to the final image because they are visible from part of the simulated lens.

Lee et al. devised a method to produce layered image-based scenes with accurate computation of depth of field blur. Instead of using a single source image, they use multiview sampling, so their technique is not directly comparable to the proposed technique.

Real-time Gaussian depth of field effects first appeared in commercial products in 2007 and can be found in games such as *Crysis* [3] and *Call of Duty 4: Modern Warfare* [6] (see Figure 4).

Figure 4: Example of depth of field in Activision's *Call of Duty 4: Modern Warfare* [6].

Although numerous approaches to creating a depth of field effect have been devised, only two have been shown to be achievable in real time on common consumer-level graphics hardware: scatter-based blur and gather-based blur.

Scatter-based blur: *Scatter-based* blur methods spread a fraction of a pixel's intensity to every pixel within its circle of confusion [13]. This can be done by drawing overlapping quads with additive blending. This approach is straight forward, but the complexity is quadratic. Epic Games (in their *Samaritan Demo*) [4] and *Capcom* (in *Lost Planet* on PCs) [15] used this approach. The massive overdraw caused by rendering thousands of overlapping polygons makes the fill cost high with this technique.

Gather-based blur: *Gather-based* blur methods produce an output value for each pixel by accumulating samples from a set of nearby pixels [6, 14, 19]. Such methods take advantage of current graphics architectures, which have high memory bandwidth and a fast texture cache optimized for clustered texture sample operations. However, the magnitude of texture sample operations required by naive gather-based methods is too large for current hardware, so they perform poorly.

In 2009, Kawase proposed a *separable*, gather-based blur algorithm to solve the problem of obtaining 2D bokeh blur effects in linear time [8]. A key insight behind the algorithm is to decompose a polygonal blur shape into a set of rhombi; this idea has also been used by McIntosh et al. [11] and mentioned by Zanuttini [20]. This decomposition allows each rhombus of the blur shape to be calculated as a separable filter (much like a typical separable box filter). For example, a hexagon can be decomposed into three rhombi. The algorithm provides an efficient means of creating a large bokeh blur, but it is limited to polygonal blur shapes. Variable-sized bokeh shapes can be accomplished through depth checks during the gather. As mentioned, the technique is restricted to polygonal blur shapes that can be decomposed into rhombi, and each additional rhombus (without a shared edge) decreases performance. This technique is used in Electronic Arts' *Frostbite 2* game engine [1].

Crytek has since developed an alternative high-performance gather-based technique [16]. Instead of decomposing the gather into multiple blur passes on different axes, they decompose it into a coarse-grained 2D pass to create the bokeh shape and a fine-grained 2D pass to fill in the gaps. Additionally, they employ a technique named *n-gon mapping*, which maps all samples into the maximum sized blur shape, to optimize the sample distribution. This approach allows the gather area to be easily changed based on depth. They also employ a low resolution maximum circle of confusion radius buffer to determine the sample area required. The approach performs relatively well and produces results of reasonably high quality. However, the small number of pixels considered in the initial gather can cause fine details to be missed, and this technique suffers from quadratic growth of complexity as either blur radius or sampling resolution are increased. This technique is used in the Xbox One game *Ryse: Son of Rome*.

3 APPROACH

The proposed approach can best be understood in contrast to a naive algorithm. We describe the naive algorithm in Section 3.1 and the proposed FLAG algorithm in Section 3.2.

3.1 Naive Approach

The naive approach to producing a high quality bokeh blur with a variable radius for the circle of confusion is to use a gather-based blur algorithm. For any pixel (called the *working pixel*), a 2D group of nearby pixels is defined as the *gather pattern* (blur shape). For example, a square of (say) 7x7 pixels, centered on the working pixel, may be used as the gather pattern. For each working pixel, the algorithm performs a 2D gather of the pixels in the pattern, and accumulates the colour value of each pixel whose circle of confusion includes the working pixel divided by the area of its circle of confusion. Instead of performing the gather at every pixel, it is performed at a spacing of every k pixels on both the horizontal and vertical axes. By multiplying the spacing by the dimensions of the gather pattern, the *gather area* can be calculated. The largest circle that can fit inside the gather area is the largest circle of confusion that can be handled by the algorithm. Therefore, half of one dimension of the gather area in pixels equals to the maximum radius of the circle of confusion.

As an example, in *Ryse: Son of Rome*, Crytek applies a spatially optimized variant of the naive approach with a 7x7 gather pattern with a spacing of perhaps 3 to 8 pixels between the samples, and then supplements the naive algorithm with an additional blur pass, which covers the artifacts.

If the naive algorithm were performed with a large gather pattern that has low spacing between the samples, the result would be of high quality. However, due to the algorithm's quadratic time complexity, the performance cost quickly becomes high. For example, a 7x7 gather pattern only requires each pixel to sample 49 neighbouring pixels, but if the size of the gather pattern is doubled or tripled on each axis, the number of samples per pixel rises to 196 or 441, respectively.

3.2   The FLAG Algorithm

The FLAG blur algorithm produces variable-sized, circular blur shapes in linear time with respect to the radius of the blur shape. Due to its linear performance scaling, it can achieve high performance while performing fine sampling. The technique depends on random access buffers, which expose the ability to perform scattered writes. (In DirectX 11, this functionality is provided by Unordered Access Views.) Like Kawase's technique, the algorithm works much like a conventional separable box filter. Many of the same advantages and limitations that apply to the polygonal decomposition technique also apply to this technique [8]. The key difference is in the horizontal pass, which writes out a 3D texture (instead of a 2D one). The vertical pass then reads from this 3D texture. The use of the 3D texture allows for bokeh shapes that cannot be decomposed into rhombi, such as circles. In total, the algorithm consists of three passes: the circle of confusion pass, the horizontal pass, and the vertical pass. Each of these passes is now described and then the complexity of the algorithm is analyzed.

3.2.1   Circle of Confusion Pass

In its first pass, the algorithm calculates the radius of the circle of confusion for each pixel in the source image from its depth value. This calculation requires several pieces of information about the optical system, namely the diameter of the aperture (A), the focal length (F), the focal plane distance (P), and the pixel depth (D). The radius of the circle of confusion (denoted r) is calculated using Equation 1 [16]:

$$r = \left| A \left(\frac{F(P-D)}{D(P-F)} \right) \right| \qquad (1)$$

The output of the first pass is stored in a 2D texture. Since the next pass only needs the r value and the RGB color value for each pixel, they should be stored together for efficiency of access. (In our implementation, we pack them together in a 64 bit RGBA value with the color in the RGB fields and the circle of confusion in the A field.)The resulting 2D texture is the only input required by the next pass.

3.2.2   Horizontal Pass

The only output of the horizontal pass is a 3D texture bound as a random access buffer for scattered writes. The output 3D texture contains all the information required by the vertical pass. The set of Z values at each {X, Y} location in the 3D texture contains the cumulative contribution of all pixels in row Y to any pixel in column X. The value at {X, Y, 0} is the contribution of row Y to the working pixel at {X, Y}, the value at {X, Y, 1} is the contribution of row Y to the first pixel directly above and below the working pixel at {X, Y ± 1}, the value at {X, Y, 2} is for the pixel 2 places above and below the working pixel, etc.

This information can be calculated efficiently because of two properties of the blur shape employed. First, the blur shape is convex, and second, the entire shape has constant intensity. If the blur shape has vertical symmetry, the memory requirements can be halved. All of these properties are physically plausible. These properties also make the calculation of the 3D texture quite simple. The example in Figure 5 shows a horizontal gather operation on a single pixel, i.e. on the working pixel located in column X, row Y. Here, the size of the gather pattern is 13x13. Three example pixels (shown for visibility as red, green, and blue) are blurring onto the working pixel in the middle. Suppose their radii happen to be as shown by the red, green, and blue circles, respectively. The amount that a circle overlaps column X depends on its radius and the nearness of the pixel to the working pixel. For example, the blue circle affects pixels in column X up to 5 positions away from the working pixel. By accumulating the contributions of the pixels in row Y to column X, the set of values shown on the far left can be calculated. These values are then written into the output 3D texture.

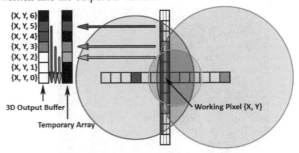

Figure 5: An example of how to calculate the 3D texture.

To maintain linear time complexity, the gather and accumulation are performed separately. While gathering for pixel {X, Y} along row Y, a temporary array is used. The cell in this array that corresponds to the point where the perimeter of the circle of confusion for each relevant pixel in row Y intersects column X is set to that pixel's intensity divided by the area of its circle of confusion. In Figure 5, the perimeter of the blue circle intersects column X in pixel {X, Y – 5}, which is 5 away from the working pixel, so position 5 in the temporary array is set to the colour value from pixel {X, Y – 5} divided by the area of the blue circle. For convenience, the affected pixel in the temporary array is shown as blue in Figure 5. After the gather operation for the working pixel is complete, an accumulation process is performed from the end of the temporary array to its start. At each consecutive pixel of the temporary array, the total accumulated so far is stored in the corresponding position of the 3D output array. In the example, the accumulated total from the last position of the temporary array is stored in position {X, Y, 6} of the output array; the total from the last two positions is stored in position {X, Y, 5}, and so forth. The overall effect is to build a rough cumulative distribution in the set of Z values for {X, Y}.

3.2.3 Vertical Pass

The vertical pass performs gathering similarly to a basic separable box filter, as shown in Figure 6. The only difference is that the gather is against a 3D texture instead of a 2D one. In the example separable box filter, shown in Figure 6(a), the values in the working pixel {X, Y} and three values on either side of it in column X are accumulated to form the sample for pixel {X, Y}. With our method, at each step, the texture is sampled using the Z value that corresponds to the difference in Y between the positions of the working pixel and the sample pixel. In Figure 6(b), the relevant samples are outlined in white. For example, for pixel {X, Y}, we accumulated values from {X, Y, 0}, {X, Y ± 1, 1}, {X, Y ± 2, 2}, etc. The effect is to find the cumulative contribution of all neighbouring pixels onto the working pixel. The final result is the total of each sample added together.

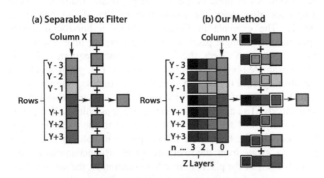

Figure 6: An example showing how the 3D texture is sampled.

3.2.4 Complexity Analysis

The circle of confusion pass has constant time complexity per pixel and both the horizontal and vertical passes have linear time complexity per pixel, so the overall time complexity is linear. Most of the cost is due to the horizontal pass, because it writes out large amounts of data. The memory cost of the 3D output buffer of the horizontal pass is linear in the gather pattern's Y dimension. For example, for a 13x13 gather pattern, the Z dimension in the 3D array is ceiling(13/2). This factor, when combined with high screen resolutions, can amount to hundreds of megabytes. A 1080p, full resolution implementation with a 41x41 equivalent gather area requires 332 MB for the 3D buffer alone. However, the memory costs of the circle of confusion pass and vertical pass are both constant per pixel, and are comparatively negligible.

4 RESULTS

The images of hoops and pillars in Figure 7 and 8, respectively, show the equivalent of a 41x41 gather pattern (1681 samples per pixel) sampling every second pixel ($k = 2$). The gather area spans an 81x81 pixel region, which allows for a maximum circle of confusion radius of 40 pixels.

Figure 8: Results for pillars image: (a) near focus, (b) mid focus.

At high screen resolutions with large gather pattern sizes, the naive approach performed inconsistently, so the following tests were run at 800x600 (on an ATI HD5870). We determined the *frame time* as the average (mean) time per frame across 500 frames. Every value reported in Figure 9 is the average of 5 runs with identical parameters.

Figure 7: Results for hoops image: (a) original, (b) blurred.

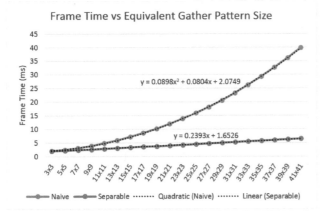

Figure 9: Frame Time versus Filter Sizes.

As the size of the gather pattern (and thus the maximum radius of the circle of confusion) increases, the total time to render each frame increases. The results show that the cost of the FLAG algorithm grows linearly with respect to the gather pattern size, while the naive approach grows at a quadratic rate. For almost all gather pattern sizes, our technique outperforms the naive implementation, and at large sizes the difference is dramatic.

The implemented naive approach samples all pixels in a complete square with a side length that is two times the maximum circle of confusion radius instead of sampling only the relevant pixels in the inscribed circle. An improved implementation could achieve the same result with approximately 20% fewer samples. Nonetheless, even with this improvement, the naive approach would still be significantly slower than the FLAG algorithm.

5 CONCLUSIONS AND FUTURE WORK

The FLAG blur algorithm produces high quality results relative to its performance costs. While similar to Kawase's approach, its use of a 3D buffer permits the FLAG algorithm to process circular blur shapes. Any convex constant intensity blur shape can be rendered. It also supports variable blur radii, which are important for creating convincing images. The theoretical time complexity of the algorithm is linear in the size of the blur radius. Experimental results show that a GPU implementation of FLAG scales up linearly with the blur radius. As expected, FLAG significantly outperforms a quadratic naive implementation. While the output is not artifact free and the memory cost is high, the blur itself is of high quality. Through further improvements to the algorithm and its implementation, it could be feasible for use in providing depth of field for real-time interactive media.

The main limitation of FLAG is its memory cost. The 332 MB buffer size for a 1080p implementation with a 41x41 gather area is too large for most applications. Also, since PC graphics drivers overlap the processing of several frames, multiple buffers of this size will be allocated simultaneously. Future research could reduce the buffer size. Half resolution or quarter resolution 3D buffers could be used, which should reduce the buffer size to 42 MB and 5.2 MB, respectively. Further memory could be saved by decreasing the precision of the 3D buffer.

Performance could potentially be improved by limiting the size of the gather area. By down-sampling the circle of confusion map to a lower resolution using a maximum operation, one could obtain a map that contains the maximum radius of the circle of confusion for each large chunk of pixels. This map could be used to reduce the size of the gather pattern with no impact on quality.

The proposed algorithm can create artifacts that are inherent to gather based blur techniques such as ours. For instance, foreground objects have sharp edges where they meet focused objects, and halos occur where background objects are occluded. Many of the techniques used to solve these problems for other blur technique could also be applied to our algorithm.

REFERENCES

[1] Colin Barré-Brisebois and John White. "More Performance!", *Advances in Real-time Rendering Course*, ACM SIGGRAPH, 2011.

[2] Joe Demers, "Depth of Field: A Survey of Techniques." In *GPU Gems*. Addison-Wesley, 375–390, 2004.

[3] Crytek, "Crysis," 2007.

[4] Epic Games, "The Technology Behind the DirectX 11 Unreal Engine 'Samaritan' Demo," *Game Developers Conference (GDC)*, 2011.

[5] Yoshiharu Gotanda, "Star Ocean 4: Flexible Shader Management and Post Processing," *Game Developers Conference (GDC)*, 2009.

[6] Earl Hammon, "Practical Post-Process Depth of Field" in H. Nguyen (ed), *GPU Gems 3*, Addison-Wesley, 583–606, 2007.

[7] Michael Kass, Aaron Lefohn, John Owens, *Interactive Depth of Field using Simulated Diffusion on a GPU*, Technical Report, UC Davis, 2006.

[8] Masaki Kawase, "Anti-Downsized Buffer Artifacts," *CEDEC 2009*. Silicon Studio Inc, 2009. http://www.daionet.gr.jp/~masa/archives/-CEDEC2009_Anti-DownsizedBufferArtifacts.ppt

[9] M. Kraus and M. Strengert, "Depth of Field Rendering by Pyramidal Image Processing," *Computer Graphics Forum*, 26(3):645-654, 2007.

[10] Sungkil Lee, Elmar Eisemann, and Hans-Peter Seidel, "Depth of Field Rendering with Multiview Synthesis," *ACM Transactions on Graphics*. 28(5), Article 134, 2009.

[11] L. McIntosh, B.E. Riecke, and S. DiPaola, "Efficiently Simulating the Bokeh of Polygonal Apertures in a Post-Process Depth of Field Shader," *Computer Graphics Forum*, 31(6):1810–1822, 2012.

[12] Jurriaan Mulder and Robert van Liere, "Fast Perception-Based Depth of Field Rendering," *Proceedings of the ACM Symposium on Virtual Reality Software and Technology*, 129–133, 2000.

[13] Michael Potmesil and Indranil Chakravarty, "A Lens and Aperture Camera Model for Synthetic Image Generation," *ACM SIGGRAPH*, 15, 3, 297–305, 1981.

[14] Przemyslaw Rokita, "Generating Depth-of-Field Effects in Virtual Reality Applications," *IEEE Computer Graphics and its Application* 16, 2, 18–21, 1996.

[15] Stefan Salzl, "CEDEC 2007: Capcom on Lost Planet, Part II," 2007. http://www.beyond3d.com/content/news/499

[16] Tiago Sousa, "CryEngine 3 Graphics Gems," *Advances in Real-Time Rendering Course*, ACM SIGGRAPH, 2013.

[17] Wikipedia, Bokeh. http://en.wikipedia.org/wiki/Bokeh

[18] Wikipedia, Depth of Field. http://en.wikipedia.org/wiki/Depth_of_field

[19] Jiaze Wu, Changwen Zheng, Xiaohui Hu, and Fanjiang Xu, "Rendering Realistic Spectral Bokeh due to Lens Stops and Aberrations," *The Visual Computer*. 29(1):41-52, 2013.

[20] Antoine Zanuttini, *Du photoréalisme au rendu expressif en image 3D temps réel dans le jeu vidéo*, PhD thesis, Université Paris 8.

[21] Tianshu Zhou, Jim X. Chen, and Mark Pullen, "Accurate Depth of Field Simulation in Real Time," *Computer Graphics Forum*, 26(1):15-23, 2007.

Casual Authoring using a Video Navigation History

Matthew Fong, Abir Al Hajri, Gregor Miller and Sidney Fels*

Human Communication Technologies Laboratory, University of British Columbia, Vancouver, BC, Canada

Figure 1: Our prototype history-based interface for casual video authoring. A history of personal video viewing provides a searchable set of intervals (*left, red*) which can be filtered to identify intervals viewed more than once (*right, red*). The video is linearly searchable using the filmstrip (*blue*). Any interval in the history can be added to the playlist (*green*), which can then be exported to a video and shared with friends.[1]

ABSTRACT

We propose the use of a personal video navigation history, which records a user's viewing behaviour, as a basis for casual video editing and sharing. Our novel interaction supports users' navigation of previously-viewed intervals to construct new videos via simple playlists. The intervals in the history can be individually previewed and searched, filtered to identify frequently-viewed sections, and added to a playlist from which they can be refined and re-ordered to create new videos. Interval selection and playlist creation using a history-based interaction is compared to a more conventional filmstrip-based technique. Using our novel interaction participants took at most two-thirds the time taken by the conventional method, and we found users gravitated towards using a history-based mechanism to find previously-viewed intervals compared to a state-of-the-art video interval selection method. Our study concludes that users are comfortable using a video history, and are happy to re-watch interesting parts of video to utilize the history's advantages in an authoring context.

Index Terms: H.5.2. [Information Interfaces and Presentation]: User Interfaces—; H.1.2. [Models and Principles]: User/Machine Systems—

1 INTRODUCTION

Casual video authoring is becoming popular with the rise of video sharing sites, such as YouTube[TM]. However, video authoring continues to be a challenging task for consumers due to a lack of tools for efficient and simple editing [14]. Part of the problem is that the 3D spatio-temporal representation of video complicates relatively simple actions such as cropping and selection. Further, video editing often taxes human memory by requiring memorization of a large quantity of digital assets. In particular, finding and selecting interesting parts has poor navigation and search support. The situation is such that recent studies have shown that unless given a significant incentive, users will avoid video editing [20]. We propose that the addition of a video history mechanism into casual video authoring will overcome some of these difficulties.

We investigate the usefulness of video history through a casual video authoring interface that supports users employing their own video navigation history to quickly retrieve previously-viewed intervals and assemble them into shareable movies. Our approach is in contrast to the commercial state-of-the-art, which requires directly linking to a start time (e.g. YouTube[TM]), with no end time given and only one clip linked at a time. Placement of temporal comments can aid navigation (e.g. SoundCloud[TM]) however this requires explicit annotation. Social navigation methods using crowd-sourced viewing patterns [21] can aid the selection of popular clips, although this does not help with home/mobile video or editing video before upload.

Current video navigation methods mostly use the familiar VCR-like controls (play, pause, seek, fast forward, rewind) and sometimes include chapter systems (e.g. DVDs) to skip to specific sections of a movie. Commercial video viewing systems have not progressed much further, despite significant research into new methods. Girgensohn et al. improved video thumbnails, allowing users to directly manipulate the preview frame by continuously moving a cursor along a timeline to find the desired clip [7]. Kimber et al. encouraged users to directly manipulate within-video content along its natural movement path to explore video [13]. These both require users to remember the temporal location of an event within the timeline (or chapters). In an attempt to summarize and show users video summaries, Christel et al. [5] developed video skims

*{mfong, abira, gregor, ssfels}@ece.ubc.ca
Graphics Interface Conference 2014
7-9 May, Montreal, Quebec, Canada

---

[1]Video and screenshots licenced under Creative Commons Attribution 3.0, © 2008, Blender Foundation

Figure 2: The filmstrip provides easy access to the entire video at once. Each thumbnail shown represents the frame of the video at the temporal location of the start of the thumbnail's interval. The red bar represents the current time being shown in the main player. Moving the cursor across each thumbnail will preview the frame that the cursor position represents. Users can drag and select video intervals, and click the "+" to add them to the playlist.

that would summarize the most important contents of a video.

We believe that the revisitation can be a useful tool for search and selection. Zipf's Law [22] and Pareto's Principle [12] both investigate the idea of natural repetition in human behaviour, under the assumption that people do not invoke more effort than needed to accomplish a task. Alexander et al. [3] use this as the basis for their work on revisitation in documents. It was found that marking user footprints on the document scrollbars yielded better performance in search. An investigation into web histories by Cockburn et al. [6] showed that over half of web page visits were previously-seen web pages. Greenberg et al. [9] investigated the reuse of commands in a command line interface, and built an interface to facilitate repeated usage. Li et al. developed smart bookmarks that can perform macro-like operations on web pages [16]; Bergman et al. created a tutorial generation system which recorded user actions and replayed it as a form of documentation for new users to follow [4]; Grossman et al. developed *Chronicle*, a system to explore workflow histories of graphical content and allow users to indicate items of interest, from which they can observe how to replicate this part of the workflow [10]. We apply a similar methodology in our work, assuming there is an element of repetition in human behaviour and that tools such as online video are supporting this. The use of a history mechanism can keep track of what is watched (and which parts have been watched more than once, or not seen at all); this leads to a new perspective on video editing which can be done directly from the viewing space, without the need for a separate tool. Our novel interface demonstrates the ease of authoring when using user-based viewing history.

Existing work that applies a history methodology to video consumption is sparse, although all demonstrate high utility for navigation, search and summarization. Yu et al. used low-level feature extraction and video interval view counts, to rank and suggest interesting scenes [21]. Mertens et al. visualized users' footprints on the video timeline and allowed users to quickly navigate to the corresponding scenes in the video [17]. Yu et al. and Syeda-Mahmood and Ponceleon used a browsing history to rank particular scenes in a video to generate video summaries [21, 19]. Although these use some form of video history, they do not provide direct access to discrete video intervals watched: the history is used internally to support the system. The first video viewing framework to provide users with direct access to a full history of their personal video navigation was recently introduced by Al Hajri et al. : they demonstrate users can find events in a video more quickly using a history than with traditional controls [1]. Al Hajri et al. later demonstrated an interface for multiple-video history with the same properties i.e. finding previously-seen content was significantly faster [2]. While their prototype demonstrated the utility of a video history for event search, we show that it can be applied successfully in an authoring context to provide a simpler mechanism than existing interactions.

The video history is more effective when users watch segments of video more than once, or use seek and search to avoid viewing portions of the video completely [8, 11, 15, 17, 18, 21]. Evidence

of this can also be shown by YouTube and Vimeo's sharing by 'link to start time'. Audience retention statistics (e.g. from YouTube) show that users do not linearly watch video (graphs have peaks and troughs, indicating different view counts across the video). Users do not currently have widespread access to video histories, and we are interested in how users react when given a history which takes advantage of the information gained from re-viewing video. We report on this aspect in the results of our user study.

In the following section we describe the methods for utilizing history to for video interval search and selection, as well as the supporting interface we designed around them; we then outline the study we performed to evaluate its effectiveness against a state-of-the-art selection method, and report on the benefits of using a history as part of a video viewing platform.

2 INTERACTION DESIGN

We envision users will watch videos differently when they have a history collection mechanism so that they may easily save clips to use later. We consider two contexts when this might be done. The first occurs when the the video in question is longer than necessary and only contains a few entertaining intervals worth sharing. This is typical in YouTube videos, for example. Using the history feature, the user watches the video and re-views interesting parts on the fly (knowing it is saved in their history): the user can then quickly share the relevant intervals with other people. Sports video provides our second example context. Here, videos are generally long, with relatively few exciting parts that are typically viewed again frequently (e.g. instant replay, highlights, etc.). Watching sports on a history-enabled viewer, the user can save the exciting parts by re-watching them. They can then add them to a playlist once the game has finished to create a personalized highlights video, and share it with friends.

The major focus of our design is to allow users to reduce video into smaller intervals using video browsing interactions; specifically, seeking (which includes re-watching video). There is one interval for each navigational action a user has taken in the history: seeking and changing videos. As soon as a user seeks within the video, the current video interval ends, and a new one is created. Within the interface, video intervals are represented by seekable thumbnails. By finding the intersections of all video intervals in the history, we can help users find intervals that have been watched more than once.

2.1 Design Guidelines

In designing our interface there were some guidelines that we tried to keep consistent throughout the interface. These guidelines include:

- To represent a video, we use thumbnails of the video itself. Each thumbnail represents an interval of video, with a distinct starting and ending time. Placing the cursor over it forces it to display the frame that corresponds to the cursor position

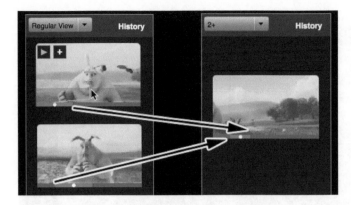

Figure 3: The history is a log of intervals the user views: in this case, the user watched a third of the video (*left, top thumbnail*), rewound via seek to approximately one quarter in, and resumed watching until stopping close to half-way through (*left, bottom thumbnail*). Using the filter (*right*), the interval the user watched twice is extracted, providing the user with a quick and simple way to store and later find intervals of interest.

on the thumbnail. Removing the cursor from the thumbnail reverts the thumbnail's frame to its original position.

- Arranging these thumbnails is also taken into consideration. We have two types of timelines: a video timeline (Figure , *highlighted in blue*), and a user timeline (Figure , *highlighted in red*). Video timelines represent how the video is playing, and is arranged horizontally, from left to right. User timelines represent the actions a user has taken and are shown vertically, from top to bottom. This is employed by the history visualization.

- To represent the entire video, video timelines stretch across the video that they are representing.

2.2 Supporting Interface

To explore how users' navigation behaviour changes in an authoring context when given access to their personal history, we designed an interface with familiar playback controls and a visualization of their history. The interface has four components: a large player to view video; a thumbnail-visualized timeline for in-video navigation (the filmstrip); a navigation history visualization; and a playlist to organize intervals.

2.2.1 Main Player

The main player, shown at the centre of Figure , displays the currently playing video. Interactions with it are limited to clicking to toggle pausing and playing the video.

2.2.2 Filmstrip

The filmstrip, shown in Figure (*highlighted in blue*), is a tool for navigating the entire video. Hovering the cursor over any point shows a preview of the corresponding frame in the video; clicking at this point will seek playback to this position. The initial preview in the thumbnail is the first frame the thumbnail represents in the interval. Intervals can be selected by click-dragging across the filmstrip. A ■ appears to let users add the selected interval to a playlist. An example of the filmstrip can be seen in Figure 2. As noted before, the previews are distributed horizontally across the screen, to represent video time. Furthermore, the filmstrip's width is the same as the main player, indicating the full length of the filmstrip is visible to the viewer as the length of the video.

2.2.3 History

The history is a collection of how a user watched a video, and it is a sequential log of all navigational actions taken by users. It is represented by a number of thumbnails which are created as a user is watching a video. There is one thumbnail for each navigational action a user has taken: video seeking and changing videos. These thumbnails represent video intervals, where each interval is the time within the video between actions. As soon as a user seeks within the video, the current video interval ends, and a new one is created. If the video is paused, this new interval represents a single frame and is essentially useless. To combat this, we check for the last interval's length and replace it if the interval is less than one second. These history interval thumbnails allow users to visually see which parts of the video they have watched.

Each thumbnail is initially a small screenshot of the frame of video that is halfway between the start and end time of the interval it represents. On the bottom of the thumbnail is a small timeline that represents the entire video, with the history interval being highlighted in red. Upon placing the cursor over the thumbnail, a popup timeline appears. Moving the cursor across the thumbnail allows users to seek across the video interval, allowing them to check the contents of the thumbnail. Again, in keeping steady with our design guidelines, the entire width of the thumbnail represents the entire length of the interval being represented. Additionally, two new buttons appear on the upper left corner of the thumbnail when the cursor is over the thumbnail. Clicking on the ▶ button will allow the user to play the video interval in the main player, and highlight the corresponding video interval in the filmstrip in blue. The same action can also be performed by clicking and dragging the thumbnail over to the main player. The ■ button allows the user to insert the video interval into the playlist. To indicate successful insertion, a ghost thumbnail is animated to fly over from the history to the playlist.

Across the top of the history, there is a drop-down selection box that allows users to filter their history, facilitating users' search for the appropriate video interval. Upon selecting one, the history widget will find the intersections of existing history intervals and use that as a basis for showing the user intervals of video that they have seen more than once. Figure 3 shows a regular history, and the results of filtering for video clips that have been seen two or more times. We would like to refer back to the sports context mentioned earlier. Watching the game, a user would like to re-watch the goals as they happen. Once they do, the history that is created would reflect the particular interval that has been re-watched. After finishing the viewing, it would be useful to be able to quickly find that particular interval to review. By using the filter, it is easy to distinguish parts of the game that were more exciting.

2.2.4 Playlist

The playlist, shown in Figure 4, stores a collection of clips, much like the history, for future viewing. It is a more explicit method for saving video intervals and requires slightly more user interaction. As noted by the other interface elements, inserting clips into the playlist can be accomplished by either selecting an interval in the filmstrip and clicking the ■ button, or by adding an interval from the history.

When the interface is started, the playlist's position is held slightly off screen to prevent distraction, as shown in Figure (*left*). It can be easily brought into view by clicking on the arrow on its left side, and subsequently hidden from view by clicking the ■ button on the right. The playlist supports saving by clicking the ■ button, as well as opening previously made playlists by clicking the ■ button. These playlists are saved as XML files for easy transport. The playlist can also be previewed by clicking the ■ button.

Figure 4: The playlist houses a collection of manually added video clips. A hovering preview is presented for easy viewing, and changes according to the cursor position. These can be adjusted by dragging the edges of each thumbnail, and both previews will change to reflect the edge being dragged. Users can also remove individual clips, and preview the entire playlist.

3 EVALUATION

We ran a comparative user study to: 1) investigate whether using a video navigation history as an interaction tool would make creating clips and adding them to playlists more efficient compared to the state-of-the-art selection method 'filmstrip'; 2) explore any differences on user behaviour when given access to their personal history; and 3) to discover if users have a positive experience with a navigation history, since this is a relatively unknown tool for video.

3.1 Participants

Eighteen volunteers participated in the experiment: thirteen male and five female, ranging in age from 19 to 50. They were monetarily compensated for their time. Each participant worked on the task individually. All were experienced computer users and watched videos at least three to five times a week, but rarely created videos.

3.2 Design and Procedure

Each subject was exposed to two interaction methods, *history* 3 and *filmstrip* 2, and six videos: each video was used once only per subject. For each video the subject created a themed playlist using one of the interactions. We divided the participants into two groups: the first group used the first set of videos with *history* and the second set with the *filmstrip*; reversed for the other group. Each set contained three two-minute videos; a variety of content was used, including sport, news, documentary and comedy.

The evaluation began with a familiarity phase: participants were shown how to use the interface and how the history is created. In the experiment, a trial involved asking the participants to watch a video and re-watch intervals they think fit one of the two themes provided (e.g. "police officers are visible" and "firefighters are visible") for each video. While participants re-watched clips for two themes, once viewing was complete, the task was to collect clips for a single theme. Using two themes ensured the history had distractors (controlling for non-relevant content, and attempting to replicate conditions of a real personal history). Participants were then asked to add clips to the playlist that fit only one theme, using the current interaction technique (either *history* or *filmstrip*); the selection method not being tested was hidden. The participants were asked to complete the task as quickly as possible and the total time taken to add the clips to the playlist was recorded. Timing began when the user clicked the 'Start' button, and stopped when the 'Share' button was clicked. Submitted clips were checked for correctness

Table 1: The mean time taken (with standard deviation, σ) to construct a new video based on the given theme, for each video and method. In all cases the History is significantly faster, with a worst-case of two-thirds the time taken by Filmstrip (comparing means).

Video	Method	Mean (seconds)	σ (seconds)
1	Filmstrip	27.61	9.25
	History	17.04	10.55
2	Filmstrip	23.04	6.92
	History	8.05	7.50
3	Filmstrip	14.55	5.54
	History	8.91	4.32
4	Filmstrip	25.70	7.91
	History	8.08	2.80
5	Filmstrip	18.59	6.89
	History	9.04	6.77
6	Filmstrip	15.24	6.13
	History	9.79	2.69

to ensure a proper evaluation among all participants. Incorrect clips were considered as errors and discarded. Once completed, participants progressed to the next video (and changed method after three video tasks were complete). Upon the completion of the six videos, participants were given two more videos, and extra time to freely experiment with both techniques at the same time (in the same interface). They then answered a questionnaire asking for their reactions to the interface. The total time taken was approximately one hour.

3.3 Results and Discussion

We would first like to note that, as explained in the design, this was a within participant study that was conducted with between elements for the method and videos. Using this design, we would be able to get more informed qualitative data from the participants who would be able to give a more accurate opinion of both techniques. The analysis was done between so that each participant was exposed to each video only once with a single method.

A two-way ANOVA analysis was used to evaluate the performance, and to explore the effect of method and video on the time needed to create a playlist. The analysis showed significant main effects of method: $F(1,96) = 66.69, p < 0.0001$; and of video:

$F(5, 96) = 5.86, p < 0.0001$. However, these main effects are qualified by a significant interaction effect - $F(5, 96) = 2.37, p = 0.045$. Simple main effects of the video at method show that for every video the time needed to create the playlist was significantly lower using the history. Participants took at most two-thirds the time of *filmstrip* when using *history*, as shown in Table 1. The interaction effect was caused by the different types of videos. Because these were real world videos, chosen to simulate real world scenarios, the location of the themes in the videos were not linearly distributed, causing some video clips to be easier to find than others.

We chose not to include viewing time into our quantitative measurements. Given the video viewing behaviour mentioned earlier in the paper, it does not fit the premise if we included the viewing time, as we do not expect users to find the video, find and rewatch the interval and share it; we expect them to find the interval in their history and share it (or combine it with others in a playlist). Our experiment uses a controlled laboratory setting to investigate this use case and the utility of a history for this purpose. Participants were required to view the videos with the same behaviour with both methods, so the viewing time is similar for both methods.

The table also shows that the video type (e.g. sports footage looks very similar) and the different strategies employed by users (described below) led to a slightly higher variation in times.

Of the six videos, we found that the history worked better for some videos than others, and the same effect can be observed in the filmstrip. These traits can generally be attributed to the content of the videos, which is why the analysis is separated for each video.

1. The first video consisted of a short hockey video of a power-play. The themes for the video were two goals, and two intervals where the defensive team had possession of the hockey puck. The participants were asked to find the two goals. In this video, it was difficult to see what was going on within the thumbnails. This was particularly difficult with the filmstrip because many participants forgot when the first goal happened, and were forced to look through the entire video in the filmstrip, whereas the history reduced the search space required, down to four short clips.

2. The second video consisted of six hockey players, three wearing blue jerseys, and three wearing white jerseys, skating around a rink and competing for the fastest time. The theme in this video is the hockey players turning the last corner. The participants were asked to find the white jerseys to insert into the playlist. Again, like the previous video, participants had to search through the entire filmstrip to find the correct clips, while the history only required participants to look through six different clips, all of which were easily distinguishable by the screenshot within the thumbnail. Furthermore, because one of the players skates in the opposite direction of the other five, using the filmstrip became slightly more difficult because the participant had to distinguish the different turns within the small thumbnail.

3. The third video was a short clip of a comedy sketch where a little girl runs around, makes smart remarks, and pulls pranks on various people. The themes to this video were the reactions to her remarks, as well as the result of the two pranks she pulled. The participants were asked to find the clips with the two pranks. This video had a slight advantage given to the filmstrip because the scene of one of the pranks was visible in the filmstrip, and the second prank was right at the end of the video, making both mental and physical retrieval relatively easy. The data reflects this condition as this was the fastest video for filmstrip.

4. The fourth video was a comedic instructional video of someone taking apart a camera. Along the way, the instructor would make mistakes that were very obvious, and he would disconnect things within the camera. The chosen theme for this video were the three mistakes made throughout the video. Like the second video, the clips were fairly spread out along the video, however they were somewhat hard to see within the filmstrip, which made it slightly more difficult using that method. Additionally, some participants forgot the location of the clips and were forced to look through the entire movie, like the first video.

5. The fifth video was a news interval on an Olympic hopeful wanting to enter the snowshoeing competition. The themes of the video were the six talking heads within the video. Of those, the participant was asked to find two specific ones. This ended up being very easy for history, as it was not visually tasking to find clips of a specific person. Again however, one of the clips appeared in the filmstrip, and the second clip was right after.

6. The last video was of a riot, and the themes of the video were of shots of fire fighters and police officers. The clips to be selected were the fire fighters. These clips were mostly within the middle 30 seconds of the video. For the filmstrip, some participants started searching from the beginning of the video, as they did not remember when the first clip appeared. They were, however, very close together within the video and allowed for quick selection once they found the first clip. They were visually distinctive from the police clips, and were also easy to find within the history.

Errors present in the experiment occurred in the selection of incorrect clips due to misinterpretation of some more complex themes. These errors occurred in both methods and were counted as mistrials and we removed them from the results. In total, there were four errors, with three made using filmstrip on videos 1 and 6, and one mistake made using history on video 2.

The questionnaire results shown in Table 2 demonstrate the positive reaction of participants to our history-based authoring interface. The overall scores for the history method were all above 5 (on a 1-7 Likert Scale). The filmstrip method scored well but participants did not find it as easy to find video clips; this is supported by the quantitative data. We performed a Wilcoxon Signed rank test on the last four questions in Table 2 but found no significant results.

Observation of users in the free play section of the study showed a strongly positive reaction to using the history. 88% of the participants changed their viewing behaviour with a history creation model in mind, and relied on this behaviour to select and add intervals to their playlists. Eleven participants deliberately watched

Table 2: The aggregated results of our questionnaire (Mean on a 1-7 Likert Scale, with standard deviation σ). Participants found the interface with the history to be useful for the creation of new videos, and their overall reaction to our mechanism was highly positive.

Question	Mean	σ
Overall usefulness	5.77	1.06
Overall ease of use	5.61	1.29
Overall reaction	5.47	1.19
History is useful	6.11	1.23
Creating usable history is easy	5.56	1.29
History filtering is useful	5.89	1.07
History filtering is intuitive	5.28	1.56
Finding history video clips is easy	5.44	1.89
Finding filmstrip video clips is easy	4.50	1.89
Inserting history video clips is easy	6.44	0.70
Inserting filmstrip video clips is easy	5.61	1.50

events twice to insert them in their history, and used the view count filter as intended. Three participants created a playlist by adding intervals from the full history and refining them in the playlist. Two participants applied a combination of *history* and *filmstrip*: they used the *history* for as much as possible, then used the *filmstrip* to find additional clips they did not re-watch. Finally, two participants were unreceptive to creating and using the *history*, and exclusively used the *filmstrip* to create the playlist. They stated that the viewing pattern required by the interface did not fit with their current viewing behaviour, and that changing their behaviour would disrupt their video viewing experience.

While these participants did not use the history, it still recorded the video as they watched: In this case, the history contained a single item for the entire video. If we extend the system to multiple videos, it would be easy to see which videos they liked, if the video was viewed more than once, and when they watched them.

While only two participants used both techniques to create their own video in the free play, it is worth noting the history works well in conjunction with the filmstrip. Enhanced integration between the two, such as placing markers in the filmstrip indicating history intervals, may further improve performance.

It may also be interesting to note that this is a fully functioning system, and the first and second videos were actually created using the interface, being pulled from a video that was two hours long. It took approximately one minute per video to create using the history.

4 CONCLUSIONS AND FUTURE WORK

Our work defines a new way to casually string video intervals together by incorporating a personal video navigation history. We demonstrated that users can simply watch videos naturally, seek or search, re-view intervals of interest and use the history to quickly share or combine them later. Our comparative user study quantitatively proved that using the history lets users more quickly find intervals and create playlists, and qualitatively demonstrated the usefulness and usability of a history-based interaction. Users were generally happy to change their video viewing behaviour in our authoring context when given an accessible history of their video watching experience. The presented method of authoring can be extended to provide access to multiple videos, which will be useful for editing collections of home movies. This also brings up the problem of scalability, since as video collections grow the history will grow as well. We also plan to observe users current viewing habits on video sites such as YouTube to establish which content types lead to specific classes of viewing behaviour (such as re-watching). This will inform on future designs of the authoring tool and the history based on the current content being viewed.

ACKNOWLEDGEMENTS

We gratefully acknowledge support from NSERC (grant provided for "Diving experiences: wayfinding and sharing experiences with large, semantically tagged video"), Bell Canada, Avigilon Corporation and Vidigami Media Inc."

REFERENCES

[1] A. Al-Hajri, G. Miller, S. Fels, and M. Fong. Video navigation with a personal viewing history. In *Human-Computer Interaction – INTERACT 2013*, volume 8119 of *LNCS*, pages 352–369. Springer, 2013.

[2] A. Al-Hajri, G. Miller, M. Fong, and S. Fels. Visualization of personal history for video navigation. In *Proceedings of the ACM CHI Conference on Human Factors on Computing Systems*, CHI'14, New York City, New York, U.S.A., April 2014. ACM.

[3] J. Alexander, A. Cockburn, S. Fitchett, C. Gutwin, and S. Greenberg. Revisiting read wear: Analysis, design, and evaluation of a footprints scrollbar. In *Proceedings of the SIGCHI Conference on Human Factors in Computing Systems*, CHI '09, pages 1665–1674, New York, NY, USA, 2009. ACM.

[4] L. Bergman, V. Castelli, T. Lau, and D. Oblinger. Docwizards: a system for authoring follow-me documentation wizards. In *Proceedings of the Symposium on User Interface Software and Technology*, pages 191–200. ACM, 2005.

[5] M. G. Christel, M. A. Smith, C. R. Taylor, and D. B. Winkler. Evolving video skims into useful multimedia abstractions. In *Proceedings of the SIGCHI conference on Human factors in computing systems*, CHI '98, pages 171–178, New York, NY, USA, 1998. ACM Press/Addison-Wesley Publishing Co.

[6] A. Cockburn and B. McKenzie. What do web users do? an empirical analysis of web use. *International Journal of Human-Computer Studies*, 54:903–922, 2002.

[7] A. Girgensohn, J. Boreczky, and L. Wilcox. Keyframe-based user interfaces for digital video. *Computer*, 34(9):61–67, Sept. 2001.

[8] C. Gkonela and K. Chorianopoulos. Videoskip: event detection in social web videos with an implicit user heuristic. *Multimedia Tools and Applications*, pages 1–14, 2012. 10.1007/s11042-012-1016-1.

[9] S. Greenberg and I. H. Witten. Supporting command reuse: Empirical foundations and principles. *International Journal of Man-Machine Studies*, 39:353–390, 1993.

[10] T. Grossman, J. Matejka, and G. Fitzmaurice. Chronicle: capture, exploration, and playback of document workflow histories. In *Proceedings of the Symposium on User Interface Software and Technology*, pages 143–152. ACM, 2010.

[11] K.-W. Hwang, D. Applegate, A. Archer, V. Gopalakrishnan, S. Lee, V. Misra, K. Ramakrishnan, and D. Swayne. Leveraging video viewing patterns for optimal content placement. In R. Bestak, L. Kencl, L. Li, J. Widmer, and H. Yin, editors, *NETWORKING 2012*, volume 7290 of *Lecture Notes in Computer Science*, pages 44–58. Springer Berlin Heidelberg, 2012.

[12] J. Juran and A. Godfrey. *Juran's Quality Handbook*. Juran's quality handbook, 5e. McGraw Hill, 1999.

[13] D. Kimber, T. Dunnigan, A. Girgensohn, F. Shipman, T. Turner, and T. Yang. Trailblazing: Video playback control by direct object manipulation. In *International Conference on Multimedia and Expo*, pages 1015–1018. IEEE, July 2007.

[14] D. Kirk, A. Sellen, R. Harper, and K. Wood. Understanding videowork. In *Proceedings of the Conference on Human Factors in Computing Systems*, CHI, pages 61–70. ACM, 2007.

[15] I. Leftheriotis, C. Gkonela, and K. Chorianopoulos. Efficient video indexing on the web: A system that leverages user interactions with a video player. In *Proceedings of the 2nd International Conference on User-Centric Media (UCMEDIA)*, 2012.

[16] I. Li, J. Nichols, T. Lau, C. Drews, and A. Cypher. Here's what i did: sharing and reusing web activity with actionshot. In *Proceedings of the Conference on Human Factors in Computing Systems*, pages 723–732. ACM, 2010.

[17] R. Mertens, R. Farzan, and P. Brusilovsky. Social navigation in web lectures. In *Proc. of the Conference on Hypertext and Hypermedia*, pages 41–44. ACM, 2006.

[18] D. A. Shamma, R. Shaw, P. L. Shafton, and Y. Liu. Watch what i watch: using community activity to understand content. In *Proceedings of the international workshop on Workshop on multimedia information retrieval*, MIR '07, pages 275–284, New York, NY, USA, 2007. ACM.

[19] T. Syeda-Mahmood and D. Ponceleon. Learning video browsing behavior and its application in the generation of video previews. In *Proceedings of the International Conference on Multimedia*, pages 119–128. ACM, 2001.

[20] S. Vihavainen, S. Mate, L. Seppälä, F. Cricri, and I. D. Curcio. We want more: human-computer collaboration in mobile social video remixing of music concerts. In *Proceedings of the Conference on Human Factors in Computing Systems*, pages 287–296. ACM, 2011.

[21] B. Yu, W.-Y. Ma, K. Nahrstedt, and H.-J. Zhang. Video summarization based on user log enhanced link analysis. In *Proceedings of the 11th International Conference on Multimedia*, pages 382–391. ACM, 2003.

[22] G. Zipf. Human behaviour and the principle of least-effort. Addison-Wesley, Cambridge, MA, 1949.

VisionSketch: Integrated Support for Example-Centric Programming of Image Processing Applications

Jun Kato, Takeo Igarashi – The University of Tokyo, Tokyo, Japan – {jun.kato | takeo}@acm.org

ABSTRACT

We propose an integrated development environment (IDE) called "VisionSketch", which supports example-centric programming for easily building image processing pipelines. With VisionSketch, a programmer is first asked to select the input video. Then, he can start building the pipeline with a visual programming language that provides immediate graphical feedback for algorithms applied to the video. He can also use a text-based editor to create or edit the implementation of each algorithm. During the development, the pipeline is always ready for execution with a video player-like interface enabling rapid iterative prototyping. In a preliminary user study, VisionSketch was positively received by five programmers, who had prior experience of writing text-based image processing programs and could successfully build interesting applications.

Keywords: Image processing, computer vision, integrated development environment, example-centric programming.

Index Terms: H.5.2. User Interfaces – GUI; D.2.6. Programming Environments – Graphical Environments, Integrated Environments.

1 INTRODUCTION

Many surveillance cameras and other kinds of monitoring cameras with fixed viewpoints are located almost ubiquitously around cities and within buildings, recording what is happening there. Time-lapse photography is also getting popular. Time-series photos taken from a fixed viewpoint highlight processes that look subtle on an ordinary time scale. It is possible to write a program that processes these recordings, detects interesting events, and extracts useful information from the real world with the help of software libraries like OpenCV [1] that provide image processing algorithms. For instance, it is possible to implement a program that monitors growth of a fungus and notifies when it has grown enough to eat. It is also possible to implement a program that monitors the rotation of a disc on a turntable being scratched by a disc jockey and creates its rotation-time graph. These examples are taken from the study reported in Section 5.

The development of such programs in conventional text-based integrated development environments (IDEs) involves two distinctive challenges. As for the first challenge, the software libraries provide various kinds of computer vision algorithms that take an image as an input parameter. Their other parameters often have visual meaning, such as four *Point* objects denoting a rectangular area in the image. These parameters cannot or (at least) are difficult to be specified in a text-based programming language. Output from the algorithms is often also an image. Conventional IDEs provide a text-based code editor and do not reflect such graphical aspect of the program. As for the second challenge, when it is necessary to monitor the behavior of the program, first, a boilerplate code is written such as that for loading an image and opening a window for visualizing the results. The code is then compiled, and the program is executed. These steps are repeated

iteratively until the processing result is satisfactory. This repetition takes long time and prevents fluent exploratory programming.

Provided the above-described issues, this paper aims to answer the research question: "How can an IDE be made usable for the development of image processing applications?" Our hypothesis was that an IDE that supports example-centric programming and integrates graphical and text-based user interfaces is usable for such purpose. VisionSketch IDE was developed to test the hypothesis and is distributed as an open-source project [2]. It first asks the programmer to select the input video to start the implementation. The selected video serves as a concrete example with which VisionSketch generates graphical feedback of the program to the programmer. Working on a concrete example is a characteristic shared with tools for end users capable of extracting information from an example in a similar manner to ImageJ [3]. The difference between VisionSketch and ImageJ is that the output of the system is an executable pipeline rather than the extracted information. VisionSketch can take another video source as an input to produce new results, and newly defined components can be reused to build another pipeline. Rapid prototyping tools for image processing, such as Light Widgets [4] and Crayons [5], provide user interfaces for tuning specific algorithms for extracting information and pass it to external applications. Instead, VisionSketch makes it possible to build general image processing pipelines. It is similar to DejaVu [6] and Gestalt [7] in that it aims to facilitate the programmer's workflow with the help of graphical representations of example data. Although VisionSketch is strongly inspired by these works, it assigns a more proactive role to graphical representations. While these systems merely use a text-based programming language, VisionSketch uses both visual and text-based programming languages to implement programs.

VisionSketch provides three interlinked interfaces (Figure 1): a *canvas* for monitoring and editing the pipeline whose graphical view is updated in real time during its execution; a *visual editor* for choosing and setting up each image processing component, which allows the programmer to draw shapes on the input image to narrow down the list of applicable components, set up their parameters, and immediately see the output of the component; and a text-based *code editor* for editing the implementation of any image processing component.

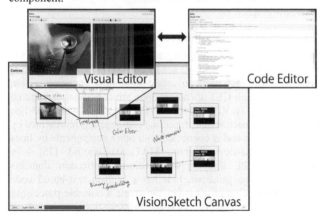

Figure 1. Overview of VisionSketch IDE.

2 RELATED WORK

2.1 Tool Support for Example-centric Programming

Early work on programming by demonstration includes systems for example-centric programming such as Pygmalion [8]. Such systems help a novice programmer to create programs with concrete examples of input data. For instance, when the programmer wants to implement a factorial function, he/she first provides an example input (such as "6") to the function. The system then tries to execute the function until it reaches the end of the code, where the further behaviour of the program is undefined. When a new code snippet is input, the system tries to execute that code again. This iterative process continues until the function returns a concrete value, in this case, 720. VisionSketch also employs the same example-driven development, where an example input to the program is given prior to the implementation of the program. Recent work on example-centric programming includes Subtext [9]. It provides a text-based code editor that allows the programmer to write an incomplete definition of a function and test cases that call the function with example input data. It automatically executes the code and shows stack traces next to the code editor, highlighting the incompleteness of the function definition. The programmer can iteratively update the code and see stack traces generated by executing the program with the example input for developing a program. VisionSketch does not show much textual information such as stack traces, but it does provide graphical representations of the under-development program to aid program understanding.

Several attempts to enhance text-based IDEs with graphical representations of example data have been made. For example, the Barista framework [10] helps to implement structured editors with graphical representations. For instance, it can be used to show a multimedia comment of an image processing operation in which images represent example input and output of the operation. Gestalt IDE [7] is designed for machine-learning applications and includes user interfaces for collecting, editing, learning, and testing examples. Picode IDE [11] is equipped with a text-based editor capable of showing inline photos representing posture data for humans and robots. The photos serve as arguments to APIs for processing posture data. Such concrete examples help the programmer to understand the program. DejaVu IDE [6] is used for developing interactive camera-based applications that add two interlinked interfaces: *timeline* is capable of recording data input to the program as examples and visualizing the history of the program state during its runtime, and *canvas* is quite similar to our own *canvas* interface in that it also provides real-time visualization of the program status. The difference between the two versions of canvas is that DejaVu's *canvas* is mere visualization while our *canvas* is a visual programming language that shows an editable data-flow graph.

2.2 Visual Programming for Image Processing

Many visual programming languages (VPLs) only visualize the structure of the program (i.e., not its contents.) VisionBlocks [12] aims to allow end users to create their own computer vision programs through GUI operations by a structured editor inspired from Scratch [13]. VIVA [14] is a VPL that adopts a box-and-line notation where each image processing component is represented by a symbolic icon and is connected with other components by lines to form a data-flow diagram. MATLAB/Simulink [15] is a commercial VPL that supports various application domains (including image processing). It has a built-in text-based code editor with which a programmer can create a reusable processing component. Some components visualize interesting data, but others are just represented by text labels and symbols. On the other hand, our *canvas* makes use of graphical representations to go beyond symbolic notation.

Some existing VPLs add more meanings to their use of visual components. For example, Agentsheets [16] provides a spreadsheet interface, whose cell shows an interactive agent that reacts to user input or information from other agents. ConMan [17] allows the user to interact with each visual component and set up parameters for rendering computer graphics. Its recorder interface is similar to our video player-like interface in that they both allow the programmer to control the program execution in a frame-by-frame manner. There are two major differences from these VPLs to VisionSketch. First, graphical representations in VisionSketch are used to build programs while those in other systems are for tuning parameters and visualizing results. Second, VisionSketch has an integrated *code editor* to edit text-based implementation of each component. This function ensures that new algorithms can be implemented at any time without leaving the IDE.

These VPLs provide a live programming experience, eliminating the gap between building and executing programs. When the programmer edits the VPL, the program is updated without explicit compilation operations and is always kept ready for execution. VisionSketch also provides a live programming environment, but it is a bit more involved since it integrates a text-based *code editor*. When the text-based code is edited, it is automatically compiled and loaded onto the program, replacing old components if any.

2.3 Tools for Image Processing

Cameras have become pervasive, and many tools to support camera-image processing have been proposed. Their target users range from end-users to novice and professional programmers. Some of these tools do not require prior knowledge of image processing algorithms. For example, Light Widgets is a system [4] that detects areas of skin in the camera images. It transforms any visible surface in everyday spaces into an interactive widget controlled by hand gestures. Vision on Tap [18] adds simple image processing features (such as motion detection) to a webcam video stream and notifies the user of interesting events through a web service. Crayons [5] allows a novice programmer to train a classifier through painting example still images. The trained classifier can later be called from the programmer's own program. *Visual editor* is inspired by the work. Eyepatch [19] is similar to Crayons but operates on video, notifies events through a network protocol, and provides multiple classifiers. While these tools provide access to a limited set of image processing algorithms, VisionSketch provides an IDE with which general image processing applications can be built.

ImageJ [3] is a standalone GUI tool with which end-users can apply image processing operations to images and videos. It requires prior knowledge of such operations, but it is used by various research projects in a broad area of natural science fields. With ImageJ, the user can draw shapes on a source image to narrow down the list of potential operations. This function is equivalent to our component filtering method in *visual editor*. It is capable of creating user-written macros and plug-ins, making the system look more like a development environment. The differences between ImageJ and VisionSketch comes from their different scopes. That is, ImageJ is a tool capable of scripting, while VisionSketch is an IDE that integrates graphical operations. For instance, the user interface for annotating the input image by drawing shapes is used for image processing operation by ImageJ and for adding a new node of a visual programming language by VisionSketch.

OpenCV [1] is a software toolkit that provides a collection of computer vision algorithms. ImageJ can also be used as a Java library. These toolkits provide well-designed APIs to support writing text-based code. The present work focuses on providing broader support for the entire workflow of the programmer. VisionSketch contains a Java wrapper of OpenCV as its default library. Within VisionSketch, any OpenCV functions can be used to implement a programmer's own image processing components.

3 VISIONSKETCH IDE

VisionSketch is an IDE for developing image processing pipelines. Design of VisionSketch benefits from the characteristics of the supported applications. The applications deal with image processing algorithms, which take an image or video (time-series images) as input. Optional arguments usually have visual meaning, such as four *Point* objects denoting a rectangular area in an image. Outputs from the algorithms are also images, videos, or a group of regions in the image. Conventional IDEs are usually equipped with a text-based code editor and debugger, which cannot present such data intuitively. It was therefore decided to implement the user interface of VisionSketch from scratch in order to better reflect the visual nature of the program.

VisionSketch has three interlinked components: the *canvas* and *visual editor* interfaces are designed to support visual programming; the text-based *code editor* interface is implemented to preserve the full expressivity of text-based programming. These interfaces for visual and text-based programming complement each other to support the programmer's entire workflow. Each interface is described in the following three subsections, followed by a concrete use case to describe how these interfaces help the programmer's workflow.

3.1 VisionSketch Canvas

Canvas is a visual programming environment in which each code element is primarily represented by an image or video rather than text (Figure 2). It is noteworthy that it is *more* visual than typical visual programming languages such as VIVA [14] and VisionBlocks [12], whose program structure is visually presented, but data are referenced by text, including file names and constants. It is the first interface that the programmer sees when opening the VisionSketch IDE. It provides an overview of the program, and although it looks like the *canvas* interface of DejaVu [6], it represents a data flow of the program in the same manner as ConMan [17] and VIVA [14].

Canvas initially has one vacant box. The programmer clicks it to choose the input data (such as a set of time-lapse photos, a video, or live camera input). Then, he/she drags a line from an existing box to another place to add a new box representing an image processing component. When he/she clicks an existing box, *visual editor* appears and allows the corresponding component to be edited. He/she can also draw freeform lines to annotate the program.

Compared to a conventional text-based editor where statements and line comments are all represented by text, VisionSketch shows a box to represent one statement and freeform drawings to comments.

Canvas contains a playback interface in its bottom part. It allows flexible control of program execution. With this playback interface, the programmer can test the program with various input data in a more casual way compared to conventional compile-and-run operations, thereby accelerating the development process. While DejaVu also provides a playback interface (named *timeline*), it is used for navigating and replaying recorded sessions of program executions. On the other hand, the playback interface of VisionSketch is used for running the program by providing example input data. Unlike general step-by-step navigation of a text-based debugger, these playback interfaces are specialized for image processing applications and allow frame-by-frame navigation.

When the input data is obtained from a camera in real time, the interface can only "play" or "pause" program execution. Frames that arrive while being paused are discarded. Otherwise, when the input data is from recorded photos or a video, the interface is also capable of jumping to a specific frame of the photos or video, going forward or backward for one frame, slowing down or speeding up the execution, which is usually done at the original frame rate (such as 30 frames per second). The "tape recorder" in ConMan has a similar role driving the computer graphics rendering pipeline, but it can only animate the computer graphics once (or forever in a loop) and does not provide as fine granularity of control as our playback interface.

3.2 Visual Editor

Visual editor is used to choose an image processing component and specify its parameters. It visually shows input and output of the component on its left and right side (Figure 3). It appears when the programmer clicks an image processing component or a vacant box before any component is assigned in *canvas*. With *visual editor*, the programmer first specifies the region of interest (ROI) by drawing shapes on the input image. Next, he/she can choose an image processing component from a list of existing components that are capable of processing the provided ROI. All the other components, which cannot be applied to the ROI, are hidden for convenience. Then, the processing result is immediately shown next to the input image. If the processing result is not satisfactory, the ROI can be edited or another component can be chosen. These operations take immediate effect and provide graphical feedback. He/she can alternatively switch to *code editor* to edit the implementation of the current component or create a new image processing component that takes the ROI of the input image as its parameter.

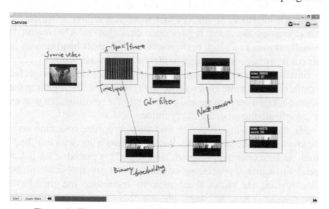

Figure 2. The *canvas* showing two algorithms in parallel.

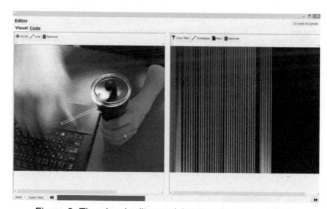

Figure 3. The *visual editor* applying time-lapse operation.

Compared to general programs, image processing pipelines tend to have components with the same or less variety of types of input and output, which often represent images. In such a case, type-based code completion of conventional IDEs do not help much in filtering the components. Instead, VisionSketch uses parameter information for the filtering, which consists of the ROI and the type of the input image. The ROI is a collection of shapes drawn on the input image. Currently, a shape is one of a circle, a line, or a rectangle. The programmer uses a shape tool (one of the "circle", "line", or "rectangle" tools) to draw a new shape or uses the "remove" tool to remove existing shapes. Every time the ROI is updated, the list is updated according to whether each component is applicable to the current parameters or not. For instance, when a circle is drawn on the input image, "linear polar conversion" appears on the list since it can be applied to a circular area. To support the parameter-based code completion, every component is required to implement a static method to check if it is applicable to the given set of parameters. In addition, when an image processing component is selected, how the ROI can be edited is limited. For instance, since "linear polar conversion" can only be applied to a circle, the "line" and "rectangle" tools are hidden. Every component is therefore also required to implement a static method to check if each tool can be used in the current context.

While conventional IDEs force necessitate running the entire program to see the result of a specific processing component, VisionSketch has a built-in interpreter that is responsible for keeping the image processing pipeline up-to-date. When a new image processing component in *visual editor* is selected, the interpreter instantiates the component, and sets up the instance by calling *parameterize(parameter)* method of the component, where *parameter* is a pair composed of the ROI and the input image. It then immediately shows its processing results next to the input image. The results are retrieved by calling *calculate (image)* method of the component. Every time the ROI is updated, the interpreter calls the *parameterize* and *calculate* methods again, as well as the *calculate* method of the subsequent components in the data-flow graph to update dependent components.

3.3 Code Editor

The text-based *code editor* is the last component used in the programmer's workflow, but it is not the least important (Figure 4). It allows the programmer to edit the implementation of any image processing component used in the VisionSketch IDE. In addition to the text-based code editor by which the programmer writes the source code, the proposed editor includes several specialized interfaces used to specify the component information used in *visual editor*. They include text boxes for specifying its function name, description, expressions (one returning acceptable input parameters

and the other returning available tools given the context information), and a combo box for selecting an icon. At the bottom of the code editor, an "update" button to save the current definition and replace all the existing components in the image processing pipeline with the updated version is provided.

As introduced in Subsection 3.2, *code editor* is shown when the programmer is not satisfied with the current processing result. Therefore, VisionSketch makes an assumption that the programmer is focusing on implementing a function for processing the current specific example rather than implementing general functions. It provides more context-sensitive support for text-based programming. In the current implementation of VisionSketch, when a new image processing component is created, *code editor* shows a template corresponding to the current ROI. For instance, when the ROI is a circle, the default expression for defining acceptable input parameters is set to "*shapes.size() == 1 && shapes.iterator().next() instanceof Circle*" checking whether the ROI is a circle or not.

When the programmer changes the code, he/she clicks the "update" button and goes back to *visual editor*, and the code is automatically compiled and reloaded to the current program. This process is technically called "hot swapping" of Java classes supported by recent text-based IDEs. Compared to the general hot swapping, the process of VisionSketch automatically feeds the reloaded component with the image of the most recent frame in the parent component. In this way, an up-to-date view of the image processing results is always provided.

3.4 Example Use Case

To describe how the three above-described interfaces can help the programmer in harmony, a concrete example use case is introduced in the following scenario (Figure 5). Bob usually grinds coffee beans, drinks a cup of espresso, and starts his work. He does not know the right amount of coffee powder for one cup, but he thinks he can estimate it by counting how many times he rotates the grinder's handle. He wants to write a program that counts the number of grinds, which applies several kinds of image processing to a recorded video of him grinding the coffee beans.

First, Bob records a video of his hand grinding the handle and loads it on VisionSketch IDE, which is shown as the source box. He can change the source to another video or live input from the camera at any time, but in this case, the loaded video will always serve as the input data to the pipeline. Using *canvas*, he drags-and-drops the mouse pointer from the source box to another arbitrary place to create a vacant box.

Next, he clicks the vacant box to open *visual editor* and starts choosing the image processing component. While *canvas* only shows thumbnails of the videos in the boxes, *visual editor* renders the video dot by dot. By playing the video in the editor with the playback interface, he notices that there is a region in which his hand crosses the same region once per rotation. The region is usually shown as a black background, but when his hand crosses it, its color prominently changes to that of his skin. He wants to create a timeline where the change in the region over time is projected spatially. To be more concrete, he wants to copy a line region in the source image every frame and paste it into the resulting image at an x-coordinate incremented every frame.

He starts drawing shapes to find the appropriate operation once he knows what he wants to do. When he draws a line with the "line" tool, such an operation (named "time-lapse") is placed in the list of predefined image processing operations that are applicable to the line region. He clicks the button to instantiate the time-lapse component. Then, he starts playing the video to cumulatively update the resulting image, showing changes over time. Next, he

Figure 4. The *code editor* for editing image processing algorithm.

goes back to *canvas* and creates another vacant box for specifying a subsequent operation. Navigating between *canvas* and *visual editor* does not interrupt the video playback.

In the case of *visual editor* for editing the newly created vacant box, the result of the time-lapse operation is treated as an input image shown on the left side. He wants to perform a contour counter operation on the input image since he thinks that the number of closed regions in the time-lapse image represents the number of grinds. However, he does not see the operation in the list, since the source image for the contour counter operation needs to be a single channel grayscale image or a binary image composed of black or white pixels. He decides to apply a color filter operation to create a grayscale image, where the skin color is highlighted in white. He highlights some time points with the rectangle tool when his hand is not crossing the line. By clicking the "color filter" button, a color filter is created with the current image and the ROI as its parameters. The resulting image is a grayscale image in which all the crossings are painted in white and everything else in black.

It is not always the case that the desired operation is in the list of predefined components. When the contour counter is applied to the result of the color filter, it outputs a much greater number of contours than expected. It seems that the result of the color filter requires some noise reduction. No such predefined operation exists, so he/she clicks the "new" button, which is the last button in the list of components, inputs the name of the operation as "noise removal," and opens *code editor* to start the implementation of a new image processing component. The code template is generated and provided to reduce the time for writing the boilerplate code. It just copies the source image to the resulting image by default, so it needs to be changed to reduce the noise. Various ways to do that are available, but simple erosion and dilation operations are thought to be sufficient. He/she replaces the original line of code that copies the image with a new line that calls up the erosion and dilation operations provided by the OpenCV library.

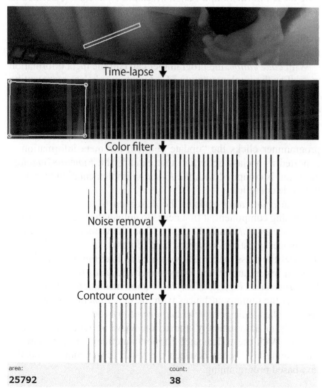

area:
25792

count:
38

Figure 5. The pipeline created in the example use case.

Once coding is completed, the programmer clicks the "update" button to save and compile the noise removal operation so it can be used in *visual editor*. If a compilation error occurs, it is shown in a message dialog. At that time, it is possible to go back to *visual editor* without any error, and the stored noise removal operation can be applied to the input image. It is noteworthy that the newly implemented operation is loaded as a Java class of an image processing operation. It runs reasonably fast for complex image processing and is reusable, which usually cannot be achieved by interpretive scripting languages.

If the programmer notices that the erosion operation is not enough by seeing the result of the image processing operation in *visual editor*, he goes back to *code editor*, changes some parameters for the erosion, clicks the "update" button and navigates back to *visual editor* to see the updated result, which is now satisfactory. This iterative cycle is enabled by the built-in interpreter and hot-swapping mechanism. Otherwise, it is necessary to compile the entire program and execute it with the source video till the program counter reaches the frame of interest. Such iterative process is cumbersome and difficult without tool support.

Finally, the contour counter operation is applied to see all the crossings highlighted in the resulting image with the total number of crossings shown below. While every image processing component is expected to return an image as a result, it can optionally return other values that are visualized in *visual editor* and can be retrieved by the child components for further processing. While VisionSketch currently supports numerical values and text for this optional visualization, its architecture is extensible enough to support other types of data for visualization.

4 IMPLEMENTATION

VisionSketch is an attempt to tightly integrate visual and text-based programming in one IDE. Since recent open-source IDEs that do the same kind of integration could not be found, it was necessary to build the IDE from scratch with help of existing low-level components such as a Java compiler, a library that implements image processing algorithms, and a text-based code editor with support of syntax highlighting and other convenient features. Its open-source distribution [2] is helpful for understanding the details.

4.1 Overview

VisionSketch runs on a computer that hosts a Java VM and the Java wrapper of the OpenCV [1] library. It currently supports both 32-bit and 64-bit Windows, Mac OS X, and common Linux distributions. It requires a video source to work on (Figure 6). The programmer can use recordings or connect to a camera device to retrieve images in real time. VisionSketch is also capable of periodically receiving images from a smartphone running the Android OS or an Internet-protocol camera.

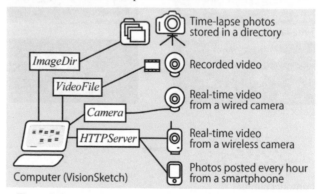

Figure 6. *Input* implementations and supported hardware setup.

119

In its current implementation, VisionSketch has five predefined image processing components as shown in Figure 7, whose details are available online [2].

4.2 VisionSketch Visual Programming Language

Canvas is a visual programming environment that graphically shows the image processing pipeline and allows it to be edited. It has a built-in interpreter that controls the execution of the pipeline. The pipeline is a directed graph without any loops, i.e., a tree whose nodes are represented by an instance of *Stmt* class (where *Stmt* stands for <u>st</u>ate<u>ment</u>). Each *Stmt* instance can have one or more child *Stmt* instances. The processing result of the instance is passed to the children as their input. Multiple children allow the programmer to compare alternatives and help him/her find the best algorithm. A *Stmt* instance always has one parent *Stmt*, except for a subclass instance (called *Input*), which is the root node in the tree and provides input data to the pipeline.

There are currently four implementations of *Input*: *VideoFile* for loading a video file, *ImageDir* for loading image files in a specified directory, *Camera* for retrieving images from a camera in real time, and *HTTPServer* for receiving images posted from external programs through the HTTP 1.0 protocol. There are currently two client implementations: one for periodically posting photos from a smartphone, and another for bypassing images from an Internet-protocol camera. When the root node is a *VideoFile* or *ImageDir* instance, the execution of the pipeline can be thought of as moving the cursor from the beginning to the end of the input set. In this case, the programmer can freely move the cursor to any arbitrary frame. Such a seeking operation is not supported by the other implementations (including *Camera* and *HTTPServer*).

All *Stmt* instances except *Input* are associated with an image processing component that is an instance of the algorithm-specific class that extends the *Function* abstract class. *Function* provides the *parameterize(parameter)* method, where *parameter* is an instance

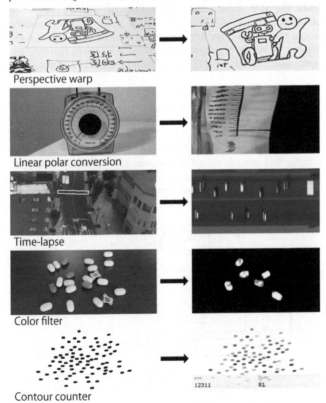

Perspective warp

Linear polar conversion

Time-lapse

Color filter

Contour counter

Figure 7. Predefined image processing components.

of the *FunctionParameter* class that holds a pair composed of the ROI and the image. The ROI is a set of shapes, each of which is a *Shape* instance. There are currently three subclasses of *Shape*: *Line*, *Rectangle*, and *Circle*. For instance, when the programmer draws a line on the input image, a *Line* instance is instantiated and added to the ROI. Then, *parameterize* method is called once upon the instantiation of the *Function* class when the component is selected in *visual editor*. It is also called whenever the programmer edits the shapes and updates the ROI. When the parent *Stmt* provides a new input image, *calculate(image)* method is called to calculate the output. For instance, *ColorFilterFunction* provides a color filter based on the histogram back projection. Its *parameterize* method calculates histogram from the ROI of the image and its *calculate* method calculates the back projection of the histogram to the current image. Through calls to these two methods, pixels in the current image with similar colors to the ROI of the parameter image are painted in white.

4.3 Integration of Visual and Text-based Programming

Visual editor is the user interface that bridges the gap between the visual and text-based programming languages. It allows the programmer to instantiate a *Function* instance, set up its parameters, and make it ready for use in the VisionSketch visual programming language. It also allows him to switch to the *code editor* to edit its text-based definition.

Implementation of an image processing component is not only responsible for processing images but also for showing and hiding relevant information in *visual editor*. For instance, when *visual editor* generates the list of *Function* subclasses, it filters the list by checking whether each subclass accepts the current set of parameters or not. Buttons in the list for instantiating *Function* instances have their own icons and text labels. Once the *Function* instance is created, some shape tools may be disabled to prevent ROIs from being invalid for the image processing. To show and hide these information, a *FunctionTemplate* subclass is defined as a singleton for each *Function* subclass. For instance, a *ColorFilter* class extends a *FunctionTemplate* abstract class and implements methods such as *getName()* and *getIconFileName()*, providing meta information about a *ColorFilterFunction* class.

With *code editor*, the programmer can edit the meta information as well as the implementation of a *Function* subclass representing an image processing algorithm. It is capable of Java syntax highlighting, code folding, and other basic features. While the *Function* implementation is directly saved as a Java source code, the meta information is saved as an XML file. When the programmer clicks the "update" button, the meta information is exported as a class definition that extends the *FunctionTemplate* class and is compiled with the *Function* implementation by a Java bytecode compiler.

When *code editor* updates the definition of an existing image processing component, it first needs to unload the old *Function* and *FunctionTemplate* implementations from the virtual machine. First, it replaces existing instances with dummy instances. Then, it disposes the class loader that was used to load the old definitions. Next, it instantiates a new class loader and loads newly compiled *Function* and *FunctionTemplate* implementations. Finally, it replaces the dummy instances with the new *Function* instances. It also invokes their *parameterize(parameter)* and *calculate(image)* methods to automatically update the view of *visual editor* and *canvas*. With these dedicated support functions, the programmer can seamlessly switch between the visual programming and the text-based programming.

5 USER EXPERIENCE

A preliminary user study was conducted to collect user feedback about VisionSketch and investigate its applications and limitations.

5.1 Setting

Five male participants, aged 23-36 years old (mean: 29.6 years old, standard deviation (SD): 4.40 years), were recruited for the study in a university laboratory of computer science. They all had professional programming experience, building applications for commercial and research purposes. They had basic knowledge of the Java programming language which is used in *code editor*. They also had prior experience of building image processing applications. Four of them had used OpenCV [1] for the purpose. Their uses of OpenCV vary from color reduction and beautifying photos to edge detection from a static image. While we did not conduct a comparative study against another IDE, we chose the participants with such experience and asked them to compare the VisionSketch experience with their past experience throughout the study.

The user study consisted of four parts. First, the participants answered a demographic questionnaire asking their age, sex, and prior experience with programming and computer vision libraries. Then, they watched a demonstration of the VisionSketch IDE, as introduced in Subsection 3.4. Next, they were provided with five pre-recorded videos which we thought interesting events could be detected; they were also allowed to bring an interesting video or use a webcam to retrieve a live video input to work on. Among these vide sources, each of them chose favourite one and used the IDE to implement an application. Finally, when they were satisfied with the processing results of their applications, they answered a post-experimental questionnaire.

5.2 Observations and User Feedback

All participants successfully created their own applications in one to two hours. The post-experimental questionnaire contained four common questions about each interface. The results are listed in Table 1, consisting of the mean, standard deviation, and percentage of positive responses (>4 on a 7-point Likert scale) for each question. We also asked to write down concrete comments on each interface. Some of the representative answers are *quoted* below.

The participants appreciated the example-centric workflow of the VisionSketch IDE that *"gives immediate graphical feedback concerning the program being developed."* Canvas and *visual editor* were favored by all participants (Q1), thought to be simple enough (Q2) and easy to use (Q3). It is *"very convenient since I could see the up-to-date overview at a glance."* In addition, *"the playback interface in the canvas allows me to control and monitor the execution interactively. It was very nice."* The shape tools in *visual editor "provide immediate graphical feedback of the ROI tuning."* One participant answered that *visual editor* was not simple (Q2) because *"it takes time to find a graphical way to do something I could do with text-based code."* He was used to low-level APIs of OpenCV, and the graphical operation typically involves several API calls. As a result, he felt overwhelmed. Another participant commented that *"existing IDEs force me to run the entire program to see a small piece of interesting results, but VisionSketch allows me to check it interactively without leaving the current context."*

All of the participants implemented new image processing components with *code editor*. While they admit the necessity of text-based programming to precisely control the algorithm logic, they were observed to prefer to stay with visual programming. One participant commented, *"It would be nice if its usage could be reduced, as the UI part is much better."* Another participant demanded, *"Code editor should come with more graphical feedback, such as a live view of the processing results, as visual editor does."* They sometimes utilized existing components and avoided text-based coding (for a concrete example, see Subsection 5.2.3). Nevertheless, they appreciated the "update" button, which *"immediately makes the newly defined or updated component available in visual editor and canvas."*

Hereafter, three applications developed by three participants in the user study are presented to showcase the real use of the VisionSketch IDE and investigate its capability and limitation (Figure 8). Two applications developed by the other two participants monitor traffic on a road and count the number of visitors in a room, respectively. Their descriptions are omitted because their usage patterns are included in the other applications.

5.2.1 Disc-jockey Analyzer

The participant retrieved a video file from an online video-sharing website that records a live session of a professional disc jockey from a ceiling-mounted camera. It is not easy for him to analyze how equipment is manipulated by the disc jockey because it contains various interfaces and the manipulation is often very quick.

To address this issue, he implemented an application with which he can analyze the actions of the disc jockey. He created multiple children of the video input to process multiple interfaces separately. For instance, two branches count the number of discs used on each turntable. Another two branches show the rotation of the discs as vertical motions. When the disc is moving clockwise, the output image scrolls down. Another branch monitors the slider's knob for controlling the left/right balance to create a time-balance graph. To monitor disc rotations and volume changes, he used linear polar conversion, perspective warp, and time-lapse components. To count the number of discs used in the session, he used perspective

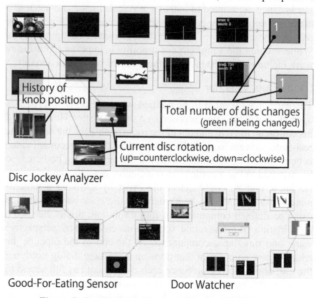

Figure 8. Applications developed by the participants.

# Question	Canvas			Visual editor			Code editor		
	Mean	SD	%	Mean	SD	%	Mean	SD	%
1 I would like to use it frequently.	5.80	0.74	5/5	5.80	0.74	5/5	3.20	1.17	3/5
2 I found it unnecessarily complex.	2.00	0.63	0/5	2.80	1.33	1/5	3.80	1.72	3/5
3 I thought it was easy to use.	6.00	0.63	5/5	5.60	1.02	5/5	3.40	1.02	2/5
4 I needed technical support to use it.	3.00	1.09	2/5	3.60	1.50	2/5	5.00	1.26	4/5

Table 1. Results of questionnaire.

warp, color filter, time-lapse, and contour counter components in addition to a new component that takes the contour counter component as its parent and displays the number of discs which is incremented when the number of detected contours gets increased and exceeds a specific threshold.

The participant looked surprised at the capability of the time-lapse operation, with which he could create various meaning graphs. He commented that the application is already very useful for analysis of the actions of the disc jockey; however, for reproducing the actions, he wants audio playback synchronized with the video. While VisionSketch currently focuses on image processing, audio-related feature is interesting future work.

5.2.2 "Good-for-eating" Sensor

The participant chose a set of time-lapse photos monitoring fungus. Photos were taken every hour under a controlled lighting condition. He wanted to create a program that analyzes the newest photo and notifies him when the fungus has grown enough for eating.

To implement such a pipeline, he decided to measure the size of the fungus area. When the size exceeds a specified threshold, the user is notified. First, he seeks an image without visible fungus and sets up the background subtraction component. When he played the video, it made the fungus area look brighter than the other area. Then, he implemented a binarization filter that binarizes each pixel (paints it white if it is brighter than the threshold; otherwise, black). To tweak the threshold, he switched seamlessly between *code* and *visual editor* with help of the "update" button. Next, he found the result a bit noisy. He implemented a median filter and inserted it right before the background subtraction to successfully remove the noise. Finally, he applied the contour counter operation, which not only counts the number of closed regions but also counts their area size. He added another component at the end that shows a coloured circle (if the size is less than the threshold, red; otherwise, green). When he switches the video source to the *HTTPServer* that receives a new image every hour, the colour tells him whether the fungus is good for eating or not.

He appreciated the *visual editor*'s capability to quickly switch and test multiple image processing components, but he commented that *"Additional interactive GUIs for tuning other parameters (such as numerical constants declared in the text-based code) are desirable,"* which was previously explored by Juxtapose [20]. Additionally, he commented that the current VPL is a bit too simple. For instance, he wanted to output a grayscale image and use it as a mask in another image processing component. This function requires the capability of a *Stmt* instance to have two input sources. While keeping the simplicity for usability is important, our future work includes such extension of the VPL for better functionality.

5.2.3 Door Watcher

The participant wanted to be notified when the door of a room is opened, so that he is not surprised by a sudden visitor. He first asked his colleague to go in and out of the room to observe the door in the real-time webcam images. Then, he noticed that the recorded video is better than live input to prevent his colleague being bothered, so he switched to the recorded video including his colleague's action. He knew that he could detect the event by applying a pattern-matching algorithm, but he hesitated to use *code editor* and tried using predefined components to find a solution; that is, he used a combination of background subtraction, color filter, perspective warp, and time-lapse components. At the end of the pipeline, he added a new component that pops up a message dialog notifying the user about the visitor. Since each component has full access to the Java API, an original GUI can be easily added. For instance, a slider interface may be provided for tuning a numerical parameter.

To get a satisfactory result, he tried various combinations of image processing components, which were effectively supported by the immediate graphical response. He commented that *canvas* should show the text label for each component as well as the graphical representation. When the pipeline grows large, mere graphical information gets confusing since it often looks similar.

6 Conclusion

The proposed VisionSketch IDE has three interlinked interfaces to facilitate example-centric workflow of building image processing applications. *Canvas* and *visual editor* interfaces show graphical representations of concrete examples to aid program understanding. They also allow graphical operations such as drawing shapes on the input image to choose and tune image processing components. The text-based *code editor* is still needed to implement new algorithms and needs interactive GUI support.

References

[1] OpenCV. http://opencv.org/

[2] VisionSketch. http://junkato.jp/visionsketch/

[3] M. D. Abràmoff, P. J. Magalhães, and S. J. Ram. Image processing with ImageJ. *Biophotonics International*, 11(7), pp.36–42, 2004.

[4] J. A. Fails and D. Olsen. Light widgets: interacting in every-day spaces. *IUI '02*, pp.63–69, 2002.

[5] J. A. Fails and D. Olsen. A design tool for camera-based interaction. *CHI '03*, pp.449–456, 2003.

[6] J. Kato, S. McDirmid, and X. Cao. DejaVu: integrated support for developing interactive camera-based programs. *UIST '12*, pp.189–196, 2012.

[7] K. Patel, N. Bancroft, S. M. Drucker, J. Fogarty, A. J. Ko, and J. Landay. Gestalt: integrated support for implementation and analysis in machine learning. *UIST '10*, pp.37–46, 2010.

[8] D. C. Smith. Pygmalion: an executable electronic blackboard. In *Watch What I Do: Programming by Demonstration*, pp.19–49, 1993.

[9] J. Edwards. Example centric programming. *ACM SIGPLAN Notices*, 39(12), pp.84–91, 2004.

[10] A. J. Ko and B. A. Myers. Barista: an implementation framework for enabling new tools, interaction techniques and views in code editors. *CHI '06*, pp.387–396, 2006.

[11] J. Kato, D. Sakamoto, and T. Igarashi. Picode: inline photos representing posture data in source code. *CHI '13*, pp.3097– 3100, 2013.

[12] A. Bendale, K. Chiu, K. Marwah, and R. Raskar. VisionBlocks: a social computer vision framework. *IEEE SocialCom '11*, pp.521–526, 2011.

[13] J. Maloney, M. Resnick, N. Rusk, B. Silverman, and E. Eastmond. The Scratch programming language and environment. *ACM TOCE*, 10(4):16, 2010.

[14] S. L. Tanimoto. VIVA: a visual language for image processing. *Journal of Visual Languages and Computing*, 1(2), pp.127–139, 1990.

[15] MATLAB/Simulink. http://mathworks.com/products/simulink/

[16] A. Repenning and W. Citrin. Agentsheets: applying grid-based spatial reasoning to human-computer interaction. *IEEE VL '93*, pp.77–82, 1993.

[17] P. E. Haeberli. Conman: a visual programming language for interactive graphics. *SIGGRAPH '88*, pp.103–111, 1988. ACM.

[18] K. Chiu and R. Raskar. Computer vision on tap. *IEEE CVPR Workshops*, pp. 31–38, 2009.

[19] D. Maynes-Aminzade, T. Winograd, and T. Igarashi. Eyepatch: prototyping camera-based interaction through examples. *UIST '07*, pp.33–42, 2007.

[20] B. Hartmann, L. Yu, A. Allison, Y. Yang, and S. R. Klemmer. Design as exploration: creating interface alternatives through parallel authoring and runtime tuning. *UIST '08*, pp.91–100, 2008.

Fast Forward with your VCR: Visualizing Single-Video Viewing Statistics for Navigation and Sharing

Abir Al-Hajri, Matthew Fong, Gregor Miller and Sidney Fels*

Human Communication Technologies Laboratory, University of British Columbia, Vancouver, BC, Canada

Figure 1: The *View Count Record* (VCR) visualization of a single video to highlight popular or unseen content using viewing statistics derived from personal or crowd-sourced histories of video consumption. The most-viewed intervals are represented by large thumbnails, with three smaller sizes to represent less-viewed content (the smallest for unseen content). The VCR is designed to be useful for fast navigation, search via seeking (*second thumbnail from left*), instant video previews (without interrupting other content) and sharing directly from the interface.[1]

ABSTRACT

Online video viewing has seen explosive growth, yet simple tools to facilitate navigation and sharing of the large video space have not kept pace. We propose the use of single-video viewing statistics as the basis for a visualization of video called the *View Count Record* (VCR). Our novel visualization utilizes variable-sized thumbnails to represent the popularity (or affectiveness) of video intervals, and provides simple mechanisms for fast navigation, informed search, video previews, simple sharing and summarization. The viewing statistics are generated from an individual's video consumption, or crowd-sourced from many people watching the same video; both provide different scenarios for application (e.g. implicit tagging of interesting events for an individual, and quickly navigating to others' most-viewed scenes for crowd-sourced). A comparative user study evaluates the effectiveness of the *VCR* by asking participants to share previously-seen affective parts within videos. Experimental results demonstrate that the *VCR* outperforms the state-of-the-art in a search task, and has been welcomed as a recommendation tool for clips within videos (using crowd-sourced statistics). It is perceived by participants as effective, intuitive and strongly preferred to current methods.

Index Terms: H.5.2. [Information Interfaces and Presentation]: User Interfaces—; H.1.2. [Models and Principles]: User/Machine Systems—

1 INTRODUCTION

Consuming video online, on mobile devices or on home computers is now a well-accepted form of communication and entertainment, shown by the rapid growth of various providers such as YouTube[TM]. Despite the volume of video available, methods for efficient navigation and sharing of in-video content have not provided users with the ease of use or level of personalization re-

quired to accommodate their needs. Constraints such as limiting the length of videos (e.g. six seconds on Vine[TM] and 15 seconds on Instagram[TM]) can simplify the problem, however these do not address the challenges with unconstrained video.

Part of the problem is that the 3D spatio-temporal representation of video complicates relatively simple actions such as search or selection. Video search often taxes human memory by requiring memorization of a large quantity of previously-seen content. In particular, finding and selecting interesting parts has poor navigation and search support. We propose that the addition of a single-video visualization mechanism using viewing statistics will overcome some of these difficulties.

We investigate the usefulness of visualizing prior viewing by either single or multiple users to support fast navigation (to popular or unseen parts), search and directly previewing content, without interrupting normal playback. We envision users will watch videos differently when they have a visualization of their personal navigation: they can implicitly tag segments of video by re-viewing (thereby increasing the view count); it would also capture their natural behaviour, such as watching a funny section multiple times in a lengthy video. This non-linear viewing behaviour is already evident, such as in YouTube audience retention graphs[2]: videos have peaks in the graphs, implying users watch different content and likely seek to find interesting parts (unfortunately these graphs are not generally public, and require voluntary publication by video owners). Viewing graphs often show a shallow negative exponential curve (i.e cold-start problem) from crowd-sourced data, which can be very simply filtered to highlight the most popular content. Likewise, viewing statistics can be used to filter out videos where only the first few seconds are watched.

2 RELATED WORK

Researchers have proposed various navigation techniques to simplify access and improve efficiency. Simple linear video navigation

---

[1] Video and screenshots licenced under Creative Commons Attribution 3.0, © 2008, Blender Foundation
[2] https://support.google.com/youtube/answer/1715160

Figure 2: The VCR is a new navigation tool based on viewing statistics which intuitively visualizes seen and unseen content. Each viewed interval is recorded and added to the view count for visualization. Playback is controlled either with the usual tools (play, pause, seek), or by using the VCR. For unwatched video, the view count is equal everywhere and the VCR gracefully becomes the familiar Filmstrip (Figure 3a).

can be accomplished through representative thumbnails (e.g. a film-strip metaphor), such that selecting a thumbnail directly positions the main video at the specific time corresponding to that thumbnail [10]. *Swifter* claimed faster video navigation by displaying a grid of thumbnails instead of a single thumbnail when scrubbing a video [15]. Map-based storyboards emerged as a video navigation tool, where different intervals are directly visualized on a map [19]. Davis [8] proposed an iconic video representation language of human actions in video. Using these iconic representation allow users to visualize, browse, annotate, and retrieve video content. Others proposed playback mechanisms to help users rapidly skim through uninteresting content and watch interesting parts at a normal pace [4]. The timeline can also be controlled by directly manipulating video content (i.e. using object motion) [9].

Video summarization aims to shorten videos to emphasize the important content and reduce time needed for viewing. For instance, Correa et al. proposed a system for generating dynamic narratives from videos where a compact, coherent and interactive poster is created for each video [6]. They use a series of spatial-temporal masks to improve the output quality of stitching foreground and background regions of video frames. Daniel et al. [7] and Nguyen et al. [18] applied computer vision algorithms to develop a 3D volume-based interface for video summarization and navigation. It enabled users to understand the content and easily navigate to the intended parts of the video. Video summarization is represented by a large body of work [1, 17, 22], however, in general these methods do not take advantage of any implicit information

gathered as users consume video, which may be used to personalize the user experience.

Video navigation histories and social navigation provide potential interaction techniques for fast navigation, event search and video summarization. People in real scenarios rewatch parts of videos that are important, interesting, affective, or hard to understand [20]. This can be seen most simply in YouTube's or Vimeo's feature for sharing a video from a specific start time, providing an exact use case of what we propose. This watching behaviour leaves digital footprints on the video frames creating a non-flat video histogram emphasizing the interest of each part of the video. Researchers have effectively employed this data for different purposes. For example, Yu et al. have used video browsing histories to rank different scenes within a video, then use the rankings to extract clips to generate video summaries [24]. Mertens et al. have used the video timeline itself to visualize users' viewing 'footprints' using different brightness levels, which lets users quickly navigate to the most viewed scenes [16]. However, this does not supply a visualization of the video, which inhibits search (when searching for a previously seen event, users need to remember its approximate location), and intervals are not defined as a whole which prevents sharing directly from the visualization. Al-Hajri et al. offered users access to their video browsing histories by visualizing the intervals a user watched as a separate thumbnail [2, 3]. Users were able to find previously-seen content more quickly than when their history was not available. However, rewatched intervals were visualized multiple times (which increased the search space) which may ham-

(a) Filmstrip (equivalent to VCR without visualization of viewing statistics)

(b) View Count Record (VCR)

Figure 3: The View Count Record (VCR) component visualizes the video viewing statistics. When no viewing history is available, the VCR presents a familiar filmstrip (a). When a history is available, our view count manipulation algorithms can be applied to visualize popular intervals within the video, leading to fast personal navigation and social navigation applications. Each thumbnail can be searched via seeking in the popup red time bar when hovering the cursor over the preview image.

per the search task.

Video navigation history can play an important role in user-based information retrieval from videos on the web. Shamma et al. [21] and Yew et al. [23] have proposed a shift from content-based techniques to user-based analysis because it provides a more promising basis for indexing media content in ways that satisfy user needs. Leftheriotis et al. used viewing statistics as a tool for extracting a representative image or thumbnail based on the most-viewed frame within a video [14]. Hwang et al. applied the viewing statistics to place the most-viewed video content in provider networks rather than using the complete video to reduce their storage and network utilization [13]. User-based viewing statistics were demonstrated to be at least as effective at detecting video events as when content-based anaylsis techniques (i.e. computer vision) were used [12]. Fong et al. [11] employed users' navigation behaviour to propose a new casual video editing interaction technique. They showed that using their technique participants took at most two-thirds the time taken by the conventional method to select video segments and create playlists.

3 SINGLE VIDEO NAVIGATION

The objective of our research is to design a visualization that supports fast in-video navigation (play most popular or unseen parts), search (seek within intervals with prior knowledge e.g. 'seen the event before' or 'never seen the event'), preview, and instant sharing (share a single interval directly). To accomplish this, we use viewing statistics (personal or crowd-sourced) as the basis for a modification to the well-known filmstrip visualization [5], to create the *View Count Record* (VCR). The VCR uses a variable thumbnail size (and variable interval length) to reflect the relative popularity of intervals. This is similar in concept to timeline footprints [16], however timeline footprints do not allow direct navigation (we do not require seeking), in-place preview or direct interval sharing. We used size instead of colour since we are representing intervals using thumbnails where colour discrimination may be confused with the thumbnail content and would be difficult to differentiate for some videos. We also piloted the visualization using a coloured frequency bar attached to each thumbnail to indicate the popularity; while the information was welcomed, the visualization was re-

ported as cluttered. The *VCR* applies a histogram visualization using thumbnails where the height of these thumbnails indicates the height of the histogram bars.

Whenever a segment of video is played, the video ID and timestamps for the interval's start and end are recorded. An accumulated view count is maintained for the video at a given resolution (e.g. 15 samples per second of video). The *VCR*, shown in Figure 3, consists of a fixed number of *video segments*[3] (described below). The duration and size of each segment is based on how often its corresponding interval has been viewed. If no viewing statistics are available, the *VCR* appears as a normal filmstrip as shown in Figure 3(a).

3.1 VCR Construction

The construction of the *VCR* starts by gathering intervals of time in which consecutive frames have equal view counts. While there are intervals less than a set threshold, the algorithm attempts to merge these intervals with one of their neighbouring intervals. The neighbour to merge with is determined by two criteria: first by the difference in view counts, and if the difference of view counts are equal, then by the duration of the neighbouring intervals. The merging process chooses the smallest difference in view counts, or the smallest interval duration. This process repeats until all intervals' duration are greater than the preset threshold.

Upon the completion of the merging process, the *VCR* contains a set of intervals with duration that are greater than the preset threshold. However, since the number of items in the visualization component is limited, we must reduce the set of intervals to match. Thus we look at the peaks of the view count graph, keep the highest peaks, and merge the other intervals until we get to the desired resolution. Conversely, if we do not have enough intervals, we linearly sample and split intervals until we have enough.

We then create our visualization by using a Video Segment component (described below) for each interval. The size of each segment is based on a ratio of the current segment's view count to the maximum view count for the video. The *VCR* updates automatically when the video is paused, based on the latest viewing statis-

---

[3]In our interface, we used 6 segments based on the width of the interface and the maximum width of a single *VCR* segment.

Figure 4: Each video thumbnail in the VCR is visualized as small video segments. Each segment is seekable and playable on mouse events. The red/gray portion at the bottom of the widget indicates the temporal location of its interval within the complete video. The yellow line illustrates the current seeking point within the thumbnail, within the zoomed interval for higher-resolution seeking.

tics (it does not update while viewing so as not to distract from the main video). It illustrates to the user how they consumed the video and which parts were viewed the most/least. This provides a simple mechanism to find or navigate back to these segments when needed.

3.2 VCR Visualization

Each interval (i.e. *video segment*) in the *VCR* is represented as a thumbnail displaying the first frame. The temporal location of the interval with respect to the video is visualized as a red line on a grey background beneath the thumbnail (the location bar) to help users spatially contextualize the temporal location of intervals within the complete video. Video segments support: seeking using a popup overlay which expands from the red line in the location bar, and the thumbnail's image updates to reflect the seeked content (see Figure 4); playing the video directly, without interrupting the main player; playing the video in the main player, either by clicking the top right arrow or dragging the interval to the main player (dragging with the seek bar active plays the interval from that specific time); and finally, sharing of the entire interval by drag-and-drop. These interactions can be easily transferred to a touch-screen device supporting today's most online video consumption platform.

3.3 VCR Scalability

The construction and visualization of the *VCR* is based on the video used, the number of peaks, and the interface size, which are independent of the platform used. It is not affected by the length or duration of the video being visualized since the algorithm as described in Section 3.1, merges (or linearly samples and splits intervals) until the *VCR* gets to the desired resolution (i.e the required number of segments). However, due to the limited space and the fixed number of video segments, some medium-height peaks may be diminished and not easily viewed in the *VCR*. To alleviate this problem, the interface supports a zoom feature (via mouse wheel) where the selected video segment expands and is represented by its own *VCR* with the same number of segments. When a segment is zoomed-in, the *VCR* updates to visualize segments within that zoomed segment only and hides any other segments. Thus the *VCR* always uses the same number of video segments.

4 EVALUATION

We designed a comparative study to investigate: 1) if our visualization of video navigation provides faster search for user-specific affective intervals, and if users prefer our visualization for this task; 2) if crowd-sourced histories provide good summaries of video. Subjects were asked to find and share their favourite intervals using either the *VCR* or *Filmstrip* visualizations. We compared against the filmstrip design instead of timeline footprints [16] for several reasons: footprints does not easily let a user directly select or share a full interval; video cannot be previewed inside the footprints visualization (*VCR* and *filmstrip* can both directly preview without seeking); *VCR* and footprints could be used together, so we believe a comparison against *Filmstrip* is more informative.

4.1 Participants

Ten paid volunteers, 6 female and 4 male, participated in the experiment. Participants ranged in ages from 19 to 35. Three of the participants were undergraduate students while the rest (i.e. 7 participants) were from the general public (non-academic). Each participant worked on the task individually. All participants were experienced computer users and have normal or corrected to normal vision. Seven participants watch online videos on a daily basis and the other three watch videos 3-5 times a week. Five of the participants watch 1-3 videos on average per day, while three watch 3-5 videos per day and two watch more than 10 videos per day on average.

4.2 Design and Procedure

Two different navigation modes were tested: *Filmstrip* and *VCR*. The case where no history was available was represented by the state-of-the-art *Filmstrip*, shown in Figure 3(a). Each participant tried both modes to navigate and share their preferred parts of the video. Participants were divided equally into two groups where Group 1 used *Filmstrip* first and *VCR* second, and Group 2 had the order reversed. Participants freely watched a set of 5 different videos (Disney short animations) between 3 and 5 minutes long. Video length does not affect the *VCR* as mentioned in Section 3.3, however, due to the time constraints of the experiment short videos were tested.

To ensure all participants had seen equivalent video, the tasks began after all videos were viewed. For each video, participants were asked to list five intervals they would like to share; these were recorded by the researcher. The researcher chose an event from those provided by the participant which they must find: the search task began by clicking 'Find', choosing a video from a grid of thumbnails, and then the navigation layout for the current mode was displayed - the participant used this to find an interval representing the event. The interval is submitted for consideration by playing it: if approved by the researcher as correct, the task is complete.

Each participant performed a total of 14 search tasks (2 modes × 7 intervals); they were asked to perform as quickly as possible. For each task, the completion time, the number of previews and the number of zoom events were recorded. The completion time was measured from when the participant clicked on a 'Find' button until the moment they found the correct interval (confirmed by the researcher). The navigation behaviour and statistics were recorded during the viewing phase. The participants were also asked to rank each mode based on speed, ease and preference.

Upon the completion of the sharing tasks, participants started the second task where they were shown a short version of each video, automatically created from crowd-sourced histories (described below). Participants were asked if they thought the shortened version was a good summarization and whether each segment in the crowd-sourced version matched their own affective segments; the experiment ended when participants had ranked all 5 shortened videos

Table 1: Results of the comparative study for the interval retrieval task, showing a significant advantage using our method (VCR) in terms of completion time. Note: SD = standard deviation; completion time measured in seconds. * $p < 0.03$

	Filmstrip		VCR		
	Mean	SD	Mean	SD	t-test
Completion Time	24.31	10.42	21.11	5.38	-2.28*
No. of Previews	40.39	35.41	35.53	27.56	0.88

and their corresponding segments. The final task was to fill out a questionnaire to rank the modes, and provide feedback on the interface, its features and their experience. The experiment lasted approximately one hour per participant.

4.3 Crowd-Sourced Data Collection

Six graduate students (2 female, 4 male, aged 24 to 37) completely separate from participants in this study, voluntarily participated in the crowd-sourced data collection. Participants were invited prior to the experiment to freely watch and navigate the same set of videos while their viewing statistics were recorded. Their data was then aggregated and visualized using the *VCR*. At least 9 peaks existed for each video. However, due to the experiment time constraints (one hour), we decided to use only the highest 5 peaks of each video in the shortened videos that were tested.

4.4 Results and Discussions

Most participants commented that they enjoyed their time using the interface and they can imagine seeing its features applied, especially in social networking websites. They foresaw its applicability as a navigation aid for un-watched videos where social navigation can be leveraged for the benefit of future viewers, as well as a summarization tool for their own videos. Participants were impressed by how closely the crowd-sourced popular intervals matched their own preferences for best intervals, confirming that in most cases this would provide an effective tool for navigating new video.

4.4.1 Search Task

The main task in the experiment was to search for previously-seen preferred intervals: each participant was able to complete each search task in less than one minute (for all 14 trials). A paired-samples t-test analysis determined the significance of the results in terms of the average completion time per search and the average number of previews per search. The analysis, shown in Table 1, demonstrated that the search task using *Filmstrip* took significantly more time than with the *VCR*. Participants were asked to rank the different modes for preference, ease and speed: they ranked the *VCR* as the most liked, easiest and fastest mode, which coincides with the quantitative results. This indicates that having access to the user's personal navigation record is useful for finding previously-seen content within video, and that our visualization cues (e.g. size) of the mostly watched segments helped users to quickly and easily navigate to the correct intervals.

In terms of the average number of previews, the results revealed no significant difference between the two modes, which we did not anticipate. This can be due to the fact that many view count peaks can exist within a single video segment of the *VCR*, and that some segments ended up much smaller in size which made it harder to navigate. When analyzing the participants' navigation history, we found that participants created 11 history segments on average per video. This means that when using heuristics some *VCR* segments had more than one peak since there are only 6 segments in the *VCR*. However, as we mentioned in Section 3.3, we added the zoom functionality to mitigate this. Participants rarely used the zoom feature

and preferred to navigate through these segments instead which explains the large number of previews.

4.4.2 Agreement With Crowd-Source

All participants agreed that the shortened video (created automatically using the crowd-sourced information) was an effective summary of the video content. Before using the interface, participants were asked whether they would use others' recommendations as a tool for navigating unseen videos; we were most interested in discovering if participants views would change after using our interface. Most said they would not use recommendations, however after using the interface and viewing the shortened video they expressed surprise at the quality of the summary. Participants mentioned that having the crowd-sourced *VCR* would save time, especially for long videos, since they can decide whether to watch the entire video or just the summary, or even just parts of the summary.

For each video, participants were asked to rank each segment derived from the crowd-sourced data. At least 8 participants out of 10 agreed that each segment represented something they liked or illustrated an affective clip. Out of a total of 25 segments, 7 segments were liked by 8 participants, 8 segments were liked by 9 subjects, while the remaining 8 were liked by all participants. The negative ranking of segments by some participants was due either to religious beliefs or perceived violent content, while other participants considered these segments to be funny. We expected the variation between participants, however, we did not predict the generally high level of agreement. This suggests implicit tagging of video from many users may serve as a valuable navigation tool for online video.

4.4.3 Ranking of Visualization's Features

From the aggregated results of the questionnaire (measuring ease-of-use and usefulness), the average ranking across all components and features was 5.82 out of 7. All features were ranked above 5 except for three items which were: getting started ($M = 4.5$), remembering how to use the interface ($M = 4.6$), and using the zoom ($M = 4.3$). The zoom scored slightly lower due to the mouse wheel sensitivity being reported as too high, which led to some participants becoming confused or frustrated. This could also explain the low usage of this feature while performing the tasks where only 2 participants used it for 4 tasks out of 140 tasks (10 participants $\times$ 2 modes $\times$ 7 tasks) when searching for events. This has been taken into account for future versions of the interface. Overall participants appreciated the zoom since it enabled them to get a more detailed view of the video's content.

4.4.4 Participants' Feedback

There were some overwhelming impressions and comments made by the participants about the interface. One participant commented that "I definitely see how this would be really helpful for long videos because I will not have to waste my time watching the whole video again to get to the important stuff. I could directly use my previous history to navigate to these intervals." Others said "I would love to see this implemented within social websites. I could see how it would save my time when viewing new videos"; "It is really cool and easy to use. When are you going to apply this to online video websites?"; and finally "I didn't expect others' history would be useful, but, you showed me it is."

5 CONCLUSION

We have presented a new way to visualize and navigate a video space using the View Count Record (*VCR*), that provides simple navigation, search, preview and sharing of video intervals. Our comparative study based on a use case of searching and sharing found significant quantitative results in favour of our method, as well as being positively perceived by the participants. Using crowd-sourced data as a tool for recommending segments within videos (i.e. social navigation) was found to be appreciated, and we confirmed that the summaries generated from crowd-popular segments were effective at communicating the content of video. The *VCR* was rated highly by users who recommend integrating this mechanism into online video websites.

We will investigate how this navigation mechanism may be extended to multiple videos, to provide users with an intuitive and fast navigation mechanism for their video collection, as well as for serendipitous discovery of new video based on crowd-sourced information. We intend to explore how users respond to these mechanisms, in conjunction with the presented *VCR*, via a field study utilizing online video; extensive data will help determine general users' current viewing behaviour for all types of video, and how it changes when given a *VCR* and other methods based on viewing statistics.

ACKNOWLEDGEMENTS

We gratefully acknowledge support from NSERC (grant provided for "Diving experiences: wayfinding and sharing experiences with large, semantically tagged video"), Bell Canada, Avigilon Corporation and Vidigami Media Inc."

REFERENCES

[1] M. Ajmal, M. Ashraf, M. Shakir, Y. Abbas, and F. Shah. Video summarization: Techniques and classification. In L. Bolc, R. Tadeusiewicz, L. Chmielewski, and K. Wojciechowski, editors, *Computer Vision and Graphics*, volume 7594 of *Lecture Notes in Computer Science*, pages 1–13. Springer Berlin Heidelberg, 2012.

[2] A. Al-Hajri, G. Miller, S. Fels, and M. Fong. Video navigation with a personal viewing history. In *Human-Computer Interaction – INTERACT 2013*, volume 8119 of *Lecture Notes in Computer Science*, pages 352–369. Springer Berlin Heidelberg, 2013.

[3] A. Al-Hajri, G. Miller, M. Fong, and S. Fels. Visualization of personal history for video navigation. In *Proceedings of the ACM CHI Conference on Human Factors on Computing Systems*, CHI'14, New York City, New York, U.S.A., 2014. ACM.

[4] K.-Y. Cheng, S.-J. Luo, B.-Y. Chen, and H.-H. Chu. Smartplayer: user-centric video fast-forwarding. In *Proceedings of the 27th international conference on Human factors in computing systems*, CHI '09, pages 789–798. ACM, 2009.

[5] M. Christel and N. Moraveji. Finding the right shots: assessing usability and performance of a digital video library interface. In *Proceedings of the 12th annual ACM international conference on Multimedia*, MULTIMEDIA '04, pages 732–739. ACM, 2004.

[6] C. D. Correa and K.-L. Ma. Dynamic video narratives. In *ACM SIGGRAPH 2010 Papers*, SIGGRAPH '10, pages 88:1–88:9, New York, NY, USA, 2010. ACM.

[7] G. Daniel and M. Chen. Video visualization. In *Proceedings of the 14th IEEE Visualization 2003 (VIS'03)*, VIS '03, pages 54–, Washington, DC, USA, 2003. IEEE Computer Society.

[8] M. Davis. Human-computer interaction. chapter Media Streams: An Iconic Visual Language for Video Representation, pages 854–866. Morgan Kaufmann Publishers Inc., San Francisco, CA, USA, 1995.

[9] P. Dragicevic, G. Ramos, J. Bibliowitcz, D. Nowrouzezahrai, R. Balakrishnan, and K. Singh. Video browsing by direct manipulation. In *Proceedings of the Conference on Human Factors in Computing Systems*, pages 237–246. ACM, 2008.

[10] S. M. Drucker, A. Glatzer, S. De Mar, and C. Wong. Smartskip: consumer level browsing and skipping of digital video content. In *Proceedings of the SIGCHI conference on Human factors in computing systems: Changing our world, changing ourselves*, CHI '02, pages 219–226. ACM, 2002.

[11] M. Fong, A. Al-Hajri, G. Miller, and S. Fels. Casual authoring using a video navigation history. In *Graphics Interface*, GI '14. Canadian Information Processing Society / ACM, May 2014.

[12] C. Gkonela and K. Chorianopoulos. Videoskip: event detection in social web videos with an implicit user heuristic. *Multimedia Tools and Applications*, pages 1–14, 2012. 10.1007/s11042-012-1016-1.

[13] K.-W. Hwang, D. Applegate, A. Archer, V. Gopalakrishnan, S. Lee, V. Misra, K. Ramakrishnan, and D. Swayne. Leveraging video viewing patterns for optimal content placement. In R. Bestak, L. Kencl, L. Li, J. Widmer, and H. Yin, editors, *NETWORKING 2012*, volume 7290 of *Lecture Notes in Computer Science*, pages 44–58. Springer Berlin Heidelberg, 2012.

[14] I. Leftheriotis, C. Gkonela, and K. Chorianopoulos. Efficient video indexing on the web: A system that leverages user interactions with a video player. In *Proceedings of the 2nd International Conference on User-Centric Media (UCMEDIA)*, 2012.

[15] J. Matejka, T. Grossman, and G. Fitzmaurice. Swifter: Improved online video scrubbing. In *Proceedings of the SIGCHI Conference on Human Factors in Computing Systems*, CHI '13, pages 1159–1168, New York, NY, USA, 2013. ACM.

[16] R. Mertens, R. Farzan, and P. Brusilovsky. Social navigation in web lectures. In *Proceedings of the seventeenth conference on Hypertext and hypermedia*, HYPERTEXT '06, pages 41–44. ACM, 2006.

[17] A. G. Money and H. Agius. Video summarisation: A conceptual framework and survey of the state of the art. *J. Vis. Comun. Image Represent.*, 19(2):121–143, Feb. 2008.

[18] C. Nguyen, Y. Niu, and F. Liu. Video summagator: An interface for video summarization and navigation. In *Proceedings of the SIGCHI Conference on Human Factors in Computing Systems*, CHI '12, pages 647–650, New York, NY, USA, 2012. ACM.

[19] S. Pongnumkul, J. Wang, and M. Cohen. Creating map-based storyboards for browsing tour videos. In *Proceedings of the 21st annual ACM symposium on User interface software and technology*, UIST '08, pages 13–22. ACM, 2008.

[20] C. A. Russell and S. J. Levy. The temporal and focal dynamics of volitional reconsumption: A phenomenological investigation of repeated hedonic experiences. *Journal of Consumer Research*, 39(2):341–359, August 2012.

[21] D. A. Shamma, R. Shaw, P. L. Shafton, and Y. Liu. Watch what i watch: using community activity to understand content. In *Proceedings of the International Workshop on multimedia information retrieval*, MIR '07, pages 275–284. ACM, 2007.

[22] B. T. Truong and S. Venkatesh. Video abstraction: A systematic review and classification. *ACM Trans. Multimedia Comput. Commun. Appl.*, 3(1), Feb. 2007.

[23] J. Yew, D. A. Shamma, and E. F. Churchill. Knowing funny: genre perception and categorization in social video sharing. In *Proceedings of the 2011 annual conference on Human factors in computing systems*, CHI '11, pages 297–306. ACM, 2011.

[24] B. Yu, W.-Y. Ma, K. Nahrstedt, and H.-J. Zhang. Video summarization based on user log enhanced link analysis. In *Proceedings of the eleventh ACM international conference on Multimedia*, MULTIMEDIA '03, pages 382–391. ACM, 2003.

Supervisor-Student Research Meetings:
A Case Study on Choice of Tools and Practices in Computer Science

Hasti Seifi*
Department of Computer Science
University of British Columbia

Helen Halbert†
School of Library, Archival & Information Studies
University of British Columbia

Joanna McGrenere‡
Department of Computer Science
University of British Columbia

ABSTRACT

Supervisory meetings are a crucial aspect of graduate studies and have a strong impact on the success of research and supervisor-student relations, yet there is little research on supporting this relationship and even less on understanding the nature of this collaboration and user requirements. Thus, we conducted an exploratory study on the choice and success of tools and practices used by supervisors and students for meetings, for the purpose of making informed design recommendations. Results of a series of five focus groups and three individual interviews yielded three themes on: 1) supervisory style diversity, 2) distributed cognition demands, and 3) feedback channel dissonance. Student-supervisor collaboration has many unexplored areas for design and as a first step our work highlights potential areas for supportive designs and future research.

Keywords: student-supervisor collaboration; supervisory meeting; tools and practices; exploratory study; thematic analysis

Index Terms: H.5.3 [Information Interfaces and Presentation (e.g., HCI)]: Group and Organization Interfaces—Computer-Supported Cooperative Work

1 INTRODUCTION

An important part of graduate research involves an inherently collaborative act of knowledge creation and problem solving between a student and his/her research supervisor. The type and nature of student-supervisor collaboration can vary significantly depending on many factors, including the culture of a community of practice and norms and expectations of the academic institution. The student-supervisor collaboration in applied sciences and engineering —and within our case study of computer science (CS)— is commonly characterized by face-to-face individual research meetings between a student and his/her research supervisor(s). This typically involves some variation of first setting a time and sharing required resources before the meeting, exchanging ideas during the meeting, and capturing the outcome of the communication after the meeting for future reference or action. The meetings are dispersed over different periods of time (e.g., one week or longer) and include the introduction of new information, as well as discussion of items already familiar to both parties. Students and supervisors are involved in multiple activities and responsibilities [12] that consume attention resources. Expectations of work habits and judgements of priorities and perceived value of research-related activities may not be made explicit. Additionally, students and supervisors' expertise and degree of involvement in the project are different; it is therefore not possible to always assume a common level of understanding between the two parties concerning the status of the research. These characteristics can increase the chance of ineffective

*e-mail: seifi@cs.ubc.ca
†e-mail:helenhalbert@gmail.com
‡e-mail:joanna@cs.ubc.ca

Graphics Interface Conference 2014
7-9 May, Montreal, Quebec, Canada

meetings, and result in miscommunications and even conflict in a student-supervisor relationship.

To handle meetings and the relationship effectively, students and supervisors use a variety of tools (e.g., email, pen and paper, Evernote) as well as practices (e.g., sending an agenda 24-hours in advance). The choice of which tools to use is based on both awareness of existing tools and practices, as well as individual differences and personal preferences [8, 15]. We suspect that developing a process that works for both the supervisor and the student takes a lot of effort and happens implicitly over time, often by trial and error, potentially compromising the efficacy of the collaboration. The purpose of our study was to understand what drives the choice of tools and practices in student-supervisor relationships, and if and how current approaches are unsupported.

Despite the importance of supervisor-student collaboration on the progression of research and success of their relationship, there is little research on supervisor-student collaboration, nor on the tools and practices supporting this relationship. Existing research on group collaboration has investigated the affordances of a set of tools such as pen and paper or physical and virtual whiteboards [26]. We believe understanding the nature of collaboration and the reasons or factors for choosing a tool is equally as important. Our study builds on the body of research within HCI that endeavours to look beyond interactions between the user and a system, and to the specific contexts and activities or practices of individuals that shape or drive the interaction [13]. Thus, instead of focusing on the specific characteristics of tools, we set out to identify the major factors affecting supervisor-student collaboration by conducting an exploratory study with students and supervisors about the selection and evaluation of tools and practices for research collaboration. Our investigation also sought to understand the nature of the supervisor-student relationship (albeit, within the specific context of CS), and determine if profiles of supervisor-student collaboration could be derived from the tools and practices used. We believe developing such an understanding is the primary step for recommending future tool and practice design to support this collaboration. To clarify the scope of our study, we considered any digital (e.g., on-line scheduling software, social networking tools) or physical (e.g., whiteboards, notebooks) tools used to facilitate a meeting. In our study, practice refers to activities, processes, or habits of students and supervisors for research, information exchange, or collaboration such as keeping a personal or shared research blog, or sending meeting minutes.

Studies suggest that the design of supportive systems for knowledge sharing would benefit from a focused investigation and a nuanced understanding of the context of the collaboration [4]. We therefore focused on the graduate level within a university department of CS. Through thematic analysis of the data collected from five focus-group interviews with supervisors and students and three individual interviews with supervisors, we developed three themes. Despite the limited population of our study, we found enough variation in the practices of our participants to suggest important implications for devising supportive tools and practices. In summary, our contributions include:

- Evidence of individual differences in supervision style as a major factor on choice of tools and practices;

- The application of distributed cognition as a theoretical framework that allows holistic analysis of student-supervisor collaboration and their tool use;

- The call for two supportive systems: 1) a system or mechanism for mutual tracking and feedback on the research and relationship progress, and 2) a dedicated tools-and-practices awareness system for the discovery of ways to address the unsupported needs of student-supervisor collaboration.

2 RELATED WORK

Research on Group Collaboration. Studies of group meetings suggest that a variety of factors impact group dynamics and the collaborative process [21, 24]. For example, seating arrangement [24] and table and group size [21] have been shown to impact the distribution of roles, coordination, and comprehension during collaborative face-to-face meetings. Various tools have been proposed and developed to account for such factors and to facilitate collocated meetings, including single display groupware [25], and note taking applications [5]. Additionally, tools have themselves been identified as a possible factor, with Verma et al. [26] studying the impact of input device affordances on collaboration and task outcome during meetings. While geographically-distributed research teams employ a variety of communication and collaboration tools to great effect, the technologies may also prove a source of stress if viewed as an additional task to manage or are not seen as appropriate platforms for conveying criticism or disagreement; Siemens [23] believes collaborators should balance their digital and non-digital tool use and plan accordingly at the onset of a research project; additionally, tools selected must support aspects of both the research and the researchers' relationship.

Research on Higher Education and IT. While pedagogical literature and higher education research agree that the supervisory relationship has a significant effect on successful experiences within academia and university attrition rates [16], there is little understanding surrounding the nature of supervisor-student relationships and collaboration, specifically how meetings are conducted, knowledge is shared, requests and recommendations are articulated, and tools and practices are used for idea exchange in meetings. In 2002, Marsh et al. [16], developed a survey instrument to assess satisfaction levels of PhD students across different universities in Australia after noting the lack of research on the quality of PhD student supervision; however, apart from a single item on the provision of university computer facilities, the Postgraduate Research Experience Questionnaire failed to explicitly address the respondents ratings and use of ICTs during their program of study. A 2004 review of the role and influence of information and communication technologies (ICTs) in graduate student supervision, indicated that technology can provide flexibility in the relationship between students and supervisors [17]. However, a 2012 survey of graduate students completing programs by distance found that they were less satisfied with their supervisory relationship than those who were not in online programs [7], leading the authors to speculate as to the exact effect the use of technology had on the relationship between students and supervisors. Based on our own literature searches, there has yet to be a comprehensive study of technological tool choice in the context of supervisor-student collaboration.

De Rezande et al. proposed a system for managing student-supervisor collaboration to support graduate thesis progression [6], however, the system was designed based on informal interviews and designers' assumptions. We think such a system could benefit from a richer study of the student-supervisor relationship. Reviews of educational technologies, like E-portfolios [14], also have focused on functionality and potential applications for graduate student supervision without closely examining if and how they are being used within a research context or relationship. The invisibility of supervision practice within the literature prevents inferences and thereby opportunities for improvement. Our qualitative formative study seeks a better understanding of users, and their practices, as a prerequisite to successful solutions and supportive systems.

3 RESEARCH CONTEXT AND METHODS

Methodology. We conducted joint supervisor-student focus groups, a student-only focus group, and individual interviews with supervisors. Each of the four focus group sessions comprised one faculty member and his/her students who were available to attend at the designated meeting time. Prior to undertaking our research, we were already familiar with the faculty members and some members of the research groups (one of us is a student in CS, and one has taken classes within the department); our experiences as members of research groups, as well as our impressions about supervisory styles and awareness of the possible diversity of participants personalities, preferences, and practices within just one research group contributed to our initial interest in the topic of study. The purpose of the joint focus groups was to highlight the variations and intragroup differences within one research group under a single supervisor. The aim of the student-only focus group was to reduce the potential influence of the supervision power dynamic on students' responses during the joint focus groups, while the individual interviews enabled supervisors to communicate their experiences more candidly while still providing a level of anonymity for their students. The student-only and the supervisor-only sessions provided an opportunity for us to member-check our findings from the joint focus groups.

Participants. We had 19 participants (7 Female) recruited from a CS department, including 13 students (8 MSc, 4 PhD, 1 undergrad), 2 postdocs, and 4 faculty supervisors for the joint focus groups; 4 of the students made up the student-only focus group and 3 (out of 4) supervisors participated in follow-up individual interviews.

Data Gathering. Because of faculty members' limited time and the difficulty of recruiting entire research groups with a general call-for-participation, we contacted six faculty members and research groups we were familiar with; we interviewed the four research groups that responded to our email. Having all participants from one department ensured that our participants came from the same academic environment and culture of CS.

For the student-only focus group, we contacted six of the students from the initial series of focus groups in order to follow up on information that they had previously shared with us. We also specifically selected students to achieve representation of at least one person from each of the four research groups and variability of both stage of research and particular supervision arrangement (e.g. co-supervision). Based on availabilities, our focus group ended up including four students. Owing to scheduling conflicts and the challenge of finding a time to meet with all supervisors at once, we individually interviewed 3 faculty supervisors who agreed to participate in our second interview.

Each focus group lasted about one hour. Two of the three authors were present and responsible for jointly conducting all of the focus groups and individual interviews. Interviews were semi-structured; discussion topics were provided to the participants in advance over e-mail and were again provided in hard-copy or by projection on a shared screen during the session. During the interview, participants were encouraged to talk about any experiences with past and current supervisors, as well as personal approaches to research and collaboration, with a particular focus on what tools and practices they used, their reasons and their degree of success. Individual interviews with supervisors were held in their offices and each took about 45 minutes. Audio files for joint focus groups were transcribed (in excerpts included here, supervisor participants and students are anonymized as Sp-G#, and St#G#, respectively, according to which research group they belonged to). We took notes by hand during the student-only focus group session and the supervisor-only interviews because of the increased sensitivity of the data.

Analysis. We used Braun and Clarke's approach to thematic analysis [3] for our qualitative dataset, which consisted of transcripts of the four joint supervisor-student focus group interviews. Thematic analysis is a research method for identifying and reporting patterns, or themes, from datasets. It differs from other approaches to qualitative analysis (for example, grounded theory) in that the findings do not need to confirm or comply with any one theoretical framework; thematic analysis is thus flexible to accommodate both essentialist (i.e. what people are actually doing) and constructionist (i.e. how people interpret and attribute meaning to their actions) analyses of practices. Our analysis sought to initially identify patterns of reported behaviour for the purpose of research collaboration, as well as evaluate their perceived effectiveness and determine which practices were either commonly shared amongst participants or unique to individuals within a supervisory relationship.

Two of the authors individually coded our transcripts by applying descriptive keywords or phrases to longer excerpts; we then reviewed codes together to discuss any deviations in our agreement on and applications of codes and refined our annotations. Excerpts annotated in the same way were collected together, and along with sets of codes that frequently co-occurred within the data, were identified as potential patterns and used to develop initial themes. Themes were later reviewed in light of the coded extracts to ensure they accurately reflected the intent of that stage of analysis. Because of the interpretive nature of this approach to analysis, we also conducted member-checking of our findings during additional interviews with the four participants of the student-only focus group and three supervisors to refine our findings and confirm that we had developed a thematic map that was representative of and consistent with the data.

4 RESULTS

We present the results of our study in three themes. As previously stated, we focused on understanding the factors that impact choice and success of tools instead of describing specific tools and their affordances in detail. We saw a variety of tool use within our case study including wikis, weblogs, physical notebooks, digital text files, Evernote, laptops, mobile devices, projectors, whiteboards, email, online calendars, and Twitter and Facebook for microupdates. Major practices included sharing a public calendar to schedule meetings, booking all regular meetings at the start of term as a 'placeholder', daily collocated or online microupdates in the research group, sending an agenda and meeting minutes, compiling meeting notes immediately after meetings, and keeping a digital or physical repository of meeting notes, like a wiki. In the first two themes, we discuss factors impacting choice and success of tools, as well as the reciprocal nature of the connection between tools used and the supervisory relationship dynamic. Theme 3 indicates that awareness of tools and practices is an important yet unsupported area of student-supervisor collaboration. Member-checking with participants confirmed and further refined the three themes.

4.1 Theme 1: Supervisory Style Diversity

A major theme developed from the data was the significance of the supervisor, and their supervision style, for determining and driving the supervisor-student relationship dynamic and choice and success of tools.

There was a large spread of individual differences among supervisors; each supervisor has his/her own preferences and personal practices already in place. The flexibility and capacity to adapt to student needs can vary between supervisors; the relative rigidness of a relationship is in turn exacerbated by each supervisor's time constraints, availabilities on campus, and concurrent supervisory responsibilities such as their current number of students.

Both supervisors and students in our study situated these individual differences in supervision style on a continuum of structure, referring to a supervision style as being more structured or less structured. Supervisors who fell on the more structured end of the spectrum typically required that their students follow or agree to certain practices (e.g., sharing meeting minutes) and expected regular communication (e.g. frequent meeting or e-mail updates) to ensure effective collaboration. The less structured supervisors, however, eschewed strict rules and rigid expectations of students in favour of having a more flexible collaboration. In this regard, the personal perceptions of 'what it meant to be a supervisor' played a role; for example, Sp-G3 recommended and Sp-G1 required all students to develop and share agendas in advance of meetings because both saw the practice as a way of training students in structuring their thoughts, which not only resulted in an effective meeting but also prepared them for professional research career.

Sp-G1: I tend to be a little more on the structured end of the scale of possible supervisory styles and like agendas...[I'm] helping you to learn this kind of discipline, because you will make progress better with this kind of structure.

Sp-G3: I think it's a very important skill for the students to figure out how they want to use the time with me, I mean it's something that I request my students do, I think it's a very good practice.

Sp-G2 and Sp-G4, on the other hand, were less structured than Sp-G1 and Sp-G3 and only articulated the worth of an agenda relative to their own needs. Specifically, because they were not always able to read them before a meeting, they did not see any point in having their students go through the effort of creating one.

Sp-G2: It kind of makes me feel guilty, asking people to send me an email [if] I'm not going to read it...I feel as a supervisor, that unless I can give quality feedback on it...it's just like "oh, I have this rule and you have to do it."

Sp-G4 reiterated this same thought, saying that it was not fair to request something of a student that would not be made use of. These expressions of consideration for the student, and mindfulness of the power dynamic inherent to the relationship is a different perspective on the role of a supervisor. In these cases, the role is understood with less emphasis on professional development which in turn enables more flexibility for the individual student and greater variation in practice within a research group. Students of Sp-G2 and Sp-G4 reported dropping by their supervisors' office if they needed while meetings with Sp-G1 and Sp-G3 were almost always pre-scheduled. For St1G2, this less structured style improved communication of both research and non-research items, such as personal life stresses. Additionally, this understanding of the supervision role may be related to the supervisor's personal interests and time constraints; Sp-G2 expressed a desire for providing more mentoring to her students and saw this as additional support the CS department should deliver.

While our analysis of the data identified a variation in supervision styles, none appeared to be categorically better or worse than any other. The relative level of structured supervision seemingly did not have much of an effect on either student research progress or relationship satisfaction. However, a mismatch between work styles and practices of a supervisor and student within a given relationship could stress the collaboration dynamic and slow research progress. Our data suggests that senior students (post-docs and senior PhD) could cope with this mismatch and adapt to their supervision style more readily than junior students.

Despite a rich variety of tool use among the students, they shared in common the behaviour of reshaping their own practices to accommodate and adapt to their supervisors. This was evidenced by shifts in behaviour for the purpose of collaboration, such as sanitizing personal notes to prepare them for the supervisor, or an adoption of scheduling or calendar tools. A change in student practice was also frequently the result of one's knowledge of supervisor practice; for example, an understanding of occasional supervisor forgetfulness might result in a habit of student-generated post-meeting reminder emails. One student (not identified for the purpose of anonymity) described adoption of a new style of directing meetings with the supervisor, in reaction to the supervisor's tendency for going on tangents, saying *"I've learned to have one thing only to discuss."* The success of this arrangement is in turn determined by the student's ability and willingness to adapt, as well as the context of the adaptation, including their stage of research, length of the relationship, and physical colocation of students and supervisors.

All supervisors reported that they rarely shifted their practices for a student and only then in exceptional circumstances. For Sp-G2 this occurred when the student was perceived to be struggling, and thus more structure was introduced by the supervisor, such as requiring an agenda or a set timetable of meetings. For Sp-G4, this happened in the absence of the regular matchmaking between supervisor and student; typically, supervisors and students choose to work together, but in situations when Sp-G4 was assigned as a supervisor and had to work with a particular student, there was more willingness to adapt research practices and communication preferences to meet the student's needs and make things work. Sp-G1 also admitted to being incapable or unwilling to change behaviour to avoid conflict with a student, citing time constraints and considerations for cognitive capacity (such as the taxing effect of being party to multiple research collaborations) as factors.

4.2 Theme 2: Distributed Cognition Demands

There is a high attention and memory demand on both students and supervisors conducting research — a process further complicated by its being distributed across multiple individuals.

The theoretical framework of distributed cognition [9] (or DCog) lends itself well to an understanding of the supervisor-student relationship. Distributed cognition theory, developed by Hutchins in mid-1980, emphasizes the social aspect of cognition. In his seminal study, Hutchins described the DCog theory within the context of navigating a US navy vessel whereby the transfer of information between crew members and various tools and external representations make the ship's navigation possible [10, 11]. In a distributed cognitive framework, the unit of analysis for cognition is not an individual but could be a small sociotechnical system comprised of individuals, their environment and its artifacts. In our case, students and supervisors, as well as their shared and personal tools and practices, can be considered as components of a cognitive system dedicated to the complex task of research. In our interviews, we found evidence of supervisors and students relying on different components of the cognitive system to perform and support tasks and distribute responsibility for execution of practices. For example, Sp-G2 mentioned a '24 hours rule', an established practice of having students be responsible for sending a reminder if they had yet to receive requested items more than 24 hours after a meeting. Sp-G1 sometimes passed on items to students to keep as their 'agenda seeds' for future meetings and, in doing so, was able to relinquish responsibility over them.

Sp-G1: I might say...let's just put it on the agenda [for] next time we meet...and then I've tossed that basketball to [the student], and I'm not gonna try and remember any more...

More intragroup awareness between members of a research collaboration, achieved through either increased use of shared workspaces or microupdate tools like Twitter and Facebook, was also identified as desirable by participants, in part because it would decrease the burden on the supervisor to be the only source of research group information. G3 also reported relying on Facebook for microupdates, but only during the summer when some group members were away or did not maintain regular hours.

According to DCog theory, the cognitive mechanisms involved

are not limited to those happening within an individual actor but involve rich interactions between internal processes and external representations and artifacts [9, 19]. Our participants' use of documents and diagrams, especially those co-created between supervisor and student, suggests that artifacts as representations of research are particularly useful for helping to remember a conversation and recover context of a past meeting (See [19] for a discussion of cognitive artifacts and the importance of external representations on cognitive functions and problem solving efficacy).

St1G1: I keep a written notebook mostly to organize my thoughts...

Sp-G1: A lot of time what's happened is that someone comes in and has already written something on a page and then we further discuss it and maybe add a layer of annotation on that page as we discuss it...I then gain some mind space on the page...

The importance of various components within a cognitive system and the information flow between components (whether it be the student, the supervisor, a shared, or a personal artifact), can vary for each supervisory relationship. Our data suggest this difference is related to the supervision style; in the case of less structured supervisors (Sp-G2 and Sp-G4), the student is the main component of the cognitive system, and thus personal (non-shared) tools and practices have a more prominent role in the success of research. In the case of those in G4, for example, sometimes the supervisor entered meetings with students without "having any idea of" what was going to be discussed; it was the role and responsibility of the students to know, not the supervisor:

Sp-G4: I tend not to [take notes], (laughs) but I ask the students, 'whoa, ok, so what happened last time?'

In the case of more structured supervisors (Sp-G1 and Sp-G3), the information exchange between the student and the supervisor is more detailed and shared tools and practices are more prominent. Consequently, these supervisors are more likely to require shared artifacts and practices such as agendas or meeting minutes. However, as previously reported, when the less structured supervisors exhibit a shift in behaviour to adapt to changing relationship dynamics, an increased or introduced dependence on tools and practices - such as regular contributions to a research wiki or requiring an agenda for every meeting - was often the outcome; with a decrease in perceived accountability of the student in the system, tools and practices became elevated components.

Additionally, the information flow among components of a supervisory Dcog system can change over time due to external factors such as sabbatical and maternity leaves or factors such as the successful transition of the student to a state of independence in their research or the adoption of a new tool or practice.

St1G3: I had some meetings with agendas and some not depending on what stage of the project we were at...

While every collaborative act implies some sort of distributed cognitive system, looking at the supervisor-student relationship as one cognitive system can help suggest which practices and tools will be useful within a given supervisory relationship and help in analyzing the temporal changes in information flow between the components.

4.3 Theme 3: Feedback Channel Dissonance

Among our participants, there appears to be little or no infrastructure in place for students and supervisors to discuss, and advise about their tools and practices. Additional evidence comes from the fact that students knew so little about their supervisors' opinions of their tools and practices that our own joint supervisor-student focus groups served as an intervention for some of the participants; St1G1, for example, came away with the knowledge of being a "master of agendas" and was appreciative of the supervisor's approval, but prior to the joint focus group had been unaware of having any aptitude for crafting them.

Supervisors also indicated uncertainty about students' viewpoints on their practices, and the value of recommending or enforcing them, as well as their effectiveness for research collaboration more generally. For example, Sp-G1 described an unawareness of the relative structure of the research group compared to others, and how it rated on "the scale of possible supervisory styles." Sp-G2 also described a difficulty with knowing if a decision not to hold group meetings was the right choice. Additionally, supervisors directly asked us to share our results as they thought it would be helpful for their future relationships.

A distinction should be noted between feedback on student projects, and feedback on practices:

St1G1: I feel I get enough feedback on what I'm working specifically on...I want to be aware of what I'm not aware of...

But while St1G1 welcomed practice feedback or performance reviews, St3G4 saw little value in this kind of information or advice, reasoning that the supervisor would be less insightful and aware of the struggles and subtleties than the student would have of their own working styles. Furthermore, there was a lack of consensus concerning how such feedback (particularly, critical feedback) ought to be communicated, especially to more sensitive or stressed students. While some students preferred a face-to-face conversation, others foresaw a discussion fraught with social pressures, in particular, a fear of offending the supervisor. On the side of the supervisor, there may also be some tension or discomfort experienced with voicing both positive and negative feedback. In the former case, Sp-G1 worried that it might seem patronizing to a student to complement them on, for example, an agenda; in the latter, both of the two less structured supervisors (Sp-G2 and Sp-G4) also expressed reluctance to critique students' research practices, partially out of fear of suppressing students' future experimentation, intellectual curiosity, and desire to explore new approaches for collaboration.

Sp-G2: I yell at my daughter to do stuff, I don't really feel like I need to yell at my student...

Perhaps not surprisingly, within the specific context of a study of CS, workflows were very much influenced by changes in technology; however, this was not strictly limited to just tool use, but how the discipline of CS itself had changed. Sp-G4 in particular discussed how the evolution and diversification of the field over the years had resulted in there no longer being a shared vocabulary among practitioners or consensus of what constituted a core knowledge that all students and supervisors would have in common. This in turn affected the assumptions one could make about tool use and awareness of technologies, for example, proficiency in LaTex, a document layout and formatting software that was once a standard tool in CS.

Our data suggests that when a feedback channel is broken or incomplete within a supervisor-student relationship, practice and tool use is transferred between peers, both within and outside a research group, but in an ad-hoc manner. For example, three students within G3 mentioned they had started using a wiki, and on a particular platform, after receiving recommendations from another student.

5 DISCUSSION

This section includes our recommendations for design followed by limitations of our work.

5.1 Implications for Design

Our study suggests that no one tool can accommodate the diverse needs of various research groups, however, we think the following implications for design can certainly benefit some, if not all, supervisory and research relationships.

1) Tracking research progress can improve awareness of research and serve as a channel for communicating relationship feedback.
As previously stated, some practices required or encouraged by supervisors were done in order to gradually transition the student into an accountable, independent state and ready the student as a professional self-directed researcher. However, there is no mechanism for tracking students' goals and progress, identifying students' professional growth over time, or communicating relationship feedback.

A mechanism that increases awareness of and promotes mutual feedback on work practices and the supervisory relationship would help with the selection, adoption, or development of tools and practices that work best for all stakeholders. Devising and committing to a feedback practice or habit could be as simple as a scheduled conversation or a more structured supervisor-supervisee performance review covering research and relationship items.

More sophisticated tools that afford data-driven tracking of the supervisor-student relationship or provide charting of its development over time with respect to selected dimensions of the collaboration (e.g., frequency of meetings, summary of submitted deliverables, and professional activities like conference presentations) can introduce a degree of centralization to distributed cognitive mechanisms of the relationship. It could additionally prove useful as indirect feedback channels that promote increased awareness of individual and relationship practices systematically, thereby avoiding having the onus on the supervisor who might forget or feel awkward to convey such information.

Supervisors in particular commented that a tracking system would be useful for recalling the stage of research for each student and resuming context; additionally, such a tool would help students visualize their progress over time more easily, which may prove helpful to more senior students, such as PhDs, who may be more in need of reminders of their accomplishments as well as indicators that it is time to move on from something they have spent a lot of effort on with little to show for it.

Customer Relationship Management (CRM) systems are examples of designs that provide related functionality, such as automatic aggregation of past activity and communications from various software applications, as well as tracking and alerts for outstanding items, and generation of a dashboard display of relevant relationship history profiles. Instances of CRM have previously been implemented within the academic environment, but typically for administrative and financial management of the student's relationship with the university [20], not with the supervisor. Unlike a typical CRM system which supports a company in tracking and management of its relations with clients, a supervisory CRM should promote a shared understanding of the research between a student and a supervisor. Thus, a supervisory CRM should support students and supervisors equally yet not identically by providing both parties with similar information while prioritizing that which is most relevant to each depending on their role within the relationship. Supervisors and students would also require different access rights and management options to support their roles. For example, supervisors must be able to manage interactions with several students working under their supervision. Another important feature for a supervisory CRM is supporting personalization to accommodate various supervisory styles, stages of research and changes in the supervisor-student relationship. For example, frequency and format of requested artifacts or updates can be increased to apply more structure or centralization to a supervisory relation as needed (e.g., supporting a new graduate student or during sabbatical).

Computational network models could also inform supportive system designs. Spatio-temporal analyses of social networks have already been used to identify emerging relationship trends, including changes in centrality of a network or increasing and decreasing network cohesiveness [22]. Similar algorithms could be applied to research groups or individual supervisor networks to analyze relationship interactions and anticipate disruptive forces. For example, in the case of a sabbatical leave, a supporting system may help to identify the increased priority of frequent student-supervisor contact, and even suggest multiple means of communications, to counteract the detrimental effect of geographical distribution.

A challenge with the implementation of such a system, however, is related to the organizational culture (or lack thereof) of graduate school. Unlike a corporate environment where employees typically have no say over what documentation software or e-mail client they use, there is a lot of individual variation and choice allowed for students and supervisors; some participants were also not in favour of the idea of forced adoption of a system. Additionally not all research communications occur through software systems which means any software modeling tool that attempted to capture the relationship and its dynamic would be incomplete. Furthermore, any new tracking support should aim for little to no additional workload and learning overhead for the students and supervisors and ideally should easily integrate with existing tools and systems. A good example is a Gmail plug-in called Streak; It provides CRM functionality and allows for easy tracking of interactions with several customers and aggregation of the customers' information all from within a person's inbox ([1]).

From our informal talks with students, we also learned about systemless or at least 'offline' practices that are currently used for relationship and project management. For example, another research group used colour-coded sticky notes on a bulletin board to represent the goals for each week; the notes, or goals, were then removed to the side of the board if they were achieved by the end of the week.

2) A dedicated tool and practice awareness mechanism can improve practice transfer among peers. We found some instances of transfer of practice and tool information among peers, including both students and supervisors. While some participants expressed a positive evaluation of this behaviour, and an appreciation for recommendations that came from those they trusted and who were working under similar demands and pressures, this behaviour seemed only to occur in a mostly happenstance ad-hoc manner, with many admitting that tool use was dependent not only on technology but awareness of it and what was available.

We think a system specifically developed for the purpose of tool and practice discovery would better ensure effective knowledge transfer and collaboration, thereby saving time and decreasing frustration for supervisors and students who otherwise must address their unsupported behaviour by experimenting with new tools or by applying a strategic combination of old ones to meet a need.

One example of system design that already supports practice transfer is an educational initiative called "This Changed My Practice." It is an online repository for health practitioners to share their most effective or newly discovered practices that support diagnosis or patient care [2]. Additional site features allow users to comment on posts, categorize and 'tag' the content, vote on practices, and refer to related evidence-based literature. A similar platform could be adapted for increasing awareness about various tools and practices among students and supervisors. Recommender systems which feature both collaborative and content-based filtering [18] may also support easy and relevant tool discovery. Further investigation is needed to establish the scope and affordances of such a system, for example whether it would be most useful as a closed system within a single research group or department, or as a completely open one to be shared among academics across disciplines.

5.2 Characteristics of Our Participants and Limitations

We limited the demographic composition of our participant pool to partially control for the wide variety of student-supervisor collaboration. However, one must note the characteristics of our chosen study group when interpreting our results. Firstly, as CS faculty and students, our participants may exhibit a better aptitude for knowledge collaboration and task management, and adoption of new tools than the population at large. While we attempted to account for the effect of the supervision power dynamic during interpretation of our data, as well as minimize its potential influence on all participants' choice to self-censor by having non-mixed (student-only or supervisor-only) member-checking sessions, we acknowledge the difficulty for participants to speak candidly about relationship satisfaction and research progress, especially within a small graduate community of a single department; however, we did specifically question participants about their experiences with communicating positive and negative feedback related to research relationships and believe this difficulty can prove an important consideration for tool and practice choice.

As previously stated, prior to undertaking our research, we were already familiar with the faculty members and some members of the research groups. This guided our sampling decisions for the initial interview requests and the student-only focus group to ensure variability among the participants. Our familiarity with the research practices in the CS department gave us the required context for interpreting participants comments. However, one of the authors is from a different department which provided us an outsider viewpoint in our analysis of the data.

Unfortunately, our demographics are skewed in terms of gender for supervisors (3 females, 1 male). We anticipate that the demographics of supervisors can impact communication styles, and relationship dynamics. Finally, we think there is an even greater variety of student-supervisor collaboration within the CS community and additional studies can further characterize this variety.

6 CONCLUSION AND FUTURE WORK

In this project, we conducted an exploratory case study on meetings between graduate students and supervisors, specifically looking at factors that impact choice and success of tools and practices to support effective collaboration. Data from focus group and individual interview sessions with faculty members and students were analyzed using thematic analysis, and resulted in three themes and two implications for design. The first two themes describe factors influencing choice and success of student-supervisor tools and practices while the last theme highlights mutual feedback on work practices as an important yet unsupported area of student-supervisor interaction. A lot is still unknown about students and supervisors' practices and intentions, and thus a lot of work needs to be done before user behavior modelling can begin. Therefore, we recommend the development of systems that will first encourage communication between students and supervisors to increase awareness about the effectiveness of tools and practices in various circumstances.

Despite the small number of participants in our study, we found ample variation in the tools and practices used by students and supervisors to suggest such diversity will be reflected in other populations within academia and geographically distributed, collaborative work environments. We recommend further study to determine how supervisory styles and practices vary between different disciplines (e.g., English Literature, Anthropology) and within alternative arrangements of semi-independent student research. We are interested in undertaking a more in-depth study of supervisors, to better model their individual differences and map them to personas of supervisory styles; for example, we might expect the gender of the supervisor to have a large influence on approaches to or preferences for communication. Also, further research into the individual differences for giving and receiving feedback in a supervisory relationship is necessary to provide guidelines to design the most effective mechanisms for this purpose. Finally, while there are likely commonalities and also differences between manager-employee supervisory relations and supervisor-student relations, a comparative study between the two would help to inform the design of general purpose supportive tools and practices.

REFERENCES

[1] Streak Gmail plugin. http://www.streak.com/.
[2] This changed my practice: A free online educational initiative. http://thischangedmypractice.com/.

[3] V. Braun and V. Clarke. Using thematic analysis in psychology. *Qualitative research in psychology*, 3(2):77–101, 2006.

[4] C.-J. Chen and J.-W. Huang. How organizational climate and structure affect knowledge management-the social interaction perspective. *International Journal of Information Management*, 27(2):104–118, 2007.

[5] R. C. Davis, J. A. Landay, V. Chen, J. Huang, R. B. Lee, F. C. Li, J. Lin, C. B. Morrey, III, B. Schleimer, M. N. Price, and B. N. Schilit. Notepals: lightweight note sharing by the group, for the group. In *SIGCHI conference on Human Factors in Computing Systems*, CHI '99, pages 338–345, New York, NY, USA, 1999.

[6] J. L. de Rezende, J. Xexeo, R. T. da Silva, M. S. Arajo, and J. M. de Souza. Supporting student-supervisor scientific collaboration. In *Computer Supported Cooperative Work in Design, 2006. CSCWD'06.*, pages 1–6, 2006.

[7] E. A. Erichsen, D. U. Bolliger, and C. Halupa. Student satisfaction with graduate supervision in doctoral programs primarily delivered in distance education settings. *Studies in Higher Education*, (ahead-of-print):1–18, 2012.

[8] M. Haraty, D. Tam, S. Haddad, J. McGrenere, and C. Tang. Individual differences in personal task management: a field study in an academic setting. In *Graphics Interface Conference. GI'12.*, pages 35–44, 2012.

[9] J. Hollan, E. Hutchins, and D. Kirsh. Distributed cognition: toward a new foundation for human-computer interaction research. *ACM Transactions on Computer-Human Interaction (TOCHI)*, 7(2):174–196, 2000.

[10] E. Hutchins. *Cognition in the Wild*. MIT press Cambridge, MA, 1995.

[11] E. Hutchins. How a cockpit remembers its speeds. *Cognitive science*, 19(3):265–288, 1995.

[12] A. Ismail, N. Z. Abiddin, and A. Hassan. Improving the development of postgraduates research and supervision. *International Education Studies*, 4(1):78, 2011.

[13] L. Kuijer, A. d. Jong, and D. v. Eijk. Practices as a unit of design: An exploration of theoretical guidelines in a study on bathing. *ACM Transactions on Computer-Human Interaction (TOCHI)*, 20(4):21, 2013.

[14] Q. Le. E-portfolio for enhancing graduate research supervision. *Quality Assurance in Education*, 20(1):54–65, 2012.

[15] P. Legris, J. Ingham, and P. Collerette. Why do people use information technology? a critical review of the technology acceptance model. *Information & management*, 40(3):191–204, 2003.

[16] H. W. Marsh, K. J. Rowe, and A. Martin. PhD students' evaluations of research supervision: issues, complexities, and challenges in a nationwide australian experiment in benchmarking universities. *Journal of Higher Education*, pages 313–348, 2002.

[17] C. McKavanagh, K. Bryant, G. Finger, and H. Middleton. Information and communication technologies and higher degree research supervision. *Higher Education Research and Development Society of Australasia, Miri, Malaysia*, pages 4–12, 2004.

[18] P. Melville, R. J. Mooney, and R. Nagarajan. Content-boosted collaborative filtering for improved recommendations. In *Eighteenth national conference on Artificial intelligence*, pages 187–192, Menlo Park, CA, USA, 2002.

[19] D. Norman. Cognitive artifacts. *Designing interaction: Psychology at the Human-Computer Interface*, pages 17–38, 1991.

[20] M. Piedade and M. Santos. Student relationship management: Concept, practice and technological support. In *Engineering Management Conference, 2008. IEMC Europe 2008.*, pages 1–5, 2008.

[21] K. Ryall, C. Forlines, C. Shen, and M. R. Morris. Exploring the effects of group size and table size on interactions with tabletop shared-display groupware. In *ACM conference on Computer supported cooperative work. CSCW'04.*, pages 284–293, New York, NY, USA, 2004.

[22] S. Shekhar and D. Oliver. Computational modeling of spatio-temporal social networks: A time-aggregated graph approach. In *Specialist Meeting-Spatio-Temporal Constraints on Social Networks*, 2010.

[23] L. Siemens. it's a team if you use reply all: An exploration of research teams in digital humanities environments. *Literary and linguistic computing*, 24(2):225–233, 2009.

[24] R. Sommer. Further studies of small group ecology. *Sociometry*, pages 337–348, 1965.

[25] J. Stewart, B. B. Bederson, and A. Druin. Single display groupware: a model for co-present collaboration. In *SIGCHI conference on Human factors in computing systems: the CHI is the limit*, pages 286–293, 1999.

[26] H. Verma, F. Roman, S. Magrelli, P. Jermann, and P. Dillenbourg. Complementarity of input devices to achieve knowledge sharing in meetings. In *ACM conference on Computer supported cooperative work. CSCW'13.*, pages 701–714, 2013.

Visualizing Aerial LiDAR Cities with Hierarchical Hybrid Point-Polygon Structures

Zhenzhen Gao*
University of Southern California

Luciano Nocera†
University of Southern California

Miao Wang‡
Microsoft Corporation

Ulrich Neumann§
University of Southern California

ABSTRACT

This paper presents a visualization framework for cities in the form of aerial LiDAR (Light Detection and Ranging) point clouds. To provide interactive rendering for large data sets, the framework combines level-of-detail (LOD) technique with hierarchical hybrid representations of both point and polygon of the scene. The supporting structure for LOD is a multi-resolution quadtree (*MRQ*) hierarchy that is built purely out of input points. Each *MRQ* node stores separately a *continuous* data set for ground and building points that are sampled from continuous surfaces, and a *discrete* data set for independent tree points. The continuous data is first augmented with vertical quadrilateral building walls that are missing in original points owing to the 2.5D nature of aerial LiDAR. The continuous data is then spatially partitioned into same size subsets, based on which hybrid point-polygon structures are hierarchically constructed. Specifically, a polygon conversion operation replaces points of a subset forming a planar surface to a quadrilateral covering the same space, and a polygon simplification operation decimates wall quadrilaterals of a subset sharing the same plane to a single compact quadrilateral. Interactive hybrid visualization is retained by adapting a hardware-accelerated point based rendering with deferred shading. We perform experiments on several aerial LiDAR cities. Compared to visually-complete rendering [10], the presented framework is able to deliver comparable visual quality with less than 8% increase in pre-processing time and 2-5 times higher rendering frame-rates.

Index Terms: Computer Graphics [I.3.3]: Picture/Image Generation—Display algorithms; Computer Graphics [I.3.5]: Computational Geometry and Object Modeling—Hierarchy and geometric transformations; Computer Graphics [I.3.7]: Three-Dimensional Graphics and Realism—Virtual reality

1 INTRODUCTION

Aerial LiDAR (Light Detection and Ranging) is cost-effective in acquiring terrain and urban information by mounting a downward-scanning laser on a low-flying aircraft. It produces huge volumes of unconnected 3D points that can be complemented by intensities, colors, and classification labels. This paper is primarily concerned with the interactive visualization of aerial LiDAR point clouds of cities, which is applicable to a number of areas including virtual tourism, security, land management and urban planning.

Interactive visualization of aerial LiDAR cities is challenging. Firstly, the large size of the data can easily exceed the memory capacity of a computer system. Secondly, points of a city contain multiple objects that possess different physical characteristics. Finally, aerial LiDAR data is 2.5D in nature [31], in that the sensor is

*e-mail: zhenzheg@graphics.usc.edu

†e-mail: nocera@usc.edu

‡e-mail:neilwa@microsoft.com

§e-mail:uneumann@graphics.usc.edu

Graphics Interface Conference 2014
7-9 May, Montreal, Quebec, Canada

only able to capture dense details of the surfaces facing it, leaving few samples on vertical surfaces such as building walls. A framework needs to leverage all these properties in order to deliver useful visualization of aerial LiDAR cities.

(a) Input points

(b) 1,195,896 pts, 46,168 quads, 29.6 fps

(c) 510,541 pts, 50,524 quads, 83.8 fps

Figure 1: A comparison between rendering of Gao et al. [10] (b) and the presented framework (c) on the data set of (a). Our framework provides comparable visual quality but with improved frame-rates. pts for points and fps for frames per second. Brown for ground; dark grey for buildings; light blue for walls; and green for trees. These terms and color scheme are used throughout the paper.

Gao et al. [10] successfully address the above challenges by introducing a visually-complete rendering framework. Their framework utilizes a hierarchical and out-of-core approach to large data management, treats points differently by classification, and completes building walls by attaching one piece of wall geometry to

137

every building boundary point. As its extension and optimization, this paper presents a new visualization framework for aerial LiDAR cities that provides comparable visual quality with greatly improved rendering performance, with the help of hierarchical hybrid point-polygon structures.

Reducing rendering load is necessary to enable interactive visualization for large data sets. One common approach is to cut down the number of rendered primitives using LOD (level-of-detail) techniques. With the support of a multi-resolution hierarchy of the scene, for each frame, the renderer selects a proper resolution with adequate details view-dependently so that only sufficient primitives are rendered. As rendering primitives, points are more efficient for displaying small details but polygons are faster for representing large flat surfaces. Therefore, to further reduce rendering load, it is desirable to support hybrid representation of both point and polygon of the scene, and to select the most efficient rendering primitive view-dependently. The presented framework is a combination of LOD and hybrid representation.

LOD employs an *MRQ* (Multi-Resolution Quadtree) hierarchy as the supporting structure. Due to lack of connectivity, points are a more efficient LOD representation than polygons. Thus the *MRQ* is built directly out of input points. In correspondence to different processing methods, each *MRQ* node separately stores a *continuous* data set for ground and building points whose latent surfaces are continuous, and a *discrete* data set for tree points that are discrete and unstructured. To complete missing building walls in the continuous data set, each building boundary point is augmented with a vertical quadrilateral connecting it to the ground.

Hybrid representation utilizes two *RPQ* (Rendering Primitive Quadtree) hierarchies as the supporting structure: one RPQ_p for input points; and one RPQ_w for augmented walls. *RPQ* structures use a hierarchically built quadtree to represent partitions of an underlying continuous space, or of data sampled from that space. Any breadth-first traversal down the tree gives a family of cells that partition the space; each cell stores the best rendering primitive (point or polygon) for an approximation to the surface represented by its data. For a cell whose entire set of points form a planar surface, the corresponding RPQ_p node stores a quadrilateral covering the same space to replace these points. Similarly, for a cell whose entire set of wall quadrilaterals approximate a planar surface, the corresponding RPQ_w node stores a simplified quadrilateral to compactly represent these walls. By sharing the same quadtree hierarchy, hybrid representations for higher levels of the *MRQ* are built through propagation from lower levels.

The framework builds supporting structures completely in pre-processing. During rendering, it traverses the *MRQ* hierarchically to locate visible nodes with sufficient details, then renders data of these nodes according to corresponding *RPQ* structures by adapting a hardware-accelerated point based rendering with deferred shading [10]. The framework also enables smooth LOD transitions by blending rendering results of two adjacent levels.

Contributions: This paper presents a framework for interactive and visually-complete rendering of aerial LiDAR point clouds of cities. The framework achieves improved rendering performance by utilizing hierarchical hybrid point-polygon structures which support both quadrilaterals converted from planar subsets of points, and simplified quadrilaterals from augmented wall quadrilaterals.

2 RELATED WORK

Considerable research efforts have been devoted to multi-resolution representation and LOD creation and management for rendering large scale data sets. There are methods designed for polygonal meshes [2, 3, 18, 23]; there are also methods customized for point sampled models [7, 11, 25, 30].

Given an object in both point and polygon representations, for small details where polygons occupy fewer screen pixels than cor-responding points, rendering as points is more efficient. But as the projected screen area grows, rendering as polygons becomes increasingly efficient. To benefit from both rendering primitives, several hybrid approaches are developed.

Known as one of the first hybrid point-polygon systems, POP [4] utilizes a multi-resolution hierarchical quadtree to store triangles only at leaf nodes and points at intermediate nodes. Those intermediate points are computed bottom-up based on bounding spheres of child nodes as QSplat [25]. The first hybrid simplification method [6] uses a triangle hierarchy based on edge collapsing. It adaptively replaces triangles with points via an error metric. The hybrid hierarchy of Coconu et al. [5] consists of original triangles and points sampled from triangle surfaces. Wand et al. [28] apply a hierarchy that is independent of mesh connectivity and topology through dynamic and random sampling of points. Zheng et al. [29] first organize the scene into a binary space partitioning (BSP) tree; and then subdivide objects in each BSP leaf node into a quadtree hierarchy, which contains both the sample points and polygon rendering information at each level. With hardware acceleration, Hao et al. [13] segment model faces into regions, store triangles and vertex point clouds of each region, and render different regions using either triangles or points according to their distances from the viewpoint. All above systems require polygonal mesh as input, which is not directly applicable to point clouds.

A few other approaches take point cloud directly as input without requiring a surface mesh. PMR [8] relies on Voronoi diagram and its dual Delaunay triangulation to convert points into triangles for the hybrid hierarchy. Wahl et al. [27] convert planar subsets of the point cloud to quadrilaterals via plane detection based on the iterative random sample consensus (RANSAC) [9]. Additionally, an octree structure is used to identify planar representations at different scales and accuracies for LOD selection during rendering. Specialized for LiDAR point clouds, Kuder et al. [15] detect continuous surfaces in points by progressively growing smooth regions, and replaces them with decimated triangle meshes. Point data is non-redundantly distributed across all levels of the hierarchy, and surfaces are triangularized into meshes for each tree node separately. Unlike these systems that take considerable efforts striving to accurately recover latent surfaces of the point cloud, the presented framework is simpler and more efficient by converting quadrilaterals only out of points in regular spacial partitions without involving expensive computation.

In the field of LiDAR point cloud visualization, Kovac et al. [14] apply a two-pass rendering to efficiently blend splats; and Kuder et al. [16] combine splatting with deferred shading [1] in a three-pass rendering algorithm. These systems laid the rendering foundation of the presented framework. The first system that addresses the 2.5D nature of aerial LiDAR points [10] introduces three ways to complete the missing building walls: point-wall augments the point cloud with missing points in pre-processing, and quadrilateral- and axis-aligned rectangular parallelepiped-walls are procedurally generated during rendering. This paper adapts quadrilateral-walls to fit in pre-processing in order to maximize rendering performance.

3 MULTI-RESOLUTION HIERARCHY

LOD rendering requires a supporting multi-resolution data structure that indexes the space of the scene. This paper uses *MRQ*, a quadtree hierarchy, since its construction is inexpensive and its domain is effectively 2.5D, which is a good match for aerial LiDAR.

The construction of the *MRQ* begins at the root node, which covers the whole area of the scene. The bounding box of the data contained in the root node is equally divided along the *x* and *y* axes into four sub-areas indexed by four children of the root node. This process continues until a predetermined maximum number of points per leaf node is reached.

Based on physical properties, point data of an *MRQ* node is

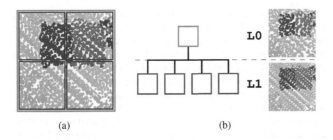

(a)   (b)

Figure 2: A two-level *MRQ*. (a) Input point data marked with bounding boxes (in red or blue). Spaces between bounding boxes are left intentionally for clarity. (b) *MRQ* of (a). Node colors correspond to colors of bounding boxes. L0 has $\frac{1}{4}$ resolution of L1.

split into two sets: one continuous data set for ground and building points that are sampled from continuous surfaces; and one discrete data set for tree points that are independent and unstructured. All points are distributed in such a way that leaf nodes represent the highest resolution of the scene, and each non-leaf node has $\frac{1}{4}$ resolution of its children, as seen in Figure 2. Consequently, we get a refinement when traversing downward, and a simplification when traversing upward.

3.1 Continuous Data Set

Because of the 2.5D characteristic, aerial LiDAR points can be represented as an elevation map without loss of information. And because the underlying surfaces of ground and building points are piece-wise continuous, interpolation-based gridding of the elevation map can preserve geometry details as long as the resolution of grids is no less than the sampling density of original point data. Compared to data structures built directly upon original 3D points, the 2D gridded elevation map (*GEM*) provides more efficient storage and neighborhood selection allowing substantial reduction of the computation complexity [17]. Therefore, we store continuous data sets of ground and building points in *GEM*s.

3.1.1 Constructing *GEM*s for *MRQ* Leaf Nodes

Given an *MRQ* leaf node, by projecting continuous data within its bounding box onto *x-y* plane, an elevation map is created. Through a gridding operation, we first convert the elevation map to a *GEM*. A filtering operation applied to the *GEM* then removes possible gaps and identifies building boundary points. Finally, vertical quadrilaterals are augmented to building boundary points to complete missing building walls.

Gridding Points of the elevation map are quantized to squares of uniform width ω_g, such that *x*, *y* positions are indexed by integers, and each (x, y) pair relates to one sample point. The quantized elevation map is a *GEM*; and each sample point of the *GEM* is referred to as a grid. To ensure the number of grids in *GEM* is approximately the same as the number of points in original data, ω_g is set to the average point spacing of the entire scene. This is reasonable as aerial LiDAR points are sampled approximately uniformly.

Each grid *g* indexed by (x_g, y_g) contains as its data an elevation value, a normal vector, and a flag indicating its classification as ground or building. *g*'s data is determined by neighbors nearest to (x_g, y_g) on the corresponding elevation map. We start with $k = 8$ nearest neighbors [19], and then select a subset of k' ($k' \leq k$) neighbors whose elevations are within ζ of the largest elevation of all *k* neighbors, in order to ensure that the subset of neighbors come from the same surface. Evaluated from these k' neighbors, *g*'s elevation takes the weighted average, its normal estimated by Principal Component Analysis (PCA), and its classification flag set as the same. ζ is the minimum elevation difference between two

roof layers as detailed in Gao et al. [10], which is proved to be effective to separate ground and different roof layers of a building. Figure 3b shows a *GEM* resulted from gridding.

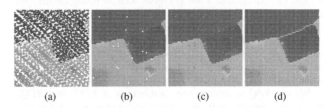

(a)   (b)   (c)   (d)

Figure 3: Gridding and filtering results on (a) The elevation map of a test data. (b) The *GEM* after gridding. (c) After applying a box filter on (b), empty grids are filled by new red points. (d) After applying a Laplace filter on (c), building boundary grids are marked in light blue.

Filtering Due to quantization errors and under-sampling of original data, a grid on *GEM* may be empty, leading to a gap in visualization. A box filter [24] is applied to effectively fill these empty grids, as shown in Figure 3c.

Following the wall completion approach of [10], building boundary points need to be distinguished. Similar to edge detection of an image [24], we apply a Laplace filter to elevations of *GEM* grids, which results in obviously larger elevations for building boundary grids than those for non-boundary grids. Thus all building boundary grids can be identified by thresholding with the same ζ for gridding, as shown in Figure 3d.

Wall Augmenting To complete missing building walls, a vertical quadrilateral is augmented offline for every building boundary grid to connect it to the ground, adapted from Gao et al. [10].

For clarity, the following sections use GEM_p (Gridded Elevation Map for Points) for the subset of *GEM* including all point data; GEM_w (Gridded Elevation Map for Walls) for the subset containing only building boundary points and their wall quadrilaterals; and *GEM* for the complete structure including both point data and augmented quadrilateral walls.

3.1.2 Constructing *GEM*s for *MRQ* Non-Leaf Nodes

We build *GEM* of an *MRQ* non-leaf node bottom-up by regularly sub-sampling $\frac{1}{4}$ of grids from its four child nodes. Specifically, the *GEM* of a non-leaf node is composed of grids on odd rows and even columns (or grids on even rows and odd columns) from *GEM*s of its child nodes. It seems that such a scheme will lead to bad aliasing, but because the LOD system only displays higher level nodes when they can provide adequate details for current frame, we don't see noticeable aliasing in practice.

3.2 Discrete Data Set

Since tree points look natural when rendered as independent separate splats, for simplicity, we apply a user-adjustable fixed splat size for tree points of any resolution in the *MRQ*. As a result, each tree point only needs to store one 3D position, and one normal vector.

An *MRQ* leaf node builds its discrete data set by including all tree points within its bounding box, as the highest resolution. An *MRQ* non-leaf node builds its discrete data set bottom-up by subsampling $\frac{1}{4}$ of discrete data sets from all its four child nodes, i.e., randomly selecting one point for every four tree points from its child nodes.

4 HYBRID REPRESENTATION

Hybrid representations are only applicable to continuous data sets that are stored in *GEM*s of each *MRQ* node. Corresponding to two types of *GEM*s, there are two types of hybrid representations in the form of *RPQ*s.

A GEM_p contains point data only, which is labeled as ground, building or building boundary. Sampled from continuous surfaces, if a subset of these points form a large flat region, the point subset can be converted to a few polygons without losing details. We construct an RPQ_p hierarchy for the GEM_p indicating whether to render an area as point or converted polygon.

Observing that a group of quadrilaterals sharing the same plane can be simplified, we also compactly decimate wall quadrilaterals. Accordingly, an RPQ_w is constructed for the GEM_w indicating whether to render an area as original or simplified quadrilaterals.

We use RPQ to refer to the combination of RPQ_p and RPQ_w hierarchies. Besides point data, the hybrid representation also supports two classes of polygons: quadrilaterals converted from planar subsets of points, and simplified wall quadrilaterals.

The following sections first introduce how to perform polygon conversion (Section 4.1) and simplification (Section 4.2) for an MRQ leaf node, then show details of propagating the hybrid representation to MRQ's non-leaf nodes (Section 4.3).

4.1 Polygon Conversion

To convert planar subsets of points into polygons, existing approaches require iterative trials of plane-fitting. The number of planes and coverage of each plane are often necessary to get satisfying results. To keep the polygon conversion fast and simple, we forfeit the idea of locating all planes with their maximum coverage. Instead, all points are spatially partitioned into subsets of the same size, and planes are only fit to these point subsets.

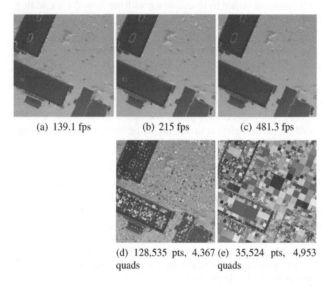

(a) 139.1 fps   (b) 215 fps   (c) 481.3 fps

(d) 128,535 pts, 4,367 (e) 35,524 pts, 4,953
quads   quads

Figure 4: Rendering effect of polygon conversion. (a) Rendered by Gao et al. [10] where ground and buildings are points. (b)-(e) Rendered by our framework with polygon conversion under different parameters: $\Lambda = 10^{-5}$ ((b)(d)) and $\Lambda = 10^{-3}$ ((c)(e)). Converted polygons in (d) and (e) are randomly colored.

RPQ_p is a quadtree hierarchy constructed similar to MRQ, but with a different termination condition. Given an RPQ_p node with $w \times h$ grids, if either w or h has no more than 3 grids, this node is a leaf node and no further splitting is needed. The number 3 comes from the fact that it requires at least 2×2 grids to form a polygon, and splitting a dimension of 3 will result in a node smaller than the minimum requirement. An RPQ_p node stores its bound on GEM_p for indexing, and a flag f_{rp} indicating its rendering primitive as either point or converted polygon.

The rendering primitive evaluation starts at leaf nodes of the RPQ_p. When all grids of a leaf node are non-empty, PCA is applied over their 3D positions. Only when the smallest eigenvalue

λ_0 of the covariance matrix is small enough (i.e., $\lambda_0 \leq \Lambda$, where Λ is a user-defined threshold that is close to 0), can points of this node be converted to a quadrilateral covering the same space whose normal is the eigenvector corresponding to λ_0. f_{rp} is set to converted polygon for this case and set to point otherwise.

The rendering primitive evaluation is then propagated bottom-up to higher levels of the RPQ_p. When four child nodes of a non-leaf node all have f_{rp} as converted polygon, PCA is applied over 3D positions of all grids from four children. A quadrilateral is fit to this node if $\lambda_0 \leq \Lambda$. In this case, f_{rp} is set to converted polygon and four child nodes are removed from the RPQ_p; otherwise, f_{rp} is set to point. Generic homogeneous covariance [22] allows efficient PCA computation for non-leaf nodes, which involves only simple additions rather than expensive outer productions.

Figure 4 shows that the rendering with polygon conversion achieves better performance without obvious quality degradation, compared to the rendering without polygon conversion.

4.2 Polygon Simplification

The construction of RPQ_w is similar to that of RPQ_p. An RPQ_w node stores its bound on GEM_w, and a flag f_{rp} indicating its rendering primitive as either original or simplified polygon.

The rendering primitive evaluation starts at leaf nodes of RPQ_w. For a leaf node with only one building boundary grid, the one original wall polygon is also the single simplified polygon, thus its f_{rp} is set as simplified polygon. For a leaf node with more than one boundary grids, PCA is applied over 3D positions of all building boundary grids. When the second smallest eigenvalue λ_1 is small enough (i.e., $\lambda_1 \leq \Lambda$), these building boundary grids approximate a straight line segment. Thus the corresponding original wall quadrilaterals can be simplified to one vertical quadrilateral defined by the line segment and the ground position with minimum elevation. The simplified quadrilateral is a conservative estimation to ensure gap-free rendering of the space covered by its original wall quadrilaterals. In this case, f_{rp} is set to simplified polygon; in all other cases, f_{rp} is set to original polygon.

The rendering primitive evaluation is then propagated bottom-up to higher levels of the RPQ_w. We apply PCA over 3D positions of all building boundary grids from four child nodes of an RPQ_w non-leaf node. If these building boundary grids form a straight line, corresponding original wall polygons are replaced by one quadrilateral, f_{rp} is set to simplified polygon, and four child nodes are removed from the RPQ_w; otherwise, f_{rp} is set to original polygon.

Figure 5 shows that polygon simplification provides comparable visual quality and with slightly improved rendering frame-rates, compared to the rendering without polygon simplification.

4.3 Hybrid Representation for MRQ Non-Leaf Nodes

Hybrid representation of an MRQ non-leaf node cannot be derived solely from its child nodes, since a parent node has different data resolution from its child nodes. It does not need to be reconstructed from scratch either, as some of the hybrid representations of higher resolutions (child nodes in the MRQ) are reusable for that of lower resolutions (parent node in the MRQ). Constructing hybrid representation of non-leaf nodes is a bottom-up propagation of RPQs of leaf nodes. As RPQ_p and RPQ_w share similar propagation process, we only demonstrate details for RPQ_p for clarity.

Given four child nodes $n_i, i \in 1,2,3,4$, each has a $GEM_p^{n_i}$ with s_{n_i} grids and an $RPQ_p^{n_i}$. The maximum height $h_{max}^{n_i}$ of $RPQ_p^{n_i}$ is $\log_4 s_{n_i}$, which is achieved when not all leaf nodes have f_{rp} as polygon. Representing $\frac{1}{4}$ resolution of these child nodes, for the parent node m with GEM_p^m, four sub-trees under the root node of its RPQ_p^m are built based on $RPQ_p^{n_i}$ as follows. When the height of $RPQ_p^{n_i}$ is $h_{max}^{n_i}$, we cut lowest level nodes from $RPQ_p^{n_i}$, and re-evaluate rendering primitives of remaining parent nodes based on GEM_p^m. The

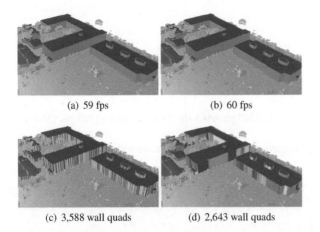

(a) 59 fps   (b) 60 fps

(c) 3,588 wall quads   (d) 2,643 wall quads

Figure 5: Rendering effect of polygon simplification. (a)(c) Rendered by Gao et al. [10]. Wall quadrilaterals are colored randomly in (c). (b)(d) Rendered by our framework with polygon simplification under $\Lambda = 10^{-4}$. Simplified walls are colored randomly in (d).

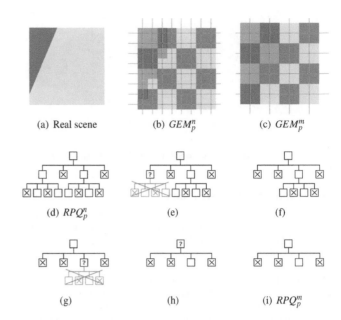

(a) Real scene   (b) GEM_p^n (c) GEM_p^m

(d) RPQ_p^n (e)   (f)

(g)   (h)   (i) RPQ_p^m

Figure 6: Building an RPQ_p sub-tree of parent node m based on a child node n. (a) Real scene. Red for buildings; and grey for ground. (b) GEM_p of node n with 64 grids. (c) GEM_p of node m covering only the region of n. (d)-(i) The propagation process of RPQ_p from child n to parent m. A node with a cross mark has f_{rp} as converted polygon; a node with a question mark needs to be re-evaluated over GEM_p^m in (c); the rest of the nodes have f_{rp} as point.

re-evaluation continues upwards until f_{rp} of a node remains unchanged, or the root of RPQ_p^n is reached. The updated $RPQ_p^{n_i}$ is a sub-tree for RPQ_p^n. When the height of $RPQ_p^{n_i}$ is smaller than $h_{max}^{n_i}$, all its leaf nodes are represented by polygons, so this $RPQ_p^{n_i}$ is taken directly as a sub-tree of RPQ_p^n. Finally, rendering primitive of RPQ_p^m's root node is evaluated over all grids in GEM_p^m. Figure 6 illustrates the above process applied to one child node.

5 RENDERING

For aerial LiDAR data sets that are larger than the memory capacity of a computer system, the presented framework applies an out-of-core scheme that processes only a manageable subset of the data at any time, similar to Gao et al. [10]. By coupling it with the MRQ hierarchy, view-dependent LOD rendering is provided. We first introduce how to perform LOD selection in Section 5.1, then present details of hybrid point-polygon rendering in Section 5.2, and finally show a simple yet effective mechanism to smooth the transitions between different LODs in Section 5.3.

5.1 LOD Selection

LOD selection is performed by hierarchical traversal of the MRQ from root (the lowest resolution) to leaves (the highest resolution). The framework applies three view-dependent selection criteria for each node: view-frustum culling, back-face culling and screen projection tolerance. The implementation of view-frustum culling is similar to Pajarola et al. [22]. Back-face culling is applied to ground and building points only, as tree points do not form surfaces. Its implementation is an efficient normal cone approach [21] that does not involve trigonometric functions. We only check screen projection tolerance for nodes that meet the first two criteria, as follows. A node n's bounding quad on x-y plane is warped to screen space covering p pixels. If p is less than the number of grids in GEM_p^n, i.e. one grid covers less than one pixel on screen, this node is selected for rendering, and downward traversal is terminated. Figure 7 shows different LODs of a scene.

As one of the major rendering expenses is the MRQ traversal, the framework utilizes the idea of coherence traversal [4] for performance consideration. At each frame, instead of traversing the MRQ from its root node, we traverse it from nodes (both displayed and culled) of the last frame either up or down to find the most appropriate nodes to display.

5.2 Hybrid Rendering

Based on a hardware-accelerated point based rendering with deferred shading approach [10], the framework integrates rendering of point splats and polygonal geometries via multiple rendering targets in three basic passes: The *visibility pass* renders all points and polygons to a depth buffer, and records only the closest depth of a pixel; the *attribute pass* renders all points and polygons again, and blends only those that are within ε offset of the recorded depth, resulting in pixels of accumulated normals and colors; and the *shading pass* applies accurate per-pixel Phong shading.

The rendering of the continuous data set of an MRQ node is actually the rendering of leaf nodes of corresponding RPQ_p and RPQ_w. For a node with f_{rp} as point, the framework displays each non-empty grid as a circular splat. The splat's diameter is at least $\sqrt{2}\omega_g$ in order to enclose the entire area covered by the grid, where ω_g is the width of quantization squares as seen in Section 3.1.1. For a node with f_{rp} as polygon, either converted, original or simplified, the framework renders the corresponding stored quadrilateral. The size of the quadrilateral is adjusted to its normal so that its projection on x-y plane can cover the entire bounding quad of the node projected on the same plane. This size is further enlarged with an offset ω_g to ensure overlapping with adjacent quadrilaterals. By using gradient colors [10], together with a blending mechanism [12], we can alleviate possible cracks between neighboring primitives.

The framework provides two rendering options for the discrete data set of an MRQ node. One is to feed tree points as splats to the above three rendering passes. It provides a unified rendering routine for all data and a smoother visualization, but it has an adverse impact on rendering performance, especially for cities with abundant trees. The other is to blend with continuous data set rendering only closest tree points that are filtered by a single pass. This provides better frame-rates, but requires additional implementation, and has obvious aliasing artifacts between neighboring tree points. Experiments of this paper utilize the first rendering option.

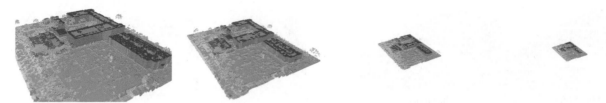

(a) 6,035 quads, 70,455 pts, 152.9 fps (b) 2,818 quads, 33,474 pts, 275.1 fps (c) 482 quads, 6,605 pts, 654.8 fps (d) 125 quads, 1,925 pts, 935.8 fps

Figure 7: A data set at different viewing distances. Converted polygons and simplified polygons are shown in red.

5.3 Smooth LOD Transitions

As the pre-computed *MRQ* has a fixed resolution per level, jumping from one level to another leads to popping artifacts. To make smooth LOD transitions, the framework blends together renderings from two adjacent levels. Given a node n that passes the screen projection tolerance test of Section 5.1, its parent node m is taken for blending. Let l_m be the resolution of m (low detail level), i.e. the number of grids in GEM_p^m; and l_n be the resolution of four child nodes (including n) of m (high detail level), where $l_n = 4 \times l_m$. Current actual resolution l takes the number of pixels of screen space warping of m's bounding quad on x-y plane. During rendering, the visibility pass renders all primitives from both node m and its four child nodes to the depth buffer, and the attribute pass blends normals and colors of all primitives from both node m and its four child nodes that are within ε depth, where the alpha of geometries of m takes $\alpha = \frac{l_n - l}{l_n - l_m}$ and the alpha of child nodes uses $1 - \alpha$.

6 Experiments

The test computer is equipped with dual-core Intel Xeon©2.0GHz CPU, 4GB RAM, NVIDIA GeForce©GTX260 896MB graphics card, Western Digital©7200RPM hard disk and Windows Vista©. All tests are rendered at 1280×800 pixels.

Table 1: Basic information of test data sets.

Data set	Denver	LA	Atlanta1	Atlanta2
File size (MB)	44.0	49.6	104.6	3,052.3
Density (pts/m^2)	6.6	0.6	22.9	20.7
# points (M)	1.6	2.6	5.5	112.6
% ground	67.1	55.9	42.2	44.1
% building	19.5	27.8	16.1	36.5
% tree	13.4	12.3	41.7	19.4
% other	0	4.0	0	0

The test data sets are from three cities as listed in Table 1. The first three data sets are of medium size, and the last data has a large size. Atlanta1 is a small part of Atlanta2. If not specified, a figure uses the LA (Los Angeles) data set.

6.1 Parameters

The framework provides a parameter Λ to adjust the error tolerance for both polygon conversion and simplification. Since Λ affects polygon conversion and simplification in the same way, we only exemplify its influence on polygon conversion for clarity. As seen in Figure 4, a larger Λ leads to larger polygons with fewer details, while a smaller Λ produces smaller polygons with more details. It also shows that the rendering speed increases with the increase of Λ, as more points are converted to polygons.

Another user-adjustable parameter is the splat radius Γ for point rendering. As seen in Figure 8, increasing the value can alleviate gaps between neighboring points with different orientations. However, since a larger Γ corresponds to more pixels on screen per

(a) $\Gamma = \frac{\sqrt{2}}{2}\omega_g$; 333 fps (b) $\Gamma = \frac{3\sqrt{2}}{4}\omega_g$; 237 fps (c) $\Gamma = \sqrt{2}\omega_g$; 153 fps

Figure 8: Speed-quality trade-off under the influence of Γ.

point, the improvement of visual quality is accompanied by the decrease of rendering performance.

By tuning Λ and Γ, users can trade off the rendering speed and quality. To get better rendering quality, a smaller Λ and a larger Γ are suggested. In a large scene where details of distant objects are not important, a larger Λ and a smaller Γ are preferred.

6.2 Performance

The presented framework is built as an extension and optimization for visually-complete rendering [10]. Among three wall primitives, the option of procedurally generated quadrilateral walls achieves the best speed and quality trade-off [10], thus this option (referred to as VRQ) is taken as the benchmark.

Table 2: Pre-processing (pp) time (in seconds) and rendering (rd) speed (in fps) comparisons of VRQ and our framework. pc for polygon conversion; and ps for polygon simplification.

Data set	Denver	Los Angeles	Atlanta1	Atlanta2
VRQ pp	125.1	238.9	404.9	8,077.2
our pp	134.2	250.6	426.5	8,252.7
VRQ rd	18.5	24.9	18.8	17.8
our rd (pc)	73.1	68.0	40.1	18.2
our rd (pc+ps)	73.4	68.5	40.3	18.3

Quality Figure 4 and 5 show that polygon conversion and simplification can preserve most of the details of small scenes under proper parameters, even though original rendering primitives are changed. Figure 1, 9a and 9b show that the quality degradation in larger scenes is negligible, as our framework provides identical visual cues to VRQ.

Pre-processing Time As shown in Table 2, the pre-processing time increases with file size and point number. It is also affected by the number of points of each class and the actual scene-architectural layout, since points of different classes are treated differently. The pre-processing time is roughly distributed as follow: 33% for disk file reading, 57% for normal estimation of

142

(a) VRQ: 1,922,328 pts, 33,482 quad, 20.4 fps

(b) Our: 707,678 pts, 80,370 quads, 108.5 fps

(c) VRQ: 3,649,426 pts, 70,269 quads, 26.4 fps; Our: 3,071,812 pts, 140,175 quads, 85.1 fps

(d) VRQ: 2,006,927 pts, 233,705 quads, 20.2 fps; Our: 1,887,311 pts, 238,770 quads, 21.0 fps

Figure 9: Rendering comparison between VRQ and our framework with $\Lambda = 10^{-3}$ and $\Gamma = \frac{\sqrt{2}}{2}\omega_g$. (a) and (b) for Denver; (c) for Atlanta1; and (d) for Atlanta2. Our framework offers comparable visual details but greatly improved rendering speed.

3D points, 2% for polygon conversion and simplification, and 8% for other operations. Compared to the pre-processing time of VRQ, our framework only adds less than 8% overhead, as in Table 2.

Rendering Speed Figure 1 and 9 list static rendering speed of three cities, by measuring average frame-rates of the displayed static images within one minute. Table 2 lists dynamic rendering speed of three cities, by adjusting the viewport to fit the entire scene, and recording average frame-rate within one minute while orbiting the camera around the scene.

The speedup of our framework over VRQ is dominated by the number of converted points and simplified polygons that are actually displayed in a frame. Because our framework is LOD based, which always displays just enough details for a view, the speedup only varies in detail level regardless of the scale of the input data set. Both static and dynamic rendering speed measurements show that our framework achieves 2-5 times speedup when data sets of medium sizes are completely fit in the display window; but the speedup is not that impressive when the entire scene of a large data set is shown. As another example, Figure 9c can be considered as a closeup of Figure 9d; while the closeup provides 322% speedup, the original scene only has a slight improvement of 3%.

Table 2 shows that the speedup by applying polygon simplification is not obvious compared to the speedup provided by polygon conversion. This is because the cost of point rendering is dominant in hybrid rendering, given the fact that the number of wall polygons is only 1.7% - 3.8% of the number of original points.

The presented framework can support hybrid rendering of colored point clouds by attaching textures to polygons. Similar to Wahl et al. [27], a theoretical speedup is estimated as

$$speedup = \frac{v_s/r_v}{(v_r + 4q)/r_v + t/r_f},$$

where v_s is the number of simplified points, q the number of quads, t the number of texel, v_r the number of remaining points, r_v the transformation rate, and r_f the fill-rate.

Considering only ambient occlusion or shadows, whose computation cost is dependent on the number of ray-object intersection tests, if points are rendered as surface splats, a theoretical speedup is given by

$$speedup = \frac{v_s}{v_r + q}.$$

Comparison with Existing Approaches Existing approaches [8, 15, 27] are also applicable to converting a planar subset of points into polygons.

Unlike these approaches that either require additional knowledge (the number of planar surfaces, plane boundaries, etc.) or involve complex computations (triangulation, iterative plane fitting, etc.), our polygon conversion is much simpler by only applying PCA over regularly partitioned subsets. Therefore, one can expect a faster pre-processing for our polygon conversion. For example, Wahl et al. [27] report the RANSAC plane fitting performance of about 33k-84k points per second on a 3.4GHz Pentium 4, while the presented polygon conversion can process about 520k-680k points per second on a 2.0GHz Xeon; taking into account that our CPU is slightly better than theirs, we can still consider that our approach is a lot faster. In addition, our approach enables more efficient texture packing for visualization of colored points, since our polygons are of known regular sizes as opposed to polygons of random sizes produced by other approaches.

On the downside, our approach may provide less speedup in hybrid rendering, because it does not necessarily produce the optimal polygonal representation, and leaves more points unconverted, compared to existing approaches that accurately recover latent surfaces of the point cloud.

7 CONCLUSION

This paper presents a framework for interactive and visually-complete rendering of aerial LiDAR point clouds of cities, by coupling LOD technique with hierarchical hybrid point-polygon structures. The hybrid representation supports both quadrilaterals converted from planar subsets of points, and simplified quadrilaterals from augmented wall quadrilaterals. Without involving expensive computation, the construction of hybrid representation is efficient, adding only less than 8% pre-processing time. Experiments show that the framework is able to provide comparable visual details with 2-5 times speedup in rendering. The framework is generic to any aerial LiDAR data regardless of sampling resolution. With appropriate modifications, e.g., patch-based representation [19], it can be applied to a variety of other data sets.

For future work, we plan to integrate point cloud quantization and compression [26] into the framework for better storage utilization. To further improve rendering frame-rates, it is desired to replace current three-pass rendering with a more efficient rendering routine (e.g., single-pass splatting [20]). Finally, by utilizing the presented hierarchical hybrid point-polygon structures, we will explore ways to perform real-time point cloud refinement in order to deliver unlimited resolution of a scene.

ACKNOWLEDGEMENTS

We appreciate the valuable comments from anonymous reviewers. We thank Eve Waterhouse and Elizabeth Chu for proofreading and editing. The LiDAR data sets are provided by Airborne 1 Corporation and Sanborn Corporation.

REFERENCES

[1] M. Botsch, A. Hornung, M. Zwicker, and L. Kobbelt. High-quality surface splatting on today's GPUs. In *Symposium on Point-Based Graphics 2005*, pages 17–24, June 2005.

[2] S. P. Callahan, J. L. D. Comba, P. Shirley, and C. T. Silva. Interactive rendering of large unstructured grids using dynamic level-of-detail. In *IEEE Visualization*, pages 199–206. IEEE Computer Society, 2005.

[3] A. Certain, J. Popovic, T. DeRose, T. Duchamp, D. Salesin, and W. Stuetzle. Interactive multiresolution surface viewing. In *Proceedings of the 23rd Annual Conference on Computer Graphics and Interactive Techniques*, SIGGRAPH '96, pages 91–98, 1996.

[4] B. Chen and M. X. Nguyen. POP: A hybrid point and polygon rendering system for large data. In *Proceedings of the Conference on Visualization '01*, VIS '01, pages 45–52, Washington, DC, USA, 2001. IEEE Computer Society.

[5] L. Coconu and H.-C. Hege. Hardware-accelerated point-based rendering of complex scenes. In *Proceedings of the 13th Eurographics Workshop on Rendering*, EGRW '02, pages 43–52, Aire-la-Ville, Switzerland, Switzerland, 2002. Eurographics Association.

[6] J. D. Cohen, D. G. Aliaga, and W. Zhang. Hybrid simplification: Combining multi-resolution polygon and point rendering. In T. Ertl, K. I. Joy, and A. Varshney, editors, *IEEE Visualization*, pages 37–539. IEEE Computer Society, 2001.

[7] C. Dachsbacher, C. Vogelgsang, and M. Stamminger. Sequential point trees. In *ACM SIGGRAPH 2003 Papers*, SIGGRAPH '03, pages 657–662, New York, NY, USA, 2003. ACM.

[8] T. K. Dey and J. Hudson. PMR: Point to mesh rendering, a feature-based approach. In *IEEE Visualization*, pages 155–162, 2002.

[9] M. A. Fischler and R. C. Bolles. Random sample consensus: A paradigm for model fitting with applications to image analysis and automated cartography. *Commun. ACM*, 24(6):381–395, June 1981.

[10] Z. Gao, L. Nocera, and U. Neumann. Visually-complete aerial LiDAR point cloud rendering. In *Proceedings of the 20th International Conference on Advances in Geographic Information Systems*, SIGSPATIAL '12, pages 289–298, New York, NY, USA, 2012. ACM.

[11] P. Goswami, F. Erol, R. Mukhi, R. Pajarola, and E. Gobbetti. An efficient multi-resolution framework for high quality interactive rendering of massive point clouds using multi-way kd-trees. *The Visual Computer*, 29(1):69–83, 2013.

[12] G. Guennebaud, L. Barthe, and M. Paulin. Splat/mesh blending, perspective rasterization and transparency for point-based rendering. In *SPBG*, pages 49–57. Eurographics Association, 2006.

[13] A. Hao, G. Tian, Q. Zhao, and Z. Li. An accelerating rendering method of hybrid point and polygon for complex three-dimensional models. In *ICAT*, volume 4282 of *Lecture Notes in Computer Science*, pages 889–900. Springer, 2006.

[14] B. Kovač and B. Žalik. Visualization of LiDAR datasets using point-based rendering technique. *Computers & Geosciences*, 36(11):1443–1450, Nov. 2010.

[15] M. Kuder, M. Šterk, and B. Žalik. Point-based rendering optimization with textured meshes for fast LiDAR visualization. *Computers & Geosciences*, 59(0):181 – 190, 2013.

[16] M. Kuder and B. Žalik. Web-based LiDAR visualization with point-based rendering. In *Proceedings of the 2011 Seventh International Conference on Signal Image Technology & Internet-Based Systems*, SITIS '11, pages 38–45, Washington, DC, USA, 2011. IEEE Computer Society.

[17] F. Lafarge and C. Mallet. Modeling urban landscapes from point clouds: a generic approach. Technical Report RR-7612, INRIA, May 2011.

[18] P. Lindstrom and V. Pascucci. Visualization of large terrains made easy. In *IEEE Visualization, 2001.*, pages 363–574, 2001.

[19] T. Ochotta and S. Hiller. Hardware rendering of 3D geometry with elevation maps. *Shape Modeling and Applications, International Conference on*, 0:1–10, 2006.

[20] T. Ochotta, S. Hiller, and D. Saupe. *Single-pass High-quality Splatting*. Konstanzer Schriften in Mathematik und Informatik. Fachbereich für Mathematik und Statistik, 2006.

[21] R. Pajarola. *Overview of Quadtree-based Terrain Triangulation and Visualization*. Technical report (University of California, Irvine. Dept. of Information and Computer Science). Department of Information & Computer Science, University of California, Irvine, 2002.

[22] R. Pajarola. Efficient level-of-details for point based rendering. In *Computer Graphics and Imaging*, pages 141–146. IASTED/ACTA Press, 2003.

[23] E. Paredes, M. Bóo, M. Amor, J. Bruguera, and J. Döllner. Extended hybrid meshing algorithm for multiresolution terrain models. *International Journal of Geographical Information Science*, 26(5):771–793, 2012.

[24] P. Rosenthal and L. Linsen. Image-space point cloud rendering. In *Proceedings of Computer Graphics International*, pages 136–143, 2008.

[25] S. Rusinkiewicz and M. Levoy. QSplat: A multiresolution point rendering system for large meshes. In *Proceedings of the 27th Annual Conference on Computer Graphics and Interactive Techniques*, SIGGRAPH '00, pages 343–352, New York, NY, USA, 2000. ACM Press/Addison-Wesley Publishing Co.

[26] R. Schnabel and R. Klein. Octree-based point-cloud compression. In *SPBG*, pages 111–120. Eurographics Association, 2006.

[27] R. Wahl, M. Guthe, and R. Klein. Identifying planes in point-clouds for efficient hybrid rendering. In *The 13th Pacific Conference on Computer Graphics and Applications*, pages 1–8, Oct. 2005.

[28] M. Wand, M. Fischer, I. Peter, F. M. auf der Heide, and W. Straer. The randomized z-buffer algorithm: interactive rendering of highly complex scenes. In *SIGGRAPH*, pages 361–370, 2001.

[29] W. Zheng, H. Sun, H. Bao, and Q. Peng. Rendering of virtual environments based on polygonal & point-based models. In *Proceedings of the ACM Symposium on Virtual Reality Software and Technology*, VRST '02, pages 25–32, New York, NY, USA, 2002. ACM.

[30] J. Zhou and Q. Ruan. Adaptive hierarchical representation of a point-sampled 3d model for fast rendering. In *Signal Processing, 2006 8th International Conference on*, volume 2, 2006.

[31] Q. Zhou and U. Neumann. 2.5D dual contouring: A robust approach to creating building models from aerial LiDAR point clouds. In *Computer Vision - ECCV 2010, 11th European Conference on Computer Vision, Heraklion, Crete, Greece, September 5-11, 2010, Proceedings, Part III*, volume 6313 of *Lecture Notes in Computer Science*, pages 115–128. Springer, 2010.

Information Visualization Techniques for Exploring Oil Well Trajectories in Reservoir Models

Sowmya Somanath*   Sheelagh Carpendale†   Ehud Sharlin‡   Mario Costa Sousa§

Department of Computer Science
University of Calgary, Calgary, Canada

ABSTRACT

We present a set of interactive 3D visualizations, designed to explore oil/gas reservoir simulation post-processing models. With these visualizations we aim to provide reservoir engineers with better access to the data within their 3D models. We provide techniques for exploring existing oil well trajectories, and for planning future wells, to assist in decision making. Our approach focuses on designing visualization techniques that present the necessary details using concepts from information visualization. We created three new visualization variations - lollipop-up, information circles and path indicator, which present well trajectory specific information in different visual formats. Our paper describes these visualizations and discusses them in context of our exploratory evaluation.

Keywords: 3D Reservoir Visualization, Reservoir Engineering, Information Visualization.

Index Terms: H.5.m [Information Interfaces and Presentation (e.g., HCI)]: Miscellaneous—; J.2 [Physical Sciences and Engineering]: Earth and Atmospheric Sciences—

1 INTRODUCTION

Oil and gas reservoirs are sub-surface portions of the earth which contain hydrocarbons. The fundamental goal of reservoir engineering studies is to assess and evaluate these entities and to design optimum ways to extract oil and gas. However, reservoir data acquisition is costly and therefore, engineers have only access to limited spatio-temporal information about the reservoirs [8]. The majority of available information comes from sensor measurements (e.g. seismic geophones, pressure transducers) and experimental results of rock samples (e.g. core measurements). These are combined with multi-disciplinary experts advice to develop a realistic 3D geological model [8]. However, complexity, size and multi-resolution data are amongst many challenges for proper data integration and efficient analysis. These require advanced visualization tools to better understand and access the data [9, 23].

In practice, the oil and gas exploration and production cycle (E&P) consist of several stages of data gathering, simulation and data analysis. Of those many stages, our work is situated at one of the last phases of the exploration cycle, called the post-processing stage. A post-processing stage of reservoir studies includes simulations of different scenarios of the reservoir models for history matching, prediction and forecasting [18]. At the history matching stage the reservoir engineer needs to manipulate some of the uncertain reservoir properties and run multiple reservoir simulations in order to provide a better match with the real production data.

*e-mail:ssomanat@ucalgary.ca
†e-mail:sheelagh@ucalgary.ca
‡e-mail:ehud@ucalgary.ca
§e-mail:smcosta@ucalgary.ca

Graphics Interface Conference 2014
7-9 May, Montreal, Quebec, Canada

This will add a further complexity as the size of the data increases rapidly. The simulation data are time varying and multi-attribute in nature, requiring techniques that support adequate exploration of those many parameters.

At the post-processing stage, a 3D cellular model, an approximation of the real reservoir, is used for exploring the various parameter configurations and fluid flows. The structure of this 3D reservoir model is usually represented by irregular corner point 3D grid [17] (irregular hexahedron geometries) consisting of thousands to millions of cells, each of which is associated with many static and dynamic properties (e.g. porosity, permeability, pressure, saturation and etc.). Apart from the cell properties, the simulation models also contain information about existing well trajectories within the reservoir (i.e. collections of perforated cells through which a 3D line passes). Thereby, the complexity of the models arising from multiple cells attributes and the 3D geometry motivates the need to invent various visual exploration techniques in order to help reservoir engineers to gain a clear picture of the relationship between these data attributes.

Among the various tasks conducted at the post-processing stage, we focus on the exploration of well trajectories. Exploring well trajectories is important as it helps in future decision making for oil well placements, a cost-intensive activity, requiring detailed analysis. In particular, we focus on a small subset of visualization tasks: learning about the existing well trajectories in a reservoir post-processing cellular model, and exploration of favorable locations for new trajectories.

During the post-processing stage, reservoir engineers analyze well performance primarily through looking at pressure curves and production rates. Reservoir production is often formulated as an optimization problem. Visual analysis with new spatial reservoir visualization tools can complement standard well production visualizations; visual tools can help develop a better understanding of the relationship between the attributes, the individual cells and the model structure as a whole. To this end, we present the design and implementation of three new information visualization techniques - lollipop-up visualization, information circles and path indicator, which present well trajectory specific information in different styles.

The fundamental contribution of our work is providing the subdomain of reservoir engineering post- processing studies with a collection of information visualization techniques that can be used for the exploration of well trajectories. Each of the visualizations was evaluated in a preliminary evaluation session with six participants and the results are presented followed by a discussion section. The big picture encompassing these efforts is to create a system wherein the engineer can study existing wells and use the learned knowledge to better predict where new wells can be placed. However, in this initial research we approach these bigger concepts by focusing on learning more from the engineers about their expectations in regards to well exploration and new well creation systems, leading to better design applications for such use cases.

2 RESERVOIR MODEL

Reservoir post-processing models are the end result of multiple simulation scenarios. The model employed in our experiment consists of the following four types of information: (a) structural information, (b) time steps, (c) cell specific information (geological property values - both static and dynamic) and (d) well trajectory specific information (type of well, length of well, perforation cells etc.). The structure of the 3D model consists of corner point cells [17], irregular hexagonal geometries, arranged along three dimensions (i, j, k). The i and j dimensions correspond to the cells in the x and y directions of the 3D space and k dimension corresponds to the layers of the 3D model. For example, the model used in our experiment (Figure 1a) consists of 33000 cells, i.e. 39x42x20 cells in the i, j and k directions respectively. The arrangement of the cells represents both spatial continuity as well as discontinuities to accommodate geological structures such as faults. The model used in this experiment consists of four dynamic properties and ten static properties. Apart from geological properties, the models also encompass well specific information. Each of the well trajectories are represented as a collection of perforated cells, and the centroids of these cells are an approximation to the 3D points of the well trajectory within the simulation grid.

2.1 Visual Mapping

To visualize geological properties, reservoir models are mapped to different color maps corresponding to the range of the property value. This mapping is usually limited to a single geological property. However, the effect of one property over another is of interest to a reservoir engineer, especially in the context of studying well trajectories [21]. Thus, to better support well trajectory exploration tasks a proof of concept protoype was developed wherein we group two geological properties (oil pressure and rock porosity) to create a color map that indicates their combined effects. Pressure and porosity were chosen as the two geological properties because in the most simple case, rock should be porous and pressure should be high in order for oil to flow. To formalize a term for regions of low pressure and low porosity (blue regions of the model in Figure 1a), we call them unfit regions, corresponding to an engineering interpretation of them being unsuitable for placement of well trajectories. Similarly, regions of high pressure and high porosity (green regions of the model in Figure 1a) correspond to regions of better fit. These types of combination values can be calculated based on many different correlation equations and ratios as per the experts discretion [16]. Depending on the calculation method employed, the resulting color pattern for the model can be different from the one shown in Figure 1. In our prototype the combined value calculation is simple and is defined as a percentage of the number of unfit cells per spatial partition (uniform spatial division) to the number of total cells per partition. Unfit cells here correspond to those cells whose porosity and pressure value lie within a threshold identified by trial and error using the given reservoir data values.

3 RELATED WORK

Data clarification is one of the major goals of visualizations in general. However, the pertinent information could either be in portions of the context or it could be correlations resulting from the analysis of the data. In particular 'focus and context' is one family of visualization techniques which can help the viewer to learn about an area of interest (pertinent parts of the whole data set) while retaining the rest of the context in intelligent ways to avoid visual clutter and occlusion in 3D volumetric data [4, 5, 6, 8, 10, 24]. Several interesting variations have been suggested for performing focus and context by using styles such as fisheye views [11], distortion [5, 19], magnification [25] and temporary displacement of context [21]. In the realm of volumetric data, concepts such as importance driven rendering [24] and illustrative rendering techniques

[4] have been suggested. Sultanum et al. [21] implemented a focus and context technique to visualize well trajectories by creating a "V" shaped opening in the region of the selected wells. Depending on the task, removing parts of the context (of the reservoir model) was suggested as not acceptable by engineers. For example, in the case of tasks such as trend analysis, the engineer is interested not just in the important entity (well trajectory), but also the entity in relation with the other parts of the context [21].

Motivated by this domain requirement, one of our visualizations (lollipop-up visualization, Figure 1) was influenced by techniques such as those proposed by Ware and Lewis [25] and Taerum et al.[22], which help to retain the context (unlike the distortion and cut-away techniques) and extract the important information to visualize them outside the context. DragMag [25] is a technique wherein the concept of offsets was used. The area of importance is displaced from the context, magnified and connected to the actual context using vertical lines for better viewing. Taerum et al. [22] used the concept of a contextual close-up to view the areas of importance. The difference between our lollipop-up visualization and these techniques is that we displace the actual 3D well blocks (i.e. no magnification) above the reservoir surface to help the viewer learn about the internal blocks. This way we are able to maintain the geometric information, continuities and discontinuities, and the actual scale of the geometric model, thus showing how the well is actually drilled underground. In the realm of reservoir engineering, offsets have been used by Lee et al. [15] in a manner similar to the bubble maps [1, 2, 13], which visualize cumulative statistical information (e.g. water injection rate over two years) using a single cube or sphere at the end of a stick for each well in the model. Lollipop-ups on the other hand, provide information about each individual perforated cell, rather than a cumulative result. Hence, they can provide insights about the underground trajectory cells both in terms of geometry and property values. Similar to offsets, the concept of lenses or 3D probes applied to seismic data survey was proposed by Castanie et al. [7].

In multi-dimensional datasets, apart from the need to focus on areas of importance, correlation between multiple instances of similar entities is also important. For example, it is important to learn about the similarities in the geological property distribution of the perforated cells for two or more trajectories. In other words, the similarities or differences between two or more well trajectories are of interest. There have been several techniques employed to visualize correlations. Some of the current research in this area includes: the volume reformation visualization technique explained by Lampe et al. to compare well trajectories [14], and the focus and context technique by Gasteiger et al. involving the use of lenses to better support correlation [12].

In our approach, we return to using visualization variables [3] to support correlation exploration. We present information circles and the path indicator visualization, which present pre-processed information allowing engineers to gain access to statistical information when needed. Our approach is to augment the 3D grid visualization of the reservoir and its contextual geology with information visualization additions representing more abstract aspects of the data using factors such as color, shape and size [3]. These visualization augmentations provide more information about single well trajectories, multiple well trajectories and individual cells of the model.

4 VISUALIZATIONS

In this section we describe the three visualization variants: lollipop-up, information circles and path indicator. All the visualizations have been implemented for the Microsoft Surface 1.0 using C# and XNA.

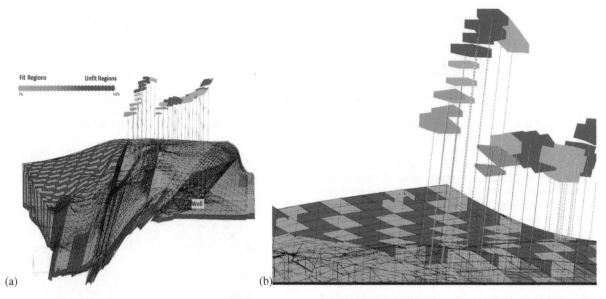

Figure 1: Lollipop-up Visualization

4.1 Lollipop-up Visualization

Lollipop-up visualization is an offset technique that provides information about existing well trajectories in the reservoir model (Figure 1). Due to the dense nature of the reservoir models it is hard to achieve a visualization that allows engineers to gain access to the well trajectories without visually removing parts of the reservoir model. Applying partial transparency as an alternative can lead to incorrect appearance of cell color in the case where all the interior layer cells are rendered. It can also lead to loss of depth perception [10]. However, using offsets we can visualize the hidden entities clearly and also maintain the entire reservoir context. Lollipop-up visualization offsets the 3D well perforated cells to a visible height for the engineer to view and learn more about the underground trajectory. It also reflects on the depth of the well point inside the model. The points closest to the surface have shorter offset lengths compared to those deeper down. The connection between the original perforated cell and the offset cell is shown using red lines. Unlike DragMag [25], in this technique we do not alter the offset entity in any way. The offset cell has the same shape, size and color as the original perforated cell within the reservoir model (Figure 1b), thus can provide insights about the underground trajectory cells both in terms of geometry and property values. The visualization also supports mapping the reservoir context to other different geological properties to enable comparing the lollipop-ups with the trend in the remaining cells of the reservoir model. For example, the reservoir model can be mapped to represent water saturation, while the lollipop-ups display the combination of oil pressure and porosity.

4.2 Single Well Information Circles

Information circles augment the lollipop-up visualizations by providing numerical information about the geological property mapping within the context of the well trajectory (Figure 2). As seen in Figure 2, the visualization appears at the position of a physical Microsoft Surface tag, thus, can be positioned anywhere on the screen. The circles are arranged in a linear fashion, sorted by size and with equal spaces between each circle. The size of the circle corresponds to the number of well cells with a particular property value (combination of pressure and porisity values). For example, if ten cells correspond to property value 40% and two cells with 60%, then the circle corresponding to 40% will be larger. As seen in Figure 2, when a viewer taps on a particular information circle, all the corre-

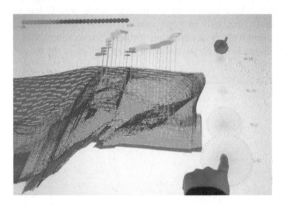

Figure 2: Single well information circles

sponding perforated cells in the lollipop-up visualization get highlighted in yellow, allowing the viewer to identify the offset cells that contribute to the particular information circle. In some situations it may happen that the perforated cells have a wide variety of property values, resulting in large number of circles. Therefore, we allow the circles list to be wrapped and unwrapped. Tapping on a particular circle causes all the circles below to be hidden (wrapping), and on sliding a finger downwards the remaining circles reappear (unwrapping).

4.3 Multiple Wells Information Circles

Information circles can also be used to compare multiple wells in the reservoir model. To facilitate this comparison the information circles of each well trajectory are 'hung' from a horizontal pole (Figure 3). Our hanging values metaphor is a twist on the classic histogram: the numbers along the vertical axis at the right represent possible geological property values of perforated cells, calculated using the combination of the two reservoir properties, pressure and porosity (see Section 2.1). Perforated cells that have specific geological property values will be represented as information circles on the hanging graph, with their position along the vertical axis corresponding to their cell value. The radius of each information circle represents the number of cells having the corresponding property value on the vertical axis (similar to the single well information circles case, Section 4.2). The information circles are all hanging on the horizontal pole, connected to each other via a spring metaphor. The spring connecting the different information circles will stretch or shorten according to the differences in their property values. This was designed to provide a quick comparison of the different distribution of property values between each of the well trajectories in the reservoir model. Consider the comparison of well A to well E. We can quickly observe from Figure 3 that the property values distribution for well A is more spread out: within the entire well A there are only a small number of cells having property value of 2% with the remaining majority having property value of 62%. In comparison, well E has cells with a smaller spread of property values (maximum number of cells having property value of 2%, followed by very few cells with value of 12% etc.), leading to the compressed regions of the spring representing well E. Being able to reflect on the differences in property values distribution between wells can help reservoir engineers to consider economic analysis aspects relating to the well placement. The pink circles at the end of the spring represent the accumulative values of all the information circles along each well trajectory, to help in overall comparison. For example, consider comparing well C to well F. From the visualization it can be observed that well F has overall higher accumulative property values (larger pink circle), meaning that more perforated cells are placed in unfit regions (more cells having higher property values/blue regions of the model), while well C has overall smaller accumulative property values (smaller pink circle), placing it in a relatively better position within the reservoir model (more cells having lower property values/green regions of the model).

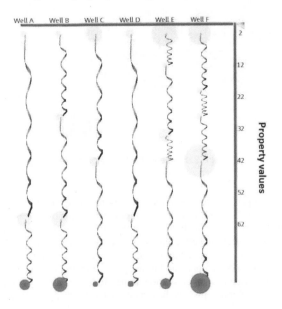

Figure 3: Multiple wells information circles

4.4 Path Indicator

Path indicator reflects on exploration of cell specific information done by sketching. This technique allows the engineer to explore the cells of the reservoir model within the context of the model. Due to the need to reach the interior cells of the reservoir model to facilitate sketching in different layers, we need to remove parts of the context. In our current prototype the sketching exploration is limited to orthogonal planes. As can be seen in Figure 4, orthogonal planes can be selected using the walls of the bounding box. Once positioned, the region in front of the plane is removed to allow visibility of sketching. Sketching exploration is augmented with an indicator bubble at the tip of the finger that grows and shrinks in

size to indicate growing path navigation through unfit or fit areas. Ideally the indicator bubble should stay small, since this reflects that the path is being placed majorly in fit regions of the reservoir model. The indicator bubble is rendered with partial transparency, to allow the engineer to see the path being sketched. The indicator bubble functions as a short-term memory aid, constantly reflecting the accumulation of the property values to that point by keeping track of the cells that have been passed through in 3D. On removing the finger, the size of the indicator bubble is reset.

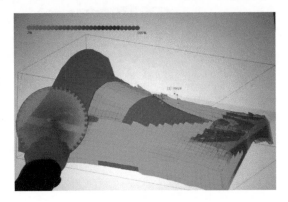

Figure 4: Path Indicator

5 EXPLORATORY EVALUATION

We conducted an exploratory evaluation through a set of semi-structured qualitative sessions. The goal of these sessions was to better understand the usefulness and the readability of these visualizations. We interviewed three domain experts and three visualization experts. The details of the study are provided in the following sections.

5.1 Participants

To learn about the usefulness, benefits, limitations and readability of our visualizations we conducted 6 qualitative semi-structured study sessions. The domain participants were graduate students in the chemical and petroleum engineering department in our university, and had both industry and academic experience with using domain specific software applications. The visualization experts were also graduate student researchers from our university and had research experience in the area of information and scientific visualization.

5.2 Method

Each study session was a one-to-one integrated demo, prototype exploration and semi-structured interview, and lasted between 60 to 90 minutes. The sessions started with a brief introduction to the dataset being explored and the visualization techniques being evaluated. As part of pre-study questionnaire, participants were asked about their research background. This was done in order to better understand their exposure and use of visualizations (in general), and their domain expertise. This was followed by a demo of each visualization technique. The participants were encouraged to interact with the visualizations and were asked to think aloud expressing their suggestions, opinions and feedback. During the discussions we asked the participants semi-structured interview questions to encourage their reflection on the usefulness of the techniques, potential advantages and problems of the techniques, and any additional suggestions for improvement. All the sessions were videotaped. Using the video recordings we transcribed the audio for every participant. We performed an open coding of the transcribed data in order to group the discussions (verbal comments) under broad categories and identify interesting observations [20]. We also used the

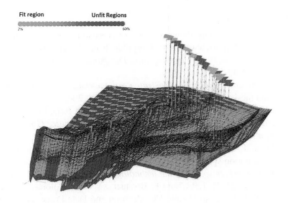

Figure 5: Offset to reflect the same shape as the actual well trajectory.

video recordings to compute the following times: (a) total interaction time - defined as the total of the spans of time the participant was interacting with the visualization either by direct interaction with the visualization or by model manipulation to view the visualization from varying viewpoints; (b) total thinking time - defined as the total of the portions of time when a participant interacted with the visualization without any verbal or physical expression for explaining their thoughts; and (c) discussion time - is the total amount of time that the participant spent discussing the visualization technique.

6 RESULTS AND DISCUSSION

In the study, 4 out of 6 participants ranked lollipop-up visualization to be most useful of the three visualizations. Two of the visualization experts mentioned liking path indicator better than lollipop-up and information circles for exploration. 4 out of 6 participants mentioned that information circles were useful for exploration, but mostly in the case where it was augmented with the lollipop-up visualization. We also observed that although all of our participants liked the visualization techniques, all of them also mentioned limitations and suggestions for improvements for each of the techniques.

From the time recordings we observed that the domain experts spent less time thinking about the lollipop-ups (domain mean rank: 2.67, vis mean rank: 4.33) but almost twice as much time discussing them (domain mean rank: 7.67, vis mean rank: 4.00). Similarly the domain experts spent close to twice as much time on discussing information circles (domain mean rank: 7.33, vis mean rank: 3.67). We also observed that when grouped as a whole, the participants had longer interaction time with the lollipop-ups (mean rank: 2.89), than with either the information circles (mean rank: 1.06) or the path indicator (mean rank: 2.06). Similarly, they spend more time discussing the information circles (mean rank: 2.56) compared to lollipop-ups (mean rank: 1.33) and indicator (mean rank: 2.11).

Below we interpret our results to highlight some of the benefits and limitations of our visualizations, and their usefulness to domain experts.

6.1 Lollipop-up Visualization

6.1.1 Benefits and Limitations

The fundamental benefit of this visualization is that it shows an overview of the hidden well trajectory without compromising the context, *"its good for a quick look"*. Secondly, it was noted that since the model could be mapped to different geological properties it allowed for quick ways to do high level comparison and correlation. Contrary to our current implementation, the shape of the offset well was found to be a limitation of this technique. The majority of our participants mentioned they would prefer to see the same shape of the well being reflected above the surface as shown in Figure 5. *"Inversion (of depth) does not help with anything, better to have regular shape (of the well)"*. Although the depth of the perforated cell is reflected by the height of the trajectory, it introduced discontinuities in the visual. This clashes with the real world modeling of well trajectories and thus was found difficult to interpret. Some of the other limitations of this technique include the overlapping well cells. Although the visualization allows for a quick overview of the geological property distribution in the well trajectory, detailed information is hard to achieve due to the overlap. As seen in Figure 1b, even though the cells are generally displaced, due to the geometric nature of unstructured corner point cells, there may be some overlap. Interactions that allow each offset cell to be separated and examined individually can remedy such situations, *"have a probe, using which you can move over the cells (offset cells) and get more information about them"*.

6.1.2 Novelty and Suggestions

Two of our domain experts mentioned that lollipop-up visualization was visually similar to bubble diagrams, a visualization available in the commercial software Petrel [1]. However, they found the lollipop-up visualization to be novel and useful as it allowed each well perforation cell to be examined. This is in contrast with bubble diagrams which show a single cumulative value for each well trajectory. Another of the domain participant mentioned that in the commercial software, well specific information can be accessed using a layer specific slicing technique. However, slicing is not easy to perform, and hence he preferred lollipop-ups, which provided an overview readily, *"In Petrel something of this sort can be done by slicing, but this (lollipop-up visualization) is better than slicing because it is not easy to select a well and go slicing"*. All our participants provided suggestions for improving this visualization. Among the many, one interesting suggestion was to use two sets of lollipop-ups in two opposite directions. Rather than collapsing two geological properties into one map, the participant suggested it would be better to have two sets of lollipop-ups each mapped to one property. The participant felt this might improve the ease of comparison and correlation.

6.2 Information Circles

6.2.1 Benefits and Limitations

One major observed benefit of this technique was the interaction between the information circles and lollipop-up visualization. With the help of this interaction, the location of well cells could be identified; this was specifically useful to identify those cells in the unfit regions requiring consideration. Another benefit of this visualization is that it gives the engineer an idea of the number of cells with a particular property value, and provides insights about where changes have to be made within the collection of well points, (*"could be useful in scenarios of economic analysis of wells"*). Some limitations of information circles included the initial training time needed to understand the technique. It was initially found to be confusing to interpret for the majority of our participants. One of the domain participant mentioned that since information circles are similar to histograms, it might be better to not introduce a new visual language. Also it was observed that the information circles strength was in interaction with lollipop-ups, *"if I knew it (interaction), maybe I could read it (information circles) without your explanation"*, *"now this (interaction) is very useful"*.

6.2.2 Novelty and Suggestions

Although static information circles were not preferred over histograms, the interaction between the lollipop- ups and information circles improved their readability and usefulness. Our domain participants found this to be something new and one mentioned that it

149

could be more useful for geologists, *"more important for geologists rather than reservoir engineers"*. One suggestion for this technique was regarding against the use of circles. Alternatively, some participants suggested arranging the perforated cells in clusters to support quick understanding of the visualization.

6.3 Path Indicator: Benefits and Limitations

6.3.1 Benefits and Limitations

Path indicator was seen as beneficial for domain tasks such as well planning, *"useful when designing new wells or to make predictions about your model"*. Because path indicator allows for somewhat free-form, sketch-based exploration, it allowed the engineer to easily explore the area of importance to them. One obvious limitation of our current protoype is the restricted orthogonal planes for sketching. To support well creation tasks, flexible drawing planes need to be supported.

6.3.2 Novelty and Suggestions

All our domain experts mentioned this visualization would be useful within the context of well planning. One of the suggestions to improve this visualization included placing the indicator bubble at an offset. While half of our participants mentioned that they preferred the indicator bubble to be at the tip of the finger for immediate feedback, the other half preferred it to be at an offset, seeing it as a distraction. Two of our visualization experts mentioned that this technique could be useful in collaborative settings, when two or more people could propose different well paths within the model and later compare their findings and strategies.

6.4 Color Scale

To facilitate distinct interpretation of the fit and unfit regions, we chose to not use rainbow color scales in this experiment. However, while this worked for some of our participants, *"I think it's nice to see the contrast between the blue and green. You can really tell that this is fit and this is unfit"*, some of the others found it difficult to read very similar shades of green and blue and preferred the use of more distinct colors.

7 CONCLUSION AND FUTURE WORK

In this paper we described the design and implementation of three visualization techniques created to support the exploration and visualization of well trajectory specific information in 3D reservoir models. We also present a discussion of our findings from two distinct groups of participants (domain experts and visualization experts) who took part in our exploratory study. From these initial set of findings we observed that all the three visualizations have potential benefits and usefulness for the domain. Part of the contribution of our work is blending concepts from scientific visualization and information visualization to come up with techniques that can provide insights about the reservoir models to the domain engineers.

In the near future, we plan to improve our visualizations based on the suggestions provided by our participants. In the long term we would like to improve our sketching techniques, and consider scenarios for creating 3D well configurations intuitively. Using these well trajectory creation scenarios as a task set we would like to conduct another set of task oriented studies to validate the usefulness and intuitiveness of these visualization variations.

ACKNOWLEDGEMENTS

We would like to thank our colleagues and reviewers for their valuable comments, suggestions and discussions. This research was supported by the Alberta Innovates Academy (AITF) / Foundation CMG Industrial Research Chair in Scalable Reservoir Visualization.

REFERENCES

[1] Schlumberger. http://www.slb.com/services/software/geo/petrel/simulation.a
[2] tecplotr. http://www.tecplot.com/products/tecplot-chorus/.
[3] J. Bertin. *Semiology of Graphics: Diagrams, Networks, Maps*. Esri Press, 2011.
[4] S. Bruckner. *Interactive illustrative volume visualization*. PhD thesis, PhD thesis, Vienna University of Technology, 2008.
[5] M. S. T. Carpendale, D. J. Cowperthwaite, and F. D. Fracchia. Extending distortion viewing from 2D to 3D. *Computer Graphics and Applications, IEEE*, 17(4):42–51, 1997.
[6] M. S. T. Carpendale and C. Montagnese. A framework for unifying presentation space. In *Proc. of the 14th annual ACM symposium on User interface software and technology*, pages 61–70. ACM, 2001.
[7] L. Castanié, B. Lévy, and F. Bosquet. VolumeExplorer: Roaming Large Volumes to Couple Visualization and Data Processing for Oil and Gas Exploration. In *Proc. of the IEEE Visualization (VIS '05)*, pages 247 – 254, 2005.
[8] R. Cosse. Basics of reservoir engineering. *Technip*, 1993.
[9] D. Dopkin and H. James. Trends in visualization for E&P operations. *First Break*, 24(3), 2006.
[10] N. Elmqvist and P. Tsigas. A taxonomy of 3D occlusion management for visualization. *IEEE Transactions on Visualization and Computer Graphics*, 14(5):1095–1109, 2008.
[11] G. W. Furnas. Generalized fisheye views. In *Proc. of the SIGCHI conference on Human factors in computing systems (CHI '86)*, pages 16–23, 1986.
[12] R. Gasteiger, M. Neugebauer, O. Beuing, and B. Preim. The FLOWLENS: A Focus-and-Context Visualization Approach for Exploration of Blood Flow in Cerebral Aneurysms. *IEEE Transactions on Visualization and Computer Graphics*, 17(12):2183–2192, 2011.
[13] IBM. Open Visualization Data Explorer, OpenDX. http://www.opendx.org/highlights.php?highlight=inaction/oil/, 2002.
[14] O. D. Lampe, C. D. Correa, K.-L. Ma, and H. Hauser. Curve-Centric Volume Reformation for Comparative Visualization. *IEEE Transactions on Visualization and Computer Graphics*, 15(6):1235–1242, 2009.
[15] S. Y. Lee, K.-W. Lee, and U. Neuman. Interactive visualization of oil reservoir data. *Geospatial Visual Analytics*, 2008.
[16] D. S. Oliver, L. B. Cunha, and A. C. Reynolds. Markov chain Monte Carlo methods for conditioning a permeability field to pressure data. *Mathematical Geology*, 29(1):61–91, 1997.
[17] D. K. Ponting. Corner point geometry in reservoir simulation. In *1st European Conference on the Mathematics of Oil Recovery*, 1989.
[18] M. J. Pyrcz and C. V. Deutsch. *Geostatistical reservoir modeling*. Oxford University Press, 2014.
[19] H. Sonnet, S. Carpendale, and T. Strothotte. Integrating expanding annotations with a 3D explosion probe. In *Proc. of the working conference on Advanced visual interfaces*, pages 63–70. ACM, 2004.
[20] A. L. Strauss and J. Corbin. *Basics of Qualitative Research : Techniques and Procedures for Developing Grounded Theory*. SAGE Publications, September 1998.
[21] N. Sultanum, S. Somanath, E. Sharlin, and M. C. Sousa. Point it, Split it, Peel it, View it: techniques for interactive reservoir visualization on tabletops. In *Proc. of the ACM International Conference on Interactive Tabletops and Surfaces*, pages 192–201. ACM, 2011.
[22] T. Taerum, M. C. Sousa, F. F. Samavati, S. Chan, and J. R. Mitchell. Real-Time Super Resolution Contextual Close-up of Clinical Volumetric Data. In *Proc. of the Eurographics/IEEE - VGTC Symposium on Visualization (EuroVis '06)*, pages 347–354, 2006.
[23] A. Tiwari and W. P. Brown. System and method for simultaneous visualization of fluid flow within well completions and a reservoir, 2011. US Patent App. 13/811,826.
[24] I. Viola, A. Kanitsar, and E. Grller. Importance-Driven Volume Rendering. In *Proc. of the conference on Visualization (VIS '04)*, pages 139–146, 2004.
[25] C. Ware and M. Lewis. The DragMag image magnifier. In *Proc. of the conference companion on Human factors in computing systems (CHI '95)*, pages 407–408, 1995.

ReCloud: Semantics-Based Word Cloud Visualization of User Reviews

Ji Wang[a,*]   Jian Zhao[b,†]   Sheng Guo[a,‡]   Chris North[a,§]   Naren Ramakrishnan[a,¶]

[a]Department of Computer Science, Virginia Tech   [b]Department of Computer Science, University of Toronto

ABSTRACT

User reviews, like those found on Yelp and Amazon, have become an important reference for decision making in daily life, for example, in dining, shopping and entertainment. However, large amounts of available reviews make the reading process tedious. Existing word cloud visualizations attempt to provide an overview. However their randomized layouts do not reveal content relationships to users. In this paper, we present ReCloud, a word cloud visualization of user reviews that arranges semantically related words as spatially proximal. We use a natural language processing technique called grammatical dependency parsing to create a semantic graph of review contents. Then, we apply a force-directed layout to the semantic graph, which generates a clustered layout of words by minimizing an energy model. Thus, ReCloud can provide users with more insight about the semantics and context of the review content. We also conducted an experiment to compare the efficiency of our method with two alternative review reading techniques: random layout word cloud and normal text-based reviews. The results showed that the proposed technique improves user performance and experience of understanding a large number of reviews.

Index Terms: H.5.2 [Information interfaces and presentation (e.g., HCI)]: User Interfaces—Natural language

1 INTRODUCTION

Many websites, such as Amazon and Yelp, provide customers with a platform for sharing product reviews, which has become a critical references resource for making decisions. However, the usefulness of those reviews is limited in practice, because reviews exist in large quantities and the detailed contents are unstructured (i.e., in plain text form). People find it tedious and time-consuming to read a large amount of text, so they either leverage the structured quantitative aspects of reviews, such as star ratings, or quickly skim the text, both of which overlook important information for decision making.

Word clouds (or tag clouds) are popular methods for visually summarizing large amounts of text, which presents the content in a space-filling, concise and aesthetically appealing manner, with the font size and color of words mapped to the word frequency, popularity or importance. Word cloud visualizations have been widely used in both business and research, e.g., Opinion Cloud [7], Tirra [15], Review Spotlight [26] and Wordle [8, 12].

However, most word clouds arrange the words randomly. Although they are useful and informative tools, the randomness of word layout does not provide a meaningful representation of the data. First, it requires significant mental demand for users to understand the review content, because users need to scan the entire visualization to gain an overview or to find specific keywords of interest. Second, it only provides one dimension of information, such as

*e-mail: wji@cs.vt.edu

†e-mail: jianzhao@dgp.toronto.edu

‡e-mail: guos@vt.edu. Sheng Guo is at LinkedIn Corp. now.

§e-mail: north@vt.edu

¶e-mail: naren@cs.vt.edu

Graphics Interface Conference 2014
7-9 May, Montreal, Quebec, Canada

word frequency, without semantic relationships among keywords, which is critical for understanding the review content [14, 26]. For example, related words in a single concept "chicken salad sandwich" or description "sushi is delicious" could be placed at different places in a random word cloud, making it difficult for users to recognize the intent.

In this paper, we present ReCloud, a word cloud visualization of user reviews, which seamlessly integrates semantic context of review keywords into the visualization layout. This provides an important additional dimension of information for users to better comprehend reviews in a quick and easy manner (Figure 1). For example, users will recognize that "delicious" goes with "sushi", and that "chicken" and "salad" and "sandwich" are a single concept. Our layout algorithm is based on grammatical dependency parsing, an effective natural language processing (NLP) approach [6] that generates a *grammatical dependency graph* (GDG) from text, which has been used in many applications to enhance users' understanding of textual sources [5, 24]. We propose a novel approach of (1) parsing user review semantics to generate a GDG, (2) clustering the GDG with a force-directed graph layout algorithm based on an energy model, and (3) embedding the clustered GDG into the word cloud. Using real review data from the Yelp Academic Dataset [27], we also conduct a formal experiment to compare ReCloud with two alternative review browsing techniques: (a) normal text reading, and (b) random layout word cloud. The results indicate that ReCloud improves user performance and experience in exploring reviews, identifying criteria, and making decisions.

2 RELATED WORK

2.1 Review Visualization

Visualization of online reviews can be categorized into two types. First, visualization of quantitative features of reviews are often used to display customer ratings, price level, and other numerical measurements of a product or service. For example, Wu *et al.* presented a system to show hotel user feedback based on quantitative review features [25]. However, many products or services cannot be simply described with quantitative values in reviews; deeper insights about actual review content are needed for users to make better decisions.

Second, visualizations of the textual content of reviews can provide a deeper view. Liu and Street first used a NLP approach to analyze reviews and then present extracted user opinions using a bar chart [14]. Along the same lines, Caternini and Rizoli presented a multimedia interface to visualize fixed features summarized from review contents that reflect a user's opinions [2]. Review Spotlight presents a word cloud based visualization by showing adjective plus noun word pairs with color-coded word sentiment [26]. Huang *et al.* proposed RevMiner, a smartphone interface that also applies NLP techniques (e.g., bootstrapping) to analyze and display user reviews in a categorical layout [10].

The major advance in ReCloud is that the NLP context is reflected in the spatial layout of the tag cloud. Thus, in general, the spatial proximity of tags in the cloud represents the frequency and path length between the tags in the NLP grammatical parse of all review text. In contrast, RevMiner uses categorical and sorted lists, and Review Spotlight uses randomized layout.

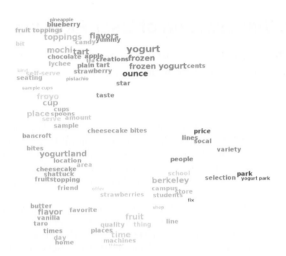

Figure 1: ReCloud of a Yogurtland store near UC Berkeley campus.

2.2 Word Cloud Layout and Evaluation

Word clouds have become very popular in showing textual content, where the font size of a keyword could reflect its frequency in the text. There exist many approaches for the layout of words. Kaser and Lemire presented an algorithm to draw word clouds in a limited space on webpages using HTML table components [11]. Viegas *et al.* proposed a greedy space-filling approach for placing words that generates more compact word clouds [8, 23].

Recently, researchers have proposed several methods for embedding text NLP results into word cloud layouts, for example, as in Spotlight [26] and RevMiner [10] mentioned above. In addition, Cui *et al.* present a context preserving tag cloud for news based on term co-occurrence in both time and text sentences, using a statistical information theoretic approach [4]. ProjCloud clusters documents into a set of polygons, then fills the polygons with high frequency keywords from those documents and arranges the keywords according to statistical co-occurrence distance metric [20]. ReCloud goes beyond simple co-occurrence metrics to semantic grammatical structure of the text and focuses on the term level, not the document level.

Moreover, several studies have been conducted to assess the effects of word clouds on text browsing tasks. For example, font size and font weight were found to catch a user's attention the most [1]. Lohmann *et al.* evaluated the effect of word cloud layouts on user task performance and found that thematic layouts were good for finding words that belonged to a specific topic [16]. However, their work was not based on real data. Rivadeneira *et al.* conducted a user study to obtain performance metrics of four types of tasks using word clouds, including search, browsing, impression formation, and recognition [21], where impression formation was later adopted in the evaluation of Review Spotlight [26].

3 RECLOUD

3.1 System Overview

We designed ReCloud following two principles summarized from the previous work [12, 20, 26]: 1) the word cloud should arrange its layout to present semantic information about the text, and 2) the word cloud should support interaction for retrieval of review content. The entire ReCloud system consists of two main parts: the back-end data processing pipeline and the front-end interactive visualization.

The back-end data processing pipeline takes raw user reviews as the input and generates a word cloud visualization. The pipeline contains the following three steps:

1. **Grammatical dependency parsing.** We first process the review content using NLP techniques to generate the grammatical dependency graph that reflects the semantic relationships between keywords in the reviews.
2. **Initial word cloud layout.** We apply the LinLogLayout algorithm [18] to the grammatical dependency graph, using an energy model to optimize the force-directed graph layout process [17]. This generates keyword clusters and their initial layout positions.
3. **Final word cloud rendering.** After the initial word placements, we then use an approach similar to Wordle [23, 8] to perform fine-grain adjustments to the word cloud. This avoids word overlapping in the final visualization.

As shown in Figure 2(c), the front-end visualization contains three main components: a main view of showing the word cloud (F), a historical view of keywords clicked by the user (G), and a detail view of review texts (H). ReCloud also supports basic user interaction for accessing review content based on keywords. When a user clicks a word tag in the word cloud, Component H shows all the reviews that contain the keyword, where the keyword is highlighted in red color.

3.2 Data

In this paper, we used the Yelp Academic Dataset [27] as our test bed. The dataset provides profiles and user reviews of 250 businesses near 30 universities, such as shopping centers and restaurants. The data includes three objects in JSON format: *business profile objects*, *user profile objects* and *review content objects*. We utilized the business profile objects to select businesses in our experiment (see Section 4) and the review content objects to generate the word cloud visualization in ReCloud.

3.3 Grammatical Dependency Parsing

In order to obtain the semantic information, we use NLP tools to compute the *grammatical dependency graph* of the review text for each business, resulting in a graph of key phrases. To construct the graph, the review content for a specific restaurant was first extracted from the raw dataset and chunked into sentences. Then, the sentences were parsed based on grammatical relations and eventually the relationship information was filtered to form a context graph. We used the Stanford Parser [6, 22] and the OpenNLP toolkits [19] to create the context graphs.

First, for each review, we broke down each sentence into typed-dependency parse graph using the Stanford Parser. In Figure 3, (a) shows the typed dependency parse for a sample sentence, and (b) shows the filtered sentence level grammatical relations. We filtered edges that represent unimportant grammatical relations such as *aux*, *auxpass*, *punct*, *det*, *cop*, etc. Because nouns, verbs, and adjectives are most important in our domain (user generated reviews), we retained only terms with those specific part-of-speech tags [6, 22], such as *VB, VBD, VBG, VBN, NN, NNP, NNS, JJ, JJR, JJS*, etc. In this first part of the process, we extracted the main grammatical relations within a sentence.

Then, for each restaurant, we concatenated the parse graphs of all the sentences of all the reviews for that restaurant into a single graph. If relations amongst different sentences shared a term, the shared term was merged as a single shared vertex. The grammatical dependency graphs for each restaurant were usually large due to the large number of reviews for each restaurant in the dataset (e.g. one restaurant had 110 reviews). Thus, we only retained the most important and meaningful types of nodes (nouns, verbs, and adjectives) in the graphs for later processing (e.g. 1500 nodes for the same restaurant).

In our final step, we assigned weight values to both the vertices and the edges for later use in the graph layout phase. The vertex weight W_i of term T_i was computed using the traditional *IDF* value:

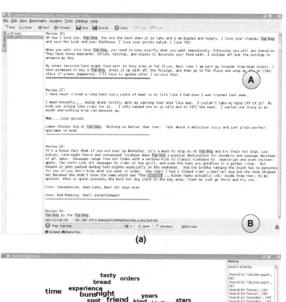

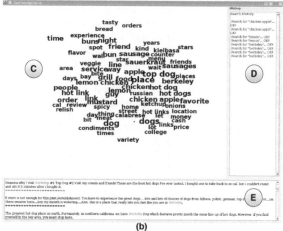

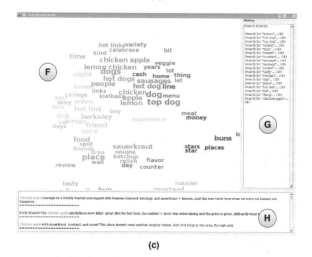

Figure 2: Different review reading techniques for showing the same Yelp review data: (a) Normal Text (NT), (b) Random Word Cloud (RW), and (c) ReCloud (RC). In the NT interface, Component A displays the raw review content and Component B is a search box for finding specific keywords. In the user interface of both RW and RC, Component C and F are the word cloud visualizations; Component D and G shows the historical keywords clicked by users; and Component E and H displays the review contents that match the currently clicked keyword highlighted in red.

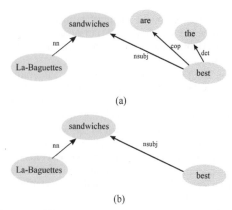

(a)

(b)

Figure 3: (a) A collapsed typed dependency parse for the sentence La-Baguettes sandwiches are the best!. (b) The sentence level graph filtered from the parse in (a).

$$W_i(T_i) = \log(N/df_i) \cdot (\log df_i + 1) \quad (1)$$

N is the number of sentences, and df_i is the document frequency which denotes the number of sentences that have this term. For weighting the edges, the same strategy as vertex weighting was used, the only difference being that the variable df_j means the number of sentences that have this edge type.

$$W_j(E_j) = \log(N/df_j) \cdot (\log df_j + 1) \quad (2)$$

3.4 Force-Directed Graph Layout with Energy Model

To create an initial two-dimensional clustered representation of the grammatical dependency graph, we applied a force-directed graph layout. Force-directed graph layout is widely used in drawing large graphs in an aesthetically pleasing way. The layout algorithm assigns "attraction forces" or "repulsive forces" between graph nodes based on edges and iteratively simulates such physical behaviors for drawing the graph. Studies have indicated that the force-directed graph layout of text semantic graph can produce easily understood representations [4, 20]. However, the force-directed graph layout has a scalability problem; the layout computation process is very time-consuming when many layout iterations are needed due to large quantities of edges and nodes.

When the graph is large, an energy model based method of performing the force-directed graph layout is better, which directly influences the layout quality and speed [18]. The essential idea of the energy model is to map the layout to an energy function, and the value of such energy is related to the optimal goal of the whole layout. Then, the algorithm iteratively searches all the possible solutions having the lowest energy of the entire layout. A good layout is considered to have the minimal energy [17]. In this paper, we used the LinLogLayout toolkit [13] as the energy model, which is fast enough to generate word clouds on-the-fly during user interaction. The resulting graph layout serves as the initial placement of words for the next phase. LinLogLayout also provides cluster label information, which we utilize in ReCloud for coloring.

3.5 Word Cloud Rendering

Based on the initial word placements output by the above force directed layout algorithm, we then performed a similar approach as [8] to generate our final ReCloud visualization. The largest difference is that the initial positions of word tags in ReCloud are not random, as opposed to traditional word clouds. We implemented this word cloud rendering process using the Java 2D Graphics library. More specifically, the fine-grain adjustment and rendering process can be described in the following steps:

1. Sort the vertex list of the grammatical dependency graph according to vertex weight (Eq. (1)) to generate the word list for rendering. High frequency (and hence large size) words are rendered first.

2. For each word in the sorted rendering list, the initial position and color is defined by the force-directed layout algorithm, and its font size is determined by the vertex weight. Unique colors are assigned to each cluster label on a simple hue scale.

3. Collision detection is performed to see whether the word spatially overlaps with previously rendered words. We use a double buffer mask for the test. We render previous words in one image buffer, render the new word in the second image buffer, and then conduct a logical AND of the bits in these two buffers to quickly check for a collision.

4. If a collision occurs, we place the word by following the Archimedean spiral [8] around the words initial position (from step 2) until there is no collision.

5. Step 2-4 are repeated until all the words are rendered, or until a predefined maximum word threshold is reached.

4 EVALUATION

The major goal of our user study was to assess the effectiveness of the ReCloud concept in decision-making tasks. The primary research question is how the grammatically semantic layout affects users' performance and satisfaction in comparison to traditional random layout and normal text reading. We chose a common daily task as our study scenario: finding good restaurants and judging restaurants based on customer review text. We specifically focus on the text content of the reviews, not the quantitative review scores, to emphasize the role of the word cloud in comprehension. These kinds of tasks are familiar to users who struggle in making informed decisions about restaurants.

4.1 Participants and Apparatus

We recruited 15 participants (7 females), aged 20 to 32 (24.4 on average), for our study. All participants were familiar with normal word clouds such as Wordle. They were all native English speakers and undergraduate (4) or graduate students (11) from our university. The study lasted about 50 minutes and each participant was compensated with $30 cash.

All the tasks were performed on a laptop with Intel Centrino 2.10GHz CPU and 4 GB RAM with Kubuntu 12.04, with an external keyboard and mouse. The display used was one 19-inch LCD monitor with 1280×1024 resolution. The entire display was used to show reviews of one given restaurant. When two restaurants were compared, users could swap freely between the reviews of the two restaurants using a keyboard shortcut (Figure 2(a)). Task completion times were measured using a stopwatch and participants' mouse cursor movement data was collected by our system.

4.2 Review Reading Techniques

During this user study, we compared three conditions: ReCloud, Random Word Cloud, and Normal Text. For the two alternative techniques, Random Word Cloud was used as a baseline for comparison because it does not embed semantics in the layout, and Normal Text was used because this is commonly how users read reviews. We also removed the review scores to let participants focus on the review content itself.

Normal Text (NT). We listed the textual content of all customer reviews for a given restaurant in a normal scrolling text editor. The quantitative ratings for each review were omitted. Users could use the search box in the text editor to find and highlight keywords in the reviews.

Random Word Cloud (RW). We used a random layout method according to the algorithm described in [8] to generate this word cloud, as shown in Figure 2(b). The user interactions were the same as described in Section 3.1.

ReCloud (RC): In this technique, participants used the aforementioned ReCloud system to read reviews using the semantic layout word cloud (Figure 2(c)).

4.3 Tasks and Design

Two types of tasks were used to assess users performance: *decision making tasks* and *feature finding tasks*. Both tasks attempt to mirror events that regularly occur in daily life. As shown in Table 1, for each of the review reading conditions, we allowed participants to perform two types of tasks as below:

Decision Making Task. The goal of this overview-oriented task is to efficiently and correctly compare and distinguish similar types of restaurants of varying quality based on review content. In this task, participants must decide between a given pair of restaurants to patronize based on the reviews. There were two sub-tasks based on restaurant quality. For the "good-good" sub-task, users compared two restaurants of good quality, meaning that both restaurants in these pairs had high ratings (4 or 5 stars on the business profiles of the Yelp dataset). For the "good-bad" sub-task, users compared two restaurants of opposite quality, meaning that the two restaurants had significant differences in their ratings (good was 4-5 stars, and bad was 1-2 stars).

The "good-good" pair serves as a difficult task. The "good-bad" pair has a correct answer, in that we assume participants would want to choose restaurants that other people highly rated quantitatively, but should be able to identify the difference in quality from the review text only. Since we carefully chose the restaurant pairs based on matching cuisine, we expect the restaurant quality to be the deciding factor, rather than menu preferences. All paired restaurants had similar price levels, locations, and cuisines. Thus we did not employ a randomized pairing process, but instead carefully chose the restaurant pairs from the Yelp Academic Dataset based on these criteria. In this study, participants were not familiar with any of the restaurants and were unaware of how the good and bad restaurants were chosen.

We selected 6 pairs of restaurants for this task, three "good-good" and three "good-bad" pairs. Each participant used all three review reading conditions. Conditions were counterbalanced in a latin-square design. For each condition they performed one "good-good" and one "good-bad" pair. Thus, in total, each participant performed all 6 pairs.

Feature Finding Task. The goal of this detail-oriented task is to efficiently identify basic non-quantitative features of a given restaurant based on review content. In this task, participants typed a list of relevant features of the restaurant based on its reviews. This task was designed to represent the process of understanding qualitative features that would be considered in deciding to patronize a particular restaurant, such as flavor, value, service, atmosphere, etc. Thus, we defined two sub-tasks: finding food features, and finding non-food features.

We selected 6 restaurants, all had high ratings (4 or 5 stars). As shown in Table 1, restaurants 1, 3, and 5 were used for non-food feature finding sub-task. Restaurants 2, 4 and 6 were used for food feature finding sub-task. The restaurants varied in number of reviews available, with 49, 65, 66, 185, 283 and 2232 reviews in restaurant 1-6 respectively. Each participant performed all three review reading conditions. Conditions were counterbalanced in a latin-square design. For each condition, the participants performed one food and one non-food feature finding sub-task. Moreover, we imposed a two-minute time limit on half of the participants, while the other half did not have any time limit. This was to investigate whether the semantic layout would be particularly helpful when users have time constraints.

Task Type	Technique	Data	Task Question
Decision Making Task	NT	Good-Good Pair 1	Which Restaurant will you go?
	NT	Good-Bad Pair 1	
	RW	Good-Good Pair 2	
	RW	Good-Bad Pair 2	
	RC	Good-Good Pair 3	
	RC	Good-Bad Pair 3	
Feature Finding Task	NT	Restaurant 1	Non-food Feature
	NT	Restaurant 2	Food Feature
	RW	Restaurant 3	Non-food Feature
	RW	Restaurant 4	Food Feature
	RC	Restaurant 5	Non-food Feature
	RC	Restaurant 6	Food Feature

Table 1: Tasks Design and Study Procedure. The three technique conditions were counterbalanced in a latin-square design.

4.4 Procedure

Before the study started, participants had time to get familiar with the three different review reading techniques using the same sample dataset. Then participants were instructed to perform the two task sets using each of the three review reading conditions according to their latin-square assignment.

For the decision making task, we measured the completion times (for all) and error rates (for good-bad pairs) in each trial. For the feature finding task, completion time was only recorded for trials of participants who were in the no time limit group. After each review reading condition in both tasks, participants completed a Likert-style questionnaire based on NASA TLX [9] to collect their ratings of mental demand, physical demand, and other metrics to measure task difficulty levels. After each of the two tasks, participants were asked to provide a ranking of preferences among the three review reading conditions, with 1 being most preferred and 3 being least preferred. At the end of the study, we conducted a short informal interview to gather general comments for each review reading condition.

5 RESULTS

5.1 Decision Making Task Results

5.1.1 Task Completion Time and Error Rate

We ran six repeated measure ANOVAs on task completion time for each review reading condition and restaurant pair sub-tasks in the decision making task. Results indicated that restaurant pairing ("good-good" vs."good-bad") had a significant effect ($F_{1,14}$=52.465, p <0.001) on task completion time, with "good-bad" being significantly faster. But there was no significant effect of review reading condition on task completion time.

A post-hoc one-way ANOVA was run for "good-good" restaurant pairs and "good-bad" restaurant pairs. The result showed that review reading technique had a significant effect on task completion time ($F_{2,42}$=3.157, p=0.05) in "good-good" restaurant pairs, but no significant effect in "good-bad" restaurant pairs ($F_{2,42}$=0.253, p=0.78). From Figure 4, we can see that participants spent less time in the decision making tasks using ReCloud compared to the other two conditions for "good-good" restaurant pairs.

In this decision making task, the error rates were calculated in good-bad restaurant pairs and we assumed that the correct answer was the good one. The error rates of RW and RC were the same (6.7%, 1 error out of 15 trials). There were no errors in NT.

5.1.2 Mouse Events Results

We recorded all mouse events when users were presented with techniques RW and RC. The metrics with which we evaluated the mouse events were: the number of word tags hovered over (for at least 0.1 sec) by the cursor, and the number of word tags clicked by the participant. The purpose of the former metric was to estimate a

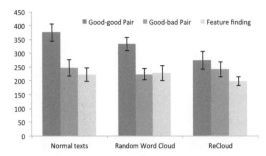

Figure 4: Completion time (seconds) for decision making task (good-good and good-bad restaurant pairs) and feature finding task.

user's amount of visual navigation, since quantity of mouse hovering likely relates to quantity of items attended to by the user. For example, Chen *et al.* [3] found a correlation between users' eye movement and their mouse cursor movement in web browsing. The latter metric could reflect how many reviews users need to read in details. We discuss the mouse movement issues further in Section 6.2.

We first compared the average number of clicked words for all 9 good restaurants (mean = 3.78, std = 0.49) and 3 bad restaurants (mean = 5.74, std = 0.41) in techniques RW and RC via one-way ANOVA. We found that the 3 bad restaurants had significantly fewer word tags clicked than the 9 good restaurants ($F_{1,22}$=5.77, p=0.02). From this, we may conclude that bad restaurants were easy to distinguish by looking at the word cloud without needing to read many reviews.

Then, we analyzed the mouse events from good-good restaurant pairs (3 pairs, 6 restaurants). Figure 5 shows the average number of hovered words (5a) and average number of clicked words (5b) of each restaurant. In Figure 5(a), RC had fewer (by at least a standard deviation) words hovered than RW for 4 of the pairs. But the average number of clicked words (Figure 5(b)) was similar in both word cloud techniques. Thus, RC required fewer mouse hovers than RW in order to accomplish similar levels of mouse clicks. Therefore, it is possible that this represents that RC users require less visual navigation to find useful search targets, perhaps due to the better semantic layout.

5.1.3 Preference Ranking

The participants preference ranking of techniques was analyzed with a Friedman test to evaluate differences in median rank across three techniques. There was a significant difference between the three based on the preferential ranking ($\chi^2(2,$ N=15)=6.533, p=0.04). The follow-up pairwise Wilcoxon tests found that NT had significantly less preferred ranking than RC (p=0.05) and RW (p=0.04). There is no significant difference in preference ordering between RC and RW. The results are shown in Figure 6(a).

5.2 Feature Finding Task Results

5.2.1 Task Completion Time

We ran a one-way ANOVA for task completion time for those participants who did not have a time limit. We did not find a significant effect on task completion time between reading conditions ($F_{2,42}$=0.253, p=0.78), as shown in Figure 4. The reason might be that all restaurants in this task had different scales of review counts (see Section 4.3).

5.2.2 Mouse Event Results

Figure 7 shows the average number of hovered words and average number of clicked words for each restaurant. The average number of clicked words was approximately 5 (for both RC and RW) in all 6 restaurants, even though the restaurants had vastly different number of reviews to read (ranging from 49 to 2,232). However, RC had

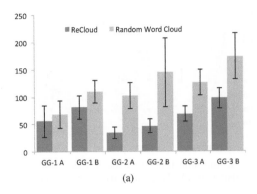

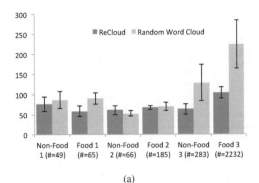

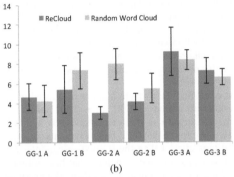

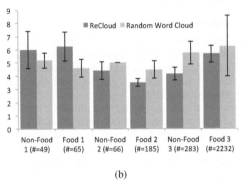

Figure 5: Mouse events data for decision making tasks (good-good pair): (a) word tag hovering data (Y-axis is average hovered word number of each restaurant) and (b) word tag clicking data (Y-axis is average clicked word number of each restaurant).

Figure 7: Mouse events data for feature finding tasks: (a) word tag hovering data (Y-axis is average hovered word number of each restaurant) and (b) word tag clicking data (Y-axis is average clicked word number of each restaurant).

(p=0.02) and RW (p=0.005), shown in Figure 6(b).

5.2.4 User Satisfaction Levels

The Likert-style questionnaire based on NASA TLX was used to acquire user feedback of the three review reading techniques from participants who had a two-minute time limit imposed on them during the feature finding task. As shown in Figure 8(b), a Friedman test was conducted to observe any differences in scores in the questionnaire. The test results showed that there were significant differences on mental demand (χ^2(2, N=8)=11.826, p=0.003), physical demand (χ^2(2, N=8)=6.5, p=0.04), temporal demand (χ^2(2, N=8)=10.129, p=0.006) and effort (χ^2(2, N=8)=7.00, p=0.03).

The follow-up pairwise Wilcoxon tests showed: for mental demand, RC is significantly lower than NT (p=0.02) and RW (p=0.03); for physical demand, RC is significantly lower than NT (p=0.04); for temporal demand, RC is significantly lower than NT (p=0.01); for effort, NT is significantly higher than RW (p=0.04) and RC (p=0.02).

In the case of the no time limit feature finding task, the Friedman test results showed there was no significant difference in any of the responses, shown in Figure 8(a). Therefore, the above results indicated that RC had better user experience and user satisfaction in time-constrained tasks. This might relate to the previous argument about efficient visual navigation for RC.

5.3 Qualitative Feedback

5.3.1 Semantic Information Retrieval

Based on feedback, we found the semantic layout provided by Re-Cloud helped people navigate and find relevant information.

"It [ReCloud] makes it much easier to look for keywords that help when deciding on which option to pick. It's well organized and groups similar words and distinguishes them by color. The black and white words [Normal Word Cloud] with no grouping make it difficult to find tags."(Subject 15)

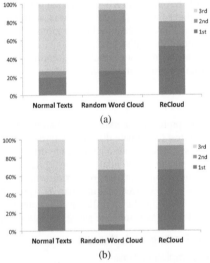

Figure 6: User preference ranking results in decision making tasks (a) and feature finding tasks (b).

significantly fewer hovered words than RW for the restaurants with large number of reviews (Non-food 3 had 283 reviews and Food 3 had 2,232 reviews). This potentially indicates that the semantic layout of RC enabled users to effectively navigate word clouds of a large number of reviews.

5.2.3 Preference Ranking

The user preference rankings of the three techniques in this task also had a significant difference across three techniques in a Friedman test (χ^2(2, N=15)=8.133, p=0.02). Follow-up pairwise Wilcoxon tests found that RC had a significantly more preferred than NT

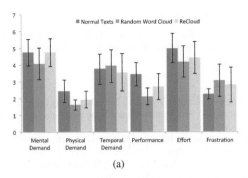

(a)

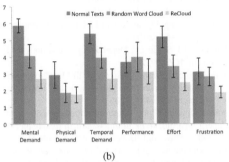

(b)

Figure 8: TLX-based Liker-style questionnaire results for feature finding tasks (where lower is better): (a) without time limit and (b) with two-minute time limit.

"...It [ReCloud] is an easy way to navigate through several reviews that use similar terminology to pinpoint specific aspects of a restaurant. It is easier to find out what I'm looking for." (Subject 14)

"Finding the keywords for 'service' or 'sandwich' was made easiest with ReCloud. It was easy to pick out the keywords that I needed to look at to make my decisions."(Subject 9)

The visual aspects of font size and color had positive impact on users' review reading process by ReCloud as well.

"The size of the words also made it easier to know what was important/more used in the reviews."(Subject 7)

5.3.2 Keywords Query by Interaction

The clickable interaction to query keywords in review content was found useful in ReCloud and Random Word Cloud.

"From these three ReCloud saves my time since I can click on the things I am interested in and quickly see them highlighted in the reviews."(Subject 2)

"The ReCloud was better because ... a good first move was to click the largest word which would give you a pretty good overview of what the place and then browse the other tags in case anything of particular interest or disinterest was there."(Subject 12)

"I still liked ReCloud over all the other techniques because it helped me find better keyword to search so I could read more details in the actual reviews."(Subject 9)

5.3.3 Natural Language Processing

There were mixed reviews on factors about our NLP techniques. A few of our participants did not feel that all the necessary word tags were presented in the word cloud.

"I would have ranked the tag clouds higher, but I was unable to finish one of the tasks because there were no tags regarding the quality of service at a restaurant. Normally, I liked ReCloud more, but I got the impression that fewer tags were included. I liked the clustering, but sometimes couldn't tell why terms were included in specific clusters."(Subject 1)

One participant wanted to assess the personality of individual reviewers based on completed reviews. But NLP based ReCloud did not provide specific information about individual review writers' personalities and interests.

"I preferred reading full reviews because I felt like I could better understand the personality and interests of the reviewers, which factors a great deal into the way I interpret the quality and reliability of the review." (Subject 8)

6 DISCUSSION

6.1 Difficulty of Decision Making Tasks

In the decision making task, we found that ReCloud had a significantly faster task completion time than the random word cloud in good-good pairs of restaurants. But there was no significant difference in good-bad pairs. We believe that these results can be explained in the following two ways:

First, good-bad restaurant pairs are easy to distinguish in all three techniques. They have lower task completion times in Figure 4. At the same time, our mouse event records also support this fact. In bad restaurants, the average number of clicked words is significantly less than that in good restaurants (see Section 5.3.2).

Second, good-good restaurant pairs are difficult to distinguish. All of them have similar high ratings, so users need more context information to support their decisions. In other words, users need to spend more time to find evidence in good-good restaurant pairs. The mouse events in Figure 5 showed that users hover less in ReCloud. Combined with users' feedback described in Section 5.3.1, we can see that the semantic layout improved the visual search process in ReCloud. Moreover, participants significantly preferred ReCloud and Random Word Cloud over Normal Text.

The error rates of the two word clouds were the same, 6.7%, and users preferred ReCloud over the random word cloud. Thus, the content discrimination and bias in NLP techniques and word cloud visualizations did not have significant negative influence on the error rates in the word clouds.

Therefore, ReCloud with semantic layout offered improved user performance in both time and mouse events, and was preferred by users, especially in difficult decision making tasks when comparing similar quality businesses.

6.2 Review Scales and Time-Constrained Situations

In the feature finding tasks, we used restaurants with different numbers of reviews (see Section 4.3), and found that ReCloud had fewer mouse hovers in cases with large number of reviews. In Figure 7(a), ReCloud in No-Food 3 (283 reviews) and Food 3 (2,232 reviews) had significantly fewer hovered words than Random Word Cloud, for similar numbers of clicked words (Figure 7(b)). That might be because the nature of the feature finding task was to perform the categorization and clustering process in people's minds. Thus, we believe that the semantic information of ReCloud helped users perform this process easier.

In the time-limited feature finding tasks, we found that users' workload ratings of ReCloud were significantly higher than that of Random Word Cloud in terms of mental demand, physical demand, temporal demand and effort. However, there was no significant difference in feature finding tasks without time limit. Furthermore, participants significantly preferred ReCloud to Normal Texts ($p=0.024$) and Random Word Cloud ($p=0.005$).

As shown above, participants hovered over few tags, yet clicked on a similar number of tags (in some of the tasks, see Figure 5(b) and Figure 7(b)), when they used ReCloud. We hypothesize that it is because the ordered layout enabled users to more easily identify tags of interest, at both the perceptual and cognitive levels. Hovering in RW might indicate a more challenging visual search process and/or greater cognitive load in considering each tag as indicated by the TLX scores. In summary, ReCloud had fewer hovered word tags and better user satisfaction in a large mount of reviews and time-constrained tasks.

6.3 NLP Technique

Our ReCloud visualization is highly dependent on the results of the NLP technique applied. Currently, ReCloud uses grammatical dependency parsing for extraction of semantics from user reviews and the resulting dependency graph to govern the layout. Although we received mixed qualitative feedback from participants on the NLP results (see Section 5.3.3), the actual statistical analysis results indicated that the overall error rates in decision making tasks were very low (see Section 5.1.1). So we believe that further improvements of the NLP algorithms can enhance our ReCloud visualization, for example, more necessary word tags would be shown, word clustering and its font size would be more accurate, and personality context information of review writers would be available.

6.4 Word Color Encoding

In ReCloud design, we used colors to represent word tags in different semantic clusters generated by the LinlogLayout force directed algorithm [18]. The goal of this color-coding was to keep semantics clusters persistent in ReCloud. Sometimes, the final word cloud rendering algorithm might jeopardize the original semantic layout suggested by NLP techniques. For example, the initial positions of some keywords in the clustered layout might overlap. Each word tag has its own font size according to its frequency in reviews (see Section 3.5). In order to avoid the collisions among other placed word tags, the process of finding new placements of the word tags might locally modify the initial layout a small amount. Finally, the word cloud might not correctly present semantics in some local areas. In this situation, the color encoding of semantic clusters can help users better understand the semantic information by visually preserving the clustering in ReCloud.

7 CONCLUSION AND FUTURE WORK

We have presented a novel visualization technique, ReCloud, based on the use of natural language processing techniques to extract a grammatical dependency graph from the raw content of user reviews. An energy based force directed graph layout algorithm was applied to the grammatical dependency graph that reflects the review semantics to create an initial layout of the keywords. Based on this initial layout, we generated a new word cloud visualization that embeds the semantic information. ReCloud also supports basic user interactions for accessing the review text, such as searching by clicking a specific word tag. We also conducted a user study to evaluate how ReCloud helps users in tasks that involve choosing and judging restaurants based on review content. We used the Yelp Academic Dataset as our testbed and designed two types of tasks in the study: decision making tasks and feature finding tasks. The results indicate that ReCloud improves user performance time in difficult decision-making, reduces unnecessary mouse hover actions, provides greater user preference, and decreased perceived workload, and produced positive user comments about the semantic layout. We believe these results indicate the value of the semantic layout in better representing context of a large amount of review text.

In the future, we plan to append more information on the clustered layout word cloud, like time-series restaurant reviews and sentiment analysis of review information. We will also apply a more sophisticated NLP technique for processing the review content data as well as enable a search box functionality for finding words easier within the word cloud. Furthermore, by manipulating the NLP algorithm, we will also try to expose keywords that previously didn't appear in the clustered layout word cloud and therefore provide a more customizable and possibly interactive review reading experience for the users.

ACKNOWLEDGEMENTS

We would like to thank all the users who participated in our study, Yelp Inc. for the award support, and the reviewers for their valuable suggestions.

REFERENCES

[1] S. Bateman, C. Gutwin, and M. Nacenta. Seeing things in the clouds: the effect of visual features on tag cloud selections. HT '08, pages 193–202, 2008.

[2] G. Carenini and L. Rizoli. A Multimedia Interface for Facilitating Comparisons of Opinions. In *IUI '09*, pages 325–334, 2009.

[3] M. C. Chen, J. R. Anderson, and M. H. Sohn. What can a mouse cursor tell us more? In *CHI '01*, 2001.

[4] W. Cui, Y. Wu, S. Liu, F. Wei, M. Zhou, and H. Qu. Context-Preserving, Dynamic Word Cloud Visualization. *IEEE CG&A*, 30(6):42–53, 2010.

[5] A. Culotta and J. Sorensen. Dependency tree kernels for relation extraction. In *ACL '04*, 2004.

[6] C. M. de Marneffe, Marie-Catherine, Bill MacCartney. Generating typed dependency parses from phrase structure parses. In *Proc. of LREC '06*, pages 449–454, 2006.

[7] Economist Opinion Cloud. http://infomous.com/site/economist/.

[8] J. Feinberg. Wordle. In *Beautiful Visualization*, chapter 3. 2009.

[9] S. Hart and L. Staveland. Development of NASA-TLX: Results of empirical and theoretical research. In *Human mental workload*. 1988.

[10] J. Huang, O. Etzioni, L. Zettlemoyer, K. Clark, and C. Lee. RevMiner: An Extractive Interface for. Navigating Reviews on a Smartphone. In *UIST '12*, 2012.

[11] O. Kaser and D. Lemire. Tag-Cloud Drawing: Algorithms for Cloud Visualization, 2007.

[12] K. Koh, B. Lee, B. Kim, and J. Seo. ManiWordle: Providing Flexible Control over Wordle. *IEEE TVCG*, 16(6):1190–1197, Nov. 2010.

[13] LinLogLayout. http://code.google.com/p/linloglayout/.

[14] B. Liu and S. M. Street. Opinion Observer : Analyzing and Comparing Opinions on the Web. In *WWW '05*, 2005.

[15] S. Liu, M. X. Zhou, S. Pan, Y. Song, W. Qian, W. Cai, and X. Lian. TIARA : Interactive , Topic-Based Visual Text Summarization. *ACM TIST*, 3(2), 2012.

[16] S. Lohmann, J. Ziegler, and L. Tetzlaff. Comparison of Tag Cloud Layouts: Task-Related Performance and Visual Exploration. volume 5726 of *LNCS*, chapter 43, pages 392–404. 2009.

[17] A. Noack. Energy Models for Graph Clustering. *Journal of Graph Algorithms and Applications*, 11(2):453–480, 2007.

[18] A. Noack. Modularity clustering is force-directed layout. *Physical Review E*, 79(2), Feb. 2009.

[19] OpenNLP. http://opennlp.apache.org/.

[20] F. Paulovich, F. Toledo, and G. Telles. Semantic Wordification of Document Collections. *Computer Graphics*, 31:1145–1153, June 2012.

[21] A. W. Rivadeneira, D. M. Gruen, M. J. Muller, and D. R. Millen. Getting our head in the clouds: toward evaluation studies of tagclouds. CHI '07, pages 995–998, 2007.

[22] Stanford Parser. http://nlp.stanford.edu/software.

[23] F. B. Viégas, M. Wattenberg, and J. Feinberg. Participatory visualization with Wordle. *IEEE TVCG*, 15(6):1137–44, 2009.

[24] M. Wang, N. Smith, and T. Mitamura. What is the Jeopardy model? A quasi-synchronous grammar for QA. In *Proc. of EMNLP-CoNLL*, 2007.

[25] Y. Wu, F. Wei, S. Liu, N. Au, W. Cui, H. Zhou, and H. Qu. OpinionSeer: interactive visualization of hotel customer feedback. *IEEE TVCG*, 16(6):1109–18, 2010.

[26] K. Yatani, M. Novati, A. Trusty, and K. N. Truong. Review spotlight: a user interface for summarizing user-generated reviews using adjective-noun word pairs. In *CHI '11*, page 1541, 2011.

[27] Yelp Academic Dataset. http://www.yelp.com/academic_dataset.

Geo-Topo Maps: Hybrid Visualization of Movement Data over Building Floor Plans and Maps

Quentin Ventura*   Michael J. McGuffin†

École de technologie supérieure

ABSTRACT

We demonstrate how movements of multiple people or objects within a building can be displayed on a network representation of the building, where nodes are rooms and edges are doors. Our representation shows the direction of movements between rooms and the order in which rooms are visited, while avoiding occlusion or overplotting when there are repeated visits or multiple moving people or objects. We further propose the use of a hybrid visualization that mixes geospatial and topological (network-based) representations, enabling focus-in-context and multi-focal visualizations. An experimental comparison found that the topological representation was significantly faster than the purely geospatial representation for three out of four tasks.

Index Terms: I.3.6 [Computer Graphics]: Methodology and Techniques—Interaction techniques

1 INTRODUCTION

Various technologies now allow people, vehicles, and other objects to be tracked over space and time. GPS is commonly used to track outdoor movements, while active badges, RFID, and security cameras can be used to track movements inside a building. Such data can be challenging to visualize and understand, even for small numbers of moving objects over short time spans.

For example, Figure 1.a shows simulated movements of just 3 people within a building. As in typical office buildings, the doorways and hallways are narrow compared to the size of rooms. This creates chokepoints or bottlenecks that people must pass through, causing trajectories to overlap each other. It is also difficult to convey the progression of time within such a 2D map. Although we can see that the red trajectory passes through all 5 rooms labelled A through E, it is difficult to see in what order these rooms are traversed, or if any rooms are visited more than once by the red trajectory. Thus, we have two main problems: first, it is difficult or impossible to see the direction of individual motions and the order in which locations are visited; and second, occlusion makes it difficult to distinguish individual trajectories. A third problem, not immediately apparent but nonetheless important, is that the user may be interested in seeing the details of activities and movements within two rooms that are far from each other, and not need to see the details of movements between these two rooms.

Figure 1.b shows a topological view that provides a solution to some of these problems. Rather than showing the detailed shape of the raw movement data, it shows transitions between nodes, where each node represents a room (or corridor), and each edge is a doorway. Movements are drawn in such a way as to disambiguate them, eliminating occlusion. The diamond icons mark the beginning of each trajectory. Furthermore, movements follow the "right-hand

---

*e-mail: quentin.ventura.1@ens.etsmtl.ca

†e-mail: michael.mcguffin@etsmtl.ca

Graphics Interface Conference 2014
7-9 May, Montreal, Quebec, Canada

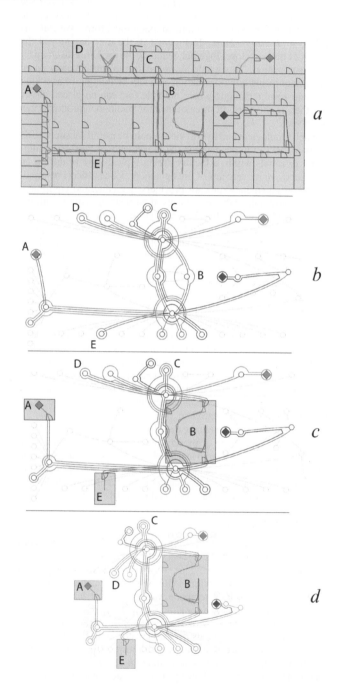

Figure 1: *a:* Movements of 3 people within a floor plan. *b:* Topological view. *c:* Hybrid view showing details and context. *d:* Rooms of interest moved closer together, reducing the visualization's total size, allowing the user to zoom in while preserving context.

traffic" rule, making the direction of every movement segment implicit. The red person travels from A, through B, C, D, back to C, and then ends at E. As long as the number of moving people or objects is not too large, and the user is more interested in the temporal ordering of transitions than detailed motion within each room, this view solves the problems of showing direction, temporal ordering, and occlusion.

Figure 1.c shows a hybrid mixture of the two previous views, yielding a focus-in-context visualization, where the user can see the details of movements in the rooms of interest, and also see the surrounding context in its simplified topological form. We call this hybrid a *Geo-Topo Map*. In Figure 1.d, the user has moved the rooms of interest closer together, reducing the total area taken up by the visualization. This would allow the user to subsequently zoom in without losing any information, and can be thought of as a kind of multi-focal technique where multiple foci can be placed closer together. In this way, all three of the aforementioned problems can be solved.

Such topological and hybrid views could be useful for supporting analytic tasks in understanding the movements of workers, equipment, or robots within a factory during typical days or during an emergency, or movements of fire fighters or police officers responding to an emergency, or care providers, patients, and equipment within a hospital, or the movements of workers or visitors within a museum or building with a mixture of public (open) and private (secure) rooms. Certain building layouts, such as airports or hospitals or campuses, may cover large geographic areas, hence a multi-focal technique could be useful in simultaneously viewing the detailed activity in two or more rooms separated by long hallways, intermediate rooms, or courtyards that are of less interest.

Our work investigates the use of these topological and hybrid visualizations of movement data. Other recent work has proposed several ways of visualizing spatio-temporal data [2], some of which use aggregation to scale up to large movement datasets [1, 17, 27, 25]. In contrast, our approach does not scale up to large numbers of moving objects, but has the advantage of showing each individual moving object or person. Our approach could thus provide an intermediate level of abstraction, in between aggregation of many objects at one extreme, and showing the detailed shape of the trajectories at the other extreme.

Our contributions are (1) the use of circular arcs around nodes to show temporal ordering of movements in topological views, (2) a hybrid mixture of geospatial and topological views, (3) a discussion of design issues, and (4) an experimental comparison of geospatial (i.e., floor plan) views and topological views that found topological views to be significantly faster for certain tasks.

2 RELATED WORK

Andrienko and Andrienko [2] present an overview of approaches for visualizing spatio-temporal data. We briefly survey a few here.

One way to analyze previous work is in the way it maps data variables to the visualization. Movement data can be characterized as having a single temporal variable and at least two spatial variables (latitude and longitude, and sometimes altitude). 2-dimensional line graphs, with a horizontal time axis, can be used to show changes in movements over time, such as in [6], where spatial position is shown as a distance (with respect to some reference location) on the vertical axis, as a function of time. Other systems use a 3D visualization, showing time, latitude, and longitude simultaneously [15]. Certain systems allow the user to interactively change the mapping of data variables to axes [13]. TripVista [11] computes multiple attributes on movement segments, and uses parallel coordinates to visualize the resulting multivariate data. Our own work maintains the familiar 2D spatial layout in the visualization, making it easy for users to relate the visualization to a floor plan, however our approach also uses graphic techniques to show

temporal information within the 2D layout.

Previous work has also provided the user with a lens for filtering or selection, or some kind of magnification or focal capability [24, 12, 16]. Our system does not implement a lens, however our hybrid visualization can be thought of as showing one or more foci within a surrounding topological view.

General techniques for aggregation are surveyed in [10]. Aggregation of many movements and/or many moving objects can provide the user with an overview of large movement data sets, and has been demonstrated in [1, 17, 27, 25]. Our current work is not focused on aggregation of multiple moving objects. However, Shneiderman's classic mantra [22] recommends that the user be able to drill down into the details of an overview, and our approach might be useful to invoke when the user wishes to drill an overview of a massive movement dataset.

Our approach is more closely related to techniques that simplify the shape of spatial trajectories, and that show movements as discrete transitions between locations. Henry Beck's London Underground Tube map is famous for having made subway maps easier to read. Such maps can be seen to discretize locations (subway stations), and have been updated in recent work [24]. However, we are unaware of previous topological maps of subways that show the movements of individuals within the subway system. Visits [23] displays two views of data: a geographic map, and a linear sequence of local maps, with the two views linked with curves. Compared to our hybrid approach, Visits has the advantages of making the linear sequence of locations very apparent, and also shows the full geographic information of the surrounding context. Our hybrid approach, however, has the advantages of embedding geospatial details within the topological view (yielding a single, integrated view), and can also show the movements of multiple individuals.

Finally, our hybrid approach is comparable to other hybrids like TreeMatrix [20], where one type of visualization is *nested* [14] within another. It can also be thought of as a focus-in-context, multi-focal visualization technique [5], with geospatial (floor plan) views providing the details, and a topological view providing the surrounding context.

3 TOPOLOGICAL REPRESENTATION

Our topological views are based on *space-portal* graphs, a term used by [26]. The space of the original movement data is partitioned into regions (such as rooms in a floor plan, or countries in a geographic map). The space-portal graph is then defined with one node for each region, and one edge for each "portal" (doorway, border crossing, etc.) Note that in the case of a floor plan, the rooms *and hallways* (corridors) each correspond to a node.

Blaas et al. [3] introduced "smooth graphs" to display transitions across 2 or more nodes as curved links with animated textures to show direction. The curved links in their system often overlap. We instead chose an approach that would eliminate all overlap between trajectories in the topological view, at the expense of requiring a band of space along each edge whose thickness is linear in the number of traversals. This band of space, within which traversals are drawn, is comparable to the space reserved for edge bundles in [18]. Figure 2 illustrates. Around each node is a local polar coordinate system. Within this coordinate system, the radius corresponds to *time of arrival* of each person or object, increasing outward. Thus, trajectories with a smaller radius arrived earlier in the room (or hallway). The angle of the trajectory within the polar coordinate system is determined simply by the direction toward the previous (or next) node in the trajectory.

This use of circular arcs of increasing radius around each node is somewhat similar to how kelp diagrams [7] increment the "thickness" (radius) of subsets around nodes to visually disambiguate them, or to how circular arcs are laid out in AlertWheel [9].

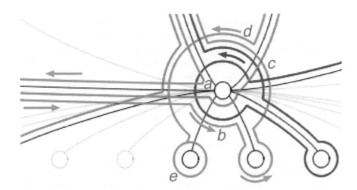

Figure 2: Enlarged view of Figure 1.b, centered on a node corresponding to a hallway. Movement along graph edges follows the "right-hand traffic" rule, and movement around nodes is always counterclockwise. Arrows were added for illustration only, and are implicit in the visualization. Movement segments farther out from graph edges or from node centers occur later in time. Green travels through points *a*, *b*, *c*, and *d* in chronological order, finally ending at *e*.

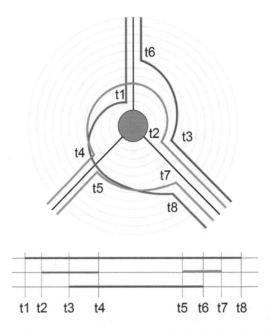

Figure 3: *Top:* a mock-up of an alternative design for the circular arcs around a node, showing progression of time within each node. *Bottom:* a gantt chart for the node.

To convey the direction of trajectories in our system, we employed a metaphor based on how cars drive on the right side of the roads in most countries. Once the user is accustomed to this, they can easily tell the direction of motion, without any arrow heads or animations being displayed. (In our user study, described later, most users appeared to understand this metaphor with little explanation.) Furthermore, trajectories always move counterclockwise around nodes. Thus, the circular arcs sometimes cover an angle greater than 180 degrees, such as the blue arc in Figure 2, to maintain this convention.

In our system, the radius of each circular arc around the nodes is held constant and determined solely by arrival time, thus the user cannot know in what order people or objects *leave* a node. An alternative design is sketched in Figure 3, where the radius of the arcs is gradually increased as time progresses. In theory, this conveys the arrival and departure time of each trajectory, and should allow the user to see if two trajectories are within the same node simultaneously. However, we found this design to be somewhat difficult to interpret, and so implemented the one in Figure 2.

3.1 Alternative Graph-Based Models of Topology

In this section, we briefly consider other kinds of graphs for modeling the topological relationships in a floor plan, that could plausibly result in simpler and easier-to-understand visualizations. The analysis that follows will help ensure that we have properly considered the potential alternatives before settling on a final choice.

As a brief reminder, given a graph of N nodes and E edges, if the graph is connected, then $E \geq N - 1$. If the graph is planar, then the embedding of the graph in the plane divides the plane into R regions (including the exterior region), where $R = E - N + 2$ (by Euler's formula).

Now, consider a floor plan with r rooms and d doors. Let $r_i < r$ be the number of rooms with i doors each, e.g., r_1 is the number of rooms with 1 door each. Also let r_{i+} be the number of rooms with i or more doors each, e.g., r_{3+} is the number of rooms with at least 3 doors each. In the example of Figure 4.a, we have $r = 11$, $d = 14$, $r_1 = 5$, $r_2 = 3$, $r_{3+} = 3$.

The space-portal graph for the floor plan is constructed with r nodes and d edges. If a pathway exists between every pair of rooms, then the space-portal graph is connected, and $d \geq r - 1$. If furthermore the floor plan is planar (e.g., the floor plan is for a single floor of a building), then the number of regions in the space-portal graph is $d - r + 2$. In the example of Figure 4.b, there are $14 - 11 + 2 = 5$ regions.

Other graphs can be constructed that contain the same information as in the space-portal graph, but that may be visually simpler. First, consider the *geometric dual* of the space-portal graph, which is constructed by replacing each region with a node, and adding an edge between two nodes if and only if the corresponding regions in the original space-portal graph are adjacent along an edge. The resulting geometric dual has $d - r + 2$ nodes, d edges (including r_1 self-loops), and r regions, i.e., the same number of edges as the original space-portal graph, but with the numbers of nodes and regions swapped. Figure 4.c illustrates.

Consider also the *hypergraph dual* of the space-portal graph, which we call the portal-space graph. The hypergraph dual is constructed by interchanging nodes and edges, yielding a portal-space graph with d nodes (each of degree 2) and r hyperedges (each incident on 1 or more nodes). In Figure 4.d, nodes are drawn as unlabelled points, and hyperedges as closed curves.

Finally, Figure 4.e shows an alternative drawing of the hypergraph dual, where rooms having 2 doors are drawn more simply as open curve segments connecting their two doors, and rooms having only 1 door are drawn only as a label near the corresponding door.

To compare the visual complexity of these graphs, we assume that small, localized elements (points, nodes, and labels) incur a negligible cost, and we only count up the number of extended curves or line-like elements in the following table.

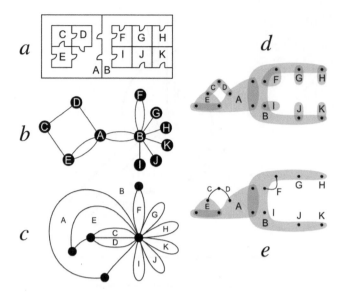

Figure 4: *a:* Original floor-plan. *b:* Space-portal graph, where each node is a room, and each edge is a door. *c:* The geometric dual of the space-portal graph, where each region is a room, and each edge is a door. *d:* The portal-space graph, where each node is a door, and each hyperedge is a room. *e:* A simpler way of drawing the portal-space graph.

	number of open curves or non-loop edges	number of closed curves (self-loops or subsets)	total
Space-Portal Graph (r nodes, d edges, ($d-r+2$) regions)	d	0	d
Geometric Dual (($d-r+2$) nodes, d edges, r regions)	$d-r_1$	r_1	d
Portal-Space Graph (d nodes, r hyperedges)	0	r	r
Simplified Portal-Space Graph (d nodes, r hyperedges)	r_2	r_{3+}	$r-r_1$

Comparing the "total" column, and keeping in mind $d \geq r-1$, we see that the simplified portal-space graph generally requires fewer curved elements to be drawn, especially if there are many 1-door rooms. In our personal experience, 1-door rooms are common in office buildings. The simplified portal-space graph may be a promising avenue for future research into simplified topological representations of floor plan data, especially large building floors with many small offices.

Despite the possible advantages of the portal-space graph, we must keep in mind that we seek not only a representation of topological relationships between rooms, but also a way to show movements through rooms without occlusion. In the portal-space graph, because the doors in it are drawn as points, it is unclear how to draw multiple trajectories traveling through doors while avoiding occlusion or overplotting. For this reason, we finally decided to stick to using normal space-portal graphs in our visualizations, where nodes represent rooms.

4 GEO-TOPO MAPS

As already discussed, Figure 1 shows how the topological and geospatial (e.g., floor plan) views can be mixed into a hybrid.

We call these hybrid visualizations *Geo-Topo Maps*. Figure 5 is a mock-up illustrating that our topological and hybrid techniques are not limited to building floor plans. They can be applied to any movement data over a space that has been partitioned into regions, whether these be rooms or countries.

4.1 Implementation

Our prototype implementation can display data in all the forms shown in Figure 1. The user can lasso select multiple nodes (or rooms) and toggle their representation between the topological style and the geospatial (floor plan) style.

In addition, a time slider allows the user to navigate through time, and see small colored diamond icons move along the trajectories to indicate the current positions of people. In the geospatial mode, these diamond icons move smoothly in response to the time slider. However, in the topological mode, the icons jump instantaneously across edges, from one node to another, because such jumps correspond to the instantaneous traversal of a doorway. In future work, we suspect it would be worthwhile to introduce piecewise "ramp" functions that cause the icons to gradually travel over edges in response to the time slider, making them easier to follow by the user, even though such smooth motion would not be a completely accurate reflection of the true movement data which moves from room to room instantaneously.

4.2 Example Applications

Hybrid Geo-Topo maps could be used to summarize the activities of a single person. For example, a typical factory worker might move between two machine rooms, a cafeteria, and a washroom, and these different rooms might be separated by many intermediate rooms where the worker does not stop. A hybrid Geo-Topo map could display detailed activities within each room of interest, and summarize the intermediate movements with the topological representation. A Geo-Topo map could also display the movements of 2 or 3 different kinds of employees, making clearer which rooms are used exclusively by one type of employee, and which ones are used by multiple types of employees, and in what order. Such visualizations might be useful for planning changes to building layout, comparing alternative layouts, or improving assembly lines. Geo-Topo maps could also be used to summarize the peculiar movements of an outlier (e.g., a thief or spy). Hospitals, campuses, and airports cover large areas and could particularly benefit from topological summarization of intermediate regions.

In certain scenarios, multiple people are involved in passing a physical item from person to person. For example, a bomb or suitcase might be passed from accomplice to accomplice throughout a large building, and being able to retrospectively visualize the meetings between one suspect and other people with detailed geospatial views could help an analyst reconstruct a chain of people and then visually summarize their analysis with a Geo-Topo map. Infections that are spread through physical contact might also be visualized with a Geo-Topo map, using geospatial views to show possible contacts between people, and topological views to summarize intermediate movements.

A purely topological view could also be used to show movements of buses within a road network, helping users to see which buses they can take to travel from one location to another.

5 EXPERIMENTAL COMPARISON

To investigate the performance advantages that the topological view might have over a geospatial view, we compared both in a controlled experiment. The hybrid mixture of visualizations was not evaluated in this experiment, since we wished to first compare each visualization technique in its "pure" (non-hybrid) form.

Four kinds of tasks were given to users. Each task required the user to answer a multiple-choice question about the dataset being

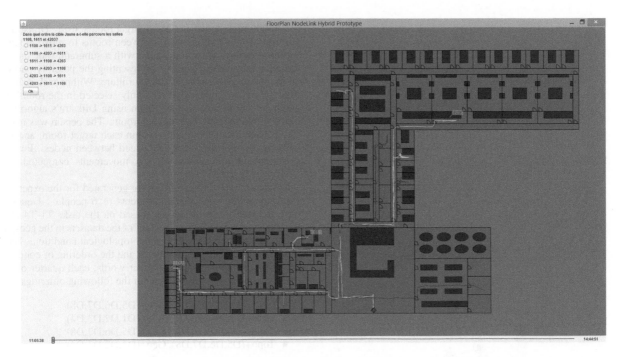

Figure 6: The user interface shown to the user during the experiment, in the geospatial (floor plan) condition. The multiple-choice question appears in the upper left corner, and the time slider widget is along the bottom. Note that the large room in the middle bottom contains virtual furniture (not displayed), requiring individuals to move around the furniture within the room.

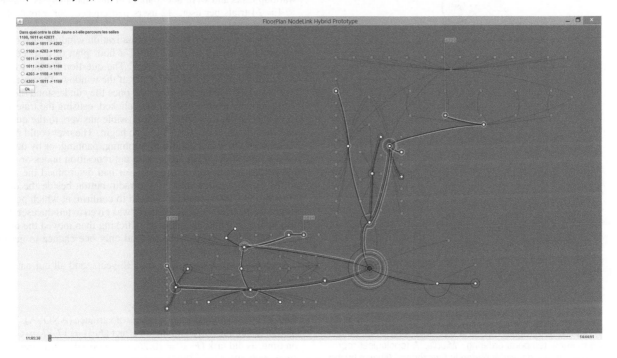

Figure 7: The user interface shown to the user during the experiment, in the topological condition.

viewed, either using the geospatial (floor plan) or topological visualization. The four tasks were based on the following template questions:

- T1: How many times did person X visit room Y? (6 possible answers, varying from "1 time" to "6 times".)
- T2: In what order did person X visit rooms U, V and W? (6 possible answers, covering all permutations such as "U → V → W", "U → W → V", etc.)

- T3: Which person arrived first in room U? (6 possible answers, covering all 6 people in the dataset.)
- T4: How many persons visited both rooms U and V? (6 possible answers, varying from "1" to "6".)

Note that the locations of rooms mentioned in the questions were indicated with red labels on the visualizations, in both conditions.

Synthetic datasets were generated for the experiment. Although this carries the risk of being less realistic as data, it has the advan-

163

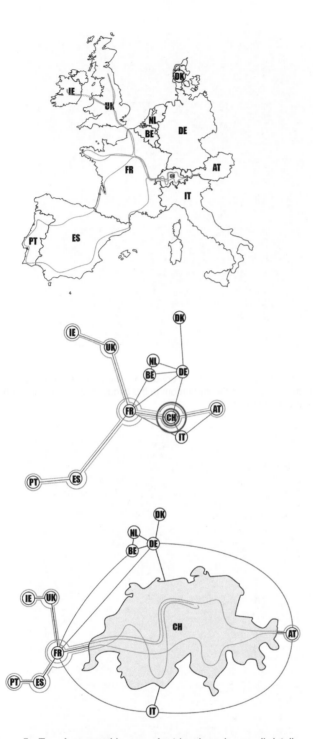

Figure 5: *Top:* A geographic map of a trip, obscuring small details and failing to show temporal ordering. *Middle:* A topological representation shows that the traveler began in Switzerland (shown by the small, dark circle around CH) and traveled through various countries to finally return to the same country (shown by the large, dark circle around CH). *Bottom:* A hybrid view allows the user to zoom in on details within Switzerland, while preserving the essential information about the surrounding contextual countries.

tage of being far more amenable to controlling the characteristics of the data, which is important for a controlled experiment. For each dataset, movements of 6 people were simulated within the building layout shown in Figures 6 and 7. Each simulated person was made

to walk through between 3 and 6 target rooms, using Dijkstra's algorithm to find shortest paths between rooms to move along. In addition, each room was modeled with a subgraph (not shown in the topological visualization), representing the possibly pathways within the room around pieces of furniture. Within each room, between 1 and 11 nodes were randomly selected in the room's subgraph for the person to visit, again using Dijkstra's algorithm to move within the subgraph of each room. The person was made to stay between 5 to 15 minutes within each target room, and move with an approximately constant speed between nodes. Finally, a small amount of noise was added to movements, computed from a *wandering* behavior [19].

8 datasets (D1 through D8) were generated for the experiment, each containing generated movements of 6 people. 4 questions were prepared for each dataset, based on the tasks T1-T4 above. Each user performed tasks with half of the datasets in the geospatial condition, and the other half in the topological condition. The assignment of datasets to conditions, and the ordering of conditions, was fully counterbalanced. In other words, each quarter of users performed tasks according to one of the following orderings:

- Geo+(D1,D2,D3,D4), Topo+(D5,D6,D7,D8)
- Geo+(D5,D6,D7,D8), Topo+(D1,D2,D3,D4)
- Topo+(D1,D2,D3,D4), Geo+(D5,D6,D7,D8)
- Topo+(D5,D6,D7,D8), Geo+(D1,D2,D3,D4)

Each user thus performed a total of 8 datasets × 4 trials/dataset = 32 trials. Of these, the tasks performed with D1 and D5 were warmup tasks and were not counted in the final analysis, leaving 6 × 4 = 24 trials per user. 12 users participated, for a total of 288 trials collected.

At the start of each trial, the visualization window showed only the building layout (in the form of a floor plan or a space-portal graph), with no visible trajectories. The question for the trial was also visible, in the upper-left corner of the window. The participant was asked to read the question, and once they understood the question and were ready to begin, they clicked, causing the trajectories to be displayed, as well as the 6 possible answers to the question, and causing the timer for the trial to begin. The user could then interact with the visualization, by zooming, panning, or by dragging on the time slider. (The user could not reposition nodes or rooms; the layout was fixed.) Once the user had determined the answer to the question, they selected the radio button beside the desired answer and clicked the "Ok" button to confirm, at which point the timer was stopped. Visual feedback was given to tell the user if they succeeded or failed the question. Clicking then moved the user on to the next trial. Thus, the user had only one chance to get each question correct.

Users ranged in age from 20 to 36 years, and all but one had a background in engineering.

5.1 Results

Results were analyzed using analysis of variance (ANOVA). Visualization technique had a significant effect ($F_{1,11} = 17.17$, $p < 0.001$) on time, as did task ($F_{3,33} = 10.26$, $p < 0.00001$). Ordering had no significant effect ($p > 0.05$) on time.

Neither the visualization technique nor the task had a significant effect on error rate ($p > 0.05$). In the geospatial condition, the error rates for the four tasks T1-T4 were 5.6, 0.0, 11.1, and 11.1%, respectively. In the topological condition, they were 5.6, 16.7, 2.8, and 5.6%, respectively.

Users were asked to give subjective ratings of the interface, and found it "intuitive" (3.91/5), "easy to learn" (4.36/5), and were "able to accomplish what [they] wanted to do" (4.82/5).

Further analyzing time, the topological visualization was significantly faster for tasks T1, T3, and T4, but significantly slower for task T2 (Figure 8).

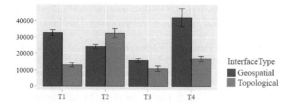

Figure 8: Median times in milliseconds, with 95% confidence intervals. Within each task type, the two visualization techniques were significantly different.

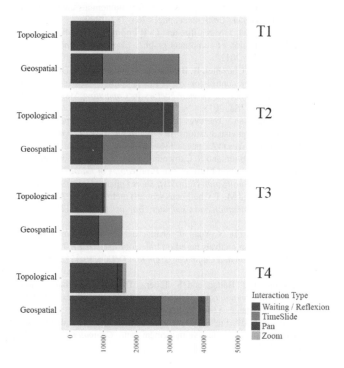

Figure 9: Average times in milliseconds, broken down by the fraction of time spent by the user not dragging on anything (red), interacting with the time slider (blue), performing pan operations (green), and zooming (yellow).

Figure 9 breaks down times by how much time the user spent performing camera or time slider operations. Notice that in the topological condition, the user spent very little time dragging on the time slider, in contrast with the geospatial (floor plan) condition. In the topological condition, tasks T1 and T3 could be performed by simply looking at the circular arcs surrounding the node mentioned in the question, and we suspect this is what users actually did, allowing them to complete the task quickly, whereas the same tasks in the geospatial condition required interacting with the time slider. Task T4 could be completed, in theory, simply by looking at the colors of trajectories present in the two rooms mentioned in the question, however in practice this was difficult to do in the geospatial condition due to occlusion hiding the trajectories.

Task T2 was the only one where the geospatial condition was faster. This task could be completed by the user in the topological condition by using one's eyes to follow the trajectory through the rooms, and from Figure 9, it seems that users made very little use of the time slider in this condition. However, using the time slider to complete this task in the geospatial condition turned out to be faster, as the user could watch the motion of the diamond icons as

they dragged on the slider.

Returning to tasks T1 and T3, and noticing the large difference in time slider use between geospatial and topological, we conjecture that the topological condition would continue to be faster even with datasets involving longer durations of time. Such datasets would presumably require more time slider scrolling when viewed in geospatial form, while not requiring more time to interpret the circular arcs around nodes in the topological form.

5.2 Potential Improvements

The experimental results suggest that the topological view may be more appropriate for summarizing activity within a single room (tasks T1 and T3), whereas the time slider in the geospatial condition was best for showing the order in which rooms are visited (task T2). With other data sets, however, dragging on a time slider to cause the diamond icons to re-enact the movements of individuals could be problematic: long time spans might make the time slider's gain too high, and individuals who spend many hours in one room could be reflected in diamond icons that are motionless for most of the user's drag and then suddenly jump to another room. Two ways this could be improved, in both the topological and geospatial views, are: (1) allowing the user to drag directly on a trajectory (either in the geospatial or topological forms) to navigate through time, similar to dragging on moving objects within videos [8] and animations [21] to implicitly move from frame to frame; and (2) displaying rapid animations of the movements of individuals whenever the user rolls their cursor over a trajectory (e.g., repeatedly "plucking" a trajectory with the cursor could cause the animation to replay over and over, giving the user a sense of the order in which locations are visited).

In the topological view, at least three avenues exist to improve scalability: (1) hallways could be broken up into shorter, simpler segments connected by virtual doors, making the topological view easier to understand and less distorted with fewer individuals traversing each part of the hallway; (2) multiple similar trajectories might be aggregated to compute a "median trajectory" [4] that is displayed to summarize the entire group or cluster; (3) rooms visited many times might be enlarged whenever the cursor passes over the room, similar to a magnification lens or popup view, making it easier to examine the multiple circular arcs surrounding the room.

6 CONCLUSIONS AND FUTURE DIRECTIONS

The topological visualization we have presented can be applied to movement data where space has been partitioned into regions, such as rooms or countries. It has the advantage of simplifying the shapes of trajectories to show the order in which regions (rooms, countries, etc.) are visited, while avoiding occlusion between multiple individuals. The direction of these trajectories can be clearly interpreted, thanks to the use of a metaphor based on the right-hand traffic rule, and the order in which each trajectory arrives at a node is also clearly shown.

Furthermore, when the topological view is mixed with the geospatial view, we obtain a hybrid visualization affording multiple foci-in-context, allowing the user to see detailed movement trajectories where desired.

Our experimental comparison established that the topological visualization is superior to the geospatial visualization for certain tasks, but not all. This further motivates the investigation of combinations of the two visualizations, to benefit from the advantages of both techniques.

As a next step, future work could experimentally evaluate different combinations of geospatial and topological visualizations. For example, a user interface with two coordinated views (one purely geospatial, one purely topological, with coordinated highlighting linking the two) could be compared against the hybrid Geo-Topo Map proposed in this paper. The coordinated view interface would theoretically have the advantage of allowing the user to quickly switch (with a fast eye movement) to whatever visual representation is best for the task (or subtask) at hand, whereas the hybrid would allow more screen space to be devoted to the one representation, and also avoid the user having to move their eyes back and forth between two views.

Other future directions include modifying the visual design of the circular arcs in the topological visualization to indicate when two people are in the same room at the same time (allowing the user to easily perceive meetings), and developing ways to scale the topological visualization up to a larger number of nodes (perhaps by allowing nodes to be collapsed into meta-nodes) and a larger number of moving people or objects.

ACKNOWLEDGEMENTS

Thanks to the participants in our study for their valuable time, and to the members of the HIFIV research group at ÉTS for their feedback. This research was supported by an NSERC Strategic Project Grant.

REFERENCES

[1] N. Andrienko and G. Andrienko. Spatial generalization and aggregation of massive movement data. *IEEE Transactions on Visualization and Computer Graphics (TVCG)*, 17(2):205–219, 2011.

[2] N. Andrienko and G. Andrienko. Visual analytics of movement: An overview of methods, tools and procedures. *Information Visualization*, 12(1):3–24, 2013.

[3] J. Blaas, C. P. Botha, E. Grundy, M. W. Jones, R. S. Laramee, and F. H. Post. Smooth graphs for visual exploration of higher-order state transitions. *IEEE Transactions on Visualization and Computer Graphics (TVCG)*, 15(6):969–976, 2009.

[4] K. Buchin, M. Buchin, M. van Kreveld, M. Löffler, R. I. Silveira, C. Wenk, and L. Wiratma. Median trajectories. *Algorithmica*, 66(3):595–614, 2013.

[5] A. Cockburn, A. Karlson, and B. B. Bederson. A review of overview+detail, zooming, and focus+context interfaces. *ACM Computing Surveys (CSUR)*, 41(1), 2008.

[6] T. Crnovrsanin, C. Muelder, C. Correa, and K.-L. Ma. Proximity-based visualization of movement trace data. In *Proceedings of IEEE Visual Analytics Science and Technology (VAST)*, 2009.

[7] K. Dinkla, M. J. van Kreveld, B. Speckmann, and M. A. Westenberg. Kelp diagrams: Point set membership visualization. *Computer Graphics Forum*, 31(3):875–884, 2012.

[8] P. Dragicevic, G. Ramos, J. Bibliowitcz, D. Nowrouzezahrai, R. Balakrishnan, and K. Singh. Video browsing by direct manipulation. In *Proceedings of ACM Conference on Human Factors in Computing Systems (CHI)*, pages 237–246, 2008.

[9] M. Dumas, J.-M. Robert, and M. J. McGuffin. AlertWheel: Radial bipartite graph visualization applied to intrusion detection system alerts. *IEEE Network, Special Issue on Network Visualization*, 26(6):12–18, 2012.

[10] N. Elmqvist and J.-D. Fekete. Hierarchical aggregation for information visualization: Overview, techniques, and design guidelines. *IEEE Transactions on Visualization and Computer Graphics (TVCG)*, 16(3):439–454, 2010.

[11] H. Guo, Z. Wang, B. Yu, H. Zhao, and X. Yuan. TripVista: Triple perspective visual trajectory analytics and its application on microscopic traffic data at a road intersection. In *Proceedings of IEEE Pacific Visualization (PacificVis)*, 2011.

[12] J.-H. Haunert and L. Sering. Drawing road networks with focus regions. *IEEE Transactions on Visualization and Computer Graphics (TVCG)*, 17(12):2555–2562, 2011.

[13] C. Hurter, B. Tissoires, and S. Conversy. FromDaDy: Spreading aircraft trajectories across views to support iterative queries. *IEEE Transactions on Visualization and Computer Graphics (TVCG)*, 15(6):1017–1024, 2009.

[14] W. Javed and N. Elmqvist. Exploring the design space of composite visualization. In *IEEE Pacific Visualization Symposium (PacificVis)*, pages 1–8, 2012.

[15] T. Kapler and W. Wright. GeoTime information visualization. In *Proceedings of IEEE Symposium on Information Visualization (InfoVis)*, 2004.

[16] R. Krüger, D. Thom, M. Wörner, H. Bosch, and T. Ertl. TrajectoryLenses: A set-based filtering and exploration technique for long-term trajectory data. *Computer Graphics Forum*, 32(3pt4):451–460, 2013.

[17] H. Liu, Y. Gao, L. Lu, S. Liu, H. Qu, and L. M. Ni. Visual analysis of route diversity. In *Proceedings of IEEE Visual Analytics Science and Technology (VAST)*, pages 171–180, 2011.

[18] S. Pupyrev, L. Nachmanson, and M. Kaufmann. Improving layered graph layouts with edge bundling. In *International Symposium on Graph Drawing (GD)*, 2010.

[19] C. W. Reynolds. Steering behaviors for autonomous characters. In *Game Developers Conference*, pages 763–782, 1999.

[20] S. Rufiange, M. J. McGuffin, and C. P. Fuhrman. TreeMatrix: A hybrid visualization of compound graphs. *Computer Graphics Forum*, 31(1):89–101, 2012.

[21] S. Santosa, F. Chevalier, R. Balakrishnan, and K. Singh. Direct space-time trajectory control for visual media editing. In *Proceedings of ACM Conference on Human Factors in Computing Systems (CHI)*, pages 1149–1158, 2013.

[22] B. Shneiderman. The eyes have it: A task by data type taxonomy for information visualizations. In *Proceedings of IEEE Symposium on Visual Languages (VL)*, pages 336–343, 1996.

[23] A. Thudt, D. Baur, and S. Carpendale. Visits: A spatiotemporal visualization of location histories. In *Proceedings of Eurographics Conference on Visualization (EuroVis), Short Papers*, pages 79–83, 2013.

[24] Y.-S. Wang and M.-T. Chi. Focus+context metro maps. *IEEE Transactions on Visualization and Computer Graphics (TVCG)*, 17(12):2528–2535, 2011.

[25] Z. Wang, M. Lu, X. Yuan, J. Zhang, and H. van de Wetering. Visual traffic jam analysis based on trajectory data. *IEEE Transactions on Visualization and Computer Graphics (TVCG)*, 19(12):2159–2168, 2013.

[26] E. Whiting, J. Battat, and S. Teller. Topology of urban environments. In *Computer-Aided Architectural Design Futures (CAADFutures) 2007*, pages 114–128. Springer, 2007.

[27] W. Zeng, C.-W. Fu, S. M. Arisona, and H. Qu. Visualizing interchange patterns in massive movement data. *Computer Graphics Forum*, 32:271–280, 2013.

How Low Should We Go? Understanding the
Perception of Latency While Inking

Michelle Annett *

University of Alberta
Microsoft Research

Albert Ng †

Applied Sciences Group,
Microsoft

Paul Dietz ‡

Microsoft Research

Walter F. Bischof §

University of Alberta

Anoop Gupta¥

Microsoft Research

ABSTRACT

Recent advances in hardware have enabled researchers to study the perception of latency. Thus far, latency research has utilized simple touch and stylus-based tasks that do not represent inking activities found in the real world. In this work, we report on two studies that utilized writing and sketching tasks to understand the limits of human perception. Our studies revealed that latency perception while inking is worse (~50 milliseconds) than perception while performing non-inking tasks reported previously (~2-7 milliseconds). We also determined that latency perception is not based on the distance from the stylus' nib to the ink, but rather on the presence of a visual referent such as the hand or stylus. The prior and current work has informed the Latency Perception Model, a framework upon which latency knowledge and the underlying mechanisms of perception can be understood and further explored.

Keywords: Latency; delay; responsiveness; stylus; pen; indirect interaction; direct interaction; perception; psychophysics; just-noticeable difference; latency perception model.

Index Terms: B.4.2 Input / Output Devices, H.5.2 User Interfaces: Input devices and strategies, H.1.2. User/Machine Systems: Human factors.

1 INTRODUCTION

While interacting with devices, whether inking, gesturing, or selecting, it is essential to receive feedback about our actions. Users readily notice whenever feedback is unavailable or delayed, adapting their behaviour or interaction styles [26]. On digital devices today, there is typically a 60 to 120 millisecond delay from when the stylus touches the screen until digital ink appears [23]. Caused by both hardware and software factors, such delays decrease user performance [3, 13, 32]. Unlike digital devices, inking with pen and paper incurs zero delay, with the ink flowing from the nib onto the paper, providing instantaneous feedback.

Until recently [3], it was assumed that the delay or latency adequate for direct interaction was on the order of 100 milliseconds [20]. Due to technological advances with high performance hardware, it is now possible to display and examine the influence and perceptibility of much smaller delays, e.g., 1 millisecond, to users [22, 23, 24]. Such hardware has been used to determine the minimum latency required for direct-touch interaction. For example, while tapping with the finger, participants could not distinguish 1 versus 63 milliseconds of delay [13]. While performing a simple box moving task, users could not discriminate

1 versus 6 milliseconds when using the finger [23], but could distinguish 1 versus 2 milliseconds while using a stylus [24].

Although we have learned a great deal about the capabilities of human perception, little is known about latency when increased task complexity and attentional demands are present. Unlike dragging or tapping a target, writing is a cognitively and visually demanding task requiring focus on character size and formation, attention to inter-word spacing, and the ability to ignore cognitive and environmental distractions. Little is known however, about the perceptual processes underlying latency perception or the influence of such conditions on the perception of latency.

In recent work, while performing a stylus-based task that requiring oscillating, scribbling movements, participants were unable to discriminate 7 from 40 milliseconds of latency [24]. Although there is an ecosystem-wide push to make systems faster, such work suggests that these efforts may not be needed. If users perceive two different latencies as being equal, while performing tasks more complex and demanding than tapping, moving a box, or scribbling, it may not be necessary to allocate resources to achieve the latency levels recommended previously. It may be beneficial to reallocate CPU or GPU cycles to improve stroke rendering, integrate pressure or tilt information from the stylus, or improve the recognition of unintended touch. If users are unable to perceive the difference in speed, but readily perceive more realistic looking strokes, delaying ink by 10 or 15 milliseconds may be acceptable if the user experience is improved in other ways.

To understand latency within the context of real-world activities and work towards an understanding of the influencing factors, two experiments were conducted. The aim was not to determine how latency influences performance or develop methods to reduce hardware or software delays, but rather to understand the human perception during real world activities. The first experiment determined the minimal perceivable latency while drawing and writing. Perceived latencies were found to be higher than those previously found with simple dragging and tapping tasks. The experiment also uncovered the importance of task demands and the strategies employed to discriminate latency. These findings motivated the second experiment, which manipulated the location and presence of visual cues and feedback. While make latency judgements, the relative motion of the hand or stylus to the ink was used instead of the distance between the ink and stylus. The results from both experiments, in addition to those from prior work, provided insight into how latency is perceived and helped to form the Latency Perception Model, which provides a blueprint for future explorations into latency perception.

2 RELATED WORK

There has been a variety of work focused on the detection and understanding of latency. Researchers within computer music have strived to determine the ideal latency for musical composition. Early work by Freed et al. and Wright et al. suggested that music controllers should have less than 10 milliseconds latency, as it is at this point that piano players notice delays [9, 34]. Many others have

* email: mkannett@ualberta.ca

† email: v-albeng@microsoft.com

‡ email: paul.dietz@microsoft.com

§ email: wfb@ualberta.ca

¥ email: anoop@microsoft.com

recommended much higher latencies, depending on the type of instrument, genre of music, and the presence of tactile feedback. Maki-Patola and Hamalainen determined that delays between 2 and 30 milliseconds were sufficient while playing a Theremin without tactile feedback [17]. Adelstein et al. found that delays of 24 milliseconds were tolerable while tapping a brick with a hammer [1]. Dahl and Bresin recommended latencies of 55 milliseconds for percussion instruments [6]. While playing collaborative music via network connection, delays of 100 milliseconds were acceptable while playing piano, but only 20 milliseconds while playing an accordion [25]. Using this work as a guide, Montag and colleagues built a low-cost multi-touch tabletop capable of providing low latency audio and haptic feedback to users for music applications [21]. The system focused on improving audio-haptic synchrony, achieving a minimum latency of 30 milliseconds. The fragmented results and recommendations from the computer musical literature demonstrate that many factors, i.e., feedback modality (e.g., tactile, audio, or visual feedback), task, and input, influence the perception of latency during musical composition [16].

Touch and stylus systems have also been used to investigate the perception of latency. Using off-the-shelf touchscreen devices, Anderson, Doherty, and Ganapthy artificially inserted latency into everyday tasks such as reading and web or photo browsing to determine that users tolerated 80 to 580 milliseconds of delay [4]. Work by Ng et al. focused not on tolerance, but on the minimum latency perceivable [23]. By integrating a high-speed DLP projector with a custom high-speed touch sensor they were capable of displaying touch latencies as low as one millisecond. Ng and colleagues determined that users were able to distinguish between one and six milliseconds of latency while dragging a box. Extensions of this work by Jota et al. examined latency while pointing and during the 'land-on' segment of a dragging task [13]. Performance degraded as latency increased during a pointing task and unlike Ng et al.'s box dragging task, participants could not distinguish between 1 and 64 milliseconds during the 'land-on' event. Although Ng and Jota's work probed the boundaries of touch-based latency perception, little information regarding the mechanisms and processes underlying latency perception was provided, nor were stylus-based interactions considered.

While working with a light-pen system, Miller hypothesized that users could tolerate delays on the order of 100 milliseconds when making slow, thoughtful strokes [20]. Although this was the first exploration of latency while using a 'stylus', little justification for this estimate is available. Due to technological limitations, stylus latency has only recently been explored again. Henzen et al. developed an electronic ink display that exhibited zero parallax and minimum latency of 40 milliseconds, but did not leave the proof of concept stage [11, 12]. Unlike Henzen and colleagues' system, our prototype High Performance Stylus System (HPSS) system exhibited zero parallax, and is capable of a one millisecond inking delay while rendering simple shapes and a seven millisecond delay while inking. In previous work with the HPSS, we examined latency perception while participants performed Ng et al.'s box dragging task [23] as well as a scribbling task [24]. We found that participants were able to discriminate between 1 and 2 milliseconds of latency while dragging and 7 and 40 milliseconds of delay while scribbling. As latency perception thus appears to be largely task-dependent and depend upon a multitude of factors, the current study extends our previous work with the HPSS to focus on real-world tasks that have added cognitive load, different loci of attention, and the presence or absence of visual feedback of the hand.

3 JUST NOTICEABLE DIFFERENCE

As the goal of this work was to determine the minimum latency perceivable, it was thus appropriate to use a just-noticeable difference (JND) methodology. With a JND methodology, participants are presented with two stimulus levels and are forced to make a judgment regarding which alternative was brighter, quieter, or in our case, faster. After repeated presentations of various stimuli, one is able to derive the minimum threshold, or *just-noticeable difference* (JND), perceivable for a given stimulus. The JND paradigm converges on a threshold that is the result of participants being unable to distinguish the minimum baseline from all latencies below the converged threshold. Because the task was constant across trials, we assume that participants would be unable to distinguish between any latencies lower than the threshold.

During our experiments, two latencies on each trial, the *baseline,* which was held constant and acted as a reference for the participant, and the *test* or *probe* that was modified on each trial. Although many methods can determine the test value, it is important to choose method that reflect the needs of the experiment. Prior work used staircase methods that have been around since the inception of psychophysics [13, 23]. Given that our experiments required repeated motor movements, a highly efficient method that mitigated fatigue and increased engagement was needed. The more modern Parameter Estimation by Sequential Testing (PEST) adaptive technique [27] met these requirements. This newer methodology produces little variance in the resulting thresholds compared to legacy methods, allows the experiment to be completed faster (30-80 trials), and reduces participant fatigue and boredom. The duration of an experiment using PEST is approximately 10 minutes.

With PEST, the Wald sequential likelihood-ratio test [33] uses the prior history of a participant's responses at a given stimulus level determined the test latency and the amount that the stimulus should increase or decrease by (step size). Once the step size reaches a minimum, in our case 1 millisecond, the experiment concluded (aka the Minimal Overshoot and Undershoot Sequential Estimation technique [18]). This ensured that participants experienced the smallest possible difference between latencies. A maximum latency upper bound was placed on the probe (i.e., 105 milliseconds) to prevent participants from experiencing higher, unreasonable levels of latency. If the probe ever reached this level, the experiment concluded.

To further increase the efficiency of PEST, an initial step size of 10 milliseconds and expected probability of 75% were used, i.e., participants correctly identified the baseline latency on 75% of trials. As the onscreen digital ink required filtering and smoothing via a moving average window, the minimum latency while inking was seven milliseconds. The baseline latency was thus set at seven milliseconds. In an ideal scenario, the baseline latency would be zero milliseconds, but as with all prior work, current technology is unable to achieve such latencies. Motivated by prior work [13, 23], the initial testing latency was set to 55 milliseconds to prevent participants from completing too many trials that would likely be too easy. Across all trials, the presentation order of the baseline and testing latencies were randomized.

4 EXPERIMENT 1: PERCEIVED LATENCY WHILE INKING

To understand latency perception during scenarios that require increased cognitive and attentional demands compared to the tasks used in prior work [24], the first experiment determined the minimum latency perceivable while participants drew simple lines, wrote a word, and sketched a simple shape.

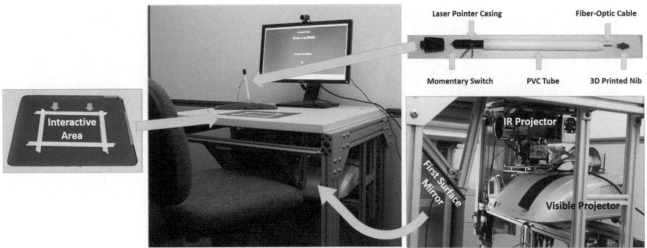

Figure 1: The prototype High Performance Stylus System, which is composed of two high-speed projectors, a first surface mirror for rear projection, and a fibre-optic based stylus. Further details about the hardware can be found in [24].

4.1 Participants

Twelve individuals (3 female) with normal or corrected-to-normal vision were recruited to participate in the study (M = 34, range 23-44 years). All participants were right handed and were naive to the purpose and goals of the experiment during recruitment to remove any bias or experience with latency from pen-enabled systems, touch enabled systems, or video games. A range of participants were recruited, some used tablets and styli daily and whereas others had limited prior exposure. In a pre-experiment questionnaire, twenty-five percent of participants were familiar with latency, through playing video or mobile phone games or through interacting with virtual environments. Each participant was provided a $10 honorarium at the conclusion of the experiment.

4.2 Equipment and Apparatus

To determine the minimum perceivable latency, the prototype High Performance Stylus System (HPSS) system from [24] was used (Figure 1). The HPSS employed two Texas Instrument Discovery 4100 high-speed projector kits [7], a first-surface mirror for rear-projection onto a diffuse surface, and a fibre-optic stylus. The Discovery kits were able to achieve high frame rates using Digital Micromirror Devices (DMD). DMD's contain arrays of micromirrors that modulate light very quickly, allowing binary frames to be projected at a rate in the tens of kHz. The first projector kit rear-projected a series of grey-coded patterns that utilized Lee et al.'s structured light technique [14]. The IR grey-coded patterns were projected at 17,000 frames per second at a resolution of 1920x1080. The patterns uniquely encoded every pixel in the image area. To provide visual feedback in the form of ink, the second Discovery 4100 kit refreshed at 23,000 binary frames per second, with a pixel resolution of 1920x1080. The stylus used a one-millimetre fibre optic cable to detect the grey-coded IR patterns. The fiber fit within a 3D printed 1.2-millimeter UV cured ABS plastic nib affixed to the end of a hollowed out laser pointer case. Opposite the nib was a momentary switch that 'activated' whenever the stylus was pressed against the screen. The stylus was close in weight and size to a Cintiq or Intuos stylus.

As operating system and application layers add latency to any system, the HPSS made use of the Discovery kits' on board Xilinx Virtex 5 FPGAs to decode the grey-code pattern sampled by the stylus and render feedback for the user via the visible projector. High-speed cameras and the method detailed in [23], in addition to

timing on the FPGAs, verified the displayed latencies. As any camera-based approach introduces delays and noise, there is likely plus or minus half of a millisecond of error on the displayed latencies.

Although the High Performance Stylus System is capable of running independently, a HP Z400 Workstation was connected to the system via a serial connection to manipulate the latency values according to PEST. A custom C# and WPF program automatically determined and sent appropriate latency values to the system, gathered latency judgments from participants, and record the JND values for each task. A 21" Dell monitor provided participants feedback about the current task and condition and prompted them for their latency decision. To advance to the next condition and indicate their latency decision, participants pressed the A, B, and space bar keys on a Microsoft Arc keyboard.

4.3 Procedure

At the start of each experiment, participants sat in an adjustable drafting chair in front of the HPSS. The concept of latency was explained to each participant to ensure that they understood the purpose and goals of our experiment. Participants were then informed that they would be performing a number of inking tasks and that we would be measuring the minimum latency that they could perceive during each task. On each trial, participants were informed that two different latencies, A and B, would be presented. Participants were asked to complete the task twice, first at latency A, then latency B. To switch from A to B, participants pressed the space bar. After each trial, participants used the A and B keyboard keys to indicate "which condition exhibited the least delay".

Although explicitly priming participants for latency could influence their behaviour, it was imperative to do so. The use of ambiguous questions probing which condition was 'most preferred' or 'better' would have left too much room for interpretation, indirectly encouraging some participants to focus on other factors or visual cues while making their decisions. It should be noted that any values determined are likely to be higher in a real-world scenario, where latency detection is not paramount in a user's mind.

4.4 Tasks

Three inking tasks were chosen based on their similarity to real world activities: line drawing, writing, and drawing.

In the first task, *line drawing*, participants drew a single vertical line, approximately 2 inches long, from the top to the bottom of the

Figure 2: Tasks used in Experiment 2, from left to right: the line drawing, writing, and drawing tasks.

screen (Figure 2). Participants drew the line wherever they wished and were told to maintain the same length and speed across trials. Such a task was included because it required a short ballistic movement, had low cognitive load, and is commonly performed while annotating or sketching diagrams, (e.g., connect two boxes, underline words, etc.). It thus provided a baseline against which the other tasks could be compared.

With the *writing* task, participants were instructed to write the word 'party' (Figure 2). 'Party' was used because it was required familiar, practised movements and included characters that contained ascending and descending elements with a variety of curved and straight line components (e.g., 'P', 't', 'y'). Although participants may have been able to make a latency judgment from a single stroke or character, they were required to write the whole word on every trial. They were also encouraged to use whichever writing style they were most comfortable with (i.e., printing, handwriting, or a hybrid of the two) and were told to write each character at whichever size they wished, but to maintain the same character size across all trials.

In the *drawing* task, participants drew a six-sided star using one continuous stroke (Figure 2). A six-sided star was used because it contained varying angles, and was less automatic and familiar than other simple shapes. The increased attention and cognitive loading that encouraged slower, deliberate movements. Participants were encouraged to start drawing the star at the same location and maintain the same size of star and general shape across all trials.

All three tasks were counterbalanced to reduce any possible effects of learning and fatigue. A 1-pixel wide line displayed 'ink' while participants performed each task. As we were interested in determining the absolute minimum latency users could perceive, we did not explicitly require participants to complete each trial at a specific speed. The experimenter did monitor each participant via web camera and provided verbal feedback to participants if they appeared to be moving at unnatural speeds. As per the requirements of any JND paradigm, participants were required to perform the same task on each trial. To test different words, shapes, or stroke directions, participants would have had to complete another JND experiment. The experiment lasted approximately 30 minutes.

4.5 Results

As the JND thresholds were not normally distributed, a non-parametric Friedman's ANOVA was performed with task as the only factor (i.e., line drawing, writing, and drawing; Figure 3). The ANOVA revealed that task did not have a significant effect on participant's ability to perceive latency ($X^2(2) = 0.809$, $p = 0.667$, $\omega^2 = 0$). Participants were able to distinguish 7 and 53 milliseconds while line drawing (range: 31-76), 7 versus 50 milliseconds while writing the word 'party' (range: 32-87), and 7 versus 61 milliseconds while drawing the six-sided star (range: 21-82). The median latency across all tasks was 53 milliseconds. The lack of significance between the tasks does not suggest that perceived latency was, or will be, identical for all stylus-based inking

activities. Rather, it suggests that other factors such as the visual cues and reference points available or the motor movements required may be more influential while perceiving latency.

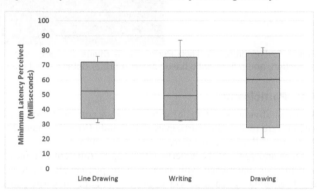

Figure 3: Median latency perceived while performing the writing, drawing, and line drawing tasks. The box boundaries represent the 5th and 95th percentiles.

4.6 Discussion

While performing everyday inking tasks, participants had a higher threshold for detecting latency than what has been found in prior work. For touch and simple box moving tasks, prior recommended target latencies were below 10 milliseconds [23] but approximately 40 milliseconds when scribbling an oscillating line [24]. While performing inking tasks at the 50-millisecond level, many participants had difficulty distinguishing between the baseline and testing latencies, believing that they were the same, "are you sure these aren't the same, they look identical to me", "I swear most of these are the same", and "oh these are impossible now". While moving a simple box to and fro or tapping on the screen, there is very little cognitive or attentional demands placed on the user, hence the lower perceptible latencies attained.

Even though sketching a shape and writing a word appear to be simple, familiar tasks, on the cognitive and attentional levels they are much more complex. The slight increase in perceptible latency found between the inking tasks used presently and those prior [24] is likely due to the present tasks being much more cognitively demanding, requiring pre- and post-planning to ensure that all strokes and characters are well formed, intra-strokes are joined, inter-stroke spacing is appropriate, and higher-level components such as characters and corners were created in the correct order and at the correct time. Such demands were not present in the scribbling task used prior, suggesting that attention and task demands likely influence the perception and detection of latency. This echoes the results found within the computer music literature and requires further investigation, especially in scenarios involving external environmental stimuli and indirect interaction.

Although not significant, there appears to be a larger range in variance as task complexity increases. As writing was more cognitively taxing then drawing the single line, participants had many opportunities and possible points of reference to use when making their latency judgments. With the line drawing task, the short, ballistic nature of the required movements left little time and a smaller set of reference points to judge latency. In the drawing task, many participants reported that they could not focus on latency as much as they could while drawing the simple line or writing because they intently focused on drawing all six points of the star. As the six sided star was an uncommon shape to draw, the increased availability of reference points (compared to the line drawing task) and focus required (compared to writing) lead to larger variability in the thresholds obtained. This observed variability may become even more prolific given a larger experimental population or different experimental stimuli.

In addition to task, post-experiment comments suggested that the natural sensorimotor processes and resulting locus of attention influenced latency perception. When asked how latency judgments were made, participants reported using a variety of strategies:

- Fixated on the eventual end location of the stylus and waited for the ink to catch up
- Fixated on one region of interest and estimated the time between the stylus / hand moving through the area and the ink appearing in the area
- Performed a pursuit movement, following the nib as it moved
- Performed a pursuit movement, following the ink as it appeared
- Alternated between the nib and ink (no saccades)
- Attended to the propagation of the ink's projected light through the translucent nib

Participants largely reported that depending on the task, they felt it was necessary to attend to different areas of the screen or visual cues. A graphic designer indicated that she focused on the global picture while inking, "intently focusing on the ink drawing the last few contour lines, not the lost, implied, or construction lines … the contour lines are the most important". Another participant commented, "when I take notes during a meeting, I rarely look at my tablet … instead I look at the speaker or their presentation. I only look at my tablet to see if I need to scroll for more paper, to fix a mistake, or to occasionally check that the pen is working". Based on such comments, it is clear that the strategy and location of focus are also implicated in the detection of latency.

5   EXPERIMENT 2: ATTENTION AND VISUAL REFERENCE

As Experiment 1 suggested, a number of factors influence the perception of latency. We thus conducted another experiment to determine the extent that the visual and motor systems work together to aid in the perception of latency. Inspired by the differing judgement strategies reported in Experiment 1, we explicitly manipulated the location of the digital ink, forcing attention away from the stylus into other areas of the screen, similar to a poorly calibrated stylus system. If participants focus on the relationship between the nib and ink to make latency judgments, offsetting the location of the ink a variety of distances, should decrease latency perception. If such information is not used, perceived latency should remain unchanged.

We were also interested in the effect of eliminating information about the motion of the stylus and hand, similar to indirect input scenarios. In such scenarios, interaction and visual attention is naturally decoupled, distributed along different planes or different devices. If latency is determined largely by the visual system, removing this reference from the visual field should impact the perception of latency. If latency is largely determined by other systems, such as audio or tactile feedback, signals from the motor system, or cognitive cues, latency perception should remain

constant. We thus manipulated the presence / absence of the hand within the visual field to mimic direct and indirect interaction scenarios.

5.1   Participants

Twelve naïve, right handed individuals (5 female) participated in the study (M = 33 years, range 24-44). Similar to the first experiment, all participants had normal or corrected-to-normal vision and had a range of experience with tablets and styli, some being experts and others complete novices. Thirty-three percent of participants were familiar with latency from playing video games or interacting with virtual environments. Participants were provided a \$10 honorarium for the 30-minute experiment. None of the participants from Experiment 1 participated in this study.

5.2   Equipment, Apparatus, and Procedure

The HPSS and procedure detailed in Experiment 1 was also used in Experiment 2.

5.3   Tasks

Four variations of the line drawing task from the first experiment were used (Figure 4). The line drawing task was chosen over the writing and drawing tasks as it was the simplest, required less time to complete, and induced the least fatigue, all of which were important given the number of conditions.

In the first condition, *no offset*, the ink appeared directly underneath the nib. This was identical to the first experiment and enabled the location of the stylus nib, stylus barrel, and hand to remain in the foveal region. In the second condition, *small offset*, the ink was offset 6.5 millimetres, or approximately one index finger width, to the left of the nib. This offset diverted attention towards the ink, forcing the nib, stylus, and hand into the parafoveal region, closely mimicked scenarios where the stylus is inaccurate. In the third condition, *large offset*, the ink was further offset to the left, approximately 65 millimetres. This condition moved the nib, stylus barrel, and hand from the parafoveal region to the periphery and required much larger saccades to see both locations. Although the third condition would likely not exist in the real world, it was included to enable a comparison with the last condition.

In the last condition, *hand not visible*, the ink was again offset 65 millimetres to the left of the nib but the hand was additionally obscured from view, using a foamboard flange placed vertically in the centre of the screen (Figure 4). Participants were instructed to attend to the left side of the screen, where they could only see the ink, not their hand. Participants did not receive visual information corresponding to the movements they were making.

Similar to the first experiment, all four tasks were counterbalanced to reduce learning and fatigue effects. A 1-pixel wide line provided visual feedback and the experimenter controlled for the speed of drawing.

5.4   Results

As the threshold distributions were not normal, non-parametric analyses were conducted. A Wilcoxon signed-rank test evaluated the influence of viewing the hand with 'hand visible' as the main factor (i.e., visible versus not visible). The results indicated that participants were able to better perceive latency when they could view the pen-wielding hand and stylus (*Mdn* = 59 milliseconds, range: 33-104) compared to not receiving this visual feedback (*Mdn* = 97 milliseconds, range: 59-105), z = -2.86, *p* < 0.005, *r* = -0.58 (Figure 5). The presence or absence of the hand and stylus is thus an important referent and influenced the perception of latency.

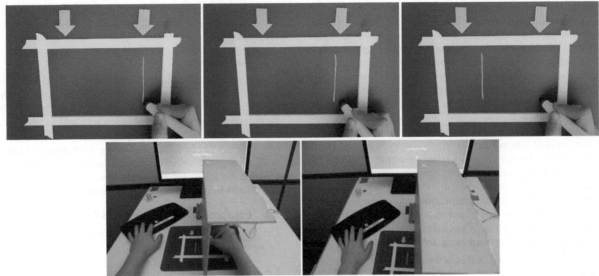

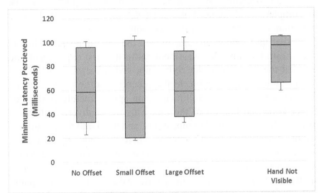

Figure 4: [Top] offsets used in Experiment 2, from left to right: no offset, small offset, and large offset. [Bottom] The hand not-visible condition. (Left) The participants placed their right arm and hand underneath the pink flange. (Right) The experiment from the perspective of the participant, wherein they could not see their hand or the stylus.

Figure 5: Median perceived latency while the ink was not offset, offset a small amount (i.e., 6.5 millimetres), offset to the opposite side of the screen (i.e., 65 millimetres), and while the hand was not visible. The box boundaries represent the 5th and 95th percentiles.

A Friedman's ANOVA examined the influence of the ink offset, (i.e., no offset, small offset, large offset). Offset distance did not have a significant effect on participant's ability to perceive latency ($X^2(2) = 4.167$, $p = 0.125$, $\omega^2 = 0.007$). Participants could distinguish 7 versus 59 milliseconds when no ink offset was present (range: 23-101), 7 versus 50 milliseconds when a small offset was present (range: 18-105) and 7 versus 59 milliseconds when a large offset was used (range: 33-104). Irrespective of the offset used, the median perceived latency was 55 milliseconds, similar to that found in Experiment 1. As there was not a significant difference between the offset conditions, participants likely did not use the distance between the nib and ink to make their judgements, instead relying on the relative movement of the stylus or hand.

5.5 Discussion

The lack of significance between the no, small, and large offset conditions suggests that the distance between the stylus and digital ink is little help while perceiving latency. Many researchers believe the gap between nib and ink is used for judging latency, but participant comments and lab-based studies from the eye-tracking literature corroborate with our results and suggest the opposite. It is actually uncommon for participants to follow the nib continually

with their eyes. Few participants actually reported explicitly focused on the nib, stylus, or distance between the nib and stylus in Experiment 2. This is surprising, given that one would assume such visual elements would be the first cues users would look towards, as the stylus initiates interaction and the ink provides feedback about the action. Scanpath analyses have found that whenever the nib is located in the parafoveal or foveal region, it is often not attended to [2], 5, 8, 19, 29]. Eye-movement patterns have also been found to be largely task and motivation dependent, some preferable for quick inking movements such as sketching, whereas others are more appropriate for reading or editing [10, 28, 29, 30, 31]. Future work is thus needed to understand the specific visual details important for latency perception and where attention is directed during natural inking tasks.

The significant differences found between the hand visible and not visible conditions, in addition to work from the eye-tracking literature, suggests that the motion of the larger elements such as the hand or stylus barrel are valuable cues. In the motor-only condition, i.e., hand not visible, performance plummeted because participants were unable to solely rely on the haptic feedback from their pen-wielding hand or the signals from their motor system to make latency judgements. Once the stylus and hand were visible, even if only in the periphery (i.e., large offset condition), they provided valuable information to participants, in the form of a large moving stimulus and increased latency discrimination. When such visual cues are not present, participants are forced to use cues from other modalities (e.g., haptic, audio, proprioceptive, or cognitive) so performance suffers.

To notice the latency inherent on stylus-enabled devices, it appears necessary for users to see their own hand in their field of view. As interaction and attention were visually and physically divided during the no-hand condition, the increased latency threshold observed from the large offset (59 milliseconds) to no-hand conditions (97 milliseconds) participants may have more difficulty perceiving latency on indirect input devices where the movement of the hand is out of view of the display. Although traditional indirect input devices separate input and output along different planes or devices, the no-hand condition mimicked such a scenario quite well. These findings suggest that. Such findings have implications for the future design and continued use of stylus devices that harness indirect interaction, such as the Wacom Bamboo Connect or Intuos devices. On such devices, sub-100 millisecond latency may not be required. A more focused study would be needed to examine other factors involved with real-world use of indirect input devices (e.g., placement relative to screen and user, size of input space, etc.).

Although there was no difference between the various offset conditions, a few users commented that they preferred the small offset condition because it was "similar to those signature pads at Home Depot or Lowes where the ink is far away from the pen location" and "allowed me to focus on the ink and still see the pen nib without having the nib occlude things or get in the way". Such comments suggest that a pixel-perfect calibration and accuracy may not be needed for a satisfying stylus experience.

Participants additionally commented that varying the speed of their strokes helped them to perceive latency, but this strategy is not supported by our results. While increased pen speeds will increase the visible gap between the pen nib and the visual ink trail, in theory, this will make it easier for participants to perceive lower latency levels. Based on the results from the second experiment, we are not convinced of this. If participants were perceiving latency based on the distance between the nib and ink, as predicted by Weber's law (i.e., the just-noticeable difference between two stimuli is proportional to the magnitude of the stimuli), performance should have decreased as the offset increased.

6 LATENCY PERCEPTION MODEL

While latency is simply the "delay between input action and the output response" [15], our previous and current explorations into latency have determined that the perception of latency is a complex, multi-faceted problem. In Experiment 2, the input action and output response remained the same, yet the perception of latency changed. Initially, participants could use visual information to make judgments but once that was removed, they were forced to use of other information streams, perhaps auditory or tactile cues from the stylus. These alternative data sources affected latency perception.

Based on our work and the prior literature, we have developed a model that describes the perceptual processes underlying latency perception in stylus and touch interaction. The model is composed of five elements: an input *action*, a *referent* stimulus, a *latency source*, output *responses*, and *contextual demands* (Figure 6). The input action can take many forms, e.g., hovering the stylus in the air, touching a finger to the screen, or pressing the stylus against the screen, and is invoked by the observer, another user, or an external system or device. Once the action occurs, it is handled by the latency source (e.g., a sensor array, operating system, application, etc.). This entity converts the input action into output responses and adds delay. The responses are most often visual (e.g., a dot, line, or simple shape), but could manifest themselves via other modalities (e.g., haptic or auditory). As our experiments demonstrated, changes in attention to and the location of responses can influence their use. Prior results using different sized boxes during dragging [13] suggest that the spatial magnitude of responses also affects latency perception.

In addition to supplying the latency source with input, the input action also generates a variety of stimuli, or referents that provide clues to the observer (e.g., stylus barrel, fingernail, hand, stylus nib). Different modalities of the referent likely influence perception as well. In prior work with tapping, the haptic sensation of the finger pad touching and moving along the surface produced an additional referent that assisted in the perception of latency [13, 23]. As the stylus naturally dampens the haptic sensations from the screen, it is likely that in stylus-based scenarios haptic referents play less of a

role. Similar to the output responses, there is spatial and temporal uncertainty about what influences the referents. The referent also need not be a physical stimulus, but may take the form of a cognitive initiation of an action (i.e., a mental 'Go' signal).

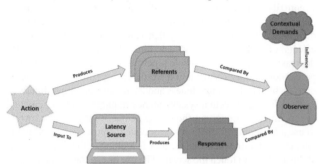

Figure 6: The Latency Perception Model, detailing the role of the input action, the resulting referent stimuli, the latency source, and the output responses. The observer compares the referents and responses when perceiving latency and is likely influenced by contextual demands such as task requirements, loci of attention, environmental factors, etc.

Once the referents or responses are available, the observer compares the original input action to the referents and responses to determine the magnitude of latency generated by the latency source. During this comparison and the decision making process, our experimentation determined that there are a variety of contextual demands influencing the observer. As suggested by Experiment 1, the judgement strategy plays a role in focusing or diverting attention from referents and responses, as does the location and amount of attention and external environmental distractions. Although we cannot make definitive comparisons, tasks that require more attention (inking versus moving a box) and increased cognitive load seem to redirect resources away from perceiving the referents and responses, making latency judgements more difficult.

Although little is known about latency perception, the model provides many avenues for future explorations. By isolating each factor in the model and examining its effects, it is possible to extend the model, such that one could predict just-noticeable difference thresholds when different referents and responses are available, without having to evaluate the role of each explicitly. The model also raises a number of questions. For example, does each modality have its own cost when judging latency? Is there a constant cost for having the referent and response in different modalities? What is the relative impact of referents versus responses? From a psychological and interaction perspective, it is imperative to understand the processes governing latency perception before recommendations for future systems are made.

7 FUTURE WORK

A great deal of attention has been devoted towards latency perception recently, but there still is a great deal open for exploration. Miller's 100 millisecond latency hypothesis focused on the issue of latency tolerance whereas our experimentation examined perceptual thresholds [20]. There is of course a difference between what users can perceive and what they will tolerate. Although we cannot provide tolerance recommendations, if users are unable to perceive delays below a certain threshold, then it is likely that they will tolerate delays at or near these thresholds. It is equally likely that they may tolerate much higher latencies as Miller predicted. Understanding the relationship between perception and tolerance thus remains an important, fruitful area of research.

This work explicitly focused on the display aspect of latency, manipulating the speed at which input was rendered. Across the experiments, participants knew that regardless of how fast or slow they interacted, all strokes would be sensed by the system and eventually appear on screen. With current devices, it is often unclear why some input is not sensed or displayed. Our experiments determined the display latency that can be perceived but not the effects of delayed or slow sampling. While we advocate for decreasing latency in the whole pipeline, it remains to be seen how perception and user satisfaction would change if devices rendered quickly but stroke completeness and accuracy were unpredictable.

As reducing the actual system latency requires many incremental improvements throughout the data pipeline, it may be worthwhile to use additional information to modulate the processing devoted to latency reduction whenever the user is looking at the display or the stylus is about to touch the screen. The use of eye tracking and 'pre-touch' information from the stylus or finger is also an interesting avenue of research. By predicating and anticipating strokes or actions before contact is made with the screen, it may be possible to decrease the perceived latency inherent in a system.

8 CONCLUSION

In our experiments, we dove further into understanding the basics of latency perception by performing simple manipulations on the tasks performed and the presence and locations of visual reference cues. By offsetting the location between the ink and stylus and removing the hand and stylus from the visual field in one condition, we determined that low-latency judgments are largely visual, using the relative movement between the stylus and ink for an accurate judgment. Participants were unable to distinguish latencies below 97 milliseconds when the hand and stylus were not visible. We additionally found that latency perception is task dependant, with inking tasks degrading one's ability to discern between various levels of latency when compared to tasks used in prior work. These results informed the Latency Perception model, a model focusing on the role of referents, responses, and additional extraneous factors on the perception of latency. Such a model provides insight into the perception of latency and forms a foundation upon which future work can be undertaken.

REFERENCES

[1]   B.D. Adelstein, D.R. Begault, M.R. Anderson, and E.M. Wenzel. Sensitivity to Haptic-Audio Asynchrony. In *Proc. of Int. Conf. on Multimodal Interfaces*, 73-76, 2003.

[2]   D. Alamargot, D. Chesnet, C. Dansac, and C. Ros. Eye and Pen: A New Device for Studying Reading during Writing. *Behaviour Research Methods*, 38(2): 287-299, 2006.

[3]   M. Annett, F. Anderson, W.F. Bischof, and A. Gupta. The Pen is Mightier: Understanding Stylus Behaviour While Inking on Tablets. In *Proc. of GI*, 2014.

[4]   G. Anderson, R. Doherty, and S. Ganapathy. User Perception of Touch Screen Latency. *Design, User Experience, and Usability Part 1*, 195-202, 2011.

[5]   R. Coen-Calgi, P. Coraggio, P. Napoletano, O. Schwartz, M. Ferraro, and G. Boccignone. Visuomotor Characterization of Eye Movements in a Drawing Task. *Vision Research*, 49(8): 810-818, 2009.

[6]   S. Dahl and R. Bresin. Is the Player More Influenced by the Auditory than the Tactile Feedback from the Instrument? In *Proc. of the COST-06 Workshop on Digital Audio Effects*, 194-197, 2001.

[7]   DLP Discovery 4100 Development Kit. http://www.ti.com/lit/an/dlpa008/dlpa008.pdf. Accessed July 2013.

[8]   M. Fayol, D. Alamargot, and V.W. Berninger. *Translation of Thought to Written Text While Composing: Advancing Theory, Knowledge, Research Methods, Tools, and Application.* Psychology Press, Taylor & Francis Group, New York, 2012.

[9]   A. Freed, A. Chaudhary, and B. Davila. Operating System Latency Measurement and Analysis for Sound Synthesis and Processing Applications. In *Proc. of Int. Computer Music Conf.*, 479-481, 1997.

[10]   E. Gowen and R.C. Miall. Eye-tracking Interactions in Tracing and Drawing Tasks. *Human Movement Science*, 25: 568-585, 2006.

[11]   A. Henzen, N. Ailenei, F. Di Fiore, F. Van Reeth, and J. Patterson. Sketching with a Low-Latency Electronic Ink Drawing Tablet. In *Proc. of 3rd Int. Conf. on Computer Graphics and Interactive Techniques in Australasia and South East Asia*, 51-60, 2005.

[12]   A. Henzen, N. Ailenei, F. Van Reeth, G. Vansichem, R.W. Zehner, and K. Amundson. An Electronic Ink Low Latency Drawing Tablet. *SID Symposium Digest of Technical Papers*, 35(1): 1070-1073, 2004.

[13]   R. Jota, A. Ng, P. Dietz, and D. Wigdor. How Fast is Fast Enough? A Study of the Effects of Latency in Direct-Touch Pointing Tasks. In *Proc. of CHI*, 2291-2300, 2013.

[14]   J.C. Lee, P. Dietz, D. Maynes-Aminzade, R. Raskar, and S. Hudson. Automatic Projector Calibration with Embedded Light Sensors. In *Proc. of UIST*, 123-126, 2004.

[15]   I.S. MacKenzie and C. Ware. Lag as a Determinant of Human Performance in Interactive Systems. In *Proc. of CHI*, 488-493, 1993.

[16]   T. Maki-Patola. Musical Effects of Latency. *Suomen Musiikintutkijoiden*, 9: 82-85, 2005.

[17]   T. Maki-Patola and P. Hamalainen. Latency Tolerance for Gesture Controlled Continuous Sound Instrument without Tactile Feedback. In *Proc. of Int. Computer Music Conf.*, 1-5, 2004.

[18]   N.A. McMillian and D.C. Creelman, *Detection Theory: a User's Guide*, Cambridge University Press, Cambridge, 1991.

[19]   R.C. Miall, H. Imamizu, and S. Miyauchi. Activation of the Cerebellum in Co-Ordinated Eye and Hand Tracking Movements: An fMRI Study. *Experimental Brain Research*, 135: 22-33, 2000.

[20]   R.B. Miller. Response Time in Man-Computer Conversational Transactions. *Fall Joint Computer Conference*, 267-277, 1968.

[21]   M. Montag, S. Sullivan, S. Dickey, and C. Leider. A Low-Cost, Low-Latency Multi-Touch Table with Haptic Feedback for Musical Applications. In *Proc. of Int. Conf. on New Interfaces for Musical Expression*, 8-13, 2011.

[22]   A. Ng and P. Dietz. The Need for Speed in Touch Systems. *SID Symposium Digest of Technical Papers,* 2013.

[23]   A. Ng, J. Lepinski, D. Wigdor, S. Sanders, and P. Dietz. Designing for Low-Latency Direct-Touch Input. In *Proc. of UIST*, 453-462, 2012.

[24]   A. Ng, M. Annett, P. Dietz, A. Gupta, and W.F. Bischof. In the Blink of an Eye: Investigating Latency Perception during Stylus Interaction. In *Proceedings of CHI 2014*.

[25]   A.A. Sawchuk, E. Chew, R. Zimmermann, C. Papadopoulos, and C. Kyriakakis. From Remote Media Immersion to Distributed Immersive performance. In *Proc. of ACM SIGMM Workshop on Experiential Telepresence*, 110-120, 2003.

[26]   S. Seow. *Designing and Engineering Time: The Psychology of Time Perception in Software*, Pearson Education, Boston, 2008.

[27]   M.M. Taylor, and C.D. Creelman. PEST: Efficient Estimates on Probability Functions. *Journal of the Acoustical Society of America*, 41: 782-787, 1967.

[28]   J. Tchalenko. Eye Movements in Drawing Simple Lines. *Perception*, 36: 1152-1167, 2007.

[29]   J. Tchalenko and R.C. Miall. Eye-hand Strategies in Copying Complex Lines. *Cortex*, 45:368-376, 2009.

[30]   N. Toyoda, R. Yamamoto, and T. Yubuta. Clarification of Transition Conditions for Eye Movement While Generating a Trajectory Using the Upper Limb. *SI International*, 106-111, 2011.

[31]   N. Toyoda, R. Yamamoto, and T. Yubuta. Eye Movement While Generating a Trajectory Using the Upper Limb. *Journal of Energy and Power Engineering*, 6: 1733-1744, 2012.

[32]   D. Vogel and R. Balakrishnan. Direct Pen Interaction with a Conventional Graphic User Interface. *Human Computer Interaction*, 25: 324-388, 2010.

[33]   A. Wald. *Sequential Analysis*, John Wiley & Sons Inc. New York, 1947.

[34]   J. Wright and E. Brandt. System-Level MIDI Performance Testing. In *Proc. of Int. Computer Music Conf.*, 318-331, 2001.

The Effect of Interior Bezel Presence and Width on Magnitude Judgement

James R. Wallace *
Wilfrid Laurier University

Daniel Vogel †
University of Waterloo

Edward Lank ‡
University of Waterloo

ABSTRACT

Large displays are often constructed by tiling multiple small displays, creating visual discontinuities from inner bezels that may affect human perception of data. Our work investigates how bezels impact magnitude judgement, a fundamental aspect of perception. Two studies are described which control for bezel presence, bezel width, and user-to-display distance. Our findings form three implications for the design of tiled displays. Bezels wider than 0.5cm introduce a 4–7% increase in judgement error from a distance, which we simplify to a 5% rule of thumb when assessing display hardware. Length judgements made at arm's length are most affected by wider bezels, and are an important use case to consider. At arm's length, bezel compensation techniques provide a limited benefit in terms of judgement accuracy.

Index Terms: H.5.2 [User Interfaces]—Graphical user interfaces (GUI);

1 INTRODUCTION

Large, interactive displays have been shown to support activities such as navigation and wayfinding [4, 27], the physical navigation of large datasets [3], and co-located, collaborative work [29]. However, when constructing physically large displays one must choose between two imperfect approaches. First, one may buy a single, contiguous display. However, these displays are costly, and are available in limited sizes, aspect ratios, and resolutions of 1080 or 4K that are inadequate at large scales. Alternatively, one may tile many smaller displays together, offering lower cost, more flexible display sizes, and significantly higher resolution, but with the trade-off of introducing visual discontinuities created by individual display frames, called *interior bezels*. These bezels are aesthetically unpleasing, and potentially disruptive to users [7].

Previous work has explored aspects of large display interaction and perception when interior bezels are present (e.g. [7, 6]) and proposed mapping techniques to compensate for bezels [13]. However, the extent to which data crossing interior bezels interferes with magnitude judgement remains unexplored. It has been suggested that existing research has lacked control over many confounds in the design and use of tiled displays [7], and that a more careful investigation of these design issues would assist in developing software that takes full advantage of their capabilities [31]. Such an understanding is very practical. For example, display manufacturers now offer panels with "ultra-thin" bezels, intended for use in video wall installations and priced at a premium compared to their desktop counterparts. Based on our current understanding of the interactions between bezels and human perception, it remains unclear how much of a benefit, if any, these displays provide.

In this work, we contribute practical results regarding the presence and width of bezels, motivated by the construction of our own

*e-mail:jwallace@wlu.ca

†e-mail:dvogel@uwaterloo.ca

‡e-mail:lank@uwaterloo.ca
Graphics Interface Conference 2014
7-9 May, Montreal, Quebec, Canada

Figure 1: Tiling many independent displays provides a means of creating large workspaces that can support activities such as data visualization and sensemaking, but introduces interior bezels.

4m wide interactive display. We present the results of two empirical studies that investigate human perception of data across bezels at a distance and at arm's length. Our results show that in most cases, introducing interior bezels has an impact on human ability to gauge the relative size of data, but once bezels are introduced, larger interior bezel width has minimal effect. However, for interactions at arm's length, we found that wider bezels more significantly impacted magnitude judgement. We also tested a 'French Window' [13] bezel compensation technique and found no reduction of overall user error. These results lead directly to practical design guidelines for large, tiled displays: (1) bezels introduce approximately 5% additional error into user magnitude judgements; (2) length judgements made at arm's length are affected by wide bezels; and (3) bezel compensation techniques have a limited effect on judgement, but may provide aesthetic improvements.

2 TILED DISPLAYS

Tiling multiple, high-resolution monitors enables researchers to create displays that offer a number of advantages when compared to projected or traditional desktop displays. For example, tiled displays can support resolutions that surpass human visual acuity [40], and allow users to view images and data an order of magnitude larger than is possible on traditional displays [38]. The large surfaces created by tiled displays provide a shared workspace for the analysis of data that can benefit users both within arms reach, and those nearby [23]. And the combination of touch interaction, and the ability to physically navigate large data sets provides opportunities to leverage new modalities of interaction such as proxemics [19, 17] to enhance interactions with these displays. In line with these opportunities, tiled displays have been constructed to support work in many fields, including analytics [31], information visualization [28, 38], and command and control [26, 24].

Despite these advantages, the literature questions whether interior bezels may interfere with tasks such as visual search [14], stereoscopic vision [18], or target acquisition [22], and whether bezels may negatively impact user experience and aesthetic [2]. For example, can users effectively interpret data when it is divided across many small screens? To mitigate these potential issues, researchers have contributed guidelines for the development of software on tiled displays [1], such as placing materials on tiled displays to avoid crossing bezels, as well as techniques to alleviate their impact on human perception and interaction. For example, de Almeida et al. [13] simulated a 'French Window' effect via head tracking data, and allowed users to 'look behind' bezels to improve their performance at a cross-display tracing task.

However not all research supports the claim that bezels negatively impact user performance. Moreland [28] notes that there is little research supporting a negative impact on user perception. McNamara et al. [27] studied their impact on navigation and wayfinding and found no difference between conditions with and without a bezel. Robertson et al. [30] reported both positive and negative effects in their investigation of visual search on large, tiled displays. Other research has suggested that bezels have little or no negative impact on tiled display usability (e.g. [34, 39, 9]), and may even be leveraged by users to *improve* their performance [4, 6, 25].

Bi et al. [7] note the difficulties in drawing strong conclusions due to the lack of experimental control in the literature and argue that it would be beneficial to further explore the impact of bezels on user interaction with tiled displays. In their work, Bi et al. explored the impact of bezels on visual search, target selection, and tunnel steering tasks using a mouse and keyboard at a distance, and controlled for the number of interior bezels present on a user's display. However, they did not experimentally control for the width of interior bezels, or investigate their impact on human perception. Grüninger and Krüger [18] explored the impact of bezel width, colour, and tile size on depth perception and found that bezels smaller than 1.2cm provided little benefit to users, however their investigation did not provide guidance for 2D displays. We aim to build on their work and determine if interior bezel presence and width may impact human perception of displayed data, both at a distance and at arm's length.

2.1 Magnitude Adjustment Tasks

To investigate any distortions introduced by the presence of interior bezels, we leveraged an approach developed by psychophysicists to explore the impact of physical phenomena on human perception: the magnitude adjustment task [15, 16]. The magnitude adjustment task consists of a series modulus and stimulus shapes, and asks participants to make estimates of their relative sizes. These tests primarily evaluate performance according to Stevens' Power Law [32], and rely on a user's ability to estimate or reproduce a displayed stimulus. Typically, stimuli representative of graphical representations such as bar, line, and pie graphs are used, as they provide a measure of how effectively users will be able to interpret common visualizations of data, as found in the scientific literature [11, 10]. A comprehensive summary of the development of magnitude judgment tasks is beyond the scope of this work. For a more recent summary of magnitude judgement studies, and meta-analysis of visual phenomenon that may impact user perception for these tasks, we direct the reader to Wagner [35].

HCI researchers have used magnitude judgement tasks to identify scenarios in which human perception of data is compromised. For example, Wigdor et al. [37] identified cases where perception of shapes on a shared, digital tabletop may be compromised. Similarly, in the context of large, tiled displays, Bezerianos et al. [6] found that the distortions caused by viewing a display at extreme angles impacted a user's ability to perceive data. By controlling the conditions under which participants engage with data, these studies are able to isolate the impact of factors of interest from confounds such as display size [31], position and angle [33], or the presence and position of other users [21], and contribute towards a funda-

mental understanding of how human perception is influenced by factors such as the presence of bezels. Magnitude adjustment tasks are particularly useful in the context of this research because they not only can help to identify potential impacts of bezels on human perception, but also provide a means of quantifying those impacts. Such quantification is useful in developing design guidelines for interfaces that take into account the capabilities of their users.

In this work, we investigated the impact of bezels from the perspective of human perception. Our goal was to build on the existing literature, and to use carefully controlled studies to quantify the effect of interior bezels on human perception. By better understanding this effect, we are able to suggest under which settings the guidelines and techniques developed to compensate for interior bezels most benefit users. This work consists of two studies. First, we studied the impact of bezels on magnitude judgement at a distance. Second, we compared the effect of bezel compensation techniques on magnitude judgement when users were able to interact with a display via touch. In both studies, we introduced bezel width as a controlled variable, allowing us to investigate the impact that bezel size has on both types of tasks. We now describe the two studies and discuss their results individually before presenting overall implications for the design of tiled displays based on their collective results.

3 EXPERIMENT 1: INTERACTION AT A DISTANCE

To begin our investigation, we aimed to understand if bezels impact human perception of elementary visual variables on tiled displays from a distance. This approach had the advantage of establishing a baseline for interaction, free from known confounds such as viewing angle [6, 37]. We also believed that interaction at a distance would be the most familiar setting for participants, resembling interactions with displays such as those in meeting spaces or theatres. Our second experiment investigates the complimentary usage case where interaction occurs at arm's length via a touch screen. We wanted to specifically test whether or not the introduction of bezels would increase error in judgements made by participants, if those judgements would take longer to make, and if different types of stimuli would be affected more significantly in the presence of bezels. Our hypotheses were:

H1 As bezel width increases, relative magnitude judgement accuracy decreases

H2 As bezel width increases, relative magnitude judgement time increases

H3 Judgement accuracy differs for different visual variables

H4 Judgement time differs for different visual variables

3.1 Experimental Design and Task

Our experiment utilized a 3 (Visual Element Type) × 5 (Bezel Width) within-subjects design that drew on that of Wigdor et al. [37], Bezerianos et al. [6], and Cleveland and McGill [10]. Rather than providing magnitude estimates, as in [37], each participant in our study was tasked with resizing a stimulus to match a corresponding modulus in each trial, thus performing a magnitude *production* task [6]. As noted by Bezerianos et al. [6], our pilot testing revealed that some participants experienced difficulty translating their perceived judgements into numerical estimates; thus, we used a magnitude production task where participants manipulated the on-screen stimulus using a keyboard to reduce the influence of estimation error. Our experiment included two independent variables: visual element type and bezel width.

3.1.1 Visual Elements

We chose a subset of three of the visual elements described by Cleveland and McGill [10] consisting of length, angle, and area

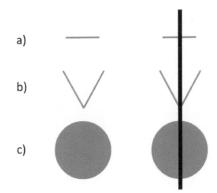

Figure 2: Participants resized three different visual element types (a) length, (b) angle, and (c) area. In conditions where a bezel was present, the stimulus was bisected (right).

Figure 3: Participants sat in a chair in front of the display and interacted via keyboard. In the second experiment, participants stood in front of the display and interacted via touch.

(Figure 2.). These three elements were also used by Bezerianos et al. [6], and have previously been found to represent shapes of varying degrees of difficulty for the judgement task through empirical studies [37, 6, 35]. For each visual variable, we asked participants to resize a stimulus element to match a presented modulus for 6 different modulus magnitudes, that were selected as multiples of 10 ranging in value from 10% to 70% of a base modulus value, depending on the type of visual element: 200 pixels for length judgements, 80° for angle judgements, and a radius of 200 pixels for area judgements.

3.1.2 Bezel Widths

We investigated 5 bezel widths, reflecting both commercially available hardware, and existing literature that investigated the effect of bezels on human perception: 0, 0.5, 1, 2, and 4cm. We surveyed available LCD and plasma displays suitable for use in video walls and found that they typically were available at different price points ranging from 0.5cm to 2cm, with smaller bezels being sold at a premium relative to larger ones. The 4cm level was included to facilitate comparisons to larger bezels studied in the literature (e.g. [7]), and is representative of panels intended for use with desktop computers, typically available at a much lower price than those intended for use in video wall installations. The width of each condition was measured to accurately reflect on-screen dimensions. The experimental design is summarized as:

15 Participants ×

5 Bezel Widths (0cm, 0.5cm, 1cm, 2cm, 4cm) ×

3 Visual Element Types (length, angle, area) ×

6 Magnitude judgements (10% to 70% of modulus)

For a total of 1350 comparisons.

Participants completed one block of trials for each of the bezel width conditions, the order of which was balanced using a latin-square design. Within each block, the ordering of visual element type and stimuli magnitudes were randomized.

3.2 Participants, Procedure, and Apparatus

15 participants (9 men and 6 women) between the ages of 22 and 35 (average age 25) were recruited to participate in this study. Participants were all Science, Technology, Engineering, and Mathematics students who were enrolled at the University of Waterloo, and received a $5 gift card for their participation.

Upon arriving, participants were seated in an adjustable chair at a conference table with a wireless keyboard and a large, projected display approximately 3m in front of them, and instructed to adjust the chair and position themselves so that they were comfortable. The display measured 2m wide by 1.5m tall, and was projected at a resolution of 1024 × 768 pixels (Figure 3). Participants were then briefed on the task, and asked to complete an informed consent form and brief demographic questionnaire. To ensure that participants understood the task and the simulated bezel, they were then presented with a series of 20 modulus/stimulus pairs in a practice period. During the practice period, participants were able to pose any clarifying questions, and were asked to confirm that they felt comfortable with the task before proceeding.

Finally, participants were instructed to complete the trials as accurately and as quickly as possible, and completed a block of trials for each bezel condition. As stimulus/modulus pairs were presented during each trial, stimuli were randomly sized within +/-20% of their corresponding modulus. Participants then resized the stimulus using the up and down arrow keys until they felt that it accurately matched the modulus, and pressed return to submit their final judgement. Both the modulus and stimulus remained visible to participants for the duration of the trial. After submitting their magnitude judgement, participants were presented with an opportunity to rest before making their next judgement, and were asked to press the space bar to proceed to the next trial. Experimental sessions lasted approximately 30 minutes in total.

3.3 Data Collection and Analysis

Participant interaction data were logged to computer files. In order to evaluate our hypotheses, our primary measures were *judgement error* and *task time*. We measured the accuracy of participant judgements based on how closely their manipulated stimulus matched the presented modulus, calculated as a percentage of the size of the modulus. As in [37, 6], judgement error was defined by:

$$error = |\text{ judged percent} - \text{true percent }|$$

We also investigated the time required to make each judgement, measured as the time starting from when the modulus and stimuli first appeared, until the participant pressed the key to submit their answer. Thus, this measure included the time required to view and adjust the stimuli. Repeated measures analysis of variance (RM-ANOVA) statistical tests were conducted to examine differences between bezel conditions, with post-hoc pairwise comparisons made using the Bonferroni adjustment. All statistical tests used an alpha-value of 0.05.

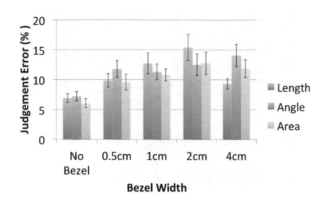

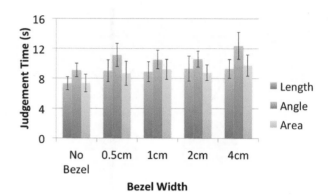

Figure 4: Judgement error results (as a percent of the modulus) for each visual element type (length, angle, and area) and bezel condition (0, 0.5, 1, 2, and 4cm). (Error bars are standard error)

Figure 5: Trial time results (in seconds) for each visual element type (length, angle, and area) and bezel condition (0, 0.5, 1, 2, and 4cm). (Error bars are standard error)

3.4 Results

Overall, participants submitted solutions with an average error of 10.8% ($\sigma = 3.41$) and took an average of 9.4 seconds ($\sigma = 4.2$) to make each judgement. Below, we discuss results relevant to our hypotheses.

3.4.1 Judgement Error

A main effect of bezel width on accuracy ($F_{4,56} = 10.704, p < 0.001, \eta_p^2 = .433$) revealed judgements made in the No Bezel condition had an average error of 6.7% and were more accurate than any condition where bezels were present: 0.5cm ($\bar{x} = 10.4\%, p = 0.004$), 1cm ($\bar{x} = 11.6\%, p = 0.001$), 2cm ($\bar{x} = 13.6\%, p = 0.005$), 4cm ($\bar{x} = 11.7\%, p = 0.006$). Our analyses did not identify any differences between conditions where interior bezels were present.

We found no effect of visual element type on accuracy ($F_{2,28} = .721, p = 0.495, \eta_p^2 = .049$). Participants' average error for length judgements was 10.8% ($\sigma = 3.9$), for angle judgements was 11.4% ($\sigma = 4.5$), and for area judgements was 10.2% ($\sigma = 3.7$). An interaction effect between visual element type and bezel was found ($F_{8,112} = 2.778, p = .008, \eta_p^2 = .166$), where accuracy error increased with bezel width, except for length judgements made with a 4cm bezel, where they decreased. Post hoc comparisons showed that length judgements made with 4cm bezels were more accurate ($\bar{x} = 9.3\%, \sigma = .884$) than angle ($\bar{x} = 14.1\%, \sigma = 1.85$) or area ($\bar{x} = 11.8\%, \sigma = 1.47$) judgements ($p < .0001$).

3.4.2 Trial Time

We found that bezel width had a significant effect on trial time ($F_{4,36} = 10.704, p = 0.026, \eta_p^2 = .433$), where magnitude judgements made in the No Bezel condition ($\bar{x} = 7.9s, \sigma = 1.79$) were faster than those made in the 4cm Bezel condition ($\bar{x} = 10.4s, \sigma = 5.4, p = 0.006$). However, we did not find differences between any of the other conditions.

Finally, our analyses revealed that shape had a significant effect on trial time ($F_{2,18} = 11.2255, p < 0.001, \eta_p^2 = .950$). Length ($\bar{x} = 8.7s, \sigma = 4.52$) and area ($\bar{x} = 8.7s, \sigma = 4.57$) judgements took less time than angle judgements ($\bar{x} = 10.7s, \sigma = 4.59, p = 0.003, p = 0.446$, respectively). No interaction effect between visual element type and bezel width was found for time ($F_{8,112} = .451, p = 0.888, \eta_p^2 = .031$)

3.5 Discussion

Our results show that the presence of interior bezels negatively affects magnitude judgements made from a distance on a large dis-

play. With significant differences between the No Bezel condition (0cm) and those where interior bezels were present (0.5, 1, 2, 4cm), we partially confirm **H1**. That is, the presence of any bezel impacted magnitude judgements, but we did not find clear evidence that increased bezel width further impacted accuracy. The average accuracy without any bezels is between 3.7% and 6.9% more accurate, or 5.1% greater than the 11.8% average accuracy across conditions with interior bezels.

Our findings partially support **H2**. Magnitude judgements in the 4cm bezel condition took 2.5s longer than the No Bezel condition, an increase of 25%. However, our analysis did not reveal any time differences between the other bezel widths. When considered together, our findings for accuracy and time suggest a small, but potentially critical effect of bezel width.

Unlike other studies [35, 6], we did not find differences in magnitude judgement accuracy for different visual element types for most of our conditions. However, for judgements made in the 4cm bezel conditions, participants' length judgements were approximately 2.5% more accurate than area judgements, and 5% more accurate than angle judgements. While these findings partially confirm **H3**, our analysis of effect size suggests that the type of visual element accounted for less than 5% ($\eta_p^2 = .049$) of the variance in accuracy. We also found that angle judgements took more time than other visual element types, partially confirming **H4**. We interpret these findings as indicative of a trade-off between judgement time and accuracy, as reported in the literature [35].

4 EXPERIMENT 2: INTERACTION AT ARM'S LENGTH

Having investigated magnitude judgements at a distance, we wanted to explore the use of tiled displays in conditions that more closely resembled those we envisioned for typical use cases on a touch-interactive tiled display. In particular, we wanted to capture interaction at arm's length to the large display, and to explore whether a user's proximity to the display may change the role that bezels play in determining the effectiveness at magnitude judgement tasks. We also wanted to investigate whether the use of bezel compensation techniques would mitigate the performance differences observed in Experiment 1. To investigate these questions, we conducted a second study that replicated the conditions of the first. Our hypotheses for this follow-up experiment are:

H5 As bezel width increases, the accuracy of relative magnitude judgements decreases

H6 As bezel width increases, the time taken to make relative magnitude judgements increases

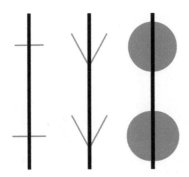

Figure 6: Participants completed trials under two bezel compensation conditions (top) bezel compensation, in which visual elements' size remained constant regardless of bezel width, and (bottom) no bezel compensation, as in Experiment 1.

H7 Judgement accuracy differs for different visual variables

H8 Judgement time differs for different visual variables

H9 Bezel compensation will improve judgement accuracy

H10 Bezel compensation will reduce judgement time

4.1 Experimental Design and Task

Our experiment utilized a 3 (Visual Element Type) × 5 (Bezel Width) × 2 (Bezel Compensation) design, where bezel compensation was a between-subjects factor and visual element type and bezel width were within-subjects factors.

4.1.1 Bezel Widths

As in the Experiment 1, we investigated 5 bezel widths: 0, 0.5, 1, 2, and 4cm.

4.1.2 Visual Elements

As in Experiment 1, visual elements consisted of length, angle, and area (Figure 6.). For each visual variable, participants made judgements for 6 different magnitudes, that were selected as multiples of 10 ranging in value from 10% to 70% of a base modulus value, depending on the type of visual element: 200 pixels for length, $80°$ for angle, and a radius of 200 pixels for area judgements.

4.1.3 Bezel Compensation

Participants completed all of their trials in one of two bezel compensation conditions: either where no bezel compensation was present, as used in Experiment 1, or in a second condition in which bezel compensation was enabled. Our bezel compensation implementation simulated the 'French Window' [13] appearance, where data is hidden behind bezels, and which has been previously shown to improve performance for physical interactions also at arm's length. With compensation enabled, their magnitude in physical space is preserved instead of their magnitude in display space. The experimental design is summarized as:

10 Participants ×

2 Bezel Compensation (Present, Absent) ×

5 Bezel Widths (0cm, 0.5cm, 1cm, 2cm, 4cm) ×

3 Visual Element Types (length, angle, area) ×

6 Magnitude judgements (10% to 70% of modulus)

For a total of 1800 comparisons.

Participants completed one block of trials for each of the bezel width conditions, the order of which was balanced using a latin-square design. Within each block, the ordering of visual element type and stimuli magnitudes were randomized.

4.2 Participants, Procedure, and Apparatus

20 participants (8 men and 12 women) between the ages of 22 and 28 ($\bar{x} = 23$) were recruited to participate in this study. Participants were all Science, Technology, Engineering, and Mathematics students who were enrolled at the University of Waterloo, and received $5 for their participation. The experimental procedure for this experiment was identical to that of Experiment 1, except for two factors: bezel compensation and touch interaction.

Unlike Experiment 1, a 'French Window' bezel compensation technique was introduced as a between subjects factor in this experiment. Unlike previous work [13], our 'French Window' implementation did not utilize head tracking technology, and replicated functionality available on commercially available graphics cards that compensates for bezels by translating the projected image by a constant amount. To ensure that participants understood the effect of bezel compensation on the stimulus/modulus pairs, we explained the bezel compensation technique to participants in lay terms before participants completed their practice session (e.g. the bezel 'covers up' part of the shape, or that they would need to account for a 'gap in the shape'). To ensure that participants understood the task and the simulated bezel, they were then presented with a series of 20 modulus/stimulus pairs in a practice period, and given the opportunity to ask questions and confirm their understanding of the display.

For each trial, participants stood in front of a large, projected display at a comfortable distance for touch interaction (determined by the participants' arm length and personal preference). Touch interaction was enabled via a PQ Labs 85" touch frame, supporting up to 12 simultaneous touch points, allowing participants to interact with a projected image at a resolution of 1920 × 1080 pixels (Figure 3). During each trial, participants resized stimuli by touching and dragging at any point within a 400 pixel radius of its projected image, with drags towards its centre reducing the stimulus' magnitude, and drags away from centre increasing magnitude. Finally, participants were instructed to complete trials as accurately and as quickly as possible, and completed a block for each bezel width condition.

4.3 Data Collection and Analysis

As in Experiment 1, our primary measures were *judgement error* and *task time*, calculated from data collected to computer log files. We measured the accuracy of participant judgements based on how closely their manipulated stimulus matched the presented modulus, calculated as a percentage of the size of the modulus. We also investigated the time required to make each judgement, measured as the time starting from when the modulus and stimuli first appeared, until the participant pressed the key to submit their answer. Repeated measures analysis of variance (RM-ANOVA) statistical tests were conducted to examine differences between bezel conditions, with post-hoc pairwise comparisons made using the Bonferroni adjustment. All statistical tests used an alpha-value of 0.05.

4.4 Results

Overall, participants submitted magnitude judgements with an average error of 11.54% ($\sigma = 7.45$), and took an average of 10.4 seconds ($\sigma = 7.08$) to make each judgement. Below, we discuss results relevant to our hypotheses.

4.4.1 Judgement Accuracy

A main effect exists for bezel width on accuracy ($F_{4,72} = 2.567, p = 0.045, \eta_p^2 = .125$). Tests revealed that No Bezel ($\bar{x} = 9.981\%, \sigma = 1.2$) and 0.5cm Bezel ($\bar{x} = 9.863\%, \sigma = 0.961$) conditions are more accurate than the 4cm bezel condition ($\bar{x} = 12.246\%, \sigma = 1.3$,

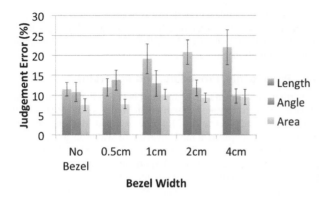

Figure 7: Judgement error results for trials without bezel compensation (as a percent of the modulus) for each visual element type (length, angle, and area) and bezel condition (0, 0.5, 1, 2, and 4cm) in the no bezel compensation conditions.

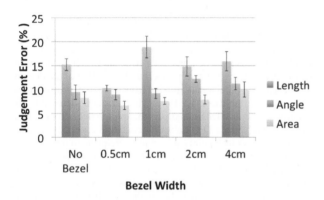

Figure 8: Judgement error results for trials with bezel compensation (as a percent of the modulus) for each visual element type (length, angle, and area) and bezel condition (0, 0.5, 1, 2, and 4cm) in the bezel compensation conditions.

$p = 0.013, 0.28$ respectively). Average judgement errors in the 1cm ($\bar{x} = 12.797\%, p = 1.25$) and 2cm ($\bar{x} = 12.808\%, p = 0.888$) bezel conditions are not significantly different from other bezel widths.

A main effect exists for visual element type on accuracy ($F_{2,36} = 14.433, p < 0.001, \eta_p^2 = 0.445$), and tests revealed that errors in length judgements ($\bar{x} = 15.148\%, \sigma = 1.2$) are less accurate then both Angle ($\bar{x} = 11.0\%, \sigma = 1.1$) and Area ($\bar{x} = 8.50\%, \sigma = 0.74$) judgements ($p = .029, .0001$, respectively). No difference was found between Angle and Area judgements ($p = .088$). An interaction effect between visual element type and bezel width is most relevant ($F_{8,144} = 3.128, p = 0.003, \eta_p^2 = .148$), and our tests reveal that length judgements are approximately 53% less accurate in 1cm, 2cm, and 4cm conditions ($\bar{x} = 17.6$) compared to the No Bezel and 0.5cm conditions ($\bar{x} = 11.5, p < .0001$).

No effect for bezel compensation was found ($F_{1,18} = 0.728, p = 0.405, \eta_p^2 = .039$). Judgements with no compensation ($\bar{x} = 12.2\%, \sigma = 1.01$) appear similar to those in the bezel compensation conditions ($\bar{x} = 10.9\%, \sigma = 1.01$). Figures 7 and 8 illustrate judgement results with and without bezel compensation data.

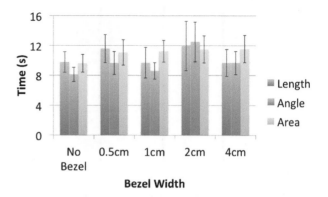

Figure 9: Trial time results in seconds for each visual element type (length, angle, and area) and bezel condition (0, 0.5, 1, 2, and 4cm).

4.4.2 Trial Time

There are no significant effects of bezel width on trial time ($F_{4,72} = 1.747, p = 0.149, \eta_p^2 = .088$), visual element type on trial time ($F_{2,36} = 1.961, p < 0.155, \eta_p^2 = .098$), bezel compensation technique on trial time ($F_{1,18} = 0.862, p = 0.365, \eta_p^2 = .046$).

4.5 Discussion

Our results show that large interior bezels have a negative effect on magnitude judgement accuracy when made at arm's length. These results are more nuanced than the clear differences between bezel and no bezel for judgements made from a distance. At arm's length, judgements with no bezel and the very small 0.5cm bezel are 2.8% more accurate than judgements made with the large 4cm bezel. Thus, we have some evidence to support **H5**, but unlike Experiment 1, we must reject **H6** given no significant differences for judgement time. An analysis of effect size suggests that bezel width plays a minor role in the accuracy of magnitude judgements ($\eta_p^2 = 0.125$) – visual element type accounted for close to half of the observed variance in our model ($\eta_p^2 = .445$).

Unlike judgements made from a distance, when at arm's length visual element types are a significant factor in accuracy, confirming **H7**. Length judgements in particular are less accurate than area and angle judgements for larger bezels (1cm, 2cm, 4cm). However, there are no differences in judgement time across visual element type, and we reject **H8**. These findings contrast with Experiment 1, where at a distance judgement accuracy is not affected by visual element type but angle judgements take more time. This difference may be attributed to differences in keyboard and touch input: fine-tuning a choice using the keyboard's precise up and down arrows in Experiment 1 could be easier than using the touch screen in this experiment.

Finally, we found no evidence that bezel compensation techniques impacted magnitude judgement accuracy or time. These results can be explained by the small effect size observed during our study, accounting for less than 3.9% and 4.6% of variance in our model. Thus, we reject hypotheses **H9** and **H10**.

5 IMPLICATIONS FOR DESIGN

Our results translate directly into practical advice for building very large display systems. If size and resolution can be achieved with a non-tiled single display, is the significant increase in price justified for the intended application? For example, at the time of writing, Panasonic manufactures a 3.9m (152 inch), 8 megapixel display – but it retails for more than USD\$500,000, compared to approximately USD\$50,000 for a 12 megapixel tiled display of comparable size. When seeking to build displays that offer even larger physical size or resolution, tiling individual displays offers even more substantial savings, and more flexibility in display size and aspect ratio. Assuming a tiled display is the only economically viable way forward, should premium thin-bezel displays be used? Are the extra expense, space, and calibration difficulties that arise when using an array of LCD projectors justified to reduce inner bezels to more subtle display seams?

Based on our results regarding the fundamental perceptual operation of magnitude judgement, we offer three design implications that inform these decisions: 1) designers should expect a 5% increase in judgement error when interior bezels are present; 2) length judgements made at arm's length are particularly prone to reduced accuracy with wider bezels; and 3) bezel compensation techniques provide a limited benefit.

5.1 When are Bezels a Design Consideration?

When viewing data from a distance, the presence of any interior bezel increases magnitude judgement error by 5.1%. When at arm's length, judgement error increases by 2.8% for very wide 4cm inner bezels compared to no bezel or thin 0.5cm bezels. Since a large display is often used both from a distance and at arm's length, the most prudent guideline is to adopt a simple rule-of-thumb to avoid bezels if a 5% increase in magnitude error is a concern. For example, maps used in military situation rooms and emergency response centres require accurate (and fast) magnitude judgements. Similarly, accurate critique of renderings for architecture and auto design may be compromised by magnitude judgement error caused by bezels. If 5% error could be detrimental, then a higher budget should be considered for displays with thin bezels or no bezel at all.

For many tasks, users, and environments, a 5% increase in accuracy error may be less critical. For example, a $1^{\circ}C$ difference in temperature is likely less sensitive to misinterpretation in the home than in a nuclear reactor. This is especially true if judgements will be made at arm's length where the effect on error is less pronounced, or data can be positioned away from interior bezels [1]. Assuming that the effect of interior bezels on mouse interaction [7], visual search [30], and target acquisition [27] is also small for the usage context, lower cost displays with wider bezels may be used. In these contexts, designers may benefit from focusing on other factors, such as viewing angle [6], that have been identified as having a larger effect on magnitude judgement.

5.2 Length Judgements made at Arm's Length

Our analyses revealed that length judgements made at arm's length were particularly prone to increased error; in these settings, accuracy error increased to 18.9% in the 4cm bezel condition, marking a 5% increase over the 13.5% error we observed in the no bezel condition. This increased error may arise due to differences in viewing angle when working close to the display [37, 6]. We anticipate that these issues will most significantly impact the interpretation of geographic maps, scientific graphs, and charts. Designers may want to provide simple tools to assist people when interpreting data close to the display. For example, allow data to be easily translated so that it does not span a bezel, or augment the visualization with numerical values to eliminate length judgements.

Alternatively, it may be beneficial for people to select data from the tiled display and then view that data on a personal device, eliminating magnitude judgements spanning inner bezels. Perhaps counter intuitively, our results suggest that interaction on personal devices may provide a more significant benefit when at arm's length from a large displays than at a distance – a consideration that is not often discussed in the literature. For example, many projects have investigated the use of personal devices to enable interaction at a distance (e.g. [5, 20]), however there may be advantages to exploring methods of displaying content [36] or relocating applications

[8] to personal devices when at arm's length.

5.3 Utility of Bezel Compensation Techniques

We did not find any benefit to using a 'French Window' [13] bezel compensation technique at arm's length. We observed only a 1.3% improvement in participant accuracy when bezel compensation was present; a difference that was not found to be statistically significant, nor is likely to have significance in practice. Further, our analysis revealed that bezel compensation technique accounted for less than 4% of the variance in our model, typically interpreted as a minimal effect [12]. Thus, we suggest implementing bezel compensation only when it is not a significant investment of resources. For example, many commercial graphics cards provide compensation as a built-in feature and can support small and medium sized tiled displays (2 – 24 displays), however, for deployments of more than 24 displays, there is currently no hardware support for bezel compensation. In this case, our results suggest that it is advisable to avoid implementing bezel compensation given its' lack of impact on magnitude judgement. However, there may be settings in which aesthetic design necessarily outweighs perceptual performance considerations, such as for artistic installations or advertising, where the representational quality of imagery is more important than its accurate lower level perception.

6 LIMITATIONS AND FUTURE WORK

By designing two experiments that carefully controlled the circumstances under which magnitude judgements were made, we reduced previously identified confounds such as viewing angle [37, 6], and focused on the effect of interior bezels on magnitude judgement. This work is only a first step in developing guidelines for tiled display design across a variety of tasks, settings, and users, and care needs to be taken in generalizing these results to a broader usage context. For example, our results differ from those of Grüninger and Krüger [18], who suggest a threshold of 1.2cm for bezels to minimally impede depth perception. Similarly, care must be taken in generalizing these results across users of different ages, heights, or with varying abilities such as visual acuity or spatial perception. An open question is how to synthesize results from these independent studies into guidelines that can inform designers as to what degree interior bezels impact higher order tasks such as reading, writing, sketching, or navigation. Given the variety of tasks, environments, and users potentially addressed by tiled displays, no single study can adequately address all questions. We reassert Bi et al.'s [7] suggestion that further studies examining the effects of interior bezels are warranted, particularly where control is leveraged to understand how physical and visual variables impact human perception.

7 CONCLUSION

This research addresses the need [7] for more focused studies that explore the impact of interior bezels on user performance with large, tiled displays. We conducted two empirical experiments that examined the impact of the presence and width of interior bezels on magnitude judgement at a distance and at arm's length, as well as the utility of bezel compensation techniques. Our results show that the presence of interior bezels impacts user performance for magnitude judgement tasks from a distance, but when at arm's length the effect is less pronounced except for length judgements. Based on our findings, we provide three practical implications for the design of large, tiled displays: (1) a 5% decreased accuracy guideline when considering budgets which minimize interior bezels in large displays; (2) length judgements made at arm's length are particularly susceptible to wider bezels; and (3) bezel compensation techniques provide only a minimal benefit for magnitude judgement tasks.

This work contributes towards an understanding of interaction and visualization on tiled displays that is grounded in the theories of psychophysics, cognition, and human-computer interaction. Our results demonstrate the importance of understanding the effect of interior bezels on human perception, and that practical design guidelines can be formed from such an understanding. As display technologies continue to become more affordable, and tiled displays become available to a variety of usage contexts, such guidelines will serve to guide designers towards appropriate hardware and software support for their target users, settings, and tasks.

ACKNOWLEDGEMENTS

The authors would like to thank Xiaojun Bi and Anastasia Bezerianos for their insight as we developed this work.

REFERENCES

[1] Andrews, C., Endert, A., Yost, B., and North, C. Information visualization on large, high-resolution displays: Issues, challenges, and opportunities. *Information Visualization 10*, 4 (2011), 341–355.

[2] Anslow, C., Marshall, S., Noble, J., Tempero, E., and Biddle, R. User evaluation of polymetric views using a large visualization wall. In *Proc. SOFTVIS 2010*, ACM (2010), 25–34.

[3] Ball, R., and North, C. Effects of tiled high-resolution display on basic visualization and navigation tasks. In *Proc. CHI 2005*, CHI EA '05, ACM (2005), 1196–1199.

[4] Ball, R., Varghese, M., Sabri, A., Cox, E., Fierer, C., Peterson, M., Carstensen, B., and North, C. Evaluating the benefits of tiled displays for navigating maps. In *Proc. IASTED-HCI 2005* (2005), 66–71.

[5] Baudisch, P., Cutrell, E., Hinckley, K., and Gruen, R. Mouse ether: accelerating the acquisition of targets across multi-monitor displays. In *CHI EA 2004*, ACM (2004), 1379–1382.

[6] Bezerianos, A., Isenberg, P., et al. Perception of visual variables on tiled wall-sized displays for information visualization applications. *IEEE Transactions on Visualization and Computer Graphics 18*, 12 (2012).

[7] Bi, X., Bae, S.-H., and Balakrishnan, R. Effects of interior bezels of tiled-monitor large displays on visual search, tunnel steering, and target selection. In *Proc. CHI 2010*, CHI '10, ACM (2010), 65–74.

[8] Biehl, J. T., and Bailey, B. P. Aris: an interface for application relocation in an interactive space. In *Proc. GI 2004*, Canadian Human-Computer Communications Society (2004), 107–116.

[9] Campbell, C. S., and Maglio, P. P. Segmentation of display space interferes with multitasking. In *Proc INTERACT 2003* (2003), 575–582.

[10] Cleveland, W. S., and McGill, R. Graphical perception: Theory, experimentation, and application to the development of graphical methods. *Journal of the American Statistical Association 79*, 387 (1984), pp. 531–554.

[11] Cleveland, W. S., and McGill, R. Graphical perception and graphical methods for analyzing scientific data. *Science 229*, 4716 (1985), pp. 828–833.

[12] Cohen, J. A power primer. *Psychological bulletin 112*, 1 (1992), 155.

[13] de Almeida, R. A., Pillias, C., Pietriga, E., and Cubaud, P. Looking behind bezels: french windows for wall displays. In *Proc AVI 2012*, ACM (2012), 124–131.

[14] Forlines, C., Shen, C., Wigdor, D., and Balakrishnan, R. Exploring the effects of group size and display configuration on visual search. In *Proc CSCW 2006*, ACM (2006), 11–20.

[15] Gescheider, G. *Psychophysics: the fundamentals*. Lawrence Erlbaum Associates, Incorporated, 1997.

[16] Gescheider, G. A. Psychophysical scaling. *Annual review of psychology 39*, 1 (1988), 169–200.

[17] Greenberg, S., Marquardt, N., Ballendat, T., Diaz-Marino, R., and Wang, M. Proxemic interactions: the new ubicomp? *interactions 18*, 1 (Jan. 2011), 42–50.

[18] Grüninger, J., and Krüger, J. The impact of display bezels on stereoscopic vision for tiled displays. In *Proc. VRST '13*, ACM (2013), 241–250.

[19] Hall, E. *The Hidden Dimension*. Anchor Books, 1966.

[20] Haller, M., Leitner, J., Seifried, T., Wallace, J. R., Scott, S. D., Richter, C., Brandl, P., Gokcezade, A., and Hunter, S. The nice discussion room: Integrating paper and digital media to support co-located group meetings. In *Proc. CHI 2010*, ACM (2010), 609–618.

[21] Hawkey, K., Kellar, M., Reilly, D., Whalen, T., and Inkpen, K. M. The proximity factor: impact of distance on co-located collaboration. In *Proc. GROUP 2005*, ACM (2005), 31–40.

[22] Hutchings, D. An investigation of fitts' law in a multiple-display environment. In *Proc. CHI 2012*, ACM (2012), 3181–3184.

[23] Isenberg, P., Isenberg, T., Hesselmann, T., Lee, B., von Zadow, U., and Tang, A. Data visualization on interactive surfaces: A research agenda. IEEE Computer Society (2013).

[24] Jiang, X., Hong, J. I., Takayama, L. A., and Landay, J. A. Ubiquitous computing for firefighters: field studies and prototypes of large displays for incident command. In *Proc. CHI 2004*, ACM (2004), 679–686.

[25] Lee, S., Kim, H., Lee, Y.-k., Sim, M., and Lee, K.-p. Designing of an effective monitor partitioning system with adjustable virtual bezel. In *Human Centered Design*, M. Kurosu, Ed., vol. 6776. Springer Berlin Heidelberg, 2011, 537–546.

[26] Mayer, T. The 4k format implications for visualization, vr, command & control and special venue application. In *Proc. EDT 2007*, ACM (2007).

[27] McNamara, A. M., Parke, F., and Sanford, M. Evaluating performance in tiled displays: navigation and wayfinding. In *Proc. VRCAI 2011*, ACM (2011), 483–490.

[28] Moreland, K. Redirecting research in large-format displays for visualization. In *Proc. LDAV 2012* (oct. 2012), 91 –95.

[29] Renambot, L., Jeong, B., Jagodic, R., Johnson, A., Leigh, J., and Aguilera, J. Collaborative visualization using high-resolution tiled displays. In *Proc. CHI Workshop on Information Visualization Interaction Techniques for Collaboration Across Multiple Displays*, ACM (2006).

[30] Robertson, G., Czerwinski, M., Baudisch, P., Meyers, B., Robbins, D., Smith, G., and Tan, D. The large-display user experience. *Computer Graphics and Applications, IEEE 25*, 4 (2005), 44–51.

[31] Shupp, L., Andrews, C., Dickey-Kurdziolek, M., Yost, B., and North, C. Shaping the display of the future: The effects of display size and curvature on user performance and insights. *Human–Computer Interaction 24*, 1-2 (2009), 230–272.

[32] Stevens, S. S. On the psychophysical law. *Psychological review 64*, 3 (1957), 153.

[33] Su, R. E., and Bailey, B. P. Put them where? towards guidelines for positioning large displays in interactive workspaces. In *Proc. INTERACT 2005*. Springer, 2005, 337–349.

[34] Tan, D. S., and Czerwinski, M. Effects of visual separation and physical discontinuities when distributing information across multiple displays. In *Proc. INTERACT 2003* (2003).

[35] Wagner, M. *The geometries of visual space*. Lawrence Erlbaum, 2006.

[36] Wallace, J. R., Mandryk, R. L., and Inkpen, K. M. Comparing content and input redirection in mdes. In *Proc. CSCW 2008*, ACM (2008), 157–166.

[37] Wigdor, D., Shen, C., Forlines, C., and Balakrishnan, R. Perception of elementary graphical elements in tabletop and multi-surface environments. In *Proc. CHI 2007*, ACM (2007), 473–482.

[38] Yamaoka, S., Doerr, K.-U., and Kuester, F. Visualization of high-resolution image collections on large tiled display walls. *Future Gener. Comput. Syst. 27*, 5 (May 2011), 498–505.

[39] Yang, X.-D., Mak, E., McCallum, D., Irani, P., Cao, X., and Izadi, S. Lensmouse: augmenting the mouse with an interactive touch display. In *Proc. CHI 2010*, ACM (2010), 2431–2440.

[40] Yost, B., Haciahmetoglu, Y., and North, C. Beyond visual acuity: the perceptual scalability of information visualizations for large displays. In *Proc. CHI 2007*, ACM (2007), 101–110.

User Adaptation to a Faulty Unistroke-Based Text Entry Technique by Switching to an Alternative Gesture Set

Ahmed Sabbir Arif, Wolfgang Stuerzlinger

York University, Toronto, Ontario, Canada

ABSTRACT

This article presents results of two user studies to investigate user adaptation to a faulty unistroke gesture recognizer of a text entry technique. The intent was to verify the hypothesis that users gradually adapt to a faulty gesture recognition technique's *misrecognition* errors and that this adaptation rate is dependent on how frequently they occur. Results confirmed that users gradually adapt to *misrecognition* errors by replacing the error prone gestures with alternative ones, as available. Also, users adapt to a particular *misrecognition* error faster if it occurs more frequently than others.

Keywords: Adaptation; errors; gesture recognition; learning.

Index Terms: H.5.2 User Interfaces: Input devices and strategies (e.g., mouse, touchscreen).

1   INTRODUCTION

Although the origin of the famous quote, "That's not a bug, it's a feature" is unknown, the computer science community is well aware of its implications [13]. It points towards a phenomenon observed in many domains, including human-computer interaction and programming languages. The quote refers to the possibility that practitioners will adapt to a non-fatal system error, if it remains in the system for long enough. Once users get accustomed to a system error they either actively avoid repeating actions that cause the error or start treating it as a feature. Such behaviour can be indirectly explained through theories of learning. Some of these theories assume that learning is a process of replacement, where incorrect response tendencies are replaced with correct ones [26]. Alternative theories describe learning as a process of accumulation, where incorrect response tendencies remain constant and correct response tendencies increase with practice [25]. Regardless of the explanation, both schools of thought imply that it is important to reduce mistakes to learn correct responses. Human errors are well studied and explained in the field of text entry, error research, and cognitive psychology. But how users deal with a faulty gesture recognizers' *misrecognition* errors is not very well studied. Based on observations from the existing literature, we can hypothesize that users' learning rates for system errors depend on how erroneous a particular system is. Also, users learn to avoid an erroneous action faster if it occurs more frequently than others. Yet, no empirical studies have been conducted to investigate this. Thus, we present two user studies that attempt to verify the above-mentioned hypothesis. We believe that a deeper insight into potential user adaptation to a faulty gesture recognizer will provide designers with guidance for future work on such technologies.

* asarif@outlook.com; wolfgang@cse.yorku.ca

Graphics Interface Conference 2014
7-9 May, Montreal, Quebec, Canada

We start with a review of gesture-based text entry techniques and the challenges they face. Based on an informal survey, we discuss the common types of errors that occur in such techniques and also how errors are handled by these systems. The use of alternative gestures is reviewed as well. The review also includes systems that allow users to perform commands with gestures. We present the software used in the user studies and elaborate on how it was designed in accordance with current trends in human and system error handling as well as provisions for alternative method usage in gesture-based techniques. Then, we present the results of two user studies that verify that users gradually adapt to *misrecognition* errors and that this adaptation rate depends on how frequently such errors occur. Finally, we conclude with practical implications and future extensions of this work.

2   RELATED WORK

Here, we briefly review related work in gesture recognition and other fields.

2.1   Unistroke Gesture Recognition

Gesture-based text entry techniques have been widely explored and aim to increase speed and accuracy over free-form handwriting methods, which support natural handwriting [30]. Gesture-based methods trade naturalness with higher recognition accuracy. Almost all gesture-based techniques limit user behaviours by permitting only a single way of drawing each character to avoid segmentation and other handwriting recognition related problems [4]. Also, many gesture-based techniques use simplified sets of characters that are drawn with a single stroke (unistroke).

One such technique, called *Unistrokes*, use a character set designed to be entered in an eyes-free manner on handheld devices with a stylus [12]. As the name suggests, each character is represented by a single stroke mark. Unistroke gestures are only somewhat similar to their printed counterparts and need to be learned [4]. A similar unistroke technique, called *Graffiti*, attempted to reduce the learning effort with strokes that resemble the equivalent printed letters more closely [14]. A later version, *Graffiti 2*, requires some characters, such as *I, K, T* and *X*, to be drawn with two strokes [16]. A longitudinal study comparing these two techniques did not find any significant difference between them [6]. *Jot System*, a technique very similar to *Graffiti 2*, includes almost all *Graffiti 2* gestures but adds multiple variants of the gestures to accommodate handwriting-like drawing [21]. *EdgeWrite* simplifies the text entry gestures to strokes between the corners of a square [34, 36]. A study showed that it requires learning effort, similar to *Graffiti* [34]. *Minimal Device-independent Text Input Method* (*MDTIM*) also simplifies the gestures to *up*, *down*, *left*, and *right* strokes [14]. Yet, significant practice is required to achieve fast entry speeds, as its gesture set is quite different from the printed counterparts [21].

A word-based technique, called *SHARK*, assigns unistroke gestures to the most frequent words based on users' finger movement pattern on a keyboard [37]. With this method, users effectively draw gestures for known words and tap on the keys for unfamiliar ones. *Swype* is similar and also permits users to enter words as gestures. It uses shape recognition to identify words, as the resulting stroke usually forms a shape that is unique to the intended word. In case the shape matches multiple words, users can select the desired word from a list. Both of these techniques are somewhat similar to the earlier *Cirrin* technique [23]. There, all characters are arranged inside the perimeter of an annulus. To input each character, users have to move the stylus into and out of the appropriate sector of that annulus. *T-Cube* was developed [33] based on marking menus [17]. It is similar to a two-level pie menu system. The main level contains nine submenus and the second level contains eight pie menus, each representing a specific character. To input a character, users first have to select an entry in the main menu. Then, users have to flick the stylus into the direction where the intended character is situated in the second level menu that appears.

Unipad augments *Unistrokes* with word prediction and auto-completion [22]. *UniGest*, in contrast, allows users to input text with pointing devices without a display [7].

2.2 Effort vs. Learning

A theory in psychology research identified the durability of episodic memory as a positive function of the degrees of semantic involvement in processing stimuli [9]. This was verified through empirical studies that showed that deeper encodings take longer to process, but that they also improve performance in tasks such as recall or recognition for words [10]. Similarly, a survey of skill acquisition research argued that manipulations that decrease the speed of acquisition might support long-term learning [28]. Encouraging active information retrieval from memory is a common and effective mechanism for skill acquisition in various domains. Motivated by this, prior work investigated the relationship between user effort and spatial memory in user interfaces. Such explorations revealed that, when interacting with effortful user interfaces, users depend more on memory retrieval than perceptually available information—a characteristic of skilled behaviour [11]. Investigations also showed that interfaces that require greater user effort improve learning for spatial tasks [8], and improve system efficiency and user experience in the long run [27]. In a recent study, Labahn et al. observed that users seemed to adapt to an error-prone recognizer after using it for about half an hour [18]. However, they did not investigate this further.

2.3 Errors in Gesture Recognition

Although gesture recognition is technically easier than online handwriting recognition, most gesture recognition techniques still suffer from notable amounts of recognition errors [24, 29]. Moreover, recent developments in gestures sets for pen, finger, and wand user interfaces on different devices have increased the overall gesture ambiguity, which further affects accuracy. A study comparing *Graffiti 2* with a virtual Qwerty keyboard showed that text entry with *Graffiti 2* is substantially slower and more error prone, even when augmented with prefix-based word prediction [16]. Yet, high accuracy is vital for a technique's success. A study showed that users find a gesture-based technique useful only when it is at least 97% accurate [19]. Another user study showed that mobile users usually abandon a gesture-based technique and start using an alternative when accuracy drops below 40% [15].

Most gesture recognizers attempt to match a performed gesture to an existing, internal gesture library and return a match score. These libraries contain templates for the supported gestures, often based on the number of strokes, their order, direction, and/or the speed associated with them [30]. When the score is above a predetermined, algorithm-dependent threshold, the system performs the action associated with the gesture that yielded the highest match score. In gesture-based text entry, this action is usually the output of a character. There are two types of errors that occur in most gesture-based techniques: *misrecognitions* and *failures to recognize*.

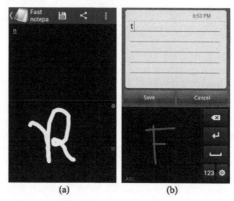

Figure 1: Misrecognition in: (a) *Touch-Writer* and (b) *DioPen*. In both cases, the user intended to input one character but the system misrecognized it as another.

A *misrecognition* error occurs when the recognition score is above the predetermined threshold, but the system misinterpreted the performed gesture, and thus, outputted an incorrect letter. A common example is that the user inputs *u*, but the system recognizes and outputs *v*. Or a gesture is too slanted relative to the template. Such errors are usually caused by some internal limitation of the system and are well known to occur in most gesture-based techniques [30]. Research on better gesture recognition algorithms attempts to reduce the potential for these. In an informal survey, we explored the error handling of five popular gesture-based techniques for handheld devices: *Path Input*, *Touch-Writer*, *DioPen*, *Hot Virtual Keyboard*, and *Gesture Go*. The first is similar to *Swype*, the next three are character-based techniques, and the last is an application launcher. Even in a short test, each of these systems misrecognized some performed gestures and output incorrect results. Figure 1 illustrates two such incidents.

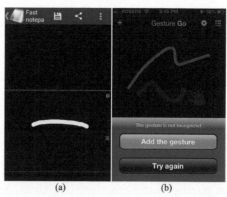

Figure 2: Error handling in: (a) *Touch-Writer* and (b) *Gesture Go*. In (a), the system displays no output when it fails to find a match for the performed gesture in the library. In (b), it asks the user to include the gesture in the library or to try again.

A *failure to recognize* error occurs when the match score for the user input is below a predetermined threshold or the length of the gesture is too short to be recognized. In our informal survey, human behaviour caused most of such errors. Common examples are the user accidently tapping the screen or aborting a gesture prematurely. Or the user inputs a gesture that is not part of the template library. The surveyed techniques deal with such errors in two different ways. They either do not display output or query the users if they want to include the new gesture in the built-in template library to enrich it. Figure 2 illustrates this.

2.4 Alternative Methods/Gestures

Some gesture-based systems permit users to input a given character with several drawing variations. *EdgeWrite* and some commercial products, such as *DioPen* and *Hot Virtual Keyboard*, provide multiple variations for drawing some characters. More relevant for our context, *Jot* permits users to indicate drawing preferences for some characters. In other words, *Jot* enables users to select less intuitive drawing variants as the dominant method for inputting some characters, if the user has problems with the recognition accuracy for those gestures [21]. Here and to distinguish between these variants, we classify the more intuitive ones as "primary" and less intuitive one as "alternative".

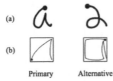

Figure 3: The primary and an alternative method for drawing 'a' with: (a) *Jot* and (b) *EdgeWrite*.

Alternative gestures are almost always *less intuitive* and *harder to discover* compared to the primary ones. Figure 3 illustrates the primary gesture and one of the alternative ones for inputting the character 'a' with *Jot* and *EdgeWrite*. Also, one has to either go to the tutorial (with *Jot*, *EdgeWrite*, and *Hot Virtual Keyboard*) or guess (with *DioPen*) to discover such alternative gestures.

3 THE EXPERIMENTAL SOFTWARE

Before we describe our user studies, we discuss the custom software we created for them. It was designed according to current trends in human and system error handling and alternative method usage among gesture-based techniques, as discussed above. The software was fine-tuned through several pilots. The design intent was to increase the external validity of this work by making the experiment software reasonably comparable to existing techniques. We also discuss technical design decisions behind the user studies.

3.1 Gesture Recognition

The software uses the $1 Unistroke Recognizer [35] to process pen-based gesture input. Similar to geometric template matchers, it recognizes gestures using a nearest-neighbour classifier with a Euclidean scoring function. This recognizer performs well for a limited number of gestures based on very few templates. A study reported 99% accuracy rate for sixteen gestures with three or more templates loaded [35]. Our implementation used fourteen gestures and loaded seven templates for each, which should make the performance of our system equivalent to other recent recognizers in the field.

3.2 The Supported Gestures

During the studies, participants inputted seven English letters, specifically *B*, *D*, *O*, *Q*, *R*, *W*, and *Y*. The custom software presented one letter at a time on the screen. Participants then had to input the presented letter with a digital pen on a graphic tablet using either *Graffiti* or *Unistrokes*. The system used *Graffiti* as the

primary method of inputting the letters, while *Unistrokes* were used as the alternative. That is, users were expected to primarily use *Graffiti* to input the letters, but were permitted to use *Unistrokes* if they felt their use necessary, such as to bypass (injected) *misrecognition* errors. We elaborate on this below.

3.3 Unistroke vs. Multistroke Gestures

We used a unistroke gesture system instead of a multistroke one, as the latter systems usually permit different variations for drawing the same letter. This makes it more challenging to recognize a performed gesture. It also makes it difficult to automatically identify human errors due to differences in gesture drawing across users. In addition, due to multiple possible drawing variations for the same letter, users often struggle to identify their mistakes and to discover the right way for drawing a letter with multistroke systems. The $N Recognizer, for example, often fails to correctly recognize a gesture when users use more strokes than the number of strokes used to define said gesture [1]. With adaptive multistroke recognizers, such as Gesture Search [20], it is difficult to isolate the human adaptation rate as the system adapts to human behaviours as well. Unistroke gesture systems usually do not suffer from such problems [30]. A more recent multistroke recognizer, $P Recognizer, resolves these issues [32], but was proposed after the completion of our studies.

3.4 Primary vs. Alternative Gestures

Graffiti and *Unistrokes* gestures were selected as *primary* and alternative method for drawing the letters for two reasons. First, a previous study did not find a significant difference between these techniques' entry speed, correction rate, and preparation time [6]. Second, *Graffiti* was selected as the *primary* method, as in almost all unistroke-based techniques the primary method is relatively more intuitive and easier to guess than the alternative one, as discussed earlier. In Figure 4, one can see how the primary *Graffiti* gestures look more like their printed counterparts. In addition, participants were encouraged to practice the *primary* gestures before the main studies, to familiarize participants (to a limited degree) with them, as also discussed below. With this experimental design we can assume that any performance effect due to switching the gesture drawing method (from *primary* to alternative and vice versa) mid-study will be attributable *predominantly* to learning.

Figure 4: The seven letters and their corresponding gestures. The *primary* gestures are from *Graffiti* and the alternatives are from *Unistrokes*. A dot indicates the start of a stroke.

3.5 Discoverability

We discussed earlier how in most gesture-based techniques alternative input methods are relatively harder to discover compared to the *primary* method. In most systems and to discover alternative gestures, one has to either go to an extended tutorial or guess. Based on this, our custom software displayed the *primary* gestures in a panel at all times and presented the to-be-inputted letters in *Graffiti*. To discover the alternative gesture for a particular letter, users had to tap or right-click on the corresponding *primary* gesture in the panel. This displayed the alternative gesture for that letter for two seconds, and then returned to the original state, that is, displaying the *primary* gestures (see Figure 5).

3.6 Errors and Error Handling

Similar to other gesture-based systems and based on several pilots, our system reported a *failure to recognize* error when the total number of recorded stroke samples was less than ten in our setup, i.e., when the stroke was much too short for a gesture. This threshold is system specific and needs to be adapted for other setups. Our pilots identified that such short gestures are almost always caused by accidental interactions. Examples include that users tapped on the graphic tablet with the pen, pressed the buttons on the pen by mistake, or stopped drawing prematurely. Similar to many gesture-based techniques, the custom software provided visual feedback on such *failure to recognize* errors. The (previously) inputted gesture field, in the top-right corner of Figure 5, displayed a special symbol (see Figure 6) in case of such accidental interactions.

If the recognized gesture did not match the presented gesture the system classified this as a *misrecognition* error. Similar to almost all gesture-based techniques, the custom software displayed the misrecognized gesture in the inputted gesture field. For example, when *O* was misrecognized as *Q*, the system displayed *Q* in the inputted gesture field. Auditory feedback, in form of a *ding* sound was provided for both *failure to recognize* and *misrecognition* errors.

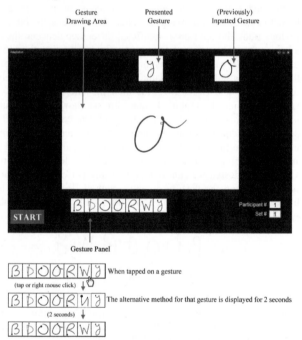

Figure 5: The custom software used during the studies. The to-be-inputted letter is presented using the *primary* gesture. To discover the alternative gesture for that letter, one has to tap on the corresponding *primary* gesture in the bottom panel.

3.6.1 Raw Recognition Error Rate

In a pilot with eight novice users, four female, average 21 years, all right-handed, where each user inputted the seven *Graffiti* gestures for forty times with the custom software **without error injection**, the system recorded 1% "system" errors, composed of 0.3% *failure to recognize* and 0.7% *misrecognition* errors. In other words, the overall accuracy rate was 99%, which matches prior work [35].

3.7 Misrecognition Error Injection

The main purpose of this work is to investigate (if and) how users adapt to *misrecognition* errors. Thus, a few *primary* gestures were randomly selected during the studies and injected with *synthetic* misrecognition errors at different rates. That is, the system intentionally misrecognized these gestures at given rates. For instance, if the *primary* gesture for the letter *D* was injected with 5% synthetic *misrecognition* error, then five out of hundred times the system would intentionally misrecognize this gesture and would randomly display a similar gesture in the inputted gesture field, such as *B*, *C*, *O*, or *Q*. The system injected *misrecognition* errors instead of *failure to recognize* errors, as *misrecognition* is the most common type of error in gesture-based techniques [24, 29]. **Only** the *primary* gestures were injected with these errors.

We accounted for any potential bias in simulated gesture recognition errors by randomly selecting a different set of letters for error injection for each participant. Another design constraint for our user studies is that with increasing gesture set size, error occurrences naturally decrease, which makes such errors then progressively harder to study. Consequently, we used only seven letters and tuned the gestures well. As mentioned above, in the absence of injected errors, users encountered only 1% "system" errors. Such a small error rate is well below what can be studies in short-term studies. Consider that 1% errors means that system errors occur only on one out of hundred letters entered. In our studies, participants entered 630 gestures within an hour or more. Thus they would see only 6-7 errors, which is too small to study adaptation.

Failed to
Recognize

Figure 6: The symbol displayed in the (previously) inputted gesture field on accidental interactions.

3.8 Bypassing Injected Misrecognition Errors

Our pilots indicate that users deal with *misrecognition* errors in two different ways [2]. They either draw a faulty gesture slowly or start using an alternative method (if available). The first approach affects one's entry speed, as it takes more time to input gestures. In contrast and assuming that the alternative method is not more complex than the *primary* one, the second approach does not compromise entry speed. Prior work provides a methodology for classifying gestures into simple, medium, and complex categories [31]. Given this, the latter approach is a better choice for experiments, as entry speed will vary less.

Besides, with only a single "faulty" gesture set (and no alternatives), users are effectively stuck. If they fail to recognize the failure patterns, they either adapt or abandon the system. In many real world situations, they would most probably abandon the system, as there are other ways to achieve their tasks. Consequently, many recent real world systems, see above, include gesture variations (alternative gestures) as a solution this problem. We chose to follow this idea.

To address the issues around speed, our studies **indirectly** discouraged participants from drawing gestures slowly. First, users were informed prior to the studies that taking more time to draw a gesture might not enhance the system's recognition rate. Second, and in the practice period prior to the main studies, most users would realize that an inputted gesture does not have to be an exact match of the displayed one for the system to recognize it—so that (subconsciously) they would be much less motivated to draw gestures slowly.

3.9 Seven Letters vs. Short English Phrases

Early on, we decided against the use of short English phrases in the studies. Two reasons motivated this. First, using English phrases would require injecting errors based on letter frequencies to maintain uniformity. This needlessly complicates and lengthens the studies. Second, a pilot study indicated that inputting English phrases with an untrustworthy gesture-based system causes a high level of user frustration, which may negatively bias study results.

We also decided against using a complete gesture alphabet. The reason is that users need to experience *enough* injected errors within 60 to 90 minutes to be able to adapt to the system. The use of seven letters assured that each letter appeared a sufficient number of times. This does not invalidate this work, as the focus here is on how users adapt to injected *misrecognition* errors and not (directly) on how text entry performance is affected.

3.10 Justification for a Short-term Study

While it is important to understand gradual adaptation over time, short-term usability is today a strong determinant in product success. If users do not see reliable enough performance in the short term, a product is likely to fail. Consequently, long-term investigations are interesting, but do not help in situations where users get frustrated up-front. This is a global issue that gesture recognizers have to contend with today.

3.11 Justifications for the Performance Metrics

The following metrics were calculated during the studies.

- **Alternative Method Usage (AMU):** The rate (%) at which the alternative method was used to input letters. As users were free to use either the *primary* or the alternative method to input/re-input a letter, this metric enable us to measure the rate at which users adapted to the alternative gestures.

- **Input Time (T^h_{input}):** This represents the average time (in milliseconds) it took to input a letter [3]. This metric captures the performance aspect of learning. We also use this to analyse performance across different *misrecognition* rates.

- **Gestures per Character (GPC):** This denotes how many gestures it took on average to input a letter [34]. As most unistroke methods have dedicated gestures for all English letters, a flawless system will require a GPC of one, providing there was no human error. This was calculated to provide an overall picture of the input process, and to check whether the more faulty letters yield higher GPCs compared to less faulty ones, as one might expect.

4 USER STUDY 1

This user study investigated users' adaptation behaviour for injected *misrecognition* error rates between 0 and 30%.

4.1 Participants

Twelve participants, aged from 21 to 30 years, average 24.5 (SD = 2.61), participated in the user study. They were recruited through online social communities, local university e-mailing lists, and by posting flyers on campus. None of them had prior experience with pen-based devices. All were unaware of the existence of *Unistrokes* and *Graffiti*. Seven of them were female and one was a left-hand pen user. They all received a small compensation for participating.

4.2 Apparatus

The custom application described earlier was used during this study. It was developed with the default *Bamboo Mini* SDK 2.1.

The application was running on a 15.4" *Compaq* Presario C700 Notebook PC at 1280×800 pixel resolution. Participants interacted with the application through a digital pen on a *Wacom* Bamboo Pen and Touch Graphic Tablet, as illustrated in Figure 7. The device's 14.73×9.14 cm active area was calibrated with respect to the application window. Its multi-touch input capability was disabled to permit participants to rest their hand on the surface while using the pen. The orientation of the tablet and the default firmware was adjusted to accommodate for left- and right-handedness. The custom application logged all interactions with timestamps and calculated user performance directly.

Figure 7: A participant drawing gestures using a digital pen on a Bamboo Pen and Touch Graphic Tablet.

4.3 Procedure and Design

The experiment setup and software was first demonstrated to users. The experimenter verified that participants understood the primary (*Graffiti*) and the alternative (*Unistrokes*) gestures, the *failure to recognize* and the *misrecognition* errors, and knew how to discover alternative gestures.

A practice period followed the demonstration. During practice, participants were asked to input the seven letters five times using the *primary* method without error injection. The intent was to familiarize them with the setup. This also gave them some experience with how similar the presented and the performed gestures needed to be for the system to recognize them accurately. Participants were able to extend the practice period (at most twice), as desired.

The main user study started roughly two minutes after the practice. In that part, participants inputted letters in random order and each of the seven letters occurred ninety times. Thus, each participant inputted in total 630 letters. Three out of the seven letters were randomly picked by the system and injected with 10, 20, and respectively 30% *synthetic misrecognition* errors. That is, in ten, twenty, and thirty out of hundred attempts the corresponding letters were intentionally misrecognized by the system. That is, the system displayed a similar letter instead of the recognized one, as discussed above. Only three letters were injected with synthetic *misrecognition* errors, to ensure that the faulty letters do not dominate the overall input process.

The letters were displayed one at a time on the screen. Participants had to input each presented letter using the pen and the graphic tablet using predominantly the *primary* method (*Graffiti*). They were informed that, unlike in the practice period, the system might not be entirely reliable. That is, it may misrecognize some of the letters, even when they were inputted correctly. However, they were not informed about error rates or the number of letters where synthetic *misrecognition* errors were injected.

A gesture was recorded from the moment one touched the graphic tablet with the pen (touch-down) to the moment it was lifted (touch-up). Upon completion of input, the recognized and the next to-be-inputted letters were displayed on the screen automatically, as illustrated in Figure 5. Participants were asked to input the gestures as fast as possible, but to focus more on the accuracy. That is, they were encouraged to reduce the *misrecognition* errors, any way they saw fit, even if it compromised their input speed. They were informed that they **could** use the alternative method (*Unistrokes*) to input a frequently misrecognized letter, if they felt that this would improve (or is improving) recognition accuracy. But they were **neither forced nor instructed** to use the alternative*s*. Users had to keep inputting a gesture until it was correctly recognized by the system. On correction attempts, no synthetic recognition errors were injected to reduce the potential for overly frustrating tasks. Thus, users who did not want to use alternative*s* could use the *primary* method on correction attempts. Auditory and visual feedback was provided, as described earlier. To minimize interruptions, participants were permitted to take at most two three-minute breaks during the study, as necessary. Given that participants entered 630 letters in the whole session, this gave them enough time to create a good mental model of the system and its errors. After all, each participant the set of faulty letters was constant for each participant. Upon completion of the study, they were asked to fill out a short questionnaire, where they were asked to list the frequently misrecognized letters.

The study used a within-subjects design, where the within-subjects factor focused on the 0, 10, 20, and 30% injected *misrecognition* rates. The dependent variables were GPC, AMU (%), and T^h_{input} (milliseconds).

4.4 Results

The whole user study lasted from sixty to ninety minutes including the demonstration, practice, and breaks. Upon completion of the study, 59% participants were able to recognize all three error prone letters, 33% had recognized the two most error prone letters, while the remaining 8% recognized only the most error prone one. Thus, about 8% of the users did not adapt to the two less faulty letters where fewer misrecognitions were injected. Consequently, they also did not use the alternative method to input those two letters.

D'Agostino Kurtosis tests on the dependent variables revealed that the data were normally distributed. Also, a Mauchly's test confirmed that the data's covariance matrix was circular in form. Hence, repeated-measures ANOVA was used for all analysis. All statistically significant results are presented with effect size (η^2).

To identify learning, the data was segmented into blocks of ten appearances of each letter during the study. That is, the average of every ten times a letter was presented to the users to input was used to observe improvements over time. As all letters appeared exactly ninety times per participant, there were nine segments for each letter. Note that we only compared different data points from the same segment to isolate the effect of *misrecognition* rates. As the learning process is gradual [25, 26], users adapt more to a (faulty) system when they spend more time with it. Hence, comparisons between different data points from different segments may be misleading or suffer from bias.

4.4.1 Alternative Method Usage (AMU)

An ANOVA on the data revealed that there was a significant effect of injected *misrecognition* rate on AMU ($F_{3,11} = 5.56$, $p < .005$, $\eta^2 = .40$). Average AMU for 0, 10, 20, and 30% injected *misrecognition* rates were 8.5, 31.85, 27.59, and 55.10%, respectively. Figure 9 illustrates this. A Tukey-Kramer test showed that the 30% injected *misrecognition* rate had significantly higher AMU than 0, 10, and 20%.

For all injected *misrecognition* error rates, power functions were fitted to the data to model the power law of practice [5]. This is illustrated in Figure 9, where the horizontal axis represents the

segments and the vertical axis represents the average AMU during that segment. Recall that there were four letters where no *misrecognition* errors were injected (0%), compared to one letter for each injected *misrecognition* rates (10, 20, and 30%). Hence, the 0% data points average the AMU of the ten appearances of the four non-faulty letters (10×4 appearances). We also tried fitting linear functions to the data (0%: $R^2 = 0.87334$, 10%: $R^2 = 0.63659$, 20%: $R^2 = 0.95331$, and 30%: $R^2 = 0.51826$), but they did not correlate as well as the power functions (0%: $R^2 = 0.92358$, 10%: $R^2 = 0.84447$, 20%: $R^2 = 0.96004$, and 30%: $R^2 = 0.73612$).

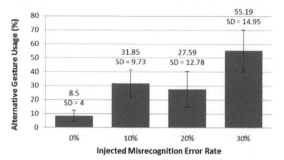

Figure 8: Average Alternative Method Usage (AMU) over all investigated injected misrecognition error rates. Error bars represent ±1 standard deviation.

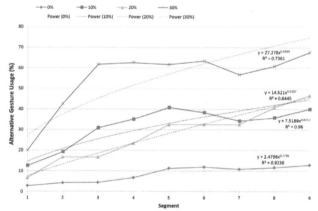

Figure 9: Average Alternative Method Usage (AMU) by injected *misrecognition* rates and segments.

4.4.2 Input Time (T^h_{input})

There was global learning, as the average time over all letters to input a gesture (T^h_{input}) correlated well with the power law of learning [5], over all letters ($y = 750.07x^{-0.109}$, $R^2 = 0.7564$). An ANOVA on the data failed to identify a significant effect of injected *misrecognition* rate on T^h_{input} ($F_{3,11} = 1.68$, $p > .05$). T^h_{input} for 0, 10, 20, and 30% injected *misrecognition* rates was 652, 627, 707, and 593 milliseconds, respectively. Figure 10 illustrates this.

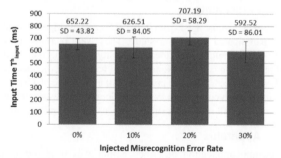

Figure 10: Average Input Time (T^h_{input}) over all investigated injected misrecognition rates. Error bars represent ±1 standard deviation.

4.4.3 Gestures per Character (GPC)

An ANOVA identified a significant effect of injected *misrecognition* error rate on GPC ($F_{3,11} = 4.39$, $p < .05$, $\eta^2 = .20$). A Tukey-Kramer test revealed that 30 and 20% injected *misrecognition* rates yielded significantly higher GPCs compared to 0 and 10%. Average GPC for 0, 10, 20, and 30% injected *misrecognition* rates were 1.11, 1.25, 1.4, and 1.37, respectively. Figure 11 illustrates this. Yet, the data over all letters did not correlate with the power law of learning [5], ($y = 1.2638x^{0.0092}$, $R^2 = 0.1001$).

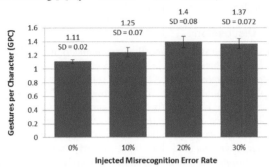

Figure 11: Average Gestures per Character (GPC) over all investigated injected misrecognition rates. Error bars represent ±1 standard deviation.

4.5 Discussion

The results show that the use of the alternative method increased over time. Figure 9 illustrated average AMU by injected *misrecognition* error rates and segments, where one can see that participants learned to use the alternative method to input those letters where synthetic *misrecognition* errors were injected, relatively faster compared to the reliable letters. A Tukey-Kramer test showed that the alternative method was used substantially more frequently for the most faulty letter (30% injected *misrecognition* rate) compared to the less faulty ones (0-20% injected *misrecognition* rates). This verifies the hypothesis that users adapt to a gesture-based technique's *misrecognition* errors and that this adaptation rate depends on how frequently they occur. That is, users adapt to an error faster if it occurs more frequently.

Note that even for letters with 0% injected *misrecognition* rate, some users chose to use the alternative gesture, see Figure 9. To investigate this behaviour, we speculated that this was due to the visual similarity between some error prone letters and alternative gesture. Consequently, we investigated if users started to use the alterative gestures for letters that were visually similar to the faulty ones, such as *D* when *B* was more error prone. Yet, we failed to find any notable relationship. One possible reason is that some users treated the whole system as faulty and thus started using alternative gestures for all letters. However, we do not have enough data to validate this hypothesis.

There was no significant effect of injected *misrecognition* rate on T^h_{input}. Instead, participants learned to input *all* letters faster with time, despite the injected *misrecognition* error rates. This validates to some degree the assumption discussed earlier that switching input methods mid-study–from primary to alternative gesture to adapt to a faulty letter - does not affect entry speed in a significant manner.

One interesting trend visible in Figure 9 is that users adapt to the 10 and 20% injected *misrecognition* rates roughly the same way, while adaptation to 0 and 30% seem distinct. One can speculate that this is because users perceive 10 and 20% injected *misrecognition* rates almost the same way, while 30% was

perceived as *too* erroneous. User feedback data also supports this, as most users responded that they were only able to differentiate between the 10 and 20% injected *misrecognition* rates towards the end of the study. This behaviour is similar to earlier results on text entry on faulty keyboards, where 10 and 20% were also not found to be significantly different [3].

A significant effect of injected *misrecognition* rate was identified on GPC. Evidently, 30 and 20% injected *misrecognition* rates yielded significantly higher GPCs compared to 0 and 10%. This is not unexpected as error correction was forced during the study. Thus, participants often had to make multiple attempts to input letters where synthetic *misrecognition* errors were injected. This is also apparent in Figure 11, where one can see the increase in average GPC with increasing injected *misrecognition* rates.

5 USER STUDY 2

We conducted a second user study to further observe user adaptation to injected *misrecognitions* and to investigate how the results apply at relatively lower error rates. This study investigated users' adaptation behaviour for injected *misrecognition* error rates from 0 to 10%.

5.1 Participants

Twelve participants, aged from 18 to 34 years, average 23.83 (SD = 4.74), took part in the study. They were recruited through online communities, local university e-mailing lists, posting flyers on campus, and by word of mouth. None of them had prior experience with pen-based devices and eleven of them had no knowledge of *Unistrokes* and *Graffiti*. One knew about these techniques, but had never used them. Six of them were female and one was a left-hand pen user. All received a small compensation for participating.

5.2 Apparatus, Procedure, and Design

The same apparatus as the first user study were used. The study also used the same procedure and design, as described earlier. The difference is that this study investigated lower injected *misrecognition* error rates (0, 5, 7.5, and 10%).

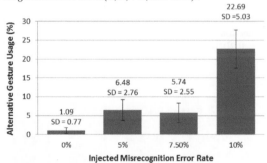

Figure 12: Average Alternative Method Usage (AMU) over all investigated injected misrecognition rates. Error bars represent ±1 standard deviation.

5.3 Results

The whole user study lasted from fifty to ninety minutes including the demonstration, practice, and breaks. Upon completion of the study, 25% participants were able to recognize all three error prone letters, 58% recognized the two most error prone letters, and the remaining 17% recognized only the most error prone one. Thus, about 17% of the users did not adapt to the two less faulty letters, where fewer *misrecognition* errors were injected. Consequently, they also did not use the alternative method to input those two letters.

D'Agostino Kurtosis tests on the dependent variables revealed that the data were normally distributed. Also, a Mauchly's test confirmed that the data's covariance matrix was circular in form. Thus, repeated-measures ANOVA was used for all analysis. All statistically significant results are presented with effect size (η^2).

As in the first study, the data was segmented into blocks of ten appearances of each letter for learning analyses.

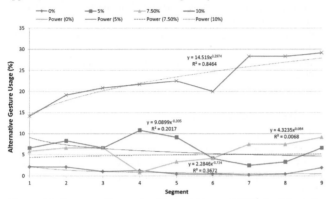

Figure 13: Average Alternative Method Usage (AMU) by injected misrecognition rates and segments.

5.3.1 Alternative Method Usage

An ANOVA revealed that there was a significant effect of injected *misrecognition* rate on AMU ($F_{3,11} = 3.52$, $p < .05$, $\eta^2 = .20$). Average AMU for 0, 5, 7.5 and 10% injected *misrecognition* rates were 1.09, 6.48, 5.74, and 22.69%, correspondingly. Figure 12 illustrates this. A Tukey-Kramer test failed to identify groupings. Yet, a (statistically somewhat weaker) Duncan's test identified two groups, 0-7.5% and 10%.

For all injected *misrecognition* rates, the data was again fit with power functions to analyse learning. Figure 13 illustrates this, where the horizontal axis represents the segments and vertical axis represents the average AMU during that segment. As above, the 0% condition is averaged across the four non-faulty letters. We also tried to fit linear functions to the data (0%: $R^2 = 0.24341$, 5%: $R^2 = 0.2467$, 7.5%: $R^2 = 0.13909$, and 10%: $R^2 = 0.83695$), yet the power functions yielded marginally better results (0%: $R^2 = 0.3672$, 5%: $R^2 = 0.20167$, 7.5%: $R^2 = 0.00681$, and 10%: $R^2 = 0.84642$).

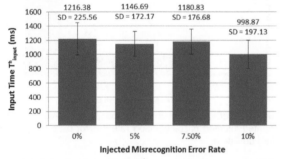

Figure 14: Average Input Time (T^h_{input}) over all investigated injected misrecognition rates. Error bars represent ±1 standard deviation.

5.3.2 Input Time (T^h_{input})

An ANOVA failed to identify a significant effect of injected *misrecognition* rate on T^h_{input} ($F_{3,11} = 1.34, p > .05$). Average T^h_{input} for 0, 5, 7.5, and 10% injected *misrecognition* rates were 1216, 1147, 1181, and 999 milliseconds, correspondingly. Figure 14 illustrates this. Similar to the first user study, the data over all letters correlates very well to the power law of learning [5], ($y = 1534.9x^{-0.22}$, $R^2 = 0.9574$).

5.3.3 Gestures per Character (GPC)

An ANOVA on the data identified a significant effect of injected *misrecognition* rate on GPC ($F_{3,11} = 5.33$, $p < .01$, $\eta^2 = .20$). A Tukey-Kramer test revealed that the 10% injected *misrecognition* rate yielded a significantly higher GPC than the 0% injected *misrecognition* rate. Average GPC for 0, 5, 7.5, and 10% injected *misrecognition* rates were 1.07, 1.16, 1.21, and 1.31, respectively, as illustrated in Figure 15. Yet and again similar to the first user study, no strong learning effect was identifiable, ($y = 1.2619x^{-0.044}$, $R^2 = 0.6529$).

5.4 Discussion

The results of the study are mostly comparable to the results of the first study: there was a significant effect of injected *misrecognition* rate on both AMU and GPC, but not on input time (T^h_{input}). Substantial learning effects were observed for AMU and input time (T^h_{input}), but not for GPC. Figure 13 illustrates average AMU by injected *misrecognition* rates and segments. Similar to the first study, one can see there that participants learned to use the alternative method to input letters, where synthetic *misrecognitions* were injected, more frequently relatively faster than the other letters. Also, the 10% injected *misrecognition* condition, common to both studies, yielded comparable AMU (32% and 23%) and GPC (1.25 and 1.31) values, which shows that the results of the two experiments are reasonably consistent. Figure 9 and Figure 13 illustrate that users adapted to the 10% *misrecognition* condition nearly the same way. Therefore, results of this study further strengthen the initial hypothesis and extend the findings towards lower injected *misrecognition* rates.

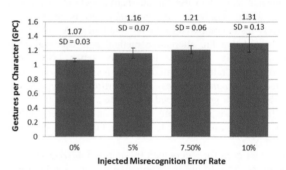

Figure 15: Average Gestures per Character (GPC) over all investigated injected misrecognition rates. Error bars represent ±1 standard deviation.

Figure 13 shows that adaptation to 0, 5, and 7.5% injected *misrecognition* rates were relatively slower than 10%. The results indicate that this is mostly due to insufficient exposure. In the post-study questionnaire, most (75%) participants responded that they managed to identify the 5 and 7.5% faulty letters only shortly before the study ended. This is also apparent in Figure 13, where one can see a distinct trend in adaptation through an increased alternative method usage for these letters during the last three segments, especially for the 5% condition. An ANOVA on the data from these segments identified a significant effect of injected *misrecognition* rate on AMU ($F_{3,11} = 3.96$, $p < .05$, $\eta^2 = .20$). A Tukey-Kramer test identified two statistically different groups for the last three segments: 0% and 5-10%. A statistically weaker Duncan's test identified three statistically different groups for the last three segments: 0%, 5-7.5%, and 10%. Note that the average input time (T^h_{input}) was higher during the second study, compared to the first. This is presumably due to the inclusion of relatively more inexperienced users.

6 OVERALL DISCUSSION AND IMPLICATIONS

Overall, we observed that users learn to use alternative gestures more quickly, if the primary gestures are faultier. This validates our primary hypothesis. It also complements findings in psychology [9, 10], skill acquisition [28], and user interface research [8, 11, 27] that imply that user interfaces requiring greater efforts from users may facilitate the transition to recall-based expert behaviour. After all, faulty gestures increase user effort to some degree. Marking menus are an example how this concept could be applied [17]. To force users to recall the direction of the intended menu item, they delay the display of the pie menu content. This affects interaction time for novices, but facilitates the transition to expert level [8]. However, this cannot be applied directly in our context, as marking menus do not provide for alternative gestures.

Our results also indicate that gesture recognizers should achieve substantially more than 90% accuracy to appear less (or maybe even in-)distinguishable from a "perfect" system. This is similar to results for keyboard based text entry [3]. The fact that users adapt to unreliable gesture recognizers by using an alternative method for inputting letters that are frequently misrecognized by the system should encourage developers to provide users with an alternative gesture set along with the primary one. Systems should also permit users to swap a primary gesture with an alternative one, and vice versa. A more advanced system could even keep track of the primary and alternative method usage for each letter and might then even propose a switch for letters that are frequently inputted with the alternative method. This may increase the overall recognition accuracy, providing that the recognition rate is higher for the alternative method than the primary one. For this, more distinct gestures would be a good choice as alternatives, as our results showed that users adapt to alternative gestures for frequently misrecognized letters, even when the alternative gestures are relatively less intuitive (and harder to discover) than the primary gestures. We speculate that such a feature can be applied not only on text entry but also to other gesture systems, such as natural user interfaces and application launchers.

Looking across both studies, one interesting observation is that about half of the users were unable to identify all faulty gestures of the system within about an hour. We speculate that this is likely due to different cognitive strategies or personality types. Investigating this is a topic for future work.

7 CONCLUSION

This article presented the results of two empirical studies that identify that users gradually adapt to *misrecognition* errors of a unistroke-based text entry technique's gesture recognizer and that this adaptation rate depends on how frequently such errors occur. That is, users adapt to an error faster if it occurs more frequently. For injected *misrecognition* rates below 10%, no clear pattern for adaptation was observed.

8 FUTURE WORK

In the future we may conduct a longitudinal study to investigate this range more closely over longer periods. Other potential future work may investigate if our results apply for multistroke recognizers as well. Finally, based on the fact that users' adaptation to *misrecognition* errors is dependent on how frequently they occur, a mathematical model could be developed to predict adaptation rates.

9 ACKNOWLEDGEMENTS

We would like to express our gratitude to NSERC, the GRAND NCE, and York University for funding the research.

REFERENCES

[1] Anthony, L. and Wobbrock, J. O. $N-Protractor: A fast and accurate multistroke recognizer. In *Proc. GI '12*, Canadian Information Processing Society (2012), 117-120.

[2] Arif, A. S. and Stuerzlinger, W. How do users adapt to a faulty system? In *CHI '12 Workshop on Designing and Evaluating Text Entry Methods*, 11-14, 2012.

[3] Arif, A. S. and Stuerzlinger, W. Predicting the cost of error correction in character-based text entry technologies. In *Proc. CHI '10*, ACM (2010), 5-14.

[4] Buxton, W. Chapter 7: Touch, gesture & marking. In *Readings in Human Computer Interaction: Toward the Year 2000*, Morgan Kaufmann, 1995.

[5] Card, S. K., Moran, T. P. and Newell, A. *The Psychology of Human-Computer Interaction*, Lawrence Erlbaum, 1983.

[6] Castellucci, S. J. and MacKenzie, I. S. (2008) Graffiti vs. Unistrokes: An empirical comparison. In *Proc. CHI '08*, ACM (2008), 305-308.

[7] Castellucci, S. J. and MacKenzie, I. S. UniGest: Text entry using three degrees of motion. In *CHI EA '08*, ACM (2008), 3549-3554.

[8] Cockburn, A., Kristensson, P. O., Alexander, J., and Zhai, S. Hard lessons: Effort-inducing interfaces benefit spatial learning. In *Proc. CHI '07*. ACM (2007), 1571-1580.

[9] Craik, F. I. M. and Lockhart, R. S. Levels of processing: A framework for memory research. *Journal of Verbal Learning and Verbal Behavior 11*, 6 (1972), 671-684.

[10] Craik, F. I. M. and Tulving, E. Depth of processing and the retention of words in episodic memory. *Journal of Experimental Psychology: General 104*, 3 (1975), 268-294.

[11] Ehret, B. D. Learning where to look: Location learning in graphical user interfaces. In *Proc. CHI '02*. ACM (2002), 211-218.

[12] Goldberg, D. and Richardson, C. Touch-typing with a stylus. In *Proc. CHI '93*, ACM (1993), 80-87.

[13] Hafner, K. Did Bill Gates really say that? *The New York Times: Bits*, Mar 25, 2008. http://nyti.ms/PFiPkO.

[14] Isokoski, P. A minimal device-independent text input method. Technical Report. University of Tampere, Finland, Report A-1999-14, 1999.

[15] Karam, M. and Schraefel, M. C. Investigating user tolerance for errors in vision-enabled gesture-based interactions. In *Proc. AVI '06*, ACM (2006), 225-232.

[16] Költringer, T. and Grechenig, T. Comparing the immediate usability of Graffiti 2 and virtual keyboard. In *CHI EA '04*, ACM(2004), 1175-1178.

[17] Kurtenbach, G. and Buxton, W. The limits of expert performance using hierarchic marking menus. In *Proc. CHI '93*, ACM (1993), 482-487.

[18] Labahn, G., Lank, E., Marzouk, M., Bunt, A., MacLean, S., and Tausky, D. MathBrush: A case study for pen-based interactive mathematics. In *Proc. SBIM '08*. Eurographics Association (2008), 143-150.

[19] LaLomia, M. User acceptance of handwritten recognition accuracy. In *Proc. CHI '94*, ACM (1994), 107-108.

[20] Li, Y. Gesture search: A tool for fast mobile data access. In Proc. UIST '10, ACM (2010), 87-96.

[21] MacKenzie, I. S. and Soukoreff, R. W. Text entry for mobile computing: Models and methods, theory and practice. *Hum.-Compute Interact.*, 17 (2002), 147-198.

[22] MacKenzie, I. S., Chen, J., and Oniszczak, A. Unipad: Single stroke text entry with language-based acceleration. In *Proc. NordiCHI '06*, ACM (2006), 78-85.

[23] Mankoff, J. and Abowd, G. D. Cirrin: A word-level unistroke keyboard for pen input. In *Proc. UIST '98*, ACM (1998), 213-214.

[24] Mankoff, J. and Abowd, G. D. Error correction techniques for handwriting, speech, and other ambiguous or error prone systems. Technical Report, Georgia Tech., Atlanta, GA, USA, GVU-99-18, 1999.

[25] Mazur, J. E. and Hastie, R. Learning as accumulation: A reexamination of the learning curve. *Psychological Bulletin 85*, 6 (1978), 1256-1274.

[26] Newell, A. and Rosenbloom, P. S. Mechanisms of skill acquisition and the law of practice. In *Cognitive Skills and Their Acquisition*, Lawrence Erlbaum, 1981.

[27] Riche, Y., Riche, N. H., Isenberg, P., and Bezerianos, A. Hard-to-use interfaces considered beneficial (some of the time). In *CHI EA '10*. ACM (2010), 2705-2714.

[28] Schmidt, R. A. and Bjork, R. A. New conceptualizations of practice: Common principles in three paradigms suggest new concepts for training. *Psychological Science 3*, 4 (1992), 207-217.

[29] Shilman, M., Tan, D. S., and Simard, P. CueTIP: A mixed-initiative interface for correcting hand-writing errors. In *Proc. UIST '06*, ACM (2006), 323-332.

[30] Tappert, C. C. and Cha, S. English language handwriting recognition interfaces. In *Text Entry Systems: Mobility, Accessibility, Universality*, Morgan Kaufmann, 123-137, 2007.

[31] Tu, H., Ren, X., and Zhai, S. A comparative evaluation of finger and pen stroke gestures. In *Proc. CHI '12*, ACM (2012), 1287-1296.

[32] Vatavu, R.-D., Anthony, L. and Wobbrock, J.O. Gestures as point clouds: A $P recognizer for user interface prototypes. In *Proc. ICMI '12*, ACM (2012), 273-280.

[33] Venolia, D. and Neiberg, F. T-Cube: A fast, self-disclosing pen-based alphabet. In *Proc. CHI '94*, ACM (1994), 265-270.

[34] Wobbrock, J. O., Myers, B. A., and Kembel, J. A. EdgeWrite: A stylus-based text entry method designed for high accuracy and stability of motion. In *Proc. UIST '03*, ACM (2003), 61-70.

[35] Wobbrock, J. O., Wilson, A. D., and Li, Y. Gestures without libraries, toolkits or training: A $1 recognizer for user interface prototypes. In *Proc. UIST '07*, ACM (2007), 159-168.

[36] Wobbrock, J.O. and Myers, B.A. Gestural text entry on multiple devices. In *Proc. ASSETS '05*, ACM (2005), 184-185

[37] Zhai, S. and Kristensson, P. Shorthand writing on stylus keyboard. In *Proc. CHI '03*, ACM (2003), 97-104.

The Pen Is Mightier: Understanding Stylus Behaviour
While Inking on Tablets

Michelle Annett *
University of Alberta
Microsoft Research

Fraser Anderson †
University of Alberta

Walter F. Bischof §
University of Alberta

Anoop Gupta ¥
Microsoft Research

ABSTRACT

Although pens and paper are pervasive in the analog world, their digital counterparts, styli and tablets, have yet to achieve the same adoption and frequency of use. To date, little research has identified why inking experiences differ so greatly between analog and digital media or quantified the varied experiences that exist with stylus-enabled tablets. By observing quantitative and behavioural data in addition to querying preferential opinions, the experimentation reaffirmed the significance of accuracy, latency, and unintended touch, whilst uncovering the importance of friction, aesthetics, and stroke beautification to users. The observed participant behaviour and recommended tangible goals should enhance the development and evaluation of future systems.

Keywords: Tablet; Stylus; User Interaction; Accuracy; Latency; Stylus Design; Palm Rejection; Unintended Touch.

Index Terms: H.5.2. User Interfaces: Input devices and strategies

1 INTRODUCTION

Over the last decade, tablets have become one of the most popular and fastest growing consumer products. Given their wireless connectivity, portability, and support for direct manipulation, tablets should be ideal devices for productivity-based activities such as note taking, sketching, or annotation. Work by Muller et al., however, demonstrated that tablets are championed for content consumption activities such as gaming, web browsing, social networking, and email instead of inking-based activities [21].

When coupled with touch, a stylus enabled tablet should afford efficient bimanual interaction, supporting the transfer of behaviours and interaction techniques commonly found with traditional pen and paper [1, 9, 10, 11, 12]. By harnessing fine motor control, styli offer increased precision and accuracy compared to the fingers [4, 13, 19, 31], allowing users to diagram, work out equations, sketch, create calligraphy, annotate, or sign their name in a manner more natural and fluid than with a mouse or keyboard [36]. Even with these benefits, consumer and educational usage of tablets for these tasks unfortunately remains low.

Some manufacturers have acknowledged the potential usefulness of pens, including styli with many newer models. Such styli typically come in two varieties, *active* and *passive*. *Passive styli* use capacitive sensing to detect touch and do not provide support for pressure, mode switching, etc. They are often after-market peripherals that mimic the properties of the finger on capacitive panels so they cannot be differentiated from touch. Although passive styli are often afterthoughts and introduce many usability

problems, they are increasingly being used with current and legacy devices. *Active styli*, however, require special digitizing hardware to detect the stylus independently from touch. Such styli are typically more precise, respond to pressure, and have barrel buttons for mode switching, making them suitable for most inking tasks. While active styli are superior in a number of respects, numerous issues prevent current widespread adoption – such as the increased cost of manufacturing, and the limited focus on pen-centric user interaction.

Although pen computing has a long history, most work has assessed specific issues with active styli such as bi-manual interaction [1, 10, 11, 12, 20] or stylus features (e.g., pressure, tilt, azimuth [2, 27]). However, exploratory work by Vogel and Balakrishnan observed pointing, selecting, and dragging tasks with a Tablet PC and identified precision, hand occlusion, and the weight and size of the tablet as problematic and frustrating for users [33]. Within the literature, there is unfortunately little empirical evidence regarding the problems users face while *inking* (e.g., drawing and writing) Similarly, the behavioural adaptations necessary to accomplish routine inking tasks, issues with passive styli, or how to best identify or evaluate inking issues remain unknown.

To understand the problems experienced by tablet users, we observed how participants used traditional pen and paper, as well as 'best' and 'worst' case digital devices, while sketching and note taking. While the digital and analog experiences are not believed to be identical, paper provides an excellent gold standard and baseline of 'frustration free' inking experiences in terms of comfort and efficiency to compare to. By observing behaviour generated from real world activities, inspecting content created by participants, and analysing questionnaires, the greatest sources of frustration while inking with styli-enabled systems were uncovered.

Specifically, this paper contributes:
- An analysis of behavioural and performance differences that occurred while inking with digital and analog media
- The description and classification of behavioural adaptations, hand movements, and grips unique to tablets while writing and sketching
- Identification and prioritization of outstanding issues prohibiting satisfying stylus experiences
- A set of tasks and quantitative measures to assess a device's suitability for inking tasks

2 RELATED WORK

Throughout the history of pen computing, much work has sought to understand the benefits of styli compared to other input modalities, the tasks styli are best suited for, observed tablet usage and behaviours, and explored pen and paper behaviour.

A number of projects explored usage patterns and behaviour with tablets. Muller, Gove, and Webb conducted a multi-method exploration of tablet usage and found that activities such as checking email, playing games, and social networking were most common [21]. Wagner and colleagues explored how users hold a tablet, observing that participants were consistent in the holds used, generally grasping the tablet between their thumb and palm or fingers and palm in consistent locations on or around the tablet [34]. Toy et al. assessed preferences for web browsing, email, drawing, and gaming on a tablet when the tablet was in the lap, inclined or flat on a desk, finding that most participants preferred to send email and browse the web while the tablet was inclined but preferred the tablet to be flat on the desk when gaming or drawing [30]. These investigations have underscored the lack of support for styli and inking tasks in the consumer tablet experience. The present work analyses why such a disparity occurs and prioritizes the of the stylus experience that are most important to users.

Many researchers have focused on identifying those tasks the stylus is most beneficial for. Device and task interactions have been largely confirmed, with the stylus being optimal for compound tasks, crossing tasks, radial steering, selection, stroke-based gestures, and shape tracing tasks [4, 8, 13, 18, 31, 35]. The stylus was also found to produce more legible notes than a finger on mobile phones [32]. Work by Briggs and colleagues and Ozok et al. investigated preferences for the different tasks and activities supported by a stylus [3, 26]. Activities such as software navigation, pointing, selecting, and sketching were found to be the most preferred, whereas writing incorporating handwriting recognition was the least preferred. Although styli have yet to be widely adopted, such work illustrates the superiority of styli for many tasks. In contrast to this work, we focus on the natural writing and sketching behaviours that occur on tablets, without the use of excessive stroke beautification or handwriting recognition.

To enhance the stylus experience, some researchers have focused on examining pen and paper usage to inform the design and features of digital devices. For example, Hinckley et al. observed participants' preferred and non-preferred hand usage of a paper notebook, pens, glue, scissors, and paper content while creating a storyboard [11, 12] to inform the interaction techniques used in Manual Deskterity. Work by Fitzmaurice and colleagues compared how often participants rotated paper, a tethered tablet, and a 6DOF tablet while completing two handwriting and three drawing tasks, using the results to inform the design of rotating user interfaces [6]. Rosner and colleagues surveyed existing literature, highlighting the importance of the physicality of paper, the folding and dog-earing of pages, the use of dust jackets, and the placement of tabs in notebooks [28]. Lim explored the differences in thinking processes and cognitive behaviour on architects' ability to compose drawings using styli versus pen and paper [16]. More time was spent inspecting and exploring the digital drawings than paper ones, calling for an increased usage of stylus-based systems within architecture. Oviatt, Arthur, and Cohen explored how cognitive load and performance was affected by using digital devices as well as pen and paper devices, and found that the more interfaces deviate from paper, the greater the cognitive load [25]. Similar to this work, we observed natural pen and paper behaviour, but in contrast, we explore behaviour and adaptations on digital devices to inform future stylus experiences. There is a need for the identification of behavioural changes that occur when one uses a tablet instead of pen and paper and an exploration of the underlying causes for these behaviours. The present work explicitly focuses on understanding the hardware and software features that should be improved to provide a satisfying digital inking experience.

3 EXPERIMENTAL METHODOLOGY

A user study was conducted to identify the behavioural, performance, and preferential differences brought about while inking with analog and digital media. The exploration was not intended to demonstrate that digital styli provide a better inking experience than pens (obviously they do not), or prove the superiority of active compared to passive styli (as active is obviously better). Rather, the goal was to understand how various tablet properties affect user behaviour and to design tasks and measures that could be used as a benchmark to determine when the tablet inking experience is 'acceptable' or 'good enough'. Paper was used as a baseline against which to compare the digital tablets because it is the 'gold standard'. The inclusion of passive styli provided verification that the tasks and measures accurately reflected the tablet experience and allowed for the exploration of the full range of behavioural adaptations made with current commercial tablets.

3.1 Participants

Thirty participants (10 female) were recruited for the study (M = 39, SD = 10 years). The Edinburgh Handedness Inventory [24] classified sixteen right handed (EHI = 73.7) and fourteen left handed (EHI = -57.4) participants. The majority of participants were novice tablet users who had little experience with stylus-enabled devices. Participants were provided with a $10 honorarium.

3.2 Experimental Apparatus

To better understand the digital versus analog experience, participants used three media: an Apple iPad 2, a Samsung Series 7 Business Slate, and 20 lbs. printer paper (trimmed to 24 x 18 cm). Although the capacitive devices are not designed for stylus input, the iPad was included as it enabled an evaluation of the 'worst case' of stylus experiences and it has an expanding ecosystem of third party passive styli. The active stylus device, the Slate, was specifically designed with stylus support in mind and it is expected to provide a better experience for the user. Other form-factors such as the Wacom Cintiq, Intuos, and Bamboo, were intentionally excluded to examine form-factors commonly used by everyday users, not niche equipment used by experts and professionals.

Three Casio ZR100 cameras were setup to capture participant behaviour (Figure 1). One camera was located above the participant and recorded the entire interaction area. As both left and right-handed participants participated, one of two side cameras were used to capture the vertical movement of the styli and hands.

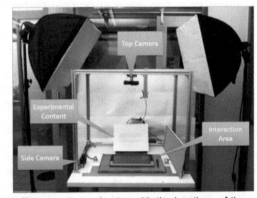

Figure 1: The experimental setup with the locations of the cameras, experimental content, and interaction areas highlighted.

To enhance ecological validity and repeatability, popular, freely available inking applications on the iPad (*Noteability*) and Slate (*PDF Annotator*) instead of custom or professional programs. For inking, participants were provided with a Wacom Bamboo Solo passive stylus with a nib thickness of 7 mm to ink and a Samsung ATIV Tablet S-Pen active stylus with a nib thickness of 2 mm. Uniball ONYX Fine pens with a nib thickness of 0.7 mm were provided for the paper-based conditions. Across all three media, the ink line thickness was approximately 0.7 millimetres and was anti-aliased on the digital devices. Participants were instructed to hold the stylus in their dominant hand and were free to reorient, move, or steady the media as necessary. Stacks of paper were placed under each media to control for the varying thicknesses.

3.3   Tasks and Procedure

To elicit natural behaviour and maintain ecological validity, participants completed two activities, *writing* and *sketching*. During the writing task, participants transcribed a paragraph of text containing a mathematical equation (Figure 2). An equation was included to capture scenarios where non-traditional, unfamiliar symbols are used. Participants completed a transcription task rather than generating their own content to ensure behaviour was comparable between participants and across media and to impose divided attention, which is common during real-world writing.

The product of a sequence is derived using the letter Π from the Greek alphabet (similar to the Σ use in summation). A product is defined as:

$$\prod_{i=m}^{n} x_i = x_m \cdot x_{m+1} \cdot x_{m+2} \cdots x_{n-1} \cdot x_n$$

The factors of the product are obtained by substituting successive integers for the index of multiplication, starting from the lower and incrementing to the upper bound.

Mathematical notation uses Σ, an enlarged form of the Greek letter Sigma, to represent the summation of many similar terms. For example, in

$$\sum_{i=m}^{n} x_i = x_m + x_{m+1} + x_{m+2} + \cdots + x_{n-1} + x_n$$

I represents the index of summation, x, is an indexed variable representing each successive term in the series, and m and n are the lower and upper bounds of summation.

If f is a continuous real-valued function defined on a closed interval [a, b], then once an antiderivative F of f is known, the definite integral of f over that interval is given by:

$$\int_a^b f(x)\, dx = F(b) - F(a)$$

Integrals and derivatives are the basic tools of calculus. They have numerous applications in computing science, mathematics, and engineering.

Figure 2: The stimuli used for the experiment: (left) The sample paragraphs containing alphanumeric and mathematical content and (right) the organic figures used for the sketching tasks.

With sketching, participants copied an organic figure, capturing as many details as possible in five minutes (Figure 2). Each figure contained strokes of varying lengths and directions and had explicit shading regions that required straight and curved lines. In pilot testing, photographs and real objects lead to huge variations in behaviour, with 30 second to 5 minute sketches. Sketching a unique shape with an explicit outline and shading ensured the task and movements were consistent between participants.

Each task was completed by every participant on the iPad, Slate, and paper, resulting in six counter-balanced experimental conditions. After each condition, participants completed Likert scales regarding their experiences with each medium. Post-experiment follow-up questions were also asked.

3.4   Measures and Data Analysis

As it is important to understand behaviour, performance, and preferences on the user experience, three measures were analysed: *hand accommodations*, *writing size*, and *user preferences*.

3.4.1   Hand Accommodations

Although there are many behaviours that participants exhibit while inking (e.g., rotating and anchoring the tablet, bimanual interaction

with dominant and non-dominant hands, etc.) easily identifiable behaviours that had a direct impact on comfort were analysed: grip and movement style. For grip, stylus grips and hand postures previously identified in the literature were consulted [15, 29]. To quantify the hand accommodations, the video data was manually analysed by one of the authors to find the 'nearest match' for each participant and each task. As hand movement styles have yet to be evaluated, the video data was used to identify how the palm and wrist were moving and stabilized while inking. The observed hand movement patterns were then clustered into groups.

This analysis resulted in 180 unique assignments for both grip and hand movement (30 participants x 3 media x 2 tasks). While a finer-grained analysis reporting on the proportion of time that each participant used each grip or movement style in each task was possible, none of the participants transitioned between grips or movement styles during a task. There were some occasions where a grip was slightly varied (e.g., the fingers were fanned more or less in the crab posture) but it remained within the same grip category during the task. To simplify the presentation of results, grip and hand-movement are provided at a per-task level.

3.4.2   Writing Size

The most appropriate measure found to quantify the effects of each device's characteristics on user behaviour during a pilot study was writing size. To compute writing size, the average height from the baseline to x-height [7] of each line was computed by averaging the height at three different points along each line (not including the larger sigma or pi characters). The writing size of the line containing the equation, *equation line*, was computed separately from the other lines, *text lines*, resulting in two measures of writing size. Writing size measures are presented in points to be consistent with common typographic conventions; twelve points are equivalent to 4.2 millimeters, as measured on-screen.

3.4.3   User Preferences While Inking

As perception and opinions towards devices are important, ratings regarding the appropriateness of using each medium were collected for both writing and sketching. Participants were asked to indicate if they felt that "the {Paper, Slate, iPad} was a good medium to complete the {sketching, writing} task with" on a 7-point Likert scale. A freeform comment section asking "Why did you provide this rating?" and "What did you like and dislike about this medium?" gathered deeper insights into the ratings.

4   RESULTS AND DISCUSSION

For each measure, the observed behaviours are detailed and followed by the statistical analysis and interpretation of the results. Where appropriate, Bonferroni corrections were applied to the post-hoc, pairwise comparisons. Note that the analyses were designed to provide insights into the features affecting tablet use. By determining which behaviours were significantly different, and to what degree, the relative importance of various tablet properties could be understood. As the study was exploratory in nature, external rather than internal validity was favoured. We do not claim to provide definitive claims regarding universal properties of active or passive devices, as there are many differences between the media aside from digitizing technology.

4.1   Hand Accommodations

Across all experimental conditions and participants, each observed grip and movement pattern was classified and multinomial regression determined if any grips or movement patterns were unique to specific media, tasks, or participant handedness.

4.1.1 Grip

Prior work on grips has identified a variety of grips common during content creation tasks (e.g., writing, drawing, painting, tool use). Levy and Reid identified one grip, the *natural* grip, and described an 'inversion' behaviour that some subjects, especially those that were left handed, performed [15]. Song et al. described five grips, i.e., *tripod*, *relaxed tripod*, *sketch*, *tuck*, and *wrap*, observed during a pilot exploration of four participants with Wacom devices [29]. These five grips are largely task dependent (e.g., the wrap grip used only for painting, the sketch grip to shade with a pencil lead) and two were similar to the natural grip previously identified by Levy and Reid (i.e., tripod and relaxed tripod).

Of these six grips identified in the literature, only one was observed during the experiment: the *natural* grip [15, 29]. Two other grips, the *knuckle* and *crab* grips (depicted in Figure 3, usage in Figure 4) were identified as novel. Across all tasks and media, the most frequent grip, *natural*, was exhibited 61% of the time. The second most common grip, used 23% of the time, was the *knuckle* grip. With this grip, the knuckles were aligned parallel to the top of the tablet and clenched around the barrel of the pen. The least common grip was the *crab* grip (12%), in which participants fanned the fingers not gripping the stylus, similar to a crab's legs. The remaining 4% of the grips were assigned to an *other* category.

Figure 3: Examples of the grips exhibited by participants. From left: the natural grip, the knuckle grip (knuckles curling in to grip the pen), and the crab grip (knuckles fanned out to support the hand).

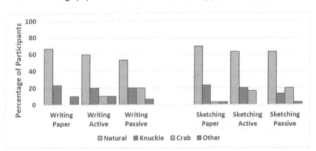

Figure 4: The grips displayed by participants while writing and sketching, presented by task and medium. Note the prevalence of the 'crab' grip while using digital devices.

A multinomial logistic regression, using *natural grip* as the reference category, evaluated the influence of medium, handedness, and task on grip. None of the factorial interactions were found influence the makeup of the model so they were removed (i.e., device x handedness $p = .781$, task x handedness $p = .941$, device x task $p = .920$, and device x task x handedness $p = .105$). In the resulting regression, the type of device ($p < 0.05$), task ($p < .001$) and handedness of the participant ($p < .001$) influenced the grip used. While writing, participants were less likely to use a crab grip than while sketching ($p < .01$). Left-handed participants were more likely to exhibit a crab grip ($p < .05$), knuckle grip ($p < .001$), and other behaviours ($p < .05$) than right-handers. Additionally, participants were more likely to use an unclassified, 'other'

behaviour with the passive stylus than with the active stylus or on paper ($p < .001$).

Across all tasks and media, the natural grip was overwhelmingly the most popular, albeit slightly less prevalent with the digital devices. Interestingly, the novel crab grip was used almost exclusively with digital devices, widely reported by participants as a method to overcome unintended touch. As passive stylus systems are more prone to stray marks (due to the lack of stylus sensing), the prevalence of crab grips with the passive system illustrates the importance of implementing palm rejection. Unlike active stylus systems, passive stylus systems cannot predict where the stylus will be, so palm rejection becomes much more difficult and encourages the use of hand accommodations when unavailable.

The grip analysis also demonstrated that left-handed participants were more likely to use the knuckle grip than right-handers. Although none of the participants exhibited the inverted, or hooked, grip commonly adopted by left-handed writers [15], those that exhibited the knuckle grip also rotated the digital media 20 - 40 degrees. Identification of the knuckle grip and the accompanying medium rotation is important for designers of unintended touch solutions to note, as the palm would likely produce a very different pattern of sensor activation that with the natural grip.

4.1.2 Hand Movement Style

Participants exhibited one of three categories of hand movement patterns: *floating*, *planting*, or *dragging* (as depicted in Figure 5). The most prominent behaviour, *floating*, was exhibited by 51% of the participants. While floating, participants held their wrist, palm, and/or fingers aloft, above the writing surface. The second most popular pattern of movement was *planting* (39%), whereby participants planted their hand on the surface and wrote or sketched until the current word or stroke was complete. Participants then picked up their hand, moved it to a more convenient location, and replanted it on the screen. The least frequent behaviour was *dragging* (10%), where the hand was placed on the media and drug across the surface until it reached the end of the line or the stroke being made. At this point, it was picked it up and moved it to the next location.

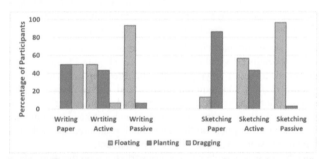

Figure 5: The patterns of hand movements used by participants while writing and sketching. Note the lack of floating with paper and the lack of dragging with digital devices.

Another multinomial logistic regression was performed using the *planting* behaviour as the reference category to determine the role of medium, task, and handedness on hand movement. None of the factorial interactions were found to influence the makeup of the model so they were removed (i.e., device x handedness $p = .212$, task x handedness $p = .713$, device x task $p = .687$, and device x task x handedness $p = .999$). The resulting regression revealed that media ($p < .001$), task ($p < .001$), and handedness ($p < .05$) influenced the movement of the hand. Participants were more likely to use a dragging movement on paper than the digital devices ($p < .01$), and more likely to use the floating behaviour with the passive than active system ($p < .001$) and active than paper ($p < .001$). Left-handed participants were also less likely to use a dragging behaviour than right-handed participants were ($p < .05$).

Hand dragging was used almost exclusively on paper, with only two participants dragging their palm on the active system while writing. On paper, participants reported that they were able to slide their hand along the surface of paper because the friction between their hand and the surface was suitable. On the digital devices, however, the level of friction was too high, leaving many participants unable to slide their hand naturally.

Although participants were encouraged to interact normally and were told that they could rest their palm, on the passive system almost all participants modified their behaviour. The difference in the floating movements on the passive versus active systems suggests that the active system's identification and rejection of unintentional touch events was unacceptable for most participants on the passive system. When touch events were improperly handled, many more extraneous touch points were created than participants were comfortable with, so they used a different movement style, i.e., the floating behaviour. The frequency of planting on paper and the active tablet indicates that participants are able to transfer their normal writing behaviours onto digital devices. It is possible that those who lifted their palm when using the active stylus and Slate were pre-conditioned to lift their palm by prior experiences with passive styli or other touchscreen devices.

4.2 Writing Size

To evaluate the character size used while writing (Figure 6), a mixed-design ANOVA was conducted, with device (levels: paper, passive, active) as the within-subjects factor and handedness as the between-subjects factor (levels: left, right). Handedness was not found to be significant (Text lines: $F(1,27) = 0.074$, $p = .788$; Equation Line: $F(1,27) = 0.207$, $p = .652$), so the handedness factor was collapsed and another ANOVA was performed without this factor. This second ANOVA determined that the device used influenced the writing size (Text lines: $F(2,50) = 9.958$, $p < .001$; Equation Line: $F(1.6,39.5) = 12.840$, $p < .001$). Post-hoc pairwise comparisons determined that participants wrote smallest on paper, slightly larger on the active device, and largest with the passive device (Table 1). When writing the equations, participants wrote substantially larger than while writing the text lines. As the equation lines contained characters that were presented and are often written larger, it is somewhat expected that this behaviour was transferred to the digital devices.

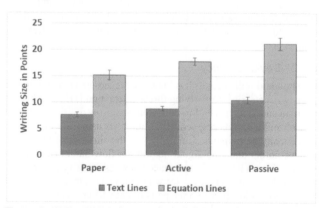

Figure 6: Writing size used on each device for the text lines and equation lines. Note the increase from paper, to active and passive. Error bars represent the standard error of the mean.

The increased writing size, from paper to active to passive, is indicative of the accuracy differences that exist between the media. Many participants believed that the passive system was "incapable of detecting any strokes smaller than a ¼ inch so [they] had to write and draw much larger than normal". With the active device, the precision of the nib and feedback provided by the hover state about the presence and location of the nib enabled participants to write at sizes very close to that of paper. This aided in the perceived accuracy of the Slate (e.g., "you can see the pen tip before you touch the tip on the surface") and improved the stylus experience, "I could actually put content where I wanted."

Table 1: Writing size pairwise comparisons (* denotes significance).

Post-hoc Comparisons	$p <$ for Text Lines	$p <$ for Equation Line
Passive vs. Paper	.001 *	.01 *
Paper vs. Active	.01 *	.25
Passive vs. Active	.05 *	.05 *

4.3 User Preferences While Inking

No significant differences were found between the handedness groups with respect to the Likert-scale ratings (Figure 7), so handedness was collapsed and a Friedman's ANOVA was performed. Participant's opinions towards each device were found to be significantly different ($p < .001$). Wilcoxon-signed rank post-hoc tests revealed significant differences for each media (Table 2), with paper being the most preferred, followed by the active and then passive system.

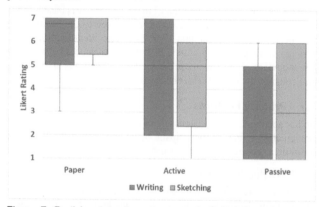

Figure 7: Participant median responses to "I feel that the {Paper, Slate, iPad} was a good medium to complete the {sketching, writing} task with". Note the decline in ratings from paper, to active and passive.

Table 2: Wilcoxon post-hoc analysis for the questionnaire data collapsing across Handedness (* denotes significance).

Post-hoc Comparisons	$p <$
Sketching passive vs. Sketching paper	.01 *
Sketching passive vs. Sketching active	.05 *
Sketching paper vs. Sketching active	.01 *
Writing passive vs. Writing active	.01 *
Writing passive vs. Writing active	.01 *
Writing paper vs. Writing active	.01 *

As expected, paper was preferred by all participants. As it has zero latency, a natural feel and texture, provides direct contact with no parallax, is lightweight and easy to manipulate, palms glide easily across its surface, ink flows easily across the page, and the nib provides audio feedback as it scratches the paper's surface, it is the gold standard. In contrast, the passive device received very poor ratings, (i.e., a median response of 'Mostly Disagree'). Passive stylus systems are not designed for productivity-based tasks and this was reflected in participants' ratings. As active stylus systems are optimized for inking, the active system was rated higher than the passive system (i.e., the median response was 'Slightly Agree').

The passive system was also rated slightly higher for sketching than writing. Although participants disliked the passive system for sketching, it is interesting that they felt it was slightly more appropriate than for writing. As sketching is inherently a messy task, the less accurate movements may have masked the passive system's other deficiencies. It is also possible that the perception many had towards the iPad as a 'finger painting' device also had an influence, along with the affordances of the passive stylus, which looks similar to a marker (e.g., "the marker-like, thicker pen gave me a much better drawing experience").

The subjective responses echo what was seen with the objective measures: paper provides the best inking experience, followed by the active device, and lastly the passive device. While this is expected, this supports the validity of the tests and measures used.

5 FEATURES INFLUENCING THE STYLUS EXPERIENCE

Our experiments uncovered many elements that influence behaviour, performance, and preferences for digital versus analog media while inking. From the observations and participant comments, many features impacting usability emerged, with participants identifying five that present substantial, pressing issues. Participants were most vocal about three *primary features*, i.e., stylus accuracy, device latency, and unintended touch, and *two secondary features*, i.e., stylus and device aesthetics and stroke beautification. The prioritization of these features was based on the number of comments each received in addition to the behavioural and performance impact that each had. The identification these primary and secondary features, as well as differences between the tablet devices, should decrease the need for adaptations in the future and enhance the design tablet hardware and software.

5.1 Primary Features

Stylus accuracy, device latency, and unintended touch resulted in the greatest effect on participant behaviour and were the most prominent features identified as problematic by participants.

5.1.1 Stylus Accuracy

A recurring theme that emerged was frustration due to inaccuracy of the stylus. Many participants were vocal about inaccuracy, as it forced them to alter their writing size. Participants had more difficulty forming and terminating letters with the passive system than the active system and paper (Figure 8). The hover information provided by the active system, mitigated the effects of inaccuracy and provided a much more enjoyable experience, "I loved the pen, and I have never used such an accurate pen before". Inaccuracy also manifested itself while sketching, where many participants made larger, straighter, seemingly haphazard strokes with the passive and active systems compared to paper (Figure 8).

The composition of the digital styli also affected the perceived accuracy and precision of strokes, with the passive styli being perceived as less accurate, "I couldn't see where I was writing because of the [passive] squishy pen so I had to write bigger" and "I couldn't tell where the lines would start or end". With the active system, however, many participants believed that "the pen tip felt almost like a real pen" and many felt that it mimicked a traditional pen quite well. Although calibration, interpolation, parallax, and sensor density influence device accuracy, the physical design of the stylus appears to be implicated as well.

As inaccuracy forced participants to write larger, in the real world, it would subsequently result in less content fitting on the

screen. It is important to consider the design implications of this. As screen real estate is already constrained by menus and UI elements, the area available for content creation is at a premium. It is thus imperative that increased accuracy, intuitive navigation methods (not accidently activated if users rest their hand or fingers on the screen), and intelligent widgets or canvases capable of reflowing or reformatting content as necessary, become integrated within stylus-supported applications.

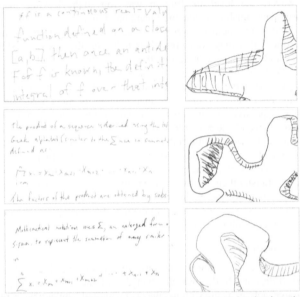

Figure 8: Inking content created using the passive stylus (top), active stylus (middle), and pen and paper (bottom) from the same participant. Note the inaccuracy of the lines on both digital devices, as well as the limited use of curved lines with the passive device. The images were cropped to show detail, and the paper image was scanned, resulting in the perceived loss of quality.

Although accuracy has long been a complaint of tablet users, it is still a problem. Based on comments and the quantitative results, accuracy appears to be influenced by many factors including the ability to detect hover, nib-size, cursor calibration, the texture of the screen, the material composition of the stylus, and the responsiveness of the device. Although third-party styli such as Project Mighty, Pencil, and Jot Pro have begun to use auxiliary input channels to improve some of these factors for passive systems, there remains much work for designers of both passive and active systems. Further experimentation is still needed to tease apart these factors to better understand the inaccuracies users can tolerate as well as how to minimize inaccuracy overall.

5.1.2 Device Latency

One hundred milliseconds has long been regarded as the minimum latency necessary for satisfying direct-interaction [[19]]. Although the iPad and Slate had end-to-end latencies below this threshold (80 and 65 milliseconds respectively, computed using the method in [23]), many participants commented on the sluggish nature of the tablets, noting that "the digital ink did not flow naturally from the stylus". The delayed ink and inaccuracy resulting in participants writing slower and larger to "see what [they] had already written so that [they] could better join the parts of each letter together instead of having to guess where they would be because of the delay". Although the active system was only 15 milliseconds faster than the passive system, some participants appreciated the difference, stating that "the [active] pen tracked as fast as I was able to write which was great" and "the Slate was much faster than the iPad, but it was of course still slower than paper".

Such comments and the increased writing size corroborate with recent work on touch-based latency perception wherein increased latency decreased performance [14]. While the experiments demonstrated that latencies as low as 25 milliseconds had an impact on performance, manufacturers are a long way from achieving such latencies with commercial products. Although we did not explicitly focus on latency, further work must investigate the relationship between latency and accuracy to determine acceptable standards and benchmarks for high accuracy tasks such as inking. Until latency is decreased across the entire pipeline, low-fidelity, high-frequency feedback should be provided. Instead of taking the time to render a smoothed, high-quality line, for example, initially rendering a quick, crude stroke and later replacing it with a smoothed line when more processing is available may be fruitful to consider. 3D modelling programs already make use of such an approach, rendering a wireframe while 3D models are manipulated and a full mesh while models are static.

5.1.3 Unintended Touch

The digital devices prevented participants from interacting naturally because participants altered their behaviour to avoid making unintended, accidental markings. Such markings were due the tablets being unable to distinguish between the intended and unintended touch events, i.e., deliberate touch actions versus those caused by resting one's palm or grazing the fingers over the surface. With the passive system, participants were "forced to write in an uncomfortable position to avoid the 'palm touch' screen" and "could not rest [their] palm on the display without disrupting it – highly unusable". With the active system, participants were "more willing to interact because [they] could rest [their] palm on the surface with no problems" and "the Slate didn't have the palm 'touchy' problems that the iPad did". Participants did not experience much fatigue, as they were only inking for 5 minutes. Inking for longer periods would have likely exacerbated fatigue and issues associated to unintended touch.

Some manufacturers have acknowledged the importance of unintended touch. While recent devices tote 'palm block' or 'palm rejection' technology, in practice, such implementations are far from robust, detecting many spurious touch points. Unintended touch will continue to be a problem whenever both pen and touch are supported, regardless of if they are used synchronously (e.g., bimanual interaction) or asynchronously (interleaved interaction). Future work should focus on palm rejection and improving the identification of unintended touch. In most applications and systems today, users do not have the opportunity to provide personalized information about their handedness or grips. The different grips that are used, especially those unique to left-handers, will produce different imprints on a sensor array and could be harnessed for palm rejection. Until unintended touch is solved, either via hardware improvements or software solutions, designers should provide mechanisms by which users can enable or disable touch input if desired and also provide feedback to alert users of any stray marks that are rendered.

5.2 Secondary Features

Surface and nib texture, stylus and screen aesthetics, and stroke beautification were also noted as being important to the stylus experience by participants, albeit to a lesser extent than the primary features.

5.2.1 Texture and Aesthetics

Interestingly, many participants had marked opinions on the texture of the digital devices and stylus aesthetics. Influenced by years of writing on paper with pens, users are accustomed to specific tactile sensations and feedback while holding a stylus. While inking with the digital devices, there was a mismatch of the friction between the hand and surface. Many participants felt that "there was not enough friction between the pen and screen to feel natural". This mismatch between skin and surface friction was also reflected in comments such as, "my hand jerked across the screen as I moved it" and in the number of participants who floated their palms above the surface of the tablets. The importance of surface texture to participants counters current thinking about tablet surfaces, i.e., that they should be made of glass because it is glossy, slick, and visually appealing. If stylus-based devices are to be taken seriously as pen and paper replacements, the texture of a device's surface and materials the stylus nib is composed of should be optimized to evoke familiar feedback patterns for the user and encourage natural movement instead of hindering it.

The aspect ratio of the active device was also problematic for some. A 16:9 ratio is well suited for watching movies, but insufficient for writing notes and sketching. Some participants mentioned the lines they writing on the Slate were "going on forever and ever" and that they had to "squish [their] sketches to fit on the Slate but not the iPad". None of the participants mentioned the increased thickness or weight of the digital devices compared to paper. This is likely because that participants did not have to support the devices themselves while performing the tasks.

A few participants also noted that end-user customization and choice is important in stylus designs. Current styli come in muted colours (i.e., black or grey) and the choice of nibs is limited (expect with active Wacom styli). Compared to traditional pens that come in a myriad of shapes, sizes, weights, and ink types, (e.g., gel, ballpoint, felt-tipped, fountain), digital styli feel impersonal. Having the opportunity to customize the stylus and appearance of ink can invoke a stronger connection to one's work, which is a natural strength of writing with a pen. Additionally, a variety of after-market gloves or surface coverings could be designed, allowing users to choose the texture they prefer, similar to the assortment of nibs available for Wacom styli.

5.2.2 Stroke Beautification

Many participants commented on the appearance of their strokes. Applications today often modify ink thickness, opacity, and path smoothing using input parameters such as pressure, velocity, and time to imitate real ink dynamics. With the passive system, participants identified that the stylus was not pressure sensitive and were unhappy that this feature was not supported, especially while sketching, e.g., "the lack of pressure sensitivity is annoying", and "without pressure sensitivity the strokes looked awful". Although the active system made use of a pressure-sensitive stylus and anti-aliased strokes, none of the participants believed it was pressure sensitive. Although many have developed stroke beautification techniques [5, 17, 37], the current beautification methods employed for inking obviously did not meet participant's expectations.

These comments highlight the value of pressure sensitivity and appropriate rendering techniques. Even if an application "fakes it", users want the illusion of pressure sensitivity, "that Paper app has pressure and I know that it's fake but I still enjoy it". As the cost of styli become cheaper and it becomes easier to integrate auxiliary communication channels into passive styli, designers should re-evaluate the role of pressure, tilt, and azimuth in ink rendering, not only within the context of pressure-based widgets or the levels of tilt, azimuth, or pressure discernible [2, 27]. Such improvements will uphold beliefs that tablets can provide experiences similar, if not more appropriate and engaging for productivity-based tasks.

6 CONCLUSION

Although pen computing has had a long history, little information is available regarding inking experiences in the analog and digital worlds. This work provided evidence of the adaptations and behaviours that occur while performing inking tasks on tablets. By comparing these behaviours to those observed with traditional pen and paper, we identified grips and patterns of hand movement unique to digital devices and left-handed users. These behaviours, as well as device characteristics, resulted in larger characters when writing, inaccurate strokes, and user frustration.

Our work identified the major features influencing the inking experience today. Stylus accuracy, device latency, device and stylus aesthetics, digital ink rendering, and the ability to distinguish between intended and unintended touch are of the utmost importance and are in need of future work. Although the devices used in the present study were not the most recent available on the market, they still represent the state of the art in terms of tablet experience. Latency, surface texture, unintended touch (palm rejection), and input resolution have not seen significant advancements in recent years. The tablet and stylus has great potential to become 'go-to' devices for inking and productivity-based activities, but many improvements are needed before tablets and styli become commonplace in everyday settings.

REFERENCES

[1] R. Balakrishnan and K. Hinckley. The Role of Kinesthetic Reference Frames in Two-Handed Input Performance. In *Proc. of UIST*, 171-178, 1999.

[2] X. Bi, T. Moscovich, G. Ramos, R. Balakrishnan, and K. Hinckley. An Exploration of Pen Rolling For Pen-Based Interaction. *In Proc. of UIST*, 191-200, 2008.

[3] R.O. Briggs, A.R. Dennis, B.S. Beck, and J.F. Nunamaker. Whither the Pen-Based Interface? *Journal of Management Information Systems*, 71-90, 1992.

[4] A. Cockburn, D. Ahlstrom, and C. Gutwin, Understanding Performance in Touch Selections: Tap, Drag, and Radial Pointing Drag with Finger, Stylus, and Mouse. *Journal of Human-Computer Studies*, 70: 218-233, 2008.

[5] J.D. Fekete, É. Bizouarn, É. Cournarie, T. Galas, and F. Taillefer. Tictactoon: A Paperless System for Professional 2D Animation. In *Proc. of SIGGRAPH*, 79-95, 1995.

[6] G. Fitzmaurice, R. Balakrishnan, G. Kurtenbach, and B. Buxton. An Exploration into Supporting Artwork Orientation in the User Interface. In *Proc. of CHI*, 167-174, 1999.

[7] Font Shop Education. *http://www.fontshop.com/education/pdf/typeface_anatomy.pdf*. Accessed August 2013.

[8] C. Forlines and R. Balakrishnan. Evaluating Tactile Feedback and Direct vs Indirect Stylus Input in Pointing and Crossing Tasks. In *Proc. of CHI*, 1563-1572, 2008.

[9] Y. Guiard. Asymmetric Transfer of Labor in Human Skilled Bimanual Action: The Kinematic Chain as a Model. *Journal of Motor Behaviour*, 19: 486-517, 1987.

[10] K. Hinckley. Input Technologies and Techniques. *The Human Computer Interaction Handbook: Fundamentals, Evolving Technologies and Emerging Applications*, Taylor and Francis Group, LLC, New York, 2002.

[11] K. Hinckley, K. Yatani, M. Pahud, N. Coddington, J. Rodenhouse, A. Wilson, H. Benko, and B. Buxton. Pen + Touch = New Tools. In *Proc. of UIST*, 27-36, 2010.

[12] K. Hinckley, K. Yatani, M. Pahud, N. Coddington, J. Rodenhouse, A. Wilson, H. Benko, and B. Buxton. Manual Deskterity: An Exploration of Simultaneous Pen + Touch Direct Input. In *Extended Abstracts of CHI*, 2793-2802, 2010.

[13] A. Holzinger, M. Holler, M. Schedlbauer, and B. Urlesberger. An Investigation of Finger versus Stylus Input in Medical Scenarios. In *Proc. of ITI*, 433-438, 2008.

[14] R. Jota, A. Ng, P. Dietz, and D. Wigdor. How Fast Is Fast Enough? A Study of the Effects of Latency in Direct-touch Pointing Tasks. In *Proc. of CHI*, 2291-2300, 2013.

[15] J. Levy and M. Reid. Variations in Cerebral Organization as a Function of Handedness, Hand Posture in Writing, and Sex. *Journal of Experimental Psychology: General*, 107(2): 119-144, 1978.

[16] C. Lim. An Insight into the Freedom of Using a Pen: Pen-Based System and Pen-And-Paper. In *Proc. of 6th Asian Design International Conference*, 2003.

[17] Y. Lu, F. Yu, A. Finkelstein, and S. DiVerdi. Helping Hand: Example-based Stroke Stylization. *ACM Transactions on Graphics*, 31(4), 1-10, 2012.

[18] R. Mack and K. Lang. A Benchmark Comparison of Mouse and Touch Interface Techniques for an Intelligent Workstation Windowing Environment. *Human Factors and Ergonomics Society Annual Meeting*, 325-329, 1989.

[19] I.S. Mackenzie, A. Sellen, and B. Buxton. A Comparison of Input Devices in Elemental Pointing and Dragging Tasks. In *Proc. of CHI*, 161-166, 1991.

[20] F. Matulic and M. Norrie. Empirical Evaluation of Uni- And Bimodal Pen and Touch Interaction Properties on Digital Tabletops. In *Proc. of ITS*, 143-52, 2012.

[21] R.B. Miller. Response Time in Man-Computer Conversational Transactions. Fall Joint Computer Conference, 267-277, 1968.

[22] H. Muller, J.L. Gove, and J.S. Webb. Understanding Tablet Use: A Multi-Method Exploration. In *Proc. of MobileHCI*, 1-10, 2012.

[23] A. Ng, J. Lepinski, D. Wigdor, S. Sanders, and P. Dietz. Designing for Low-Latency Direct-Touch Input. In *Proc. of UIST*, 453-462, 2012.

[24] R.C. Oldfield. The Assessment and Analysis of Handedness: The Edinburgh Inventory. *Journal of Neuropsychologia*, 9: 97-113, 1971.

[25] S. Oviatt, A. Arthur, and J. Cohen. Quiet Interfaces that Help Students Think. In *Proc. Of UIST*, 191-200, 2006.

[26] A.A. Ozok, D. Senson, J. Chakraborty, and A.F. Norcio. A Comparative Study between Tablet and Laptop PCs: User Satisfaction and Preferences. *Journal of Human Computer Interaction*, 329-352, 2008.

[27] G. Ramos and R. Balakrishnan. Pressure Marks. In *Proc. of CHI*, 1375-1384, 2007.

[28] D. Rosner, L. Oehlberg, and K. Ryokai. Studying Paper Use to Inform the Design of Personal and Portable Technology. In *Proc. of CHI*, 3405-3410, 2008.

[29] H. Song, H. Benko, F. Guimbretière, S. Izadi, X. Cao, and K. Hinckley. Grips and Gestures on A Multi-Touch Pen. In *Proc. of CHI*, 1323-1332, 2011.

[30] K.J. Toy, S.C. Peres, T.Y. David, A. Nery, and R.G. Phillips. Examining User Preferences in Interacting with Touchscreen Devices. In *Proc. of the Human Factors and Ergonomics Society Annual Meeting*, 1862-1866, 2012.

[31] H. Tu, X. Ren, and S. Zhai. A Comparative Evaluation of Finger and Pen Stroke Gestures. In *Proc. of CHI*, 1287-1296, 2012.

[32] E. del Carmen Valderrama Bahamóndez, T. Kubitza, N. Henze, and A. Schmidt. Analysis of Children's Handwriting on Touchscreen Phones. In *Proc. of MobileHCI*, 171-174, 2013.

[33] D. Vogel and R. Balakrishnan. Direct Pen Interaction with a Conventional Graphical User Interface. *Journal of Human Computer Interaction*, 324-388, 2010.

[34] J. Wagner, S. Huot, and W. Mackay. BiTouch and BiPad: Designing Bimanual Interaction for Hand-held Tablets. In *Proc. of CHI*, 2317-2326, 2012.

[35] S. Zabramski. Careless Touch: A Comparative Evaluation Of Mouse, Pen, And Touch Input In Shape Tracing Task. In *Proc. of OzCHI*, 329-332, 2011.

[36] R. Zeleznik, T. Miller, A. Van Dam, C. Li, D. Tenneson, C. Maloney, and J.J. LaViola. Applications and Issues in Pen-Centric Computing. *Multimedia*, 15(4):14-21, 2008.

[37] L. Zitnick. Handwriting Beautification Using Token Means. *ACM Transactions on Graphics*, 32(4): 53, 2013.

Computation of Polarized Subsurface BRDF for Rendering

Charly Collin*
EECS
University of Central Florida

Sumanta Pattanaik†
EECS
University of Central Florida

Patrick LiKamWa ‡
CREOL
University of Central Florida

Kadi Bouatouch §
IRISA
Université de Rennes 1

ABSTRACT

Interest in polarization properties of the rendered materials is growing, but so far discussions on polarization have been restricted only to surface reflection, and the reflection due to subsurface scattering is assumed to be unpolarized. Findings from other field (e.g. optics and atmospheric science) show that volumetric interaction of light can contribute to polarization. So we investigated the polarized nature of the radiance field due to subsurface scattering as a function of the thickness of the material layer for various types of materials. Though our computations shows negligible polarization for material layers of high thickness, thin layered materials show significant degree of polarization. That means polarization cannot be ignored for subsurface component of reflection from painted surfaces (particularly painted metal surfaces) or from coated materials. In this paper we employ the vector radiative transfer equation (VRTE), which is the polarized version of the radiative transfer equation inside the material. We use a discrete ordinate based method to solve the VRTE and compute the polarized radiance field at the surface of the material layer. We generate the polarimetric BRDF from the solutions of the VRTE for incident irradiance with different polarizations. We validate our VRTE solution against a benchmark and demonstrate our results through renderings using the computed BRDF.

Index Terms: I.3.0 [Computer Graphics]: General—; I.4.1 [Image Processing and Computer Vision]: Digitalization and Capture—Reflectance

1 INTRODUCTION

Accurate modeling of the bidirectional reflection distribution function (BRDF) of materials is important for realistic rendering. The BRDF of most real world materials is composed of two components: (a) the *surface* BRDF, the component due to surface only interaction of light, and (b) the *subsurface* BRDF, the component due to subsurface interaction of light as defined by Hanrahan and Krueger [6, 7]. Both of these components may have significant directional dependence. The Fresnel equation models the surface BRDF component for smooth surfaces and is often extended to rough surfaces by modeling the surface by a microfacet distribution [14]. Subsurface BRDF computation requires the simulation of light interaction inside the medium. Radiative transport equation (RTE) models this interaction [5]. Solution of RTE is expensive and is particularly so for BRDF computation. In the Computer Graphics literature, various approximation methods (for example: diffuse approximation [10]) have been proposed for computing this subsurface component. In this paper we use a discrete ordinate based solution method (DOM) of solving RTE for accurately computing the subsurface component of BRDF. Our simulations are done on plane-parallel media composed of spherical or randomly oriented symmetric particles.

Light, as an electromagnetic wave, exhibits polarization. The human visual system cannot directly detect the polarization state of light, which is the reason why it is often omitted in rendering. However, the polarization state of light affects the interaction between light and matter, and hence must be taken into account for accurate global illumination computation [16, 18]. The Fresnel equation explicitly models polarization. So polarized surface reflection components have been used in global illumination computation. The subsurface interaction of light is assumed to create a randomly polarized (or unpolarized) radiation field, and consequently subsurface BRDF is assumed to be unpolarized as well. In this paper we use the vector radiative transport equation (VRTE) to simulate polarization effects due to subsurface interaction of light and to show that radiation field and BRDF due to subsurface interaction can be significantly polarized. We carry out an experiment and show the evidence for polarization in the subsurface component of BRDF. We solve VRTE to compute polarized subsurface BRDF for real world materials and use those in global illumination computation to show their effect on the polarization of a scene.

The organization of the paper is as follows. After a brief overview of Stokes vector representation of polarized light, and of RTE for modeling light transport in plane-parallel media, we introduce the vector radiative transfer equation (VRTE) to model the subsurface transport of polarized light and its discrete ordinate (DOM) based solution for subsurface BRDF computation. We validate our implementation of the DOM based VRTE solution method against a benchmark, and study the polarization property of the subsurface BRDF as a function of various parameters. We describe an experiment to verify the evidence of polarization in subsurface BRDF. Using our polarized path tracer, we show that polarized BRDF is important for accurate light transport in a scene, particularly so when polarizing reflectors or filters and/or polarizing source are present in the scene. Finally, we show some renderings to visualize the polarization components of the light transport in a scene.

2 BACKGROUND

2.1 Polarized light

Light polarization is explained by the electro-magnetic wave nature of light, and describes the orientation of the electric wave at any point in space. This wave may be oriented in a single direction perpendicular to the direction of propagation (linear polarization), or it may rotate as light propagates (circular polarization). Any propagated light may have a combination of these polarizations.

Among the possible formalisms describing the polarization state of light, Stokes vector [8] is a popular choice for its simplicity to understand and because its components are measurable. It is a four component vector:

$$\mathbf{I} = [I, Q, U, V]^t.$$

In this representation, I is the radiance and is exactly the same quantity that is used in the scalar representation. Q is the difference between the linearly polarized components of radiance along the horizontal and vertical axis, U is the difference of radiance between the linearly polarized components at 45 degrees and 135 degrees, and V is the difference of radiance between the right circularly and left

*e-mail: charly.collin@bobbyblues.com
†e-mail: sumant@cs.ucf.edu
‡e-mail: patrick@creol.ucf.edu
§e-mail: kadi@irisa.fr

Graphics Interface Conference 2014
7-9 May, Montreal, Quebec, Canada

circularly polarized components. The four components satisfy the following relation: $I^2 \geq Q^2 + U^2 + V^2$, and the degree of polarization (DOP) of light is expressed as:

$$DOP = \frac{\sqrt{Q^2 + U^2 + V^2}}{I}. \quad (1)$$

While I, the first component of the Stokes vector is always positive, the other three take their values in the range $[-I, I]$. For example, a Stokes vector with $V = -I$ represents light with full left circular polarization. For unpolarized light only the I component is non zero, and hence its Stokes vector representation is $[I, 0, 0, 0]^t$. In the rest of this paper we use symbols I and $\mathbf{I}$, to represent the scalar and vector forms of radiance respectively.

For simpler tracking of the orientation of the linear polarization, a Stokes vector is associated with a local reference frame (XYZ) whose Z-axis is defined along the propagation direction of the light and the other two axes are in a plane perpendicular to that direction. While the choice of the orientation of X,Y axes is arbitrary, it defines the components Q and U. When adding two Stokes vectors, one has to make sure that their reference frames are the same, which can be achieved through rotation. For two Stokes vectors whose X-axes (or Y-axes) are separated by an angle σ, the corresponding rotation matrix is:

$$Rotation(\sigma) = \begin{bmatrix} 1 & 0 & 0 & 0 \\ 0 & \cos 2\sigma & -\sin 2\sigma & 0 \\ 0 & \sin 2\sigma & \cos 2\sigma & 0 \\ 0 & 0 & 0 & 1 \end{bmatrix}. \quad (2)$$

Light-matter interaction (e.g. reflection or scattering) may have different effect on the radiance and the polarization. One element of the Stokes vector could increase while another one decrease for example. A single scalar factor is then not enough to represent those changes and a 4×4 matrix, called Mueller matrix, is used to describe such interactions [4]. That means the optical property of the matter must be specified by its characteristic Mueller matrix $\mathbf{M}$. Optical properties of particular importance to Computer Graphics are reflection and scattering, and both of those must be specified as Mueller matrix functions of incident and outgoing directions. A Mueller matrix is defined for incident and outgoing Stokes vectors with their specific reference frames. Changing the reference frame of any of those vectors changes the Mueller matrix as well. Therefore, given a Mueller matrix, one has to rotate carefully the incident and outgoing Stokes vector to match the desired reference frames. During the propagation of light its reflection or scattering is computed through multiplication between the Mueller matrix and the Stokes vector. We refer the reader to previous work [4, 19] for more details on Stokes vectors and Mueller matrix operations.

2.2 Radiative Transport Equation

The volumetric interaction of light is modeled by the radiative transfer equation (RTE) that expresses the radiance field in the medium as a function of the incident radiance. If we assume that the subsurface material volume is a plane-parallel medium, meaning that its scattering and absorption properties vary only along the depth (the direction perpendicular to the horizontal plane), then the radiance $I(\tau, \mu, \phi)$ in a non-emitting volume at an optical thickness τ along the direction (μ, ϕ) due to light incident (I_{inc}) from a single direction (μ_{inc}, ϕ_{inc}) (see Figure 1), is expressed by the RTE as follows:

$$\mu \frac{\partial}{\partial \tau} I(\tau, \mu, \phi) + I(\tau, \mu, \phi) - J(\tau, \mu, \phi) = Q(\tau, \mu, \phi), \quad (3)$$

where μ is the cosine of the outgoing direction's zenith angle and ϕ its azimuth angle. The function Q accounts for the radiance due

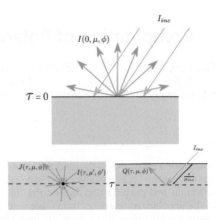

Figure 1: 2D cross section of a material composed of plane-parallel volume. The computation of the radiance at an optical thickness of τ in a direction (μ, ϕ) requires solving RTE in the volume.

to the direct scattering of I_{inc} (illustrated in the bottom right image of Figure 1) and is expressed as:

$$Q(\tau, \mu, \phi) = \frac{\omega(\tau)}{4\pi} Z(\tau, \mu, \mu_{inc}, \phi - \phi_{inc}) I_{inc}(\mu_{inc}, \phi_{inc}) e^{-\tau/\mu_{inc}}, \quad (4)$$

with ω as the single scattering albedo and Z as the phase function of the volume layer at the optical thickness τ. Note that the RTE used here is defined according to the optical thickness τ instead of the more classic euclidian distance. The optical thickness between two points x and x' is defined as:

$$\tau(x, x') = \int_x^{x'} \sigma_t(t) dt, \quad (5)$$

with σ_t being the extinction coefficient. In equations 3, 4 and 6 we assume that the medium is composed of spherical or randomly oriented particles and so the phase function is rotationally invariant. Moreover, because of the plane-parallel representation of the medium, we assume without loss of generality that the entering and exiting points of the light in and out the medium are the same. The function J in equation 3 accounts for the indirect radiance due to the multiple scattering of light (illustrated in the bottom left image of Figure 1) and is expressed as:

$$J(\tau, \mu, \phi) = \frac{\omega(\tau)}{4\pi} \int_{-1}^{1} \int_0^{2\pi} Z(\tau, \mu, \mu', \phi - \phi') I(\mu', \phi') d\phi' d\mu', \quad (6)$$

with (μ', ϕ') as the cosine zenith angle and azimuth angle of the in-scattering directions. Our goal in this paper is to compute and study the polarization properties of the radiance field due to subsurface interaction of the incident light, and compute polarized subsurface BRDF from this computed radiance field. In the next section we introduce VRTE, the extended RTE that supports polarization and discuss a solution method specific to this VRTE.

3 POLARIMETRIC SUBSURFACE BRDF AND ITS COMPUTATION

3.1 Vector RTE

In section 2 we described the Stokes vector representation $\mathbf{I}$ for polarized radiance. We can write the RTE for this vector representation as[12]:

$$\mu \frac{\partial}{\partial \tau} \mathbf{I}(\tau, \mu, \phi) + \mathbf{I}(\tau, \mu, \phi) - \mathbf{J}(\tau, \mu, \phi) = \mathbf{Q}(\tau, \mu, \phi), \quad (7)$$

where $\mathbf{J}$ and $\mathbf{Q}$ are respectively the polarized components of the indirect and direct radiances and are expressed as:

$$\mathbf{J}(\tau, \mu, \phi) = \frac{\omega(\tau)}{4\pi} \int_{-1}^{1} \int_0^{2\pi} \mathbf{Z}(\tau, \mu, \mu', \phi - \phi') \mathbf{I}(\tau, \mu', \phi') d\phi' d\mu', \quad (8)$$

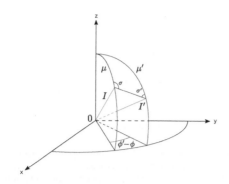

Figure 2: Main frame of reference and various angles.

$$\mathbf{Q}(\tau,\mu,\phi) = \frac{\omega(\tau)}{4\pi}\mathbf{Z}(\tau,\mu,\mu_{inc},\phi-\phi_{inc})\mathbf{I}_{inc}(\mu_{inc},\phi_{inc})e^{-\tau/\mu_{inc}}. \tag{9}$$

These equations are similar to their scalar counterpart and the Z phase function is replaced by the phase matrix $\mathbf{Z}$. We elaborate on the incident and scattered reference frames of $\mathbf{I}$ and $\mathbf{Z}$ in the next few paragraphs.

3.2 Reference frame of the Stokes Vector

As mentioned earlier, Stokes vectors are defined with respect to their reference frames. The reference frame that we use for solving the VRTE is described as follows. The Z axis of a ray's Stokes vector reference frame has to match its propagation direction (μ,ϕ). We define both of this frame's X and Y directions in reference to the *meridional* or *meridian* plane, which is defined as the plane containing the light ray and the Z axis of the coordinate frame (see the vertical circular sectors in Figure 2 containing Z-axis of the world coordinate frame, and the ray direction vectors of the rays $\mathbf{I}$ and $\mathbf{I}'$).The X axis of the reference frame lies in that plane while the Y axis is perpendicular to it such that XYZ forms a right handed coordinate system.

3.3 Scattering matrix

A scattering event in the volume scatters light in all direction around the point of interaction. The amount and the polarization of the scattered light is specified by the scattering matrix $\mathbf{F}$, which is a function of the scattering angle Θ between incident and scattered direction. Scattering depends on the size, shape and orientation of the interacting particles inside the volume of interaction, and in general all the 16 elements of the scattering matrix could be nonzero and each of the element is a scalar functions of Θ. As mentioned earlier, our discussion is restricted to the scattering of light inside volume composed of spherical or randomly oriented symmetric particles. As a consequence, the scattering matrix is rotationally invariant, and has eight non-zero elements, of which only six elements are unique [9].

$$\mathbf{F}(\Theta) = \begin{bmatrix} a_1(\Theta) & b_1(\Theta) & 0 & 0 \\ b_1(\Theta) & a_2(\Theta) & 0 & 0 \\ 0 & 0 & a_3(\Theta) & b_2(\Theta) \\ 0 & 0 & -b_2(\Theta) & a_4(\Theta) \end{bmatrix} \tag{10}$$

The phase functions are assumed to be normalized, that means:

$$\frac{1}{4\pi}\int_{S^2} a_1(\Theta)d\omega = 1.$$

The elements in (10) may be tabulated for a discrete set of Θ values, or alternatively, may be expressed as coefficients of expansion in some orthogonal basis set.

Being a function of the scattering angle Θ only, the scattering matrix's reference frames are not expressed using the same rule as

in section 3.2. Instead, the local X-axes of the incident and outgoing directions of the scattering matrix lie in the scattering plane, the plane formed by the two directions (see Figure 2). So the X axis of the reference frames of both the incident and scattered ray must lie on that plane for the scattering matrix to be valid.

3.4 Phase matrix

For convenience, we would like our Mueller matrix for scattering to have the incident and scattered reflection frames to be the same as the reference frames of the incident Stokes vector and scattered Stokes vector. So instead of scattering matrix ($\mathbf{F}$) we use phase matrix ($\mathbf{Z}$) that has the latter property. Both matrices carry the same information (i.e. the amount of light scattered from incident direction ot scattered direction), only their reference frames differ. Phase matrix is related to scattering matrix as:

$$\mathbf{Z}(\mu,\mu',(\phi-\phi')) = Rotation(\pi-\sigma) \times \mathbf{F}(\Theta) \times Rotation(-\sigma')$$

$$= \begin{bmatrix} 1 & 0 & 0 & 0 \\ 0 & \cos 2\sigma & \sin 2\sigma & 0 \\ 0 & -\sin 2\sigma & \cos 2\sigma & 0 \\ 0 & 0 & 0 & 1 \end{bmatrix}$$

$$\times \begin{bmatrix} a_1(\Theta) & b_1(\Theta) & 0 & 0 \\ b_1(\Theta) & a_2(\Theta) & 0 & 0 \\ 0 & 0 & a_3(\Theta) & b_2(\Theta) \\ 0 & 0 & -b_2(\Theta) & a_4(\Theta) \end{bmatrix}$$

$$\times \begin{bmatrix} 1 & 0 & 0 & 0 \\ 0 & \cos 2\sigma' & \sin 2\sigma' & 0 \\ 0 & -\sin 2\sigma' & \cos 2\sigma' & 0 \\ 0 & 0 & 0 & 1 \end{bmatrix}, \tag{11}$$

where (μ',ϕ') and (μ,ϕ) represent the incident and scattered directions, σ' and σ are the angles between the scattering plane and the reference planes of incident Stokes vector and scattered Stokes vector respectively. See Figure 2 for the symbols.

Using spherical trigonometry, the scattering angle can be defined as

$$\cos\Theta = \mu'\mu + \sqrt{(1-\mu'^2)(1-\mu^2)}\cos(\phi-\phi'),$$

and the angles σ' and σ can be related to μ',ϕ',μ,ϕ as

$$\cos\sigma' = \frac{\mu - \mu'\mu}{\sqrt{(1-\mu'^2)}\sqrt{(1-\cos^2\Theta)}},$$

$$\cos\sigma = \frac{\mu' - \mu\cos\Theta}{\sqrt{(1-\mu^2)}\sqrt{(1-\cos^2\Theta)}}. \tag{12}$$

Finally, using simple trigonometric relations we can express $\cos 2\sigma$ and $\sin 2\sigma$ as:

$$\cos 2\sigma = 2\cos^2\sigma - 1 \tag{13}$$

$$\sin 2\sigma = \begin{cases} 2\sqrt{(1-\cos^2\sigma)}\cos\sigma & \text{for } 0 < \phi-\phi' < \pi \\ -2\sqrt{(1-\cos^2\sigma)}\cos\sigma & \text{otherwise}. \end{cases}$$

3.5 Solution of the VRTE

Most numerical solution methods of RTE proceed by first removing the azimuthal dependency of the functions involved by expanding them in Fourier series. We expand the phase function in Fourier series as [12]:

$$\mathbf{Z}(\mu,\mu',\phi-\phi') = \frac{1}{2}\mathbf{Z}^{c,0}(\mu,\mu') \tag{14}$$

$$+ \sum_{m=1}^{L}(\mathbf{Z}^{c,m}(\mu,\mu')\cos[m(\phi-\phi')] + \mathbf{Z}^{s,m}(\mu,\mu')\sin[m(\phi-\phi')]),$$

where L is the maximum order of expansion and depends on the complexity of the phase function, $\mathbf{Z}^{c,m}(\mu,\mu')$ and $\mathbf{Z}^{s,m}(\mu,\mu')$ are computed by integrating the phase function with the cosine and sine basis respectively. Similarly, we expand the vector radiance function in Fourier series as:

$$\mathbf{I}(\tau,\mu,\phi) = \frac{1}{2}\mathbf{I}^{c,0}(\tau,\mu) + \sum_{m=1}^{L}(\mathbf{I}^{c,m}(\tau,\mu)\cos m\phi + \mathbf{I}^{s,m}(\tau,\mu)\sin m\phi).$$

Using these expansions, we can write VRTE equation for the m-th order Fourier coefficients of $\mathbf{I}$ as a pair for m $\geq$ 1:

$$\mu\frac{\partial}{\partial\tau}\mathbf{I}_k^{c,m}(\tau,\mu) + \mathbf{I}_k^{c,m}(\tau,\mu) - \mathbf{J}_k^- = \mathbf{Q}_k^{c,m}(\tau,\mu)$$

$$\mu\frac{\partial}{\partial\tau}\mathbf{I}_k^{s,m}(\tau,\mu) + \mathbf{I}_k^{s,m}(\tau,\mu) - \mathbf{J}_k^+ = \mathbf{Q}_k^{s,m}(\tau,\mu) \quad (15)$$

where the $\mathbf{J}_k$ terms are defined as:

$$\mathbf{J}_k^- = \frac{\omega(\tau)}{2}\sum_{l=m}^{L}\int_{-1}^{1}(\mathbf{Z}_l^{c,m}(\tau,\mu,\mu')\mathbf{I}_k^{c,m}(\tau,\mu') - \mathbf{Z}_l^{s,m}(\tau,\mu,\mu')\mathbf{I}_k^{s,m}(\tau,\mu'))d\mu',$$

$$\mathbf{J}_k^+ = \frac{\omega(\tau)}{2}\sum_{l=m}^{L}\int_{-1}^{1}(\mathbf{Z}_l^{c,m}(\tau,\mu,\mu')\mathbf{I}_k^{c,m}(\tau,\mu') + \mathbf{Z}_l^{s,m}(\tau,\mu,\mu')\mathbf{I}_k^{s,m}(\tau,\mu'))d\mu',$$

and the inhomogeneous terms $\mathbf{Q}_k$'s are defined as follows:

$$\mathbf{Q}_k^{c,m}(\tau,\mu) = \frac{\omega(\tau)}{2}\sum_{l=m}^{L}\mathbf{Z}_l^{c,m}(\tau,\mu,\mu_{inc})\mathbf{I}_{inc}(\mu_{inc})e^{-\tau/\mu_{inc}},$$

$$\mathbf{Q}_k^{s,m}(\tau,\mu) = \frac{\omega(\tau)}{2}\sum_{l=m}^{L}\mathbf{Z}_l^{s,m}(\tau,\mu,\mu_{inc})\mathbf{I}_{inc}(\mu_{inc})e^{-\tau/\mu_{inc}}.$$

To obtain the complete solution of the radiance field in the volume and at the boundary, we solve the collection of inhomogeneous equations defined by (15) for a specified boundary condition. The boundary conditions of our interest are as follows:

- No incident radiance at the top of the layer from any direction other than μ_{inc}, i.e. $\mathbf{I}_k^m(0,\mu) = \mathbf{0}$ for $\mu \leq 0$ and $\mu \neq \mu_{inc}$.

- For the material layer placed on the top of a black-body base, there is no entering radiance from the bottom of the layer. i.e. $\mathbf{I}_k^m(\tau_0,\mu) = \mathbf{0}$ where τ_0 is the thickness of the material layer, and $\mu > 0$. For the material layer placed on the top of a reflector, $\mathbf{I}_k^m(\tau_0,\mu)$ must be computed by integrating the known BRDF of the base reflector with $-\mu'\mathbf{I}_k^m(\tau_0,\mu')$ where $\mu' < 0$.

We use a discrete ordinate based method (DOM) for solving the inhomogeneous equations. Following the standard practice in DOM solutions, we assume a layer of the plane parallel medium to be homogeneous, that means the phase function, scattering and absorption coefficients and the single scattering albedo are constants in the layer (i.e. independent of τ inside the layer), and the optical thickness in a layer is simply the product of actual thickness in the layer and its extinction coefficient. We model the inhomogeneity of the material by decomposing the plane-parallel medium by multiple layers of homogeneous media (see figure 3). We refer the reader to previous work from Thomas and Stamnes [13] for more details on a DOM based solution method.

3.6 Computing Mueller Matrix for Subsurface BRDF

The Mueller matrix of the polarimetric BRDF ($\mathbf{F}_r$) must satisfy the following relation:

$$\mathbf{F}_r(\mu,\mu_{inc},\phi - \phi_{inc})\mathbf{E}_{inc}(\mu_{inc}) = \mathbf{I}(0,\mu,\phi), \quad (16)$$

where $\mathbf{E}_{inc}$ is the irradiance incident from direction (μ_{inc},ϕ_{inc}), and $\mathbf{I}(0,\mu,\phi)$ is the radiance due to subsurface scattering at the surface (i.e. $\tau=0$) of the material.

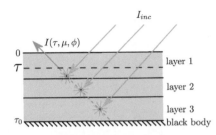

Figure 3: Material composed of three plane-parallel layers. The computation of the radiance at an optical thickness of τ in a direction (μ,ϕ) requires solving RTE for each layer. It involves the computation of the scattered radiance along (μ',ϕ') from all direction (small arrows) and the scattering of the attenuated incident radiance (long arrows).

We compute this matrix by computing radiance field for four linearly independent irradiance Stokes vectors, for every incident direction, and using the following relation:

$$\mathbf{F}_r(\mu,\mu_{inc},\phi - \phi_{inc}) = [\mathbf{I}^{(1)}(0,\mu,\phi),\cdots,\mathbf{I}^{(4)}(0,\mu,\phi)] \quad (17)$$

$$\times[\mathbf{E}_{inc}^{(1)}(\mu_{inc}),\cdots,\mathbf{E}_{inc}^{(4)}(\mu_{inc})]^{-1}.$$

We choose the following irradiance stokes vector values for our BRDF matrix computation:

$$\mathbf{E}_{inc}^{(1)} = \begin{bmatrix}1\\0\\0\\0\end{bmatrix}, \quad \mathbf{E}_{inc}^{(2)} = \begin{bmatrix}1\\1\\0\\0\end{bmatrix}, \quad \mathbf{E}_{inc}^{(3)} = \begin{bmatrix}1\\0\\1\\0\end{bmatrix}, \quad \mathbf{E}_{inc}^{(4)} = \begin{bmatrix}1\\0\\0\\1\end{bmatrix}.$$

The inverse matrix for (17) for this set of irradiance vectors is:

$$\begin{bmatrix}1 & -1 & -1 & -1\\0 & 1 & 0 & 0\\0 & 0 & 1 & 0\\0 & 0 & 0 & 1\end{bmatrix}. \quad (18)$$

We compute the BRDF matrices by solving the VRTE for each of these four incident irradiance stokes vectors for each incident direction. Note that parts of the solution are independent of the incident direction and therefore do not need to be repeated four times. The resulting BRDF matrices are expressed in their reference frames following the definition in section 3.2, i.e. in reference to a meridional plane containing the direction and the vertical axis Z. As we assumed our material to be composed of horizontal layers, when applied to a scene for rendering, the meridional plane becomes the one containing the direction and the normal at the surface.

4 IMPLEMENTATION, VALIDATION AND RESULTS

We implemented our VRTE solver using C++ and the EIGEN library [1]. This solver takes the following input: the incident irradiance vector, a set of incident zenith angles, a set of outgoing azimuth and zenith angles defining the radiance field directions, the bottom boundary condition, and finally the number of layers, and information for each layer: layer optical thicknesses and material information. The solver accepts phase function coefficients and single scattering albedo of the layer as input material information. The solver outputs the Mueller matrix for the polarized BRDF for each pair of incident and outgoing direction, and optionally outputs the polarized radiance field at the specified optical thickness for each incident direction. The latter is used mostly for validation purposes. The tabulated BRDF were then used for renderings using our own polarized ray tracer written in OpenCL [19, 20].

We compute the Fourier expansion coefficients for equation 14 using the analytic expansion from [12]:

$$\mathbf{Z}^{c,m}(\mu,\mu') = \mathbf{A}^m(\mu,\mu') + \mathbf{D}\mathbf{A}^m(\mu,\mu')\mathbf{D}, \quad (19)$$

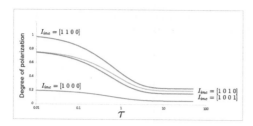

Figure 4: Degree of polarization as function of the optical thickness of the layer. From top to bottom, the incident light is horizontally polarized ($I_{inc} = [1100]$), polarized along 45 degrees ($I_{inc} = [1010]$), circularly polarized ($I_{inc} = [1001]$) and unpolarized ($I_{inc} = [1000]$)

$$\mathbf{Z}^{s,m}(\mu, \mu') = \mathbf{A}^m(\mu, \mu')\mathbf{D} - \mathbf{D}\mathbf{A}^m(\mu, \mu'), \qquad (20)$$

$$\mathbf{A}^m(\mu, \mu') = \sum_{l=m}^{L} \mathbf{P}_l^m(\mu) \mathbf{B}_l \mathbf{P}_l^m(\mu'). \qquad (21)$$

$\mathbf{D}$ in the equations is the diagonal matrix $diag\{1, 1, -1, -1\}$, and $\mathbf{B}_l$ defines the scattering property of the medium in matrix:

$$\mathbf{B}_l = \begin{bmatrix} \beta_l & \gamma_l & 0 & 0 \\ \gamma_l & \alpha_l & 0 & 0 \\ 0 & 0 & \zeta_l & -\varepsilon_l \\ 0 & 0 & \varepsilon_l & \delta_l \end{bmatrix}. \qquad (22)$$

where β, α, ζ, δ, γ, and ε are the coefficients of expansion of the functions $a_1(\Theta)$, $a_2(\Theta)$, $a_3(\Theta)$, $a_4(\Theta)$, $b_1(\Theta)$, and $b_2(\Theta)$ from equation 10, and are computed using Mie theory, $\mathbf{P}_l^m$ is a 4×4 matrix composed of the normalized associated Legendre polynomials P_l^m and generalized spherical polynomials $P_{m,n}^l$ [11]:

$$\mathbf{P}_l^m(\mu) = \begin{bmatrix} P_l^m(\mu) & 0 & 0 & 0 \\ 0 & R_l^m(\mu) & -T_l^m(\mu) & 0 \\ 0 & -T_l^m(\mu) & R_l^m(\mu) & 0 \\ 0 & 0 & 0 & P_l^m(\mu) \end{bmatrix}, \qquad (23)$$

with R_l^m and T_l^m defined as:

$$R_l^m(\mu) = -\frac{1}{2}(i)^m [P_{m,2}^l(\mu) + P_{m,-2}^l(\mu)],$$

$$T_l^m(\mu) = -\frac{1}{2}(i)^m [P_{m,2}^l(\mu) - P_{m,-2}^l(\mu)].$$

For computing scattering coefficients using Mie theory, we use wavelength dependent refractive index data from publicly available SOPRA [3] and filmetrics [2] optical databases. The refractive indices used for our results can be found in table 2. Our implementation supports three types of base materials: a black body (no light is reflected from the bottom), a depolarizing Lambertian surface and a metallic surface whose reflection is modeled by the Fresnel equation. Figure 9 shows the rendering of a single layer of material composed of rust particles on top of those three base layers.

4.1 Validation

For validation, we applied our solver to the problem specified in the benchmark from Wauben and Hovenier [15]. This benchmark tabulates the polarized radiance field for several plane-parallel media illuminated by an unpolarized incident light source from direction ($\mu_{inc} = -0.6, \phi_{inc} = 0$). Figure 5 shows the plot of the first two elements of the Stokes vectors at two different τ values for the problem #2 of the benchmark, as a function of μ at $\phi = 0$. The results from our solver (continuous curves) are in perfect agreement with the

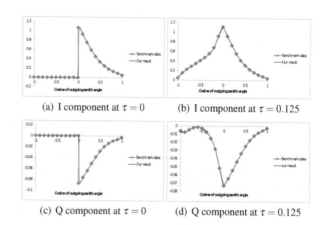

(a) I component at $\tau = 0$ (b) I component at $\tau = 0.125$

(c) Q component at $\tau = 0$ (d) Q component at $\tau = 0.125$

Figure 5: Comparison between our results (continuous curves) and the tabulated data from Wauben and Hovenier benchmark [15] (dots). We plot the I and Q elements of the radiance Stokes vector.

tabulated values from the benchmark (dots). The radiance field at $\tau = 0$ for negative μ values are zero because the incident field is zero (except for $\mu = \mu_{inc}$) at the top boundary.

In order to validate our BRDF computation approach from section 3.6, we used our solver to compute the radiance field for five different incident vectors. We used four of them to compute the BRDF matrix, and verified that multiplying that matrix with the fifth incident vector would give the same result as our solver. The results matched for all the outgoing directions.

4.2 Experimental Evidence of Polarizing Subsurface reflection

Preliminary tests with our solver indicated that the reflected radiance field due to subsurface scattering could exhibit polarization, particularly for thin layers of materials. We verified this finding through measurements of reflection from a thin layer of paint. For this experiment, we applied a thin layer of metallic car paint (Naple Gold Metallic YR524M Honda) on the top of a chromium metal disc. For our incident light, we used a vertically polarized laser beam from a Helium-Neon laser device. The beam is then passed through a half-wave plate. This arrangement allowed us to rotate the plane of polarization of the beam. The resulting beam then hits the paint surface. A narrow beam of the reflected light is passed through a beam splitter to separate the horizontally polarized and vertically polarized components of the reflected light. The separated components are measured through a light meter. Figure 6 summarizes the setup of the measurement. This setup allowed us to measure only the proportion of horizontal and vertical polarization components of the reflected field. After completing the measurement for a number of polarization states of the incident light, we added liberal amounts of the paint on the top of the sample to create a very thick layer, and repeated similar measurements. We subtracted the light meter readings for reflection from the thick layer, from the reading of the thin layer. Assuming that the final thick layer contributed negligible polarizing effect due to subsurface reflection, this latter step was carried out to remove the polarizing effect due to the surface reflection. Our results are shown in table 1. The reflected value for all measurements exhibited polarization. The ratio between the horizontal and vertical components of the measurements correlated with the ratio of the incident light, but were never the same. To compare the measurement with the result from our solver, we carried out an equivalent simulation. Note that

Input Incident light		Measured Reflected light		Finding from Simulation	
Horizontal	Vertical	Horizontal	Vertical	Horizontal	Vertical
0%	100%	11%	89%	28%	72%
7%	93%	19%	81%	32%	68%
25%	75%	24%	76%	41%	59%
50%	50%	37%	63%	54%	46%
75%	25%	63%	37%	66%	34%
93%	7%	98%	2%	74%	26%
100%	0%	86%	14%	77%	23%

Table 1: Percentage of horizontal and vertical linear polarization after reflection of different polarized incident light. The first two columns correspond to the percentage of horizontally and vertically polarized light of the incident beams. Columns 3 to 4 are the same percentages for the reflection from a thin layer of paint from the measurement. The final two columns show the results obtained from our solver for a simulated reflection from a layer of paint containing thin layer of aluminum particles (0.5 optical thickness) placed on the top of chromium metal. The incident stokes vector and the wavelength for the μ measurement and for the simulation are kept same.

the content of the actual paint material was entirely unknown. As a best guess we used a thin layer of material containing aluminum particles over chromium metal base. The Stokes vector for the incident light were computed to match exactly with the experiment input. The result of the simulation (the rightmost column of the table) showed a reasonably good agreement with our measured observation.

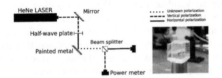

Figure 6: Schematic of our experimental setup. The vertically polarized light beam exiting the laser goes through the half-wave plate to let us control the angle of polarization, reflects on the painted metal and passes through the beam splitter to separate the vertically (red beam) and horizontally (green beam) polarized components of reflection and are each measured using a power meter. The image on the right is the picture of the beam splitter.

4.3 Comparison of BRDF computed using RTE and VRTE solver

Subsurface light transport involves scattering of light, modeled through the phase matrix, and each scattering event changes the polarization properties of the scattered light. Scalar computations omit these changes, and thus introduce errors into the computed radiance field and hence into the computed BRDF. To demonstrate this, we computed subsurface BRDF for different materials both with and without polarization properties, and computed the error

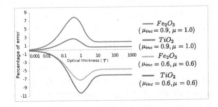

Figure 7: Percentage of error between scalar and polarized computations as a function of optical thickness of the layer. Each curve corresponds to a different pair of incident and outgoing angles (μ_{inc}, μ). The first and third curves (from top to bottom) are for layers of Iron oxide with angles (0.9, 1.0) and (0.6, 0.6) respectively. The other two curves correspond to titanium dioxide particles for the same direction pairs.

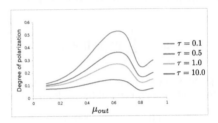

Figure 8: Degree of Polarization as a function of the outgoing angle μ. Each curve corresponds to a layer of Titanium dioxide particles with different optical thicknesses τ.

between the two results. For this error computation, we used the top left element of the computed BRDF matrix. In the subsequent text, we refer to it as F_v, and BRDF from scalar computation as F_s. The error $e = 1 - \frac{F_s}{F_v}$ depends on several factors, such as the material, the wavelength, the incident and reflected directions, and the thickness of the material. The figure 7 plots e for material layers composed of titanium dioxide particles and iron oxide particles and various layer thicknesses. The radius of the particles used is set at $0.2 \mu m$, which is the size that the manufacturer try to maintain in titanium dioxide based paints for optimal light reflection. We can see from the plot that for very thin layers (optical thickness below 0.001), e is negligible, but it increases to a maximum of 11% (for a layer of titanium dioxide at optical thickness around 1.0) and remains relatively high (ex: 7% for layers of titanium dioxide at larger thicknesses) for certian incident angles.

4.4 Polarizing properties of BRDF

In this section we show how the polarization of the radiance field and hence the polarization properties of BRDF varies as a function of thickness of the pigment layer and the type of pigment. Figure 8 plots the degree of polarization of light after reflection of the light ray on a layer of titanium dioxide paint as a function of the outgoing μ direction.

Thus we demonstrated that, scalar computations lead to approximations, and accounting for polarized interaction of light is essential for accurate BRDF computation.

For this plot we used $0.2 \mu m$ as the particle size. The reflected radiance was computed for $\mu_{inc} = -0.6$, and each curve corresponds to a different optical thickness. As expected, the curves show that the degree of polarization reduces with the thickness of the paint layer. Indeed, the thicker a layer, the more subsurface scattering events occur, randomizing more and more the polarization state of light. However in this example case, the degree of polarization was never less than 5% even for the thickest paint layer. Figure 10 shows a rendering of 4 spheres covered with those same layers of paint,

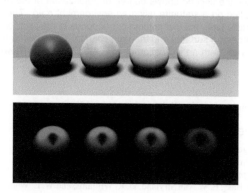

Figure 9: Rendering of a layer of rust particles over a black-body sphere (left), a white sphere (middle) and a silver sphere (right). Rust particles have a size of $0.2\mu m$ and the layer has an optical thickness of 1.

Figure 10: Rendering of spheres covered with a layer of Titanium dioxide paint.The optical thickness of the paint layers are (from left to right): 0.1, 0.5, 1.0 and 10.0. The bottom image shows the corresponding degree of polarization.

with increasing thickness from right to left. At the top we can see the resulting image while the bottom image shows the degree of polarization. We use here the visualization technique suggested by Wilkie et al. [17]. The more red a pixel, the stronger the degree of polarization of the light received by the camera through that pixel. Once again, we see that the thicker the material, the less is the degree of polarization. The walls and floor used in the rendering act as depolarizer and therefore do not have any polarization.

Figure 11: Rendering of spheres with different paints (on the left) and corresponding degree of polarization (on the right).

The degree of polarization is a function of optical thickness and the type of particles that compose the paint. Figure 11 shows several spheres painted with different materials, as well as the associated degree of polarization. From left to right, the paints used were alluminium gallium arsenide over a white depolarizing surface, thick layer of gold paint, thick layer of rust particles, gold paint over white depolarizing surface, and rust over a white depolarizing surface. All the particles composing the paints used here have a size of $0.2\mu m$. We can see that polarization differs between the materials as some spheres present important polarization effects while the others show very little.

In figure 8, we show that relatively thick layers, which are more likely to be seen in real life, are responsible for some but not much

polarization. It does not mean however that they act as depolarizer. Figure 4 shows the DOP of light reflected on the same titanium dioxide paint as a function of the optical thickness τ. Each curve

Figure 12: Rendering of a scene with different light sources. Images on the top row were rendered using a desk lamp as an unpolarized light source. Images at the bottow row have a monitor as a right circularly polarized light source. The first column gives a global view of the scene and the last two colums show the rendering of the spheres and the associated degree of polarization.

corresponds to incident light at a different state of polarization (unpolarized, horizontal and vertical linear polarization and right circular polarization). While those states may not correspond to real-life light sources, it permits us to see how the material affects an already polarized light. As in the previous case, the unpolarized light sees its DOP decrease as the material gets thicker, but when considering fully polarized incident light, the degree of polarization never goes below 20% after reflection even for layers with an infinite optical thickness. Figure 12 shows a scene illuminated by a desk lamp casting unpolarized light, and a computer screen casting circularly polarized light. The figure shows the rendering and the associated degree of polarization using these sources. Though little polarization is present when the light source is the desk lamp, all the three spheres exhibit polarization when the monitor screen is used, thus showing that even materials not creating polarization can convey important polarization information in global illumination.

Material	450nm		550nm		650nm	
	n	k	n	k	n	k
TiO_2	3.141	0.000	2.954	0.000	2.860	0.000
Gold	1.509	1.879	0.350	2.714	0.168	3.118
Iron oxide	0.253	0.692	0.260	0.383	0.023	0.218
AlGaAs	3.832	0.183	3.411	0.000	3.239	0.000
Silver	0.151	2.470	0.125	3.339	0.139	4.129

Table 2: Real and complex components of the refractive indices of the particles used in this paper

Figure 13 shows the BRDF lobes for paint layers composed of different materials. Each paint layer was placed on top of three different base layers: black body, a white depolarizing Lambertian surface and a metallic silver base acting as a polarizing mirror. The BRDF of the paint layers exhibited similar trends. The Lambertian base made the BRDF lobe bigger (visible on the first row), but reduced the degree of polarization of the reflected light significantly (shown on the second row). Using silver base however not only increased the BRDF, but also created a lobe along the mirrored light direction, adding to the material specular effect. Metallic bases plays also a big role on polarization as they clearly change the shape of the degree of polarization lobe as seen on the second row. The rendering of each BRDF applied to a statuette using an environment map is shown on the last row of (13) and agree with the previous observations. Middle rendering are more pale than the

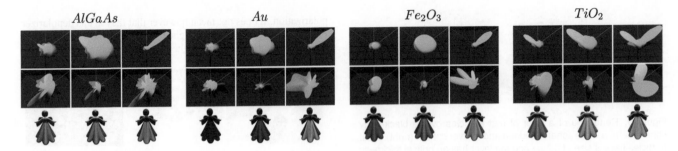

Figure 13: BRDF lobes for different materials. The first row shows the BRDF lobe, the second shows degree of polarization of the reflected unpolarized incident light and the third row shows the rendering of the BRDF applied on a statuette using an environment map. The optical thickness of the layers are kept at 1.0, and the particle size at $0.6\mu m$. For each particle type, the first column corresponds to the layer on top of a black body, the middle column is for the layer on top of a white depolarizing Lambertian surface, and the right column is on top of a metallic Silver base. The lobes correspond to an incident light coming from the top left corner, with an inclination of $45°$. AlGaAs lobe is shown for a wavelength of $550nm$ while the others are for a wavelength of $650nm$.

left ones, because of the white base, while most of the color on the right side renderings come from the reflection of the environment map itself. A rendering of a statuette with a visible environment map is shown on figure 14.

Figure 14: Rendering of an Angel Statuette using a material composed of a layer of iron oxide particles on top of a silver base. The environment map used corresponds to Florence's Uffizi gallery.

5 CONCLUSION AND FUTURE WORK

Light transport during subsurface interaction involves multiple changes of the polarization state of the light, which depends on the types of pigment particles that make up the subsurface medium. Though the polarization properties are not visually important, they are needed for accurate computation of light transport, and hence must be accounted for in the BRDF computation and in global illumination computation.

We described vector radiative transport equation (VRTE) for modeling polarizing light interaction in media. We described a discrete ordinate based method for solving VRTE and used it to compute BRDF due to subsurface interaction of light.

Our VRTE solver, though complete, is slow. Depending on the complexity of the scattering medium, a single BRDF computation for $51 \times 51 \times 61$ directions takes 5 to 10 minutes. We are working towards parallelizing the computation steps and porting to GPU to speed up the computation.

Our preliminary experimental study supports the polarizing behavior of the subsurface BRDF. In future we would like to improve our experimental setup, to support both polarized and unpolarized input, to make full Stokes measurements and to measure the full reflection field. This will allow us to make full scale validations and better understand some of the observed optical behavior.

ACKNOWLEDGEMENTS

This work was supported by NSF grant IIS-1064427.
Environment maps were taken from University of Southern California high-resolution light probe image gallery.

REFERENCES

[1] Eigen library: http://eigen.tuxfamily.org.

[2] Filmetrics: http://filmetrics.com/.

[3] Sopra: http://www.spectra.com/sopra.html.

[4] M. Bass, E. W. Van Stryland, D. R. Williams, and W. L. Wolfe. *Handbook of optics*, volume 2. McGraw-Hill, 2001.

[5] S. Chandrasekhar. *Radiative transfer*. Dover publications, 1960.

[6] J. Dorsey, H. Rushmeier, and F. Sillion. *Digital Modeling of Material Appearance*. Morgan Kaufmann Publishers Inc., San Francisco, CA, USA, 2008.

[7] P. Hanrahan and W. Krueger. Reflection from layered surfaces due to subsurface scattering. In *Proceedings of the 20th annual conference on Computer graphics and interactive techniques*, SIGGRAPH '93, pages 165–174, New York, NY, USA, 1993. ACM.

[8] E. Hecht and A. Zajac. *Optics*, volume 4. Addison Wesley San Francisco, CA, 2002.

[9] J. Hovenier and C. Van der Mee. Fundamental relationships relevant to the transfer of polarized light in a scattering atmosphere. *Astronomy and Astrophysics*, 128:1–16, 1983.

[10] H. W. Jensen, S. R. Marschner, M. Levoy, and P. Hanrahan. A practical model for subsurface light transport. In *Proceedings of the 28th annual conference on Computer graphics and interactive techniques*, pages 511–518. ACM, 2001.

[11] C. Siewert. On the equation of the transfer relevant to the scattering of polarized light. *The Astrophysical Journal*, 245:1080–1086, 1981.

[12] C. Siewert. A discrete-ordinates solution for radiative-transfer models that include polarization effects. *Journal of Quantitative Spectroscopy and Radiative Transfer*, 64(3):227 – 254, 2000.

[13] G. E. Thomas and K. Stamnes. *Radiative transfer in the atmosphere and ocean (Chapter 8)*. Cambridge University Press, 2002.

[14] K. E. Torrance and E. M. Sparrow. Theory for off-specular reflection from roughened surfaces. *JOSA*, 57(9):1105–1112, 1967.

[15] W. Wauben and J. Hovenier. Polarized radiation of an atmosphere containing randomly-oriented spheroids. *Journal of Quantitative Spectroscopy and Radiative Transfer*, 47(6):491 – 504, 1992.

[16] A. Wilkie, R. Tobler, C. Ulbricht, G. Zotti, and W. Purgathofer. An analytical model for skylight polarisation. In *Eurographics Symposium on Rendering*, volume 25, pages 53–69. Citeseer, 2004.

[17] A. Wilkie and A. Weidlich. A standardised polarisation visualisation for images. In *Proceedings of the 26th Spring Conference on Computer Graphics*, pages 43–50. ACM, 2010.

[18] A. Wilkie and A. Weidlich. How to write a polarisation ray tracer. In *SIGGRAPH Asia 2011 Courses*, page 8. ACM, 2011.

[19] A. Wilkie, A. Weidlich, and A. Ghosh. Polarised light in computer graphics. In *SIGGRAPH Asia 2012 Courses*, page 8. ACM, 2012.

[20] L. B. Wolff and D. J. Kurlander. Ray tracing with polarization parameters. *Computer Graphics and Applications, IEEE*, 10(6):44–55, 1990.

Spectral Global Intrinsic Symmetry Invariant Functions

Hui Wang*
Shijiazhuang Tiedao University

Patricio Simari†
The Catholic University
of America

Zhixun Su‡
Dalian University
of Technology

Hao Zhang§
Simon Fraser University

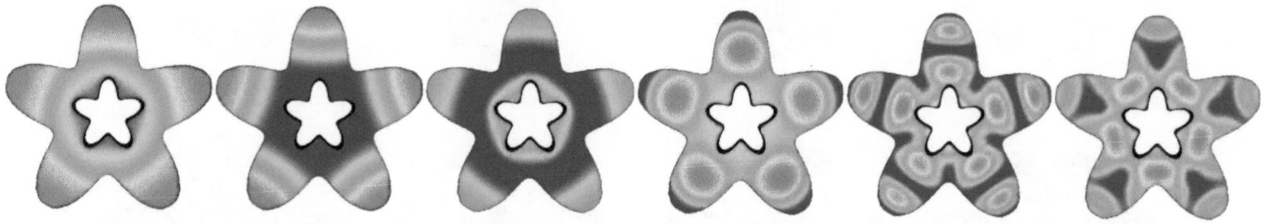

f_{2_3} f_{4_5} f_{6_6} f_{16_17} f_{49_50} f_{72_75}

Figure 1: Spectral Global Intrinsic Symmetry Invariant Functions (GISIFs) computed on a five-point star with rotational symmetries; f_{i_j} denotes a GISIF computed using eigenfunctions of the Laplace-Beltrami operator corresponding to repeated eigenvalues i through j (see Eq. 7).

ABSTRACT

We introduce spectral Global Intrinsic Symmetry Invariant Functions (GISIFs), a class of GISIFs obtained via eigendecomposition of the Laplace-Beltrami operator on compact Riemannian manifolds, and provide associated theoretical analysis. We also discretize the spectral GISIFs for 2D manifolds approximated either by triangle meshes or point clouds. In contrast to GISIFs obtained from geodesic distances, our spectral GISIFs are robust to topological changes. Additionally, for symmetry analysis, our spectral GISIFs represent a more expressive and versatile class of functions than the classical Heat Kernel Signatures (HKSs) and Wave Kernel Signatures (WKSs). Finally, using our defined GISIFs on 2D manifolds, we propose a class of symmetry-factored embeddings and distances and apply them to the computation of symmetry orbits and symmetry-aware segmentations.

1 INTRODUCTION

Symmetry is ubiquitous in both naturally-occurring and human-manufactured shapes. Thus, detecting symmetries and finding symmetry invariants represents an important research problem in computer graphics with many applications [12], especially for global intrinsic symmetries [6, 15, 18].

Global Intrinsic Symmetry Invariant Functions (GISIFs), which are functions defined on a manifold invariant under all global intrinsic symmetries, have received much attention in the context of shape analysis [6, 9, 14]. For example, the critical points of the GISIFs obtained via geodesic distances form symmetry invariant point sets for the generation of candidate Möbius transformations [6]. GISIFs such as the classical Heat Kernel Signature (HKS) [22] and Wave Kernel Signature (WKS) [1] are also used as symmetry invariant descriptors for shape correspondence [14].

In this paper, we propose a new class of GISIFs over compact Riemannian manifolds via spectral methods, where each eigenvalue

*e-mail:wangh@stdu.edu.cn; this research work was initially conducted when the first author visited Simon Fraser University.

†e-mail:mail:simari@cua.edu

‡e-mail:zxsu@dlut.edu.cn

§e-mail:haoz@cs.sfu.ca
Graphics Interface Conference 2014
7-9 May, Montreal, Quebec, Canada

of the Laplace-Beltrami operator, either repeated or non-repeated, corresponds to a GISIF. Our spectral GISIFs have advantages over those which have been previously-proposed. First, spectral GISIFs demonstrate a robustness to topological changes, a property not found in GISIFs based on geodesic distances. Furthermore, the HKS and WKS are linear combinations of our spectral GISIFs. The key difference between the HKS, WKS, and our spectral GISIF is that the HKS and WKS combine all eigenfunctions of the Laplace-Beltrami operator, while we define a spectral GISIF for each eigenvalue, either repeated or non-repeated, using its corresponding eigenfunctions. As such, the new GISIFs represent a broader and more versatile class of functions.

We generate symmetry-factored embeddings from spectral GISIFs and apply them to compute symmetry orbits and symmetry-aware segmentations. In contrast to previous works, which use only non-repeated eigenvalues [9], we use eigenfunctions of the Laplace-Beltrami operator corresponding to both repeated and non-repeated eigenvalues. We will show this allows our embeddings to better capture rotational symmetries, not only reflectional symmetries.

2 RELATED WORK

Global Intrinsic Symmetry Invariant Functions. Symmetry detection and analysis are fundamental problems in computer graphics, image processing, and computer vision [3, 12]. Recent works in computer graphics focus mainly on analyzing global and partial intrinsic symmetries and on leveraging symmetries in shape processing and analysis [6, 11, 15, 25]. For an in-depth survey of such methods and applications, we refer the interested reader to a recent state-of-the-art survey [12]. In this section, we will focus on overviewing previous work in the area of GISIFs.

To the best of our knowledge, Kim et al. are the first to propose a class of GISIFs based on geodesic distances, and they use the critical points of these GISIFs as sampling points for the generation of candidate Möbius transformations [6]. In this paper, we introduce a new class of GISIFs based on the spectral method. Compared to GISIFs obtained with geodesic distances, our spectral GISIFs are more robust to topological changes, as illustrated in Figure 8.

Lipman et al. [9] introduce the concept of a symmetry-invariant function space, and use a symmetry correspondence matrix to symmetrize functions on shapes. However, for their global intrinsic symmetry dissimilarity measure, they only use those eigenfunctions which correspond to non-repeated eigenvalues of the Laplace-Beltrami operator, making it difficult to handle shapes with rota-

f_{2_4} $\qquad$ f_{5_9} $\qquad$ f_{10_12} $\qquad$ f_{13_15}

f_{23_24} $\qquad$ f_{38_39} $\qquad$ f_{48_49} $\qquad$ f_{94_100}

Figure 2: Spectral GISIFs on a filigree triangle mesh.

tional symmetries. In contrast, our spectral GISIFs utilize eigenfunctions corresponding to both repeated and non-repeated eigenvalues, allowing better capture of such symmetries.

The classical Heat Kernel Signature (HKS) [22] and Wave Kernel Signature (WKS) [1] are also GISIFs and can be used as symmetry invariant descriptors for shape correspondence [14]. The Auto Diffusion Function (ADF), in turn, is used for skeletonization and segmentation [5]. Interestingly, all three of these signatures are linear combinations of our spectral GISIFs so our approach can be viewed as a generalization of these and other such global symmetry invariant functions.

Spectral methods using Laplace-Beltrami Operator. The Laplace-Beltrami operator and its spectra are widely used in computer graphics for shape processing and analysis [7, 8, 23], with applications including shape retrieval [19], intrinsic embedding [21], global intrinsic symmetry detection [15], heat kernel signature [22], and shape correspondence [13].

In this paper, we propose spectral GISIFs, a class of GISIFs based on the spectra of the Laplace-Beltrami operator. Our work is inspired by spectral global intrinsic symmetry detection [15], which uses only the eigenfunctions corresponding to non-repeated eigenvalues of the Laplace-Beltrami operator. However, if a compact manifold has a symmetry T such that $T^2 \neq I$, then the eigenvalues of the Laplace-Beltrami operator of the manifold must have repeated eigenvalues, as pointed out in [16]. Here, we take a first step toward using the eigenfunctions corresponding to the repeated eigenvalues of the Laplace-Beltrami for symmetry analysis.

3 SPECTRAL GISIFs ON RIEMANNIAN MANIFOLDS

In this section, we define global intrinsic symmetry and GISIFs and then construct a class of GISIFs over compact Riemannian manifolds via the eigendecomposition of the Laplace-Beltrami operator.

3.1 Global Intrinsic Symmetry

A global intrinsic symmetry on a particular manifold is a geodesic distance-preserving self-homeomorphism [15, 18].

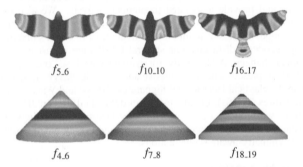

f_{5_6} $\qquad$ f_{10_10} $\qquad$ f_{16_17}

f_{4_6} $\qquad$ f_{7_8} $\qquad$ f_{18_19}

Figure 3: Spectral GISIFs on a bird and cone point cloud.

Definition 1: A self-homeomorphism $T : M \to M$ that preserves all geodesic distances on manifold M is called a global intrinsic symmetry; i.e., it holds that

$$g(\mathbf{p}, \mathbf{q}) = g(T(\mathbf{p}), T(\mathbf{q})), \tag{1}$$

for all $\mathbf{p}, \mathbf{q} \in M$, where $g(\mathbf{p}, \mathbf{q})$ is the geodesic distance from $\mathbf{p}$ to $\mathbf{q}$.

The set of all global intrinsic symmetries on the manifold M forms a group $G(M)$ called the symmetry group with composition as the group operation. Obviously the identity mapping I on the manifold M is an element of the group $G(M)$.

3.2 Global Intrinsic Symmetry Invariant Function

Definition 2: Suppose $f : M \to \mathbb{R}$ is a function defined on the manifold M. If every global intrinsic symmetry T on M satisfies $f \circ T = f$, that is

$$f \circ T(\mathbf{p}) = f(T(\mathbf{p})) = f(\mathbf{p}), \tag{2}$$

for all $\mathbf{p} \in M$, then f is a global intrinsic symmetry invariant function. Note that this definition is the same as that of Kim et al. [6]. The following useful propositions can be easily obtained:

1. Constant functions $f(\mathbf{p}) = c$, for all $\mathbf{p}$ in manifold M are GISIFs.

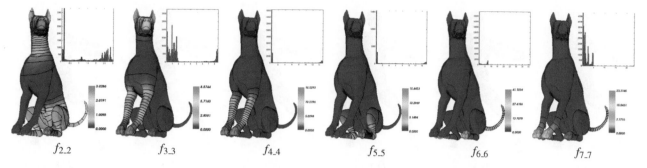

Figure 4: Level sets and histograms of our spectral GISIFs on a dog model. The large blue areas without contours along with the histograms of each field (above), which show a large fraction of values to be near-zero, illustrate the sparsity of the fields.

2. If f is a GISIF on manifold M, then $c * f$ (where c is a constant) is also a GISIF on M.

3. If functions f and g are GISIFs on manifold M, then $f + g$, $f - g$, $f * g$, $f/g (g \neq 0)$ are GISIFs on M.

Based on the above propositions, all of the GISIFs defined on M form a linear space $F^+(M)$ called the global intrinsic symmetry invariant function space, which is a subspace of the functional space $F(M)$ on M. Further, if $G : (F(M), F(M), \dots, F(M)) \to F(M)$ is a linear operator, then $G(F^+(M), F^+(M), \dots, F^+(M)) \subseteq F^+(M)$.

3.3 Spectral GISIFs via the Laplace-Beltrami Operator

We propose a new class of GISIFs based on the eigendecomposition of the Laplace-Beltrami operator on compact Riemannian manifolds without boundaries. Each GISIF corresponds to an eigenvalue, repeated or non-repeated, of the Laplace-Beltrami operator.

Theorem 1: Suppose M is a compact Riemannian manifold without boundary, λ_i is an eigenvalue of the Laplace-Beltrami operator Δ on M with a k-dimensional eigenfunction space. If $\phi_{i1}, \phi_{i2}, \dots, \phi_{ik}$ is an orthogonal basis of the corresponding eigenfunction space of λ_i, then the following function

$$f(\mathbf{p}) = \sum_{j=1}^{k} \phi_{ij}^2(\mathbf{p}), \qquad (3)$$

for all $\mathbf{p} \in M$, is a GISIF on M.

Proof: $\phi_{i1}, \phi_{i2}, \dots, \phi_{ik}$ is an orthogonal basis of the k-dimensional eigenfunction space of eigenvalue λ_i of Δ on M. Then

$$< \phi_{ij}, \phi_{il} > = \delta_{jl} = \left\{ \begin{array}{ll} 1, & j = l \\ 0, & j \neq l \end{array} \right. \quad j, l \in \{1, 2, \dots, k\}.$$

For every global intrinsic symmetry $T : M \to M$, $\phi_{i1} \circ T, \phi_{i2} \circ T, \dots, \phi_{ik} \circ T$ are also eigenfunctions corresponding to the eigenvalue λ_i [15, 20], satisfying the following equation

$$< \phi_{ij} \circ T, \phi_{il} \circ T > = \delta_{jl} = \left\{ \begin{array}{ll} 1, & j = l \\ 0, & j \neq l \end{array} \right. \quad j, l \in \{1, 2, \dots, k\}.$$

That is, $\phi_{i1} \circ T, \phi_{i2} \circ T, \dots, \phi_{ik} \circ T$ is also an orthogonal basis of the corresponding eigenfunction space of the eigenvalue λ_i. Then, there exists a k-dimensional orthogonal matrix $\mathbf{A}$ ($\mathbf{A}\mathbf{A}^T = \mathbf{A}^T\mathbf{A} = \mathbf{I}$, where $\mathbf{I}$ is the k-dimensional identity matrix) such that:

$$(\phi_{i1}(T(\mathbf{p})), \phi_{i2}(T(\mathbf{p})), \dots, \phi_{ik}(T(\mathbf{p})))$$
$$= (\phi_{i1}(\mathbf{p}), \phi_{i2}(\mathbf{p}), \dots, \phi_{ik}(\mathbf{p})) * \mathbf{A},$$

for all $\mathbf{p} \in M$. So we have

$$f \circ T(\mathbf{p}) = f(T(\mathbf{p})) = \sum_{j=1}^{k} \phi_{ij}^2(T(\mathbf{p}))$$
$$= (\phi_{i1}(T(\mathbf{p})), \phi_{i2}(T(\mathbf{p})), \dots, \phi_{ik}(T(\mathbf{p}))) *$$
$$(\phi_{i1}(T(\mathbf{p})), \phi_{i2}(T(\mathbf{p})), \dots, \phi_{ik}(T(\mathbf{p})))^T$$
$$= (\phi_{i1}(\mathbf{p}), \phi_{i2}(\mathbf{p}), \dots, \phi_{ik}(\mathbf{p})) * \mathbf{A} * \mathbf{A}^T * (\phi_{i1}(\mathbf{p}), \phi_{i2}(\mathbf{p}), \dots, \phi_{ik}(\mathbf{p}))^T$$
$$= (\phi_{i1}(\mathbf{p}), \phi_{i2}(\mathbf{p}), \dots, \phi_{ik}(\mathbf{p})) * \mathbf{I} * (\phi_{i1}(\mathbf{p}), \phi_{i2}(\mathbf{p}), \dots, \phi_{ik}(\mathbf{p}))^T$$
$$= (\phi_{i1}(\mathbf{p}), \phi_{i2}(\mathbf{p}), \dots, \phi_{ik}(\mathbf{p})) * (\phi_{i1}(\mathbf{p}), \phi_{i2}(\mathbf{p}), \dots, \phi_{ik}(\mathbf{p}))^T$$
$$= \sum_{j=1}^{k} \phi_{ij}^2(\mathbf{p}) = f(\mathbf{p}).$$

Therefore, the function defined in Equation (3) is a global intrinsic symmetry invariant function on M. □

4 DISCRETIZATION ON 2-MANIFOLDS

In this section, the spectral GISIFs proposed in the above section are discretized on 2D manifolds approximated either by triangle meshes or point clouds. We also illustrate some examples of our spectral GISIFs and show their properties and advantages.

4.1 Implementation

Discretization on Triangular Meshes. A 2D compact manifold M can be approximated by a triangle mesh TRI = $(\mathbf{V}, \mathbf{E}, \mathbf{F})$, where $\mathbf{V} = \{\mathbf{v}_1, \mathbf{v}_2, \dots, \mathbf{v}_n\}$ denotes the set of vertices, $\mathbf{E} = \{(i, j) \mid \mathbf{v}_i$ and $\mathbf{v}_j \in \mathbf{V}$ linked by an edge$\}$ denotes the set of edges, and $\mathbf{F} = \{(i, j, k) \mid \mathbf{v}_i, \mathbf{v}_j, \mathbf{v}_k \in \mathbf{V}$ linked by a face$\}$ denotes the set of faces. $N(i) = \{j \mid (i, j) \in \mathbf{E}\}$ is the set of vertex indices of the 1-ring neighbors of $\mathbf{v}_i$. A function $f : M \to \mathbb{R}$ on M is approximated by a piecewise-linear scalar function defined by linearly interpolating the values of f at the vertices $\mathbf{f} = (f(\mathbf{v}_1), f(\mathbf{v}_2), \dots, f(\mathbf{v}_n))^T$ of TRI.

For the approximation of the Laplace-Beltrami operator Δ on triangle meshes, different methods have been introduced [24]. In this paper, we use the cotangent scheme originally proposed by [4, 17], where Δ is discretized as an n-dimensional Laplacian matrix $\mathbf{L}$. This matrix is represented as $\mathbf{L} = \mathbf{S}^{-1}\mathbf{M}$, where $\mathbf{S}$ is a diagonal matrix whose i-th diagonal element is the Voronoi cell area of vertex $\mathbf{v}_i$ proposed in [4], and $\mathbf{M}$ is a symmetric matrix holding the well known cotangent weights:

$$\mathbf{M}_{ij} = \left\{ \begin{array}{ll} \sum_{k \in N(i)} w_{ik}, & i = j \\ -w_{ij}, & j \in N(i) \\ 0, & otherwise \end{array} \right. , \qquad (4)$$

where $w_{ij} = \frac{cot\alpha_{ij} + cot\beta_{ij}}{2}$, α_{ij} and β_{ij} are angles opposite edge (i, j).

211

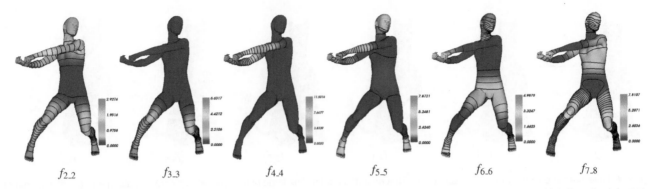

f_{2_2} f_{3_3} f_{4_4} f_{5_5} f_{6_6} f_{7_8}

Figure 5: Level sets of our spectral GISIFs on a human model. The large blue areas without contours showing a large fraction of values to be near-zero illustrate the sparsity of the fields.

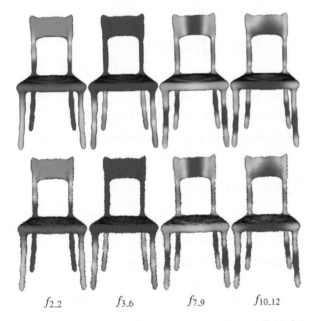

f_{2_2} f_{3_6} f_{7_9} f_{10_12}

Figure 6: The spectral GISIFs corresponding to the smallest eigenvalues are insensitive to noise. **Top:** results on the original mesh. **Bottom:** results on the mesh corrupted with Gaussian noise with variance set to 20% of the mean edge length. Note the visual similarity despite the noise.

The eigendecomposition $\Delta f = \lambda f$ of the Laplace-Beltrami operator can be discretized as the following problem,

$$\mathbf{Lf} = \lambda \mathbf{f}, \qquad (5)$$

where $\mathbf{f} = (f(\mathbf{v}_1), f(\mathbf{v}_2), \ldots, f(\mathbf{v}_n))^T$ is a vector with elements sampling the values of f at the vertices. Equation (5) can be converted into a generalized eigenvalue problem, i.e.,

$$\mathbf{Mf} = \lambda \mathbf{Sf}. \qquad (6)$$

Discretization on Point Clouds. A 2D compact manifold M can also be approximated by a point cloud P, where $\{\mathbf{p}_1, \mathbf{p}_2, \ldots, \mathbf{p}_n\}$ denotes the set of points in P. A function $f : M \to \mathbb{R}$ on M is approximated by a vector $\mathbf{f} = (f(\mathbf{p}_1), f(\mathbf{p}_2), \ldots, f(\mathbf{p}_n))^T$, which samples the values of f at the vertices. There are several approaches for computing the discrete Laplace-Beltrami operator on point clouds [2, 10, 26]. Although any of these methods could be used to compute our spectral GISIFs, we use the approach proposed in [10], where the Laplace-Beltrami operator is discretized as an $n \times n$ matrix $\mathbf{L} = \mathbf{GD}$, where $\mathbf{D}$ is a diagonal matrix and $\mathbf{G}$ is a symmetric

matrix. The eigendecomposition $\mathbf{Lf} = \lambda \mathbf{f}$ can also be converted into a generalized eigenvalue problem (see Section 3.2.1 in [10]).

Computation of GISIFs. In our experiments, we use MATLAB's *eigs* solver to solve the generalized eigenvalue problems on both triangle meshes and point clouds. Let us denote the eigenvalues as $\lambda_1 \le \lambda_2 \le \ldots \le \lambda_n$, and their corresponding eigenvectors as $\phi_1, \phi_2, \ldots, \phi_n$. While the computed eigenvalues are, in practice, seldom exactly equal, if the differences ε between λ_i, λ_{i+1}, ..., and λ_{i+k} are sufficiently small, we regard λ_i as a repeated eigenvalue, and the GISIF f_{i_i+k} corresponding to λ_i is defined as follows

$$f_{i\_i+k}(\mathbf{v}_l) = \sum_{j=0}^{k} \phi_{i+j}^2(l), l \in \{1, 2, \ldots, n\}. \qquad (7)$$

In practice, ε is dependent on the input model, and automatically choosing this threshold for all models is difficult.

4.2 Spectral GISIF Results

All scalar functions on triangle meshes and point clouds in this paper are displayed using colormaps where the low, middle, and high function values are represented as blue, green, and red respectively.

We illustrate several spectral GISIFs across different triangle meshes (Figures 1 and 2) and point clouds (Figure 3). It can be seen that the spectral GISIFs corresponding to the first smallest eigenvalues are smoothest. This is because the eigenfunctions of the first smallest eigenvalues represent the lowest frequencies. For most applications, the spectral GISIFs corresponding to the first 100 smallest eigenvalues, either repeated or non-repeated, of the Laplace-Beltrami operator suffice.

Sparsity property. In practice, we empirically find that most of our spectral GISIFs are sparse; that is, most of the function values of a particular GISIF are close to zero. Figures 4 and 5 show the level sets of our spectral GISIFs on two mesh models, and Figures 4 also displays their histograms. It can be seen that the sparsity property holds for most of the GISIFs in these two figures.

Robustness to noise. Figure 6 illustrates that the spectral GISIFs corresponding to the first smallest eigenvalues are robust to noise. This is because the noise lies in the higher frequencies, which do not affect the GISIFs built from the lower frequencies.

Comparisons with the Heat Kernel Signature. As previously noted, the classical Heat Kernel Signature (HKS) [22] and Wave Kernel Signature (WKS) [1] are widely used in shape analysis, where HKS is defined with a time scale

$$HKS_t(\mathbf{v}_i) = \sum_{j=1}^{n} e^{-\lambda_j t} \phi_j^2(i), i \in \{1, 2, \ldots, n\}. \qquad (8)$$

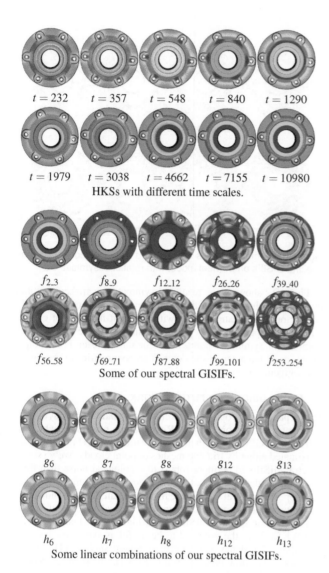

HKSs with different time scales.

Some of our spectral GISIFs.

Some linear combinations of our spectral GISIFs.

Figure 7: Comparisons of our spectral GISIFs with the HKSs [22]. It can be seen that the HKSs across different time scales (**top**) do not exhibit much variation, while our spectral GISIFs (**center**) and some of their linear combinations (**bottom**) differ significantly from each other, capturing more information.

The HKS and WKS are linear combinations of our spectral GISIFs and so are also GISIFs. In Figure 7, our spectral GISIFs (the center two rows) are compared with with HKSs (the top two rows) across different time scales, where the time scales are the default values in [22]. It can be seen that the HKSs across different time scales do not exhibit much variation, while our spectral GISIFs differ significantly from each other, capturing more information.

Furthermore, for symmetry analysis, our spectral GISIFs are more general (and therefore more flexible) than the symmetry invariant descriptors of HKSs and WKSs. We can use our spectral GISIFs to form other GISIFs rather than HKSs or WKSs. The bottom two rows of Figure 7 show some simple linear combinations of our GISIFs, where g_i, $i \in \{6,7,8,12,13\}$ is the the difference between the GISIF corresponding to the i-th and $(i+1)$-th smallest eigenvalue, and $h_i = -g_i, i \in \{6,7,8,12,13\}$.

Comparisons with the Average Geodesic Distances. Kim et al. pioneered work on GISIFs and propose a class of GISIF based on geodesic distances [6], i.e., Average Geodesic Distances (AGDs) and Minimal Geodesic Distances (MGDs).

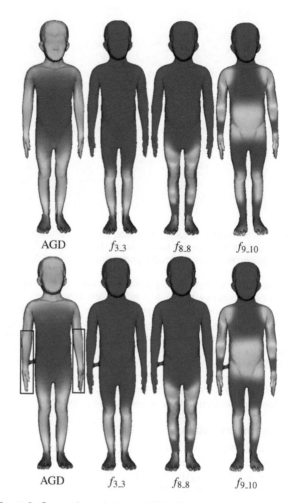

Figure 8: Comparisons between AGDs (**Column 1**) and our spectral GISIFs (**Columns 2, 3, and 4**). **Top:** results on the original mesh. **Bottom:** results on the mesh corrupted by topological noise. Note how the AGD is significantly altered while corresponding GISIFs remain largely unaffected.

In Figure 8, we compare the spectral GISIFs with the AGDs, illustrating that the AGD is sensitive to topological noise while our GISIFs are much more robust. This is due to the fact that small changes in topology, such as the closing of gaps between otherwise geodesically distant limbs, can have a relatively large effect on the AGDs, while the Laplace-Beltrami operator and its corresponding eigenfunctions remain largely unchanged [21].

5 APPLICATIONS

For a 2D manifold M, in Section 3 we can construct a class of spectral GISIF $f_1, f_2, \ldots, f_n, \ldots$, where f_i corresponds to the i-th smallest eigenvalue (repeated or non-repeated) of the Laplace-Beltrami operator. As in [9], based on these components we can obtain a *Symmetry-Factored Embedding* (SFE) of M as follows

$$\text{SFE}(\mathbf{p}) = (\tilde{f}_1(\mathbf{p}), \tilde{f}_2(\mathbf{p}), \ldots, \tilde{f}_n(\mathbf{p}), \ldots), \qquad (9)$$

for $\mathbf{p} \in M$ where $\tilde{f}_i = f_i / \sqrt{\int_M f_i^2(\mathbf{p}) d\mathbf{p}}$ is the normalization of f_i.

The *Symmetry-Factored Distance* (SFD) between points $\mathbf{p}$ and $\mathbf{q}$ on M is defined as the Euclidean distance between their SFEs; i.e.,

$$\text{SFD}(\mathbf{p}, \mathbf{q}) = \sqrt{\sum_{i=1}^{\infty} (\tilde{f}_i(\mathbf{p}) - \tilde{f}_i(\mathbf{q}))^2}. \qquad (10)$$

The SFDs between a point and its symmetric points are zero.

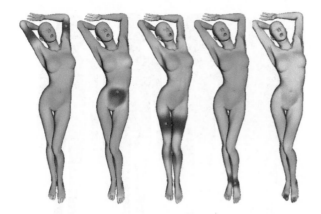

Figure 9: Symmetry-factored distances (SFDs) computed using spectral GISIFs from the red points shown. Note how the SFDs between each point and its symmetric points are near zero (blue).

As stated in Section 4, in practice, we only use the spectral GISIFs corresponding to the first m smallest eigenvalues of the Laplace-Beltrami operator, except for the first eigenvalue whose value is zero and its corresponding GISIF is constant. These selected GISIFs represent the lowest frequency information of the shape. In this paper we use a default value $m = 15$. Figure 9 shows examples of SFDs from different source points, where the SFDs between a point and its symmetric points are close to zero. In the following subsections, we use the above SFEs and SFDs to compute symmetry orbits and symmetry-aware segmentations as in [9].

5.1 Symmetry Orbits

As stated in [9], given a 2D manifold M and its global intrinsic symmetry group $G(M)$, the *Symmetry Orbit* (SO) of a point $\mathbf{p}$ on M is defined as $SO(\mathbf{p}) = \{g(\mathbf{p}) | g \in G(M)\}$. The SFDs from the source point $\mathbf{p}$ form a scalar function on M as follows

$$D_{\mathbf{p}}(\mathbf{q}) = SFD(\mathbf{p}, \mathbf{q}) = \sqrt{\sum_{i=1}^{\infty} (\tilde{f}_i(\mathbf{p}) - \tilde{f}_i(\mathbf{q}))^2}, \qquad (11)$$

for $\mathbf{q} \in M$. The function values at the symmetric points of $\mathbf{p}$ are zero, so we can use the points with zero values of the function of Equation (11) to find the symmetry orbit of $\mathbf{p}$. In practice, the function values of Equation (11) on the symmetry orbit of $\mathbf{p}$ are not exactly zero, so we use the local minima of $D_{\mathbf{p}}(\mathbf{q})$ whose function values are close zero to find the symmetry orbit of $\mathbf{p}$. However, the threshold that defines which local minima belong to the symmetry orbit of vertex $\mathbf{p}$ is dependant on the functional values of $D_{\mathbf{p}}(\mathbf{q})$. In practice, it is difficult to give a fixed threshold for all vertices.

Figures 10 and 11 display the symmetry orbits from some source points. The five-point star in Figure 11 has five rotational symmetries and six reflectional symmetries, including the front-back one. The number of points in symmetry orbits of the red points in Figures 11 (a)-(d) are 5, 10, 20 and 20, respectively.

5.2 Symmetry-aware Segmentation

Symmetry is an important cue for segmentation of shapes into functional parts [9, 25]. In this paper, the symmetry-aware segmentation is obtained by performing the standard k-means clustering algorithm on the points in the symmetry-factored embedding space, and then segmenting the input shape based on the resulting clusters. The reason is that the symmetry-factored distance between two points measures how close the two points are to being symmetric, so clusterings of the symmetry-factored embedding in Equation (9) would obtain symmetry-aware segmentations, dividing a point and its symmetric points into the same segment [9].

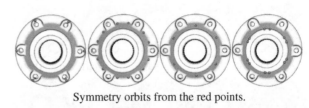

Symmetry orbits from the red points.

Symmetry-factored distances from the same red points.

Figure 10: Symmetry orbits and factored distances computed using spectral GISIFs on a wheel model with rotational symmetries.

Figure 12 shows some results of symmetry-aware segmentation by k-means clustering on the symmetry-factored embedding of a point cloud and triangle mesh with different numbers of clusters without any optimization or postprocessing. It can be seen that each point and its symmetric points are in the same cluster. For example, the cusps of tentacles of the octopus are symmetric, so they are in one segment.

6 CONCLUSION AND FUTURE WORK

In this paper, we propose a new class of global intrinsic symmetry invariant functions on compact Riemannnian manifolds, which we call spectral GISIFs, and their discretization onto 2D manifolds approximated either by triangle meshes or point clouds. We've shown spectral GISIFs to be more robust to topological noise than those based on geodesic distances. Furthermore, for symmetry analysis, the proposed spectral GISIFs are more general, flexible, and appear to capture more information than the classical HKSs and WKSs. Generally, our spectral GISIFs, with higher rank than the HKSs and WKSs, have the potential to be useful as symmetry invariant descriptors for shape matching via quotient spaces [14]. As applications, we show how spectral GISIFs can be used to compute symmetry orbits and symmetry-aware segmentations.

There are two main limitations of spectral GISIFs. First, they cannot be computed on non-manifold shapes, a characteristic that is inherited from the Laplace-Beltrami operator not being defined in such cases. Second, it may be difficult for a user to decide which spectral GISIFs to use out of the full available spectrum.

There are several open avenues for future work. First, we would like to investigate automatic methods for choosing the most informative GISIFs, possibly based on entropy. Second, we would like to study the relation between global intrinsic symmetry and the multiplicity of eigenvalues of the Laplace-Beltrami operator. Third, we plan to investigate principled heuristics for automatically setting the threshold ε for deciding whether an eigenvalue is repeated or not. Fourth, while we have shown that the sparsity property holds empirically in the datasets we have worked with, we will investigate if this property is theoretically derivable from the properties of the manifold. Finally, we would like to investigate more applications of spectral GISIFs, including symmetry aware skeletonization, texture synthesis, denoising, repair, and processing and analysis of high-dimensional manifolds.

ACKNOWLEDGEMENTS

We thank the anonymous reviewers for their valuable comments and suggestions. We are also grateful to Maks Ovsjanikov for sharing the models used in Figure 8. This research is supported in part by the National Natural Science Foundation of China (61173103,

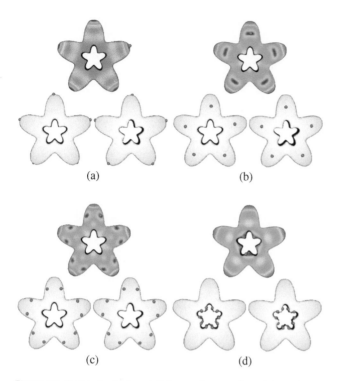

(a)   (b)

(c)   (d)

Figure 11: Symmetry factored distances from some points and symmetry orbits of these points on the five-pointed star. In each result, the **top** shows the symmetry factored distance from the red point, and the **bottom** shows the front and back viewpoints of the symmetry orbit of the corresponding red point.

$k = 3$ $k = 6$ $k = 9$

$k = 3$ $k = 4$

Figure 12: Symmetry-aware segmentations: we use k-means clustering on the SFE of the point cloud of a cone (**top**) and octopus triangle mesh (**bottom**).

F0208), the Natural Sciences and Engineering Research Council of Canada (611370), the Natural Science Foundation of Hebei Province (F2014210127), and Scientific Research Foundation of Shijiazhuang Tiedao University (Z110205).

References

[1] M. Aubry, U. Schlickewei, and D. Cremers. The wave kernel signature: a quantum mechanical approach to shape analysis. In *Computer Vision Workshops*, pages 1626–1633, 2011.

[2] M. Belkin, J. Sun, and Y. Wang. Constructing Laplace operator from point clouds in R^d. In *Nineteenth Annual ACM-SIAM Symposium on Discrete Algorithms*, pages 1031–1040, 2009.

[3] M. Chertok and Y. Keller. Spectral symmetry analysis. *IEEE Transactions on Pattern Analysis and Machine Intelligence*, 32(7):1227–1238, 2010.

[4] M. Desbrun, M. Meyer, P. Schröder, and A. H. Barr. Discrete differential-geometry operators for triangulated 2-manifolds. In *Proceedings of Visualization and Mathematics*, pages 35–57, 2002.

[5] K. Gębal, J. A. Bærentzen, H. Aanæs, and R. Larsen. Shape analysis using the auto diffusion function. *Computer Graphics Forum*, 28(5):1405–1413, 2009.

[6] V. G. Kim, Y. Lipman, and X. Chen. Möbius transformations for global intrinsic symmetry analysis. *Computer Graphics Forum*, 29(5):1689–1700, 2010.

[7] B. Lévy. Laplace-Beltrami eigenfunctions: Towards an algorithm that understands geometry. In *Shape Modeling and Applications, invited talk*, 2006.

[8] B. Lévy and H. Zhang. Spectral mesh processing. In *ACM SIGGRAPH Asia Courses*, 2009.

[9] Y. Lipman, X. Chen, I. Daubechies, and T. A. Funkhouser. Symmetry factored embedding and distance. *ACM Transactions on Graphics*, 29(4):439–464, 2010.

[10] C. Luo, I. Safa, and Y. Wang. Approximating gradients for meshes and point clouds via diffusion metric. *Computer Graphics Forum*, 28(5):1497–1508, 2009.

[11] N. J. Mitra, L. J. Guibas, and M. Pauly. Partial and approximate symmetry detection for 3D geometry. *ACM Transactions on Graphics*, 25(3):560–568, 2006.

[12] N. J. Mitra, M. Pauly, M. Wand, and D. Ceylan. Symmetry in 3D geometry: extraction and applications. *Computer Graphics Forum*, 32(6):1–23, 2013.

[13] M. Ovsjanikov, Q. Mérigot, F. Mémoli, and L. J. Guibas. One point isometric matching with the heat kernel. *Computer Graphics Forum*, 29(5):1555–1564, 2010.

[14] M. Ovsjanikov, Q. Mérigot, V. Pătrăucean, and L. Guibas. Shape matching via quotient spaces. *Computer Graphics Forum*, 32(5):1–11, 2013.

[15] M. Ovsjanikov, J. Sun, and L. Guibas. Global intrinsic symmetries of shapes. *Computer Graphics Forum*, 27(5):1341–1348, 2008.

[16] M. Ovsjanikovs. *Spectral methods for isometric shape matching and symmetry detection*. PhD thesis, Stanford University, Stanford, 2011.

[17] U. Pinkall and K. Polthier. Computing discrete minimal surfaces and their conjugates. *Experimental Mathematics*, 2(1):15–36, 1993.

[18] D. Raviv, A. M. Bronstein, M. M. Bronstein, and R. Kimmel. Symmetries of non-rigid shapes. In *International Conference on Computer Vision*, pages 1–7, 2007.

[19] M. Reuter, F.-E. Wolter, and N. Peinecke. Laplace-Beltrami spectra as a shape-DNA of surfaces and solids. *Computer-Aided Design*, 38(4):342–366, 2006.

[20] S. Rosenberg. *The Laplacian on a Riemannian Manifold*. Cambridge University Press, 1997.

[21] R. M. Rustamov. Laplace-Beltrami eigenfunctions for deformation invariant shape representation. In *Eurographics Symposium on Geometry Processing*, pages 225–233, 2007.

[22] J. Sun, M. Ovsjanikov, and L. J. Guibas. A concise and provably informative multi-scale signature sased on heat diffusion. *Computer Graphics Forum*, 28(5):1285–1295, 2009.

[23] B. Vallet and B. Lévy. Spectral geometry processing with manifold harmonics. *Computer Graphics Forum*, 27(2):251–260, 2008.

[24] M. Wardetzky, S. Mathur, F. Kälberer, and E. Grinspun. Discrete Laplace operators: No free lunch. In *Eurographics Symposium on Geometry Processing*, pages 33–37, 2007.

[25] K. Xu, H. Zhang, W. Jiang, R. Dyer, Z. Cheng, L. Liu, and B. Chen. Multi-scale partial intrinsic symmetry detection. *ACM Transactions on Graphics*, 31(6), 2012.

[26] X. G. Yang Liu, Balakrishnan Prabhakaran. Point-based manifold haronics. *IEEE Transactions on Visualization and Computer Graphics*, 18(10):1696–1703, 2012.

First Person Sketch-based Terrain Editing

Flora Ponjou Tasse[1]* Arnaud Emilien[2,3]† Marie-Paule Cani[2]‡ Stefanie Hahmann[2]§

Adrien Bernhardt[2]¶

[1] University of Cambridge
[2] Laboratoire Jean Kuntzmann (Grenoble University, CNRS) and Inria
[3] LIGUM, Dept. I.R.O., Montreal University

ABSTRACT

We present a new method for first person sketch-based editing of terrain models. As in usual artistic pictures, the input sketch depicts complex silhouettes with cusps and T-junctions, which typically correspond to non-planar curves in 3D. After analysing depth constraints in the sketch based on perceptual cues, our method best matches the sketched silhouettes with silhouettes or ridges of the input terrain. A specific deformation algorithm is then applied to the terrain, enabling it to exactly match the sketch from the given perspective view, while insuring that none of the user-defined silhouettes is hidden by another part of the terrain. As our results show, this method enables users to easily personalize an existing terrain, while preserving its plausibility and style.

Keywords: First person editing, terrain, sketch-based modelling, silhouettes

Index Terms: I.3.7 [Computer Graphics]: Three-Dimensional Graphics and Realism—

1 INTRODUCTION

Terrain is a key element in any outdoor environment. Applications of virtual terrain modelling are very common in movies, video games, advertisement and simulation frameworks such as flight simulators. Two of the most popular terrain modelling methods are procedural [9, 20, 17, 21] and physics-based techniques [21, 25, 4, 22, 24, 16]. The former are easy to implement and fast to compute, while the latter produce terrains with erosion effects and geologically sound features. However, the lack of controllability in these methods is a limitation for artists.

Sketch-based or example-based terrains have been very popular recently in addressing these issues [5, 28, 29, 10, 12, 27, 11]. However, many of these methods assume that the user sketch is drawn from a top view, which makes shape control from a viewpoint of interest very difficult. Others only handle a restricted category of mountains, with flat silhouettes. Lastly, terrains fully generated from sketches typically lack details. Dos Passos et al. [6] recently presented a promising approach where example-based terrain modelling and a first person point-of-view sketch are combined. However their method does not support local terrain editing and cannot handle typical terrain silhouettes with T-junctions. Moreover, terrain patches are often repeated which may spoil the plausibility of the results from other viewpoints.

---

*e-mail: flora.ponjou-tasse@cl.cam.ac.uk
†e-mail:arnaud.emillien@inria.fr
‡e-mail:marie-paule.cani@inria.fr
§e-mail:stefanie.hahmann@inria.fr
¶e-mail:adrien.bernhardt@inria.fr

Graphics Interface Conference 2014
7-9 May, Montreal, Quebec, Canada

Figure 1: A typical artist sketch (top left), is used to edit an existing terrain (right). Results are shown on the second row from the same two viewpoints. Note the complex silhouettes with T-junctions, matched to features of the input terrain. The bottom image shows a rendering of the resulting terrain, from a closer viewpoint.

In this work, we address the problem of intuitive shape control of a terrain from a first person viewpoint, while generating a detailed output, plausible from anywhere. To achieve the intuitive shape control goal, we stick to the sketch-based approach, but allow the user to input complex silhouettes with cusps and T-junctions, as those typically used to represent terrains (see Figure 1). To get plausible, detailed results from anywhere, we focus on editing an existing terrain rather than starting from scratch. This approach captures the coherent small details from the existing terrain, while avoiding the patch blending and repetition problems that are typical of example-based methods. The use of an existing terrain also enables matches of sketched silhouettes with plausible, non planar curves on the terrain.

In practice, the user edits the input terrain by over-sketching it from a first person viewpoint. The user strokes, forming a graph of curves with T-junctions, represent the desired silhouettes for the ter-

217

rain. The input terrain is then deformed such that its silhouettes exactly match the strokes in the current perspective view. This means that each stroke segment is to be some silhouette of the output terrain, and that no other part of the deformed terrain should hide them. Previous sketch-based modelling methods have successfully use feature curves to deform surfaces [26, 30]. Our work explores the use of terrain features for sketch-based terrain editing.

First, we order the sketched strokes by inferring their relative depth from the height of their end-points and from the T-junctions detected in the sketch. Next, features of the input terrain such as silhouette edges and ridges are assigned to each stroke and extended if necessary, to cover the length of the stroke. This assignment is the solution of a minimization problem expressing the similarity between a terrain feature and a stroke in the drawing plane, and the amount of deformation caused by their matching. The selected features then become constraints for an iterative diffusion-based terrain deformation method. Our main contributions are:

- An algorithm for ordering strokes in a complex, perspective sketch with respect to their distance from the camera.

- A method for matching terrain features with user-specified silhouettes, drawn from a given first-person viewpoint.

- A deformation method for matching silhouette constraints while preventing them from being hidden by other parts of the terrain.

Related work is discussed in Section 2. Then we present an overview of our solution in Section 3. This is followed by a description of stroke ordering in Section 4, generation of feature constraints in Section 5 and terrain deformation in Section 6. We discuss results in Section 7 before concluding.

2 RELATED WORK

Most terrain modelling systems use one or a combination of the following: procedural terrain generation, physics-based simulation, sketch-based or example-based methods. See [23] for a detailed survey.

Procedural terrain modelling methods are based on the fact that terrains are self-similar, i.e. statistically invariant under magnification [18]. These methods are the popular choice for landscape modelling due to their easy implementation and efficient computation. They mainly consist of pseudo-randomly editing height values on a flat terrain by using either adaptive subdivision [9, 20, 17] or noise [20, 21]. Adaptive subdivision progressively increases the level of detail of the terrain by iteratively interpolating between neighbouring points and displacing the new intermediate points by increasingly smaller random values. Noise synthesis techniques are often preferred because they offer better control. Superposing scaled-down copies of a band-limited, stochastic noise function generates noise-based terrains. For more information on fractal terrain generation methods, see Ebert et al. [7]. Fractal-based approaches can generate a wide range of large terrains with unlimited level of details. However, they are limited by the lack of user control or non-intuitive parameter manipulation, and the absence of erosion effects such as drainage patterns. To address the last issue, fractal terrains can be improved using physics-based erosion simulation [21, 25, 4, 22, 16]. Alternatively, river network generation can be incorporated in the procedural method [15, 11]. In particular, Genevaux et al. [11] create procedural terrains from a hydrographically and geomorphologically consistent river drainage network, generated from a top-view sketch. However, this method only captures terrains resulting from hydraulic erosion, and there is no mechanism for controlling their silhouettes from a first person viewpoint.

Physically-based techniques generate artificial terrains by simulating erosion effects over some input 3D model. Musgrave et al. [21] present the first methods for thermal and hydraulic erosion based on geomorphology rules. Roudier et al. [25] introduce a hydraulic erosion simulation that uses different materials at various locations resulting in different interactions with water. Chiba et al. [4] generate a vector field of water flow that then controls how sediment moves during erosion. This process produces hierarchical ridge structures and thus enhances realism. Nagashima [22] combines thermal and fluvial erosion by using a river network pre-generated with a 2D fractal function. Neidhold et al. [24] present a physically correct simulation based on fluids dynamics and interactive methods that enable the input of global parameters such as rainfall or local water sources. Kristof et al. [16] propose fast hydraulic erosion based on Smooth Particle Hydrodynamics. The main drawback of all these methods is that they only allow indirect user-control through trial and error, requiring a good understanding of the underlying physics, time and efforts to get the expected results.

Sketching interfaces and more generally feature-based editing have been increasingly popular for terrain modelling. These methods can be combined with some input terrain data to generate terrains with plausible details.

Cohen et al. [5] and Watanabe et al. [28] present the first terrain modelling interfaces that take as input a 2D silhouette stroke directly drawn on a 3D terrain model. They only handle a single silhouette stroke, interpreted as a flat feature curve. McCrae and Singh [19] use stroke-based input to create paths which deform terrains. However user strokes are interpreted as path layouts and not as terrain silhouettes. Multi-grid diffusion methods enable generation of terrains that simultaneously match several feature curves, either drawn from a top view [12] or from an arbitrary viewpoint [2]. The main limitation is that generated terrains typically lack realistic details.

In contrast, Zhou et al. [29] use features (actually, sketch maps painted from above) to drive patch-based terrain synthesis from real terrain data. Closer to our concerns, Gain et al. [10] deform an existing terrain from a set of sketched silhouettes and boundary curves. The algorithm deforms the terrain based on the relative distance to the feature-curves in their region of influence, and on wavelet noise to add details to the silhouettes. In this work we rather use a diffusion-based deformation method to propagate feature constraints, avoiding the need for boundary curves. Lastly, Tasse et al. [27] present a distributed texture-based terrain generation method that re-uses the same sketching interface. Unfortunately, all these methods interpret each sketched silhouette as a planar feature curve, which reduces the realism of the result.

Dos Passos et al. [6] propose a different approach to address this issue. Given a set of sketched strokes drawn from a first person point-of-view, copies of an example terrain are combined such that the silhouettes of the resulting terrain match the strokes. This gives a realistic, varying depth to silhouettes. To achieve this, the algorithm assumes each stroke represents a terrain silhouette. A stroke is matched with a portion of a silhouette, selected from a set of silhouettes viewed from several standing viewpoints around the example terrain. Terrain slices representing portions of matched silhouette are cut from the example terrain and then combined through a weighted sum to produce a smooth terrain. A drawback of this method is that it does not handle complex sketches with T-junctions, which are common in landscape drawings. Moreover, the matching process may select the same silhouette portions for different strokes, thus producing unrealistic repeating patterns in the final result. Finally, the weighted sum function used for merging may fail to remove the boundary seams produced by combining different terrain slices. In this work, we address these issues by presenting a sketch-based method that handles T-junctions in complex sketches and deforms an input terrain to match the sketch rather than copy-pasting parts of it.

3 OVERVIEW

Let us describe our processing pipeline. As in many terrain modelling and rendering methods, our terrains are represented by a *height field*, namely a greyscale image storing elevation values. This representation cannot emulate features such as overhangs and caves, but it is the most prevalent format in terrain generation because of its simplicity and efficient use of storage space. For rendering purposes and silhouette detection, a 3D triangular mesh is constructed from the height field by connecting adjacent terrain points $(x, y, altitude(x, y))$. Users are able to navigate on a 3D rendering of the existing terrain, possibly flat, with a first-person camera always at a standing viewpoint. A sketch is created by drawing one or multiple strokes from the same camera position. The drawn strokes represent silhouettes that should be visible from that position. Our main goal is to deform the terrain such that these user constraints are respected. The following requirements should be satisfied:

- Every sketched stroke should be a terrain silhouette, in the current perspective view from the first-person camera viewpoint.

- Each of these terrain silhouettes should be visible, i.e. not hidden by any other part of the terrain.

- The deformed terrain should not have artifacts nor contain unrealistic deformations, from any other viewpoint.

Our solution consists of five main steps, illustrated in Figure 2:

1. We order strokes according to their depth, from front to back with respect to the camera position. This order is used when we generate constraints for terrain deformation, so that a curve constraint is not occluded by another, when viewed from the first-person viewpoint.

2. Terrain features such as silhouettes and ridges are detected. Deforming existing terrain features to match the desired silhouettes results in a more realistic terrain since no extra features are added and thus, the nature of the existing terrain is best preserved.

3. For each stroke, we select a terrain feature that will be deformed to fit the stroke, when seen from the camera position. These deformed features represent the positional constraints that we use in the diffusion-based terrain deformation. A key idea of our framework is the expression of this feature selection step as an energy minimization problem, in which we penalize features with large altitude differences compared to their corresponding stroke as well as features that would result in too large deformations.

4. We use a multi-grid Poisson solver for diffusion-based terrain deformation. It solves for altitude differences instead of absolute terrain positions, thus preserving the small-scale features of the input terrain.

5. After terrain deformation, other parts of the terrain may hide the user-specified silhouettes. To address this issue, we run the following iterative process: we detect terrain silhouettes that do not fit any user stroke and yet hide one of the sketched silhouettes. Extra deformation constraints are constructed to enforce lowering these protruding silhouettes until the user-sketched silhouettes are no longer occluded. The terrain is deformed with a combination of previous constraints and the newly constructed constraints. We repeat this process until there is no longer protruding silhouette.

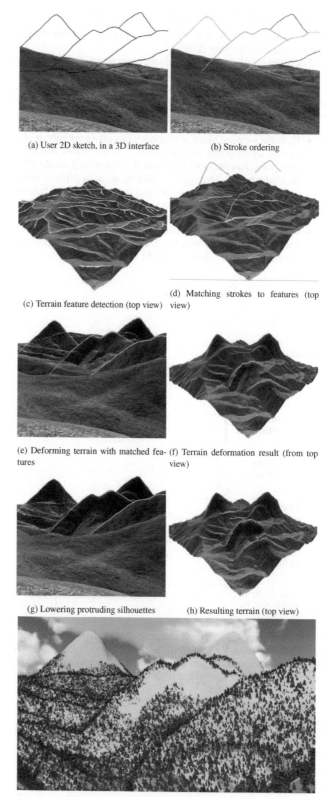

(a) User 2D sketch, in a 3D interface

(b) Stroke ordering

(c) Terrain feature detection (top view)

(d) Matching strokes to features (top view)

(e) Deforming terrain with matched features

(f) Terrain deformation result (from top view)

(g) Lowering protruding silhouettes

(h) Resulting terrain (top view)

(i) Closer view of the generated terrain

Figure 2: Overview of our terrain editing framework. In (b), stroke colour indicates stroke ordering: blue indicates that a stroke is closer to the camera position and red indicates that it is the furthest. (c) illustrates detected terrain features in white and (d) shows the subset of terrain features that have been assigned to user strokes. In (f) the terrain features are deformed so that they match the strokes from the user viewpoint. The final result in (h) is obtained after removing some residual artifacts.

4 ANALYSING COMPLEX TERRAIN SKETCHES

In this section, we explain how depth ordering of silhouette strokes is extracted from the user sketch.

The different silhouette strokes in the input sketch first need to be ordered, in terms of relative depth from the camera viewpoint. This will enable us to ensure, when they are matched with features, that they will not be hidden by other parts of the terrain. Our approach to do so is based on two observations:

- If, in the viewing plane, a silhouette lies above another, it obviously corresponds to a mountain A farther away from the viewpoint than the other mountain B. Otherwise A would hide B. Using height coverage for ordering them in depth is however not sufficient, since some strokes may overlap in height, as for the green and blue strokes in Figure 3.

- Furthermore, the terrain being a height field, the projection of each stroke onto the horizon (x-axis of the viewing plane) is injective (no more than one height value per point).

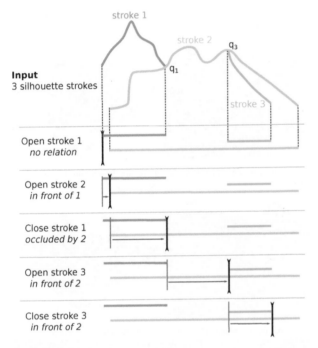

Figure 3: An input sketch (top) and the different steps of the sweeping algorithm used for scanning the sketch, labelling T-junctions and ordering strokes (bottom). As a result, stroke 3 is detected to be in front of stroke 2, which is itself in front of stroke 1.

These two observations allow us to solve the relative stroke ordering problem thanks to a new sweeping algorithm (see Figure 3): We consider the projections of all the strokes onto the horizontal x axis (depicted in the bottom part of the Figure) and sweep from left to right, examining the extremities (starting and endpoints in sweeping direction) and junction points of the silhouette strokes. While doing so, we label the strokes' extremities and the junction points in the following way: an extremity q_s of stroke s is a T-junction if its closest distance to another stroke r is smaller than a threshold. An endpoint q_s is labelled (*occluded-by*, r) if the oriented angle, measured counterclockwise, between the tangent[1] of s

---
[1] Strokes are always oriented clockwise. Hence, stroke tangents are independent of the direction in which the stroke was sketched. When labelling a starting point q_s as T-junction, we flip its tangent.

at q_s and the tangent of r at q_s, $\angle(t_s, t_r) < 180°$. This indicates that s is occluded by, and thus behind, r. Otherwise, s is in front of r and we label q_s as (*in-front-of*, r).

If a stroke s has no T-junctions, then it is behind a stroke r either if the projection of s completely contains the projection of r or if the smallest height value of s's endpoints is larger than the smallest height value of r's endpoints.

While scanning the sketch from left to right, we insert each stroke in a sorting structure, at a relative depth position determined by the cues above. This results in a relative ordering of the user strokes.

5 POSITIONING STROKES IN WORLD SPACE

The key idea of our approach is to create a 3D terrain that matches the user drawing, by deforming an existing one. More precisely, we deform the features of the existing terrain, like its ridgelines, to match the user silhouette strokes. Because a terrain has many features, we first have to compute to which one of them it is the most appropriate to apply a deformation. In this section, we detail how we compute the set of terrain features (Section 5.1), how we affect one of them to each of the user strokes (Section 5.2) and we present a feature completion algorithm that infers the hidden parts of the silhouettes, enabling a more realistic terrain deformation result (Section 5.3).

5.1 Feature detection: silhouettes and ridgelines

Silhouette detection on the existing terrain is based on a common and naive algorithm for computing the exact silhouettes of a 3D mesh. Silhouette edges are detected by finding all visible edges shared by a front face and a back face in the current perspective view. Neighbouring silhouette edges are then linked to form long silhouette curves.

Ridge detection is based on the profile-recognition and polygon-breaking algorithm (PPA) by Chang et al. [3]. The PPA algorithm marks each terrain point that is likely to be on a ridge line, based on the point height profile. Segments, forming a cyclic graph, connect adjacent candidate points. Polygon-breaking repeatedly deletes the lowest segment in a cycle until the graph is acyclic. Finally, the branches on the produced tree structure are reduced and smoothed. The result is a graph where nodes are end points or branch points connected by curvilinear ridgelines. An improvement of the PPA algorithm connects all the terrain points into a graph using a height-based or curvature-based weighting and computes the minimum spanning tree of that graph [1]. Because we are mainly concerned with performance and detection of large-scale ridges, we simply connect candidate terrain points as in the original PPA algorithm and replace the polygon-breaking with a minimum spanning forest algorithm.

5.2 Stroke - Feature matching

In this section, we discuss a method for determining, for each stroke, the terrain features which can be used to construct deformation curve constraints. Viewed from the first person camera, these curve constraints should match the user-sketched strokes. To achieve this, we first construct a features priority list for each stroke and then select features for each priority list such that the sum of their associated cost is minimized.

5.2.1 Features priority list per stroke

For a stroke s, we project all terrain features on the sketching plane (i.e. we use the 2D projection of the feature from the first-person viewpoint) and select feature curves that satisfy the following condition: the x interval they cover matches the one of the stroke s. We deform the selected feature curves, and if necessary extend their endpoints, such that viewed from the camera position, they cover the length of s. This deformation is simply achieved by displacing the feature curve points according to their projection on the 2D stroke in the sketching plane, and their distance to the camera position. Let f be a terrain feature and f_p its projection on the stroke plane. If a portion of f_p is below or above s, f is truncated to that portion. Moreover, for each point $q \in f$, its altitude is modified as follows:

$$q.z = q.z + k * ||q_p - q_p^s|| * \frac{||q - eye||}{||q_p - eye||}$$

where eye is the camera position, $k = -1$ if f_p is below s and $k = 1$ otherwise, q_p the projection of q on the stroke plane, and q_p^s the intersection of s and the vertical line passing at q_p.

We used this deformed version of the feature to associate the following cost $E(f,s)$ to each feature f with respect to stroke s:

$$E = E_{dissimilarity} + E_{deformation} + E_{sampling} + E_{extension} \quad (1)$$

$$E_{dissimilarity}(f) = \frac{w_1}{curvelength(f_p)} * \int_{f_p} h_{f_p} dt$$

$$E_{deformation}(f) = \frac{w_2}{curvelength(f)} * \int_f h_f dt$$

$$E_{sampling}(f) = w_3 * \frac{longestedgelength(f)}{\max_{g \in prioritylist(s)} longestedgelength(g)}$$

$$E_{extension}(f) = w_4 * \frac{extendedcurvelength(f)}{curvelength(f)}$$

where, w_i are weights, f_p is the projection of f on the stroke plane, h_f is the altitude difference between f and f's projection on the terrain, and h_{f_p} is the altitude difference between f_p and the stroke s. $E_{dissimilarity}$ represents the dissimilarity between f and s, $E_{deformation}$ expresses the amount of deformation along f, $E_{sampling}$ penalizes features with long edges and $E_{extension}$ penalizes features that were extended to fully cover s when viewed from the camera position. All the results shown here were generated with $w_1 = w_2 = w_3 = w_4 = 1.0$.

All features are sorted in a priority list according to their cost. Figure 4 illustrates this process for a single stroke (in this simple case, the feature of minimal cost is selected).

5.2.2 Energy minimization

The goal here is the selection of a feature curve f from the priority list of each stroke s_i, to construct deformation constraints for terrain deformation. In addition to the feature order within the different priority lists, we need to take into account the depth ordering for silhouette strokes computed in Section 4.

Therefore, this selection process can be seen as a minimization problem. Let $S = \{s_i : i = 1,...,n\}$ be the stroke list (ordered by depth) and f^i denote a feature in the priority list $L(s_i) = \{f_k^i : k = 1,...,m_i\}$ for a stroke s_i. We are looking for $\{f^i : i \in 1...n\}$ such that $f^i < f^j$ if $i < j$ and $\sum E(f^i)$ is minimized. Here, $f^i < f^j$ means that f^i should not be occluded by f^j, so that all deformation curve constraints are visible from the first person viewpoint. We process the ordered stroke list from front to back, and after each stroke, we remove from the priority list of the next strokes, features that will be occluded if selected. We chose to process strokes from front to back for two main reasons. Firstly, strokes that are closest to the eye are processed first and due to $E_{deformation}$, the algorithm attempts to select constraints that will minimize the terrain deformation. Thus, features closer to the eye are more likely to be selected. Secondly, if all the features of interest for a given stroke s_i were already selected, and therefore its priority list was empty, an arbitrary curve on the terrain would be used instead. If this ever occurs, we prefer it to be for background silhouettes.

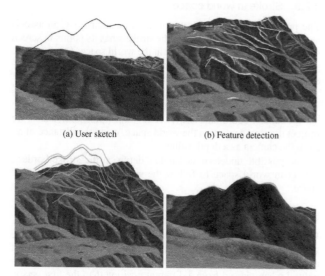

(a) User sketch   (b) Feature detection

(c) Detect possible candidate matches   (d) Terrain deformation using best match

Figure 4: Computing possible features to match with a user stroke. Images (a) and (d) show the terrain from the first person viewpoint used for editing, while image (b) and (c) use a higher viewpoint to better show features on the input terrain. Feature colour indicates cost: blue for the lowest cost and red for the highest.

In practice, feature selections that cause any stroke to have an empty priority list are penalized with a very high cost. Thus, a configuration that guarantees a non-empty priority list for each stroke is always selected, if it exists. If no such configuration exists and s_i has an empty priority list, we automatically compute a 3D embedding of the 2D stroke s_i and use the resulting curve as a deformation constraint. To easily compute this 3D embedding, we take the two strokes lying just in front and just behind s_i. Then we place s_i halfway between the terrain features assigned to these two strokes. If there is no stroke restricted to lie behind s_i, we place it behind the furthest stroke from the viewpoint. If there is no stroke restricted to lie in front of s_i, we place it in front of the closest stroke to the viewpoint. With this approach, each stroke is represented by a deformation constraint even if it was not matched to a terrain feature during the energy minimization.

The energy minimization problem we have described so far is NP-hard. We use a branch-and-bound algorithm to efficiently discard all partial solutions that have a cost higher than the current best cost, without having to explore the whole solution tree. The branch-and-bound algorithm consists of two steps: a *branching* step and a *bounding* step. The branching step consists of exploring possible choices for s_{i+1} once we have made a feature selection for s_i. In other words, we split the node (s_i, f^i) into multiple nodes (s_{i+1}, f_k^{i+1}), where f_k^{i+1} are features in the priority list of s_{i+1}. The bounding step allows the algorithm to stop exploring a partial solution if the total cost of features in the solution is higher than the cost of the best solution found so far.

It is possible for a feature to be the first choice in the priority lists for two or more strokes. To handle this, when exploring a possible solution, a feature curve assigned to a stroke is no longer considered for subsequent strokes. Our branch and bound algorithm will explore other solutions with the feature curve assigned to different strokes as long these solutions are guaranteed to have a smaller cost than the current best solution.

5.2.3 Stroke in world space

The previous minimization gives us, for each stroke s, an associated terrain feature f. However, the stroke s has its points in screen space, whereas the points of f are in the world space. Our goal is to place the stroke in the world space, in order to deduce terrain constraints, i.e. find the distance of their projection from the camera.

For each point of the stroke $q_s = (x_s, y_s)$, we check if there exists a feature point q_f whose projection on screen $q_p = P(q_f) = (x_p, y_p)$ has the same x-coordinate as q_s, i.e. $x_s = x_p$. If this point exists, we project the stroke point on the world space, using the distance of q_f from the camera as a depth value.

The possible undetermined points depth, at the stroke borders, are set in world space to follow the stroke tangent, in the world space.

5.3 Completing selected 3D features

Using user-specified endpoints of an occluded stroke during the generation of deformation constraints would create silhouettes that appear to start exactly at these endpoints. This can look quite unnatural when viewed from a different position than the first person camera position used for sketching: indeed, the endpoint of the occluded stroke (a junction) is typically above the terrain and thus, a sharp deformation will be created at that point.

We address this problem by simply extending 3D features assigned to strokes at both endpoints along their tangents, until they reach the surface of the terrain. An example of this feature completion is presented in Figure 5. More sophisticated contour completion methods such as the one presented in SmoothSketch [14] could alternatively be used, but this simple method was sufficient in our case, and is proposed as an optional step in the editing process.

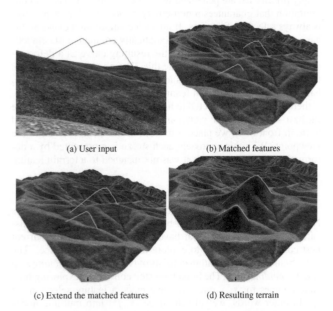

      (a) User input   (b) Matched features

 (c) Extend the matched features   (d) Resulting terrain

Figure 5: Completing selected features: after matching 2D strokes to terrain features, we extend these features until they reach the surface of the terrain, to ensure a smooth transition from specified silhouettes to the terrain.

6 TERRAIN DEFORMATION

In the previous section, we analysed terrain features and used them to position the strokes in the world space. We present in this section how we use them as constraints to deform the existing terrain.

6.1 Diffusion-based equation solver

Our deformation algorithm relies on iterative diffusion of displacement constraints, which are computed from the 3D strokes positioned in the world space.

The diffusion method, first introduced by the authors in [8], consists in computing the difference of the curve height and the terrain height $\mathcal{H}$, and to diffuse these differences (instead of absolute height values) using a multi-grid Poisson solver similar to the one in [12].

More precisely, for each point $p = (x, y, z)$ of the stroke in the world space, we compute $\delta = z - \mathcal{H}(x, y)$, and set it as a displacement constraint. The constraints are rasterised on a grid, whose resolution is equal to the terrain resolution. After having set the constraints of all strokes, we perform the diffusion, which gives the displacement map $\mathcal{M}$.

The displacement is finally applied on the terrain height field $\mathcal{H}$, whose feature line silhouettes are now matching the user strokes, when seen from the first-person viewpoint used for sketching. The deformation only consists of adding the two heights, $\mathcal{H}'(x, y) = \mathcal{H}(x, y) + \mathcal{M}(x, y)$, where $\mathcal{H}'$ is the resulting terrain. Because height differences are propagated, instead of absolute heights, the terrain preserves fine-scale details during the deformation.

6.2 Lowering protruding silhouettes

After deformation, the user-defined silhouettes may be hidden by other parts of the terrain. To address this issue, we detect the unwanted protruding silhouettes and constrain them to a lower position so that the user-defined silhouettes become visible.

6.2.1 Detecting most protruding silhouette edges

First, all visible silhouettes are detected, with the algorithm discussed in Section 5.1. These silhouettes are projected onto the sketching plane. Let s be a silhouette of the deformed landscape, inherited from the example terrain. The mountain of silhouette s hides a user-specified silhouette g if s is closer to the camera than g and the projection s_p of s in the sketching plane has a higher altitude than g_p, the projection of g. In this case, s is an unwanted protruding silhouette. Determining how much s should be lowered is done as follows: Let h be the maximum height difference between s and a silhouette g hidden by s. h is the minimum altitude by which s should be lowered to ensure the silhouettes it hides become visible. Our solution is simply to uniformly lower s by an offset h. This method is applied to all unwanted protruding silhouettes and we use the set of lowered silhouettes to form new deformation constraints.

6.2.2 Updating deformation constraints

The new deformation constraints from the lowered protruding silhouettes are added to the set of constraints associated to the sketched silhouettes, and the terrain is deformed once again using the method of section 6.1. This operation maintains the user-specified silhouettes while lowering areas around the unwanted protruding silhouettes, so that user specifications are satisfied.

The process of detecting protruding silhouettes and using this information to further constrain the terrain is repeated until protruding silhouettes are no longer detected. In practice, a single iteration is usually sufficient to make all user-specified silhouette strokes visible.

7 RESULTS

Validation examples : The examples below and the joined video illustrate the results of our method in a variety of cases. In particular, Figure 6 shows editing of a terrain with a complex sketch containing 5 T-junctions. Our method is also able to handle complex mountains where ridges are not as well-defined as they are on smooth landscapes. An example of this is presented in Figure 7. Our proposed approach differs from other sketch-based methods in that non-planar silhouettes can be generated from planar user-sketched strokes. This is illustrated in Figure 8. Moreover, the method is robust enough to support terrains with few or no features, as shown in the example given in Figure 9. This complex sketch-based editing framework comes with interactive rates, as illustrated in the attached video, which makes it a very attractive alternative to other terrain generation/editing techniques discussed in Section 2.

User tests: We performed an informal user test with two experienced computer artists. The system was briefly introduced to the users, who had no prior knowledge about it. They were then asked to draw sketches to deform existing terrains. Both of them reported that our system was very easy to take in hand and use, and where able to quickly create new sceneries. Their feedback indicates that the approach is original, and seems a promising way to create a scene that matches their artistic intend. However, they had some difficulties for predicting the result of their sketch. This could have been improved by manually tuning the feature matching weights, which was not among their skills. These first users also asked for the ability to move within the scene and edit the terrain from multiple viewpoints. Note that this is not a technical issue: we simply did not implement it since this editing mode was already provided by previous methods. Lastly, the users insisted on the natural aspect of the resulting terrain, and noted that it matched their sketches in the expected way.

Limitations: Although our system succeeds in matching a complex user-sketch through a natural deformation of the terrain, based on its existing features, the lack of predictability of the stroke-feature solver may be a problem. A full user study would be useful to understand the user intent when sketching over the existing terrain, and identify the ranges of weight values allowing us to better match this intent. We could also improve our matching method using extra error functions.

Another limitation comes from our deformation solver. The diffusion-based deformation method sometimes creates small declivities around the extremity of a constraint curve, when the slope of the curve is high and the extremity is located on the terrain: in this case, the terrain locally inflates, except at this end-point where the deformation is zero, which causes the problem. Using an inverse distance to deform a terrain [13] does not work either, because of our use of curves as constraints. Future work still needs to be done on terrain deformation, especially for curve-based deformations.

8 CONCLUSION

We presented the first sketch-based modelling method enabling the deformation of a terrain from a single viewpoint. The user sketches a few silhouette strokes forming a graph with T-junctions, similar to the silhouette representations used in artistic terrain sketching. A key feature of our method is that sketched silhouettes are matched with existing terrain features: this enables our technique to both match silhouette strokes with a non-planar curve, and produce a deformation that does not spoil plausibility, since the structure of ridges and valleys typically remains unchanged. This work could easily be extended to a multiple-view editing interface, where the user can move over the terrain and iteratively edit it from different points of view, while keeping his other sketches as constraints.

ACKNOWLEDGEMENTS

This work was conducted during an internship of Flora Ponjou Tasse at Inria Rhône-Alpes in Grenoble. It was partly supported by the ERC advanced grant EXPRESSIVE.

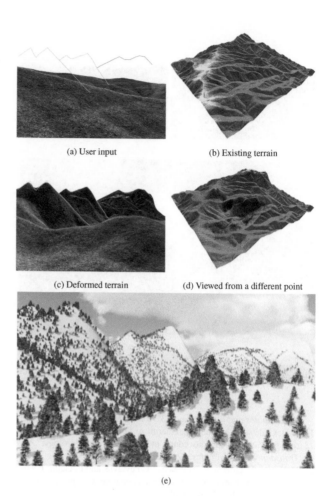

(a) User input   (b) Existing terrain

(c) Deformed terrain   (d) Viewed from a different point

(e)

Figure 6: Terrain editing with a complex user sketch.

REFERENCES

[1] S. Bangay, D. de Bruyn, and K. Glass. Minimum spanning trees for valley and ridge characterization in digital elevation maps. In *Proceedings of the 7th International Conference on Computer Graphics,* *Virtual Reality, Visualisation and Interaction in Africa*, AFRIGRAPH '10, pages 73–82, New York, NY, USA, 2010. ACM.

[2] A. Bernhardt, A. Maximo, L. Velho, H. Hnaidi, and M.-P. Cani. Real-time Terrain Modeling using CPU-GPU Coupled Computation. In *XXIV SIBGRAPI*, Maceio, Brazil, Aug. 2011.

[3] Y.-C. Chang and G. Sinha. A visual basic program for ridge axis picking on dem data using the profile-recognition and polygon-breaking algorithm. *Computers and Geosciences*, 33(2):229–237, 2007.

[4] N. Chiba, K. Muraoka, and K. Fujita. An erosion model based on velocity fields for the visual simulation of mountain scenery. *Journal of Visualization and Computer Animation*, 9(4):185–194, 1998.

[5] J. M. Cohen, J. F. Hughes, and R. C. Zeleznik. Harold: A world made of drawings. In *Proceedings of the 1st International Symposium on Non-photorealistic Animation and Rendering*, NPAR '00, pages 83–90, New York, NY, USA, 2000. ACM.

[6] V. Dos Passos and T. Igarashi. Landsketch: A first person point-of-view example-based terrain modeling approach. In *Proceedings - Sketch-Based Interfaces and Modeling, SBIM 2013 - Part of Expressive 2013*, pages 61–68, 2013.

[7] D. S. Ebert, F. K. Musgrave, D. Peachey, K. Perlin, and S. Worley. *Texturing and Modeling: A Procedural Approach*. Morgan Kaufmann Publishers Inc., San Francisco, CA, USA, 3rd edition, 2002.

[8] A. Emilien, P. Poulin, M.-P. Cani, and U. Vimont. Interactive procedural modeling of coherent waterfall scenes. *Computer Graphics Forum*, 2014. to appear.

[9] A. Fournier, D. S. Fussell, and L. C. Carpenter. Computer rendering of stochastic models. *Commun. ACM*, 25(6):371–384, 1982.

[10] J. Gain, P. Marais, and W. Straer. Terrain sketching. In *Proceedings of I3D 2009: The 2009 ACM SIGGRAPH Symposium on Interactive*

(a) User input   (b) Result

(c)

Figure 7: Editing a complex rocky mountain with a complex sketch.

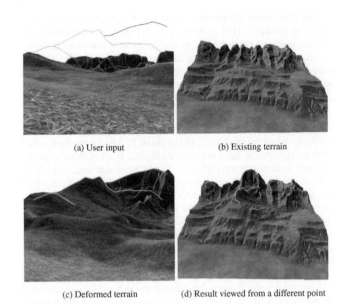

(a) User input   (b) Existing terrain

(c) Deformed terrain   (d) Result viewed from a different point

Figure 8: Terrain editing produces non-planar silhouettes in the output, from 2D planar strokes.

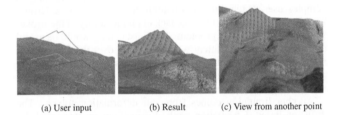

(a) User input   (b) Result   (c) View from another point

Figure 9: Adding deformation constraints automatically: the stroke furthest away from the user did not have an assigned feature to it and so one was automatically generated, and positioned on a plane orthogonal to the view direction, such that stroke ordering is respected.

3D Graphics and Games, pages 31–38, 2009.

[11] J.-D. Genevaux, E. Galin, E. Guerin, A. Peytavie, and B. Benes. Terrain generation using procedural models based on hydrology. *ACM Transactions on Graphics*, 32(4), 2013.

[12] H. Hnaidi, E. Guerin, S. Akkouche, A. Peytavie, and E. Galin. Feature based terrain generation using diffusion equation. *Computer Graphics Forum*, 29(7):2179–2186, 2010.

[13] H. Jenny, B. Jenny, W. E. Cartwright, and L. Hurni. Interactive local terrain deformation inspired by hand-painted panoramas. *Cartographic Journal, The*, 48(1):11–20, 2011.

[14] O. Karpenko and J. Hughes. Smoothsketch: 3d free-form shapes from complex sketches. In *ACM SIGGRAPH 2006 Papers, SIGGRAPH '06*, pages 589–598, 2006.

[15] A. D. Kelley, M. C. Malin, and G. M. Nielson. Terrain simulation using a model of stream erosion. *Computer Graphics (ACM)*, 22(4):263–268, 1988.

[16] P. Kristof, B. Benes, J. Krivanek, and O. Stava. Hydraulic erosion using smoothed particle hydrodynamics. *Computer Graphics Forum*, 28(2):219–228, 2009. Cited By (since 1996):27.

[17] J. P. Lewis. Generalized stochastic subdivision. *ACM Trans. Graph.*, 6(3):167–190, July 1987.

[18] B. B. Mandelbrot. *The fractal geometry of nature*. W. H. Freeman, New York, 1983.

[19] J. McCrae and K. Singh. Sketch-based path design. In *Proceedings of Graphics Interface 2009*, GI '09, pages 95–102, Toronto, Ont., Canada, Canada, 2009. Canadian Information Processing Society.

[20] G. S. P. Miller. The definition and rendering of terrain maps. *SIGGRAPH Comput. Graph.*, 20(4):39–48, Aug. 1986.

[21] F. K. Musgrave, C. E. Kolb, and R. S. Mace. The synthesis and rendering of eroded fractal terrains. In *Proceedings of the 16th Annual Conference on Computer Graphics and Interactive Techniques*, SIGGRAPH '89, pages 41–50, New York, NY, USA, 1989. ACM.

[22] K. Nagashima. Computer generation of eroded valley and mountain terrains. *Visual Computer*, 13(9-10):456–464, 1997.

[23] M. Natali, E. M. Lidal, I. Viola, and D. Patel. Modeling terrains and subsurface geology. In *Proceedings of EuroGraphics 2013 State of the Art Reports (STARs)*, pages 155–173. Eurographics, Eurographics 2013 - State of the Art Reports, May 2013.

[24] B. Neidhold, M. Wacker, and O. Deussen. Interactive physically based fluid and erosion simulation. *Natural Phenomena*, pages 25–32, 2005.

[25] P. Roudier, B. Peroche, and M. Perrin. Landscapes synthesis achieved through erosion and deposition process simulation. *Computer Graphics Forum*, 12(3):375–383, 1993.

[26] K. Singh and E. Fiume. Wires: A geometric deformation technique. In *Proceedings of the 25th Annual Conference on Computer Graphics and Interactive Techniques*, SIGGRAPH '98, pages 405–414, New York, NY, USA, 1998. ACM.

[27] F. Tasse, J. Gain, and P. Marais. Enhanced texture-based terrain synthesis on graphics hardware. *Computer Graphics Forum*, 31(6):1959–1972, 2012.

[28] N. Watanabe and T. Igarashi. A sketching interface for terrain modeling. In *ACM SIGGRAPH 2004 Posters*, SIGGRAPH '04, pages 73–, New York, NY, USA, 2004. ACM.

[29] H. Zhou, J. Sun, G. b. b. Turk, and J. b. b. Rehg. Terrain synthesis from digital elevation models. *IEEE Transactions on Visualization and Computer Graphics*, 13(4):834–848, 2007.

[30] J. Zimmermann, A. Nealen, and M. Alexa. Silsketch: Automated sketch-based editing of surface meshes. In *Proceedings of the 4th Eurographics Workshop on Sketch-based Interfaces and Modeling*, SBIM '07, pages 23–30, New York, NY, USA, 2007. ACM.

Coordinated Particle Systems for Image Stylization

Chujia Wei*
Carleton University

David Mould†
Carleton University

ABSTRACT

Our paper provides an approach to create line-drawing stylizations of input images. The main idea is to use particle tracing with interaction between nearby particles: the particles coordinate their movements so as to produce varied but roughly parallel traces. The particle density varies according to the tone in the input images, thereby expressing bright and dark areas. Using procedural distributions of particles, we can also generate smooth abstract patterns.

Index Terms:

I.3.3 [Computer Graphics]: Picture/Image generation—Line and curve generation

1 INTRODUCTION

Using only black and white lines, artists can create stylized images which depict objects clearly; Figure 1 shows an example. The darker parts of the image use more strokes, while the brighter parts use fewer. The shape of the objects is communicated in part by the local orientation of the strokes.

Figure 1: An artistic drawing with details shown on the right. Engraving by Gustave Doré [2].

We identify three main characteristics of this drawing:

- First, strokes are almost parallel to their neighbors.

- Second, strokes have different individual directions.

- Third, strokes change their directions and spacings smoothly without sharp or sudden turns. This is especially noticeable on the clothes.

Many algorithms can produce stylized images akin to those created by artists. We present an algorithm inspired by the natural yet irregular style illustrated in the figure; our goal was to create strokes possessing the three characteristics listed above. In our line drawing approach, individual lines are smoothly curved and the collection of lines fills space.

---

*e-mail: chujiawei@cmail.carleton.ca
†e-mail: mould@scs.carleton.ca

Graphics Interface Conference 2014
7-9 May, Montreal, Quebec, Canada

The method we describe is further inspired by a particular style of artistic pen-and-ink drawings, where strokes are mostly parallel and tones are produced by different line spacings. Figure 2 shows an example of this kind of pattern: several groups of lines are used to draw a head of hair. The lines in each group are approximately parallel, generating a sense of unity within a group; lines change their directions and spacings gradually, except at the intersections between two groups, and the visible intersections provide a sense of the 3D structure of the surface. We would like to create both representational images based on input photographs and more abstract images based on procedural or user-designated arrangements of curves. Our image synthesis method is based on a particle system [14], where the particles' trajectories are the curves drawn in the final image. Our process is automatic: the logic of the particle system creates the image without human intervention. The method creates smooth, parallel curves with added irregularity for a more natural look. The density of curves matches the tone in the input image.

Figure 2: Left: A hairstyle created by Maria Gil Ulldemolins. Right: An abstract hair style drawn by Rachael Bartram. Images from Flickr.

A set of rules guides the behaviour of particles. All particles move and leave traces in a coordinated way, obtaining information from an input image. Each particle tracks the distance to its neighbors and adjusts its direction so that all particles can remain approximately evenly spaced and parallel. See Figure 3 for an example. The approach is reminiscent of flocking [15], but used here for drawing rather than animation. We also add small random perturbations to particle orientation to increase the variety and naturalness of the trajectories.

A local target particle density is computed from an input image, so that dark areas have more closely packed lines and lighter areas have wider spacing. New particles can be spawned to increase density, and similarly, particles can be terminated when the density is too high. Guptill [10] advises that textures of parallel lines look better when the line endings match up with other lines, rather than having lines terminate in empty space; we take some trouble to ensure that particle birth and death events are matched up with line intersections.

Our minimum line density is not very low, so it is difficult to portray very dark tones. To increase contrast, we use a second layer of particles to create a cross-hatching effect with the first; we construct a foreground map that governs where this second layer operates. The foreground map can be created by various means, but thresholding the input image is one simple and moderately effective mechanism.

Figure 3: Particles leave parallel curves which can smoothly change spacing.

This paper is organized as follows. Having mentioned the problem of line drawing with coordinated particle systems in this introduction, we give more background and discuss related work in the next section. Next, we provide details of our method. A gallery of results and comparisons to similar methods follows; finally, we conclude and give some suggestions for possible future directions.

2 PREVIOUS WORK

Over the years, there has been considerable attention paid to algorithms for creating line art and for image stylization with line and curve primitives. In the following, we describe some highlights of previous work in the area.

Winkenbach and Salesin introduced a system to produce pen-and-ink style images [18], capable of rendering with different stroke styles and various outlines and tones. They also presented a technique of "controlled-density hatching" [19] to generate lines that can appear and disappear gradually to convey tone and shape, and generate various textures. Salisbury et al. also proposed a method to produce quality pen-and-ink illustrations with various texture styles [16]. Some user interaction is needed for choosing and placing stroke textures.

Kang et al. [9] explored a method to create a coherent line drawing style. They compute a smooth edge tangent flow (ETF) and then apply a flow-based difference of Gaussians filter to produce stylized images in a line drawing style. Aiming at a different visual effect, Curtis [1] proposed a method to produce loose and sketchy animations. With limited user intervention, it can create expressive line drawings and animations showing the silhouette edges of the input. Curtis used a particle system but the particles did not coordinate except indirectly through using the same input edge map.

Ostromoukhov [12] proposed a technique to produce engraving-style images. This method shares some similarities with our work, such as parallel lines and different groups of lines for different objects. Inglis et al. proposed algorithms to create an Op Art effect with groups of parallel lines [7, 8]. The technique of Xu and Kaplan [20] shows mazes built with almost parallel lines based on input images. Pedersen and Singh [13] synthesize labyrinths and mazes with a set of curves which evolve through simulated forces. By controlling solution paths, boundaries, and other factors, this system computes maze curves showing input image details.

Elber and Cohen presented a scheme to cover free-form surface with isoparametric curves [5], later improved with variable density [3] and real-time rendering [4]. Hertzmann and Zorin [6] mentioned that the computation of directions for hatching in Elber's work is not reliable, and proposed a more robust technique to find the directions of hatching curves, used for line-drawing renderings of geometric models. The disadvantage of this work is the rendering time, which can be minutes depending on the density and the

complexity. The systems of Elber and Cohen and of Hertzmann and Zorin operate on 3D models, while our approach is intended to work with input images.

Li and Mould used particle tracing to draw tessellation boundaries [11]. The main idea of this method is to release particles with different positions and directions, and track the path of each particle until it reaches another curve or a region boundary. The spacing between particles and the length of paths are controlled so that no narrow or short strokes can be drawn. The approximately parallel lines in their results are not shaped by coordination between particles but by a careful choice of initial particle placement and direction and by removing curves that are poorly spaced.

Schlechtweg et al. proposed an approach to render stroke-based non-photorealistic images with a multi-agent particle system [17]. In their method, intelligent agents called RenderBots produce different effects, such as edging, hatching, and painting, simultaneously in one image. Among their different agents, the "Hatching-Bots" are similar to our particles; these bots draw almost parallel lines and stop when they are too close to other bots or edges. However, the HatchingBots do not change direction and the authors did not attempt to make naturalistic curved strokes using these agents.

While the techniques we discussed above have been largely successful at achieving their goals, none of them precisely addresses the problem we sought to solve. Many techniques involve significant user effort, which is an extra cost. Approaches designed for 3D models are not applicable when the input is an image. Few techniques attempted to fill the image plane with curves; Inglis et al.'s Op Art, which is an exception, pursues a significantly different style from ours. In the following sections, we describe the details of our algorithm and show some results.

3 ALGORITHM

Our objective is to cover the image plane with irregular but approximately locally parallel curves. As an aesthetic choice, prompted by Guptill [10], we decided not to allow curves to begin or end in empty space: a curve should end either at the image boundary or at an intersection with another curve. Curves should not change directions suddenly. The patterns created by the curves can be either abstract or representational; if representational, they can be guided by an input image, in which case we approximate the input tone by tracing more curves in the darker areas and fewer in lighter areas.

We refer to our solution as a *coordinated particle system*. Commonly, the particles in a particle system are noninteracting. In the coordinated system, they interact by informing their neighbors about their location and direction; in this way, the method is similar to flocking. Unlike flocking, but like other particle systems, particles can be added to or removed from the simulation during runtime, depending on the local particle density and collisions with other particle trajectories. The coordinated particle system can create natural-looking patterns and engraving-like images; coordinating the movement and density of particles while tracing particle trajectories, we can create smooth, near-parallel curved tracks.

Beginning with an input image, we divide the image plane into foreground and background regions, possibly by thresholding the intensity. The foreground area will be covered by two sets of curves, and the background only one. We assign particle groups to regions of the image; by default, there are only two groups – one for the entire image and another restricted to the foreground region – but in principle there can be any number. Each group of particles is organized into a chain, linearly ordered. The chains are placed at their initial locations, possibly along an image boundary, and each particle is assigned its initial values. Subsequently, the particles move across the image plane, seeking to maintain even spacing with their neighbors in the chain. Particles are created or added as needed to maintain an appropriate local particle density along the chain, guided by monitoring the input image intensity. The simulation ends and the image is complete when all remaining particles have left the image region.

In our implementation, particles are a key data structure, with each particle possessing many attributes: position $\vec{x}$, bearing b, and other properties including state flags (such as whether a particle is presently visible or invisible) and a base threshold value describing the local desired interparticle spacing. The particles themselves are stored in a linked list and each particle stores the IDs of the adjacent particles, previous and next in the list.

A particle will move alongside its two neighbors. During the simulation, some particles will be removed and some new ones will be generated and inserted into the list, but we maintain the ordered structure. Particles seek to equalize their distances with their neighbors, always moving closer to the more distant one; they also try to maintain the same directions as their neighbors. Together, these two effects produce nearly parallel trajectories. The parallelism is disturbed by deliberately added randomness and by the particle chains' responses to the input image, creating and removing particles to achieve a desired density.

New particles are born when the local particle density becomes too low, as measured by distance between adjacent particles. Particles die when the local particle density becomes too high or when a particle collides with a previously drawn trajectory. While living, the particles move, coordinating with their neighbors, according to rules which will be described next.

The coordinated particles follow sigmoidal paths, which ensures the smoothness of the particle traces. When particles are born or killed, following sigmoidal paths also allows them to turn smoothly. Our sigmoid is based on the tangent function; we provide details below. Each particle's position $\vec{x}$ is updated using Euler integration with unit velocity along the particle's direction $\vec{d}$.

We want particles to have stable directions, so that they will turn smoothly; we want particles to be evenly spaced out; and we want the traces to be parallel, meaning that neighbouring particles have the same bearings. Note the similarity to Reynolds's flocking algorithm [15], where boids should be evenly spaced and share the same orientation as their flockmates. These desires led us to an equation for the bearing that includes a term for each factor mentioned. A new bearing b_{new} is computed from the old one b_{old} as follows:

$$b_{new} = (1 - \alpha)b_{old} + \alpha(b_{aver} + b_{sig}), \qquad (1)$$

where b_{aver} is the average of the two neighbors' bearings and b_{sig} is a bearing computed to produce sigmoidal movement towards the midpoint of the two neighbours. The parameter α is a small value governing the rate of change of bearing. The larger α is, the faster a particle's bearing will be changed, and the sharper the particle will turn.

To compute b_{sig}, we use the tangent function to approximate a sigmoid. By following a sigmoidal curve, particles will smoothly change directions.

For example, as shown in Figure 4, a particle, say C, moves in cooperation with its two neighbours A and B. Assume C is closer to A: we obtain an angle θ for the particle, interpolating between $-\pi/2$ and $\pi/2$ depending on the particle's position between A and the AB midpoint. The particle's bearing is then $\tan(\theta)$. If the particle is closer to B, we do the same, but reversing the direction of the interpolation so that θ is $-\pi/2$ near B, $\pi/2$ near the midpoint. More formally,

$$\theta = \begin{cases} \pi \times S_{AC}/S_{CB} - \pi/2, & AC < CB \\ \pi/2 - \pi \times S_{CB}/S_{AC} & \text{otherwise,} \end{cases} \qquad (2)$$

where S_{AC} is the distance from A to C and similarly S_{CB} is the distance between C and B.

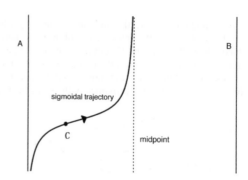

Figure 4: The path of a sigmoidal curve which leads a particle C towards the middle of its neighbours A and B.

3.1 Particle Birth and Death

Tone matching between the input image and the output curves is accomplished by varying the particle count locally. We do not attempt to strictly match tone, but to loosely approximate the input tone by placing more curves in dark areas and fewer curves in lighter areas. Our method manages the number of particles with continuous particle birth and death – when two neighbouring particles get too close, one of them will be terminated, and if they move too far away from each other, a new particle will be generated.

Each pair of neighbouring particles constantly monitors their separation distance. If the distance exceeds a threshold T_b, particle birth is triggered; if the distance is smaller than a threshold T_d, one of the particles is terminated. The thresholds T_b and T_d are computed based on a deviation from a base distance that is linearly interpolated from the local image intensity. Details are given later in this subsection.

Figure 5 shows the procedure of particle birth. The distance S_{AB} of neighbouring particles A and B is checked. When $S_{AB} > T_b$, a new particle C is created from the path of B with a direction inherited from B's direction and rotated slightly towards A. Once the particle enters the simulation, the sigmoidal component of its bearing updates will cause it to move towards A; at the same time, particle B will follow a sigmoidal path carrying it away.

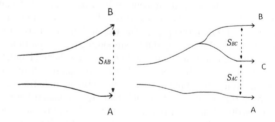

Figure 5: Left: Particles A and B move too far from each other; right: a new particle C spawns from B adding one more line to the image.

When particles enter a lighter area of the image, requiring a larger spacing to match the tone, it is difficult or impossible for them to push their neighbours away quickly enough to match the desired spacing. The solution is to remove some particles; particle death is triggered when the interparticle spacing becomes sufficiently smaller than the desired spacing. Figure 6 depicts a typical case. Particle B observes a small distance S_{BC} with neighbour C: formally, $S_{BC} < T_d$ where T_d is the death threshold. B and C are then marked as dying, and gradually merge their paths. Merging is accomplished by pushing each particle towards the midpoint of the outside neighbours, using the sigmoidal trajectory illustrated in Figure 4; in Figure 6, the relevant neighbours are particles A and D. Once the paths of B and C converge, one of the particles is killed and the other one continues the coordinated movement with its neighbors. After some time, the three surviving particles reach the desired spacing and have approximately the same bearings.

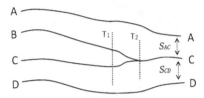

Figure 6: At time T_1, particles B and C are too close to each other and they are forced to merge; at T_2, the paths of B and C overlap. B is killed.

The birth and death thresholds are computed with respect to base threshold values stored on a per-particle basis. For each particle pair, their base thresholds are averaged, producing a base threshold for the gap, say T_g; the birth threshold T_b is $1.5 \times T_g$ and the death threshold T_d is $0.5 \times T_g$. The constants 0.5 and 1.5 were chosen somewhat arbitrarily, but empirically seem effective. This choice of constants ensures that the particles do not get closer than half the desired distance without triggering a termination, and that a gap that exceeds the desired spacing by 50% triggers a new particle. Note that the death threshold could be larger or the birth threshold smaller, making the particle set more stable, but the tradeoff is a greater variation from the desired separation distance. Conversely, making a smaller death threshold or larger birth threshold incurs the tradeoff in the opposite direction: the separation distance is in principle better matched, but there will be more birth and death events. These values can be changed for a particular input image based on the perceived aesthetics of the birth and death events and on the necessity of matching tone.

The base thresholds T_g are stored on a per-particle basis because they depend on the set of tones the particle has passed over. At every timestep, a target spacing is computed from the image tone at each particle's location, linearly interpolating between a user-specified minimum and maximum particle spacing. Particles update their current base threshold in the direction of the local target spacing, incrementing or decrementing by a parameter β depending on whether the current threshold is below or above the target. We used $\beta = 0.001$ in this paper. The use of dynamic, per-particle thresholds makes the spacing stable, smoothing out the particle trajectories; tiny features of the image do not cause sudden changes in the particle behaviour. In effect, the dynamic per-particle thresholds are equivalent to smoothing the image along the particle trajectory.

The base threshold stored in each particle is updated based on image intensity. The input image is converted to grayscale and a target spacing computed for each intensity level by linearly interpolating between a user-specified minimum and maximum spacing. There is no practical upper bound to the maximum spacing, although spacings that approach the image size are unlikely to be useful. However, by default, our implementation uses the original pixel resolution to perform calculations such as collision detection with previously drawn curves; accordingly, the minimum spacing should not be set to a value smaller than 2 pixels. With a minimum spacing set smaller than this, particles may die due to accidental collisions with others, creating a lot of unappealing short lines. In practice, we try to avoid settings smaller than about 8 pixels. If more closely packed lines are desired, we can upsample the grid before processing and downsample afterward; the downsampling is optionally facilitated by using vector instead of raster output.

In addition to particle spacing, we use multiple particle groups for cross-hatching to indicate tone and to show the structure of the input image. A segmentation of the input image divides the image plane into regions; we can assign different particle groups to different regions, each with a different direction, to indicate different image elements. Alternatively, we can divide the image into two regions, darkening one by drawing over it a second time with a second particle group with a different direction than the first. In principle, we could add further layers with yet more directions, but our initial experiments in this regard were unpromising and we did not pursue this idea: two groups are sufficient to distinguish between darker and lighter areas, and intermediate areas can be further distinguished by varying particle spacing. In almost all examples in this paper, we obtained a binary map by thresholding the intensity: dark areas will be crosshatched and light areas will be covered only with one set of lines. We refer to the map obtained by thresholding as a *foreground map* even though it does not always specifically separate foreground and background, and indeed is not guaranteed to have any semantic information when produced by thresholding.

3.2 Additional Details

We would like to apply some random variation to the particle directions to increase the variety and naturalness of the resulting images. However, simply applying a random perturbation to each particle's bearing each timestep does not produce a suitable result; under this regime, the particles simply acquire a high-frequency shivering motion but do not change their overall trajectories very much, since the long-term mean perturbation is zero.

Instead, we suggest a technique to increase the stability of the randomness. Each particle has a flag saying in which direction it should turn. At each timestep, a random value is added to the particle's bearing, causing it to turn slightly in the desired direction. Each particle also has a timer, counting down; when the timer reaches zero, it is reset to a random value and the turn flag is flipped to the other side. The magnitude of the random increment is between 0 and a parameter r that governs the size of the fluctuations. The second-derivative discontinuities from the timer resets are sometimes visible, and there is still room to improve this technique. Figure 7 shows some examples.

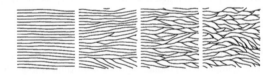

Figure 7: Different levels of randomness. From left to right: $r = 0.01$; $r = 0.03$; $r = 0.05$; $r = 0.09$.

The most interesting aspect of this scheme is the interaction between the randomness and the coordinated movement of multiple neighbouring particles. Because the particles' timers are not synchronized, particles will sometimes share a turn direction with one or both neighbours, and sometimes attempt to turn in opposite directions. However, particles seeking to turn towards each other are prevented by the coordination, where the particle directions are averaged. Conversely, when adjacent particles have the same turn flag, several particles turn simultaneously in the same direction. This behaviour is most apparent in flat-colored regions of the image plane, and we exploit the behaviour to create strong illusions of surface shape in abstract images, seen in the next section.

Our bearing calculations (equations 1 and 2) assume that all particles are approximately arranged in a line and their motion is roughly perpendicular to the line's direction, locally aligned with the vectors to the neighbours. However, because of randomness, variation in distance traveled owing to changing separation distance, or other factors, some particles may fall behind or move ahead compared to the local average. This may mean that the bearing calculations previously described no longer make sense; we need to take some steps to forestall the problem and ensure that the particles do not depart much from the linear structure. Our approach is to decide, for each particle pair, which one is ahead and which one is behind; then, the leading particle is dragged back and the lagging particle pushed ahead. Particles that are close together in progress will tend to alternate being pushed and dragged; although the resulting stuttering movement does not look very appealing in animation, the trajectories are not much affected in this case, especially since the magnitude of pushing or dragging will be near zero.

Consider a pair of particles A and B. Let ω be the projection of A's direction vector $A.\vec{d}$ on the displacement $\vec{s}_{AB}$. If $\omega > 0$, A is lagging; if $\omega < 0$, A is leading. We adjust the positions of A and B proportional to ω: $A.\vec{x}$ is incremented by $\Phi \times \omega \times A.\vec{d}$ and $B.\vec{x}$ is decremented by the same amount. Here Φ is a parameter controlling the magnitude of pushing or dragging; we used $\Phi = 0.005$. This calculation and correction is done for every pair of neighbouring particles at every timestep.

A compact summary of our method appears in the following pseudocode. The particle group in this code can travel over the entire image, i.e., not restricted by the foreground map.

Algorithm 1 Pseudocode for main simulation

Each particle P_i has properties: pointers *prev* and *next*, a position vector $\vec{x}$, a bearing b, and a spacing threshold T. Designate the distance between P_i and P_{i-1} as $S_{P_iP_{i-1}}$.
Input: Spacing map A; array P consists of particles.
Output: the array P of particles updated.
1: **for** each particle P_i **do**
2:     Take the spacing value at $P_i.\vec{x}$ from map A, say $A(P_i.\vec{x})$;
3:     **if** $P_i.T > A(P_i.\vec{x})$ **then**   ▷ Update P_i's spacing threshold
4:         $P_i.T \leftarrow P_i.T - \beta$;
5:     **else if** $P_i.T < A(P_i.\vec{x})$ **then**
6:         $P_i.T \leftarrow P_i.T + \beta$;
7:     Designate the base threshold as T_g;
8:     $T_g \leftarrow (P_i.T + P_i.next.T)/2$;   ▷ Update base threshold
9:     $T_b \leftarrow T_g \times 1.5$; $T_d \leftarrow T_g \times 0.5$;▷ Birth and death thresholds
10:    **if** $S_{P_iP_i.next} > T_b$ **then**   ▷ Particle birth
11:       Create a new particle P_m;   ▷ See Section 3.1
12:       $P_m.\vec{x} \leftarrow P_i.\vec{x}$;
13:    **else if** $S_{P_iP_i.next} < T_d$ **then**   ▷ Particle death
14:       Start killing $P_i.next$;   ▷ See Section 3.1
15: **for** each particle P_i **do**   ▷ Collision detection
16:     Get a list L_i of all colliding particles;
17:     Kill all the particles in L_i;
18: **for** each particle P_i **do**   ▷ Position and bearing update
19:     Update $P_i.b$ and $P_i.\vec{x}$;   ▷ See Algorithm 2

---

4 DISCUSSION AND EVALUATION

In this section, we present some results from our coordinated particle system. We first illustrate the overall process, then show the results of applying the process to a few example images. Then, we show some results of purely abstract images with no guidance from any input image. Lastly, we compare our results with those of previous algorithms. Original images for the results shown are found in Figure 12.

4.1 Complete Procedure of Rendering

We begin with an input image, and compute a foreground map, possibly by thresholding. We then release two particle groups: the first group covers the whole canvas, while the second group only draws

---

Algorithm 2 Pseudocode for bearing and position update

Designate Δt as the timestep, $\vec{d}$ as the direction vector, and b_{new} as the new bearing.
Input: Particle P_i.
Output: P_i with its bearing and position updated.
1: $P_i.\vec{x} = P_i.\vec{x} + \Delta t \times P_i.\vec{d}$;
2: **if** P_i is ahead of $P_i.next$ **then**   ▷ Let particles travel in a line
3:     Push $P_i.next$ forward and drag P_i backward;
4: **else if** P_i is behind $P_i.next$ **then**
5:     Push P_i and drag $P_i.next$;   ▷ See Section 3.2
6: Add randomness to $P_i.b$;   ▷ See Section 3.2
7: Compute b_{new};   ▷ See Equation 1
8: $P_i.b \leftarrow b_{new}$;

---

the black areas in the foreground map. The combination of lines drawn by both groups is our final result.

An overview of the rendering process appears in Figure 8. The first group of particles begins on the left side of the canvas traveling right, and the second group of particles travels from bottom to top. The second group only draws the trajectories when the particles are within the foreground area, as marked in the foreground map.

The first group of particles is shown in the first two subimages. Particle density is adjusted depending on image intensity, showing the dark landscape and ruin. Note that the particles approximately maintain the same pace, having been pushed or dragged to maintain the desired line formation. The second particle group is released on the bottom edge of the canvas; it darkens the landscape and the ruin even further. Notice how the output is able to portray different gray levels: the mountain has an impression of distance, apparently standing behind the ruin owing to the difference in particle spacing.

Figure 8: The procedure of creating a stylized image with our coordinated particle system.

4.2 Application to Images

In this section we show some results from applying the method to photographic images. As described previously, tones from the input image are approximately matched by varying particle spacing; also, we cross-hatch the darker portions of the image with a second set of particles. In principle, we could also vary line thickness depending on the underlying image tone; however, our vector rendering code does not presently support variable line width.

Overall, the large-scale structure of the input image is usually discernible in the output. For example, in Figure 9, the ship itself is nicely presented with the overlapping particle groups generating a darker tone, while the lighter area has only one group of particles and hence the output tone is also lighter. In this example, the particle traces shape a smooth, waving texture for the sky region, suggesting a complex surface despite no surface being actually modeled. The lighter clouds are somewhat suggested by the variation in line spacing; even in the relatively uniform region of the sky, interest has been increased by the fill of varied lines. Unfortunately, the sun is not shown: its tone is too low for our method to distinguish it easily from the surrounding clouds, and both tone values are outside the range separated by our thresholding. Since the water's surface is covered in dark waves, this area is populated by intermittent cross-hatching, suggesting the uneven surface and distinguishing it from the sky. In the line-drawing version of the image, the actual horizon is lost, but there is an apparent horizon that lines up with the bottom of the ship, so the main context of the image remains clear. We encourage the reader to view the digital version of the image and to zoom in so as to best appreciate the structure of the lines. Additional examples are given in the appendix.

Our system is most effective when the input image has high contrast or is otherwise easily able to be divided into foreground and background. Consider Figure 10. The wings and body of the butterfly are much darker than the background, allowing them to be emphasized with cross-hatching while the nearby regions are covered only by a single layer of lines. The flower is made indistinct, and hence deemphasized. The background, mostly quite unremarkable in the original image, has been replaced by a smooth and largely abstract texture. We consider this outcome to be a success.

One limitation of our system is that it is easy to miss some fine details when tracing out features. For example, the smallest branches in Figure 11 are not well portrayed, even though the branch edges are present in the foreground map. The process has succeeded to a large extent, and the bird itself and the thickest branches are portrayed nicely, but the numerous short strokes do not entirely resolve into a coherent depiction of the branches. The image also contains a suggestion as to how the situation can be improved: when the traces follow the branch direction, as is the case in the upper middle, the line is quite clear. The contrast in direction is sufficient to show the feature, even leaving aside the change in tone. It might be possible to improve on our results by having particles follow the structures in the input image, perhaps by exploiting the edge tangent field.

Figure 10: Stylized image: butterfly.

Figure 11: Stylized image: bird.

Figure 9: Stylized image: sailboat with sunset.

4.3 Abstract Patterns

In the previous subsection, we demonstrated that our system is capable of reproducing images with a natural smooth line-drawing style. It can also create compelling abstract images, such as the examples in Figure 13 where particles in multiple groups are used. We first draw a single curve on the canvas, and then release a particle

Figure 12: Original images used in this section.

group perpendicular to the curve. Each particle has an initial direction randomly changed from the perpendicular direction. The group undergoes the usual simulation process, with coordinated movement and particle birth and death, until the particles have either left the image or have collided with previously drawn trajectories. The curves traced by the head and tail of the group are tracked for later use: particles distributed along these curves are released once the main group has finished. In turn, the head and tail trajectories of later particle groups themselves form the basis of new groups. The process halts after nine groups have been processed; the number nine is quite arbitrary but generally fills most of the image plane, and the balance between filled and unfilled regions of the image is itself a source of interest in the final results.

Various abstract patterns are shown in Figures 13 and 14. By changing the randomness values that modify particles' directions, we can obtain curving lines which give an illusion of complex structure. For example, the patterns in the upper left of Figure 13 resemble braids. The upper right image seems to show a surface, such as desert dunes or water waves. The lower left image is a tangled structure reminiscent of the hairstyle drawings in Figure 2. On the lower right is a complex abstraction with many different elements. The larger example in Figure 14 also has many complexities; the wavering parallel lines occasionally give the impression of cloth or some other flexible material. There are small gaps where the particle systems have not filled the canvas; we found these interesting and did not seek to eliminate them, but if desired, they could be covered by additional groups of particles.

The overall appearance of the abstract images are controlled by the placement and shape of the initial thread line, the particle spacing (here constant over the entire canvas), the randomness parameter, and the number of groups to be released. We tried to choose examples that showed some variety, but due to the heavy use of random factors, all abstract images have some unexpected aspects.

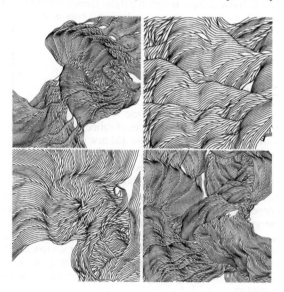

Figure 13: Some random abstract patterns.

5 COMPARISON AND DISCUSSION

So far we have presented various results using coordinated particle system, and provided some suggestions and solutions for possible problems. In this section, we will compare our results with some previous work.

Li and Mould's method [11] to tessellate images using a particle system is algorithmically the most similar past work to ours. Figure 15 shows a comparison with our result. In Li and Mould's work,

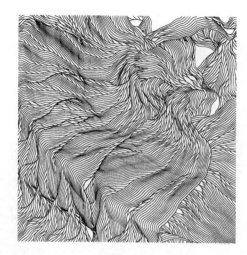

Figure 14: An abstract image.

the growing curves successfully sketch the outline of the lotus and create a smooth texture with long continuous lines. The area below the lotus is drawn with straighter lines, which allows the viewer to distinguish the background and the flower. Our result focuses both on the texture and the tone. The tone is conveyed both by the crosshatching in the darker areas and by the spacing. The structure of the lotus petals can be seen in our result because of the occasional crosshatched areas marking the shadows; contrast with the dark areas behind the flower is produced by small line spacing. As with other examples, a texture is introduced into the uniform area by the collection of lines. Our texture is smoother and less distracting than the chaotic flow seen in the artistic tessellation image.

Figure 16 is another example. We reproduced the lion in our black-and-white line-drawing style. The light and shadow are well managed, especially around the eye and mouth. Recall that we do not use the original image color to fill in the regions, as was done with artistic tessellation: the dark areas, such as the left-hand side, are made dark by cross-hatching with small spacing. The style is particularly good for this kind of image, where the flow of lines can suggest the texture of the lion's fur; additional suggestions of detail are given by the small foreground areas in the lion's mane, which are crosshatched with only a few short strokes.

Like the Op Art method proposed by Inglis et al. [7], our system is also able to convey different color sections with parallel lines moving in different directions. A generalization of the foreground map can indicate different segments to be drawn with different particle groups; each group is initialized with its own direction and only drawn within its designated segment.

As shown in Figure 17, the bottom left image of our result has a smooth appearance somewhat similar to the result generated by Op Art rendering. Both Op Art and our results applied parallel lines with different directions, and the features are successfully depicted without drawing the outlines. The Op Art, with its structured linewidth and directions, produces the characteristic shimmering perceptual effect; our does not, or at least not to as great an extent. However, the shape of the heart is as or more apparent in our result.

There are numerous small differences between the results of Op Art and our method. In our system, the two particle groups trace out features separately, and two lines in different groups do not link with each other to form a single line. Our results contain lines with variable, smoothly changing directions. In the Op Art method, the lines are continuous across segment boundaries, with lines carrying on from one section to another. Moreover, instead of using strictly parallel lines, our system reproduced the heart in the input image

Figure 15: Top left: original image – lotus; top right: reproduced with tessellations [11]; bottom: our result.

Figure 16: Top left: original image – lion; top right: reproduced with tessellations [11]; bottom: our result.

with some irregularities. We are also able to control the brightness by changing the line spacing – more lines appear in darker areas and less are shown in light areas. The Op Art method did not seek to reproduce tone at all.

Since we are interested in managing particles to create natural, irregular lines, we generated another result with more randomness values added to particles' directions. See the bottom right image where a lot of birth and death are triggered. With a high level of randomness, the heart looks "furry" and lively, compared to the one in the bottom left example.

Figure 17: Top left: input image; top right: created with Op Art [7]; bottom left: our result with low randomness; bottom right: our result with high randomness.

6 CONCLUSION AND FUTURE WORK

We presented a coordinated particle system which is capable of tracing out images with parallel lines of varied directions. To match tones and generate parallel lines, we add new particles to areas that have too few, and terminate particles when collisions occur or when particles are packed too closely together. Natural yet irregular patterns are achieved by randomly perturbing particle directions.

One of the disadvantages of our system is that the quality of results depends on the original image. Sometimes fine details cannot be portrayed because of the limitation of particles' spacings; our reliance on tone is also problematic, and using direction to convey features would also be useful. One possible approach will be adding a force to a particle's direction which is tangent to edges. By doing so, particles will be able to leave traces that conform to image content.

As we described before, particles in a group all start with the same direction. No doubt user interaction is one possibility to obtain textures with desired directions; however, we also want to have an option to find the best orientation for each group automatically. Furthermore, with the ability to classify the texture orientations, we can have a new way to create foreground maps.

We would like to explore more in the area of abstract patterns. If we can arrange the threads properly, the particles traces will imitate a recognizable pattern such as waves or smoke. However, we also want to create abstract patterns without manual control, placing threads automatically.

ACKNOWLEDGEMENTS

Thanks to Hua Li and other GIGL members for their advice. Thanks to the anonymous reviewers for their helpful comments.

Many source images were taken from Flickr and are used under a Creative Commons license; thanks to photographers Garry Wilmore, Storm Crypt, Barbara Miers, Richard Skoonberg, Per Ola Wiberg, Andrew Krizhanovsky, Tambako the Jaguar, and Zuhair Ahmad for images of the butterfly, volcano, bird, sailboat, lotus, winter bridge, cat, and girl respectively. Financial support for this work was provided by the GRAND NCE.

REFERENCES

[1] C. J. Curtis. Loose and sketchy animation. In *ACM SIGGRAPH 98 Electronic art and animation catalog*, SIGGRAPH '98, page 145, New York, NY, USA, 1998. ACM.

[2] G. Davidson. *The Drawings of Gustave Doré: Illustrations to the Great Classics*. Metro Books, 2008.

[3] G. Elber. Line art rendering via a coverage of isoparametric curves. *IEEE Transactions on Visualization and Computer Graphics*, 1(3):231–239, Sept. 1995.

[4] G. Elber. Interactive Line Art Rendering of Freeform Surfaces. *Eurographics 1999*, 18:1–12, 1999.

[5] G. Elber and E. Cohen. Tool path generation for freeform surface models. In *Proceedings of the second ACM symposium on Solid modeling and applications*, SMA '93, pages 419–428, New York, NY, USA, 1993. ACM.

[6] A. Hertzmann and D. Zorin. Illustrating smooth surfaces. In *Proceedings of the 27th annual conference on Computer graphics and interactive techniques*, SIGGRAPH '00, pages 517–526, New York, NY, USA, 2000. ACM Press/Addison-Wesley Publishing Co.

[7] T. Inglis, S. Inglis, and C. S. Kaplan. Op art rendering with lines and curves. *Computers and Graphics*, 36(6):607–621, 2012.

[8] T. C. Inglis and C. S. Kaplan. Generating op art lines. In *Proceedings of the International Symposium on Computational Aesthetics in Graphics, Visualization, and Imaging*, CAe '11, pages 25–32, New York, NY, USA, 2011. ACM.

[9] H. Kang, S. Lee, and C. K. Chui. Coherent line drawing. In *Proceedings of the 5th international symposium on Non-photorealistic animation and rendering*, NPAR '07, pages 43–50, New York, NY, USA, 2007. ACM.

[10] A. L. Guptill. *Rendering in Pen and Ink: The Classic Book On Pen and Ink Techniques for Artists, Illustrators, Architects, and Designers*. Watson-Guptill, 1997.

[11] H. Li and D. Mould. Artistic tessellations by growing curves. In *Proceedings of the ACM SIGGRAPH/Eurographics Symposium on Non-Photorealistic Animation and Rendering*, NPAR '11, pages 125–134, New York, NY, USA, 2011. ACM.

[12] V. Ostromoukhov. Digital facial engraving. In *Proceedings of the 26th annual conference on Computer graphics and interactive techniques*, SIGGRAPH '99, pages 417–424, New York, NY, USA, 1999. ACM Press/Addison-Wesley Publishing Co.

[13] H. Pedersen and K. Singh. Organic labyrinths and mazes. In *Proceedings of the 4th International Symposium on Non-photorealistic Animation and Rendering*, NPAR '06, pages 79–86, New York, NY, USA, 2006. ACM.

[14] W. T. Reeves. Particle systems - a technique for modeling a class of fuzzy objects. *ACM Trans. Graph.*, 2(2):91–108, Apr. 1983.

[15] C. W. Reynolds. Flocks, herds and schools: A distributed behavioral model. *SIGGRAPH Comput. Graph.*, 21(4):25–34, Aug. 1987.

[16] M. P. Salisbury, S. E. Anderson, R. Barzel, and D. H. Salesin. Interactive pen-and-ink illustration. In *Proceedings of the 21st annual conference on Computer graphics and interactive techniques*, SIGGRAPH '94, pages 101–108, New York, NY, USA, 1994. ACM.

[17] S. Schlechtweg, T. Germer, and T. Strothotte. Renderbots – multi agent systems for direct image generation. *Computer Graphics Forum*, 24(2):283–290, 2005.

[18] G. Winkenbach and D. H. Salesin. Computer-generated pen-and-ink illustration. In *Proceedings of the 21st annual conference on Computer graphics and interactive techniques*, SIGGRAPH '94, pages 91–100, New York, NY, USA, 1994. ACM.

[19] G. Winkenbach and D. H. Salesin. Rendering parametric surfaces in pen and ink. In *Proceedings of the 23rd annual conference on Computer graphics and interactive techniques*, SIGGRAPH '96, pages 469–476, New York, NY, USA, 1996. ACM.

[20] J. Xu and C. S. Kaplan. Image-guided maze construction. *ACM Trans. Graph.*, 26(3), July 2007.

SUPPLEMENTAL IMAGES

T - #0440 - 101024 - C250 - 280/216/14 - PB - 9781482260038 - Gloss Lamination